Morocco,
Algeria & Tunisia
a travel survival kit

Geoff Crowther
Hugh Finlay

Morocco, Algeria & Tunisia – a travel survival kit

2nd edition

Published by
Lonely Planet Publications
Head Office: PO Box 617, Hawthorn, Vic 3122, Australia
Branches: PO Box 2001A, Berkeley, CA 94702, USA and London, UK

Printed by
Singapore National Printers Ltd, Singapore

Photographs by
Geoff Crowther (GC)
Hugh Finlay (HF)

Front cover: Doorway: Sidi Bou Said, Tunisia (HF)

First Published
July 1989

This Edition
April 1992

Although the authors and publisher have tried to make the information as accurate as possible, they accept no responsibility for any loss, injury or inconvenience sustained by any person using this book.

National Library of Australia Cataloguing in Publication Data

Crowther, Geoff, 1944–
Morocco, Algeria & Tunisia – a travel survival kit.

2nd ed.
Includes index.
ISBN 0 86442 126 5.

1. Morocco – Description and travel – 1981– – Guide-books. 2. Algeria – Description and travel – Guide-books. 3. Tunisia – Description and travel – 1981– – Guide-books. I. Finlay, Hugh. II. Title.

916.4045

Geoff Crowther

Born in Yorkshire, England, on the Ides of March, Geoff took to his heels early on in the search for the miraculous, eschewing what he had been assured was a promising career in biochemistry. The lure of the unknown took him to Kabul, Kathmandu and Lamu in the days before the overland bus companies began digging up the dirt along the tracks of Africa. His experiences led him to join the now legendary but sadly defunct alternative information centre BIT in the late '60s.

In 1977, he wrote his first guide for Lonely Planet – *Africa on the Cheap*, since renamed *Africa on a shoestring*. He has also written *South America on a shoestring* as well as travel survival kits for *Korea* and *East Africa*. Geoff has also co-authored travel survival kits for *India*, *Kenya* and *Malaysia, Singapore & Brunei*.

In an effort to keep these books up to date, Geoff still spends much of his time overseas, often assisted by Choe Hyung Pun, whom he met in Korea in 1981, and their demolition derby son, Ashley. When not gazetting the globe, Geoff beavers away at a word processor in the rainforests of northern New South Wales, Australia, in a cramped, book-lined 'office' in the basement of a shingle-roofed fantasy house which he and his brothers-in-arms constructed over a three-year period. When not writing travel guides, Geoff continues to pursue noxious weeds and brew passion-fruit wine.

Hugh Finlay

After deciding there must be more to life than a career in civil engineering, Hugh first took off around Australia in the mid-'70s, working at everything from parking cars to prospecting for diamonds in the back blocks of South Australia, before heading further afield. He spent three years travelling and working in three continents, including a stint on an irrigation project in Saudi Arabia, before joining Lonely Planet in 1985.

Hugh has also written the Lonely Planet guide *Jordan & Syria – a travel survival kit* and has contributed to others including

Africa on a shoestring and *India – a travel survival kit*.

Hugh and Linda are now finding life considerably enlivened by their daughter, Ella. When not travelling and writing, Hugh spends a good deal of time striving for the perfect home-brew beer.

From the Authors

Thanks must go to all those travellers who have written in with ideas and comments, and to those we met on the road during the course of researching this book. They include:

Dave Brooks & Sarah Bunce (UK), Ann Brooks, Sarah Nicholson & Jackie Berber (UK), Edwin Buis & Jaap Vink (Nl), Rick Dubbeldam (Nl), Paloma Engel (USA), Michael Grove (Aus), Cathy & Alan Hook (UK), Aaron Kitchen (UK), Bob Lassen (NZ), David Lubkurt (USA), Phil Nelson (UK), Paul Olai-Olssen (N), Michael & Liliane Perefais (Aus), Jo Pott (UK), Simon Shepheard (UK), Joaquin Olaso Samper (Sp), Per Storksen (Dk), Jim Taylor (UK), Tim Woodward (UK).

From the Publisher

This edition of *Morocco, Algeria & Tunisia* was edited by Michelle Coxall under the excellent supervision of Michelle de Kretser. Thanks to Jeff Williams for impeccable proof reading and to Sue Mitra for editorial guidance.

Jane Hart was responsible for the cover design, layout and illustrations. Thanks to Vicki Beale for moral support and artistic expertise, and also to Dan Levin, our resident computer whiz extraordinaire.

To all those travellers (apologies if we've misspelt your names) who wrote to tell us of their experiences in North Africa – thanks! If you are not immortalised here, don't despair. Your contributions may be acknowledged in *Africa on a shoestring*.

Hemmadi Ahmed, Teppo Arell (Fin), Debi Arnoni (C), Chris Barton (UK), J Eric Bauwens (USA), Philippe Bovet (F), Adrian Boyle (UK), Debra Brief (USA), Dave Brooks (UK), Sally & Lennert Carlsen (Dk), Mark Chapman (UK), Rick Dubbeldam (Nl), Arne & Unni Eggen (N), Appie Engelaar (Nl), Maria Alvarez Folgado (Sp), Lennart H Forsell (Sw), Jona-

than France (UK), Madame Galland Alexander Groenewege (Nl), Michael Grove (UK), Peter Hoffman (Can), Cathy & Alan Hook (UK), Walter Hunt (USA), Norman Inglis, Mr Jan L H Ippen (Nl), Esthel Issa (C), Iain Jackson (UK), Julie Jones (UK), Robin Kerr (UK), Bart Kleyer (Nl), Erik Klingzell (Sw), Alan Knight (Aus), Bestel Knudsen (Dk), Tom & Eva Kuiper (Nl), Martin Lavers (UK), Abdelkrim Maamri (UK), Alistair MacNab (UK), Runar Mathisen (N), Mark Moore (USA), Chanouk Nap (Nl), Paul Olai-Olssen (N), Frank Patris (USA), David Porter (UK), Gillian Price, Yvonne Pyott (Aus), Andrea Radic (It), Jane Reynolds (UK), Anna Robbins (UK), Lucy Robertson (UK), Erica Rynsburger (Nl), Joaquin Alaso Samper (Sp), Nigel Sawyer (UK), M Scherb (USA), Jane Sillman, David Stanley (C), D L Stevens (USA), Per Storksen (Dk), Bas Suverkropp (Nl), Arjen Talsma (Nl), Tomasz Torbus (D), William van den Olden (Nl), L Villata (Aus), Finn Volstrup (Dk), Florence Vuillet (F), Samantha Wake (UK), Jan White (UK).

Aus – Australia, C – Canada, D – Germany, Dk – Denmark, F – France, Fin – Finland, It – Italy, N – Norway, Nl – Netherlands, NZ – New Zealand, Sp – Spain, Sw – Sweden, UK – United Kingdom, USA – United States of America

Warning & Request

Things change – prices go up, schedules change, good places go bad and bad places go bankrupt – nothing stays the same. So if you find things better or worse, recently opened or long since closed, please write and tell us and help make the next edition better!

Your letters will be used to help update future editions and, where possible, important changes will also be included as a Stop Press section in reprints.

All information is greatly appreciated and the best letters will receive a free copy of the next edition, or any other Lonely Planet book of your choice.

Contents

STOP PRESS
Recent political events in North Africa, including the breakdown of the UN-supervised ceasefire in Western Sahara and the aborted second round of the Algerian general elections, have made it necessary to add stop press sections to this book. For more details, see the following chapters on the pages as indicated:

Morocco 79
Algeria 261

Introduction

For most people, a trip to this region is one of two things: seeing the splendours of the imperial Moroccan cities, or crossing the greatest desert of them all – the Sahara. Without doubt, these are the two principal attractions of the area, but there is also much much more for the traveller, especially if your interest extends to Roman history and Islamic architecture.

Morocco is, of course, the star attraction, far overshadowing its Arab neighbours to the east. It's a fascinating mix of African, Islamic, Arab, Berber and even European influences and this, combined with its accessibility from Europe, makes it a popular and memorable place to visit. As well as the four imperial cities – Fès, Meknès, Marrakesh and Rabat – there are the natural attractions of the Atlantic beaches and the remote villages of the High Atlas and Rif mountains. The contrasts are great – poverty and opulence, hospitality and aggression. Love it or hate it, you are unlikely to quickly forget a trip to Morocco.

Algeria is the lumbering socialist giant of the Maghreb. While most people set out to conquer the Sahara, in itself a once-in-a-lifetime experience, few people take the time to explore the rich diversity of the north of the country. As a result, sites of great historical importance and areas of superb natural beauty are both unspoilt and uncrowded. The people of the country, too, go out of their way to make the visitor welcome – an invitation to have a meal or spend the night in a local home is not at all uncommon. Really it's a

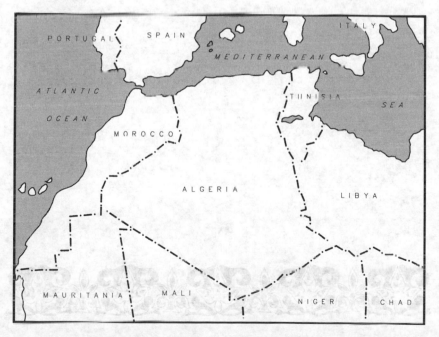

country which more than amply rewards the traveller who wants to get off the beaten track.

Tunisia is very much the 'little brother' of the three countries as far as size goes. Because it has embraced the West so openly it has a well-developed tourist industry, helped in no small measure by the fact that the country has some of the best beaches in the Mediterranean. For most foreign visitors Tunisia comes as a neat package, which means that for the enterprising traveller who wants to get away from the resorts, there is plenty of scope for exploration in an unspoilt environment. Distances are small, transport is fast and efficient, and the variety of things worth seeing would do justice to a country many times bigger – ruined Roman towns, holy Islamic cities, Berber strongholds, underground villages, desert oases and sand seas, and of course the beaches.

Facts about the Region

Prehistory

Although archaeological finds in the region date back to well over 200,000 years ago, it was not until around 3000 BC that human settlement became well established throughout the Maghreb (the Arab term for 'west' and now taken to include Morocco, Algeria and Tunisia). Prior to this, various groups of hunter-gatherers had existed in patches throughout the area, leaving behind traces such as the remarkable rock paintings in the Hoggar and Tassili ranges in the southern Sahara. These date from around 6000 BC and show mainly animals, many now extinct or found only much further to the south of the continent.

Around the 10th century BC a race of light skinned invaders arrived from western Asia and by the 2nd century BC they had spread right across the north of the continent. This race is known as Capsian Man, after finds made at ancient Capsa (present-day Gafsa) in Tunisia. The finds are mainly of stone axes and other implements which were more sophisticated than anything else in the area at the time. It is from these people that the Berbers as a race are believed to be descended.

Carthaginian Dominance

The Phoenicians first came cruising the North African coast around 1000 BC. They were looking for staging posts for their trade vessels making the journey from the eastern Mediterranean shores to the Atlantic coast of Spain, a major source of raw metals. On the whole these ports remained largely undeveloped and little was done to exploit the interior of the continent. By about the 7th century BC settlements had been established at Utica, Carthage, Hadrumetum (Sousse) and Hippo Diarrhytus (Bizerte) in Tunisia; Hippo Regius (Annaba), Saldae (Bejaia) and Cesare (formerly Iol) (Cherchell) in Algeria; and Tamuda (Tetouan), Lixus, Mogador (Essaouira) and Tingis (Tangier) in Morocco.

The foundation of Carthage is traditionally given as 814 BC and, in the traditional manner, it remained totally dependent on the mother culture in Tyre (modern-day Lebanon). Although the emergence of Carthage as an independent power came about partly as the power of Tyre was weakened by the Babylonians from the east, closer to the scene it was the Greeks in southern Italy who forced the Carthaginians to defend their outposts there as well as their trade routes in the Mediterranean.

By the 4th century BC, when Tyre had long been taken over by the Persians and had ceased to be actively involved in the Mediterranean, Carthage had become a major regional power controlling the coast all the way to the Atlantic in Morocco. The Carthaginians had developed the hinterland, particularly the fertile Cap Bon peninsula, and did their utmost to guard the trade routes. This led to a clash with the Greeks in Sicily in 396 BC in which the Carthaginians were defeated. In 310 BC, successful Greek raiders led by Agathocles, the ruler of Syracuse, landed in North Africa and left a trail of destruction for some three years before finally being defeated by Carthaginian mercenaries. It was also in Sicily that Carthaginian and Roman interests clashed, which led to the famous Punic Wars and, ultimately, the downfall of Carthage itself.

The first of the Punic Wars was a long-drawn-out affair lasting some 22 years from 263 to 241 BC. It saw the Carthaginians defeated in numerous naval battles, although they did defeat and capture the Roman general Regulus. Having lost their navy in a final skirmish, and being close to broke, they finally accepted Roman terms and gave up their hold in Sicily, followed soon by Sardinia and Corsica. They were soon to face troubles at home, however: there was no money in the coffers to pay the mercenaries,

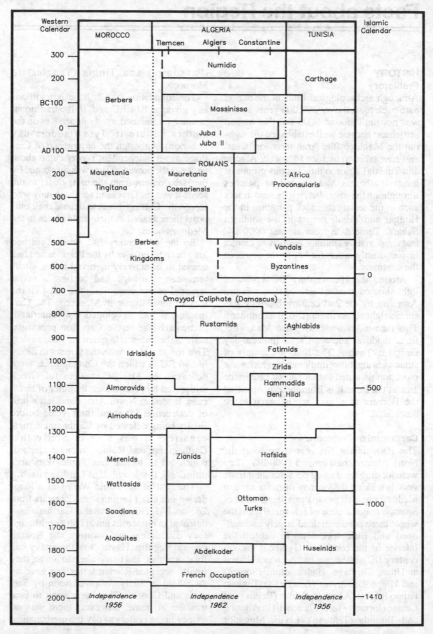

who promptly revolted and were only starved into submission after a prolonged period of brutality and a final stand-off. This came to be known as the Truceless War; it later inspired Gustave Flaubert's memorably bad novel *Salammbô*.

After the First Punic War, Carthage set about consolidating its position in Africa and establishing itself in Spain under the leadership of Hamilcar. His son, Hannibal, ignored Roman threats aimed at discouraging any Carthaginian expansion. At the age of 29 he led the now famous trek with elephants across the Alps, invading Italy in 218 BC and inflicting crushing defeats at Lake Trasimene (217) and Cannae (216). This became known as the Second Punic War. Rome seemed to be powerless. Only after Hannibal had been stranded in southern Italy for some seven years waiting for support were the Romans able to forget about the

Punic stele

threat of being overrun by him and his 300-odd elephants.

The Roman emperor Scipio retook Spain and landed in Africa at Utica in 204 BC. Carthage was teetering; Hannibal was recalled from Italy in 203 in an attempt to halt the Romans but was resoundingly beaten at Zama (near Le Kef) in 202. Carthage capitulated and paid an enormous price, giving up its fleet and overseas territories. Hannibal fled to Asia minor where he eventually committed suicide to avoid capture in 182.

For the next 50 or so years Carthage managed to hang on in North Africa despite incessant threats from the Numidian king Massinissa, who was based at Cirta Regia (Constantine in Algeria) and had previously allied himself with the invading Scipio. Although Carthage was no longer a major power, many Romans felt that as long as it existed, it was a potential threat. Among these people was Cato the Elder, an eminent statesman and writer who became well known for his vehement opposition to Carthage. So, in the Third Punic War, the Roman army once again landed in Utica, this time in 149 BC. For the next three years the Romans laid siege to Carthage, and it finally fell in 146. Such was the Roman thoroughness that the city was utterly destroyed and the site symbolically sprinkled with salt and damned forever.

Overall, the Carthaginians were great traders and merchants. However, they were never particularly adept at getting the right people on side or fostering any sort of loyalty, even at home among the Berbers who, although not reduced to outright slavery, were forced to pay them heavy tribute and supply them with troops. The armies of Carthage consisted for the most part of paid mercenaries.

The Carthaginians greatly influenced the area by introducing advanced agricultural techniques; this was to lead to the Berbers changing from a seminomadic life style to a much more settled one.

The Romans

Roman settlement in Africa was brought about not through a desire to expand but just as a matter of survival when waging war with Carthage. Once Carthage had fallen, the area was ruled by a governor for over a century. Then the emperor Augustus refounded Carthage in 44 BC and installed a proconsul there to govern the new colony, which indicates the increasing importance of the area.

The areas to the west were still controlled by the Numidian rulers. It was Massinissa's grandson, Jugurtha, who got them into hot water by massacring some Italian opponents who were helping a Roman ally, Adherbal, defend the town of Cirta Regia. Alarm bells rang in Rome, but Jugurtha managed to resist a couple of attempts to uproot him; however, he was finally betrayed by Bocchus I, a Mauretanian king, in 105. The boundaries of the Roman colony were extended and some settlers (mostly veterans) were given land in the area.

For a period of 50 or so years there was just a trickle of Roman settlers moving in of their own accord. Then state expansion went ahead in a big way, when the last of the formidable Numidian kings, Juba I, backed the wrong side in the Roman civil war and was defeated by Julius Caesar in 46 BC at Thapsus (near Mahdia). The new province of Africa Nova was amalgamated with the old and renamed Africa Proconsularis.

When the Mauretanian king Bocchus II died in 33 BC, Augustus installed Juba II, a renowned scholar married to Cleopatra Selene (the daughter of Mark Antony and Cleopatra), as king. After the murder of Juba II's son and successor Ptolemy, the western kingdom was split into the two provinces of Mauretania Caesariensis, which extended roughly from what is now Sétif to the Moroccan border, and Mauretania Tingitana from there to the Atlantic coast.

From here on until the decline of the Roman Empire in the 4th century AD, Roman North Africa proved to be a stable and integral part of the empire. Agriculture was all important, and by the 1st century AD, Africa was supplying more than 60% of the empire's grain requirements. Animal husbandry and fishing were also widely practised; from Africa too came the majority of the wild animals used in amphitheatre shows.

The period of Roman rule saw a great spread in urbanisation throughout Tunisia and the North African coast. Colonies of veterans and civilians were established all the way along the coast. Many indigenous communities prospered and their members were granted Roman citizenship; many upper-class Roman citizens were actually of African origin. Several went on to hold high office and in fact in the 3rd century they made up the majority of Roman senators. The African colonies also provided a line of African emperors, the most notable being Septimus Serverus. It was these wealthy citizens who donated the monumental public buildings which graced the Roman cities of the region.

Even in the 4th century there were signs that all was not well in North Africa. Landowners rebelled against increasingly harsh economic policies and there were tribal uprisings in Mauretania. Christianity spread rapidly, especially with the conversion of the emperor Constantine in 313 AD. It was hoped that this might give the empire's flagging fortunes a boost, but the Donatist controversy emerged in Carthage to spoil any such hopes. This controversy centred around a schism named after Donatus, a priest of Carthage, who split from the orthodox church. The movement gained popularity and, despite some banning and persecution, it is estimated that in the 4th century Donatists made up about 50% of all Christians. Following vigorous support for orthodoxy by St Augustine of Hippo Regius (Annaba, Algeria), laws were formulated at a conference in Carthage regarding religious unity which the Donatists were forced to obey, and the schism was healed.

The Vandals & the Byzantines

With Rome in a state of weakness, the Germanic Arian Vandals invaded from the north. They took Spain and wasted no time in crossing to Africa in 429 under the leadership of Gaiseric; by the end of the following year they were sitting pretty in Carthage. They confiscated large amounts of property and their exploitative policies only served to accelerate the general economic decline of the area. The Berbers became increasingly rebellious and, as the borders of the Vandal Empire receded, independent kingdoms became established, particularly in Mauretania and the west.

The Byzantine emperor Justinian, who was based in Istanbul, had revived the eastern empire and had similar plans for the lost western territories. His general Belisarius defeated the Vandals in 533; there followed a century of fairly ineffective Byzantine rule, which saw increasing Berber uprisings and the loss of territory under Byzantine control.

The Arabs

Following successes in Asia the Arabs looked westward for more areas to conquer, arriving in Tunisia in the middle of the 7th century. After numerous forays, Kairouan was founded by Aqbar ibn Nafi in 670; by 711 Islam had spread to the Atlantic coast despite some stubborn Berber resistance. One of the most famous instances was the defiant stand of the princess Kahina who, according to tradition, made her last stand in the amphitheatre at El Jem in Tunisia.

It seems that even once Islam became well established, the Berbers, although accepting the religion, were not to be pacified. A mass rebellion inspired by the Muslim heresy of Kharijism set out from Morocco in 740 and conquered the Omayyad armies west of Kairouan.

With the shift of the caliphate from the Omayyads in Damascus to the Abbasids in Baghdad, the Muslim west (North Africa and Spain) split from the east. Although there was a great deal of unrest, there finally emerged three major Islamic kingdoms: the Idrissids in Fès, the Rustamids in Tahart and the Aghlabids in Kairouan.

Idriss was a *sherif* (a descendant of the Prophet) who, due to persecution from the

Abbasids, fled to northern Morocco; here, on receiving support from the Berbers, he established the Idrissid kingdom. He and his son, Idriss II, founded the Islamic city of Fès (present-day Fès el-Bali) – a place of diverse influences from both Andalusia and Kairouan.

In 800 the Aghlabids were appointed by the caliph of Baghdad to promote religious orthodoxy in the Maghreb. This they did with some success, and the dynasty founded by Ibrahim ben Aghlab lasted until 909. This period saw the construction of the Great Mosque in Kairouan (their capital) and of the *ribats* (monastic forts) at Sousse and Mahdia.

The only people to embrace the Shiite sect of Islam to any great extent were the Berbers of the Kabylie region of northern Algeria. Led by Obeid Allah, who declared himself *Mahdi* (Chosen One) they defeated the Aghlabids and installed themselves in Kairouan. The Fatimids, as they were called, built their new capital, Mahdia, on a small, easily defended headland on the coast. Obeid Allah's great ambition, however, was to be the caliph of Islam; if he was ever to achieve this he needed a stronger base, so he set his sights on Egypt. After several unsuccessful attempts, Emir al-Mu'izz, a new Fatimid leader, defeated the Egyptians and founded Cairo in 972.

Before leaving for Egypt, however, the Fatimids entrusted their North African territory (by now known as Ifriqiya) to the rule of the Berber Zirids. They and their neighbours to the west, the Hammadids, were unable to resist pressure for religious orthodoxy from within and officially returned to Sunnism in open defiance of the Fatimids in Cairo. The reply from Cairo was devastating: the Beni Hilal and Beni Sulaim tribes of upper Egypt were ordered to invade the Maghreb, and North Africa was reduced to ruins. The Zirids managed to hang on to a few coastal cities until 1148, while the Hammadids retreated to the coastal town of Bejaia.

These invading tribes were the first major influx of Arabs into the Maghreb; until that time the vast majority of people had been of Berber descent.

Berber Empires

In the south of Morocco, the Sanhaja confederation of Berber Touareg tribes comprised the Lemtunas, the Gudalah and the Massufah. It was a Lemtuna chief, Yahia ibn Ibrahim, who made the pilgrimage to Mecca and brought back with him a Moroccan scholar, Ibn Yasin, to reform the rather slack Islam of the desert tribe. This was the start of the Almoravid dynasty. Under the leadership of Ibn Tachfin the Almoravids had overrun the region as far east as Algeria by 1069 and had founded their new capital city, Marrakesh. By the end of the 11th century the Almoravids had conquered the Christians in Spain in response to pleas for assistance by the Spanish Muslims.

They were rulers who won support by making popular decisions such as abolishing taxes not sanctioned by the Koran and by presenting themselves as liberators from corrupt rule. They didn't win everyone over, however. In fact in the High Atlas a young Berber, Mohammed ibn Tumart, feeling that the Almoravids were corrupting the oneness of God, went to study in Tunisia and there developed his doctrine of the divine unity. On his return to Morocco his followers adopted the name *al Muwahadin* ('those who affirm the unity of God', ie the Unitarians).

He retreated to the High Atlas and there preached and rallied support against the Almoravids. Although he died in 1130, by 1147 his successor, Abd el Moumen, had conquered the whole Maghreb and all Andalusia in the name of the Almohads. This marked the high point of Berber Islam and was the first and last time that the whole of the Maghreb would be a single Berber kingdom.

For over a century the Almohads were able to rule successfully. However, with increasing pressure from both the Christians in Spain and the Bedouin in the east, the caliph Mohammed an-Nasr was forced to split his government in two and appointed a member of the Hafsid family to govern in Tunisia. This was the beginning of the end for the Almohads. Before long, anarchy reigned; at the end of the 13th century the empire split into three kingdoms under the Hafsids in Tunisia and eastern Algeria, the weak Abd el Wadids based in Tlemcen in the centre and the powerful Merenids in Morocco.

The Hafsids managed to hang on until the middle of the 15th century, when Tunisia became the scene for rivalry between the Spanish and the Turks. In Morocco the Merenids prospered for a full century and a half before falling under the sway of the Wattasid dynasty of viziers in 1459. It was under the Merenids that Morocco really went through a golden age, which saw the establishment of Fès el-Jedid (Fès the New) and the building of fine *medersas* and mosques, many of which still stand today. The Abd el Wadids formed an alliance with Granada in an effort to survive, but fell to the greater power of the Merenids in 1352 and then to the Turks in 1555.

The Wattasids' biggest mistake was to allow Portuguese traders and raiders to settle at various points along the coast. It was ostensibly in opposition to the Portuguese that the Saadians rose from the Drâa oases in a holy war. In fact, they used the opportunity to conquer Morocco and set themselves up in Marrakesh.

The Saadian sultan Ahmed el Mansour made only one major raid – against the Muslims of the southern Sahara in 1591 – in the course of which he captured Timbuktu, from where he obtained slaves and massive wealth in gold. Marrakesh became a rich and decadent city and so was ripe for overthrow.

Enter the Alawi sherifs (the Alaouites), who took Fès in 1666 under the leadership of Moulay Rashid. He was assassinated in 1672 and, after a struggle for power between his sons, Moulay Ismail emerged on the top of the pile and was the last of the imperial rulers of any import. Although he built a splendid new capital at Meknès, he is probably best remembered for being extremely unpredictable and cruel; such was the state of the country, however, that ruthlessness was necessary to the survival of the dynasty.

Ibn Khaldoun

Ibn Khaldoun is, without any doubt, the greatest Arab historian who has ever lived. He developed the first philosophy of history which wasn't based on religion. Called the *Muqaddimah* (Introduction to History), it is regarded as a classic. The 20th-century historian Toynbee has called it 'a philosophy of history which is undoubtedly the greatest work of its kind that has ever yet been created by any mind in any time or place.' Ibn Khaldoun also wrote a definitive history of Muslim North Africa.

He was born in Tunisia in 1332 and spent the early years of his life there, but by the age of 23 he had become a secretary to the Sultan of Fès. After being imprisoned for two years on suspicion of being involved in a palace rebellion, Ibn Khaldoun moved to Granada, then Bejaia, Tlemcen, Biskra and Fès before ending up back in Granada.

In 1375 he gave up the world of business and politics and retired to the village of Frenda in Algeria where, under the protection of the local emir, he spent the next four years writing the *Muqaddimah*.

He spent the later years of his life as a professor at the great Islamic university, Al Ahzar, in Cairo, and was appointed chief judge by the Mamluk ruler, Sultan Barquq.

When the Mongol emperor Tamerlane invaded Syria in 1400, Ibn Khaldoun found himself in besieged Damascus with the new Egyptian sultan, Faraj. Tamerlane asked to meet Ibn Khaldoun who, after filling Tamerlane in on North Africa, was able to secure permission to return to Egypt, where he died in 1406.

The Ottoman Turks

In the early 16th century, the pirate Barbarossa (or Khair Ed Din) and his brother Aruj, sons of a Turk from the Greek island of Lesbos, were permitted to settle in Jerba (Tunisia). Aruj captured Algiers from the Spanish, but they retook the city and killed Aruj in 1518. Thereupon Khair Ed Din decided to ally himself with the Turks in order to protect his Barbary (from Barbarossa) possessions. The Ottomans jumped at the chance, conferred on him the title of *beylerbey* (governor) and sent him 6000 artillery men. In 1529 he managed to boot the Spaniards out of Algiers once again and five years later was in control of Tunis as well. However, the following year saw Spain's Charles V take that city and the

Hafsid ruler Moulay Hassan installed as a Spanish vassal.

There was a flurry of activity for a while as Spaniards and Turks fought for supremacy in North Africa. A Turkish pirate and associate of Barbarossa settled in Jerba and controlled Kairouan; Tunis was taken for the Turks in 1569 but it fell to Don John of Austria the next year. The Turks rallied and retook Tunis in 1574 and Tunisia, like Algeria, became an Ottoman province.

In both places piracy played a particularly important role, and the Barbary pirates were the scourge of Europe.

The two provinces had a complex system of government whereby the head man, the *pasha*, was assisted by a *dey*, who was the administrative chief, and a *bey*, who was in charge of the military. Power in fact resided more in the dey in Algeria and the bey in Tunisia, and the pashas were little more than figureheads. Deylical power declined in Algeria with the assassination of the last dey elected directly from Turkey in 1671.

In Tunisia, the beylical line carried on strongly until the beginning of the 19th century. Husein bin Ali, a Greek soldier from Crete, founded the last of the Tunisian dynasties, the Huseinids, when he had himself elected bey by the Turkish janissaries (the Ottoman army elite) in 1705.

Meanwhile, Back in Morocco...

After being enthroned, Moulay Ismail's first move was to raise an army of Black slaves and Arab troops to assert his authority at home and to repel the Christian invaders who had set themselves up at various places on the coast. In both pursuits he was only partially successful: the mountain tribes refused to be pacified, and he only managed to drive out the European Christians from Tangier, Larache and Mahdia, while reducing the Spanish presence to the small enclaves of Melilla and Ceuta. The unrest at home was due in no small measure to the high rates of taxation which he levied on the people in order to finance his lavish palaces and military undertakings.

After a 30-year period of decline following the death of Moulay Ismail in 1712, Morocco's fortunes revived somewhat under his grandson Sidi Mohammed. The latter kicked the Portuguese out of El Jadida and started trading with Europe. Again chaos followed, but order of a kind was restored by Moulay Sliman who ruled from 1792 to 1822. However, by this stage there was little left to govern and the British, French and Spanish were all looking to grab a bit of the action in North Africa.

The French

The French overran Algeria in 1830. Tunisia and Morocco were made protectorates in 1881 and 1912 respectively. The three countries' struggles for independence followed different paths, with Morocco getting it first in 1956, followed by Tunisia later the same year and Algeria (after a bitter and bloody six-year war) in 1962. The 19th-century colonial era, independence and modern history to the present day are dealt with in the individual country chapters.

RELIGION

Islam is the predominant religion in the Maghreb. Muslims are called to prayer five times a day and, no matter where you might be, there always seems to be a mosque within earshot.

In the early 7th century in Mecca, having received the word of Allah (God), Mohammed called on the people to turn away from pagan worship and submit to the one true God. His teachings appealed to the poorer levels of society and angered the wealthy merchant class. By 622 life had become sufficiently unpleasant to force Mohammed and his followers to migrate to Medina, an oasis town some 300 km to the north. This migration – the Hejira – marks the beginning of the Islamic calendar, year 1 AH or 622 AD. By 630 Mohammed had gained a sufficient following to return and take Mecca.

With seemingly unlimited zeal the followers of Mohammed spread the word, using force where necessary, and by 644 the Islamic state covered Syria, Persia, Mesopotamia, Egypt and North Africa; in following

decades its influence would extend from the Atlantic to the Indian Ocean.

Islam is the Arabic word for submission, and the duty of every Muslim is to submit themselves to Allah. This profession of faith (the *Shahada*) is the first of the Five Pillars of Islam, the five tenets in the Koran which guide Muslims in their daily life:

Shahada 'There is no God but Allah and Mohammed is his prophet' – this profession of faith is the fundamental tenet of Islam. It is to Islam what The Lord's Prayer is to Christianity, and it is often quoted (eg to greet the newborn and farewell the dead).

Salah is the call to prayer. Five times a day – at dawn, after midday, mid-afternoon, after sunset and nightfall – Muslims must face Mecca and recite the prescribed prayer.

Zakat was originally the act of giving alms to the poor and needy and was fixed at 2.5% of one's income. It has been developed by some modern states into an obligatory land tax which goes to help the poor.

Ramadan is the ninth month of the Muslim calendar when all Muslims must abstain from eating, drinking, smoking and sex from dawn to dusk. It commemorates the month when Mohammed had the Koran revealed to him; the purpose of the physical deprivation is to strengthen the will and forfeit the body to the spirit.

Hajj is the pilgrimage to Mecca, the holiest place in Islam. It is the duty of every Muslim who is fit and can afford it to make the pilgrimage at least once in their life. On the pilgrimage, the pilgrim *(hajji)* wears two plain white sheets and walks around the *kabbah*, the black stone in the centre of the mosque, seven times. Other ceremonies such as sacrificing an animal and shaving the pilgrim's head also take place.

According to Muslim belief, Allah is the same as the God worshipped by Christians and Jews. Adam, Abraham, Noah, Moses, David, Jacob, Joseph, Job and Jesus are all recognised as prophets by Islam. Jesus is not, however, recognised as the son of God. According to Islam, all these prophets partly received the word of God but only Mohammed received the complete revelation.

In its early days Islam suffered a major schism that divided the faith into two streams: the Sunnis (or Sunnites) and the Shiites. The prophet's son-in-law, Ali, became the fourth caliph following the murder of Mohammed's third successor, and he in turn was assassinated in 661 by the governor of Syria, who set himself up as caliph. The Sunnis, who comprise the majority of Muslims today, are followers of the succession from this caliph, while the Shiites follow the descendants of Ali.

Islam & the West

Unfortunately, Islam has been much maligned and misunderstood in the West in recent years. Any mention of it usually brings to mind one of two images: the 'barbarity' of some aspects of Islamic law such as flogging, stoning or the amputation of hands; or the so-called fanatics out to terrorise the West.

For most Muslims, however, Islam provides stability in a very unstable world. They are not aware that they are seen as a threat to the West; in fact they see the inroads that Western culture is making into their society as a threat to them.

While the West is offended by the anti-Western rhetoric of the radical minority, the Muslims see the West, especially its support of Israel, as a direct challenge to their struggle for Islamic rights and political independence.

The Western media condemn the political violence of 'fanatics' in Lebanon, while similar violence in Afghanistan was applauded because it was directed at the Soviet Union. Similarly, it is emphasised that political terrorism in the Middle East is motivated by religion, while in the coverage of similar events in Northern Ireland, for instance, the religious element barely rates a mention.

Just as the West receives a distorted and exaggerated view of Muslim society, so too are Western values distorted in Islamic societies. The glamour of the West has lured those able to embrace it (usually the young, the rich and the well educated); for others, the West is the bastion of moral decline and it is easier for them to reassert their faith in Islam than to seek what they cannot attain. Often what is being accepted or rejected by Muslims is a mishmash of Western values which may bear little relation to life in the West.

As long as these misunderstandings exist, the fact that Islam offers many people a code of religious and political behaviour that they can apply to their daily lives, making an often difficult life tolerable, will be overlooked. Instead, it'll be thought that the majority of Muslims, rather than a very small minority, are extremists, or radicals bent on revolution.

Islamic Customs

When a baby is born, the first words uttered to it are the call to prayer. A week later this is followed by a ceremony in which the baby's head is shaved and an animal is sacrificed.

The major event of a boy's childhood is circumcision, which normally takes place sometime between the ages of seven and 12.

Marriage ceremonies are colourful and noisy affairs which usually take place in summer. One of the customs is for all the males to get in their cars and drive around the streets in a convoy making as much noise as possible. The ceremony usually takes place in either the mosque or the home of the bride or groom. The partying goes on until the early hours of the morning, often until sunrise.

The death ceremony is simple: a burial service is held at the mosque and the body is then buried with the feet facing Mecca.

When Muslims pray, they must follow certain rituals. First they must wash their hands, arms, feet, head and neck in running water before praying; all mosques have a small area set aside for this purpose. If they are not in a mosque and there is no water available, clean sand suffices; and where there is no sand, they must just go through the motions of washing.

Then they must face Mecca (all mosques are oriented so that the *mihrab* (prayer niche) faces the right direction) and follow a set pattern of gestures and genuflections – photos of rows of Muslims kneeling in the direction of Mecca with their heads touching the ground are legion. You regularly see Muslims praying by the side of the road or in the street as well as in mosques.

In everyday life, Muslims are prohibited from drinking alcohol and eating pork (as the animal is considered unclean), and must refrain from gambling, fraud, usury, and slander.

ISLAMIC HOLIDAYS

As the Hejira (Islamic) calendar is 10 days shorter than the Gregorian (Western) calendar, Islamic holidays fall 10 days earlier each year. Islamic years are numbered from the Hejira – the flight of Mohammed to Medina in 622 AD. The actual dates given below may vary, as they depend upon the sighting of the moon.

Ras al Sana
New Year's Day, celebrated on 1 Moharram (1 August 1992, 22 July 1993).

Mulid al Nabi
The Prophet Mohammed's birthday, celebrated on 12 Rabi al-Awal (9 September 1992, 30 August 1993).

Ramadan
The ninth month of the Muslim calendar and the fourth pillar of Islam. During Ramadan pious Muslims who have reached puberty abstain from eating, drinking, smoking and sex during daylight hours for the whole month (6 March to 1 April 1992, 24 February to 22 March 1993). There are no public holidays, but it is difficult to deal with officialdom because of unusual opening hours.

These prohibitions don't apply to travellers, but it would be insensitive to openly flaunt them and you might very well generate anger if you do. If you must do any of these things during Ramadan then be discreet. Better still, do what the locals do, because travelling at this time of year isn't really the feat of endurance which the above might suggest.

While it's true that most Muslims become a little

frazzled by the end of the month, each evening when the sun goes down people pour onto the streets to eat, drink and promenade up and down. There's a feeling of relief and festivity in the air, and the cafés and restaurants stay open until very late. It's better to enter into the spirit of it than attempt to fight it. Why are you visiting the area if not to experience fully what it is like to live there?

Eid al Fitr
The end of the Ramadan fast, celebrated on 1 Shawwal (1 April 1992, 22 March 1993).This is one of the major celebrations in Islam and is marked by feasting and attendance at the mosque. It is also a time of animal sacrifice, and in the days leading up to the festival many doorways have a sheep tied up outside; the bleating of the hapless animals can be heard all over the place.

Eid al Adhah
The time when Muslims fulfil the fifth pillar of Islam – the pilgrimage to Mecca. This period is between 10 and 13 Zuul Hijja (11 July 1992, 1 July 1993). The day is also celebrated by those who are not fortunate enough to be in Mecca.

LANGUAGE

Arabic is the official language of all three Maghreb countries, though most travellers make little effort to learn any. Unfortunately North African Arabic is difficult to learn, as it differs from the more common and accessible Classical (or Levantine) Arabic (which comes from the Middle East).

Obviously, French is the most commonly used European language, and a basic knowledge of it is extremely helpful if you are going to be in Tunisia and, particularly, Algeria. Most people you come across will be bilingual in Arabic and French. Very few people speak more than a couple of words of English at most, so learn a bit of Arabic or French before you arrive if possible. At the very least you should learn the French words relevant to filling out visa applications and other forms, as these are nearly *always* in French (and Arabic).

In Morocco the situation is a little bit different: not only do the touts and guides speak French, Arabic and Berber, many of them are proficient in English, German and Spanish as well.

There are several Berber languages

spoken in the Maghreb. Tamahaq is the language of the Touareg, Kabyle comes from the Kabylie region of northern Algeria, while Rif and Tamazight are spoken in Morocco.

For a comprehensive guide to the Arabic spoken in the Maghreb, get hold of Lonely Planet's *Moroccan Arabic Phrasebook*, by Dan Bacon with Abdennabi Benchehda & Bichr Andjar.

Arabic Basics
Greetings & Civilities

hello	salaam wa laykoom
How are you?	labas?
goodbye	ma'salaama
please	afak
thank you	shukran

Useful Words & Phrases

I/you	ana/inta(i)
yes/no	eeyeh/la
left/right	leesar/leemon
why?	laish?
now	daba
Is there...?	wash kayn...?
big/small	kabeer/sigheer
open	mehlool

Time

What is the time?	shahal fessa'a
today	alyoum
tomorrow	ghedda
yesterday	lbareh
morning	fessbah
afternoon	felsheeya
day	nhar
on time	felweqt
when?	emta?
late	m'ettel

Days of the Week

Monday	nhar ithneen
Tuesday	nhar talata
Wednesday	nhar arbiya
Thursday	nhar khamees
Friday	nhar jumah
Saturday	nhar assabt
Sunday	nhar ahad

Months

The Islamic year has 12 lunar months and is 10 days shorter than the Western calendar, so important Muslim dates fall 10 days earlier each (Western) year.

When the Western calendar is being used, which is often the case, the French names are used. The Hejira months, however, have their own names:

1st	Moharram
2nd	Safar
3rd	Rabi al-Awal
4th	Rabi al-Akhir
5th	Jumada al-Awal
6th	Jumada al-Akhir
7th	Rajab
8th	Shaaban
9th	Ramadan
10th	Shawwal
11th	Zuul Qaada
12th	Zuul Hijja

Shopping

How much?	bish-hal?
too much	ghalee
Do you have...?	wash indkom...?

Getting Around

here	hona
where?	feen?
bus	ottobees
train	el masheena
boat	el baboor
bus station	lmehetta dyal ottobeesat
ticket	werqa

Around Town

bank	baanka
money	faloos
post office	bosta
stamps	tanber

Accommodation

hotel	ootail
youth hostel	ooberzh
campsite	moxeyyem
room	beet
bed	namooseeya
shower	doosh

key	*saroot*
roof	*staah*
full	*'amer*
blanket	*b'taneeya*
sheet	*eezar*
hot water	*mai sxoon*

Arabic Numbers

Arabic numerals are simple enough to learn and, unlike the written language, run from left to right.

0	•	*sifr*
1	١	*wahid*
2	٢	*ithneen or zoosh*
3	٣	*thalatha*
4	٤	*arba'a*
5	٥	*khamsa*
6	٦	*sitta*
7	٧	*sabah*
8	٨	*tamanya*
9	٩	*tissa*
10	١٠	*ashera*

11	*wahidash*
12	*ithna'ash*
13	*tamantahsh*
14	*arba'atahsh*
15	*khamstahsh*
16	*sit'tahsh*
17	*sabahtahsh*
18	*thamantahsh*
19	*tissa'atahsh*
20	*ashreen*
21	*wahid wa ashreen*
22	*ithneen wa ashreen*
30	*talateen*
40	*arba'een*
50	*khamseen*
60	*sit'teen*
70	*saba'een*
80	*tamaneen*
90	*tissa'een*
100	*mia*
101	*mia wa wahid*
125	*mia wa khamsa wa ashreen*
200	*miatayn*
300	*talata mia*

400	*arba'a mia*
1000	*alf*
2000	*alftayn*
3000	*talat talaf*
4000	*arba'a talaf*

French Basics

Greetings & Civilities

hello	*bonjour*
How are you?	*comment ça va?*
goodbye	*au revoir*
please	*s'il vous plaît*
thank you	*merci*

Useful Words & Phrases

yes/no	*oui/non*
I/you	*je/vous*
he/she	*il/elle*
why?	*pourquoi ?*
big/small	*grand/petit*
open/closed	*ouvert/fermé*
Is/are there...?	*il y a...?*

Passport/Document Details

surname	*nom*
given names	*prénoms*
date of birth	*date de naissance*
place of birth	*lieu de naissance*
date of issue	*date de déliverance*
date of expiry	*date d'expiration*
visa	*visa*
passport	*passeport*

Directions

left/right	*gauche/droite*
here/there	*ici/là*
next to	*à côté de*
opposite	*en face*
behind	*derrière*
which?	*quel ?*
where?	*où?*

Time

when?	*quand?*
now	*maintenant*
at what time?	*à quelle heure?*
what is the time?	*quelle heure est-il?*
today	*aujourd'hui*
tomorrow	*demain*

yesterday	*hier*
after	*après*
morning	*matin*
afternoon	*après-midi*
evening	*soir*
day/night	*jour/nuit*
week/year	*semaine/an*
quickly	*vite*
slowly	*lentement*

Shopping

How much?	*combien?*
more/less	*plus/moins*
too much	*trop*

Getting Around

bus	*car, autobus*
railway	*chemin de fer*
train	*train*
boat	*bâteau*
ferry	*bac*
station	*gare*
bus station	*gare routière*
ticket	*billet*
rucksack	*sac*
left-luggage office	*consigne*

Around Town

bank	*banque*
money	*argent*
post office	*poste*
stamps	*timbres*
parcel post office	*colis posteaux*

Accommodation

hotel	*hôtel*
youth hostel	*auberge de jeunesse*
room	*chambre, salle*
bed	*lit*
shower	*douche*
washbasin	*lavabo*
key	*clé*
roof	*terrasse*
full	*complet*
blanket	*couverture*
sheet	*drap*
hot water	*eau chaude*

French Numbers

1	*un*
2	*deux*
3	*trois*
4	*quatre*
5	*cinq*
6	*six*
7	*sept*
8	*huit*
9	*neuf*
10	*dix*
11	*onze*
12	*douze*
13	*treize*
14	*quatorze*
15	*quinze*
16	*seize*
17	*dix-sept*
18	*dix-huit*
19	*dix-neuf*
20	*vingt*
21	*vingt et un*
22	*vingt deux*
23	*vingt-trois*
30	*trente*
40	*quarante*
50	*cinquante*
60	*soixante*
70	*soixante-dix*
80	*quatre-vingts*
90	*quatre-vingt dix*
100	*cent*
101	*cent et un*
125	*cent vingt-cinq*
200	*deux cents*
300	*trois cents*
400	*quatre cents*
1000	*mille*
2000	*deux mille*
3000	*trois mille*
4000	*quatre mille*

Facts for the Visitor

HEALTH

Travel health depends on your predeparture preparations, your day-to-day health care while travelling and how you handle any medical problem or emergency that does develop. While the list of potential dangers can seem quite frightening, with a little luck, some basic precautions and adequate information few travellers experience more than upset stomachs.

Travel Health Guides

There are a number of books on travel health: *Staying Healthy in Asia, Africa & Latin America*, Volunteers in Asia. Probably the best all-round guide to carry, as it's compact but very detailed and well organised.

Travellers' Health, Dr Richard Dawood, Oxford University Press. Comprehensive, easy to read, authoritative and also highly recommended, although it's rather large to lug around.

Where There is No Doctor, David Werner, Hesperian Foundation. A very detailed guide intended for someone, like a Peace Corps worker, going to work in an undeveloped country, rather than for the average traveller.

Travel with Children, Maureen Wheeler, Lonely Planet Publications. Includes basic advice on travel health for younger children.

Predeparture Preparations

Health Insurance A travel insurance policy to cover theft, loss and medical problems is a wise idea. There are a wide variety of policies and your travel agent will have recommendations. The international student travel policies handled by STA or other student travel organisations are usually good value. Some policies offer lower and higher medical expenses options but the higher one is chiefly for countries like the USA which have extremely high medical costs. Check the small print:

1. Some policies specifically exclude 'dangerous activities' which can include motorcycling and even trekking. If such activities are on your agenda you don't want that sort of policy.

2. You may prefer a policy which pays doctors or hospitals direct rather than you having to pay on the spot and claim later. If you have to claim later make sure you keep all documentation. Some policies ask you to call back (reverse charges) to a centre in your home country where an immediate assessment of your problem is made.

3. Check if the policy covers ambulances or an emergency flight home. If you have to stretch out you will need two seats and somebody has to pay for them!

Another thing to check is that the policy covers any money you might lose by forfeiting a booked flight, and that it will cover the cost of flying both you and a travelling companion back home with you in the event of you becoming seriously ill.

Remember that if you have to make a claim against your insurance policy, then you will have to furnish proof of any money spent or any losses incurred. This will include a doctor's certificate (if you required medical assistance or hospitalisation) or a police report (in the case of loss or theft). In the event of loss or theft, they may also insist on you furnishing receipts for the articles you claim were lost or stolen.

Getting recompense for a cancelled flight or for medical expenses is usually quite straightforward, but the same cannot be said for loss or theft. This is frequently a can of worms. Even with all the requisite documentation, insurance companies are very reluctant to pay up without a major hassle. Their standard excuse is that you didn't exercise sufficient care to prevent the loss or theft or that you should have been aware of the hazards and not exposed your belongings to the attentions of a thief. In many cases, a company's reasons for refusing to pay are nothing short of pure, unadulterated sophistry, but that isn't the impression they give you when you buy a policy.

Medical Kit A small, straightforward medical kit is a wise thing to carry. A possible kit list includes:

1. Aspirin or Panadol – for pain or fever.
2. Antihistamine (such as Benadryl) – useful as a decongestant for colds, allergies, to ease the itch from insect bites or stings or to help prevent motion sickness.
3. Antibiotics – useful if you're travelling well off the beaten track, but they must be prescribed and you should carry the prescription with you.
4. Kaolin preparation (Pepto-Bismol), Imodium or Lomotil – for stomach upsets.
5. Rehydration mixture – for treatment of severe diarrhoea; this is particularly important if travelling with children.
6. Antiseptic, Mercurochrome and antibiotic powder or similar 'dry' spray – for cuts and grazes.
7. Calamine lotion – to ease irritation from bites or stings.
8. Bandages and Band-aids – for minor injuries.
9. Scissors, tweezers and a thermometer (note that mercury thermometers are prohibited by airlines).
10. Insect repellent, sunscreen, suntan lotion, chap stick and water purification tablets.

Ideally antibiotics should be administered only under medical supervision and should never be taken indiscriminately. Overuse of antibiotics can weaken your body's ability to deal with infections naturally and can reduce the drug's efficacy on a future occasion. Take only the recommended dose at the prescribed intervals and continue using the antibiotic for the prescribed period, even if the illness seems to be cured earlier. Antibiotics are quite specific to the infections they can treat: stop immediately if there are any serious reactions and don't use an antibiotic at all if you are unsure whether you have the correct one.

In the countries covered by this book, medicines are generally available over the counter without a prescription and are usually cheaper than in the West. In smaller places, however, you should check that the expiry date has not passed. You should also be aware that drugs which are no longer recommended, or have even been banned, in the West may still be being dispensed in some places.

Health Preparations Make sure you're healthy before you start travelling. If you are embarking on a long trip make sure your teeth are OK; there are lots of places where a visit to the dentist would be the last thing you'd want to do.

If you wear glasses take a spare pair and your prescription. Losing your glasses can be a real problem, although in many places you can get new spectacles made up quickly, cheaply and competently. This is especially so in the large cities of Morocco.

If you require a particular medication take an adequate supply, as it may not be available locally. Take the prescription, with the generic rather than the brand name (which may not be locally available), as it will make getting replacements easier. It's a wise idea to have the prescription with you to show you legally use the medication – it's surprising how often over-the-counter drugs from one place are illegal without a prescription, or even banned, in another.

Immunisations Vaccinations provide protection against diseases you might meet along the way. No vaccinations are required of visitors to Morocco. Algeria demands vaccination against yellow fever for visitors arriving within six days from an infected area or for those planning to cross the Sahara desert by road. Tunisia, likewise, demands yellow fever vaccinations for visitors arriving within six days from an infected area. Infants under one year old are exempt from this requirement in both countries.

Though not compulsory, vaccination against typhoid, cholera and polio is recommended for Morocco, Algeria and Tunisia, though the risks of contracting these diseases in any of these three countries is minimal. If you are intending to spend any amount of time off the beaten track in the Sahara desert where you will often be reliant on water from local wells, you would be advised to be vaccinated against hepatitis.

All vaccinations should be recorded on an International Health Certificate, which is available from your physician or government health department.

Plan ahead for getting your vaccinations: some of them require an initial shot followed by a booster, while some vaccinations should not be given together. Most travellers from Western countries will have been immunised against various diseases during childhood, but your doctor may still recommend booster shots against measles or polio, diseases which are still prevalent in many developing countries. The period of protection offered by vaccinations differs widely and some are contraindicated if you are pregnant.

In some countries immunisations are available from airport or government health centres. Travel agents or airline offices will tell you where. The possible list of vaccinations includes:

Cholera Some countries may require cholera vaccination if you are coming from an infected area, but protection is not very effective, only lasts six months and is contraindicated for pregnancy.

Tetanus & Diptheria Tetanus and Diptheria boosters are necessary every 10 years and protection is highly recommended.

Typhoid Protection lasts for three years and is useful if you are travelling for long in rural, tropical areas. You may get some side effects such as pain at the injection site, fever, headache and a general unwell feeling.

Infectious Hepatitis Gamma globulin is not a vaccination but a ready-made antibody which has proven very successful in reducing the chances of hepatitis infection. Because it may interfere with the development of immunity, it should not be given until at least 10 days after administration of the last vaccine needed; it should also be given as close as possible to departure because of its relatively short-lived protection period of six months.

Yellow Fever Protection lasts 10 years and is recommended where the disease is endemic, chiefly in Africa and South America. You usually have to go to a special yellow fever vaccination centre. Vaccination is contraindicated during pregnancy but if you must travel to a high-risk area it is probably advisable.

Basic Rules

Care in what you eat and drink is the most important health rule; stomach upsets are the most likely travel health problem but the majority of these upsets will be relatively minor. Don't become paranoid; trying the local food is part of the experience of travel after all.

Water The number one rule is *don't drink the water* and that includes ice. If you don't know for certain that the water is safe always assume the worst, though in most urban areas of Morocco and Tunisia tap water will be chlorinated. Reputable brands of bottled mineral water or soft drinks are generally fine and are readily available from even the smallest stores, although in some places bottles refilled with tap water are a possibility. Take care with fruit juice, particularly if water may have been added. Outside urban areas, milk should be treated with suspicion, as it is often unpasteurised. Boiled milk is fine if it is kept hygienically, and yoghurt is always good. Tea or coffee should also be OK, since the water should have been boiled.

Water Purification The simplest way of purifying water is to boil it thoroughly. Technically this means boiling for 10 minutes, something which happens very rarely! Remember that at high altitudes water boils at a lower temperature, so germs are less likely to be killed.

Simple filtering will not remove all dangerous organisms, so if you cannot boil water it should be treated chemically. Chlorine tablets (Puritabs, Steritabs or other brand names) will kill many, but not all, pathogens. Iodine is very effective in purifying water and is available in tablet form (such as Potable Aqua), but follow the directions carefully and remember that too much iodine can be harmful.

If you can't find tablets, tincture of iodine (2%) or iodine crystals can be used. Two drops of tincture of iodine per litre or quart of clear water is the recommended dosage; the treated water should be left to stand for 30 minutes before drinking. Iodine crystals can also be used to purify water but this is a more complicated process, as you have to first prepare a saturated iodine solution. Iodine loses its effectiveness if exposed to air or damp, so keep it in a tightly sealed container. Flavoured powder will disguise the taste of treated water and is a good idea if you are travelling with children.

Food Salads and fruit should be washed with purified water or peeled where possible. Ice cream is usually OK if it is a reputable brand name. Thoroughly cooked food is safest but not if it has been left to cool or if it has been reheated. Take care with shellfish or fish unless you know it's fresh and avoid undercooked meat. If a place looks clean and well run and if the vendor also looks clean and healthy, then the food is probably safe. In general, places that are packed with travellers or locals will be fine, while empty restaurants are questionable.

Nutrition If your food is poor or limited in availability, if you're travelling hard and fast and therefore missing meals, or if you simply lose your appetite, you can soon start to lose weight and place your health at risk.

Make sure your diet is well balanced. Eggs, beans, lentils and nuts are all safe ways to get protein. Fruit you can peel (bananas, oranges or mandarins for example) is always safe and a good source of vitamins. Try to eat plenty of grains – rice or bread. Remember that although food is generally safer if it is cooked well, overcooked food loses much of its nutritional value. If your diet isn't well

balanced or if your food intake is insufficient, it's a good idea to take vitamin and mineral pills.

If travelling during the summer months, make sure you drink enough – don't rely on feeling thirsty to indicate when you should drink. Not needing to urinate or very dark yellow urine is a danger sign. Always carry a water bottle with you on long trips. Excessive sweating can lead to loss of salt and muscle cramp. Salt tablets are not a good idea as a preventative, but in places where salt is not used much, adding salt to food can help.

Everyday Health A normal body temperature is 98.6°F or 37°C; more than 2°C higher is a 'high' fever. A normal adult pulse rate is 60 to 80 per minute (children 80 to 100, babies 100 to 140). You should know how to take a temperature and a pulse rate. As a general rule the pulse increases about 20 beats per minute for each °C rise in fever.

Respiration (breathing) rate is also an indicator of illness. Count the number of breaths per minute: between 12 and 20 is normal for adults and older children (up to 30 for younger children, 40 for babies). People with a high fever or serious respiratory illness (like pneumonia) breathe more quickly than normal. More than 40 shallow breaths a minute usually means pneumonia.

Many health problems can be avoided by taking care of yourself. Wash your hands frequently – it's quite easy to contaminate your own food. Clean your teeth with purified water rather than straight from the tap in out-of-the-way places. Avoid climatic extremes: keep out of the sun when it's hot, and dress warmly when it's cold. Avoid potential diseases by dressing sensibly. You can get worm infections through walking barefoot. You can avoid insect bites by covering bare skin when insects are around, by screening windows or beds or by using insect repellents. Seek local advice before swimming in the sea. If you're told there are jellyfish around, don't go in. Bilharzia is absent from the countries of the Maghreb.

Medical Problems & Treatment
Potential medical problems can be broken down into several areas. First there are the climatic and geographical considerations – problems caused by extremes of temperature, altitude or motion. Then there are diseases and illnesses caused by insanitation, insect bites or stings, and animal or human contact. Simple cuts, bites or scratches can also cause problems.

Self-diagnosis and treatment can be risky, so wherever possible seek qualified help. Although we do give treatment dosages in this section, they are for emergency use only. Medical advice should be sought before administering any drugs.

An embassy or consulate can usually recommend a good place to go for such advice. So can four and five-star hotels, although they often recommend doctors with five-star prices. (This is when that medical insurance really comes in useful!)

Climatic & Geographical Considerations
Sunburn In the tropics, the desert or at high altitude you can get sunburnt surprisingly quickly, even through cloud. Use a sunscreen and take extra care to cover areas which don't normally see sun – eg, your feet. A hat provides added protection, and you should also use zinc cream or some other barrier cream for your nose and lips. Calamine lotion is good for mild sunburn.

Prickly Heat Prickly heat is an itchy rash caused by excessive perspiration trapped under the skin. It usually strikes people who have just arrived in a hot climate and whose pores have not yet opened sufficiently to cope with greater sweating. Keeping cool but bathing often, using a mild talcum powder or even resorting to air-conditioning may help until you acclimatise.

Heat Exhaustion Dehydration or salt deficiency can cause heat exhaustion. Take time to acclimatise to high temperatures and make sure you drink sufficient liquids. Salt deficiency is characterised by fatigue, lethargy, headaches, giddiness and muscle cramps and

in this case salt tablets may help. Vomiting or diarrhoea can deplete your liquid and salt levels. Anhydrotic heat exhaustion, caused by an inability to sweat, is quite rare. Unlike the other forms of heat exhaustion, it is likely to strike people who have been in a hot climate for some time, rather than affecting newcomers.

Heat Stroke This serious, sometimes fatal, condition can occur if the body's heat-regulating mechanism breaks down and the body temperature rises to dangerous levels. Long, continuous periods of exposure to high temperatures can leave you vulnerable to heat stroke. You should avoid excessive alcohol or strenuous activity when you first arrive in a hot climate

The symptoms are feeling unwell, not sweating very much or at all and a high body temperature ($39°C$ to $41°C$). Where sweating has ceased, the skin becomes flushed and red. Severe, throbbing headaches and lack of coordination will also occur, and the sufferer may be confused or aggressive. Eventually the victim will become delirious or convulsive. Hospitalisation is essential, but meanwhile get patients out of the sun, remove their clothing, cover them with a wet sheet or towel and then fan continually.

Fungal Infections Hot weather fungal infections are most likely to occur on the scalp, between the toes or fingers (athlete's foot), in the groin (jock itch or crotch rot) and on the body (ringworm). You get ringworm (which is a fungal infection, not a worm) from infected animals or by walking on damp areas, like shower floors.

To prevent fungal infections wear loose, comfortable clothes, avoid artificial fibres, wash frequently and dry carefully. If you do get an infection, wash the infected area daily with a disinfectant or medicated soap and water, and rinse and dry well. Apply an antifungal powder like the widely available Tinaderm. Try to expose the infected area to air or sunlight as much as possible and wash all towels and underwear in hot water as well as changing them often.

Cold Too much cold is just as dangerous as too much heat, particularly if it leads to hypothermia. If you are trekking at high altitudes or simply taking a long bus trip over mountains, particularly at night, be prepared. In the mountains of the Maghreb you should always be prepared for cold, wet or windy conditions even if you're just out walking or hitching.

Hypothermia occurs when the body loses heat faster than it can produce it and the core temperature of the body falls. It is surprisingly easy to progress from very cold to dangerously cold due to a combination of wind, wet clothing, fatigue and hunger, even if the air temperature is above freezing. It is best to dress in layers; silk, wool and some of the new artificial fibres are all good insulating materials. A hat is important, as a lot of heat is lost through the head. A strong, waterproof outer layer is essential, as keeping dry is vital. Carry basic supplies, including food containing simple sugars to generate heat quickly and lots of fluid to drink.

Symptoms of hypothermia are exhaustion, numb skin (particularly toes and fingers), shivering, slurred speech, irrational or violent behaviour, lethargy, stumbling, dizzy spells, muscle cramps and violent bursts of energy. Irrationality may take the form of sufferers claiming they are warm and trying to take off their clothes.

To treat hypothermia, first get the patient out of the wind and/or rain, remove their clothing if it's wet and replace it with dry, warm clothing. Give them hot liquids – not alcohol – and some high-kilojoule, easily digestible food. This should be enough for the early stages of hypothermia, but if it has gone further it may be necessary to place victims in warm sleeping bags and get in with them. Do not rub patients, place them near a fire or remove their wet clothes in the wind. If possible, place a sufferer in a warm (not hot) bath.

Altitude Sickness Acute Mountain Sickness or AMS occurs at high altitude and can be fatal. The lack of oxygen at high altitudes affects most people to some extent. Take it easy at first, increase your liquid intake and eat well. Even with acclimatisation you may still have trouble adjusting – headaches, nausea, dizziness, a dry cough, insomnia, breathlessness and loss of appetite are all signs to heed. If you reach a high altitude by trekking, acclimatisation takes place gradually and you are less likely to be affected than if you fly straight there.

Mild altitude problems will generally abate after a day or so but if the symptoms persist or become worse the only treatment is to descend – even 500 metres can help. Breathlessness, a dry, irritative cough (which may progress to the production of pink, frothy sputum), severe headache, loss of appetite, nausea, and sometimes vomiting are all danger signs. Increasing tiredness, confusion, and lack of coordination and balance are real danger signs. Any of these symptoms individually, even just a persistent headache, can be a warning.

There is no hard and fast rule as to how high is too high: AMS has been fatal at altitudes of 3000 metres, although 3500 to 4500 metres is the usual range. It is always wise to sleep at a lower altitude than the greatest height reached during the day.

Motion Sickness Eating lightly before and during a trip will reduce the chances of motion sickness. If you are prone to motion sickness try to find a place that minimises disturbance – near the wing on aircraft, close to midships on boats, near the centre on buses. Fresh air usually helps; reading or cigarette smoke doesn't. Commercial anti-motion-sickness preparations, which can cause drowsiness, have to be taken before the trip commences; when you're feeling sick it's too late. Ginger is a natural preventative and is available in capsule form.

Diseases of Insanitation
Diarrhoea A change of water, food or climate can all cause the runs; diarrhoea caused by contaminated food or water is more serious. Despite all your precautions you may still have a bout of mild travellers'

diarrhoea but a few rushed toilet trips with no other symptoms is not indicative of a serious problem. Moderate diarrhoea, involving half-a-dozen loose movements in a day, is more of a nuisance. Dehydration is the main danger with diarrhoea, particularly for children, so fluid replenishment is the number one treatment. Weak black tea with a little sugar, soda water, or soft drinks allowed to go flat and diluted 50% with water are all good. With severe diarrhoea a rehydrating solution is necessary to replace minerals and salts. You should stick to a bland diet as you recover.

Lomotil or Imodium can be used to bring relief from the symptoms, although they do not actually cure the problem. Only use these drugs if absolutely necessary – eg, if you *must* travel. For children Imodium is preferable, but do not use these drugs if the patient has a high fever or is severely dehydrated.

Antibiotics can be very useful in treating severe diarrhoea, especially if it is accompanied by nausea, vomiting, stomach cramps or mild fever. Ampicillin, a broad spectrum penicillin, is usually recommended. Two capsules of 250 mg each taken four times a day is the recommended dose for an adult. Children aged between eight and 12 years should have half the adult dose; younger children should have half a capsule four times a day. It should be noted that if the patient is allergic to penicillin, ampicillin should not be administered.

Three days of treatment should be sufficient and an improvement should occur within 24 hours.

Giardia This intestinal parasite is present in contaminated water. The symptoms are stomach cramps, nausea, a bloated stomach, watery, foul-smelling diarrhoea and frequent gas. Giardia can appear up to several weeks after you have been exposed to the parasite. The symptoms may disappear for a few days and then return; this can go on for several weeks. Metronidazole, known as Flagyl, is the recommended drug, but it should only be taken under medical supervision. Antibiotics are of no use.

Dysentery This serious illness is caused by contaminated food or water and is characterised by severe diarrhoea, often with blood or mucus in the stool. There are two kinds of dysentery. Bacillary dysentery is characterised by a high fever and rapid development; headache, vomiting and stomach pains are also symptoms. It generally does not last longer than a week, but it is highly contagious.

Amoebic dysentery is more gradual in developing, has no fever or vomiting but is a more serious illness. It is not a self-limiting disease: it will persist until treated and can recur and cause long-term damage.

A stool test is necessary to diagnose which kind of dysentery you have, so you should seek medical help urgently. In case of an emergency, note that tetracycline is the prescribed treatment for bacillary dysentery, metronidazole for amoebic dysentery.

With tetracycline, the recommended adult dosage is one 250 mg capsule four times a day. Children aged between eight and 12 years should have half the adult dose; the dosage for younger children is one third of the adult dose. It's important to remember that tetracycline should be given to young children only if it's absolutely necessary and only for a short period; pregnant women should not take it after the fourth month of pregnancy.

With metronidazole, the recommended adult dosage is one 750 to 800 mg capsule three times daily for five days. Children aged between eight and 12 years should have half the adult dose; the dosage for younger children is one third of the adult dose.

Cholera Cholera vaccination is not very effective. However, outbreaks of cholera are generally widely reported, so you can avoid such problem areas. The disease is characterised by a sudden onset of acute diarrhoea with 'rice water' stools, vomiting, muscular cramps, and extreme weakness. You need medical help – but treat for dehydration, which can be extreme, and if there is an appreciable delay in getting to hospital, then begin taking tetracycline. See the Dysentery section for dosages and warnings.

Viral Gastroenteritis This is caused not by bacteria but, as the name suggests, by a virus. It is characterised by stomach cramps, diarrhoea, and sometimes by vomiting and/or a slight fever. All you can do is rest and drink lots of fluids.

Hepatitis Hepatitis A is the more common form of this disease and is spread by contaminated food or water. The first symptoms are fever, chills, headache, fatigue, feelings of weakness and aches and pains. This is followed by loss of appetite, nausea, vomiting, abdominal pain, dark urine, light-coloured faeces and jaundiced skin; the whites of the eyes may also turn yellow. In some cases there may just be a feeling of being unwell or tired, accompanied by loss of appetite, aches and pains and the jaundiced effect. You should seek medical advice, but in general there is not much you can do apart from resting, drinking lots of fluids, eating lightly and avoiding fatty foods. People who have had hepatitis must forego alcohol for six months after the illness, as hepatitis attacks the liver and it needs that amount of time to recover.

Hepatitis B, which used to be called serum hepatitis, is spread through sexual contact or through skin penetration – it could be transmitted via dirty needles or blood transfusions, for instance. Avoid having your ears pierced, tattoos done or injections where you have doubts about the sanitary conditions. The symptoms and treatment of type B are much the same as for type A, but gamma globulin as a prophylactic is effective against type A only.

Typhoid Typhoid fever is another gut infection that travels the faecal-oral route – ie, contaminated water and food are responsible. Vaccination against typhoid is not totally effective and it is one of the most dangerous infections, so medical help must be sought.

In its early stages typhoid resembles many other illnesses: sufferers may feel like they have a bad cold or flu on the way, as early symptoms are a headache, a sore throat, and a fever which rises a little each day until it is around 40°C or more. The victim's pulse is often slow relative to the degree of fever present and gets slower as the fever rises – unlike a normal fever where the pulse increases. There may also be vomiting, diarrhoea or constipation.

In the second week the high fever and slow pulse continue and a few pink spots may appear on the body; trembling, delirium, weakness, weight loss and dehydration are other symptoms. If there are no further complications, the fever and other symptoms will slowly go during the third week. However, you must get medical help before this because pneumonia (acute infection of the lungs) or peritonitis (burst appendix) are common complications, and because typhoid is very infectious.

The fever should be treated by keeping the victim cool, and dehydration should also be watched for. Chloramphenicol is the recommended antibiotic but there are fewer side effects with ampicillin. The adult dosage is two 250 mg capsules, four times a day. Children aged between eight and 12 years should have half the adult dose; younger children should have one third of the adult dose.

Patients who are allergic to penicillin should not be given ampicillin.

Worms These parasites are most common in rural, tropical areas and a stool test when you return home is not a bad idea. They can be present on unwashed vegetables or in undercooked meat and you can pick them up through your skin by walking in bare feet. Infestations may not show up for some time, and although they are generally not serious, if left untreated they can cause severe health problems. A stool test is necessary to pinpoint the problem and medication is often available over the counter.

Diseases Spread by People & Animals

Tetanus This potentially fatal disease is found in undeveloped tropical areas. It is difficult to treat but is preventable with immunisation. Tetanus occurs when a wound becomes infected by a germ which lives in the faeces of animals or people, so clean all cuts, punctures or animal bites. Tetanus is known as lockjaw, and the first symptom may be discomfort in swallowing, or stiffening of the jaw and neck; this is followed by painful convulsions of the jaw and whole body.

Rabies Rabies is found in many countries and is caused by a bite or scratch by an infected animal. Dogs are a noted carrier. Any bite or scratch from a mammal should be cleaned immediately and thoroughly. Scrub with soap and running water, and then clean with an alcohol solution. If there is any possibility that the animal is infected, medical help should be sought immediately. Even if the animal is not rabid, all bites should be treated seriously as they can become infected or can result in tetanus. A rabies vaccination is now available and should be considered if you are in a high-risk category – eg, if you intend to explore caves (bat bites could be dangerous) or work with animals.

Meningococcal Meningitis Sub-Saharan Africa is considered the 'meningitis belt' and the meningitis season falls at the time most people would be attempting the overland trip across the Sahara – the northern winter before the rains come. This very serious disease attacks the brain and can be fatal. A scattered, blotchy rash, fever, severe headache, sensitivity to light and neck stiffness which prevents forward bending of the head are the first symptoms. Death can occur within a few hours, so immediate treatment is important.

Treatment is large doses of penicillin given intravenously, or, if that is not possible, intramuscularly (ie, in the buttocks). Vaccination offers good protection for over a year, but you should also check for reports of current epidemics.

Tuberculosis Although this disease is widespread in many developing countries, it is not a serious risk to travellers. Young children are more susceptible than adults and vaccination is a sensible precaution for children under 12 travelling in endemic areas. TB is commonly spread by coughing or by unpasteurised dairy products from infected cows. Milk that has been boiled is safe to drink; the souring of milk to make yoghurt or cheese also kills the bacilli.

Diphtheria Diphtheria can be a skin infection or a more dangerous throat infection. It is spread by contaminated dust contacting the skin or by the inhalation of infected cough or sneeze droplets. Frequent washing and keeping the skin dry will help prevent skin infection. A vaccination is available to prevent the throat infection.

Sexually Transmitted Diseases Sexual contact with an infected sexual partner spreads these diseases. While abstinence is the only 100% preventative, using condoms is also effective. Gonorrhoea and syphilis are the most common of these diseases; sores and rashes on the genitals and pain when urinating are common symptoms. Symptoms may be less marked or not observed at all in women. Syphilis symptoms eventually disappear completely but the disease continues and can cause severe problems in later years. The treatment of gonorrhoea and syphilis is by antibiotics.

There are numerous other sexually transmitted diseases, for most of which effective treatment is available. However, there is no cure for herpes and there is also currently no cure for AIDS. The latter is common in parts of Africa though its incidence in the Maghreb is still relatively low. Using condoms is the most effective preventative.

AIDS can be spread through infected blood transfusions, so if you need a transfusion, enquiring whether the blood has been screened may be a matter of life or (a slow) death. It can also be spread by dirty needles – vaccinations, acupuncture and tattooing can potentially be as dangerous as intravenous drug use if the equipment is not clean. If you do need an injection it may be a good idea to buy a new syringe from a pharmacy and ask the doctor to use it.

Insect-Borne Diseases

Malaria This serious disease is spread by mosquito bites. If you are travelling in endemic areas it is extremely important to take malarial prophylactics. Symptoms include headaches, fever, chills and sweating which may subside and recur. Without treatment malaria can develop more serious, potentially fatal effects.

Antimalarial drugs do not actually prevent the disease but they do suppress its symptoms. Chloroquine is the usual malarial prophylactic for the Maghreb; a tablet is taken once a week for two weeks prior to arrival in the infected area and six weeks after you leave it.

Chloroquine is quite safe for general use: side effects are minimal and it can be taken by pregnant women. Maloprim can have rare but serious side effects if the weekly dose is exceeded and some doctors recommend a checkup after six months of continuous use. Fansidar, once used as a Chloroquine alternative, is no longer recommended as a prophylactic, as it can have dangerous side effects, but it may still be recommended as a treatment for malaria. Chloroquine is also used for malaria treatment but in larger doses than for prophylaxis. Doxycycline is another antimalarial for use where Chloroquine resistance is reported; it causes hypersensitivity to sunlight, so sunburn can be a problem.

Mosquitoes appear after dusk. Avoiding bites by covering bare skin and using an insect repellent will further reduce the risk of catching malaria. Insect screens on windows and mosquito nets on beds offer protection, as does burning a mosquito coil. Mosquitoes may be attracted by perfume, aftershave or certain colours. The risk of infection is higher in rural areas and during the wet season.

In general, it's safe to assume that the risk of catching malaria in the Maghreb is absolutely minimal between October and May and only slight during the rest of the year, except in the more remote southern provinces of Morocco and Algeria. Many travellers dispense with prophylaxis entirely during the winter months.

Cuts, Bites & Stings

Cuts & Scratches Skin punctures can easily become infected in hot climates and may be difficult to heal. Treat any cut with an antiseptic solution and Mercurochrome. Where possible avoid bandages and Band-aids, which can keep wounds wet.

Bites & Stings Bee and wasp stings are usually painful rather than dangerous. Calamine lotion will give relief or ice packs will reduce the pain and swelling. Scorpion stings are notoriously painful; be particularly careful in rural areas of the Maghreb when dressing in the morning by checking footwear and clothing, which is where scorpions often shelter.

Snakes To minimise your chances of being bitten always wear boots, socks and long trousers when walking through undergrowth where snakes may be present. Don't put your hands into holes and crevices, and be careful when collecting firewood.

Snake bites do not cause instantaneous death and antivenenes are usually available. Keep the victim calm and still, wrap the bitten limb tightly as you would for a sprained ankle, and then attach a splint to immobilise it. When you have done this, seek medical help, and if possible, bring the dead snake for identification. Don't attempt to catch the snake if there is even a remote possibility of being bitten again. Tourniquets and sucking out the poison are now comprehensively discredited.

Bedbugs & Lice Bedbugs live in various places, but particularly in dirty mattresses and bedding. Spots of blood on bedclothes or on the wall around the bed can be read as a suggestion to find another hotel. Bedbugs leave itchy bites in neat rows. Calamine lotion may help.

All lice cause itching and discomfort.

They make themselves at home in your hair (head lice), your clothing (body lice) or in your pubic hair (crabs). You catch lice through direct contact with infected people or by sharing combs, clothing and the like. Powder or shampoo treatment will kill the lice, and infected clothing should then be washed in very hot water.

Women's Health

Gynaecological Problems Poor diet, lowered resistance due to the use of antibiotics for stomach upsets, and even contraceptive pills can lead to vaginal infections when travelling in hot climates. Keeping the genital area clean, and wearing skirts or loose-fitting trousers and cotton underwear will help to prevent infections.

Yeast infections, characterised by a rash, itch and discharge, can be treated with a vinegar or even lemon-juice douche or with yoghurt. Nystatin suppositories are the usual medical prescription. Trichomonas is a more serious infection; symptoms are a discharge and a burning sensation when urinating. Male sexual partners must also be treated, and if a vinegar-water douche is not effective medical attention should be sought. Flagyl is the prescribed drug.

Pregnancy Most miscarriages occur during the first three months of pregnancy, so this is the most risky time to travel. The last three months should also be spent within reasonable distance of good medical care, as quite serious problems can develop at this time. Pregnant women should avoid all unnecessary medication, but vaccinations and malarial prophylactics should still be taken if necessary. Additional care should be taken to prevent illness and particular attention should be paid to diet and nutrition.

DANGERS & ANNOYANCES

Anyone with any amount of common sense is going to have no trouble travelling in the Maghreb. Sure, you do hear of people getting ripped off, drugged and ripped off, or worse, and these things *do* happen; but they also happen in London, Melbourne and New York, and probably a lot more frequently. If you exercise caution and discretion, you shouldn't have any problems.

As for less serious rip-offs and annoyances, often when relating their experiences in a country, people will tell you first about the *worst* things that happen. The fact that they were invited into someone's house to have a meal or were helped when lost may often be completely overshadowed by the fact that they got 'overcharged' $10 by a wily carpet dealer who's had years of practice at squeezing the absolute maximum out of a deal. This they will invariably describe as a 'rip-off'.

Hassles

Morocco has the worst reputation for this, but a distinction has to be made between enterprise (and even opportunism) and theft. They are not the same thing. It's more often than not the gullibility of tourists out to make a purchase or fix a price for someone's services which gives rise to such accusations, rather than the supposed dishonesty of Moroccans,

It's also very important to remember that unemployment, particularly among young people, is very high in Morocco. Guiding tourists is one way to make ends meet, though you can hardly describe it as lucrative. These sort of 'touts' you will meet in all the main tourist areas and you may even want to hire them occasionally. If you don't, then remember that 'no' is always interpreted, initially at least, as 'maybe'. If you continue to be firmly negative about wanting their services then most will leave it at that. Display the slightest ambivalence and you're lost. All manner of subterfuges will be used to get you to agree, including accusations of 'racism'. Stay firm, but on no account, get abusive. If you do, you may very well find yourself in trouble – as you would anywhere else in the world. Moroccans are proud people and abuse will be interpreted as the challenge which it undoubtedly is.

Theft

As far as theft itself goes, be sensible and

don't leave your belongings unattended except where you know they will be safe. Fools deserve to be ripped off. And don't leave your gear unattended for any length of time (even if not visible) in a locked vehicle. If you do, someone, somewhere will have noticed who is driving it and you'll return to find a window smashed and your belongings gone.

You should never, of course, leave money or passports lying around anywhere. The place to carry such things is in a pouch against your skin, around either your waist or your neck. Neither method is foolproof, but both give a good measure of security and make it much harder to lose things. Leather pouches are far more comfortable to have against your skin than nylon and the moisture from perspiration is far less of a problem. Cameras are also best kept with you or left at your hotel reception, though I've left my own in many a hotel room and never had any problems.

Having said that, I find Moroccans, on the whole, to be a remarkably honest people, interested to strike up conversations with you, and generally helpful. Persistent they certainly are and superb negotiators at business, but 'dishonest' they are not.

The people in Algeria and Tunisia, particularly in Algeria where they see so few tourists, are some of the most hospitable you'll find anywhere. Getting invited into a house for a meal is not uncommon and people will invariably go out of their way to help.

Physical Violence

Violence against tourists is extremely rare and only in certain remote areas of the Rif Mountains is there a possibility of encountering this. It's suggested you avoid the area around Ketama in this respect.

The Evil Weed

Morocco is famous (or infamous – depending on your point of view) for its cannabis; Ketama became a household word among dope freaks in the 1970s. Dope is, however, illegal in Morocco, although judging from the number of people who smoke it, you wouldn't know that. Since alcohol is prohibited for strict Muslims, cannabis is the most widely used recreational drug and is available just about everywhere.

As a tourist, however, you need to be very discreet about using it. Blatant public use is going to land you in a heap of trouble involving possible jail. If you're a user, don't jump at the first offer. Take your time. Be especially careful in the north around Tetouan and Ketama. There's plenty of money to be made selling you cannabis and then shopping you to the police. Many travellers have learnt this to their cost.

The quality of dope in Morocco is generally good and the cost very modest in comparison with Europe.

Ever since the northern European dealers descended upon Ketama in the early 1970s, the Rif has acquired a reputation for hassles. If you don't want those hassles, then avoid the area like the plague. Chechaouen is still sweet but Tetouan and Ketama can be very bad news. We get letters all the time from travellers who have been relentlessly pursued by hustlers wanting to sell them vast quantities of the stuff.

In Tunisia and Algeria there is not the tradition of smoking that there is in Morocco. Penalties are much stiffer and the law is enforced with much less flexibility. If you bring any dope with you from Morocco and get caught, the consequences could be disastrous. Algerian officials at the Moroccan border are looking specifically for two things – drugs and dinar. If they find the latter, it will be confiscated, if they find the former, you are in deep shit.

WOMEN TRAVELLERS

Women travellers in the Maghreb face an additional problem – sexual harassment. It *is* extremely constant, particularly in Algeria, the most conservative of the three countries. The harassment we're talking about may be limited to being stared at in ways that leave little to the imagination, or it may take other forms such as being followed or touched. Such harassment is uncomfortable and annoying, but it probably won't go any further than this.

If you're a woman travelling solo, in Morocco you'll find that you have local men as constant companions, in Algeria you'll get stared at and in Tunisia they won't exactly ignore you, but things are much more relaxed.

Even women travelling with a male companion are not immune: it's quite possible that an Arab man will ask the male in a Western couple if he can take liberties with his partner! It's pretty bizarre and indeed unfortunate that Arab men (especially Muslims) have this stereotyped idea that Western women are promiscuous and ready to jump into bed at the drop of a hat. Western films and TV soapies only help to reinforce these ideas.

Despite all this, women are travelling, both alone and in pairs, throughout the Maghreb and are still having a great time. There are certain things you can do to minimise the friction. Modest dress is the first and most obvious thing. By tradition, Muslims are modest people when it comes to dress and Westerners who travel in a Muslim country with no regard for the local customs are asking for trouble.

Women should wear tops that keep at least the shoulders covered, and dresses or pants which come at least to the knee. A scarf is not necessary but adds greatly to your respectability. A wedding ring too will increase your respectability in North African eyes. Dress modestly at all times but particularly in smaller towns, which are likely to be more conservative than the cities. The only exceptions to this general rule are the chic areas of Casablanca and Rabat where the more revealing and sexually suggestive Parisian fashions appear to have taken off in a big way amongst young women. Tight miniskirts are not at all unusual in these places and the trend appears to be spreading to the *ville nouvelle* areas of other major Moroccan towns and cities. Finally, you should avoid eye contact with a man you don't know, and ignore any rude remarks and act as if you didn't hear them. Women travelling alone or in pairs

should experience few problems if they follow these tips.

The best way for female travellers to meet and talk to local women is to go to a *hammam* (bathhouse). Every town has one, and if there is not one that is exclusively for women there are times set aside each day for women and men.

TRAVELLING WITH CHILDREN

Geoff and Hyung Pun took along their 1½-year-old son on the last research trip to Morocco and have a few observations and comments which might be useful for others contemplating the same thing.

The three biggest considerations with children of this age are finding suitable food and bathroom facilities and keeping them amused on long journeys. Ours had been off the breast and onto solid food for about half a year before arrival in the Maghreb, and we found he was quite happy eating the same food that we ate. He had no problems with diarrhoea, though we were pretty fastidious about what we fed him – street-stall food, for example, was essentially out. So it came down to soups, tajines (stews), couscous (a semolina dish), fried or grilled fish, omelettes/boiled eggs and fruit (washed and peeled, of course). We even fed him (unwashed) dates without mishap. For liquids, we bought a large tin of proprietary powdered baby milk from a supermarket in Casablanca and mixed it up with bottled mineral water. Where it wasn't possible to do this – on long journeys, for example – he seemed quite happy with neat mineral water.

As for nappies (diapers), it was obviously impractical to take along more than half a dozen of the washable variety if only because of the logistics of where to put them when they were full of crud and where to hang them to dry once washed. Disposable nappies, despite their environmentally unfriendly nature, were the only practical solution. These we found were readily available in general stores and supermarkets all over Morocco but they certainly weren't cheap – Dr 38 to Dr 40 (about US$4.50) for a packet of 10. As far as brands went, the only ones worth buying were Babidou. None of the others were worth considering, though we had to use them on occasion.

Keeping him and his clothes clean was what constrained us most. Though we did stay in quite a few hotels with shared bathroom facilities, we found this generally impractical and so most of the time stayed in hotels with private showers and hot water.

The biggest plus about travelling in Morocco with a child was the attitude of the Moroccans themselves – they just love children. They have all the time in the world for them, and go out of their way to help you. Having a child with you is an instant introduction to just about any Moroccan – man or woman. Hotels do their best to give you a room with an extra bed or provide a cot, usually at no extra cost. And no-one cares what they get up to. Kids will be kids and you'll never encounter a disapproving glance or comment even when they're bawling their head off. The only thing I was never able to find was a child restraint chair in hired cars.

FOOD

The Maghreb ought to be an area of gastronomic delights given the peoples and civilisations which have come and gone over the centuries here. That's true but, with some notable exceptions, only if you're prepared to pay over the odds for a meal. You can still eat well and cheaply but the lack of variety at this level can become tedious after a while. The places where you get the biggest variety and the best quality food are the places with the most tourists, so in parts of Tunisia and Morocco the choices are good.

The most basic local eateries barely warrant being called restaurants. These places will usually have just one or two dishes, and will often run out by early evening. As might be expected, the further south you go, the more basic the restaurants become and the less variety they have. Vegetables become rarer and the emphasis is on meat and starch, so soups and salads disappear and basically what you get is meat and couscous, spaghetti or bread.

In the larger towns there are restaurants which have a set menu, which will get you soup, salad, main course and dessert, though in southern Algeria such places are often out of the range of the budget traveller.

If you're on a strict budget and get tired of eating in basic restaurants, you may well have to splurge occasionally and go to a decent restaurant. This won't always guarantee you a better or more tasty meal but you might welcome the change. In Morocco and Tunisia, for example, there are quite a few such places to splurge, though you'll be looking at around US$8 to US$10 per person in the more modest restaurants and up to US$35 to US$40 in the very best.

The French influence is still very noticeable. Except in Morocco where traditionally baked bread is still widely available, 'French sticks' are virtually the only bread eaten, and every town has at least one *patisserie* which sells all manner of sticky cakes and often has a coffee bar at the back. Menus, where they are supplied, are always in French and/or Arabic. Croissants are available everywhere and, with a cup of coffee, make a reasonable breakfast.

The food is fairly uniform throughout the Maghreb, but there are a few specialities which are served in one country only.

Snacks

Tunisia The great invention here is the *casse-croûte*. It consists of a large hunk of French bread which is stuffed with any or all of the following: olives, tuna, egg, sausage, chips and oil; it always includes a generous slathering of *harissa*, a spicy chilli sauce which varies in strength but is often hot enough to bring tears to your eyes and have you reaching for a drink.

Many patisseries, particularly in Tunis, serve individual pizzas and savoury pastries. These are very rich and filling and can be a meal in themselves.

Morocco One of the biggest growth industries here is the proliferation of kebab and kefta fast-food outlets. These parallel the growth of Greek doner kebab and souvlaki outlets in the West during the 1970s and 1980s. What you get is a serving of barbecued kebab or kefta wrapped in bread with or without salad, and a dose of hot sauce plus chips. They're very popular, essentially a meal in themselves, and cost as little as US$1.

Soups & Starters

Soups (chorba, or harira in Morocco) are usually tasty and filling. Based on a meat stock, they have macaroni and vegetables as the other main ingredients. Any flavours these might impart are often cunningly concealed by a hefty dose of pepper or chilli. Moroccan harira is far and away the best and is based on lentils. With a chunk of bread, it makes a pretty good meal in itself. It's usually only available in the late afternoon/early evening.

Salad is a great catch-all that can include anything from a limp piece of lettuce and a tired tomato right through to a tasty mix of chopped vegetables and herbs, olives, anchovies, tuna and spicy dressing. Unfortunately it's the former that you are most likely to encounter in cheap restaurants. Coriander leaves and parsley are the most common herbal ingredients. It is generally unwise to eat salads if you have just arrived from Europe, as the ingredients are unlikely to have been washed thoroughly, if at all. After a while, when your stomach has had a chance to acclimatise, you should be able to handle them without any problem.

Tunisia One speciality (peculiarity?) here is the brik à l'oeuf. This is a strange creature: it consists of a thin crisp pastry which is fried like a pancake, has an egg dropped in the middle and is folded in half. The result varies from a horrible greasy mess to a tasty snack. It should be tried at least once, and if the first one you get doesn't impress you try one more at a later date; a good one is really excellent.

Whether you've got a good or bad brik they are awkward things to eat, as the egg invariably oozes everywhere, the pastry cracks into dozens of pieces and you get oil over everything.

Another delight in Tunisia (and to a certain extent Algeria) is shakshuka. This is rather like a thick vegetable stew and consists of onions, peppers, tomatoes and egg all fried up in a spicy tomato sauce; it's usually excellent.

Main Courses

Most of the dishes are starch based, which usually means couscous, spaghetti or rice.

Couscous is the staple food of the region and is an enormous bowl of steamed semolina topped with a meat and vegetable sauce. It is available virtually everywhere and varies tremendously. It's actually the sauce which varies and can make the difference between a good meal and a plate of dry couscous not unlike sawdust. Fortunately there is enough variety most of the time for you not to have to live off it. Having said that, almost every Moroccan will assure you, in no uncertain terms, that the couscous prepared in private homes is a totally different species from that served in restaurants and that it's absolutely delicious. This may well be true, and it's what you will be offered if you're invited for dinner.

Regarding couscous ordered at a restaurant, if you want to cut costs and aren't too bothered about not eating meat, ask how much the dishes are without meat (sans viande), as you still get the rest of the sauce and the price drops significantly.

Chicken has taken off in a big way right across North Africa and is often the only meat available. It is usually roasted and served with chips, which, unless you ask specifically, are often cold. There's something about cold chips which really make you feel as though you've hit rock bottom.

Brochettes are one of the most basic meals and are available just about everywhere. They're essentially kebabs – pieces of meat on a skewer barbecued over hot coals. A chilli sauce is usually provided, though not always.

Seafood is big in the coastal regions of Tunisia and Morocco and there are many restaurants which specialise in it. Some do nothing else. At the better restaurants in

Tunisia, a tray of fresh fish is usually brought to your table and you select what you want. Elsewhere you take your chances, but it is rare to get one that doesn't taste fine.

In Moroccan coastal towns, you can be sure that the seafood is fresh; also, the culinary traditions of Portugal and Spain have long been assimilated into the art of preparing dishes so you're looking at something far more exotic than just plain fish and chips (though, if that's what you want, you can get that too).

Morocco Other than couscous, the big dish here is *tajine*. This is basically a meat and vegetable stew cooked very slowly in an earthenware dish over hot coals. The meat used is usually lamb, goat or chicken, but you can also find beef or rabbit.

The vegetables usually cooked with the meat are potatoes, onions, carrot and squash, but it's not unusual for fruits such as prunes, apricots and raisins to be included, and you would definitely expect this in a better class restaurant. Tajines vary, depending on the restaurant, from being absolutely delicious to almost tasteless.

The other dish worth trying, although not widely available, is *pastilla (b'stila* in Arabic). It is a delicious and incredibly rich pigeon pie, which is made in layered *ouarka* pastry (like filo pastry) with nuts and spices and is then coated with sugar and baked. It is common in Fès, where you just get a chunk

from a stall, but it is also served in some restaurants in other cities.

Desserts
Desserts and sweets are more often available from patisseries than in restaurants, but things such as *ordma oaramol*, cakes and fruit are often served in the better restaurants.

Fruit
In season there's a great variety of fruit available, particularly in the north of Tunisia, including apples, pears, peaches, grapes, melons, watermelons, figs, dates, cactus fruit and pomegranate. In Morocco, the usual fruits are mandarins, grapes, dates and watermelons.

English	Arabic	French
Soup		
soup	*chorba*	*potage*
spicy lentil soup	*harira*	

Salads & Vegetables

English	Arabic	French
carrots	*gazar*	*carottes*
chips		*frites*
cucumber	*khiyaar*	*concombre*
green beans	*fasooliya*	*haricots verts*
haricot beans		*haricots blancs*
lentils	*'aads*	*lentilles*
lettuce	*kahss*	*salade*
mixed salad		*salade tunisienne/marocaine*
olives	*zitoun*	*olives*
onions	*bassal*	*oignons*
peas	*baseela*	*petits pois*
potatoes	*batatas*	*pommes de terre*
tomatoes	*tamatin*	*tomates*

Meat

English	Arabic	French
camel	*lahma gamil*	*chameau*
chicken	*farooj*	*poulet*
kidneys	*kelawwi*	*rognons*
lamb	*lahma danee*	*agneau*
liver		*foie*
meat	*al-luhum*	*viande*

Fruit

apple	toofa	pomme
apricot	meesh-meesh	abricot
banana	mohz	banane
dates	tamr	dattes
figs	tiin	figues
fruit	fawaka	fruits
grapes	einab	raisins
orange	burtuaan	orange
pomegranate	ruman	grenade
watermelon	bateeq	pastèque

Miscellaneous

bread	khobz	pain
butter	zibna	beurre
cheese	gibna	fromage
eggs	bayd	oeufs
oil	zit	huile
pepper	filfil	poivre
salt	mehal	sel
sugar	sukur	sucre
yoghurt	labanee	yaourt

DRINKS
Tea & Coffee

Tea and coffee are the national obsessions in all three countries and are drunk in copious quantities. They are also extremely strong and, when your body is not used to them, drinking either in the evening is usually a recipe for a sleepless night.

The main pastime for men is sipping tea or coffee in a café while reading the paper, chatting or playing cards or backgammon. Every town has at least one café; they are the social centres and are a good place to meet the local men. Local women don't frequent these places but Western women can enter. Often the tables and chairs are set out on the footpath, and are a good spot to sit and watch the world go by.

Tea is served in large glasses and is heavily sweetened. In Morocco it also comes complete with a substantial sprig of mint. Indeed, mint tea is almost synonymous with Morocco. It's what you will be served (free of charge and without any obligation to buy) whenever you get down to the serious business of negotiation in any shop in a *souk* (market).

Coffee is always strong and is served the French way: small black or large white. Sugar is optional and served in cubes on your saucer. A glass of water is invariably served at the same time.

Soft Drinks

Morocco and Tunisia both have those pillars of multinationalism – Coca-Cola and Pepsi. Algeria makes its own and, for the most part, these are quite OK, although it does depend on the quality of the water used. In places like In Salah, where the ground water is very salty, the drinks are quite unpalatable.

Alcohol

Despite the fact that Islam prohibits the consumption of alcohol, it is widely drunk and readily available.

In Algeria and Tunisia there are few bars and most of the drinking goes on in the hotels, usually the more expensive places. The few bars in Tunis are hard-drinking places with a sleazy, smoky atmosphere.

Morocco is far more liberal in its attitudes to alcohol and you'll have no problem finding a bar or a shop selling beer, wines and spirits (often part of a general store). Likewise, almost all the better class of hotels and restaurants will either have a bar and/or be licensed to sell it though you'll pay considerably more for it in these places. The only problem with most bars in Morocco, outside such cosmopolitan places as Casablanca, Rabat and Tangier, is that the clientele is all male. If it's mixed company you are looking for then you can largely forget them. The only place you'll find this is in a discotheque and you'll pay an arm and a leg for a drink here, though the entry fee (usually Dr 50), frequently includes the first drink.

Beer All three countries brew their own beer. In Tunisia, Celtia is a very weak and watery drop which really isn't that flash, no matter how many times you drink it.

Algerian beer comes in an anonymous bottle and is similar to what you get in Tunisia. The biggest problem is that about

one in four bottles are dead flat, and the usual custom is to drink it nevertheless.

Morocco devotes much more loving care to the amber nectar and its favourite brew, Flag Speciale, is comparable with the world's best. Flag is actually brewed in most of the francophone West African countries. The other beer on sale here is Stork, which is not quite as good but definitely palatable. A beer costs around US$1 in a public bar; more in a hotel bar.

Wine Connoisseurs of premium wines from Europe, California or Australia may well tell you that North African wines don't quite measure up to the standards of those countries, but, for most people, they'd be splitting hairs. Moroccan wines, in particular, have come a long way over the last few years. Try a few and judge for yourself. I certainly found a few reds which compared very favourably with those from the more established wine-producing areas. Prices vary from around US$3.50 to US$10 a bottle if bought from a store, though if you buy them in a restaurant you'll be paying up to double and triple this price.

WHAT TO BRING

Bring the minimum. When you have gathered all the stuff you think you're going to need, throw half of it out and you'll probably be close to a sensible amount. There is nothing worse than having to lug loads of excess stuff around, but once you've brought something it is much harder to throw it away and the longer you carry it the less inclined you are to throw it out. Unless it's absolutely essential, *leave it at home*!

A rucksack is far more practical than an overnight bag and is much more likely to stand up to the rigours of African travel. It is worth paying for a good quality one, as a cheap one is a liability: buckles and straps start falling off and before long all you have is a worthless bit of junk.

What type of pack you take is largely a matter of personal preference. I find that the internal-frame types are much less hassle than those with an external frame, the ends of which constantly get snagged on things. Berghaus, Lowe and Karrimor are three recommended brands. One of the best stockists in London is the YHA Adventure Centre, 14 Southampton St, London WC2.

A sleeping bag and closed-cell foam mat are essential for sleeping out in the Sahara, but if your route is confined to the north they are unnecessary. A youth-hostel-type sleeping sheet can be handy to keep the mosquitoes off when it is too hot to use a sleeping bag. In southern Algeria the climate is such that sleeping out is a viable option for much of the year, so a sleeping bag is invaluable. It also comes in handy to pad hard seats on long bus or truck journeys. If you are doing any sleeping out, a waterproof groundsheet is also well worth carrying.

Depending on your itinerary and the season, you are going to need clothes for all climates. Although much of this area is desert and the desert is supposed to be hot, many people underestimate the severity of the colder months right across the north of the Maghreb. Snow is common, and bitterly cold winds can make life unbearable if you don't have a decent sweater to keep out the cold. A windproof and waterproof knee-length jacket also comes in handy, even if only to keep your pack dry.

Clothes must not only be practical but should also take local sensibilities into account. This is Muslim territory and large areas of exposed flesh are certainly frowned on. Women especially need to be careful about what they wear (particularly when you take a look at the women in central Algeria, who have everything covered except for one eye peering through a gap in the cloth). Tops should cover at least the shoulders, and skirts or pants should reach at least to the knee. Lightweight fabrics are often see-through, so be aware of that also. For men, long pants are preferable; if you really want to wear shorts this won't be a problem, even though some of the locals will think that you are so dense you have forgotten to put your pants on and are wandering around in your underwear!

Some people take a stove and tent. If you are heading further south this is worth considering, but for just the Maghreb the extra weight and inconvenience aren't justifiable.

Overlooked by many people, but absolutely indispensable, is a good pair of sunglasses. The glare in the desert is not only uncomfortable but can damage your eyes. A hat which shades your face and neck is also worth considering, but then you have the inconvenience of trying to pack it when you are not using it. Straw hats are as good as any. For my money, a water bottle is worth its weight in gold, despite the inconvenience of having an extra piece of luggage. It needs to be unbreakable, have a good seal, a carry-strap and, preferably, be insulated. Anything which holds less than a litre is not worth bothering with.

Most important are the little things which take up little room but make life just that little bit more comfortable: a Swiss Army knife, a small sewing kit (including a few metres of fishing line and a big needle for emergency rucksack surgery), contraceptives, tampons, a few metres of nylon cord (what are you going to use for a washing line?), and half a tennis ball (which makes a good fits-all washbasin plug).

Most toiletries – soap, shampoo, toothpaste, toilet paper, washing powder – are available all over Tunisia and Morocco, though tampons can usually only be found in supermarkets. In Algeria, toilet paper is not hard to find, but the others can be difficult to obtain and even then the quality may not be all that good, so you need to carry some supplies.

Getting There & Away

The Maghreb is a popular place for a holiday, mainly because it is so easily accessible from Europe. Not only are there regular air connections with Europe from over a dozen North African cities, there is also a choice of at least as many ferry routes from Spain, France and Italy.

Since many travellers visit the Maghreb as part of a longer journey through Africa, often with a vehicle, these ferries are popular (especially with the overland route through Sudan being closed) and, obviously, are cheaper than flying.

AIR
To/From Europe
With the ferry connections being so good there is little need to fly from Europe to North Africa, but if you are short on time it may be the way to go.

There is little discounting to destinations north of the Sahara, so you will probably end up paying close to the full fare. The so-called bucket shops are the place to look for the best deal. These are travel agencies which sell discounted tickets, often at real bargain rates.

If you can't find a discounted fare, another option before paying full fare is an advance purchase excursion ticket, which is usually discounted by up to 40%. The discount is offered because there are restrictions, such as buying the ticket at least 21 days before departure, staying away for a minimum period and returning within a certain time (usually six months). Another disadvantage is that there are often penalties to pay if you want to change the dates. Check carefully that the restrictions on an advance purchase ticket are not going to disadvantage you.

Another possibility is getting a seat on a charter flight. There are many operating in the summer to Tunisia and Morocco; although the seats are mostly reserved for people on package deals, they can be incredibly cheap if you can get on. Often an operator will sell tickets cheaply at the last minute to fill empty places. Good travel agents should be able to point you in the right direction.

To/From North America
The best way to find cheap travel deals is by checking the Sunday travel supplements in major newspapers such as the *Los Angeles Times* or the *San Francisco Examiner-Chronicle* in the west and the *New York Times* in the east.

It is unlikely that you will find any real bargains to North Africa from either the USA or Canada. It will probably work out cheaper to take a cheap flight to Europe with a company like Virgin Atlantic (for around US$780 return) and then either fly or head overland from there.

To/From Australasia
There are no direct connections between North Africa and Australia or New Zealand. Again, the most convenient way is probably to go to London and then hunt around there for a cheap flight; otherwise go overland through Europe.

If you do specifically want to go direct to North Africa, the cheapest deal costs around US$1500 return to Tunis or Casablanca from the Australian east coast. This fare uses Royal Jordanian between Singapore and North Africa. The flights go via Amman and you may have to stop over there for a day or two, as the connections aren't that great. There is only one flight a week from Jordan to Tunisia and Morocco.

LAND
To/From West Africa
If you are coming north from West Africa, the only way to enter North Africa is to go from either Mali or Niger to Algeria. The crossing points are at In Guezzam on the route from Niger, and at Borj Mokhtar if coming from Mali.

The western routes down through

43

Morocco and western Algeria to or from Mauritania are out of the question as long as the war in Western Sahara between the Polisario guerrillas and Morocco continues. A UN-supervised ceasefire in the disputed area which went into effect in September 1991 could herald changes in the not to distant future.

See the Algeria Getting There & Away chapter for details of the routes.

Taking Your Own Vehicle

Carnet A *carnet* (short for *carnet de passage en douane* and sometimes known as a *triptique*) is not required for Morocco, Algeria or Tunisia, but if you are heading through to West Africa and beyond they are mandatory. You also don't need to prearrange them for most West African countries (Nigeria is an exception); documentation can be arranged at the Niger or Mali borders. At the Niger border they'll charge you CFA 5500 per month and the documents will cover you for all CFA countries.

The purpose of a carnet is to allow you to take a vehicle into a country without paying the duties which would normally apply. It's a document which guarantees that if a vehicle is taken into a country but not exported, then the organisation which issued it will accept responsibility for payment of import duties. Carnets can only be issued by one of the national motoring organisations (in the UK, this is the AA or RAC; in Australia, the AAA). Consult one of these organisations if you plan on taking a vehicle into any other African country.

Full details regarding carnets and related matters can be found in the Lonely Planet guides to the relevant areas, such as *Africa on a shoestring*.

It is important to note the following: though you don't need a carnet to take a foreign-registered vehicle into Algeria, if you have to abandon it in the desert, you'll be up for import duties. And they won't let you out of the country until you pay. You might think this is unfair, since you haven't sold the car – you've simply been forced to abandon it. Tough luck! As far as the customs officials are concerned, you've sold it and they are not prepared to go out into the desert to confirm that it had to be abandoned. Your only option for getting around paying the import duties is either to get the vehicle going again or have it towed in. The latter would cost a fortune.

The amount of import duty can vary considerably but, generally speaking, it's between one and 1½ times the new value of the vehicle. There are exceptions to this where duty can be as high as three times the new value.

The road between Tamanrasset and the Algeria-Niger border is littered with abandoned cars, so you won't be the first. The moral of the story is simple: make sure your vehicle is in top mechanical condition before you set off, carry sufficient spare parts and be able to fix it if anything goes wrong.

Insurance If you're going to be driving in Morocco, make sure you have a green card proving that you have third-party insurance. The police there can fine you Dr 35 (about US$4) if you can't produce one.

Legislation about compulsory third-party insurance varies considerably from one country to another. It is compulsory in all three Maghreb countries and you must buy it at the border.

The liability limits on these policies are often absurdly low by Western standards and if you have any bad accidents you could be in deep water. Also, you can only guess whether or not the premium is simply pocketed by the person collecting it or is actually passed on to the company, although this is more of a problem further south than in the Maghreb.

If you want more comprehensive and reliable cover then you will have to arrange this before you leave. If you're starting from the UK, the company that everyone recommends for insurance policies and for detailed information on carnets is: Campbell Irvine Ltd (☎ (071) 937 9407), 48 Earls Court Rd, London, W8 6EJ. The people who work here are very friendly, will give you personal attention, and, since they've been handling these kinds of enquiries for years, they know the business inside out. Most of the overland tour companies use them too. Write to them for a copy of their Overland Insurance leaflet or call round there and discuss it with them.

Books Taking a vehicle to Africa requires thorough preparation, and the detailed information and advice you need is really outside the scope of this book. An excellent guide which discusses all aspects of this is the *Sahara Handbook* by Simon & Jan Glen (Lascelles, London, 1987).

Another book, which has been recently updated and doesn't confine itself to the Sahara, is *Overland & Beyond* by Jon & Theresa Hewatt (Lascelles, London). If you understand German a very good book is *Dürch Afrika* by K & E Darr (Touring Club Suisse, Zürich, 1977).

Selling Cars in West Africa For years now large numbers of French, German and Swiss travellers and small entrepreneurs have been buying second-hand cars in northern Europe, driving them across the Sahara Desert and selling them in West Africa. For most travellers this is a one-off affair, the object of which is to reduce the costs of an Africa trip, but there are quite a few people who do it full-time for a living by taking several cars at once on the back of a truck. It's still possible to make a reasonable profit on the transaction, but don't expect too much by the time you've deducted expenses and the wear and tear which a car inevitably goes through when it's driven through the desert. You'll certainly still cover your costs (including the purchase price of the car).

For the full details, see the Lonely Planet guide *Africa on a shoestring*, by Geoff Crowther .

Fuel Costs (per litre)			
	Regular	Super	Diesel
Algeria	AD 3.10	AD 3.75	AD 0.95
Morocco	Dr 6.85	Dr 7.10	–
Tunisia	TD 0.470	TD 0.490	TD 0.290

SEA

Which ferry you want to take depends largely on where you want to travel and how much you want to pay. Obviously the shorter the route, the cheaper the fare, which makes the Spain-Morocco ferries the cheapest. Next on the fare scale are those from southern Italy to Tunis, the cheapest being from Trapani in Sicily which costs US$65 per person and around US$100 for a vehicle. A more convenient route may be the one from Genoa to Tunis (which costs US$120 per person and US$180 for a vehicle), as you don't have to drive right down through Italy.

There are also direct ferries from France to Algeria, but these are not that cheap at US$150 per person and US$320 for a vehicle from Marseilles to Algiers.

Whichever route you want to take, *all* are heavily subscribed in the summer months. If you plan to take a vehicle across it is imperative that you book well in advance, especially for the Tunisian and Algerian crossings. The situation is not quite as bad for Morocco, as there are many more crossings.

For full details of routes, schedules and operators, check the Getting There & Away chapters for each country.

MOROCCO

Facts about the Country

HISTORY SINCE 1830

Unlike its neighbours to the east Morocco was able to retain its independence right through the 19th century, although this was due mainly to rivalry between the European nations rather than to Moroccan effort.

The British secured trade privileges in 1856. In 1894, the new sultan, Abd el Aziz, came to power at the age of 10 and set about surrounding himself with expensive toys and European advisors, the latter whose life style and customs he adopted. Naturally this disgusted the populace, particularly the religious leaders, and his rule became tenuous at best.

The European powers saw this period of uncertainty and weakness as an opportunity to further their own interests in the country and in Africa as a whole. In 1904, Britain gave France a free rein in Morocco in exchange for an assurance that the French wouldn't interfere in Egypt; France pacified the Spanish by giving them north Morocco and the Italians were kept happy with Libya.

The end came for Abd el Aziz when his brother, Abd al-Hafid, led a rebellion against him in 1907, claiming that he (Abd el Aziz) had betrayed his Muslim origins. Abd al-Hafid installed himself in Fès but soon found himself besieged by hostile tribespeople and was forced to turn to the French for assistance. After the French had bailed him out, he had little choice but to accede to French terms. These were ratified by the 1912 Treaty of Fès, which saw Morocco become a French protectorate with provision for Spanish control of the north and the desert province of Tafaya in the south. Tangier became an international zone in 1923.

The terms of the protectorate recognised the Sultan of Morocco, but in practice his power was minimal. However, unlike the experience in Algeria where local culture was systematically wiped out, the first French Resident-General, Marshal Lyautey, had a deep-seated respect for the Arabs. As a consequence, he didn't destroy the existing Moroccan towns, but built new French towns (*villes nouvelles*) alongside them. A new capital was built on the Atlantic coast and the port of Casablanca was developed.

Marshal Lyautey's successor was a good deal less sympathetic. Local interests became less and less important in the administration of the protectorate, and French settlement went ahead at a great pace. One of the few problems faced by the French was an uprising in the Rif Mountains led by the Berber scholar Abd el-Krim. This revolt led to the declaration of the Republic of the Rif. The Rif was finally overrun in 1926 by a combined Spanish-French force of over 250,000, and Abd el-Krim surrendered to the French.

By 1934, the last of the mountain tribes had been 'pacified', and from here on nationalist feeling was channelled away from violence, into moves towards gaining political concessions.

In 1943 the nationalist movement had become the Istiqlal ('independence') party and had put forward proposals demanding independence. Not only were the proposals ignored, the French reacted by detaining the party leaders.

After serving with distinction with the French in WW II, the Moroccans hoped (in vain, as it turned out) that their demands for independence might be treated more favourably. Violence by nationalist guerrilla groups increased and was met with equal violence by some of the 300,000 French settlers.

In a climate of increasing tension it became clear to the French that their governing days were numbered unless they could stem the growing nationalist tide. Their last hope was to try and scare the nationalists with the threat of getting the mountain tribes to invade. To this end they cooperated with a Berber chieftain called Thami el-Glaoui, who ruled briefly in 1953 when the French exiled the Alaouite sultan Sidi Mohammed (Mohammed V). The sultan immediately became a national hero and was allowed back in 1955.

Full independence was granted in 1956 by France, and Mohammed V formed a government. The Spanish withdrew at about the same time but held on to Ifni in the south, and Ceuta and Melilla in the north. Ifni was handed back to Morocco in 1970, but Ceuta and Melilla continue to this day as Spanish enclaves.

Independent Morocco

With the French gone, Mohammed V was free to resume his autocratic rule and was succeeded by his son Moulay Hassan (Hassan II) in 1961 following the former's sudden death.

Parliamentary elections were held in 1963, but Hassan II had to resume personal control when, after only one year, the opposition Istiqlal and the FDIC (the party supporting the king) came to a deadlock.

Attempts to introduce a new constitution in 1970 and 1972 both met with attempted coups against the monarchy. The leader of this second attempt, General Mohammed Oufkir, had been implicated in the kidnapping and assassination in 1963 of Mehdi Ben Barka; Barka, the former leader of the Istiqlal party, had been exiled after being implicated in a plot to overthrow Hassan II. Oufkir committed suicide after his coup failed.

Western Sahara

Hassan's popularity soared in 1975 following the well-publicised 'Green March' into Spanish Western Sahara. This quickly led to the handover by the Spanish of this part of Africa to Morocco and Mauritania and, while it's true that Morocco has a semilegitimate historical claim to the area, the issue was to plague relations between the countries of the Maghreb for the next 15 years.

The colony of Western Sahara had been of little interest to Spain right up until the discovery of enormous phosphate reserves there in the 1960s. Once discovered,

however, the Spanish saw their opportunity and went full bore into developing and exploiting the deposits. It didn't all go smoothly, however, and Spain rapidly found itself up against growing nationalist feeling among the resident Saouarhis.

In an attempt to head off this challenge, Spain promised to hold a referendum on the colony's future as early as 1966. When this failed to eventuate by 1973 the Saouarhis formed the Popular Front for the Liberation of Saguia el Hamra and Río de Oro – Polisario – and started attacking the Spanish.

The Spanish found themselves hard pressed and their phosphate extraction facilities and associated infrastructure were frequently disrupted by this guerrilla activity. Their problems didn't go unnoticed by King Hassan II. Beset by problems at home and seeking an issue which would boost his popularity and, at the same time, unite the many disparate groups squabbling for political power, Hassan seized his opportunity. In 1975, claiming that the area was historically part of Morocco, he organised some 350,000 volunteers and marched them off across the border into Western Sahara. The ploy succeeded perfectly. Spanish forces offered no resistance and shortly afterwards Spain agreed to withdraw all its forces, leaving Morocco and Mauritania to sort things out between them.

This flood of Moroccans into the Western Sahara came to be known as the Green March, and it provided the country with a rallying cause whose bloom has not completely faded even now.

The carve-up saw Morocco take the northern two-thirds of the area and Mauritania the southern third. To Polisario, of course, this was just exchanging one set of colonial overlords for another, and the guerrilla war continued unabated.

Morocco, because of its far larger, better trained and better equipped army, was able to contain this onslaught, but for Mauritania it was a disaster. By 1979, Mauritania had had enough and came to an agreement with the Polisario guerrillas whereby they (Mauritania) pulled out of the area. Morocco

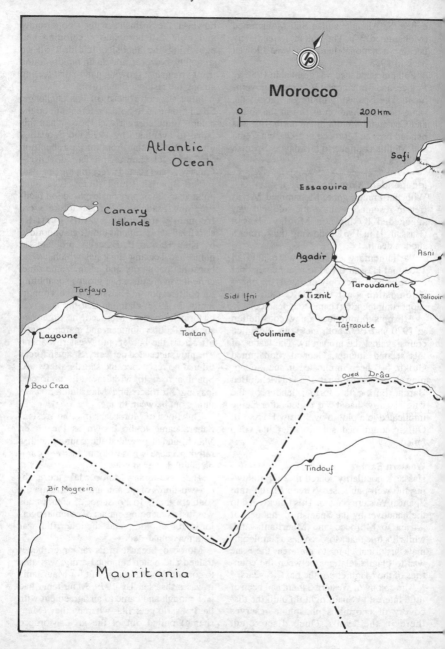

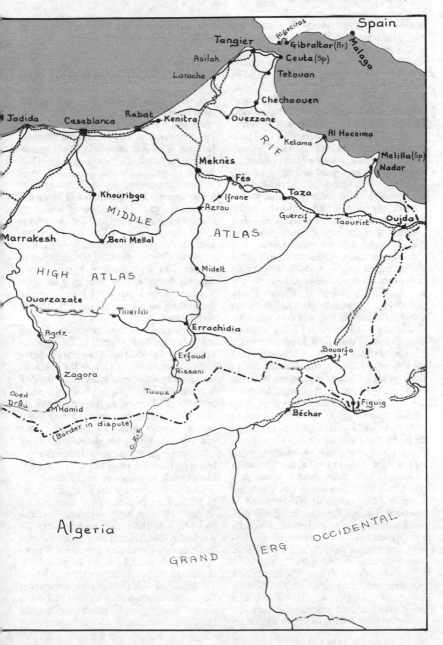

immediately jumped into the breach and took over what Mauritania had vacated.

The war continued with renewed vigour, with Polisario, strongly supported by Algeria and, for a while, Libya, operating out of its base at Tindouf in south-western Algeria. Ranged against its estimated 25,000 guerrillas were 100,000 regular Moroccan troops. Though able to keep the Moroccan forces under pressure, Polisario quickly found their freedom of action severely restricted following the construction by the Moroccans of an enormous defensive sand wall cquipped with high-tech detection aids, stretching the whole length of the Western Sahara. Meanwhile, the continued refusal of the Moroccans to budge on the question of sovereignty over the area frequently brought them to the brink of war with Algeria.

Diplomatically, Morocco didn't have everything its own way, and in 1984 came under increased pressure from both the UN and the Organisation of African Unity (OAU) over its claim to Western Sahara. As a result, Hassan not only withdrew from the OAU but also entered into a treaty of union with Colonel Gaddafi of Libya, the main purpose of which was to stop Libyan support for Polisario. This Hassan achieved, but at the expense of harming relations with the USA which, along with the French, had been bankrolling Morocco's war effort. The nascent 'union' quickly came to an end in 1986 following a visit to Rabat by the Israeli Prime Minister Shimon Peres.

An attempt to patch up relations with Algeria was made in 1987 at the instigation of King Fahd of Saudi Arabia. It was proposed that the Western Sahara would become a separate Saharan state, but federated to Morocco. Though Hassan rejected this proposal at the time, relations between Morocco and Algeria have since improved considerably, and normal diplomatic relations have been restored at ambassadorial level.

In September 1991, a UN-supervised ceasefire went into effect in the Western Sahara. This is apparently the first stage of a peace plan designed to give inhabitants the choice between independence or Moroccan rule. It remains to be seen what the outcome of the ceasefire will be.

The Present

While the king's grip on power certainly appears to be more secure than ever, with the army fully occupied with the war in Western Sahara and the trade unions and press restricted, it remains to be seen how long he can continue to outmanoeuvre the dissident factions in Moroccan society. These groups have so far failed to attract mass support but, as the economic climate gets worse, their influence is growing, especially in the shanty towns around the large cities and in the traditional villages of the Rif Mountains.

It is estimated that half the population lives below the poverty line, and unemployment levels are unacceptably high. The number of highly educated but unemployed people you will meet in Morocco is a national disgrace. Jobs there may be in the Western Sahara but most people regard going there as a form of personal, cultural and political exile.

Resentment is inexorably growing against the privileges and standard of living of the elite who inhabit the Casablanca-Rabat region, particularly in view of the effects of the austerity measures demanded by the IMF which have made life much harder for many millions of Moroccans. There have already been riots in the main cities (during 1984) following price rises of staple foods. And that's not all. With a population growth rate of 3% per year, which will double the population by the early years of the 21st century, there clearly are major problems ahead.

On the other hand, it's probably true to say that Morocco is a relatively conservative society. It is in no hurry to jettison its centuries-old traditions and embrace radical political philosophies. This is another reason for Hassan's continuing popularity. Claiming direct descent from the Prophet, he is revered by the people as their spiritual leader, and among his titles is that of Commander of the Faithful. Add to that the fact that many of his countrypeople believe he has the *baraka* – a form of charismatic power usually associated with *marabouts* (holy men or saints) – as a result of surviving several coup attempts, and you have a formula for longevity in power.

GEOGRAPHY

Morocco is one of Africa's most geographically, socially and culturally diverse areas. Only in parts of East Africa and southern Africa is it possible to find similar diversity. It is also spectacularly beautiful.

The country is traversed by four distinct ranges of mountains – some of them the highest in Africa. From north to south, they are the Rif, the Middle Atlas, the High Atlas and the Anti-Atlas. Certain peaks of the High Atlas remain snow-capped year round.

Between the mountain ranges themselves, and between these ranges and the Atlantic Ocean, are plateaus and plains. These are often fertile and well watered, since they are fed by the melting snow on the mountain slopes, but this is not always the case.

On many of the plains further south agriculture is tenuous to say the least, except along river courses. In the extreme south, at the edge of the Anti-Atlas, the country is characterised by vast, eroded gorges which, like the rivers that flow at their bases, gradually peter out into the endless sand and gravel wastes of the Sahara Desert. The two major rivers of the extreme south, the Drâa and Ziz, for instance, are eventually soaked up by the sands of the Sahara, and only in exceptional years of heavy rainfall has the Drâa ever been known to reach the Atlantic Ocean.

Deforestation, and its associated soil erosion, is a major problem in many areas. Between Ouezzane and Meknès and Fès and Taza, for instance, you could easily imagine yourself to be on the moon in many areas. The main reasons are the demand for firewood and vast, modern agricultural monoculture.

CLIMATE

The climatic variations in a country like this are endless. However, it's generally true to say that in winter the lowlands are pleasantly warm to hot (30°C) during the day and cool to cold (15°C) at night. In summer, it's very hot during the day (45°C) and uncomfortably warm at night (23°C).

Winter in the higher regions demands clothing suitable for Arctic conditions; this is true of anywhere in the vicinity of the High Atlas, since bitterly cold winds sweep down from the peaks at this time of year. In summer, it's hot during the day and cool at night.

Passes over the High Atlas can be blocked with snow during winter. Snowploughs usually clear them by the following day, but this can mean that you spend a bitterly cold night stuck in a bus in the snow without heating.

The main rainy season is between November and April but it brings only occasional light rain, which falls mainly on the coastal regions and on the high peaks. Rain rarely falls on the eastern parts of the country. Given the low rainfall, humidity is generally low.

GOVERNMENT

Morocco has been ruled by sultans ever since the Arab conquest and, until very recently, the power of the sultan was absolute – at least in theory. Just how far any sultan's writ extended, however, varied greatly from one reign to another and was dependent on the degree of control which he exercised over the always rebellious local chieftains.

Although King Hassan II, the present ruler, acts as the undisputed head of state and spiritual leader of the nation, the country remains a patchwork of ethnic and tribal groups. So far, the king has displayed considerable political acumen in maintaining at least a semblance of unity by playing off one region against another, the towns against the countryside and one political party against another. The war in Western Sahara has also been used to enhance his position by inspiring a sense of Moroccan nationalism and diverting attention from more pressing domestic problems. It will be interesting to see if this focus will change in the wake of the recent ceasefire in the disputed region.

It has not all been plain sailing for the monarchy, which has been forced to come to terms with the political developments of the 20th century and the aspirations of its subjects for a voice in government. The present constitution (the country's second since independence from France), which was adopted by referendum in 1972, provides for a 'constitutional and presidential monarchy' together with a multiparty national assembly.

There are five main political parties in Morocco. The oldest is Istiqlal, a nationalist conservative party founded in 1943, which draws its support from the middle classes. It previously had a much broader appeal, but was weakened when many of its left-wing members split off to form the Union Nationale des Forces Populaires (UNFP) under the leadership of Ben Barka in 1959. Istiqlal came out badly in the 1984 general elections, losing half of the seats it had previously held.

Another party which enjoys a great deal of support – this time from the Berbers and other rural dwellers – is the promonarchist Mouvement Populaire (MP). Also close to the monarchy is the Mouvement Populaire Constitutionnel et Démocratique (MPCD), a splinter group of the Mouvement Populaire. Other parties with representatives in the national assembly include the Union Socialiste des Forces Populaires (USFP), which draws its main support from the working classes, students and intellectuals, and the Communist MPP (formerly the Parti du Progrès et du Socialisme) which was banned until 1983.

Until 1985, the ruling coalition was made up of the MP, MPCD, USFP, the Rassemblement National des Indépendants (RNI), the Union Constitutionelle (UC) and the Parti des Indépendants Démocrates (PID). The last three are all right-wing, proroyalist parties and, together with the MP, they control 206 seats in the national assembly.

As a result of the war in Western Sahara, in 1985 the king demanded that the prime minister form a Government of National Unity. Both Istiqlal and the USFP refused to join, so parliament is currently controlled by a centre-right coalition comprising the UC, RNI and PID.

There are 306 members of parliament, two-thirds of whom are elected by universal suffrage. The remainder are nominated by an electoral college consisting of municipal councillors, representatives of the Chambers of Commerce and Agriculture, artisans' guilds and labour unions.

On a provincial and local level, Morocco is divided into 40 provinces, each headed by a governor. Provinces are subdivided into *préfectures* headed by *chefs de cercle*. In turn, each préfecture is divided into *caidates* under the direction of *caids*. Caids have much the same powers as *pashas*, who are responsible for the administration of urban municipalities.

Despite Morocco's flirtation with democracy and the monarchy's apparently constitutional status, it is the king and a small circle of trusted advisors who make all the real decisions. The king retains the right to appoint or dismiss prime ministers and their cabinets, and also to dissolve the national assembly.

There have been serious confrontations in the past (centred on the universities) and two attempted coups (involving the armed forces). There are also occasional disturbances involving left-wing and Islamic fundamentalist groups but they have been suppressed, though Hassan only narrowly escaped death in the attempted coup of 1972.

ECONOMY

Morocco's economy has been going through hard times in recent years. The country has been forced to adopt austerity measures prescribed by the IMF in order to have its external debts rescheduled and to secure bridging loans. The austerity programme has had serious social and political repercussions including rising unemployment and riots, the latter brought on by the reduction of subsidies on staple foods.

The main reasons for the downturn in the economy are droughts which have plagued the agricultural sector, a collapse of the world phosphate market, sluggish industrial growth and heavy dependence on imported oil, which accounts for some 80% of national energy requirements.

The war in Western Sahara has also been a serious drain on the economy, costing an estimated US$2 million per day.

Much of the debt with which Morocco is now saddled was run up in the 1970s, when the country was able to borrow heavily to fund an ambitious development programme on the strength of a boom in phosphate prices.

The mainstays of the economy are mining, agriculture, tourism, industry and remittances from Moroccans working overseas.

Morocco is the world's third largest producer of phosphates (15% of world production) but its largest exporter, with estimated reserves of around 60 billion tonnes. Exports of phosphates and their derivatives (mainly fertilisers and phosphoric acid) account for up to 60% of foreign earnings. Since the world price for phosphates plummeted in the early 1980s, however, production has been cut back by a factor of about one quarter.

Small deposits of other minerals – mainly anthracite, iron ore and barytes – are also being exploited but they account for only 8% of the mining sector. It was hoped at one time that large deposits of oil might be found; this has not been the case, and most of the companies involved have suspended drilling operations.

Agriculture employs over 50% of the workforce and accounts for about 25% of exports. The main crops are wheat, barley and maize, citrus fruits, beans and other legumes, tomatoes, potatoes and olives. Date palms line the banks of the southern valleys such as the Drâa, Dadès and Ziz and are the mainstay of the local economy. However, they are suffering heavily from a virus which is killing them by the thousand.

Unfortunately, agricultural practices have remained relatively primitive in many areas because the majority of the holdings are small and owners are unable to invest in new techniques which might produce surplus. Continuing drought has not helped either; there are some areas, particularly in the south, where you'll find it hard to imagine how the local people manage to feed themselves at all, so sparse is the vegetation.

There are other areas, however, where dramatic progress has been made in agriculture with government assistance for irrigation, introduction of new techniques and financial incentives to farmers. This applies to virtually all the land stretching from Meknès to the coast and north to Tangier, as well as to the area around Beni Mellal in the Middle Atlas.

The fishing fleet is also being modernised but the potential for export is hampered by strong competition from France, Spain and Portugal and limited access to the EEC.

Industrial development is concentrated around Casablanca, Sidi Kacem and Mohammedia but its contribution to exports remains small. Products include cement, textiles, paper, rubber, refined fuels, plastics and vehicles.

Morocco's most buoyant economic sector is tourism. Although it accounts for only 5% of the gross domestic product, tourism provides hundreds of thousands of jobs either directly or indirectly and is a major source of foreign revenue. Currently, over 1½ million tourists visit Morocco each year; around 90% of them are European and a good quarter of that percentage are French.

Another important source of foreign revenue are the remittances from the million or so Moroccans who work overseas, mainly in Europe. These amount to over US$1.5 billion each year.

POPULATION

The population stands at about 24 million but, at present growth levels, is expected to double by the end of the century. Some 55% of the population is aged 20 or under. In 1982, an incredible 65% of the population were still illiterate.

The largest city by far is Casablanca, with a population of around 3½ million. It's followed by Rabat-Salé (825,000), Marrakesh (450,000), Meknès (330,000) and Tangier (280,000).

RELIGION

The basics of Islam are dealt with in the Facts about the Region chapter. Morocco, however, is far from being a strictly orthodox Muslim nation of the sort you might expect to find in the Middle East. Still, the differences between Moroccan and Middle Eastern Islam are less accentuated in the cities than they are in the countryside.

There are several reasons for these differences: the remoteness of Morocco from the religion's origin; the nature of its fiercely independent indigenous tribes (the Berbers); the long period of benign interaction which North African Islam had with Christianity in El Andalous (Spain and Portugal), and with the Normans in Sicily, Libya and Tunisia; and the effect which Islam's major schism – between Sunnis and Shias – had on the religious and political forces at work within Morocco.

There's probably much the same degree of

difference between the Islam of Morocco and that of the Middle East as there is between the Hinduism of Bali and that of India, or between the Roman Catholicism of Spain and Peru.

The principal difference centres around the worship of local saints and holy men (marabouts), which itself is a sort of resurgence of pre-Islamic religious traditions. The whitewashed *koubbas* (tombs) of the marabouts can be found all over the Maghreb and down through the Sahara into Mauritania, Mali and Niger. Orthodox Islam, while it naturally venerates the Prophet, does not regard Him as God incarnate but simply as His messenger. Nothing in Islam resembles the Christian concept of the Holy Trinity (God the Father, God the Son and God the Holy Ghost), since such a division would constitute a heresy. Likewise, the worship of individual holy men is counter to orthodox Islam but has a very strong following in Morocco, especially in the rural areas.

Where these local saints have accumulated large numbers of followers, prosperous individuals have endowed the koubba with educational institutions known as *zaouias*, which offer an alternative to the educational facilities available in the urban (and orthodox) *medersas* (theological colleges) attached to the mosques.

Such cults naturally posed a threat to the maintenance of orthodoxy and would probably have been vigorously suppressed in countries nearer to the centre of the caliphate (variously at Damascus, Baghdad, Cairo and Istanbul), but in the difficult mountainous terrain of Morocco this was impossible.

Certainly there have been many attempts to 'purify' Islam in this corner of the Muslim world; the Almoravids were only the first of such crusaders. However, the main thrust has always been directed against urban material decadence as opposed to the individualistic interpretation of Islam by the tribal people of the mountains.

Not only that, no Moroccan king, with the possible exception of the present ruler, has ever been able to claim total control over the country. It has always been a patchwork of alliances, and toleration of local cults has always been an important factor in maintaining the allegiance of the mountain tribes. Perhaps the nearest parallel can be found in the highlands of Peru and Bolivia, where local Inca and Aymara pre-Christian cults were grafted wholesale onto those of the Catholic Church at a time when the Spanish conquerors were militarily too weak to oppose such syncretism.

It's also an historical fact that Islam coexisted with Christianity in the Iberian peninsula as well as in Sicily and southern Italy, until the advent of the Crusades. This sort of liberal interaction must have had profound effects on both religions.

None of this is to suggest that Islam in Morocco is in any way profoundly heretical. It isn't, but it has been tempered by regional sensibilities. Nevertheless, whenever it has been perceived as diverging too far from its basic tenets, there has been a fundamentalist reaction. This is as true of the present as it is of the past. Iran and Egypt are not the only Islamic nations which are either ruled by or have to deal with Islamic fundamentalism. Such forces exist in Morocco too and are perceived as a serious political issue. As a traveller you should be aware of this. It's conceivable that part of the growth of hardline fundamentalism is directly related to the disrespect shown by many tourists to Islamic customs and strictures.

Certain local cults in Morocco extended their influence so far that they acquired national significance; their saints were endowed with real or imaginary lineages going back to the Prophet. The descendants of such saints acquired the title of *sherif* and many of them enjoyed a high political profile. The foremost of these was Moulay Idriss, whose tomb stands in the town of the same name outside Meknès. In the 8th century he founded the first Moroccan dynasty, which held sway until the advent of the Almoravids. He is held in such high esteem that, even today, non-Muslims are prohibited from staying overnight in the town and are only barely tolerated near his tomb.

Such cults later developed into brotherhoods not unlike those of the Sufis in the Middle East and, like them, they shared a mystical interpretation of Islam. Their magical powers and the trance-like states which they induced through dancing became legendary. Though active until fairly recently, these brotherhoods are now officially frowned upon and their more extreme rituals outlawed. Nevertheless, loyalty to a particular saint's family remains an important part of Moroccan society.

Apart from the regionalism described above, almost everyone in Morocco is Muslim, and Sunni Muslim at that. While it is true that the Berber tribes took advantage of the great schism in Islam in the 7th century to reassert their independence, they quickly rejoined the Sunni mainstream.

Until the establishment of Israel, Morocco was the home of many Jews. Traditionally, they lived in the *mellahs* (Jewish sections) of the main cities and were an important economic force in the life of the nation. Very few now remain, most of them having emigrated to Israel.

One last important facet of Islam which travellers should be aware of is that it is incumbent upon Muslims to help the poor. It's not that you are going to encounter many beggars in Morocco, except in central Casablanca, since they are few and far between, but unemployment is high, so well-heeled tourists (ie virtually all foreigners) are regarded as employment opportunities. Hence the hassles at the entrance to most large city *medinas* (the Arab part of modern towns and cities in the Maghreb). In your dealings with these people, remember that they have no access to welfare payouts. Such things do not exist in Morocco. If you refuse to help out by hiring them for the day then don't be too surprised if you get treated with contempt. It's not quite as simple as that, of course, so be sure to read the section on Bargaining in the Facts for the Visitor chapter.

LANGUAGE

Arabic, Berber, French and Spanish are the

main languages. English is also spoken in many places. Spanish is more common in the north and French along the Atlantic coast and in the south. The country's official languages are Arabic and French, and both of these are taught in every school – even in the smallest villages.

Moroccans must be among the world's most accomplished linguists. There is probably no other country in the world where you will come across so many people – even children – who can speak so many different languages passably. The motivation – unemployment amid hordes of well-heeled tourists – might be obvious but their skill can only be admired. Even dishwashers at food stalls can manage one or two sentences of passable Japanese, not to mention any European language you can think of. Most of the people in this category are, naturally, involved in the tourist trade. Don't expect much beyond Moorish Arabic and French outside the main cities and popular tourist spots.

Although Arabic may be one of the official languages, its spoken form – Maghrebi Arabic – is considerably different from that which you hear in the Middle East. It's basically a regional dialect and is not radically different from the Arabic which you hear in Algeria and Tunisia. The written language, however, remains uniform.

Berber is widely spoken in the countryside and particularly in the mountains. Though related to Arabic, it's a language whose roots go back to prehistoric times. Prior to the Arab conquest of North Africa, it was spoken over much of the area between the Moroccan Atlantic coast and the Egyptian border. The original script of the language has disappeared but was probably not too dissimilar to that used today by the Touareg in the Sahara Desert. Berber is now rendered in Arabic script.

Berber has many dialects – some of them almost different languages – and this is especially true in Morocco. The country is, after all, one of the extremities of the Arab world, so it's not surprising that regional languages and dialects should have survived in the way they have done on the western extremities of Europe.

Moroccan Berber falls into three main colloquial groups – Riffian, Braber and Chleuh. The first and the last are almost mutually unintelligible but Braber contains elements of both.

Riffian, as the name implies, refers to the dialect spoken by the inhabitants of the Rif Mountains. It is also spoken in the Middle Atlas and as far south as the oases around Figuig on the Algerian border.

Braber is the dialect spoken by the transient pastoralists of the Middle Atlas, the eastern High Atlas and the valleys which connect the High Atlas to the Sahara – the Ziz, Todra and Dadès.

Chleuh is the dialect spoken by the settled tribes of the High Atlas, the Anti-Atlas, the Sous Valley and the south-western oases; it can also be found in the Ziz, Todra and Dadès valleys.

Unlike Basque, Breton and Welsh, however, the dialects which these people speak do not mark them off as belonging to any particular race or tribe. Most Berbers are bilingual (Berber and Arabic) and many are trilingual (Berber, Arabic and French).

Facts for the Visitor

VISAS & EMBASSIES

Visas are not required by the following: nationals of West European countries (with three exceptions – Belgium, the Netherlands and Portugal), Australia, Brazil, Canada, Chile, Japan, Mexico, New Zealand, Peru, the Philippines, the USA, Venezuela and most Arab countries. All other visitors must have a visa.

Nationals of Israel and South Africa are not admitted. What is more, if you do need a visa it's advisable not to have an Israeli stamp in your passport or you may be refused a visa. Visas are not available at land borders or ports of entry.

Visas cost US$3 or the equivalent and are valid for a stay of up to 90 days.

Moroccan immigration officials not only do not believe that 'hippies' are an endangered species, they still subscribe to the enduring myth that hippies are the offal of Western society. They represent a moral pollutant which must be turned back before it corrupts the fibre of Moroccan society. A 'hippie' is any male with long hair (and preferably an untidy beard) or untidy/outlandish clothes. Women face no such discrimination. And if a male fits the above description, the rules are applied with a frustrating capriciousness: some people get through; others are refused.

The ferry from Algeciras to Tangier is notorious for arbitrary refusals. The one from Algeciras to Ceuta doesn't have this problem, since Ceuta is Spanish territory and its border with Morocco is usually controlled in an easy-going fashion.

The Melilla border (Spain's other Moroccan enclave), on the other hand, is often staffed by officials whose main qualification for the job appears to be obnoxiousness. If you are planning on entering Morocco here, make sure you have on your Sunday best and that your razor was sharp that morning.

Men who have left their Sunday best at home, but who plan to fly into Casablanca, Tangier or Agadir, shouldn't experience any problems. If you can afford to fly, you must have money.

Moroccan Embassies

Visas and related information can be obtained at Moroccan diplomatic missions in the following countries:

Algeria
    8 Rue des Cèdres, Parc de la Reine, Algiers (☎ 60 7737)
    26 Rue Cheikh Larbi Tebessi, Oran (☎ 33 1784)
Australia
    Suite 2, 11 West St, North Sydney, NSW 2060 (☎ 957 6717)
Canada
    1455 Rue Sherbrooke, Montreal H3 GIL2 (☎ 937 9460)
Cameroun
    BP 1629, Yaoundé (☎ 22 5092)
Central African Republic
    Immeuble Sabbagh, Ave Barthélèmy, Boganda (☎ 61 3951)
Côte d'Ivoire
    24 Rue de la Cannebière, Cocody, Abidjan 01 (☎ 44 5873)
Egypt
    10 Rue Salah Eddine, Zamalek, Cairo (☎ 40 9677)
France
    19 Rue Saulner, Paris 75009 (☎ 423 3740)
    8 Rue Tête d'Or, Lyons (☎ 93 1802)
    22 Allées Léon Gambetta, 13001 Marseilles (☎ 62 6420)
Germany
    Gotenstrasse 7-9, Bonn 2 (☎ 35 5044)
Holland
    Oranje Nassaulan 1, 1075 AH Amsterdam (☎ 73 6215)
Italy
    Via Lazzaro Spallanzani, 8/10, Rome (☎ 85 5432)
Mali
    Badalabougou BP 2013, Bamako (☎ 22 2123)
Mauritania
    BP 621, Nouakchott (☎ 51 411)
Niger
    BP 12403, Niamey (☎ 73 4085)
Portugal
    Avenida Joao Crisostomo, Lisbon (☎ 52 1644)

Sénégal
  Route de Ouakam, Angle Bourguiba, Dakar
  (☎ 21 6927)
Spain
  Rambla de Cataluna 78, Barcelona 8 (☎ 215 3470)
  Ave de Las Fuerzas Armadas No 4, Algeciras
  (☎ 66 1803)
  Ave de Andalucia 15, Malaga (☎ 32 9962)
  Calle Serrano 179, Madrid 2 (☎ 458 0950)
  Ave Mesa Y Lopez, Las Palmas (☎ 26 2859)
Tunisia
  39 Rue du 1 Juin, Tunis (☎ 78 0257)
UK
  49 Queens Gate Gardens, London SW7 5NE
  (☎ (081) 581 5001)
USA
  1601 21st St NW, Washington DC 20009 (☎ 462 7979)

Visa Extensions

Visa extensions are free of charge but you may need a letter of recommendation from your own embassy. In theory, extensions are obtainable from the *gendarmerie* (police) headquarters in any regional capital but, in practice, you'll be told you have to go back to Rabat to get them. In Rabat you have to go to the Sûreté Nationale, Rue Soekarno. You can collect your extension the same day (at 6 pm) if you get there early.

If you intend to stay more than three months, you must apply for permission to do this within 15 days of arrival. Nationals of France and Spain are allowed an unlimited stay so long as they report to the police within three months of arrival.

Travel Restrictions

It is prohibited to travel south of Dakhla in Western Sahara without a special permit from the military authorities. It's unlikely you'll get this and, in any case, there's not much point since the road is mined.

Foreign Embassies & Consulates in Morocco

Most of the developed nations of the world maintain embassies in the capital, Rabat. There are foreign consulates in Agadir, Casablanca, Oujda, Tangier and Tetouan.

Rabat Following are a list of the foreign embassies in Rabat:

Algeria The Algerian Embassy in Rabat (☎ 76 5474), is at 10-12 Rue d'Azrou, just off Ave de Fas. The offices are open Monday to Friday from 8.45 to 11.45 am. The cost of visas varies depending on your nationality but is from Dr 60 to Dr 87.50. Likewise, the number of photographs required varies from two to four. They are generally issued the following day, though sometimes it can take 48 hours so long as your application does not have to be referred to Algiers. Visas are for a stay of one month.

If you have a German passport *do not* apply for your visa in Morocco. You may be refused. I even met a German man married to an Algerian woman who was refused a visa in Rabat. Apply for your visa in Bonn before leaving. Much the same applies to Dutch nationals, who also should get their visas in Europe.

During the Gulf crisis of early 1991 visas were being refused to Australians and Brits – but this should have been remedied by now.

France The French Embassy is on Ave Mohammed V at Chellah but there is also a consulate, which deals with visas, on Ave Allal ben Abdallah. They cannot issue you with a visa for Niger, despite the fact that there's no Niger embassy in Rabat.

Mauritania The embassy in Rabat is at 9 Zankat Taza, just off the Rue de Tunis and one block back from the road which fronts onto the Mohammed V Mausoleum. Visas cost Dr 50 and can be issued the same day, but you need a letter of introduction from your own embassy. Two photographs are required. At the UK Embassy (on the same street) these cost Dr 75. Australian and New Zealand interests in Morocco are handled by the UK Embassy but the Mauritanian Embassy is apparently unaware of this, so passport holders of those countries can save themselves money by saying they have no diplomatic representation in Rabat.

Niger Niger does not have an embassy in Rabat and the French Consulate in Rabat cannot issue Nigerian visas. The nearest Niger diplomatic missions are in Algiers or Tamanrasset (Algeria).

Senegal The embassy here does not issue visas – you must go to the consulate in Casablanca.

UK The UK Embassy (☎ 72 0905) in Rabat is on Blvd de la Tour Hassan (though the street sign says Charia Saomaat Hassan).

Other embassies in Rabat include:

Canada
13 bis, Rue Jaafar Assadik, Aghdal (☎ 77 1375)
Egypt
31 Ave d'Alger (Charia al Jazair), Place Abraham Lincoln (☎ 73 1833)
Germany
7 Zankat Madnine (☎ 76 9692)
Italy
2 Rue Zankat Driss em Azhar (☎ 72 2698)
Netherlands
40 Rue de Tunis (☎ 73 3512)
Spain
3 Rue Madnine (☎ 76 8988)
Tunisia
6 Ave de Fas (☎ 73 0636)
USA
Ave de Marrakech (☎ 76 2265)

Casablanca There are the following foreign consulates in Casablanca:

Algeria
159 Blvd Moulay Idriss (☎ 28 8435)
France
Rue Prince Moulay Abdallah (☎ 26 5356)
Senegal
6 Rue de la Tours (☎ 30 3325). Three-month visas are issued on the spot, cost Dr 31 and require three photos.
Spain
29 Rue d'Alger (☎ 22 0752)
UK
60 Blvd d'Anfa (☎ 22 1653)
USA
8 Blvd Moulay Youssef, (☎ 26 4550)

There are also consulates in Casablanca for Austria, Belgium, Côte d'Ivoire, Denmark, Finland, Germany, Greece, Guinea, Italy, Japan, the Netherlands, Norway, Pakistan, Poland, Portugal, Switzerland and the USSR.

Tangier The following countries have diplomatic representation in Tangier:

Algeria
10 Rue Ibn Zaïdoune (☎ 94 7013)
Belgium
124 Blvd Sidi Mohammed ben Abdallah (☎ 93 1218)
Denmark
3 Rue ibn Roch (☎ 93 8183)
Finland
3 Ave de Lisbonne (☎ 94 2985)
France
Place de France (☎ 93 2039)
Portugal
9 Place des Nations (☎ 93 1708)
Germany
47 Ave Hassan II (☎ 93 8700)
Italy
35 Rue Assad ibn al Farrat (☎ 93 7647)
Netherlands
47 Ave Hassan II (☎ 93 1245)
Norway
3 Rue Regnault (☎ 93 8183)
Spain
85 Rue Habib Bourguiba (☎ 93 5625)
Sweden
31 Rue du Prince Héritier (☎ 94 8730)
Switzerland
Rue Regnault (☎ 93 4721)
UK
Rue d'Angleterre (☎ 93 5895)
USA
Rue El Achouak (☎ 93 5904)

Agadir There are consulates in Agadir for Belgium, Finland, France, Italy, Norway, Spain, Sweden and the UK.

Oujda There is an Algerian Consulate (☎ 68 3740) on Blvd Bir Anzarane. It is open Monday to Thursday from 8 am to noon for visas. Ten-day visas (extendable in Algiers) cost Dr 100 and are issued in 24 hours; three photos are required. The staff are not particularly helpful, and have the unpleasant habit of refusing to issue visas. If this happens, you'll have to trek back to Rabat – Algerian visas are not available at the border.

Tetouan There is a Spanish Consulate in Tetouan on Ave Massira. It's open daily except Thursday from 9 am to noon. Visas can be issued on the spot, although none of the staff speak English.

MONEY
Currency

The unit of currency is the dirham. A dirham is made up of 100 centimes. The import or export of local currency is officially prohibited. There's no black market as such, though you will occasionally be made an offer. Even if you are, it will only be a few cents above the bank rate, so it's hardly worth the effort unless you're desperate to change.

Exchange Rates

US$1	=	Dr 8.78
UK£1	=	Dr 15.19
FFr1	=	Dr 1.53
DM1	=	Dr 5.20
Y100	=	Dr 6.77
A$1	=	Dr 6.99
NZ$1	=	Dr 4.99
C$	=	Dr 7.81

Some banks (eg Banque Marocaine du Commerce Extérieur (BMCE)) charge commission on travellers' cheques amounting to between 0.35% and 0.6% but others (eg Bank Al-Maghrib and Société Générale Marocaine de Banques (SGMB)) charge no commission. Banking services are usually quick and efficient.

Avoid bringing Scottish pound notes with you as they won't be accepted.

A lot of travellers have run into hassles changing money at Tangier Airport. Quite often, they refuse to take travellers' cheques and insist on cash. There are no such hassles at Casablanca's Mohammed V Airport but the service is as slow as a snail.

Credit Cards

Credit cards are widely accepted in the main cities but not in the smaller places or in the countryside. American Express is represented by the travel agency Voyages Schwartz, which can be found in Agadir, Casablanca, Marrakesh, Rabat and Tangier.

Visa, MasterCard and Access cards are accepted by most banks including the

BMCE, Interbank, Banque Crédit du Maroc and Banque Populaire. The principal banks in all the main cities now have automatic telling machines (*guichet automatique*) from which you can withdraw money using your card. Alternatively, you can go into a bank which takes the cards and withdraw up to US$100 per day without reference to your bank. The transaction takes about as long as changing a travellers' cheque since virtually all banks are now computerised. If you need more than US$100 they have to refer to your bank, which naturally takes longer.

The use of a credit card for purchases in the various medinas of Moroccan cities often attracts a 5% surcharge – that's what the vendor will tell you the bank charges them as commission. Officially they're not supposed to do this, otherwise the credit card company will withdraw their franchise, but what are you going to do about it?

Costs

Whether you are coming from Europe, America or Australasia, you'll find Moroccan prices refreshingly reasonable. A basic (ie unclassified) hotel with shared bathroom costs around US$4.50 a single and US$8 a double. A hot shower in such a hotel costs extra (up to US$1). In a one-star hotel, a room with its own bathroom costs around US$8.50 to US$11 a single and US$11 to US$12.50 a double, and will usually include hot water. Two-star hotels cost around US$11.50 to US$15 a single and US$15 to US$17.50 a double.

Food is good and relatively cheap, and a standard meal of tajine or couscous costs around US$2.50, though the latter is usually slightly more expensive. European-style food costs more, but is rarely over US$5 a meal, so long as you aren't eating in an expensive restaurant or hotel. US$10 would buy you a three-course Moroccan-style meal at a mid-range restaurant.

The only things which are relatively expensive are alcoholic beverages (beer and wine). You will pay around US$1 for a small beer and US$5 and up for a bottle of Moroccan wine.

Transport is a bargain, particularly by bus or train (the latter even in 1st-class), though taxis cost up to half as much again as buses. For instance, a long bus journey (eg 500 km) costs around US$14.

So, adding on a few small tips here and there plus a few entry charges to museums and the like (a standard US$1.20), you could get by on US$17 a day per person so long as you stay in cheap hotels, eat at cheap restaurants and are not in a hurry. If you'd prefer some of life's basic luxuries like hot showers or the occasional splurge at a good restaurant, and don't mind taking a taxi if it's going to increase your enjoyment of a particular journey, then plan on US$25 to US$30 per day per person.

Obviously, some cities are more expensive than others, and the countryside is usually considerably cheaper than the cities, so your expenses will vary. The only other major expense which you need to bear in mind is the cost of all those crafts which you are going to buy when you get into the *souks* (markets). Few people can resist purchasing at least two or three articles. There's no way of suggesting an approximate budget for these things, since it all depends on when and where you buy them, how good you are at haggling, whether you want quality or are happy with semi-trash, and the nature of the article. One thing's certain: money speaks and an empty pocket gets you nothing.

Stock up on petrol in Ceuta or Melilla if you have your own vehicle, as they are both duty-free ports. Petrol in Morocco costs Dr 6.85 (regular) and Dr 7.10 (super) per litre – less than US$1.

Bargaining

Contrary to what a lot of people would like to believe, most prices in Morocco are more or less fixed. This includes hotel accommodation, meals at a restaurant or café and transport.

On the other hand, there is no such thing as a fixed price for crafts bought in the souks, where haggling is the name of the game. In some places, especially Marrakesh, this is becoming less and less the slow, relaxed process which it used to be: too many well-heeled tourists with more money than brains, no sense of values and little time to spare have been through before you. If you're not prepared to pay what local people would regard as ridiculous prices then there's always another mug around the corner who will. If you run up against this, go somewhere else.

Fortunately, there are still many places where you can enjoy the process of haggling and where it isn't just a charade put on to give you the illusion that you're getting a bargain. Traditionally, sellers would start off at around double the price they were actually prepared to accept and buyers would start off at less than half that amount. Gradually, over several glasses of mint tea, a mutually acceptable price would be reached.

These days it's no longer quite so predictable. Sellers frequently start at triple the price they are prepared to accept, so you need to start off at around one-quarter of the price they propose. The price will quickly drop to not far from what the trader is prepared to accept, so you'll mostly end up haggling over a few dirham.

A major constraint on your bargaining power will be the 'guide' who accompanies you around the souks. The people who act as 'guides' make a lot of their income from commissions which they receive from shopkeepers when you buy something. This can be up to 10% of the price you pay, so they're naturally very keen to see you buy a lot of things, and your tour around the souks can rapidly degenerate into being hustled through an endless succession of shops.

If you wish to maximise your bargaining powers, avoid buying anything whilst you are with a 'guide'. This isn't always easy, as you'll be subjected to high-powered sales tactics; some 'guides' actually get abusive once it appears you are not going to buy anything. Don't get sucked in and react in the same manner: it's just a ruse to browbeat you, though many people fall for it. Even better, make it clear to the 'guide' before you set off that you may not be buying anything.

The 'guides' hang around the entrances to the souks and are incredibly tenacious. In some places – Marrakesh being notorious – it's virtually impossible at times to get past them without accepting one, until your face gets known. On the other hand, taking a 'guide' is probably a good idea for your first and second visits, as it's an opportunity to familiarise yourself with the layout of the souks. Agree on a price for their services before you set off. Base your price on the fact that you can hire an official guide from the tourist office or local *syndicat d'initiative* for Dr 35 per half day. Many unofficial 'guides' will accept less than this.

Refusing a 'guide's' services can be a harrowing experience. Many of them are expert at manipulating the conversation to suit their ends. This is the major source of the bad-news stories with which many travellers come away from Morocco. The trouble usually starts because the traveller doesn't want a guide, and eventually loses patience in the face of the extreme persistence of the guide who wants to be taken on. There's no easy answer to this but anger isn't the solution: the guide will simply get angry too, and you'll end up having a full-on blue.

Remember that unemployment amongst young people is very high in Morocco and you can generally assume that the people who are trying to sell their services are otherwise unemployed. So while you might regard their persistence as a 'hassle', they regard it as 'enterprise'. They probably also regard you as 'rich' even if only in relative terms. After all, how is it that you can afford to visit their country while they cannot afford to visit yours? And how can you do it without having a job? And so why is it that you can't afford a few dollars to help them out? After all, they're offering a service, not begging. And when it comes down to it, one of the tenets of Islam is the giving of alms to the poor.

You're entitled to see things differently, of course, but it helps if you're aware of local circumstances.

Unemployed youth apart, another ruse is becoming more and more common. What happens is that two or three stations before you arrive in either Fès or Marrakesh, someone comes into your carriage on the train and strikes up a very engaging conversation with you. Naturally, they live in the town you are proposing to visit, and are on their way home. How nice to invite you to their home on arrival! See the real Morocco? Why not! You don't know the place and don't know where you're going to stay. It turns out that your 'friend' owns a carpet warehouse and that's where you end up, being worked on vigorously by a bevy of salespeople. You're caught. You don't want to get up and walk out since there's that lingering feeling that you are being offered genuine hospitality. If you do go to walk out, everyone affects extreme umbrage. The truth is, you've been conned, subtly of course, but conned nevertheless. If you find yourself in this position, recognise it for what it is, and get out immediately.

The following letter gives an account of how the situation was dealt with by one traveller:

On the subject of hustlers, hasslers, guides and touts (I never quite sorted out the distinction among these), we had, I'm sure, a fairly typical number and range of encounters with these folks. Although we never worked out a fail safe way of parting with a mutual smile without buying something, the overall tone of these encounters certainly improved over the course of our stay. In other words, I think I learned something about dealing with this (to me) very new and potentially stressful type of relationship.

To start with, I think all first-time travellers to such a place could use some preventive medicine against the defensive, stiffly armoured, trust-nobody attitude they're likely to pick up from concerned relatives and friends. I also think this is a pretty natural reaction for many people coming into a situation which can seem threatening in its total unfamiliarity.

Initially I resolved that I wouldn't trust people who approached me, and that I'd simply try to ignore them until they went away. This is clearly the wrong attitude in Morocco. The only nasty verbal abuse I received during my stay was in response to what must have seemed to them my contemptuous silence. One fellow snarled hateful imprecations at me ('Jew', 'Zionist', 'Nazi') when I ignored him after getting off a bus; another lectured me angrily on the necessity of interacting with the people ('We are not animals in a zoo!') when I ignored his invitation to come and take a look at his factory.

The point of travelling is not to stand behind a glass wall and watch, but to interact with people, get beyond first appearances, get a personal feel for what life is like in such a place. So I started smiling, always at least acknowledging, and often responding to, the constant calls, invitations and greetings, and trying to tuck my caution away somewhere where it would be less visible and offensive. That worked a lot better. Even those who were more persistent were less annoyingly so when I made clear that my lack of interest in their wares or services did not arise from contempt or fear.

Clearly, openness and amiability need to be tempered with caution, as there are a lot of apparently friendly people who are primarily interested in one's cash. On the other hand, it is misleading to try to divide people rigidly into those whom one can trust, who are genuinely interested in friendship, and those who cannot be trusted as their interest is financial. From what I gathered of Moroccan microeconomics, the interdependence of family industries and businesses makes relationships that are based on a mixture of personal and economic exchange, even among Moroccans, considerably more common than in our culture. If this is true, it should be expected that genuine offers of companionship, hospitality and friendly conversation might imperceptibly combine with a bit of public relations for a friend's carpet concern.

This does not mean that whatever rapport might have been established must be dismissed as a put-on; rather, it simply means that other cultures do not enforce the strict division of personal and economic matters that we supposedly do. It might be helpful to keep in mind as well that, apart from word of mouth, many or most of the businesses one is invited to patronise have no advertising at their disposal. There are no yellow page listings, no neon glitz, freeway billboards or garish shop signs. Hopefully visitors can appreciate this difference, and respect the far more personal and straightforward local alternative.

David Porter

WHEN TO GO

The most pleasant seasons to explore Morocco are spring (April to May) and autumn (September to October). Midsummer can be very pleasant on the coast but viciously hot in the interior. Likewise, winter can be idyllic in Marrakesh and further south as far as the Algerian border during the day, but you can be chilled to the bone at night.

TOURIST OFFICES
Local Tourist Offices

Morocco is well geared for tourism. The

national tourist body, ONMT, has offices in Agadir, Casablanca, El Jadida, Fès, Layoune, Marrakesh, Meknès, Ouarzazate, Oujda, Tangier and Tetouan.

Each office usually has a fair stock of glossy brochures and maps of the major places, but they do vary quite a lot in the degree of extra effort which their employees put into their work. If they were all as keen as the man who runs the Ouarzazate office, they'd be excellent.

The offices of the national tourist body are complemented in many towns by local tourist offices, known as syndicats d'initiative. These often have much the same range of literature as the ONMT offices but the staff are usually more clued up on local matters. Some of them, such as the one in Casablanca, are excellent.

Overseas Reps

The ONMT also maintains offices overseas and these are good places to contact if you need any information before you go.

Australia
  11 West St, North Sydney, NSW 2060 (☎ 957 6717)
Austria
  1010 Wien, Elisabeth Strasse 4/5/6/16 (☎ 2256 8356)
Belgium
  66 Rue du Marché aux Herbes, 1000 Brussels (☎ 512 2182)
Canada
  2001 Rue Université Suite, 1460 Montreal (☎ 842 8111)
France
  161 Rue St Honoré, Place du Théâtre Français, 75001 Paris (☎ 4260 6350)
Germany
  Graf Adolf Strasse 59, Düsseldorf 4000 (☎ (211) 37 0551)
Italy
  Via Larga 23, 20122 Milan (☎ 5830 3633)
Japan
  Owariya Building 4, 8th Floor, Banchi-1-chome, Kandacho, Chiyoda-ku, Tokyo 101 (☎ (03) 251 7781)
Netherlands
  150 Roking 1er, 1012 Amsterdam (☎ 24 0025)
Portugal
  Rua Artilharia Un 79 85, Lisbon (☎ 68 5871)

Spain
  Calle Quintana 2, 28008 Madrid (☎ 542 7431)
  There are branch offices in Torremolinos and Las Palmas.
Sweden
  Sturegatan 16, 11436 Stockholm (☎ 660 9913)
Switzerland
  Schifflände 5, 8001 Zürich (☎ 252 7752)
UK
  205 Regent St, London W1R GHB (☎ (071) 437 0073)
USA
  20 East 46th St, Suite 1201, New York, NY 10017 (☎ 557 2520). There are branch offices in Los Angeles and Orlando.

BUSINESS HOURS & HOLIDAYS
Banking Hours
Banking hours are Monday to Thursday from 8.15 to 11.30 am and 2.15 to 4.30 pm. On Fridays it's 8.15 to 11.15 am and 2.45 to 4.45 pm. During Ramadan, hours are 9.30 am to 2 pm. In the main tourist cities there will be at least one bank which has late opening times for its change section.

Public Holidays
The main public holidays are:

New Year's Day
  1 January
Feast of the Throne
  3 March
Labour Day
  1 May
Anniversary of the Green March
  6 November
Independence Day
  18 November

These holidays are tied to the Western calendar and, therefore, can be accurately predicted. On these days all banks and post offices are closed, as are most shops.

CULTURAL EVENTS
In addition to secular holidays there are many national and local religious holidays and festivals (known as *moussems* or *amouggars*). Some of these are national affairs celebrated countrywide, but others are less elaborate local events. They are all tied to the lunar calendar, so their approxi-

mate dates can be worked out if you know the phases of the moon; however, their exact dates cannot be predicted, since that decision rests with the religious authorities in Fès. The dates for local festivals are even less predictable, as they are generally set by local caids, who take the weather into account.

Probably the most important religious festival is that of Eid al Fitr which comes at the end of the month-long Ramadan fast. Ramadan takes place during the ninth month of the Muslim calendar and is a sort of parallel to the Christian Lent, with the difference being that it is strictly observed by Muslims.

Another very important national festival is that of Aid el Kebir, which coincides with the beginning of the Islamic year. It commemorates Abraham's submission to God through the offer of his son Isaac for sacrifice. It takes the form of a traditional family gathering and those who can afford it slaughter a sheep for the occasion.

The third main religious festival, known as Mouloud, celebrates the Prophet Mohammed's birthday.

Local festivals are usually held in honour of marabouts. They are often no more elaborate than an unusually lively and more extensive market day, though quite a few have taken on regional and sometimes national importance. These sorts of festivals are common amongst the Berbers and are usually held during the summer months. It's worth making enquiries to determine when they are due to take place. The most important, in chronological order, are:

March
> *Moussem of Moulay Aissa ben Driss* in Beni Mellal

May
> *Fête des Roses* (rose festival) at Kelaâ des M'Gouna in the Dadès Valley. It is held late in the month.
> *Moussem of Sidi Bou Selham* south of Larache. This festival sometimes takes place in June.

June
> *National Folklore Festival* in Marrakesh. This festival runs for 10 days and is held early in the month.
> *Fête des Cerises* (cherry festival) in Sefrou

July
> *Moussem* at Mdiq, north-east of Tetouan. This festival takes place early in the month.

August
> *Moussem of Moulay Idriss* in Zerhoun, north of Meknès
> *Moussem of Moulay Abdallah* south of El Jadida. The festival takes place late in the month.
> *Moussem of Setti Fatma* in the Ourika Valley, south of Marrakesh
> *International Arts Festival* in Asilah

September
> *Fête des Fiancés* in Imilchil. The festival is held late in the month.
> *Moussem of Sidi Moussa Ou Quarquour* near El Kelas du Straghna, north of Marrakesh

October
> *Moussem of Moulay Idriss* in Fès
> *Fête du Cheval* (horse festival) in Tissa, north-east of Fès. These two festivals take place in early October.
> *Fête des Dattes* (date festival) in Erfoud. This takes place in late October.

The Folklore Festival at Marrakesh is essentially a tourist event these days (even though it also attracts large numbers of Moroccans). Nevertheless, it's very colourful and well worth attending, since groups of dancers, musicians and other entertainers are invited from all over the country.

MARKETS

In common with most African countries (and many others around the world), Moroccan towns and villages have a special weekly market day (sometimes twice a week) when people from the surrounding area come to sell their wares and buy goods which they cannot produce for themselves.

These markets are different from the permanent covered markets which most towns have where fruit, vegetable and meat sellers have their shops and stalls. The open markets are usually lively affairs and a good place to observe the customs and distinctive clothing of local tribespeople. They often take place on what is essentially just a patch of open ground reserved for the purpose. Some of the most interesting include:

Agadir: Sunday
Figuig: Saturday
Ifrane: Sunday

Khenifra: Sunday
Larache: Sunday
M'Hamid: Monday
Midelt: Sunday;
Moulay Idriss: Saturday
Ouarzazate: Sunday
Ouezzane: Thursday
Oujda: Wednesday and Sunday
Sefrou: Thursday
Tafraoute: Wednesday
Taroudannt: Thursday and Sunday
Tinerhir: Monday
Tinzouline: Monday
Zagora: Wednesday and Sunday

POST & TELECOMMUNICATIONS

The Moroccan post is reliable, and you shouldn't have any problem receiving letters posted to you care of poste restante. There's a small charge for collecting letters – Dr 1.35. Post offices can be distinguished by the 'PTT' symbol.

Parcel Post

Parcels posted back to your home address have to be inspected by customs (at the post office) before you seal the parcel and pay for the postage, so don't turn up at a post office

with a sealed parcel – you'll just waste time and money. And although you will be handed what might appear to be a somewhat dubious receipt for a parcel, it will get there. The days when the contents might have been stolen or the stamps steamed off belong to the distant past. However, as in many countries around the world, it might not be a good idea to send money through the post.

Some post offices have a packing service on offer operated by private individuals but, if you're not sure whether this is available, bring all the requirements with you.

Telephone

The telephone service is similarly reliable, and you shouldn't have to wait too long for an international connection. Telephone directories, on the other hand, are a different matter. Last time I was in Rabat, the only Rabat directory available at the main telephone office was 10 years out of date. In that time all the numbers had changed, as a new system had been installed, so it was completely useless. The staff at the enquiry desk were about as useful as the directory.

The other thing you need to bear in mind if calling a number in Morocco is that the numbers in most of the larger cities are being changed to increase the number of lines available. The way this is being done, in most cases, is simply to add a number to the beginning of the original one – and it's always one particular number for each particular city. So, if you're calling a number and getting a continuous tone, but know the number which is being used as a prefix in that particular city, then try again using that number. Most of the time you'll get through. Telephone numbers in most of the larger cities now consist of six numbers.

TIME

Moroccan time is GMT plus one hour all year round.

ELECTRICITY

Morocco has both 240 and 110 volts AC, depending on which area you are in, so check before plugging in any appliances.

BOOKS & MAPS
People & Society
Morocco – Its People & Places by Edmondo de Amicis, translated by C Rollin-Tilton (Darf, London, 1985). This book, first published in Italian in 1882, was written by a man who accompanied an Italian diplomatic mission to the sultan's court at Fès. It's a delightfully fresh and lively account of life in Morocco at that time and is illustrated with the original sketches executed by the artist who was attached to the mission. I'd nominate this book as one of the best travelogues I've ever read.

The Moors – Islam in the West by Michael Brett & Werner Forman (Orbis, London, 1985). This large-format book, filled with superb colour photographs, details the impact and development of Islam on Morocco and Spain when Moorish civilisation was at its height, and follows through to the Spanish *reconquista*. It's not just a history book, however: it includes chapters on topics such as the social framework and the Muslim mind, and examines social, economic and political issues relevant to the times.

Doing Daily Battle by Fatima Mernissi, translated by Mary Jo Lakeland (The Women's Press, London, UK£5.95). This is a collection of interviews with 11 Moroccan women which gives a valuable insight into their lives and aspirations. Fatima Mernissi is also the author of the classic study *Beyond the Veil: Male-Female Dynamics in a Modern Muslim Society*.

Morocco (Insight Guides, APA Publications (HK) Ltd, 1990). This is a typical well-produced APA photographic-cum-descriptive essay of the country which is well worth reading before you go to get an idea of what is worth seeing and visiting.

History
The Conquest of Morocco by Douglas Porch (Cape, London, 1986) can be recommended. Another good book, also by Porch, is *The Conquest of the Sahara* (Cape, London, 1985).

Architecture
Islamic Architecture of North Africa by Antony Hutt (Scorpion, London, 1977). This book is mainly for those interested in the architecture of North Africa and is essentially a photographic essay. Unfortunately, most of the photographs are black and white, so much of the richness of the decoration is lost.

Cookbooks
The Taste of Morocco by Robert Carrier (Century, London, 1987) is a brilliant hardback on Moroccan cuisine complete with recipes; colour photos throughout.

Maps
The only map which really makes the grade in terms of detail is the Michelin *Morocco* No 169 (Scale 1:1,000,000).

For minute detail of routes within Morocco, you can't do better than buy the Michelin *Guide de Tourisme – Maroc*. The maps (and the descriptions of places) in this book are excellent. Unfortunately this guide is only available in French. As a consequence, few bookshops in the UK stock it, but you can find it in the bookshops along Charing Cross Rd or Tottenham Court Rd in London, and in major bookshops in Morocco. Otherwise, it's available from Michelin, 46 Ave de Breteuil, 75341 Paris, France.

FILM & PHOTOGRAPHY
Colour negative and slide film is readily available in all large Moroccan cities and towns, but it's usually Kodak or Fuji. If you prefer Agfa bring your own because you won't find it in Morocco.

Kodak or Fuji film of 64, 100 and even 200 ASA is available in most photography shops, but don't expect to find 400 or 800 ASA film. They'd probably order it for you, but if you're not going to be hanging around for several weeks then forget about it.

As prices go, there's not a great deal in it, but if you want to be sure, bring your own supply with you.

As with most hot, dry countries, remember that photographs are best taken in the early morning or late afternoon. Unless you know a lot about photography and your camera has manual override, most photographs taken in the middle of the day will be 'washed out', especially in summer.

The reverse is true of photographs taken in the medinas of places like Fès, Marrakesh and Meknès. Even in the middle of the day it can be relatively dark in the narrow streets, and without fast film (400 to 800 ASA) you'll just end up with a lot of silhouettes or, more usually, nothing but indistinct rubbish.

Urban Moroccans are generally easy going about foreigners taking photographs – most middle-class Moroccans, after all, own cameras. In the countryside, however, this isn't necessarily the case and you should ask permission beforehand. It isn't that country people are hostile to having their photographs taken: they just like to know who's taking them. And that can take half an hour of exchanging pleasantries, talking about where you come from and what life is like there, what you are doing in Morocco, or anything else they feel like asking you about. One thing is guaranteed: if you spare the time for this sort of exchange you'll end up with superb shots instead of furtive and very grainy garbage taken from a great distance with a zoom lens. Moroccan country people are very earthy and don't know how to pose, so you'll lose nothing, photographically speaking, by telling them what you want to do.

However, if you ever run into a situation where people don't want to be photographed, respect their right to privacy and don't take photos.

ACCOMMODATION
Camping
You can camp anywhere in Morocco so long as you have the permission of the site's owner, but there are a large number of official campsites which vary in price depending on the facilities provided. Most provide shower and toilet facilities (though there's not always hot water) and there's usually a shop and a simple restaurant. Tourist offices

Classified Accommodation Costs

Category	Type of Room	Shower & Toilet	Shower & Shared Toilet
One-star B	Single	Dr 67	Dr 58
	Double	Dr 86	Dr 70
One-star A	Single	Dr 85	Dr 85
	Double	Dr 98	Dr 98
Two-star B	Single	Dr 92	Dr 75
	Double	Dr 112	Dr 92
Two-star A	Single	Dr 119	Dr 94
	Double	Dr 138	Dr 110
Three-star B	Single	Dr 151	Dr 119
	Double	Dr 186	Dr 151
Three-star A	Single	Dr 175	Dr 138
	Double	Dr 212	Dr 174
Four-star B	Single	Dr 234	Dr 191
	Double	Dr 292	Dr 235
Four-star A	Single	Dr 280	Dr 230
	Double	Dr 358	Dr 300

A third bed in any of the above costs between Dr 33 (one-star) and Dr 76 (four-star). Breakfast, likewise, is extra, ranging from Dr 14 per person (one-star) to Dr 31 (four-star).
Tourist tax must be added to the above prices and ranges from Dr 4 per person in the lower classes to Dr 8 per person in the higher classes.

have details of their location. In most cases you're looking at Dr 5 to Dr 10 per person plus Dr 5 for a car. At some you can rent tents (usually Dr 10); at others you must have your own. The amount of shade provided by trees varies considerably. Some campsites are just patches of bare earth; others are like the sylvan glades of Greek myths.

Youth Hostels

There are a number of youth hostels (auberges de jeunesse) in Morocco and, if you're travelling alone, they are among the cheapest places to stay. The charge is usually Dr 20 per night with a youth hostel card or Dr 25 without. Breakfast is often available at hostels but you will have to buy other meals elsewhere. Most hostels have (free) cold showers but you have to pay extra for hot showers. There are hostels at Asni, Casablanca, Chechaouen, Fès, Ifrane, Marrakesh, Meknès, Mohammedia and Rabat.

Where there is no youth hostel, there is usually a Centre Sportif or a Centre de Jeunesse, where basic accommodation can be found for a small charge. Sometimes it's just floor space; at other times you get a bed.

In mountain walking/climbing areas, such as Toubkal, there are also a series of refuges (buildings similar to youth hostels which offer dormitory accommodation and basic cooking facilities) and associated gîtes (mountain huts). They are generally operated by the Club Alpin Français and cost Dr 10 per bed for members, Dr 15 for youth hostel members and Dr 20 for others.

Hotels

Youth hostels are fine if you don't mind dormitory accommodation and if you're not carrying valuables which might attract the attention of thieves. On the other hand, a cheap (ie unclassified) hotel will often cost not much more than a bed at a youth hostel. It's certainly cheaper to rent a room at a hotel if you're sharing, rather than paying for two (separate) beds at a youth hostel.

Only occasionally will you find a dirty room or dirty sheets, even in the cheapest hotels. The vast majority are remarkably clean and reasonable value. The communal toilets and bathrooms are generally in the same state, though not always. Hot showers are the exception rather than the rule and, if you want one, there's usually a small additional charge for it (in most cheap hotels hot showers are run off bottles of propane gas).

The rest of the hotels in Morocco are all classified according to a set of government guidelines and there's a fixed maximum price which they're allowed to charge according to the facilities which they provide. The charges are listed in the table called Classified Accommodation Costs.

The five-star luxury hotels have no ceiling on their prices and are not regulated by the government.

Baggage left in hotel rooms is generally safe. I never had a single thing stolen and found the level of honesty to be very high indeed.

THINGS TO BUY

For centuries, Moroccan crafts have been justifiably world famous, both for their variety and their quality. There's probably no other country of a similar size which can boast so many different craft guilds. The sale and export of these crafts is an essential pillar of the Moroccan economy even though, in the 20th century, mining and agriculture have overtaken this in importance. Virtually no-one returns home from a trip to Morocco without carrying with them one or more examples of the crafts which are produced here.

The extensive souks of Fès, Meknès, Marrakesh and, to a lesser extent, Rabat and Tangier offer a full range of crafts. Naturally, styles vary from region to region and the price of any particular object is usually lowest in its place of origin.

Wooden boxes, marquetry and chessboards are best bought in Essaouira, where the range is enormous. Cedar-wood screens assembled into intricate patterns are best sought in Fès or Meknès, whereas brightly painted chests and cradles are a speciality of Fès and Tetouan. Chased copper and brass trays, vases, candlesticks and the like are best bought in Casablanca, Fès, Marrakesh and Tetouan, and they range from items costing only a couple of dollars to trays on which you could literally stage a banquet.

Silver-inlaid sabres and muskets are best sought in Tiznit and Taroudannt. Tiznit, Rissani and Tantan are famous for their range of silverwork, since silver jewellery is worn by the nomads of the south. Gold jewellery, on the other hand, is at its best in Fès, Essaouira and Tangier.

Be careful when buying jewellery. At the cheaper end of the scale, what is sold as solid silver is nothing of the sort: it's merely plated. The same thing goes if you're offered cheap amber: put a lighted match to it and you'll quickly discover that it's plastic – albeit skilfully crafted to appear genuine.

Leatherwork is another of Morocco's famous crafts. Its quality and softness is legendary. The best wallets, desk sets, slippers *(babouches)* and embossed poufs are found in Fès, Meknès and Rabat, whereas elaborate leather bags are a speciality of the Riffian towns of Tetouan, Chechaouen and Taghzout. Camel saddles should be sought in Marrakesh.

Fès, Meknès, Marrakesh and Rabat all have their carpet souks, which stock a wide range of styles and sizes. You need to spend a considerable amount of time examining what is available before buying, as the quality varies and the colours in the cheaper examples have a tendency to fade rapidly.

What was an extravaganza of colour when you first bought it can quickly lose its vividness. Enquire about the dyes used and make an effort to see the genuine article in a museum before doing the rounds of the carpet souks. Styles and patterns are as varied as the tribes and some are hard to find outside their region of origin. You won't, for instance, come across many of the brightly coloured and delightfully naive patterns which are found on the carpets woven in Ouarzazate and Zagora outside these areas except, perhaps, in Meknès.

Pottery – vases, plates, tajine dishes and the like – is best bought in Fès or Safi, where there are famous potteries, though many other areas have now realised how good the market is for these products and you'll come across plenty of road-side stalls offering similar goods.

Stoneware is at its best in Taroudannt, where you will find boxes, lamps and paperweights. Outside Taroudannt, along the mountain roads of the High Atlas, you will come across numerous stalls where semiprecious and ornamental stones are sold. These include amethyst, rock crystal, quartz and many others. Fossils – especially large ammonites – are also a feature of this region. There are even large polished slabs of rock containing many different types of fossil available in many places. You'd need your own transport to take them home – they're *heavy*! Prices are very reasonable indeed.

Getting There & Away

AIR

Although most travellers arrive by ferry from Spain or Gibraltar, Morocco is well served by air from Europe, the Middle East and West Africa, and has international airports at Tangier, Casablanca and Agadir. There are also direct flights from Paris to Ouarzazate and Marrakesh.

Airlines which fly to Morocco include: Aeroflot, Air Afrique, Air Algérie, Air France, Alitalia, Balkan, British Airways, GB Air, Iberia, KLM, Lufthansa, Royal Air Maroc (RAM), Royal Jordanian, Sabena, Saudia, Swissair and Tunis Air.

To/From Europe

Depending on the time of year that you want to travel, there may well be some very cheap charter flight tickets available to Morocco from northern European cities such as Amsterdam, London, Manchester or Paris. They're always return tickets and generally must be paid for in advance. However, some agents will sell you a one-way ticket a few days before the flight or even on the day itself if they have a deal with the charter companies and there are spare seats going.

The same goes for flights to Madrid and Malaga. A one-way London-Malaga ticket, for instance (UK£45 to UK£50 if you're lucky), followed by the ferry to Melilla (about UK£10) is cheaper than flying direct to Morocco. These charter tickets are often tied to a minimum number of nights at a specific hotel and, in theory, you can't buy a ticket without also paying for the accommodation. In practice, most agents will sell you the air ticket and provide you with a bogus voucher for the accommodation so that it all looks normal in case you're questioned by officials. Naturally, you can't use the bogus voucher.

Even if you have to buy a return charter ticket, they're often so much cheaper than a regular one-way ticket that you can afford to throw away the return half. A London

Agadir return charter ticket can cost as little as UK£100. Finding these tickets can involve a lot of leg and phone work, and they get snapped up quickly. Trying to arrange them through provincial agents is usually a waste of time.

A regular return flight ex-London to Tangier or Casablanca on Royal Air Maroc or Air France should cost you around UK£225 but fares can drop to around UK£180 in the low season.

To/From North America

With no direct flights between North America and Morocco, the cheapest way to go is on a cheap flight to London and then a separate flight to Morocco from there.

To/From Australasia

As with the USA and Canada, there are no direct flights between Australia or New Zealand, and Morocco. The cheapest fare quoted was A$1600 return and this was with Royal Jordanian going via Amman and Singapore. It wouldn't work out much more expensive to fly to London and then hunt around for a cheap ticket to Morocco from there.

LAND

To/From Europe

Bus The Moroccan national bus line, CTM (Compagnie de Transports au Maroc), operates buses between Brussels, Paris, Toulouse, Marseilles and Lyons to most of the largest Moroccan towns including Tangier, Rabat, Casablanca, Meknès, Fès, Agadir, Taroudannt and Errachidia.

To Paris (via Tours and Bordeaux) the service varies from five times per week for the largest cities (Casablanca) to once per week from the smaller places (Errachidia). The fare is a standard Dr 1080 (US$123) one way. The service to Lyons (via Beziers, Perpignon, Nîmes, Montpellier and Avignon), Marseilles (via Avignon) and Toulouse (via

Bordeaux and Montauban) is less frequent, usually only once per week, and only connects the major cities.

To Brussels (via Lille, Vallenciennes, Liège and Ghent) the service is usually twice weekly but only connects with the major Moroccan cities. The fare is Dr 1375 (US$156) one way.

Train Buses are fine if you can handle them over long distances but with a train you have the option of *couchettes* and therefore a good night's sleep. The Moroccan rail system is part of InterRail and the cheapest fare from London is UK£162 return, which compares very favourably with the above CTM bus fares.

To/From Algeria

Road There are two crossing points between the two countries: between Oujda and Tlemcen in the north near the coast and between Figuig and Beni Ounif some 300 km further south.

In the past, it used to be necessary for people bringing their own vehicle into Morocco to have a telex from their embassy in Rabat guaranteeing that they would take the vehicle out of the country. This may now have lapsed but it's worth checking out well in advance, as getting such a telex used to take up to a couple of weeks. This telex was in addition to a carnet or green card.

For full details of the two crossings, see the Algeria Getting There & Away chapter.

There are no direct buses between Morocco and Algeria. You must change at the border.

Train The rail link between Morocco and Algeria and on to Tunisia was suspended for many years due to tension between Morocco and Algeria but the service has now been restored. The schedule is shown in the Trans-Maghreb Express table below.

It should be clear from this table that a change of train and an overnight stay in Algiers are necessary if you're travelling from Tunis to Morocco. The service is sometimes suspended during the winter months.

Moroccan customs and immigration are at Oujda station.

SEA
To/From Spain

There's a whole variety of car ferries operated by Compania Transmediterranea, Compagnie Marocaine de Navigation, Limadet, Transtour and Catsline. The most popular of these is the Algeciras-Tangier route; the others are Algeciras-Ceuta (Spanish Morocco), Almeria-Melilla (Spanish Morocco) and Malaga-Melilla. Others include Cadiz-Tangier and Tarifa-Tangier. The majority of the ferries are car ferries of the drive-on and drive-off type.

There's also a high-speed catamaran service between Gibraltar and Tangier operated by Gibline.

Algeciras-Tangier There are up to eight crossings per day in either direction on this route (less in the low season). The crossing takes 2½ hours and fares, depending on class, range from 2700 to 3440 Ptas or Dr 196 (half price for children under 12 years of

Trans-Maghreb Express						
Casablanca	Oujda	Oran	Algiers	Constantine	Annaba	Tunis
21.50	09.30	16.20	20.25 (arr)	02.45	08.15 (arr)	18.00
			21.00 (dep)		09.30 (dep)	
Tunis	Annaba	Constantine	Algiers	Oran	Oujda	Casablanca
12.00	20.15 (arr)	01.06	09.14 (arr)	14.00	18.55	08.00
	22.15 (dep)		07.30 (dep)			

age). A car up to six metres long costs 8500 Ptas or Dr 618.

Algeciras-Ceuta (Spanish Morocco)
There are four crossings per day in either direction (three only on Sundays) on this route.

The trip takes 1½ hours and the fare is 1190 Ptas. Cars up to six metres long cost 1170 Ptas.

Almeria-Melilla (Spanish Morocco)
There are departures three times a week, from Almeria on Tuesday, Thursday and Saturday at 2 pm, and from Melilla on Monday, Wednesday and Friday at 11.30 pm by Compania Transmediterranea. The crossing takes 6½ to eight hours and the fare, depending on class, costs 2290 to 5870 Ptas. Cars up to six metres long cost 2060 Ptas.

Malaga-Melilla (Spanish Morocco)
Also operated by Compania Transmediterranea, ferries leave Malaga on Monday, Wednesday and Friday at 1 pm and Melilla on Tuesday, Thursday and Saturday at 11.30 pm.

The journey time is 7½ to 10 hours and the fare, depending on class, is 2290 to 5780 Ptas. Cars up to six metres long cost 2060 Ptas.

Tarifa-Tangier
The Transtour hydrofoil service operates daily except Sunday in either direction at 10 am from Tarifa and 3 pm from Tangier.

The crossing takes one hour and the fare

is 2700 Ptas or Dr 196 (children half price). This is not a car ferry.

To/From Gibraltar
Gibraltar-Tangier The only service which operates between these two places is a high-speed catamaran which does not take vehicles.

The Gibline catamaran leaves Gibraltar at 9.30 am on Tuesday, Thursday and Saturday, 11 am on Sunday and 6.30 pm on Monday and Friday, and Tangier at 10.30 am on Monday, 3.30 pm on Wednesday and Friday, 5.30 pm on Sunday and 7.30 pm on Monday and Friday.

The trip takes 1¼ hours and costs UK£19 (children half price).

The same company also operates from Gibraltar to Mdiq but schedules depend on demand. Mdiq is just north of Tetouan and there are regular buses between the two.

To/From France
Sète-Tangier This car ferry service is operated by the Compagnie Marocaine de Navigation and the crossing is made between six and seven times per month, usually once every four to five days.

The trip takes 38 hours and the fare, depending on class, is between UK£110 and UK£300 (children half price). Cars under four metres long cost between UK£130 and UK£220.

Sète-Nador The frequency of these ferries is much the same as those between Sète and Tangier, and the journey time and fares are the same.

Getting Around

AIR

If your time is very limited and you want to see as much of Morocco as possible, it's worth considering the occasional internal flight offered by Royal Air Maroc or its subsidiary, Royal Air Inter. If you're 26 years of age or under it works out particularly cheap, as they offer 30% 'youth fare' discounts on the normal prices. You can only get this discount at a Royal Air Maroc office, not through travel agents.

Internal airports serviced by the above are Agadir, Al Hoceima, Casablanca, Dakhla, Errachidia, Fès, Kenitra, Layoune, Marrakesh, Oujda, Ouarzazate, Rabat, Smara, Tangier, Tantan and Tetouan.

BUS

There is a good network of buses all over the country; departures are frequent. Most Moroccan cities and towns now have a central bus terminal, though this isn't always the case. Where there is no central terminal, the various bus companies are usually clustered together in the same area.

CTM is the largest and the preferred company. Along the main routes it generally offers two classes of buses: 'Mountaz' (deluxe) and 1st-class. 'Mountaz' is very comfortable and is preferable for long distances. Fares in this class are about 25% more than in 1st-class. On less important routes there's generally a choice between 1st and 2nd-class buses. Second-class buses often do quite a lot of stopping, which is fine unless you're only interested in getting from one place to another. Seats on 'Mountaz' buses are in high demand so advance booking is advisable.

The other bus companies are all privately owned. Some of them (eg SATAS) operate nationally along the same routes as CTM; others only operate regionally. Most of them have 1st and 2nd-class buses but some only have 2nd-class vehicles. On the main routes,

they're just as fast as CTM and sometimes slightly cheaper.

Even where a city has a central bus terminal, CTM often maintains its own separate terminal. Where this is the case, the CTM terminal is indicated on the street maps. Sufficient leg room is no problem on 1st-class CTM buses but the width of the seats is another matter. On non-CTM buses you're usually looking at being squeezed both ways. On well-subscribed routes and those which have only one bus a day, try to book your ticket in advance.

Bus transport is cheap and isn't going to be one of your major expenses. Some examples of bus fares on CTM 'Mountaz' class include:

Agadir to:	Dakhla (Dr 275)
	Layoune (Dr 154)
Marrakesh to:	Fès (Dr 95)
	Ouarzazate (Dr 45)
Casablanca to:	Agadir (Dr 105)
	Chechaouen (Dr 65.50)
	Errachidia (Dr 123.50)
	Essaouira (Dr 70)
	Marrakesh (Dr 50)
	Oujda (Dr 137)
	Tangier (Dr 80)
Tangier to:	Fès (Dr 67.50)
	Tiznit (Dr 205)

Take about 25% off these fares and you have the approximate 1st-class fare.

There are no official charges for baggage placed either on the roof or in the side compartments but, if it goes on the roof, the baggage handlers will demand a tip however much help you offer. They're usually happy with Dr 1, though local people pay less. On dusty journeys your gear is better placed on the roof, where it won't end up the colour of the road, since tarpaulins are pulled over roof-top baggage. You shouldn't have any problems with theft of baggage, though it might be wise to keep an eye on it if the bus is standing for any length of time at an intermediate terminal.

Don't expect anything other than a 'Mountaz' CTM bus to have heating, even on the journeys over the Atlas Mountains in winter; they often don't. Warm clothing is, therefore, essential and particularly if there's any chance of being stranded on the passes due to snow drifts. The Marrakesh-Ouarzazate road is prone to this. It's extremely unlikely you'll be stranded for longer than overnight, as snowploughs usually clear a path by early morning.

CTM also operates international buses from all the main Moroccan cities to Paris and Brussels. See the Getting There & Away chapter for details.

TRAIN

As with the bus system, there is a good network of railways connecting all the main population centres. Trains are the best method of transport in Morocco if you have the choice. A lot of money has been spent on upgrading the railways and rolling stock in recent years, so trains are comfortable, fast and reliable. Also, even if you travel 2nd-class the fares cost very little more than the equivalent bus fares would. Third-class (known as Economique) is cheaper than going by bus, though it can be overcrowded. First-class is definitely luxurious and an unnecessary expense. Second-class consists of separate compartments with six seats and is usually air-conditioned. It would be the equivalent of 1st-class on trains anywhere else in Africa and is the one most travellers seem to go for.

On the fringes of the railway system – Meknès or Fès to Oujda, for instance – you may come across 2nd-class carriages which are of the old type, in which case they won't be air-conditioned (or heated in winter). The Rabat-Casablanca line is an experience all of its own. The track is electrified and super fast, and the journey takes only 55 minutes (nonstop).

Most trains offer a choice of all three classes, but there are some which offer only 1st and 2nd-class. Sleepers are available on night trains. A refreshment trolley usually does the rounds of the carriages offering hot coffee, soft drinks and snacks and, on the longer journeys, there is a buffet car with lunch and dinner available.

Timetables are prominently displayed in the railway stations. If you want to plan ahead, get hold of the small booklet entitled 'Horaire des Trains' which is available from the ticket offices and railway bookstores at major railway stations.

Advance booking is advisable for 1st-class, though it's probably true to say that it would be rare for all the trains to be booked out on any particular day. For 2nd and 3rd-class you just roll up and buy the ticket before departure. You can in fact buy the ticket in advance, but as there is no seat reservation there seems little point in this.

You are allowed unlimited stopovers between the point of origin and your final destination, as long as the entire journey is completed within five days. When you get off at an intermediate station, get a Bulletin d'Arrête from the ticket window.

The Moroccan railway system is contiguous with that of Algeria and there are through trains except at certain times of the year. Details can be found in the Getting There & Away chapter.

TAXI

Shared taxis (grands taxis) are worth considering on some routes – particularly along scenic routes which buses might cover partially after sunset. They cost about 50% more than the equivalent bus fare, but make sure you know what local people are paying beforehand. There's often an attempt to conceal this so that you end up paying more. As a rule of thumb, fares are approximately Dr 1 per three km.

Shared taxis are a particularly good idea if there are enough of you to fill one. An added bonus is that you can ask the driver to stop occasionally so you can take photographs or walk around for five or 10 minutes. It will cost you more if you want the driver to do this, so negotiate a price before you set off. They won't stop if you are sharing with local people. The Ziz and Drâa valleys and the Tizi-n-Test Pass particularly lend themselves to shared taxis, and there are many other scenic routes.

Shared taxis are frequently older Mercedes Benz, bought by their owners whilst they were 'guest workers' in France and Germany in the days when those countries were short of manual labourers.

City taxis *(petits taxis)* are very useful in urban areas and will save you a lot of time getting from one place to another. They're very cheap by European standards – rarely more than Dr 10 for an average journey.

CAR RENTAL

There are many out-of-the-way places in Morocco which you simply won't be able to get to if you don't hire a taxi or haven't got your own transport. Car rental is not cheap, but with four people it's affordable. The cheapest cars are Renault 4 and Fiat 127. Charges vary only slightly among the major international companies (Hertz, Budget, Avis, Europcar/InterRent) but there are any number of local companies which will rent you the same cars for much less so check things out thoroughly before renting.

It isn't true that cars rented from a major company are any better than those from a local company. What does differ is the degree of service or help you can get in the event of a breakdown. Major companies will replace a car from their nearest depot if there are problems; local companies often don't have branch offices so there isn't much they can do. *Always* haggle for a discount when renting a car, especially if it's for an extended period of time. Most companies offer excellent discounts for rentals over one month.

As examples of the costs you are looking at for car rental, compare the prices shown in the table called Car Rental. It's clear from the table that, in some cases, what you gain on the swings you lose on the roundabout because of differing mileage charges. Most of the savings are on rentals for seven days or more.

The rates in the table below do not include a government tax of 19% which you must pay on all rentals regardless of the company. It's also advisable to take out Collision Damage Waiver insurance (around Dr 40 per day), otherwise you'll be liable for the first Dr 3000 in the event of an accident. You may also want to take out personal insurance (around Dr 25 per day).

Most companies demand a (returnable) deposit of Dr 3000 when you hire the car, unless you're paying by credit card in which

Car Rental

Major Companies

Category	Models	Cost with Mileage		Unlimited Mileage	
		Per Day	Per Km	3 Days	7 Days or More
A	Renault 4	Dr 195	Dr 2	Dr 1380	Dr 2415
B	Fiat Uno	Dr 235	Dr 2.45	Dr 1900	Dr 3300
C	Peugeot 205	Dr 265	Dr 2.85	Dr 2270	Dr 3970
D	Renault 12	Dr 350	Dr 3.50	Dr 2900	Dr 5000
E	Peugeot 309	Dr 370	Dr 3.70	Dr 3000	Dr 5250
F	Peugeot 405	Dr 480	Dr 4.80	Dr 4000	Dr 6950

Local Companies

Category	Models	Cost with Mileage		Unlimited Mileage	
		Per Day	Per Km	3 Days	7 Days or More
A	Renault 4	Dr 140	Dr 1.75	Dr 1300	Dr 2300
B	Fiat Uno	Dr 180	Dr 2.10	Dr 1650	Dr 2900
C	Peugeot 205	Dr 220	Dr 2.40	Dr 2050	Dr 3400
D	Peugeot 309	Dr 300	Dr 3.25	Dr 2700	Dr 4500
E	Peugeot 405	Dr 450	Dr 5	Dr 3700	Dr 6500

case this is waived. Minimum age for drivers is 21 years, with at least one year's driving experience. An international driving licence is usually required, though most agencies will accept your national driving licence.

Virtually all cars take premium petrol ('super') which costs around Dr 7 per litre (more in country areas).

HITCHING

Hitching is OK, but demands a thick skin and considerable diplomatic expertise in the north due to aggressive hustlers. They simply won't take 'no' for an answer and feign outrage if you express lack of interest in whatever it is that they're trying to sell you – usually drugs. It's particularly bad on the road between Tetouan and Tangier.

It goes without saying that women attempting to hitch without a male companion are placing themselves at risk.

The Mediterranean Coast & the Rif

From those two bastions of Spanish tenacity, the enclaves of Ceuta and Melilla, to the cosmopolitan hustle and hassle of Tangier and the contrasting laid-back ambience of Chechaouen in the Rif Mountains, the northwestern region of Morocco manages to offer, in a relatively small geographical area, a diverse range of experiences for the independent traveller.

Tangier

All the various peoples who have settled here at one time or another have left their mark on the city, so it has an atmosphere which is very different from that of other Moroccan cities. However, there's little left of the sophisticated decadence for which it was notorious during the 1930s and 1940s.

As a result of Tangier being the major port of entry for tourists, the sleaze and the opulence have been replaced by hordes of the world's best hustlers. Pick any language, any situation, any time of day or night, and they'll find you like flies find shit. Nothing you say is going to make any difference to the persistent patter which will accompany you all the way from the ferry to the inside of the hotel room which you choose. Even if you know exactly which hotel you are heading for and its exact location, and require no 'help', they'll claim they found it for you. Naturally, you'll want to 'reward' them. Every subterfuge in the book will be used to get you to pay. Getting into the first available taxi is no guarantee of shaking them off either – they'll just muscle their way into the taxi!

That unemployment in Morocco is high cannot be denied – hence there's some justification for this behaviour. But these hustlers are rivalled only by those who hang around the entrance to the medina in Marrakesh. There's no way through this cobweb that's

guaranteed to succeed, but patience, politeness, minimal interaction and firmness can go a long way to reducing any 'claim' they have on you. You'll just have to treat it as your first introduction to Morocco. Things do get better!

History

Tangier has been coveted for millennia as a strategic site for a fortress commanding the Straits of Gibraltar. The area was certainly settled by the ancient Greeks and Phoenicians, for whom it was a trading port. The name which the latter gave to it – Tingis – has, more or less, remained the same. It also gave rise to the name of the citrus fruit tangerine, though the tree was imported by either the Romans or the Arabs at a later date.

Since those early days, the site has been one of the most contested in the Mediterranean world. Among those who have occupied it at one time or another are the Romans (1st to 5th century), Vandals (5th century), Byzantines (6th), Arabs (8th), Berbers (8th), Fatimids (10th), Almoravids (11th), Almohads (12th), Merenids (13th), Portuguese (15th and 16th), Spanish (16th), British (17th) and French (19th).

During the Roman period, Diocletian made it the capital of what remained of the province of Mauretania; incredible as it may seem, it was garrisoned by British (ie Celtic) cavalry. Not long after, it became part of the Christian episcopal see of Spain, and in fact may actually have been the seat of the bishops.

Following the break up of the Roman Empire and the arrival of the Vandals from Spain in 429 AD, there was a long period of strife between the Barbarians and the Byzantine Empire for control of the site. Actually, the Byzantines only ever occupied Tangier for short periods of time, contenting themselves with their strongly fortified outpost at Ceuta.

The Byzantines remained for only a short

while and, once they had withdrawn, little was recorded about the area until the coming of the Arabs in 705 AD. Possibly one of the reasons for this was the smallpox epidemic which wrought havoc throughout Europe and North Africa not long afterwards; another may have been the continual warfare between the indigenous Berber tribes and the conquering Arabs.

Once Arab supremacy had been established, however, Tangier became a bone of contention between the Omayyads of Spain and the Idrissids of Morocco, and was eventually occupied by the Fatimids of Tunis in 958. A little over 100 years later, it was taken by the Islamic fundamentalist Almoravids as they swept across Morocco from their Mauretanian desert strongholds; it eventually passed to the Almohads in 1149. As the Almohad regime gradually reached its nadir the city elected to be ruled by the Hafsids of Tunis, but passed to Merenid control shortly afterwards in 1274.

A few centuries later, following the victories of the Christian armies in the Iberian peninsula, the Portuguese attempted to take Tangier in 1437. Unsuccessful at first, they finally made it in 1471. Tangier was passed to Philip II of Spain in 1580 when Spain and Portugal were united; it reverted to Portugal when that country regained its independence, only to be passed to England in 1661 as part of Catherine of Braganza's dowry to Charles II (she also brought with her the Portuguese enclave in India which would eventually become Bombay).

The English were not to remain long. Tangier was besieged by Moulay Ismail in 1679 but the English only abandoned the city seven years later (after destroying the port and most of the city), following a dispute between parliament and the king in which the former refused funding for the reinforcement of the garrison in Tangier.

From that point on, the Moroccans were left in control until the mid-19th century, when Tangier became the object of intense rivalry between the French, Spanish, Italians, British and Germans. The situation was partially resolved by the Treaty of Algeciras, whereby the British were bought off with Egypt and the Italians with Libya, leaving the remaining three European powers intriguing for the spoils. The status of the city was finally resolved only in 1923, when Tangier and the surrounding countryside was declared an 'international zone' controlled by the resident diplomatic agents of France, Spain, Britain, Portugal, Sweden, Holland, Belgium, Italy and the USA; however, Italy and the USA refused to recognise the arrangement for a while. Even the Moroccan sultan was represented by an agent, though the latter was appointed by the French Resident-General (by this time France and Spain had divided Morocco between them).

Tangier was to remain an 'international zone' until a few months after Morocco became independent, when it was reunited with the rest of the country. In the meantime it became one of the most fashionable Mediterranean resorts, as well as a haven for freebooters, artists, writers, refugees, exiles and bankers; it was also renowned for its high profile gay and paedophile scene. Each of the countries represented in Tangier maintained its own banks, post offices and currency, and took a share in the policing of the city. Banks, in particular, made fortunes out of manipulating the currency markets. All this came to an end in 1956, but the legend of notoriety lingers on.

Orientation

The square known as the Grand Socco is the centre of things and is the link between the medina and the new city. From here the medina covers the hillside below, and the crowded main street, Rue es Siaghin, leads down to the Petit Socco. This smaller square forms the heart of the medina. To the southeast of the medina, the port, bus offices and train station are all within easy walking distance. The kasbah occupies the north-west corner of the medina and is built in a dominating position on the top of the cliff. The whole medina is fairly small and, although it is the usual tangle of twisting narrow lanes, it is very easy to find your way around in it.

The new city lies to the west and south of

1 Hotel de Grand Socco
2 Pensions Mauritania & Becerra
3 Ave Mokhtar Ahardan
  (Pensions Palace, Amal,
  Karlton, Hotel Mamora etc)
4 Great Mosque
5 Old Bus Terminals
6 Rue de la Plage
  (Pensions Miami, Détroit etc)
7 National Tourist Office (ONMT)
8 Post Office (PTT)
9 CTM Office
10 Restaurant Africa
11 Voyages Schwartz (Amex)

the medina and, as is usually the case, it contains the bulk of the banks, the main post office, the consulates and the middle and top-end accommodation. The main streets of interest to travellers in this part of the city are the Blvd Pasteur, the Blvd Mohammed V and the Avenue des FAR. A new bus station has been built on the Place Jamia el Arabia at the end of Ave Louis van Beethoven and should soon replace the chaos in front of the train station. If you arrive here, you'll need to take a taxi into the centre as it's a long way from both the main hotel areas.

Information

Tourist Office The tourist office, at 29 Blvd Pasteur, has a limited range of maps and brochures and the staff speak several languages (you can usually rely on English, French, German and Spanish). Otherwise, it's of marginal use – they didn't even know where the Algerian Consulate was despite the fact it was in the fortnightly publication, *La Quinzaine du Maroc*. This booklet is available from most tourist offices in Morocco as well as the large hotels.

Money There are plenty of banks along both Blvd Pasteur and Blvd Mohammed V as well as one on the bottom side of the Grand Socco at the junction with Rue d'Italie which is quick and efficient. Mid-range hotels can also usually change money at much the same rate as the banks. Outside banking hours, any of the big hotels should be able to help.

The agent for American Express is Voyages Schwartz (☎ 93 7546), 54 Blvd Pasteur. Thomas Cook/Wagons Lits (☎ 93 1640) is at 86 Rue de la Liberté.

Post The main post office is on Blvd Mohammed V, 15 to 20 minutes walk from the Grand Socco.

Foreign Consulates Quite a few countries have diplomatic representation in Tangier. See the Morocco Facts for the Visitor chapter for details.

Books The *Rogue's Guide to Tangier* is a humorous and well-written alternative guide to the city. It's well worth buying but is only sporadically available from some of the larger hotels.

Medina

The Petit Socco, with its cafés and restaurants, is very much the centre of things; it's easy to sit for an hour or so, sipping a mint tea and watching the world go by. In the days of the international zone this was the sin and sleaze centre of the city, and today it retains something of its seedy air. The whispers in your ear of 'Something special, my friend?' (or the equivalent phrase in French, German or Spanish) are amazingly constant.

The narrow Rue des Chrétiens takes you to the kasbah. When you take a walk along here you really have to run the gauntlet past the shopkeepers, who practically leap out and grab you to come and have a look.

Kasbah The kasbah is built on the highest point of the city; you enter from Bab el Assa at the end of Rue ben Raissouli in the medina. The gate gives onto a large open courtyard which leads to the Dar el Makhzem, the former sultan's palace and now quite a good museum.

The palace itself was built by Moulay Ismail in the 17th century and enlarged at various stages by the later sultans. The interior has some beautifully carved wooden ceilings and a marble courtyard. You can leave via the garden and visit the Café Detroit on the 2nd floor in the walls. It was set up by Brian Gysin, the 1960s writer and friend of the Rolling Stones, and was called The Thousand & One Nights. It became famous for the trance musicians who played here in the 1960s and released a record produced by Brian Jones.

Musicians still play here, but today it's a tourist trap nonpareil. The tour groups are all brought here, and after the obligatory mint tea they file out while the musicians play European songs of the 'Roll Out the Barrel' variety. It's worth a trip up here just for the fantastic views over the port, but the tea and traditional cakes are expensive. The museum is open daily, except Tuesday, from 9 am to 3.30 pm in summer and 9 to 11.45 am and 3 to 6 pm in winter; entry is Dr 10.

Places to Stay – bottom end

Most of the traditional Moroccan-style hostelries are to be found in the medina around the Petit Socco and along the Ave Mokhtar Ahardan (formerly the Rue des Postes), which connects the Petit Socco and the port area. They run the gamut from flophouses to two-star hotels.

If you're arriving by ferry from Spain or Gibraltar, walk out of the port area until you pass through the main gates and arrive at a square with the railway station on your left and bus offices on your right. Then take the road on the extreme right-hand side, which goes uphill until you get to a set of steps just past the junction with Rue de Portugal. Go up the steps and you'll find yourself at the bottom of the Ave Mokhtar Ahardan (see the Tangier-Medina (Budget Hotel Area) map).

If you'd prefer more European-style hotels on your first night(s) or don't want to stay in the medina area then, once out of the port gates, carry on past the railway station and take the first street on your right, Rue de la Plage (also called Rue Salah Eddine el Ayoubi), or the (narrower) fourth street on your right (Rue Magellan) where there's also a good choice of unclassified, one and two-star hotels (see the Tangier-Centre Ville Nouvelle map).

Medina Area Almost all the hotels in this area are either on or just off the Petit Socco and along the Ave Mokhtar Ahardan. There are plenty of cheap pensions to choose from here. Most of them are very basic and you won't get much more than a bed and shared bathroom facilities, though some of them do offer hot water (for a small extra charge). Prices vary only slightly and you're looking at Dr 15 for a dormitory bed (where available) and Dr 30 to Dr 40 for singles and Dr 50 to Dr 60 for doubles. Some are grubby; some are well maintained. They include the

Hotel Esaada and the Pensions *Becerra, Larache, Fuentis, Amal, Fès, Karlton, Maarifa, Tan Tan* and *Victoria*.

Recommended here is the recently refurbished *Pension Palace* (☎ 93 6128), 2 Ave Mokhtar Ahardan, which offers pleasant, airy rooms without own shower for Dr 40/80 for singles/doubles and Dr 120 a double with own shower. Many of the rooms front onto a quiet internal courtyard. Also worth checking out is the *Hotel de Grand Socco*, in the square of the same name, which is friendly and has singles/doubles/triples with shared

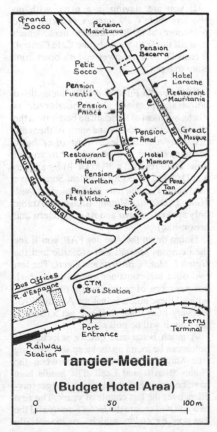

Tangier-Medina

(Budget Hotel Area)

bathroom facilities for Dr 42/55/88 plus taxes.

Somewhat better accommodation can be found at the one-star *Hotel Olid* (☎ 93 1310), 12 Ave Mokhtar Ahardan, which has singles/doubles with shower but shared toilet for Dr 66/85 and Dr 85/98 with own shower and toilet. Taxes are extra.

If you prefer a modicum of luxury but still want to stay in the medina area then the place to stay is the two-star *Hotel Mamora* (☎ 93 4105), 19 Ave Mokhtar Ahardan, which offers excellent, spotlessly clean singles/ doubles with shower for Dr 94/110 or Dr 119/138 with shower and toilet.

If you are staying in a place with no showers there's a *hammam* (Turkish-style bathhouse) at 80 Rue des Chrétiens, which runs off the Petit Socco by the Café Central. It costs Dr 5 for a shower, and it's open from 8 am to 8 pm.

Ville Nouvelle First up are the unclassified hotels and pensions along the Rue de la Plage, but most of these are no better than the cheapies in the medina and some of them are decidedly characterless. Most offer basic accommodation with shared bathroom and toilet facilities for Dr 30 to Dr 40 for singles and Dr 50 to Dr 60 for doubles. Some have hot water. They include the pensions *Royal, Madrid, Détroit, Miami, Talavera* (Arabic only spoken), *Playa* and *Atou* (modern and prison-like).

Going down the Ave des FAR you'll see the Pensions *Mendez* and *Majestic* and the *Hotels L'Marsa, Biarritz* and *Cecil*. The last two offer self-contained rooms (for which you pay more, of course) but the only trouble with all these hotels is that the Ave des FAR is a very busy road, so if you get a room at the front it will be noisy.

A much better and quieter selection of hotels can be found up the steep and winding Rue Magellan, which starts between the Hotels Biarritz and Cecil. The hotels here have become very popular with budget travellers over the last couple of years. The first two you will see are the *Hotel Family* and the *Pension Excelsior*, which are essentially flophouses. Go further up and around the corner and you will get to the *Hotels l'Amor* and *Magellan*, which both offer clean, well-maintained rooms with own shower but shared toilet for Dr 40/80 for singles/doubles. The Magellan advertises hot water '24 hours a day'.

Further up again brings you to the *Hotel El Muniria/Tanger Inn* and the *Hotel Ibn Batuta* (☎ 93 7170), opposite one another just before you reach a flight of steps. They're both one-star hotels and offer spotlessly clean singles/doubles with own bathroom for Dr 85/98 plus taxes. The El Muniria is where William Burroughs wrote *The Naked Lunch*, if that makes any difference to you. It's also a popular place to take an evening beer and many of the rooms have a good view of the harbour.

Very close by and a hotel with even better views over the harbour (assuming you get a front room) is the one-star *Hotel Massilia* (☎ 93 5009), on the corner of Rue Ibn Joubair and Rue Targha. The staff here are very friendly and a double room with own shower, toilet and hot water costs Dr 130 including breakfast.

Continuing on up to the top of what is essentially Rue Magellan you arrive at the junction of Blvd Mohammed V and Blvd Pasteur. Right opposite the tourist office here is the *Hotel de Paris* (☎ 93 8126), 42 Blvd Pasteur, a popular one-star hotel with airy rooms and friendly staff. It costs Dr 45/65 with shared bathroom facilities, Dr 66/85 with own shower but shared toilet and Dr 85/98 with own shower and toilet for singles/doubles. Taxes are extra. On the next street up, parallel to Blvd Pasteur, are the unclassified *Pension Al Hoceima* and the *Pension Atlal*.

It's unlikely you will have to go further afield than this to find budget-priced accommodation but, if you do, there is the *Omar Khayam Annexe* on the Rue Antaki, which is off the Ave des FAR further down the road from the Cecil.

Camping Campers have a choice of two sites. The cheaper and more convenient of

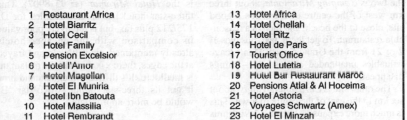

1 Restaurant Africa	13 Hotel Africa
2 Hotel Biarritz	14 Hotel Chellah
3 Hotel Cecil	15 Hotel Ritz
4 Hotel Family	16 Hotel de Paris
5 Pension Excelsior	17 Tourist Office
6 Hotel l'Amor	18 Hotel Lutetia
7 Hotel Magollan	19 Hotel Bar Restaurant Maroc
8 Hotel El Muniria	20 Pensions Atlai & Al Hoceima
9 Hotel Ibn Batouta	21 Hotel Astoria
10 Hotel Massilia	22 Voyages Schwartz (Amex)
11 Hotel Rembrandt	23 Hotel El Minzah
12 Hotel Tanja Flandria	

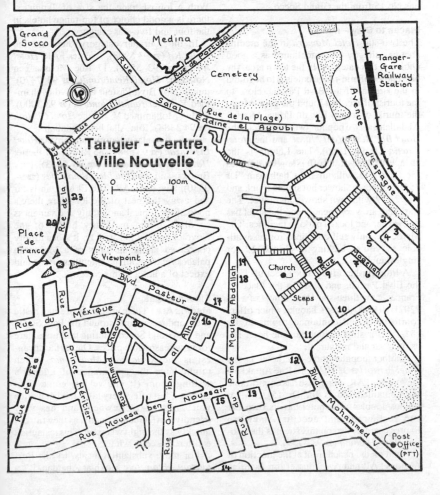

the two is *Camping Miramonte*, about three km west of the centre of town. It's a good site, close to the beach, and there's a reasonable restaurant. To get there, take bus Nos 1, 2 or 21 from the Grand Socco. Don't leave valuables unattended at this site – things disappear.

The other site is *Caravaning Tingis*, about six km to the east of the centre of town. This is much more expensive but includes a tennis court and swimming pool. To get there, take bus No 15 from the Grand Socco.

Places to Stay – middle

The two-star *Hotel Mamora* in the medina area has already been mentioned as a good choice in this category. In the town area, the best choice of mid-range hotels is to be found in the streets off the Blvd Pasteur, close to the tourist office. Just round the corner from the tourist office on Rue du Prince Moulay Abdallah are two popular two-star hotels, the *Hotel Bar Restaurant Maroc* and the *Hotel Lutetia* (☎ 93 1866). The Lutetia is the cheaper of the two and offers singles/doubles for Dr 61/75 without own bathroom, Dr 75/92 with own shower but shared toilet, and Dr 92/112 with own shower and toilet. The staff here are very friendly and the hotel has its own bar and locked parking facilities. The Maroc has only self-contained rooms available so you're looking at Dr 92/112 for singles/doubles.

A little further afield, one street up from the Blvd Pasteur and close to the Place de France, is the three-star *Hotel Astoria* (☎ 93 7202), 10 Rue Ahmed Chaouki, which offers comfortable self-contained rooms at Dr 151/186 for singles/doubles. The hotel has its own bar and restaurant.

Another popular three-star hotel is the *Hotel Bristol* (☎ 93 1070), 14 Rue Antaki off the Ave des FAR, which also has comfortable self-contained rooms for Dr 151/186 for singles/doubles. The hotel has its own bar and restaurant and accepts American Express cards. Also on this street is the two-star *Hotel Djenina* (☎ 93 4759).

Right on the beach front at the junction of Ave des FAR and Ave Youssef Ibn Tachfine is the *Hotel Miramar* (☎ 93 8907). This three-star hotel has singles/doubles for Dr 175/212 plus tax, but is relatively poor value in comparison with the cheaper hotels already mentioned, since it's old and frayed at the edges, there's no bar and the restaurant is mediocre. It's difficult to understand how it got its three-star rating – two-star 'B' would be more appropriate.

Places to Stay – top end

With a tourist trade the size of Tangier's, there is a good choice of top-range hotels in the four and five-star category.

In the four-star category there are the *Hotel Rif* (☎ 93 5908), Ave des FAR; *Hotel Africa* (☎ 93 5511), 17 Rue Moussa ben Noussair; *Hotel Rembrandt* (☎ 93 7870), junction of Blvd Pasteur and Blvd Mohammed V; *Hotel Tanjah Flandria* (☎ 93 3000), 6 Blvd Mohammed V; and the *Hotel Chellah* (☎ 94 3388), Rue Allal ben Abdallah.

In the five-star category there are the *Hotel El Minzah* (☎ 93 5885), 85 Rue de la Liberté; *Hotel Intercontinental* (☎ 93 6053), Park Brooks; and the *Hotel les Almohades* (☎ 94 0330), Ave des FAR. The El Minzah is far and away the best of the lot. Here there's none of the typical anonymity and sameness so often found in luxury hotels of the Novotel and Sofitel variety. It's beautifully conceived along the lines of a Moroccan palace, yet it has all the amenities you would expect of a hotel in this category.

Places to Eat

Medina Area There are plenty of small rustic cafés and restaurants around the Petit Socco and the Grand Socco offering traditional fare for very reasonable prices. One of the cheapest is the *Restaurant Mauritania*, which might have the appearance of Lucifer's waiting room (if you've just come from Europe), but offers very tasty food at a price you can't beat elsewhere and has very friendly staff. Get there early, as they run out quickly as the night wears on. This restaurant is often closed in winter.

For more substantial meals, try the *Restaurant Ahlan*, Ave Mokhtar Ahardan. It's a popular place and offers excellent chicken and olive tajines with soup for around Dr 15. Also good value is the cosy *Restaurant Moderne* at No 21 on the same street.

There are a couple of food stalls at the bottom of the steps at the end of Ave Mokhtar Ahardan. The one closest to the port looks a bit rough, but does excellent fried fish with a tomato sauce and bread for just a few dirham; three or four make a fair meal.

Ville Nouvelle At 83 Rue de la Plage, almost on the corner of Ave d'Espagne, is the *Restaurant Africa*, which has good set menus for Dr 30 for three courses as well as good individual dishes. There are restaurants on either side of the Africa which are also worth investigating.

Somewhat more expensive meals with a more European flavour can be found in the restaurants and cafés around the Place de France. If you're staying in one or other of the hotels on Rue Magellan or Blvd Pasteur then the Rue du Prince Moulay Abdallah, just around the corner from the tourist office, is an excellent street to find anything ranging from Moroccan/European takeaways to a full-on Moroccan banquet complete with belly dancers. Obviously, you get what you pay for, but the takeaways are excellent value and very tasty. If you want to splurge in one of the classier restaurants here, then check out prices and opening hours during the day to get an idea of what your options are. Restaurants on this street include *Les Ambassadeurs, Damascus, Brenda's Tea Shoppe, Pizzaria, Romero* (seafood) and the *Morocco Palace* (belly dancers) as well as a number of unnamed sandwich bars.

Things to Buy

Tangier is not the ideal place to buy souvenirs – the place sees too many people coming over from Spain on day trips and the prices are generally way over the top. It is possible to get things for a reasonable price but it involves a lot of hard work. If you have to buy something here, keep clear of Blvd Pasteur and shop in the medina.

Getting There & Away

Air The following airlines have offices in Tangier:

Air France
    7 Rue du Méxique (℅ 93 6477)
British Airways
    Rue de la Liberté (☎ 93 5211)
GB Airways
    83 Rue de la Liberté (☎ 93 5877)
Iberia
    35 Blvd Pasteur (☎ 93 6177)
KLM
    Rue du Méxique (☎ 93 8926)
Lufthansa
    7 Rue du Méxique (☎ 93 1327)
Royal Air Maroc
    Place de France (☎ 93 5505)

Bus By the time you read this, all bus companies should be operating from the new bus station on the Place Jamia el Arabia at the end of Ave Louis van Beethoven. It is too far to walk from the medina/Blvd Pasteur area so you'll have to take a petit taxi.

There are regular CTM departures to Casablanca (Dr 80), Fès (Dr 67.50), Rabat (Dr 59), Tetouan (Dr 12), and other smaller places.

Train There are two railway stations – Tangier Gare and Tangier Port. Most trains start from the Port station out at the port and stop at the Gare.

The main departures are to:

Marrakesh (4.02 pm, 8 pm (Gare only), 11.30 pm, 10 hours)
Meknès and Fès (12.30 am, 9.02 am, (both Gare only), 4.02 pm, five and six hours)
Oujda (same times as those to Meknès and Fès, 12 hours)
Rabat and Casablanca (7.22 am (Gare only), 4.02 pm, four and 5½ hours)

Taxi Grands taxis leave from around the square in front of the station/port entry gate; there are regular departures to Tetouan (Dr 20), Asilah and Rabat.

Sea If you're heading to Spain or Gibraltar by boat you can buy tickets from the company offices down at the dock (closed on weekends), or from virtually any travel agency around town. The Wasteel agency by the port entrance is a popular one.

Ferry is the cheapest way to travel between Europe and Morocco. When arriving in Tangier, it's only a few minutes' walk from the ferry terminal to the medina; it will no doubt seem a lot longer as you will be accompanied by persistent touts.

There are ferries to both Algeciras (Spain) and Sète (France). In summer there are also hydrofoils to Algeciras and Gibraltar. See the Morocco Getting There & Away chapter for more details.

Getting Around

To/From the Airport Tangier Airport is 15 km from the town centre. From here you can arrange taxis into town.

Petits Taxis The price for a standard petit taxi journey around town is Dr 8.

Spanish Morocco

CEUTA

One of the two tiny Spanish enclaves on the northern coast of Morocco, Ceuta came under Spanish control in the late 15th century and, when the rest of Morocco attained independence in 1956, was retained by Spain. Like Melilla, it's an intensely Andalusian city, but is regarded by the Moroccans in much the same way as the Spanish regard Gibraltar. Campaigns are occasionally mounted for the enclave's return to Morocco, but so far they have all fallen on deaf ears, and the colony is likely to remain Spanish for a long time to come.

Known as Sebta in Arabic, Ceuta's raison d'être is as a supply and service centre for the military base here; its duty-free status helps it to prosper. You're not going to find any great bargains, but if you are heading for Algeria it's worth picking up a bottle of whisky for sale later on. Fuel is also worth buying, as it's cheaper here than in Morocco; stock up if you're driving.

Ceuta doesn't offer the visitor a great deal. There's nothing to keep you here, especially as it's not particularly cheap. If you're heading for Morocco, your best bet is to catch an early ferry from Algeciras and move straight through to Tetouan or Chechaouen.

A lot of people enter Morocco via Ceuta as a way of avoiding the hundreds of touts who hang around in Tangier, just waiting for the ferries to arrive so they can attach themselves to the new arrivals.

Information

Tourist Office The small tourist office (☎ 51 1379) is right by the ferry terminal, so you can pick up the useful brochure, map and accommodation list. The guy staffing the office speaks reasonable English and is helpful with any enquiries. It is open from 8 am to 2 pm and 4 to 6 pm Monday to Saturday; closed Sunday. Outside these hours, the ferry times, maps and other handy info are displayed in the window.

Money There are plenty of banks along the main street, Paseo del Revellin, and its continuation, Calle Camoens. It's sometimes possible to buy Moroccan dirham, even though they're a non-exportable soft currency. Outside business hours you should be able to change small amounts of foreign currency at the four-star Hotel La Muralla at Plaza de Africa.

There are moneychanging facilities at the border in the form of a bank on the Moroccan side and informal moneychangers on the Spanish side. The latter deal almost exclusively in dirham and pesetas but the rate is only average. If you want to change other currencies, the rates are worse.

Post The main post office (*correos y telégrafos*) is the big yellow building at Plaza de España, a square just off Calle Camoens, in the centre of town.

Archaeology Museum

This tiny museum, set in a small park just off the busy Avenida de España, is not really worth bothering with but it will kill five minutes if you are waiting for a ferry. There is just one tiny room, with a few bits and pieces from Palaeolithic times through to Spanish. The museum has a subterranean gallery, but it has been closed off. Opening hours are 9 am to 1 pm and 5 to 7 pm; closed Monday.

Legión Museum

The Museo de la Legión is dedicated to this highly regarded special unit of the army created in 1920. It holds a staggering array of weapons, uniforms and other military paraphernalia – quite interesting if you like that sort of thing, although the glass-eyed dummies are a bit bizarre. The museum is on Paseo de Colón and is open only on Saturdays, Sundays and public holidays from 11 am to 2 pm and 4 to 6 pm.

Peninsula

If you have a couple of hours to spare, it's easy to walk around the peninsula, which is capped by Monte Acho. From the convent of Ermita de San Antonio there is an excellent view over the Mediterranean, and Gibraltar is plainly visible on a clear day.

At the convent itself, originally built in the 17th century and reconstructed in the 1960s, a large festival is held annually on 13 June to mark San Antonio's Day.

Places to Stay – bottom end

There is no shortage of *fondas* and *casas de huéspedes*, easily identifiable by the large blue-and-white F or CH on the entrances. Cheapest of these is the small *Pensión Charito* (☎ 51 3982), on the 1st floor at 5 Calle Arrabal, about 15 minutes' walk along the waterfront from the ferry terminal. The only indication that it is a guesthouse is the 'Chambres' sign above the footpath, and the CH sign on the wall. There are only eight rooms and they cost 500/900 Ptas for singles/doubles. There are no hot showers in this place but otherwise it is quite adequate. Just around the corner from the Charito, and right on the waterfront, is the *Pensión Marina* (☎ 51 3206), on the 3rd floor at 26 Marina Española. It is a tiny place with only

three double rooms, which go for 1200 Ptas each. It's basic but OK.

Conveniently situated right in the centre, the *Pensión Revellin* ☎ 51 6762) is on the 2nd floor at 2 Paseo del Revellin. The doorway is right in the middle of the busy shopping street and again can be identified by the CH sign. It is directly opposite the Banco Popular Español. Rooms cost 800/1500 Ptas for singles/doubles, and hot showers are available for an extra 150 Ptas.

Youth Hostel The *Youth Hostel* is the cheapest place to stay, but unfortunately it only operates during the school vacation periods of July and August. It's hidden away on the Plaza Rafael Gilbert, just off Paseo del Revellin where you see a big red sign for the Restaurant China – stairs lead up through an arch to the Plaza, and the hostel is in the corner to the right.

Places to Stay – middle

Those looking for comfort should try the *Atlante* (☎ 51 3548), at 1 Paseo de las Palmeras, right on the waterfront and handy to the boat terminal. It is a two-star *hostale residencia* and charges 2000/2600 Ptas for singles/doubles with washbasin.

Places to Stay – top end

The four-star *Hotel La Muralla* (☎ 51 4940) is at 15 Plaza de Africa. It'll set you back around 6200/10,300 Ptas for singles/doubles with private bath. Breakfast is an extra 600 Ptas.

Places to Eat

Finding a good cheap meal is a real problem in Ceuta. There are plenty of cafés which just have snacks, but these are still quite expensive and not really very filling.

Things get cheaper as you get further from the centre along Calle Real. The *Café La Imperial* at No 27 has some set menus for 400 Ptas.

Getting There & Away

To/From Morocco Buses to the border run every 15 minutes or so from Plaza de la

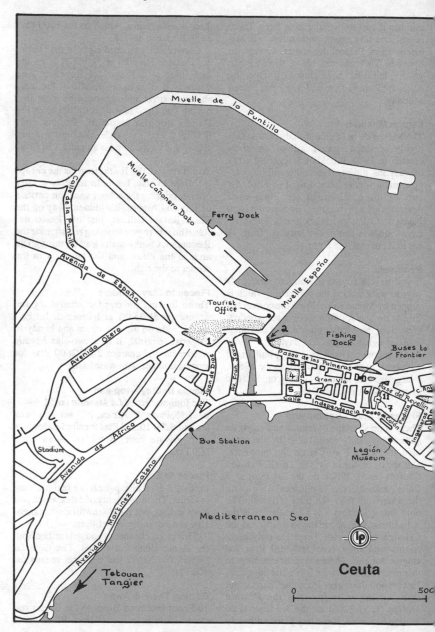

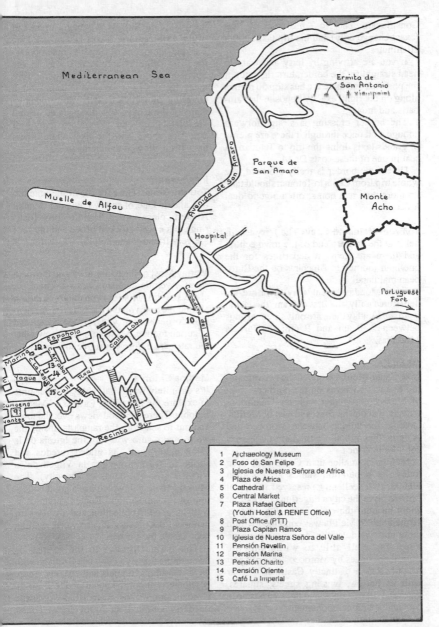

1   Archaeology Museum
2   Foso de San Felipe
3   Iglesia de Nuestra Señora de Africa
4   Plaza de Africa
5   Cathedral
6   Central Market
7   Plaza Rafael Gilbert
    (Youth Hostel & RENFE Office)
8   Post Office (PTT)
9   Plaza Capitan Ramos
10 Iglesia de Nuestra Señora del Valle
11 Pensión Revellin
12 Pensión Marina
13 Pensión Charito
14 Pensión Oriente
15 Café La Imperial

Constitucion. The No 7 bus costs 40 Ptas (exact change only) and the trip takes about 20 minutes.

If you are arriving by ferry and want to head straight for the border, turn right out of the port area and there is a bus stop 50 metres along on the right, exactly opposite the ramparts and moat.

The border crossing is straightforward enough, and once through it there are plenty of grands taxis doing the trip to Tetouan. A seat in one of these costs Dr 14.

Unless the border is really crowded, the whole trip from Ceuta to Tetouan should take no more than two hours; often a good deal less.

To/From Mainland Spain The ferry terminal is at the western end of the town centre, and there are frequent departures for the one-hour journey to Algeciras on the European mainland.

From Monday to Saturday there are six departures daily, the first at 8 am, the last at 9 pm; on Sunday there are only three sailings between 9.30 am and 9 pm; the fare is 1100 Ptas.

MELILLA

Like Ceuta, Melilla is one of the two remaining Spanish enclaves on the northern coast of Morocco. Together with the Chafarinas Islands, just off the coast and east of Melilla, close to the border between Morocco and Algeria, they are all that remain of Spain's colonies in Africa.

Melilla is smaller than Ceuta and, even today, its population stands at less than 80,000. Its excellently preserved medieval fortress gives the city a lingering fascination. Right up until the end of the 19th century virtually all of Melilla was contained within these massive defensive walls; the garrison here was well able to withstand the occasional sieges by Morocco. This old part of town has a distinctly Castilian flavour with its narrow, twisting streets, squares, gates and drawbridges, and the area has been declared a national monument.

Construction of the new part of town, to the west of the fortress, was begun at the end of the 19th century; it was laid out by Don Enrique Nieto, one of Gaudí's contemporaries. The original architecture was in the Spanish modernist style, and there were many façades of stucco and gypsum with a covering of Sevillan tiles. Unfortunately, many of these have now disappeared behind the plate glass and aluminium frames of duty-free shops and the like, while others have been allowed to deteriorate.

Information

Tourist Office The office is at the junction of Calle de Querol and Avenida del General Aizpuru, close to the Plaza de Toros (bullring). It's a well-stocked office and the staff are very friendly and helpful.

Money Most of the banks are along the main street, Avenida de Juan Carlos I. There are always a lot of moneychangers hanging around the cafés on the Plaza de España who will do deals with you for Moroccan and Algerian money. Make sure you know what the rates are before you agree to a deal.

Medina Sidonia

It's definitely worth half a day of your time to explore the incredible fortress of Medina Sidonia. There are good views over the town and out to sea from the ramparts. Inside the walls, make sure you visit the Iglesia de la Concepción, with its gilded reredos and shrine to Nuestra Señora la Virgen de la Victoria (the patroness of the city). The Museo Municipal, which has a good collection of Phoenician and Roman ceramics as well as a coin collection and displays of historical documents, is also worth visiting once inside the fortress.

The main entrance to the fortress is through the massive Puerta de Santiago with its drawbridges, tunnels and chapels. There is another entrance, known as the Foso de Hornabeque, on the eastern flank opposite the ferry terminal; this provides vehicular access via a stone tunnel under the walls.

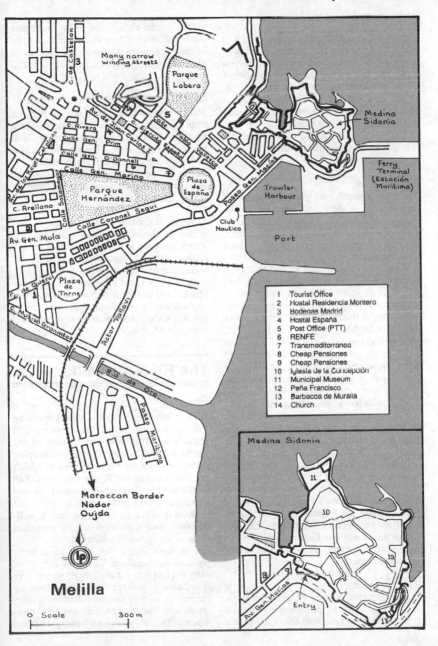

1 Tourist Office
2 Hostal Residencia Montero
3 Bodegas Madrid
4 Hostal España
5 Post Office (PTT)
6 RENFE
7 Transmediterranea
8 Cheap Pensiones
9 Cheap Pensiones
10 Iglesia de la Concepción
11 Municipal Museum
12 Peña Francisco
13 Barbacoa de Muralla
14 Church

Melilla

0   Scale   300m

Places to Stay

There's not a lot of cheap accommodation in Melilla, so you may find yourself staying in a one or two-star hotel, especially if you arrive late in the day. There are a couple of cheap pensiones on the Calle de Jardines, which runs parallel to the Paseo General Macías, but these are pretty rough and ready and function mainly as brothels.

The other option is one of the three-star hotels – these cost around 4000 Ptas for a double with bath.

Places to Eat

There are a number of good restaurants to choose from in the streets bounded by the Avenida de Juan Carlos I, the Avenida de los Reyes Catolicos and the Parque Hernández, but check prices before you eat, as most are quite expensive.

A better hunting ground for budget travellers is the Calle de Castelon. Here you'll find a number of rustic bar/restaurants, most of which open only in the evenings (though some open at lunch time too). They all have a range of fresh seafood, meat and salads on display, and you can eat very well indeed at a reasonable price. All of them offer cheap Spanish wines and beer and, by early evening, they are packed out by revellers. Highly recommended is the *Bodegas Madrid* with its old wine casks for tables.

For a splurge, you can't beat the *Barbacoa de Muralla*, inside the fortress on top of the Foso de Hornabeque. The restaurant is in a refurbished building which retains all its original features, including the barred windows overlooking the port. If you're not sure you can afford a meal here, pop in first, order a beer and have a look at the menu.

Also inside the fortress are a number of small bar/restaurants where you can get simple meals and snacks and drink away to your heart's content. They're open lunch times and evenings.

Entertainment

You could spend your evenings in the many bars around town or promenading up and down the main street. Other than that, there's a folk music club – the Peña Francisco, inside the fortress (see map) which is open in the evenings – as well as a number of discotheques (addresses in the tourist leaflet).

Getting There & Away

To/From Morocco There are local buses from the Plaza de España to the border which run from about 7.30 am to late evening. From where the buses stop, it's about 150 metres to the Spanish customs and then another 200 metres to the Moroccan customs. On the other side of the Moroccan customs there are frequent buses to Nador.

To/From Mainland Spain Melilla is connected to Spain by ferries from Malaga. There is usually at least one per day, though sailings are occasionally cancelled in the winter due to rough weather.

Both RENFE and Transmediterranea have offices in town (see map for location) where you can buy ferry tickets. Otherwise, tickets can be purchased at the ferry terminal itself (Estación Maritima).

The Rif Mountains

TETOUAN

With its interesting medina, dramatic setting and nearby beaches, Tetouan isn't a bad place, especially since the creation of the pedestrian mall along the main shopping street, between the Place Moulay el Mehdi and the Place Hassan II. The city also has an unmistakable Spanish-Moroccan flavour which you won't find elsewhere.

Several years ago, Tetouan had a well-deserved bad reputation for its persistent touts which generally induced most travellers to leave after a day in search of more pleasant surroundings. This is no longer the case, but just why it has changed so radically is not clear – perhaps there was a purge by the police, or they simply killed the golden goose and had to seek 'employment' elsewhere. So, if you hear nasty stories,

Top: Djemaa el Fna, Marrakesh, Morocco (GC)
Left: Water seller, Rabat, Morocco (HF)
Right: Dar el Makhzen, Tangier, Morocco (HF)

Top: Todra Gorge, Morocco (GC)
Left: Fès el-Bali, Morocco (HF)
Right: Tanneries, Fès, Morocco (HF)

remember that reputations die hard, and don't strike Tetouan off your itinerary.

History

Tetouan was a Mauretanian city founded in the 3rd century BC; it was destroyed in the 1st century AD by the Romans, following a revolt against their annexation of the country. Other than a Roman military camp which remained for about 200 years, the site was not resettled until the advent of the Merenids in the early 14th century.

The Merenids needed Tetouan as a base from which to attack a rival claimant to the Moroccan throne who was supported by the Spanish. Though the town initially became prosperous, it was destroyed by the Christian king of Castille in 1399 and not reoccupied until the 16th century.

The new occupants of the town – mainly Arab-Berber and Jewish refugees from Spain – made their living from piracy in the western Mediterranean. They eventually incurred the wrath of the Spanish monarchy, which led to the blockading of the pirates' port of Martil on the coast which, in turn, led to another decline in the city's fortunes. Tetouan prospered once more under Moulay Ismail; however, it was captured again by the Spanish in 1862. They stayed for some three years and, although they evacuated the town, they effectively remained in control until they reoccupied the town in 1913 at the beginning of the Spanish protectorate.

Information

Tourist Office The tourist office is on Rue Mohammed V, just near the corner of Rue ben Tachfine. The guy here is helpful and speaks quite a bit of English. Don't be talked into hiring a guide (unless, of course, you want one), as the medina is small and manageable on your own. Even if you get lost, it's never long before you come to the walls or a gate.

Money There are plenty of banks along the main street, Rue Mohammed V, and around the roundabout known as Place Moulay el Mehdi, in the Spanish-built new city.

Post The post office can also be found on the roundabout known as Place Moulay el Mehdi.

Foreign Consulates There is a Spanish Consulate in Tetouan. See the Morocco Facts for the Visitor chapter for details.

Medina & Around

As is often the case in Morocco, the place which links the old and new cities is the real centre of the city. In this case it is Place Hassan II, the town's showpiece. The square recently underwent a massive 'beautification' project, and the Ave Mohammed V was converted into a pedestrian precinct. These are now popular places for the young men and women from the university campus in town to promenade in the evenings.

The busiest medina entrance is Bab er Rouah, to the right of the old Spanish Consulate. It's an interesting and surprisingly busy medina, great for just wandering at random. The area towards the eastern gate, Bab el Okla, was the up-market end of town; some of the fine houses built by the city's residents in the last century still stand here. At least one has been turned into a carpet showroom. There are plenty of touts hanging around who will take you to one if you're interested.

Museum of Moroccan Art Just inside Bab el Okla is the excellent Museum of Moroccan Art, built in an old bastion in the town wall – there are still cannon in place in the garden. The exhibits of everyday Moroccan and Andalusian life are well presented. It's a pity that the staff rush you through as fast as they can, switching lights off before you have finished and generally trying to hustle you through so they can go back to their seat at the door. It is open daily, except Tuesday, from 9 am to noon and 2 to 6 pm, and the entry fee is Dr 10.

Artisan School Just opposite Bab el Okla is the artisan school, where you can see children being taught traditional crafts such as

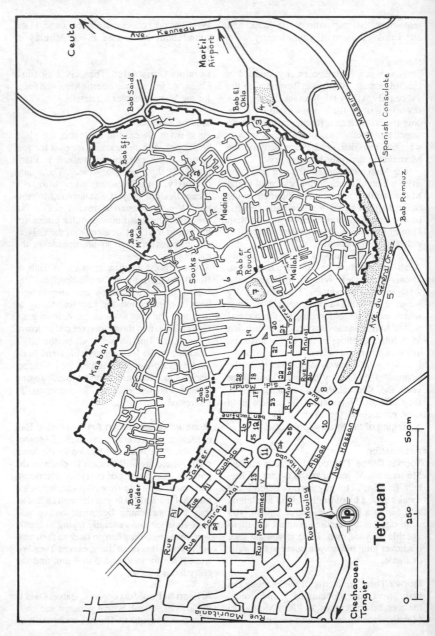

Tetouan

PLACES TO STAY

13 Pensions Fés, Bienvenida & Florida
14 Pension Rio Jana
17 Hotel Regina
18 Pension Cosmopolita
21 Hotel Bilbao
22 Hotel Nacional
24 Pension Iberia
25 Hotel Príncipe
28 Hotel Persa
29 Hotel Oumaima
30 Hotel Paris

PLACES TO EAT

20 Restaurant Granada
23 Restaurant Restinga
26 Sandwich Ali Baba
27 Restaurant Saigon

OTHER

1 Saidi Mosque
2 Great Mosque
3 Museum of Moroccan Art
4 Artisan School
5 Artefact Emporium
6 Royal Palace
7 Place Hassan II
8 Bus Station
9 Taxis to Ceuta
10 Taxis to Tangier
11 Place Moulay el Mehdi
12 Tourist Office
15 Post Office
16 Men's Hammam
19 Museum

leatherwork, woodwork and the making of enamel *zellij* tiles. The building itself is worth a visit. The school is open from 9 am to noon and 2.30 to 5.30 pm; closed Tuesday and Saturday. Entry is Dr 10.

Archaeology Museum There is a small archaeology museum opposite the end of Rue Prince Sidi Mohammed but it is only for the dedicated. They have a few prehistoric stones, some Roman coins and a number of small mosaics and other artefacts from

Lixus. It is open Monday to Saturday from 9.30 am to noon and 2.30 to 5.30 pm; closed Sunday. Entry costs Dr 10 but the enclosed gardens in front of the museum, where many of the larger exhibits have been set up, are free.

Places to Stay – bottom end
There are plenty of cheap, basic pensions available in Tetouan, all at the usual price, but some are decidedly better than others in terms of facilities, views and character. Some, for instance, could be straight out of Spain with their wrought-iron balconies overlooking the street. Others are located on noisy streets or are basically just flophouses. The pensions *Fès, Bienvenida, Florida* and *Rio Jana* are reasonable, but basic. Likewise, the *Pension Rif*, opposite the Bilbao, might be a pleasant place to stay if you had a front room but is otherwise very basic.

One pension which can be recommended is the *Pension Iberia*, on the 3rd floor above the Banque Marocaine du Commerce Extérieur (BMCE) on Place Moulay el Mehdi. Though there are only a few rooms, it has a homely atmosphere and great views over the square. Rooms here cost Dr 30/50 for singles/doubles with shared bathroom facilities. Hot showers are Dr 5 extra.

The *Hotel Bilbao* (☎ 96 7939), 7 Rue Mohammed V, is a good cheap alternative to the pensions and has a lot of character, especially if you can get one of the front rooms. It costs Dr 26/49 for singles/doubles with shared bathroom and cold showers. They also have one room which is of a better standard for Dr 65.

If you're looking for something better, but not too expensive, try the one-star *Hotel Príncipe* (☎ 96 2795), 20 Rue ben Tachfine; the front rooms, however, can be noisy because it's right at the place where the grands taxis queue up. The staff are friendly and singles/doubles cost Dr 56/66 with shared bathroom.

Camping The nearest campsite is by the beach at Martil, about eight km away. There's also a site not far from the Club Med, about halfway between Tetouan and the (Ceuta) border.

Places to Stay – middle

One of the best places to stay in this category is the one-star *Hotel Regina* (☎ 96 2113), 8 Rue Sidi Mandri. Doubles with own shower and toilet here cost Dr 108 and there's hot water in the mornings. The hotel has its own restaurant and tea salon. Similar is the *Hotel Nacional* (☎ 96 3290), 8 Rue Mohammed ben Larbi Torres, which has singles/doubles with own shower and toilet for Dr 71/108 including taxes. Going up in price, there is the *Hotel Persa*. This two-star hotel is a fairly old place with some character, and offers doubles with own shower and toilet for Dr 70.

Better, but considerably more expensive and devoid of character, is the *Hotel Paris* (☎ 96 6750), 11 Rue Chakib Arsalane, where singles/doubles with own shower, toilet and hot water are Dr 124/148 including taxes. The management are friendly but you'll need to hassle for soap and toilet paper. The *Hotel Oumaima* (☎ 96 3473), Rue Achrai Mai, costs the same but would be preferable.

Place to Stay – top end

The five-star *Hotel Safir* (☎ 96 7044), Ave Kennedy, is the only top-range hotel in Tetouan. It has 98 rooms, a swimming pool, tennis courts and a nightclub, but is a long way out of the centre of town.

Places to Eat

The best cheap place is *Sandwich Ali Baba* on Rue Mourakah Anual. Despite the name, they also do chicken, chips, soups and tajines. It's a very popular place, and you practically have to fight through the crowd at the front to get to the seating area in the back.

Far less frantic and excellent value is the *Restaurant Restinga*, which you get to through a small alley off Rue Mohammed V. You can't miss it as there's a large sign outside on the main street. The restaurant is set up under tents in a small open courtyard and it's a popular place to eat both at lunch

times and for dinner, though it doesn't stay open late in the evenings. They offer seafood, meat dishes, soups, salads and cold beers. Service is fast and the staff are friendly.

Despite the name, there's nothing Asian about the *Restaurant Saigon* on Rue Mohammed ben Larbi Torres. The food is OK and, like the Restinga, it's a popular place to eat. The menu is limited but prices are low.

The *Restaurant Granada*, on Rue Mohammed V at Place Al Jala, is clean and cheap and serves the usual tajines, couscous and soups.

Things to Buy

To the south of the medina on Ave du Général Orgaz is a government-run artefact emporium, where you can get an idea of the real prices of things. Bear in mind, however, that what you would pay here is definitely the top end of the price scale. Upstairs, and out the back downstairs, you can see young men and women making all sorts of handicrafts. The emporium is open daily from 9.30 am to 1 pm and 3.30 to 6.30 pm.

Getting There & Away

To/From Ceuta (Spanish North Africa)

The Spanish border is about 33 km to the north at Fnideq. Grands taxis leave frequently from the corner of Rue de Mouquauama and Rue Sidi Mandri, just up from the bus station. A seat costs Dr 15 for the 20-minute trip. Although the border is open 24 hours, transport dries up from about 7 pm to 5 am.

On the Spanish side of the border, the No 7 public bus runs every half hour or so to the centre; 40 Ptas, exact change only.

The border is fairly easy-going, although crowded at times. It is possible to visit Ceuta in a day trip from Tetouan, but it's hard to think why anyone would want to, unless it's to buy a bottle of duty-free liquor. This is quite cheap and there's a good selection.

Bus The bus station for all buses is at the junction of Rue Sidi Mandri and Rue Moulay

Abbas. It is a dark and gloomy old place with the ticket windows upstairs and the buses downstairs.

There are CTM departures to Al Hoceima (four times daily), Casablanca (twice daily), Ceuta (eight times daily), Chechaouen (six times daily), Fès (once daily), Ouezzane (once daily), Rabat (once daily) and Tangier (four times daily). Plenty of other bus companies in Tetouan have buses to the same places, as well as to other towns. Book in advance where possible and check around the different windows to find out all the possibilities.

Tickets for buses to the beaches at Martil and Cabo Negro are available from window 12 at the bus station.

Taxi There are plenty of grands taxis in the two ranks, with frequent departures to Fnideq (for Ceuta, Dr 15) and Tangier (Dr 25).

CHECHAOUEN

Also called Chaouen, Chefchaouen and Xauen, this delightful town in the Rif Mountains is a favourite with travellers for obvious reasons: the air is cool and clear, the people are noticeably more relaxed than down by the coast, there's more *kif* than you can poke a stick at, and the town is small and manageable. All this makes it a great place to hang out for a few days.

Founded by Moulay Ali ben Rachid in 1471 as a base from which to attack the Portuguese in Ceuta, the town prospered and grew considerably with the arrival of Muslim refugees from Spain. It was these refugees who built the whitewashed houses with blue painted doors and window frames, tiny balconies, tiled roofs and patios with a citrus tree planted in the centre, which give the town its distinctive Hispanic flavour. The obvious intention was to recreate what they had been forced to leave behind in Spain.

The town remained very isolated – almost xenophobic – until occupied by Spanish troops in 1920, and right up until that time the inhabitants continued to speak a variant

of medieval Castilian. The Spanish were briefly thrown out of Chechaouen by Abd el-Krim between 1924 and 1926 during the Riffian rebellion but returned to stay until independence in 1956.

Today the town is firmly on the tourist circuit but is still remarkably easy-going. The touts are relatively few except around the bus station and the Hotel Asma. Elsewhere, even in the medina and the Place de Makhzen (the main square of the medina), they keep a low profile – a refreshing contrast to some other places, such as Tangier.

Information
Post & Money Both the post office and a branch of the BMCE are on Ave Hassan II – the main street, which runs from Place Mohammed V to Bab el Ain and curves around the south of the medina.

Market
The market is on Ave Al Khattabi (see map). It is very much the centre of things on market days (Monday and Thursday), when merchants come from all over the Rif to trade. The emphasis is on food and second-hand clothes, although there are sometimes a few things of interest in the way of souvenirs.

Medina
The old medina is small, uncrowded and very easy to find your way around in. For the most part, the houses and buildings are a blinding blue-white and, on the northern side especially, you'll find many with tiny ground-floor rooms crowded with weaving looms. These are a legacy of the days when silkworms were introduced by Andalusian refugees and weaving became the principal activity of the families living here. You'll find the people working these looms generally very friendly and, to break the monotony of their work, they may well invite you in for a smoke and a chat.

There is also a fair smattering of tourist shops, particularly around Place de Makhzen and Place Outa el Hammam – the focal points of the old city.

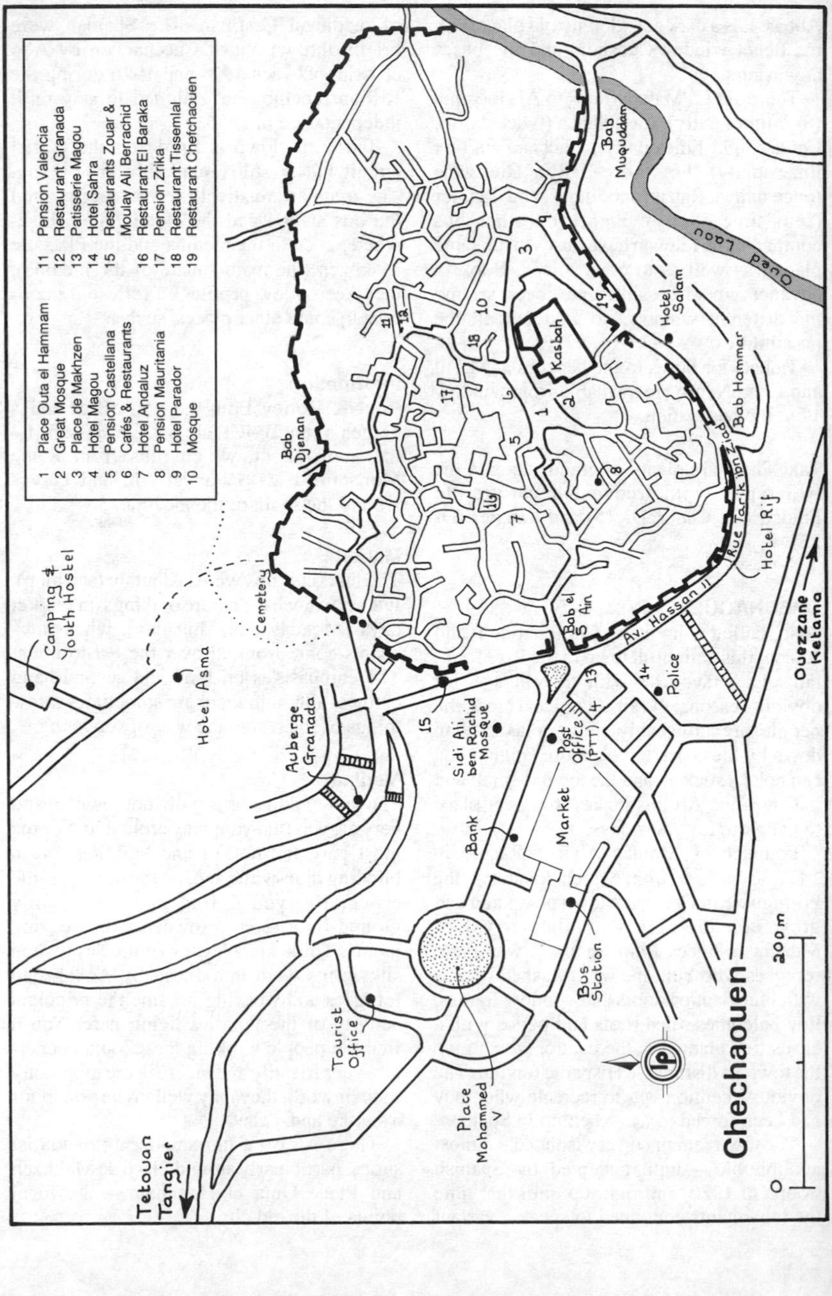

Key to map:

1 Place Outa el Hammam
2 Great Mosque
3 Place de Makhzen
4 Hotel Magou
5 Pension Castellana
6 Cafés & Restaurants
7 Hotel Andaluz
8 Pension Mauritania
9 Hotel Parador
10 Mosque
11 Pension Valencia
12 Restaurant Granada
13 Patisserie Magou
14 Hotel Sahra
15 Restaurants Zouar &
   Moulay Ali Berrachid
16 Restaurant El Baraka
17 Pension Zrika
18 Restaurant Tissemlal
19 Restaurant Chefchaouen

Chechaouen

Tetouan
Tangier

Ouezzane
Ketama

Oued Laou

Bab Muqaddam
Hotel Salam
Bab Hammar
Bab Rif
Hotel Rif
Av. Hassan II
Police
Bab el 5 Ain
Rue Tarik ibn Ziad
Bab Djenan
Kasbah
Camping & Youth Hostel
Hotel Asma
Cemetery
Auberge Granada
Sidi Ali ben Rachid Mosque
Bank
Post Office (PTT)
Market
Bus Station
Tourist Office
Place Mohammed V

200 m

Place Outa el Hammam & Kasbah The shady, cobbled Place Outa el Hammam with the kasbah along one side is at its busiest in the early evening, when everyone starts to get out and about after the inactivity of the afternoon. It's a great time to sit in one of the many cafés opposite the kasbah and relax. The atmosphere is sedate and almost medieval; it's just a pity that cars are still allowed in.

The ruins of the 15th-century kasbah dominate the square and its walls now enclose a beautiful garden. An entrance fee of Dr 10 is charged, but this gives you access to the museum, where you'll be shown the cells, complete with neck chains at floor level, where Abd el-Krim was imprisoned in 1926.

In the corner of the garden opposite the prison is a small pavilion, which has been restored to house a small display of traditional crafts, utensils, musical instruments and clothes.

Place de Makhzen The Place de Makhzen is the lesser of the two town squares; it has a large old gum tree in the centre. Instead of cafés, it has mostly tourist shops. However, on market days you still get people squatting under the tree selling bundles of mint and vegetables grown in the surrounding area.

If you take the lane heading east from the square you'll eventually come out at Bab Onsar; after this comes the river, with a couple of very agreeable shady cafés on its banks. This is also where the women come to slave away doing the washing while the men busy themselves drinking tea.

Places to Stay – bottom end
The cheapest places are the pensions in the medina. For the most part they are OK, if a little gloomy and claustrophobic at times. It all depends on what you are offered, but some of them are very popular with budget travellers so, if you want a good room, get there early in the day.

The *Pension Castellana*, just off the western end of Place Outa el Hammam, is the cheapest of the lot at Dr 10/20 for singles/doubles, but it is very basic and there

are cold showers only. The rooms are arranged around a small central courtyard. Somewhat better is the *Hotel Andaluz*, which costs Dr 30 a double; there are no singles. The rooms all face an internal courtyard and while those on the upper floor are light and airy, the ones on the ground floor are dark and gloomy. Hot showers are available for Dr 5 extra.

Another very popular place with travellers is the *Pension Mauritania*, which offers singles/doubles for Dr 25/45 including a very good breakfast. The staff are friendly and there's a beautiful traditional lounge area. Also excellent value is the brand new *Pension Znika* which is spotlessly clean, light and airy and costs Dr 15/30 for singles/doubles. Hot showers are available on the ground floor.

Up in the higher reaches of the medina with good views and the chance of a breeze is the *Pension Valencia*. The doubles and triples are clean, simple and good value at Dr 30/45, but the singles are glorified cupboards and not even worth considering. The communal showers and toilets are clean and well maintained. To find the Valencia, take the lane off to the north from Place Outa el Hammam; it twists back and forth up the hill but after a few minutes you come to the Restaurant Granada – the pension is around the back and to the right.

Outside the medina area below the Bab el Ain is the *Hotel Sahra* which also has singles/doubles for Dr 15/30, but it's a little gloomy and doesn't have the atmosphere of the pensions in the medina.

Going up in price, there is a choice of two one-star hotels. The first is the popular *Hotel Rif* (☎ 98 6207), just below the city walls on Rue Tarik ibn Ziad. This is good value at Dr 60 a double with shared bathroom or Dr 90 with own shower and toilet. The showers have hot water. Equally good value is the *Hotel Salam* (☎ 98 6239), further around from the Rif towards the Place de Makhzen. The rooms are bright and clean and some look right out over the valley. Both the comfortable lounge and the shady rooftop terrace also have good views. Singles/doubles here cost Dr 26/52 with shared bathroom facilities. There's hot water in the showers, and the hotel has its own reasonable restaurant.

Youth Hostel & Camping Right up on the side of the hill, behind the Hotel Asma, is the campsite and *Youth Hostel*. They are only really worth considering if you have your own vehicle, as it's quite a hike to get to them, especially if you have a rucksack. It's a steep 30-minute walk by the road (just follow the signs to the Hotel Asma), or a 15-minute scramble up the hill through the cemetery; you shouldn't attempt the latter on a Friday, as the locals don't take kindly to it.

The camping area is pleasantly shady and cheap at Dr 5 per vehicle and the same per person. The hostel is extremely basic and relatively poor value at Dr 15 per person.

Places to Stay – middle
The best choice in this category is the two-star *Hotel Magou* (☎ 98 6275), 23 Moulay Idriss, close to the market and bus station. It is often used by small tour groups and if you are looking for modest comfort it's good value at Dr 60/77 for singles/doubles without own shower and toilet and Dr 123/146 with own bathroom. There's hot water all day if demand warrants it; otherwise mornings only.

Places to Stay – top end
The cheapest of the top-end hotels is the three-star *Hotel Asma* (☎ 98 6002), a huge concrete structure overlooking the town above the cemetery. It has 94 very pleasant, self-contained rooms, a bar and restaurant, though meals in the restaurant are very pricey at Dr 83 for lunch and Dr 100 for dinner. The rooms are Dr 175/212 for singles/doubles plus taxes. The disadvantage of staying here is the distance from town and the lack of involvement in the activities there. The advantage is the views – especially at night. Avoid having laundry done here – the rates are extortionate.

The most expensive hotel in town is the four-star *Hotel Parador* (☎ 98 6324), on the Place de Makhzen, which costs Dr 234/292 for singles/doubles plus taxes. The hotel has its own bar and restaurant and all the usual facilities you would expect of a hotel at this price.

Places to Eat
Amongst the cafés on Place Outa el Hammam are a number of small restaurants which serve good local food. Up near the Pension Valencia, the *Restaurant Granada* is run by a cheery character who cooks a variety of dishes at reasonable prices. Also worth checking out inside the medina are the *Restaurant el Baraka*, near the Hotel Andaluz, and the *Restaurant Assada*, just inside the Bab el Ain to the left.

Excellent value outside the medina, just up the hill from the Bab el Ain, are the *Restaurant Moulay Ali Berrachid* and the *Restaurant Zouar* – take your pick. For just Dr 32 two of us had soup, mixed salad, fried fish, bread and mineral water. You can't beat that for price, and the food was tasty and the kitchens at both restaurants spotless.

For something of a splurge, try the *Restaurant Chefchaouen* on the street leading up to the Place de Makhzen. It's a new place and pleasantly designed in traditional style, but don't come here for breakfast as it will take forever to arrive. A full meal (soup, tajine/couscous and fruit) for lunch or dinner costs Dr 32.

More expensive is the *Restaurant Tissemlal*, 22 Rue Targui, just up from the Place Outa el Hammam and off to the right. Like the Chefchaouen, this restaurant has been beautifully conceived and even has an upstairs balcony running the whole way around. The service is quick but the food, unfortunately, only average. You're looking at Dr 45 for a full lunch.

The *Patisserie Magou* on Ave Hassan II has good pastries and fresh bread.

Most of the cafés on Place Outa el Hammam have seedy rooms upstairs where the hard smoking goes on – you can just about cut the air with a knife in some of them – and there are certainly worse ways to pass a few hours than to sit around playing dominoes with the locals.

Getting There & Away

Bus The bus station consists of an open yard next to the market. All buses leave from here and there are daily departures to Tetouan (two hours), Meknès (five hours) and Fès (seven hours). There are also buses to Tangier but all of them stop in Tetouan for 1½ hours, so it's far better to take a bus first to Tetouan and then another from there to Tangier to avoid the wait.

It's well worth booking in advance as far as possible (at least 24 hours ahead), as transport from here, especially to Meknès, is in high demand. Buses coming from Tetouan are much quicker in getting to Meknès but there's no guarantee of getting a seat – in fact in summer you can be fairly well assured that there *won't* be seats.

Taxi Grands taxis to Tetouan, Meknès, Fès, Ketama, Al Hoceima and Ouezzane also leave from the bus station. Things are much busier in the mornings.

The Atlantic Coast

The capital of Morocco, Rabat, is, naturally enough, an important administrative centre. Despite, or perhaps, because of this, Rabat offers a great opportunity for hassle-free exploration. A trip to Rabat can also take in an excursion to the old city of Salé, just across the estuary.

Casablanca, the other major city on the Atlantic coast, defies Hollywood stereotypes. It's a surprisingly modern city, a legacy of the period of the French protectorate, but it has a heritage dating back over 10 centuries, when it was the capital of a Berber state.

The small port of Asilah, on the northern coast, boasts good beaches, interesting architecture and a chequered history. South of Asilah are the ancient ruins of Lixus – also well worth a visit.

The towns of Azemmour and El Jadida are two more good reasons to spend some time exploring the Atlantic coast.

Rabat

All the different influences and building styles which have swept through Rabat have left an interesting legacy, and it's well worth spending a few days here.

Though it definitely retains a distinctive Moroccan flavour, the city is unlike many others in Morocco in that few of its people are involved in the tourist trade. Most are government and office workers. That being so, you are in for a treat: this is one of those rare Moroccan cities where there's no hassle. You can even walk through the souk without having to steel yourself against high-pressure sales tactics.

History
Rabat has been the capital of Morocco only since the days of the French protectorate. However, it has a long and interesting history

which goes back over 2500 years to the days when the Phoenicians were exploring the North African Mediterranean and Atlantic coasts and setting up colonies and trading posts.

The Phoenicians were followed by the Romans, who built a settlement here known as Sala. This, like Volubilis, lasted long beyond the break-up of the Roman Empire and eventually gave rise to an independent Berber kingdom. This kingdom, though it quickly accepted Islam with the arrival of the Arabs in the 7th century, retained a high degree of independence both in secular and religious terms. Its unorthodox interpretation of Islam prompted the Arab rulers of the interior to build a ribat (a kind of fortified monastery) on the present site of the kasbah in an attempt to bring them into line.

The orthodox authorities were relatively successful in this venture so that by the time a new settlement was established at Salé on the opposite side of the estuary in the 11th century, the original town had been all but abandoned.

Next on the scene were the Almohads, who arrived in the 12th century. They built a new kasbah on the site of the ribat and used it as their base for the conquest of Spain. The city was further expanded by Yacoub el Mansour, who was responsible for the building of the magnificent Oudaia Gate of the kasbah and for the Hassan Mosque (the Tour Hassan) which was never finished. This period of glory was, however, brief and, on the death of Mansour in 1199 AD, the city declined rapidly in importance.

It was to remain that way until the beginning of the 17th century, when it was resettled by Muslims who had been expelled from Spain. With the settlers' numbers augmented by renegade Christians, Moorish pirates and adventurers of many nationalities, the settlement asserted its independence once more. The stage was set for the most colourful era of Rabat's history – that of the

Sallee Rovers. The pirates who set sail from here attacked and plundered thousands of merchant vessels returning to Europe from Asia, West Africa and the Americas throughout much of the 17th and 18th centuries, and were feared far and wide. Certain sultans, despite the Rovers' threat to their authority, even encouraged their activities so as to ensure a constant supply of both slaves to work on the sultans' extravagant building activities, and booty to finance them. The Rovers' demise came only in the early 19th century with the rise of industrialised northern Europe and the desire of the Moroccan sultans to bring their errant, semiautonomous peripheries into line.

Rabat's genesis as the capital of Morocco dates from the French protectorate and it was chosen to be so because of its only tenuous connection with the imperial dynasties of Morocco, in contrast to such cities as Marrakesh, Fès and Meknès.

Orientation

Rabat is best approached by rail, since the railway station lies on the city's main thoroughfare, the wide, tree-lined Ave Mohammed V, which becomes thronged with promenaders each evening. Arrival by bus is quite inconvenient as the bus station lies some three km outside the centre and you will need to take a bus (No 30) or taxi into the centre – not always an easy task because of the competition.

All the main administrative buildings and most of the hotels lie on or just off Ave Mohammed V, though there are others further afield. Most of the embassies are scattered around the streets to the east between Ave Mohammed V and Place Abraham Lincoln.

The medina itself is divided from the ville nouvelle by the wide and busy Blvd Hassan II, which follows the line of the medina walls to the Oued Bou Regreg (an *oued* is a river).

Rabat is an easy and pleasant city to walk around, and you probably won't need public transport unless you plan to visit the twin city of Salé.

Information

Tourist Office At the syndicat d'initiative, Rue Lumumba, you can pick up information and maps on Rabat and Salé. Even so, you shouldn't expect too much.

Money The banks are concentrated along Ave Mohammed V. The BMCE is open from 8 am to 8 pm Monday to Friday; weekends from 10 am to 2 pm and 4 to 8 pm.

Post & Telecommunications Poste restante is not in the main post office building but in the telephone office across the road. Go in through the door marked 'Permanence Télégraphique et Téléphonique' and ask at the desk inside. You need to show your passport as proof of identity, and there's a charge of Dr 1.35 for each letter collected.

Foreign Embassies The main embassy area is around Place Abraham Lincoln and Ave de Fas ('Fas' is the same as 'Fès' and is the way it appears on the street signs). See the Morocco Facts for the Visitor chapter for a full list of embassies in Rabat.

British Council The British Council is at Sharia Tanja, about 200 metres from the American Bookstore. As well as a library, they have feature films twice a week. It is open from 9.30 am to 12.15 pm and 2.30 to 5.45 pm Tuesday to Friday; closed Monday morning and weekends.

Bookshops There's a good English-language bookshop at 7 Zankat Alyamama, behind the British Council, run by Mohammed Belhaj. He's a very friendly person and stocks a good selection of mainly second-hand English and American novels, guides, language books, dictionaries, etc. Books taken back in under two weeks can usually be swapped for another for a small service charge. The American Bookstore, Rue Tanja at the junction with Rue Lumumba, also has a good selection of similar material.

Medina

The walled medina here is far less interesting

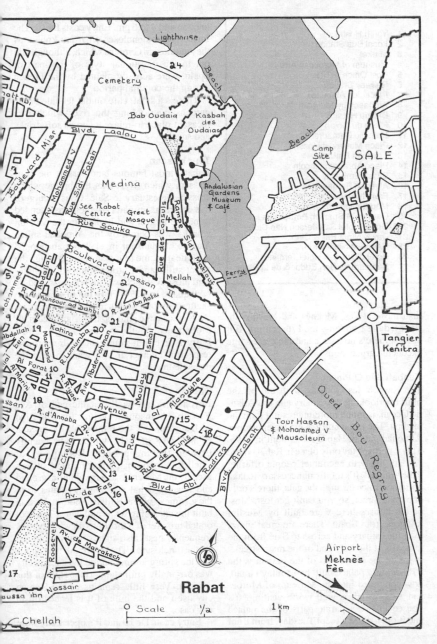

Rabat

0   Scale   ½   1 km

1	Youth Hostel
2	Local Bus Station
3	Market
4	Museum of Moroccan Arts
5	Post Office (PTT)
6	Railway Station
7	Place des Alaouites
8	Archaeology Museum
9	Balima Hotel
10	Place du Golan
11	Catholic Cathedral
12	Place Moulay al Hassan
13	Egyptian Embassy
14	Place Abraham Lincoln
15	British Embassy
16	Algerian Embassy
17	French Embassy
18	Mauritanian Embassy
19	German & Spanish Embassies
20	Grand Hotel & Jefferson Nite Club
21	Day & Night Bar & Club
22	L'Avenue Night Club
23	Hotel d'Orsay & Hotel Terminus
24	Restaurants Borj Eddar & de la Plage

than those at Fès, Meknès and Marrakesh, since it dates from only the 17th century. But at least there's no hassle and there are some excellent carpet shops.

Kasbah des Oudaias

The Kasbah des Oudaias, built out on the bluff overlooking the estuary and the Atlantic Ocean, is much more interesting than the medina. The usual entry is via the enormous Almohad gate of Bab Oudaia, built in 1195. This is perhaps the only place in Rabat where you are likely to encounter people offering to be 'guides'. It's totally unnecessary to take one since, once through the gate, there's only one main street, so you can't get lost. Most of the houses here were built by Muslim refugees from Spain. There are great views over the estuary and across to Salé from the ramparts at the very end of the main street.

Inside the lower part of the kasbah is the 17th-century palace built by Moulay Ismail, now converted into the Museum of Moroccan Arts, which is well worth visiting. It's housed in two separate parts of the palace and is open daily, except Tuesday, from 8 am

to noon and 4 to 6 pm. Entry costs Dr 10. The former palace encloses what are known as the Andalusian Gardens which, although laid out in the traditional style of that part of Spain, were actually planted by the French during the colonial period.

There's a small café on the far side of the gardens overlooking the river which is a pleasant place to relax. It serves soft drinks and snacks.

Tour Hassan

Rabat's most famous landmark is the Tour Hassan, which overlooks the bridge which crosses the estuary to Salé. Construction of this enormous minaret – which was intended to be the largest and highest in the Muslim world – was begun by the Almohad sultan Yacoub el Mansour in 1195 but abandoned at his death some four years later. Though the tower still stands, little remains of the adjacent mosque which was all but destroyed by earthquake in 1755. Only the re-erected but shattered pillars of this mosque now remain.

On the same site is the Mausoleum of Mohammed V, the present king's father. Entry is free, but you must be dressed in a respectful manner if you want to visit the mausoleum.

Chellah

Beyond the city walls, at the end of Ave Yacoub el Mansour at the junction with Blvd ad Doustour, are the remains of the ancient Roman city of Sala, which subsequently became the independent Berber city of Chellah. When abandoned in 1154, it was used by the Merenids as a royal burial ground and most of what stands today dates from those times, when Sultan Abou el Hassan built the enclosing walls and gates. The decorated minaret of a mosque (on which storks frequently nest) also stands near the bottom of the enclosure. The Merenid necropolis and the spring around which the ancient city was originally built stand to the right of this minaret. Very little remains of the Roman city itself and the bulk of it is fenced off in any case.

Entry costs Dr 10 and it's open daily from

8.30 am until sunset. You'll probably run into a few touts offering to be guides but it isn't necessary to take one.

Archaeology Museum

This museum, not far from the Grande Mosquée (Great Mosque) on Place Djemaa Assouna, is well worth a visit. It has excellent collections of Phoenician, Carthaginian and Roman relics. Some of the Roman exhibits were collected from Volubilis and Lixus but others were found at Chellah. It's here that you'll find the famous bronze head of Juba II, the Berber king of Mauretania who ruled this part of the world prior to the imposition of direct Roman rule in AD 42. The museum is open daily, except Tuesday, from 8.30 am to noon and 2.30 to 6 pm. Entry costs Dr 10.

Places to Stay – bottom end

There are several basic budget hotels to choose from on or just off the continuation of Ave Mohammed V as it enters the medina. Few make any concessions to creature comforts and some of them don't even have showers, cold or otherwise, so they're not such good value for money. An extra dollar or two will buy you far better accommodation outside the medina.

Perhaps the best of the cheapies is the *Hotel Marrakesh*, Rue Sebbahi just off Ave Mohammed V, which costs Dr 40/70 for singles/doubles. The staff are friendly and cold showers are available. The *Hotel des Voyageurs*, just off Ave Mohammed V, is similar and costs Dr 60 a double but there are no showers and it's often full. The *Hotel du Centre*, on the right just as you enter the medina, also costs Dr 60 a double (no singles). The rooms are clean and provide bed, table and chair, and handbasin but there are no showers.

Others in this immediate area which you might like to try are the *Hotel el Alam* (Dr 60 a double; no singles), *Hotel Regina*, *Hotel Magreb al Jadid*, *Hotel du Midi* and the *Hotel d'Alger*.

Just outside the medina, the one-star *Hotel Majestic* (☎ 72 2997), 121 Blvd Hassan II,

offers better value at Dr 58/70 for singles/doubles with own shower but shared toilets and Dr 67/86 with own shower and

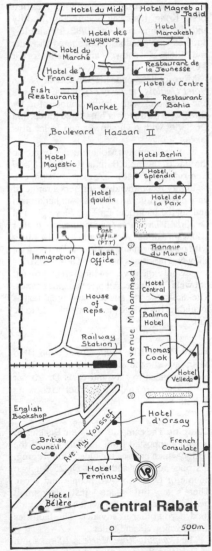

Central Rabat

toilet plus Dr 3 tax per person. Hot water is available between 5 am and noon. Close by on Ave Mohammed V, the *Hotel Berlin* is also reasonable value. It's on the 2nd floor, above the Vietnamese restaurant called Hong Kong. It's clean, secure and friendly and the rooms cost Dr 60/82 for singles/doubles with handbasin but shared showers and toilets. Hot showers are available for Dr 5 extra.

More or less opposite the Berlin is the *Hotel Gaulois* (☎ 72 3022), 1 Rue Hims, a one-star hotel with singles/doubles for Dr 66/85 with own shower but shared toilets and Dr 85/98 with own shower and toilet plus taxes.

Further along Ave Mohammed V opposite the side of the large Balima Hotel, the *Hotel Central* (☎ 76 7356), 2 Zankat al Basra, can be highly recommended. It offers a range of very clean, large, airy rooms with handbasin and shared bathroom for Dr 57 a single and Dr 72/84/93 a double (depending on whether you want a double bed or twin beds. Doubles with own shower and toilet cost Dr 105. Hot showers (mornings only) are Dr 8.50 extra – somewhat expensive, but there are gallons of hot water available. All prices include taxes. The staff are very friendly and breakfast is available. It's a large place and unlikely to be full.

Youth Hostel The *Youth Hostel* is on Blvd Misr, opposite the walls of the medina. It's a pleasant place to stay and costs Dr 20 per night. There are cold showers but no cooking facilities.

Camping The campsite is at Salé Beach and is well signposted from the Salé end of the bridge which crosses the Oued Bou Regreg. It's open all year and costs Dr 25 for two people or Dr 30 for two people and a car. There's very little shade – just a few small trees – but a snack bar which can provide food if you order in advance. The facilities include showers and toilets.

The *Camping Rose Marie* is 20 km south of Rabat on the coastal road to Casablanca.

It's not a bad place and is right next to the beach.

Places to Stay – middle
There can be few people who would not be satisfied with the standard of accommodation offered by the Hotel Central. However, if it's not to your liking there are two two-star hotels on Rue de Ghazzah, around the corner from the Hotel Berlin. They are the *Hotel Splendid* (☎ 72 3283) and the *Hotel de la Paix* (☎ 72 2926). The Splendid offers large, clean doubles without own shower for Dr 97 and doubles with own shower and toilet for Dr 116 including taxes. Hot showers are Dr 8 extra. The hotel has a very pleasant internal courtyard. The Hotel de la Paix also has doubles with own shower (including hot water) and toilet for Dr 116 including taxes. Neither hotel has single rooms.

Further afield, but also two-star, are the *Hotel Velleda* (☎ 76 9531), 106 Ave Allal ben Abdallah and the *Hotel Royal* (☎ 72 1171), 1 Rue Amman. The Velleda offers singles/doubles with shower but without toilet for Dr 75/92, and Dr 92/112 with own shower and toilet, plus taxes. Singles/doubles at the Royal are Dr 94/110 with shower but without toilet and Dr 119/138 with own shower and toilet plus taxes.

Going up in price, there are two three-star hotels just above the railway station at the junction of Ave Mohammed V and Ave Moulay Youssef. The cheaper of the two is the *Hotel d'Orsay* (☎ 73 1895), 11 Ave Moulay Youssef. This is a small hotel with only 30 rooms at Dr 89/123 for singles/doubles with shared bathroom and Dr 154/192 with own shower and toilet. Round the corner, the *Hotel Terminus* (☎ 73 1895), 384 Ave Mohammed V, has singles/doubles with own shower and toilet for Dr 178/218. Both these hotels are a good choice in this category.

Further along Ave Mohammed V is the huge *Balima Hotel* (☎ 76 7755), which has self-contained singles/doubles for Dr 151/186 plus taxes, but it's a very poor choice. The plumbing is falling apart, the beds collapsed years ago under the strain, windows won't open and the lifts work only reluctantly. There's a gulag-style restaurant on the ground floor which does good salads but lousy omelettes and soups, and the 'breakfasts' are a rip-off at Dr 23 per person. There's also a bar and nightclub. Visa cards are accepted.

Better value, but further afield, is the *Grand Hotel* (☎ 72 7285), 19 Rue Lumumba, which offers self-contained doubles for Dr 176 including breakfast. The hotel has its own bar and restaurant.

Lastly, there is the *Hotel Les Oudayas* (☎ 76 7820), 4 Rue Toubrouk. Self-contained singles/doubles here cost Dr 175/212 plus taxes.

Places to Stay – top end

At the lower end of this category, the *Hotel Bélère* (☎ 76 9901), 33 Ave Moulay Youssef, and the *Hotel Chellah* (☎ 76 0209), 2 Rue d'Ifni, would be good choices. They're both four-star hotels and offer self-contained singles/doubles for Dr 280/358 plus taxes. All the rooms are air-conditioned.

Best of all is the five-star *Hotel La Tour Hassan* (☎ 72 1401), 26 Rue du Chellah, which has 148 air-conditioned rooms and all the facilities you would expect of a hotel in this league.

Places to Eat

Rabat abounds with coffee shops, where office workers, business people, students and travellers pass the time of day. Some of these places serve snacks but most are not restaurants as such. Good, cheap restaurants are surprisingly few and far between, but there are a few places which can be recommended.

Perhaps cheapest of all are the collection of seafood restaurants (eight in total) under a common roofed area directly opposite the Hotel Majestic on the medina side of Blvd Hassan II. These are all open 24 hours a day and offer freshly fried fish, salads and the like. You can eat here for as little as Dr 8, though you'd have to spend more than that if you were hungry.

Equally cheap are the restaurants close to the market on Ave Mohammed V. One which has been popular with travellers for years is the *Restaurant de la Jeunesse*, where you can pick up a meat tajine for around Dr 12 or a full meal of, say, kebabs and chips, salad and bread for Dr 20. On the ground floor they offer even cheaper takeaways.

Also very popular is the *Restaurant Bahia*, Blvd Hassan II, close to the junction with Ave Mohammed V, which is actually built into the walls of the medina. This has a shady open-air section surrounding a fountain, as well as a very comfortable, traditional Moroccan-style section upstairs. The staff are friendly and the food is remarkably cheap but very tasty. A delicious tajine (among the best you will taste in Morocco) costs just Dr 18 or you can eat couscous for Dr 20. They also have kebabs (various prices depending on what you want), salads, omelettes and harira (just Dr 4) as well as many other dishes.

Another good place is the *Café Restaurant Mona Lisa*, in a small square called l'Passage Derby at 258 Ave Mohammed V; there's a sign on the footpath pointing to it. Although the place is used more as a coffee shop by the locals, the food is good and the prices reasonable – excellent tajines and salads.

The *Restaurant La Koutoubia*, at 10 Rue Pierre Parent, is not cheap at around Dr 60 for a main course, but the food is excellent and includes such things as pigeon tajine. Further afield near the Grand Hotel, try the *Café Restaurant Chantilly*, which offers *plats du jour* and fish specialities. It's a minor splurge.

Restaurants and cafés tend to close by 9.30 pm, except during Ramadan when they stay open much later.

Entertainment

Bars are few and far between but there are two good ones at the junction of Zankat al Basra (on which the Hotel Central is situated) and Ave Allal ben Abdallah (which runs parallel to Ave Mohammed V – the Bar Tanger and Bar La Reve.

There's a good choice of nightclubs in

Rabat, some of them attached to the more expensive hotels, and they're all very popular with well-heeled young people. The music is standard international disco fare. The normal entry fee is Dr 50 which includes the first drink but be sure you know, before ordering, what are the prices of subsequent drinks, because they can be as high as Dr 50! Some of the best nightclubs are Jefferson, Day & Night and L'Avenue, and the disco at the Hotel Bélère. You need to be suitably dressed to get into any of these places, and, at the Jefferson and L'Avenue, if you're a man, you may not even be allowed in at all without a member of the opposite sex. L'Avenue has a 'happy hour' daily from 6 to 8 pm when drinks cost Dr 20 (whisky or local beer), or Dr 30 (imported beer) though just how happy you will feel paying up to 2½ times the normal amount for a beer is up to you. Discos close around 3 am.

Getting There & Away
Air Royal Air Maroc (☎ 76 9710), Air France and Iberia are all on Ave Mohammed V.

Bus The bus station is inconveniently situated quite a distance from the centre of town on Place Mohammed Zerktouni – a major roundabout with a huge illuminated crown in the middle.

All the various bus companies have their offices here, but *everything* is in Arabic except for the CTM Casablanca ticket office. If you arrive here, you'll need to take either a public bus (No 30) or a shared taxi (Dr 8) into the centre. The taxi rank is chaotic, and it's hard to get a cab if you have a backpack.

CTM has buses to Azrou (once daily at 1.30 pm), Casablanca (seven times daily), Ceuta (once daily at 11 pm), Errachidia (once daily at 9 pm), Fès (four times daily), Marrakesh (once daily at 7.30 pm), Oujda (once daily at 9.30 pm), Tangier (five times daily), Tetouan (twice daily) and Tiznit (via Agadir once daily at 7.50 pm).

The local bus station is on Blvd Hassan II adjacent to the Hotel Bou Regreg. There are buses from here to the long-distance bus station and to Salé.

The grand taxi rank is also along Blvd Hassan II close to the local bus station.

Train If possible, this is the best way to arrive in Rabat, as the Rabat Ville station is right in the centre of town on Ave Mohammed V at Place des Alaouites. (Don't get off at Rabat Agdal.)

There are nonstop express trains virtually every hour to Casablanca from 6.30 am to 8.25 pm on weekdays (less at weekends and on public holidays) which take 50 minutes and cost Dr 25 one way. Other main daily departures are to El Jadida (7.15 pm, two hours); Marrakesh (4.41, 8.45 and 11.05 am and 6.22 pm, four hours); Meknès and Fès (7.20 and 9.06 am, 1.33, 2.09, 3.57, 6.15, 9.51 and 11.04 pm, four hours); Oujda (9.06 am, 2.09, 9.51 and 11.04 pm, 10 hours); and Tangier (8.16 am, 6.53 pm and 12.22 am, six hours).

Getting Around
To/From the Airport Buses between Rabat and Mohammed V International Airport leave from outside the Hotel Terminus on Ave Mohammed V at 5, 6.30, 8.30 and 10 am, and 12.30, 3.30 and 6.30 pm. From the airport they leave for Rabat at 6.45, 8.15 and 10.45 am, and 1.30, 4.30, 7.30 and 9.30 pm. The fare is Dr 50 and the journey takes 90 minutes.

SALÉ
Though only just across the estuary from Rabat, the white city of Salé has a distinctive character all its own as a result of centuries of jealously guarded independence followed by a long isolation from mainstream Morocco. Here you have the opportunity to experience the sights, smells and sounds of the Morocco of yesterday before the arrival of the tourist hordes. Indeed, you're very unlikely to see another tourist within the walls of Salé except around the Great Mosque and Medersa. Because of this, there are no touts and you're free to wander undisturbed through its narrow, winding alleyways and souks, which haven't changed for centuries.

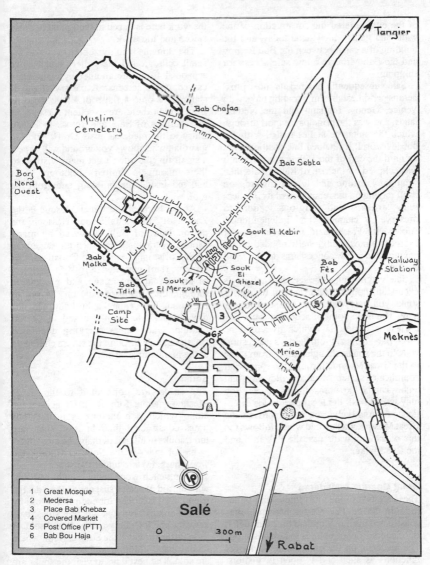

1 Great Mosque
2 Medersa
3 Place Bab Khebaz
4 Covered Market
5 Post Office (PTT)
6 Bab Bou Haja

Salé

0   300m

Salé's genesis as a walled city dates back to the early 13th century following a daring raid by the Spanish. Taking advantage of a revolt against the Merenid sultan by the gov-

ernor of Salé, the Spanish were able to attack Salé and make off with a large amount of valuable booty. To prevent a recurrence of this, the sultan, once he had regained control of the city, ordered the construction of the walls and gates which stand today, and the building of a canal between the Bou Regreg and the Bab Mrisa to allow safe access for shipping.

Salé subsequently entered its most prosperous period, establishing trading links with Venice, Genoa, England and the Netherlands, and was the principal seaport through which the sultanate at Fès traded with the outside world. It retained this position right up until the end of the 16th century when it was eclipsed by the rise of Rabat. Salé then went into decline and turned inwards on itself relying on the reputation of its intellectuals, artisans and religious leaders to preserve its character and independence. Along with Fès el-Bali, it remains one of Morocco's most traditionally minded cities, having made few concessions to the 20th century.

Salé's sights can all be seen in a half day's excursion though if you have a liking for souks you may well want to spend longer here. The main point of access into the city is via the Bab Bou Haja which gives onto the Place Bab Khebaz. From here it's just a short walk to the souks, though getting from these to the Great Mosque through the somewhat complicated system of narrow alleyways and arches can be like unravelling a puzzle. You may need to ask the local people for directions. Alternatively, you can approach the Great Mosque via the road which follows the line of the city walls past the Bab Jdid and the Bab Malka.

Great Mosque & Medersa

These are two of the most interesting buildings in Salé. The Great Mosque was constructed during Almohad times though it is, of course, out of bounds to non-Muslims. The medersa, on the other hand, no longer functions as such and is open to visitors. Constructed in 1333 by the Merenid sultan, Abou el Hassan, it's a superb example of lavishly carved and decorated Muslim artistry and, though smaller, certainly the equal of the Medersa Bou Inania in Fès. Much of

the work here is in cedar, though there's also stucco and tile work.

The students who lived here occupied the small cells around the gallery and they're separated from one another by elaborately carved cedar screens. A narrow flight of stairs leads onto a flat roof above the cells from which there are excellent views over the rooftops of Salé and across to Rabat. Entry to the medersa costs Dr 10, and the guardian who shows you around will expect a small tip (they don't get many visitors so their income is limited). Photography is allowed inside the building and from the roof.

At the back of the Great Mosque is the Zaouia of Sidi Abdallah ibn Hassoun, the patron saint of Salé. Revered by many Moroccan travellers in much the same way as St Christopher is among Christians, this respected sufi, who died in 1604, is the object of an annual pilgrimage and procession through the streets of Salé on the eve of Mouloud, the Prophet's birthday. On this day, local fishermen dressed in period costume and others carrying decorated candles parade through the streets ending up at the marabout's shrine.

Souks

The souks are connected to the Great Mosque via the Rue de la Great Mosque along which rich merchants in previous times constructed their houses. There are three souks in all, but perhaps the most interesting of them is the Souk el Ghezel, the wool market. Here under the shade of trees you can watch wool being bought and sold with the aid of scales suspended from a large tripod, as it has been for centuries. Close by is the Souk el Merzouk where textiles, basketwork and jewellery are made and sold. A little further afield is the Souk el Kebir where second-hand clothing and household items are sold. The best days to visit the souks are Thursday and Friday.

There are plenty of hole-in-the-wall cafés in the souks and in the surrounding streets where refreshments and good cheap meals can be found, and it's worth calling into one or more of them to soak up the unhurried atmosphere of this timeless place.

Getting There & Away

The easiest and most pleasant way of getting to Salé from Rabat is to take one of the boats across the Bou Regreg from just below the mellah. They run all day and leave when full. On the far side, simply follow the rest of the people up the rise to the Bab Bou Haja. Alternatively, there are local buses between Rabat and Salé or you can take a petit taxi.

Casablanca

With a population of 3½ million, Casablanca is Morocco's largest city by far and its largest industrial centre, and it's still growing at the rate of some 50,000 people per year. This growth is a fairly recent phenomenon, however, dating from the early days of the French protectorate, when Casa was chosen as the administrative centre. As a result, it was laid out in grand style according to current ideas of French urban planning, with wide boulevards, public parks and fountains and imposing Mauresque civic buildings. It's the place to which any Moroccan (and many others from the Muslim world) aspiring to fame and fortune or simply a better living gravitate.

The massive influx of hopefuls from the countryside in search of a job has naturally led to the creation of slums as in any other huge conurbation. As a visitor staying within striking distance of the centre, however, your only experience of this poverty will be the sight of abandoned mothers begging around the Place Mohammed V. Instead, what will strike you most is the gleaming white medium high-rise 1930s architecture, the pedestrian precincts thronged with speedy, fashion-conscious young people dressing and behaving in a manner which might well be frowned on in the more traditionally minded cities of the interior, and the pace of life.

Yet, despite its outward liberalism and apparent ready acceptance of Western cultural values and ideas, Casablanca is still a recognisably Moroccan and Muslim city. Morocco's window on the world it certainly is, but then Morocco, because of its geographical position and long involvement with the Iberian peninsula, has had an interchange with the West for well over 2000 years. In that respect, it's inevitable that at least one Moroccan city would become a melting pot for a synthesis of different ideas and customs.

For this reason alone, it's worth spending a few days here to get an appreciation of the contrast between this fast-paced cosmopolitan city and the rest of Morocco. This is where trends are created; this is where modernism departs company with traditionalism or tries to blend them; this is where ideas and developments are discussed with sceptical precision. With the possible exception of Cairo, Casablanca would have to be one of the world's most interesting and open Muslim cities. Don't be mesmerised by the superficialities. Morocco is alive and well here and firmly in touch with the 20th century. And, despite the pressures of urban living, it's easy to strike up conversations and to make friends in Casablanca. In this respect, it beats London, Paris, New York and Sydney hands down.

History

Settlement of the Casablanca area has a long history. Prior to the Arab conquest, what is now the western suburb of Anfa was the capital of a Berber state set up by the Barghawata tribe. The Almoravids failed to bring this state into their ambit and it was not until 1188, during the time of the Almohads, that it was finally conquered. Some 70 years later Anfa was taken by the Merenids, but when that dynasty became weak the area reasserted its independence, taking to piracy, as well as trading directly with England and Portugal.

By the second half of the 15th century, the Anfa pirates had become a serious threat to the Portuguese. A massive military expedition, consisting of some 10,000 men and 50

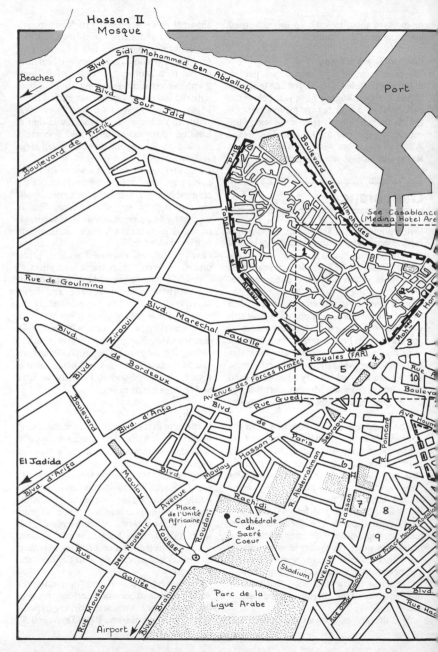

Casablanca

1 Chleuh Mosque
2 Great Mosque
3 Touring Club du Maroc
4 Place Mohammed V
5 Hyatt Regency Hotel
6 Main Post Office (PTT)
7 Place des Nations Unies
8 Law Courts
9 French Consulate
10 Wagons Lits/Thomas Cook
11 Central Market
12 CTM Bus Station
13 Syndicat d'Initiative &
    Post Office (PTT)

Pedestrian Precinct

Docks

Gare du Port
(Casa-Port Railway
Station)

Rabat

Boulevard Moulay Abderrahmane

Boulevard du Forbin

Avenue des Forces Armées Royales (FAR)

Avenue Pasteur

Vidal

Rue Mohammed Smiha

Rue Seghir

Blvd de la Résistance

Blvd Mohammed V

Blvd Emile Zola

Main Railway Station (Casa-Voyageurs)

Abdallah

Hassan

Fetouaki

R. Strasbourg

Boulevard Abdallah ben Yacine

Blvd de Khouribga

Blvd Ibn Tachfine

Rue d'Oujda

R. E. Barathon

Place de la Victoire

Strasbourg

Route des Oulad Ziane

Libourne

Rue de

Meskini

Blvd Lahcen Ider

New Medina

Marrakesh

ships, was launched from Lisbon. Anfa was sacked and left in ruins. It wasn't long before the pirates were active again, however, and, in 1515, the Portuguese were forced to repeat the operation. Sixty years later they arrived to stay, renaming the port Casa Branca and erecting fortifications.

Though harried by the tribes of the interior, the Portuguese stayed until 1755, when the colony was abandoned following a devastating earthquake (which destroyed Lisbon too). Sultan Sidi Mohammed ben Abdallah subsequently had the area resettled and fortified. However, its importance had declined rapidly, and by 1830 it was little more than a village of some 600 inhabitants.

It was about this time, however, that the industrialised nations of Europe began casting their nets for ever-increasing quantities of grain and wool – two of the main products of the Chaouia hinterland. To secure these products, European agents gradually established themselves in Casablanca (or Dar el-Baïda as the Moroccans had renamed the port). Prosperity began to return, but the activities and influence of the Europeans caused much resentment among the indigenous population. By the turn of the century and with the encouragement of the sultan, the resentment finally boiled over into open revolt, during which seven French port workers were beaten to death and the French Consulate was ransacked.

This was the ideal pretext for intervention which the procolonialist faction in the French Chamber of Deputies had been waiting for. A French warship, along with a company of marines, was dispatched to Casablanca and proceeded to bombard the town. With the fortifications breached, the marines poured into the town, bayoneting and shooting everyone in sight; they were soon joined in the fray by the Spanish. The real slaughter began, however, with the arrival of 2000 Senegalese troops and Foreign Legionnaires, the latter thoroughly undisciplined. Within days, the town of 25,000 inhabitants had been reduced to a few thousand terrified people hiding in the ruins of their former houses. The Jews of the mellah were a particular target – in this case of the Arab tribes, who had taken advantage of the situation to rape and pillage.

The French and Spanish action led to a whole train of events culminating in the Chaouia campaign, the dethronement of the sultan, Abd el Aziz, his replacement by Abd al-Hafid, and the declaration of the French and Spanish protectorates in 1912. Marshall Lyautey, previously the French commander of Oran, was appointed the first French Resident-General; it was he who decided to establish Casablanca as the administrative centre of the new protectorate. It was largely his ideas on public works and the layout of the new city which made Casablanca what it is today.

Orientation

Although Casablanca is a huge modern metropolis, most places of interest to travellers are within walking distance of each other. The heart of the city is Place Mohammed V, a large traffic roundabout at the southern end of the medina, from which the city's main boulevards branch out – Ave des Forces Armées Royale (FAR), Ave Moulay Hassan I, Ave Hassan II and Blvd Mohammed V.

Casa-Port railway station lies about 200 metres north of this main square, at the end of Blvd Mohammed el Hansali. The main bus station is to be found about 300 metres east of the square on Rue Vidal. The city's main administrative buildings are clustered around the large Place des Nations Unies to the south of the main square.

Most of the budget hotels are to be found in the narrow streets close to the southeastern end of the medina; the mid-range hotels are concentrated in the area bounded by Ave des FAR, Ave Hassan II, Ave Lalla Yacout and Blvd Hassan Seghir.

Information

Tourist Offices The national tourist office (ONMT) is at Rue Omar Slaoui and the syndicat d'initiative is at 98 Blvd Mohammed V. The staff at the latter are friendly and helpful, and have a range of literature and print-outs on Casablanca, which are far more informative than anything you will find at the national tourist office. If you need information, come here. It's open Monday to Saturday from 8.30 am to noon and 3 to 6.30 pm and on Sundays from 9 am to noon.

Money American Express is represented by Voyages Schwartz (☎ 22 2946), 112 Rue Prince Moulay Abdallah. Thomas Cook is represented by Wagons Lits (☎ 20 3051), 60 Rue Foucauld.

Post & Telecommunications The central post office is at the Place des Nations Unies. This building can be confusing because the front entrance is closed. Postage stamps have to be bought in the post box hall to the left as you face the front entrance. The poste restante counter, however, is in the same section as the international telephones. The entrance is the third door along the right-hand side of the building as you face it. There is a packing service available for parcels outside this door. Negotiate costs beforehand.

Touring Club de Maroc This is at 3 Ave des FAR. It's open Monday to Friday from 9 am to noon and 3 to 6.30 pm, and on Saturday from 9 am to noon.

Foreign Consulates The main consulates are in the area to the south-west of Place Mohammed V. See the Morocco Facts for the Visitor chapter for a full list of consulates in Casablanca.

Medina

The old medina is worth wandering through, though it has seen more dynamic days. Most of the surviving craft industries are concentrated along the Blvd Mohammed el Hansali, which is where they catch sailors on shore leave and tourists coming out of the railway station. Under these circumstances prices, as you might imagine, are relatively high. On the other hand, one of the advantages of exploring this medina is that there are no hassles with 'guides'.

Ville Nouvelle

Some of the best examples of Mauresque architecture are to be found around or close to the Place des Nations Unies. They include the law courts, post office, French Consulate and the Sacré Coeur Cathedral.

Hassan II Mosque

With the possible exception of the pyramids and Houphouet-Boigny's basilica at Yamoussoukro (Côte d'Ivoire), no greater monument to a monarch's ego has ever been built. Going up on the shoreline just beyond the northern tip of the medina, and nearing completion, is the world's largest mosque and certainly its tallest minaret.

Beautiful it will no doubt be, having consumed the labours of some 10,000 of Morocco's best artisans for over 10 years, but the cost has been astronomical – around US$800 million – to which everyone has been required to contribute. Perhaps one shouldn't be churlish about such things. After all, what did it cost Saddam Hussein to fight Iran for a few km of territory in the 1980s and the USA and its allies to throw him out of Kuwait in 1991? With such comparisons in mind, it's perhaps not a lot to pay for finally achieving what the Almohad sultan, Yacoub el Mansour, attempted to do in the 12th century. He, too, set out to build the world's largest mosque, at Rabat (the Tour Hassan), but construction was abandoned at his death. This time around it seems Morocco will finally make the Guinness Book of Records.

Beaches

Casablanca's beaches are to the found to the east of town along the Blvd de la Corniche, at the end of which (where it becomes the Blvd de Biarritz) the very affluent have their exclusive suburb. It's a very trendy area, lined with four-star hotels, up-market restaurants, bars, coffee shops and nightclubs, and you're going to feel very much out of place unless you dress accordingly and have a wallet to match.

Personally, unless you're desperate, I'd give them a miss as there are better beaches both north and south of here. Bus No 9 goes all the way along the Blvd de la Corniche; otherwise take a petit taxi.

Places to Stay – bottom end

All the hotels in the medina are unclassified and, although they are the cheapest, they have seen better days. Generally speaking, there's not a lot to choose between them. None of them have hot showers and many of them have no showers at all. Quite a few of them are essentially just flophouses. They're pretty poor value at around Dr 35/70 for singles/doubles without own shower and

toilet, when you consider that for a dollar or two extra you can get much better accommodation outside the medina area. Nevertheless, the lure of staying in the medina lives on and travellers do shack up in this area.

The most convenient approach to the hotels in the medina is from the entrance on Place Mohammed V.

The hotels to choose from here, all of which are marked on the map, include the *Genève, Helvetia, Widad, Brésil, Soussi, Gibraltar, des Amis, de Medine, Candice, de la Reine* and the *Hotel Central*.

Casablanca (Medina Hotel Area)

0 — 200m

1   Hotels des Amis,
    de Medine & Gibraltar
2   Hotel Candice
3   Hotel Soussi
4   Hotel de la Reine
5   Hotel de Brésil
6   Hotel Helvetia
7   Hotel de Widad
8   Hotel Genève
9   Plaza Hotel
10 Hotel George V
11 Hotel el Mansour
12 Touring Hotel
13 Hotel Excelsior
14 Hotel de Foucauld
15 Hotel du Périgord
16 Hotel Kon Tiki

Boulevard des Almohades

Casa-Port Railway Station

Youth Hostel

Post Office (PTT)

Hotel Central

Rue Centrale
Rue Anfa
Rue de Fès
R. du Marché aux Grains
Boulevard Mohammed el Hansali
Rue Chakab Arsalane

Place Mohammed V

Avenue des Forces Armées Royales (FAR)

Hyatt Regency Hotel

Ave. Mly Hassan I
Ave. Hassan II

Rue Allal ben Abdallah

Boulevard Mohammed V

Outside the medina area there are also a number of unclassified hotels to choose from, and most are better than those in the medina. One of the best if you can get in – it's frequently full – is the *Hotel du Palais*, 68 Rue Farhat Hached, which costs Dr 62 for a single or double with shared bathroom. Another which has been popular for years, but which is also frequently full, is the *Hotel du Périgord*, 56 Rue Foucauld, which offers singles/doubles for Dr 35/52 with shared bathroom. Hot showers are extra. Virtually next door is the one-star *Hotel de Foucauld* (☎ 22 2666), 52 Rue Foucauld, which has singles/doubles with shared bathroom for Dr 45/66 and Dr 61/85 with own shower.

Close by is the *Hotel Kon Tiki*, 88 Rue Allal ben Abdallah, another unclassified hotel, and the *Touring Hotel* (☎ 31 0216), 87 Rue Allal ben Abdallah, a one-star hotel with singles/doubles for Dr 66/85 with shared bathroom, and Dr 85/98 with own shower and toilet. Round the corner from these, opposite the entrance to the covered market, is the one-star *Hotel Colbert* (☎ 31 4241), 30 Rue Colbert, which has similar prices to those at the Touring Hotel.

Just south of the market is the *Hotel Gallia*, another unclassified hotel, with a range of rooms available from Dr 39/54 for singles/doubles without bathroom, Dr 51/63 with own shower but shared toilet, and Dr 59/77 for rooms with own shower and toilet. Similar, and a nice quiet place to stay, is the one-star *Hotel Louvre* (☎ 27 3747), 36 Rue Nationale. This offers singles for Dr 44, Dr 58 and Dr 65 and doubles for Dr 58, Dr 70 and Dr 86, plus tax. The higher priced rooms have their own shower.

Further afield and more or less opposite one another are the unclassified *Hotel de Mamora* (☎ 31 1511), 59 Rue ibn Batouta, and the *Hotel Volubilis*. Both have singles/doubles for Dr 38/52 with shared bathroom. Up on the Blvd de Paris is the one-star *Hotel Lafayette*, 40 Blvd de Paris, which has doubles for Dr 85 with shared bathroom, and Dr 106 with own shower and toilet. Between here and the Place Mohammed V is the *Hotel Lausanne* (☎ 26 8690),

24 Rue Poincaré. From the outside, you might think this is an expensive hotel, but it has singles/doubles with own shower and toilet for Dr 85/98 plus taxes.

Lastly, in this price range, there's the one-star *Hotel Majestic* (☎ 31 0951), 57 Ave Lalla Yacout, which is thoroughly overpriced but where quite a few travellers stay. Doubles with own shower and toilet here cost Dr 170. The plumbing is falling apart and the beds are terrible but it does have clean sheets. Downstairs there's a tea salon and brasserie.

Youth Hostel The cheapest place to stay if you're happy with dormitory accommodation is the *Youth Hostel* (☎ 22 0551), 6 Place Admiral Philbert, which faces a small, leafy square at the northern end of the medina adjacent to Blvd des Almohades. It's a fairly large hostel, comfortable and clean, and costs Dr 20 per person including breakfast. It's closed daily between 10 am and noon and from 2 to 5 pm. From Casa-Port railway station, walk out to the first major intersection and turn right along the Blvd des Almohades. Turn left when you get to the second opening in the medina wall. Go through it and the hostel is on the right.

Camping Campers should head for *Camping Oasis*, Ave Mermoz (the main road to El Jadida). It's a long way from the centre, so unless you have your own transport it's hardly worth it. Bus No 31 from the CTM terminal will take you there.

Places to Stay – middle
In this range you're unlikely to do better than stay at the two-star *Hotel Guynemer* (☎ 27 5764), 2 Rue Pegoud, which offers singles/doubles without own bathroom for Dr 66/85, and Dr 80/102 with own bathroom. They also have other rooms for Dr 122 a double. It's great value, quiet, clean and secure.

Facing the Place Mohammed V is the *Hotel Excelsior* (☎ 27 6513), 2 Rue Nolly, which has doubles with own bathroom for Dr 168. There are no singles and you need to

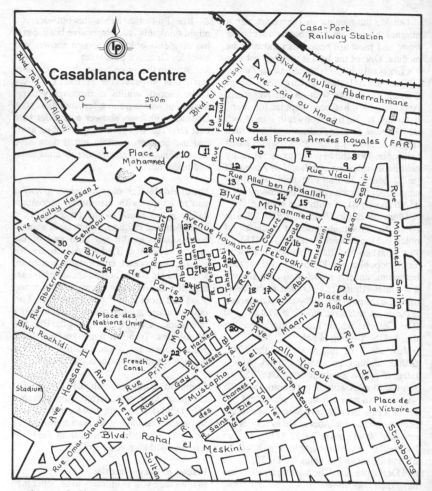

Casablanca Centre

get there early if you want a room, as it's a popular place to stay. Just a stone's throw away is the *Hotel George V* (☎ 31 2448), 1 Rue Sidi Belyout, which is similarly priced.

Going up in price, the three-star *Hotel de Paris* (☎ 27 3871), 2 Rue Branly, on the Prince Moulay Abdallah pedestrian precinct, is superb value. Recently refurbished to a very high standard, I'd rate this as one of the best hotels in Morocco. Very comfortable, self-contained rooms here with hot water and balcony go for Dr 151/186 for singles/ doubles plus taxes. It has 34 rooms so it's unlikely to be full. If it is, try either the nearby *Hotel Noailles* (☎ 27 0585), 22 Blvd du 11 Janvier, just off the Ave Lalla Yacout, or the *Hotel Plaza* (☎ 22 1262), 18 Blvd Mohammed el Hansali, just off the Place Mohammed V. Both of these are three-star hotels with singles/doubles for Dr 175/212 plus taxes.

1	Hyatt Regency Hotel
2	Hotel Plaza
3	Hotel George V
4	Hotel el Mansour
5	Hotel Marhaba
6	Royal Air Maroc
7	Hotel Sheraton
8	Hotel Safir
9	CTM Bus Terminal
10	Hotel Excelsior
11	Hotels de Foucauld & du Périgord
12	Touring Hotel
13	Hotel Kon Tiki
14	Hotel Colbert
15	Central Market
16	Hotel Gallia
17	Hotel de Mamora
18	Hotel Volubilis
19	Hotel Majestic
20	Hotel Champlain
21	Hotel Noailles
22	Hotel du Palais
23	Hotel Lafayette
24	Hotel de Paris
25	Hotel Guynemer
26	Hotel de Seville
27	Hotel du Louvre
28	Hotel Lausanne
29	Central Post Office (PTT)
30	Hotel al Mounia

Places to Stay – top end

Most of Casablanca's top-end hotels are to be found on the Ave des FAR. They include the *Hotel Sheraton* (☎ 31 7878), *Hotel Safir* (☎ 31 1212), *Hotel el Mansour* (☎ 31 3011) and the *Hotel Marhaba*. All are five-star hotels. Close by on Place Mohammed V is the *Hyatt Regency Hotel* (☎ 22 4167), also five-star. A little further afield is the *Hotel Al Mounia* (☎ 26 0727), 50 Blvd de Paris, close to the main post office.

The bulk of the other top-end hotels are to be found overlooking the beaches along the Blvd de la Corniche. Most of them are four-star. They include the *Hotel Tropicana* (☎ 36 7595), *Hotel Tarik* (☎ 36 7073), *Hotel La Corniche* (☎ 36 3011), *Hotel Karam* (☎ 36 7314), *Hotel Anfa Place* (☎ 36 7566), *Hotel Suisse* (☎ 36 0202) and the *Hotel Riad Salam* (☎ 36 3535).

Places to Eat

There are quite a few cheap restaurants around the Place Mohammed V entrance to the medina. No particular place stands out, but one that is clean, bright and good is the *Restaurant Widad*, attached to the hotel of the same name. They serve good Moroccan food and the servings are generous. A similar place, but outside the medina, is the *Café Restaurant Point Central*, at 89 Rue Allal ben Abdallah, right next door to the Hotel Touring. Another good place in the new city is the kitsch *Restaurant de l'Etoile Marocaine*, at 107 Rue Allal ben Abdallah, not far from the Hotel Touring. It's a very friendly place, the food is good and they have individual serves of delicious pastilla (pigeon pie) for Dr 40. Round the corner from here, opposite the entrance to the covered market, is a restaurant serving mainly barbecued chicken, where you can eat reasonably well for around Dr 20 to Dr 25.

If you're staying anywhere near the pedestrian mall (Rue Prince Moulay Abdallah), there are quite a number of Moroccan fast-food cafés along the Ave Lalla Yacout which are extremely popular with local people both at lunch times and in the early evening. One which stands out is *Kwiki Sandwich*. You can get a ketta sandwich with salad and chips here for just Dr 8.50.

On the pedestrian mall itself, diagonally opposite the Hotel de Paris, try the *Snack Manhattan*. It's actually situated inside a small courtyard, but it's signposted on the mall. The service can be slow, but they do excellent cheap fruit juices, omelettes, kebabs, sausages and salads.

For something a little better, *Las Delicias*, at 168 Blvd Mohammed V, has a good range of tajines such as chicken with prunes and onions, or beef with raisins. Watch out for the service charge and taxes here which amount to 20%. Also good in this area is the *Restaurant Le Cardinal*, very close to Place Mohammed V.

For seafood, try one or other of the restaurants along Blvd Mohammed el Hansali or, for a splurge, head out to the lighthouse on the way to the beaches. Here there's a cluster of three up-market restaurants, *Le Cabestan*, *La Mer* and *La Petite Roche*.

Entertainment

Without a lot of money to spend, the possibilities for nightlife in Casablanca are very limited. One thing which won't cost you an arm and a leg is to join the promenading throng up and down the pedestrian mall (Rue Prince Moulay Abdallah) each evening or to sit down at one of the cafés along it and watch life go by.

There are few bars in this area, but one which is popular in the evenings – and where it won't be the usual all-male company – is that opposite the Hotel de Paris on the pedestrian mall.

The best of the nightclubs (and there are quite a few of them) are out at the beaches, but remember that the clientele will be very ritzy and the prices will reflect this. You'd be looking at Dr 50 to Dr 100 entry (including first drink) and subsequent drinks at Dr 50.

Getting There & Away

Air From Casa's Mohammed V Airport there are regular connections to most of the countries of Western Europe, as well as to West Africa, Algeria, Tunisia, Egypt and the Middle East.

Airlines flying into and out of Mohammed V International Airport include:

Air Algérie
    1 Rue Nolly (☎ 26 6995)
Air France
    15 Ave des FAR (☎ 29 4040)
Aeroflot
    27 Ave des FAR (☎ 31 0521)
Alitalia
    4 Ave des FAR (☎ 27 7535)
Air Afrique
    Tour des Habous (☎ 31 2866)
British Airways/GB Airways
    Place Zellaqa (☎ 30 7629)
Iberia
    17 Ave des FAR (☎ 27 9600)
KLM
    6 Blvd Mohammed el Hansali (☎ 27 2729)
Lufthansa
    Tour des Habous (☎ 31 2371)
Royal Air Maroc
    44 Ave des FAR (☎ 31 1122)

Royal Jordanian
    Place Zellaqa (☎ 30 6273)
Swissair
    Tour des Habous (☎ 31 3280)
Sabena
    41 Ave des FAR (☎ 31 3991)
Tunis Air
    10 Ave des FAR (☎ 27 3914)

Bus The CTM bus terminal is on Rue Vidal at the back of the Hotel Safir, which is on the Ave des FAR. There are other bus stations scattered around, but most of them use the terminal on the Rue Strasbourg, two blocks down from the Place de la Victoire. The latter terminal is some way from the centre of the city, so it might be better to take a taxi from the Place Mohammed V.

There are regular CTM departures to Agadir (four times daily); Chechaouen (once daily at 8.30 am); Essaouira (twice daily at 5.30 am and 5 pm); Errachidia (once daily at 7.30 pm); Fès (six times daily); Marrakesh (five times daily); Meknès (six times daily); Oujda (twice daily at 8 and 8.30 pm); Rabat (19 times daily); Safi (seven times daily); Tangier (five times daily); Taza (once daily at 1 pm) and Tetouan (three times daily).

CTM also operates international buses to France and Belgium from Casablanca. See the Morocco Getting There & Away chapter in the introductory sections for further details.

Train Most departures are from Casa-Voyageurs station, which is a Dr 15 taxi ride from the centre, or 30 minutes' walk. Departures include: Fès (five daily at 6.05 am, and 12.52, 2.40, 5.18 and 9.55 pm, 5½ hours); El Jadida (8.07 pm, 1¼ hours); Marrakesh (six daily at 1.28, 7.45 and 9.40 am, and 12.10, 5.34 and 7.15 pm, four hours); Oujda (12.52 and 9.55 pm, 11½ hours); and Tangier (11.15 pm, seven hours).

Departures from the much more convenient Gare du Port ('Casa-Port' on the platform signs) on Blvd Mohammed el Hansali are as follows: Fès (8.05 am, and 12.32 and 8.50 pm, 5½ hours); Marrakesh (1 am); Oujda (8.05 am and 8.50 pm, 10¼ hours); and Tangier (7.15 am and 5.57 pm, seven hours)

All trains going north call at Rabat and you can use the mainline trains to get there, but the quickest and most convenient way is to take one of the nonstop express trains which ply only between Casa-Port and Rabat Ville. These depart virtually every hour between 6.50 am and 8.35 pm on weekdays (less at weekends and on public holidays). The journey takes 50 minutes.

All trains to Fès call at Meknès.

Car Rental Most of the main agencies are in the centre on Ave des FAR: Avis (☎ 31 2424), 19 Ave des FAR; Budget (☎ 31 3945), Tour des Habous; Europcar/InterRent (☎ 31 3737), 44 Ave des FAR; and Hertz (☎ 31 2223), 25 Rue Foucauld.

There are plenty of other local car rental agencies in the same area which are considerably cheaper than the above, and many of them employ runners so expect to be approached by them when you leave any of the above offices. They're well worth checking out before you decide whom to rent from.

If you do rent a car then you should be aware of Casablanca's horrendous parking problems. It is virtually impossible to find a park in the centre between the hours of 8 am and 6 pm. During these hours, cars will be literally parked nose to tail in every conceivable spot. How they disentangle themselves at the end of the day is anyone's guess.

Getting Around
To/From the Airport There are departures every 30 minutes from 5.30 to 8 am and every hour from 9 am to 11 pm daily from the CTM bus terminal to Mohammed V Airport. The fare is Dr 20 and the trip takes 40 minutes.

Taxi There's no shortage of petits taxis in Casablanca, but you'll usually find drivers unwilling to use the meters so negotiate the fare before getting in, especially if going a long way. Expect to pay Dr 10 for a ride in or around the city centre.

A grand taxi to Mohammed V Airport will cost you Dr 200.

North Coast

ASILAH
About 46 km south of Tangier along a magnificent sweep of Atlantic beach is the small port of Asilah. Small it may be but, over two millennia, it's had a tumultuous history far out of proportion to its size.

The first settlers here were the Carthaginians, who named the port Zilis. Next on the scene were the Romans. Faced with the prospect of having to deal with a population which had unfortunately backed the wrong side in the aftermath of the Punic Wars, the Romans forcibly moved the inhabitants to Spain and replaced them with people from that country.

Asilah featured again in the 10th century, when it successfully held Norman raiders from Sicily at bay; it was also prominent in the 11th century, when it became the last refuge of the Idrissids. Asilah's most turbulent period, however, followed the Christian victories over the forces of Islam on the Iberian peninsula in the 14th and 15th centuries. In 1471 it was captured by the Portuguese; the walls around the city date essentially from this period, though they have been repaired from time to time.

In 1578 King Sebastian of Portugal chose Asilah as the base for an ill-fated crusade against the Muslims. Despite the immense army which he landed, which included the flower of the Portuguese nobility, his forces were defeated by the Saadian sultan Abd el-Malik on the banks of a tributary of the River Makhazen. Some 26,000 Portuguese were killed or taken prisoner, Sebastian himself was killed and the sultan died of a heart attack in the early stages of the battle.

The defeat of the Portuguese had radical consequences far beyond the shores of Morocco. Since Sebastian died childless,

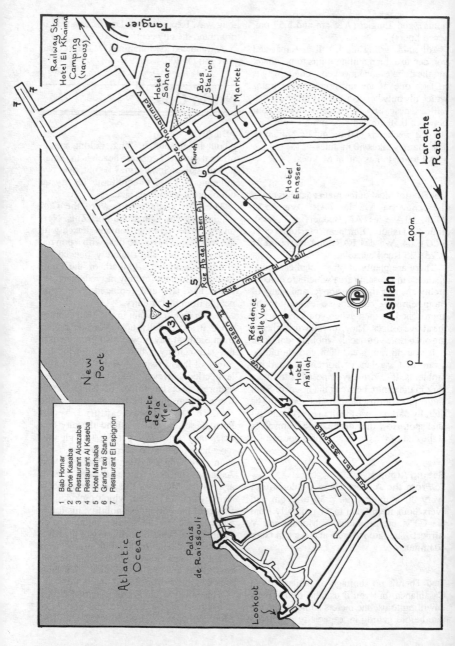

Key
1 Bab Homar
2 Porte Kasaba
3 Restaurant Alcazaba
4 Restaurant Al Kaseba
5 Hotel Marhaba
6 Grand Taxi Stand
7 Restaurant El Espignon

Asilah

Top: Moulay Idriss, Morocco (HF)
Left: Moulay Idriss, Morocco (HF)
Right: Todra Gorge, Morocco (GC)

Top: Berber kasbah, Drâa Valley, Morocco (GC)
Left: Chechaouen, Morocco (HF)
Right: Ruins of ancient granaries, Meknès, Morocco (HF)

Spain inherited his kingdom along with all of Portugal's overseas possessions (including Asilah). Portugal regained its independence only in the following century. In the meantime, the balance of trade with Morocco passed into the hands of the English and Dutch.

Asilah was recaptured by the Moroccans in 1589, lost again to the Spanish for a while and then recaptured again by Moulay Ismail in 1691. In the 19th century, as a result of pirate attacks on their shipping, the city was bombarded by both the Austrian and Spanish navies.

At the beginning of the 20th century, Asilah became the base of a famous brigand and kidnapper, Raissouli, who also had pretensions to becoming pasha. Arrogant and ruthless, but with a peasant's wily intuition, and credited with considerable baraka by his followers, his relations with the sultan varied from one extreme to the other – from being made governor of the province to being thrown in jail. The Spanish, preferring to have him on their side in their bid for influence within Morocco, confirmed his governorship but soon found themselves quarrelling with him. For the next eight years, Raissouli fought a running battle with the Spanish forces but successfully eluded capture. That honour fell instead to Abd el-Krim, who was later to lead the revolt against the Spanish and French forces in the Rif.

By intriguing among the consuls of the warring European powers in Tangier, Raissouli was able to return to his palace in Asilah and his governorship between 1914 and 1918. However, at the end of WW I, his influence waned; he died in 1925, largely abandoned and forgotten.

Asilah seems to have found its vocation in the late 20th century as a bijou resort town. Money has been poured into restoring and gentrifying the houses within the city walls by both affluent Moroccans and Europeans. Consequently, its streets gleam with fresh whitewash, ornate wrought-iron work adorns windows and chic craft shops have sprouted along virtually every alley. A new enclosed harbour is under construction and should soon be providing berths for pleasure yachts as well as the small fishing fleet based here.

A little further north along the beaches, camping resorts have mushroomed. These are very popular with Europeans who flock here in summer hoping to find something a little cheaper and more authentic than what is on offer along the Spanish Costa Brava.

Despite the changes which mass tourism has brought, it is worth visiting and staying in Asilah for a while, especially in the low season when there are hardly any tourists around.

Ramparts

The impressive 15th-century Portuguese ramparts are essentially intact, though there has been a considerable amount of restoration done on them in recent years. Unfortunately, access is very limited since many private houses abut against them; the two prongs which jut out into the ocean, however, can be visited at any time and these are where you get the best views in any case. It's very reminiscent of the old towns enclosed between the walls of El Jadida and Essaouira and there are plenty of photographic opportunities here.

Raissouli Palace

Undoubtedly one of the most interesting places to see is the Palais de Raissouli (Raissouli Palace). This beautifully preserved three-storey building was constructed in 1909 and includes a main reception room with a glass-fronted terrace overlooking the sea. It's from this terrace that Raissouli forced convicted murderers to walk to their deaths onto the rocks 30 metres below. Unfortunately, all the furniture has been removed from the palace so it's hard to get an idea of what sort of life style Raissouli used to lead here. Entry to the palace is free and you're allowed to wander around at will though, if it's locked up, you may have to ask around before you find someone with the key to let you in. The palace is the venue for an international arts festival held in August each year.

Beaches

Other than the old town, the beaches to the north of town are the main attraction. During the summer months they are awash with tourists from Europe. A whole service industry has grown up to cater for the needs of these people, including campsites, restaurants, discos and the like. It's Agadir revisited at this time of year and you can meet people from as far afield as Brisbane and Bremen.

Places to Stay – bottom end

Probably the cheapest place is the *Hotel Enasser*, which offers basic, simple small rooms with shared bathroom for Dr 25 (less if you intend to stay for a week or so). Somewhat more comfortable are the *Hotel Asilah* (☎ 91 7286) and the *Hotel Marhaba*, both right outside the ramparts. The Asilah is a one-star hotel so you're looking at Dr 58/70 for singles/doubles with own shower but without toilet and Dr 67/86 for singles/doubles with own shower and toilet. During the low season, this hotel is often closed between noon and 3 pm. The Marhaba overlooks the Place Zelaka, in front of the main entrance (Porte Kasaba) to the old town, and is quite adequate for most travellers. It costs Dr 55 for a single or double. Each room has a double bed with clean sheets and a handbasin but you share the bathroom. Hot showers are Dr 5 extra.

Another similarly priced hotel is the *Hotel Sahara* (☎ 91 7185), 9 Rue Tarfaya, which one traveller described as having 'pokey little rooms with back-breaking beds and weird staff who never spoke' but which I found to be quite clean and pleasant. It's a one-star hotel and costs the same as the Marhaba.

Camping For campers, there are a number of resorts/sites along the beach, all of them north of town. They include *Camping Es Saida, Camping Sahara, Camping L'Ocean* and *Hotel Camping*. During the summer months and the Christmas/New Year period, they all cater essentially for package tour groups from Europe and individuals with their own vehicles so, at these times, which one you choose will very much depend on what language you speak. At other times of the year, you'll virtually have the place to yourself. They all have guarded camping facilities, shower and toilet blocks, and restaurants and bars, and are all situated right on the beach.

Places to Stay – middle

The only middle-range hotel in Asilah at present is the *Résidence Belle View*, Rue Al Khansaa, which opened its doors in late 1990 and has friendly staff and a range of different rooms. Those with shared bathroom cost Dr 40/65 for singles/doubles, and self-contained apartments with lounge, kitchen and refrigerator cost Dr 165 (small) and Dr 225 (large). The hotel has hot water, its own restaurant and a roof terrace.

Places to Stay – top end

The three-star *Hotel El Khaima* (☎ 91 7230) is right beside the road heading north just out of town on the right-hand side. Rooms here cost Dr 175/212 for singles/doubles plus taxes. Many of the rooms face the sea and the beach is just across the road.

Long-Term House Rentals

Due to the fact that many people have bought up houses in the old town and converted them into holiday homes, it is possible to find long-term rentals outside the high season. Simply ask around if there's anything going. The grapevine will do the rest. What you pay for these houses will obviously depend on the standard of accommodation which they offer, but they won't be cheap. References and/or a substantial deposit for wear and tear/breakages would be normal.

Places to Eat

Restaurant facilities in Asilah are surprisingly limited. Essentially it's down to the one or two cheap cafés in front of the ramparts at the beginning of Ave Hassan II, or a semi-splurge at either the *Restaurant Al Kaseba* or the *Restaurant Alcazaba*, outside the Porte Kasaba. These restaurants are owned by the same people and, most of the time, what you order from the Alcazaba actually gets cooked at the Al Kaseba. The food at both restaurants is good, but not exceptionally cheap at Dr 54 for fried seafood, chips and salad. Another place to splurge at is the more expensive *Restaurant El Espignon*, at the end of the seafront boulevard.

Getting There & Away

You can get to Asilah by either rail or road from Tangier or by road from Larache. Asilah is on the main Tangier-Rabat/Meknès line and there are at least six trains per day in either direction which stop at Asilah. The journey from Asilah to Tangier takes between 45 and 55 minutes.

Buses and grands taxis run regularly between Tangier and Asilah and between Larache and Asilah.

LARACHE

Most people come to Larache to visit the Roman ruins of Lixus, some four to five km out of town to the north, but it's worth staying here for a night or two just for its own sake. Like Asilah, but considerably larger and a far more substantial fishing port, Larache is a pleasant, tranquil town where you'll have few hassles. The old town was once walled but the kasbah and ramparts are now in almost total ruin. What remains intact are the old medina, a fortress known as the Casbah de la Cigogne and a pocket-sized, Spanish-built citadel which these days houses the Archaeological Museum. The heart of the new town – the Place de la Libération (formerly the Plaza de España) – is a typical example of grandiose Spanish colonial urban planning.

What makes Larache interesting, however, is not so much the crumbling ruins as the nightlife. It's a long time since the Spanish left but, somehow, the social institution of the evening stroll lives on. Between the hours of 5.30 and 9 pm virtually everyone who lives here emerges from the woodwork to promenade, drink coffee or beer, play cards and talk about the day's events. And if you have something to contribute, even if it's

just the fact that you're not Moroccan, then you can join a conversation anywhere. Spanish is widely spoken though you can also get by in English, French or even Korean – there's a large fishing fleet here, so the fishermen meet people from all over the world. Naturally, there's plenty of excellent seafood available in the restaurants.

Archaeological Museum

The collection here, though small, is very well organised, well labelled and interesting. Most of the artefacts are from Lixus and anyone who wants to explore those ruins would appreciate more about them by first visiting this museum. There are two floors to the museum, which is housed in a Spanish citadel bearing the arms of Charles V above the main door. Entry costs Dr 10 and it's open daily except Tuesday from 9 am to noon and 3 to 5 pm.

The Old Town

The only remaining intact fortification here, the Casbah de la Cigogne, is out of bounds to visitors. Likewise, the old city walls and the ruined kasbah (the Kebibat), built by the Portuguese in the 16th century, while not actually out of bounds, are dangerous because of the possibility of falling masonry. It's up to you if you want to explore this area.

The old cobbled medina, on the other hand, is alive and well and, though not comparable with the medinas of the imperial cities, is well worth exploring. No-one here is going to hassle you about 'guide' services and there are good photographic possibilities. The best place to enter the medina is through the large Mauresque arch on the Place de la Libération. Going through here you come immediately into a colonnaded market square which was built by the Spanish during their first occupation of Larache in the 17th century. You can also get into the heart of the medina through a similar arch opposite the Archaeological Museum.

The Beaches

The nearest beaches are north of Larache, across the other side of the Loukkos estuary.

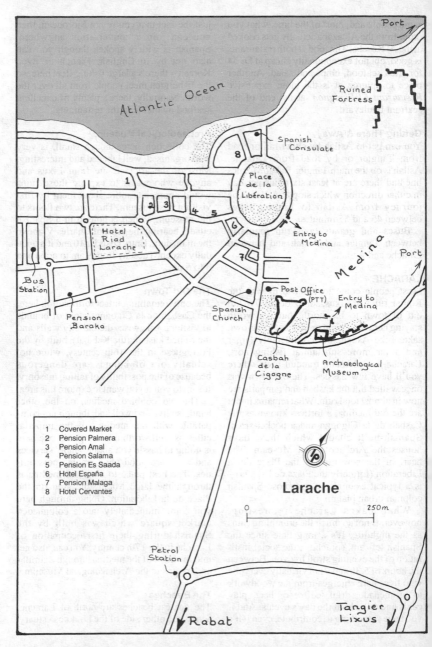

1 Covered Market
2 Pension Palmera
3 Pension Amal
4 Pension Salama
5 Pension Es Saada
6 Hotel España
7 Pension Malaga
8 Hotel Cervantes

Larache

0   250m

Atlantic Ocean

Port

Ruined Fortress

Spanish Consulate

Place de la Libération

Entry to Medina

Medina

Port

Hotel Riad Larache

Bus Station

Pension Baraka

Post Office (PTT)

Entry to Medina

Spanish Church

Casbah de la Cigogne

Archaeological Museum

Petrol Station

Rabat

Tangier Lixus

To get there, you can either take a small boat directly across the estuary from the port or take the more circuitous road route (seven km) using the No 4 bus which you can also pick up from the port. The buses run approximately every hour throughout the day. There are a number of simple restaurants at the beach offering the usual range of seafoods.

Lixus

Four to five km north of Larache, alongside and above the main Larache-Tangier highway, on a hillock overlooking the Loukkos estuary are the Roman ruins of Lixus. Though not as substantial or as well excavated as those at Volubilis, they are definitely worth a visit if you are passing through this area. An hour or so is sufficient time for most people to explore these ruins. To get there, take bus No 4 (the same one as for the beach) and ask to be dropped at the turn-off. The site is not enclosed and you're at liberty to wander around on your own. There's no entry fee and, if you exercise some discretion about where you enter the ruins, no-one will hassle to be your 'guide'. Otherwise, there'll be the inevitable unemployed youth offering their services.

The site was originally occupied by a megalithic sun-worshipping people about whom little is known except that they left a number of stones in the vicinity of the acropolis. The positioning of these stones suggests that these people were in touch with developments in astronomy and mathematics which led to the building of stone circles in places as far apart as The Gambia and Scotland during the megalithic period.

Next on the scene were the Phoenicians, who set up a colony here, known as Liks, around 1000 BC or even earlier, at about the same time they settled Cadiz, or Gadera as it was known to them. Trade here, and through the later established colonies of Tingis (Tangier), Tamuda (Tetouan), Rusadir (Melilla) and Chella (Rabat), was principally in gold, ivory and slaves.

Nevertheless, the Atlantic colonies were never very important economically to the Phoenicians until the destruction of the mother city of Tyre by Nebuchadnezzar in the 6th century BC, and the subsequent rise of the city-state of Carthage.

As a result of explorations as far south as the mouth of the Niger River about this time by the Carthaginian Hanno, Carthage was able to monopolise the trade in gold from West Africa and to keep its source a secret. Liks was a key base from which this trade was organised and equipped, and even when Carthage fell to the Romans in 146 BC, Liks continued to exert a civilising influence on this area of the Maghreb until the setting up of the Roman vassal state of the Berber king, Juba II, in 25 BC.

Direct Roman rule over this part of the world came in AD 42 under the emperor Claudius and it was at about this time that Lixus entered upon its second period of importance. Instead of gold as its economic cornerstone, however, its most important exports during Roman times were salt, olives, garum (an aromatic anchovy paste) and wild animals for the various amphitheatres of the empire.

Lixus rapidly declined in importance following the Roman withdrawal north under Diocletian but was not finally abandoned until sometime in the 5th century AD when the Roman Empire fell apart.

Most of the ruins at Lixus date from the Roman period and include the garum factories alongside the highway. Just beyond these (at the end of a line of green-painted railings), a gravel track leads up the hillside past a number of minor ruins to the public baths and amphitheatre. Restoration has recently been done on these and they're undoubtedly the most impressive of the ruins here. Also to be found is a mosaic of the Sea God – the only such mosaic to be seen at Lixus.

Carrying on to the top of the hill you come to the acropolis where most of the civic buildings were located, including the main temple and associated sanctuaries, an oratory, more public baths and what remains of the city walls. The view over the estuary of the Loukkos from here is excellent, but most of the antiquities are in an advanced

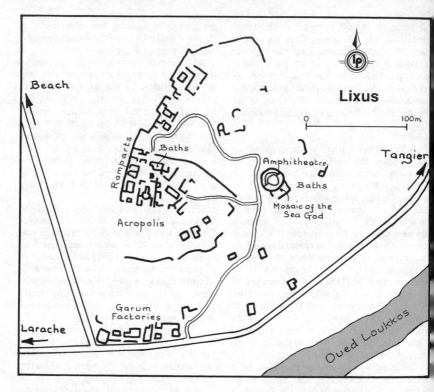

state of decay and there's been some woefully amateurish restoration done on them.

It's a pity Lixus has been allowed to decay to the degree that it has, whereas attention has been lavished on Volubilis. Were it to be found in Europe, it would be regarded, no doubt, as an important national monument.

Places to Stay – bottom end
There's a good choice of budget accommodation in Larache, and, ignoring a couple of very basic places in the medina, all but one of the pensions are along the same street. They include the *Pension Es Saada, Pension Salama, Pension Amal* and the *Pension Palmera*. Not on this street, but closer to the bus station, is the *Pension Baraka*, and

there's also the *Pension Malaga* just off the Place de la Libération. There's not much to choose between any of these places, though I'd suggest you try the Amal first. Prices are the usual Dr 40/60 for singles/doubles with shared bathroom.

Places to Stay – middle
Once the chosen place to stay during Spanish colonial times, the two-star *Hotel España* (☎ 91 3195), which fronts onto the Place de la Libération, still exudes an air of grandness. It has a total of 50 rooms, some with their own bathroom and balcony. The cost is Dr 92/112 for singles/doubles with own bathroom and Dr 75/92 without own bathroom plus taxes. Also in this league is the *Hotel Cervantes* just off the north-west side of the

Place de la Libération. Some of the rooms at the Cervantes have sea views.

Places to Stay – top end
The only top-end hotel in town is the three-star *Hotel Riad Laruche* (☎ 91 2626), Rue Mohammed ben Abdallah, which was apparently once the private home of French nobility. It's now part of the KTH hotel chain. Set in its own luxuriantly formal grounds complete with swimming pool and tennis courts, it offers very spacious self-contained rooms at Dr 175/212 for singles/doubles plus taxes. As well as a beer garden, there's an internal bar and restaurant which offers three-course dinners for Dr 80 as well as (expensive) breakfasts.

Places to Eat
There are a number of small eateries around the Place de la Libération as well as in the colonnaded market square just inside the medina where you can get cheap Spanish-style meals, especially those based on sardines.

Other than this, one of the best places to eat is the *Restaurant El Pozo*, opposite Hotel España.

Some two km south of Larache on the Rabat road is a Spanish-style bistro called the *Paco y Pili* which might be worth a visit if you have your own transport and plenty of money to spend. It's beautifully conceived and the food is excellent, but portions are small and at around Dr 110 per person for soup and main course plus a beer, it's a lavish way to pretend you're somewhere else.

Getting There & Away
There are frequent bus and grand taxi services between both Rabat and Tangier, and Larache, and less frequent services between Fès and Larache. Buses between Tangier and Larache usually call at Asilah, but not always, so if that's where you're heading, you need to check this out before boarding the bus.

Buses and grands taxis share the same terminus in Larache.

Central Coast

EL JADIDA
History
El Jadida was founded by the Portuguese in 1513, in the days when these seafaring people were undertaking their voyages of discovery around the world and pouring what meagre resources they had into establishing a maritime trading empire which quickly stretched as far as China and Japan. They were to hold on to El Jadida (which, in those days, was known as Mazagan) until 1769 when, following a siege by Sultan Sidi Mohammed ben Abdallah, the Portuguese were forced to evacuate the fortress. Although they took little more than the clothes they stood in, the ramparts were mined and, at the last moment, blown to smithereens, taking with them a good part of the besieging army.

The walls of the fortress lay in ruins until 1820, when they were rebuilt by Sultan Moulay Abderrahman. The Moors who took over the town after the Portuguese withdrawal preferred to settle outside the walls of the fortress. The medina inside the walls was largely neglected until the mid-19th century, when it was recolonised by European merchants following the establishment of a series of 'open ports' along the Moroccan coast.

A large and influential Jewish community became established at this time. The Jews controlled trade with the interior and particularly with Marrakesh. Not only that but, contrary to the practice in most Moroccan cities, the Jews of El Jadida were not confined to living within their own separate quarter (the mellah).

The massive bastioned fortress with its enclosed medina, churches and enormous cistern is still remarkably well preserved. Indeed, despite having been reconstructed by the Moroccans, it's one of the most spec-

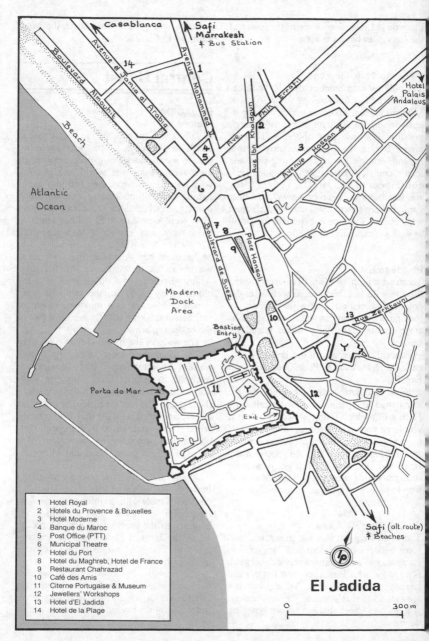

1   Hotel Royal
2   Hotels du Provence & Bruxelles
3   Hotel Moderne
4   Banque du Maroc
5   Post Office (PTT)
6   Municipal Theatre
7   Hotel du Port
8   Hotel du Maghreb, Hotel de France
9   Restaurant Chahrazad
10 Café des Amis
11 Citerne Portugaise & Museum
12 Jewellers' Workshops
13 Hotel d'El Jadida
14 Hotel de la Plage

El Jadida

0   300 m

tacular European-style fortresses to be found anywhere in the world.

These days, El Jadida is a very popular Moroccan beach resort.

Portuguese Fortress

The old Portuguese fortress (known as the Cité Portugaise) is the focal centre of town. Although its enclosed medina has suffered from neglect, it's still inhabited and well worth exploring. There are two entrance gates to the fortress; the northernmost one, which is more convenient, opens onto the main street through the medina. The street ends at the Porta do Mar, which is where ships used to discharge their cargo in the Portuguese era.

Citerne Portugaise

About halfway down the main street of the Portuguese fortress is the famous Citerne Portugaise (Portuguese Cistern). Though the Romans built water collection and storage cisterns similar to this, it remains a remarkable piece of architecture and engineering which has stood the test of time and is still functional. The reflection of the roof and arched pillars in the water covering the floor creates a dramatic and beautiful effect. This hasn't escaped the attention of various film directors, who have staged scenes for several movies here. The cistern is open on weekdays from 8 am to noon and 2 to 6 pm (sometimes later). Entry costs Dr 10 and includes a guide who will show you around. Photography is permitted at no extra charge. There's also a small museum next to the cistern (free) but it's not up to much.

Medina

Being zealous Catholics, the Portuguese naturally constructed a number of churches within the medina. Unfortunately, they're all closed, except for what remains of one on top of the ramparts at the extreme southern seaward side. Even if it were possible to visit them, however, it's unlikely that they would still retain their original features, since they were taken over and used for secular purposes long ago. The Great Mosque, adjacent to the largest former church close to the entrance, used to be a lighthouse.

Ramparts

Entry to the ramparts, which you can walk all the way around, is through the large door at the end of the tiny cul-de-sac which is first on the right after entering the fortress. The man with the key for this is usually hanging around and, if not, he won't be far away. There's no charge, but he'll expect a tip when he lets you out at the far side (you may have to hammer on the door for several minutes before he arrives).

Beaches

There are beaches to both the north and south of town, though the ones to the north occasionally get polluted by oil. They're pleasant enough out of season but can get very crowded during July and August, during which time you'd do better to head for Essaouira.

Places to Stay – bottom end

Hotel rooms can be very hard to find in the summer months, as there's heavy demand, so you may have to stay at a relatively expensive hotel if you arrive late in the day.

Three convenient budget hotels right in the centre of town and all in the same block are the *Hotel du Maghreb*, *Hotel de France* and, round the corner on the Blvd de Suez, the *Hotel du Port*. All these hotels are relatively old and their interiors cavernous, but the first two offer better value for money. The Hotel du Port is essentially a brothel. At all of them you're looking at Dr 25/36 for singles/doubles plus Dr 15 if you want an extra bed in any room. They're simple and basic, and there are cold, communal showers but the staff are friendly and helpful.

Another which you can try, which costs exactly the same, is the *Hotel d'El Jadida*, Rue Zerktouni, but this is basically a flophouse and there are no showers whatsoever (though there is a hammam next door).

A little more expensive is the *Hotel Moderne*, Ave Hassan II, which has a friendly manager and costs Dr 62 a double. It's not particularly good value since the rooms are small and dimly lit and only cold showers are available.

Places to Stay – middle

Going up in price, there are two hotels adjacent to each other which are excellent value. They are the *Hotel du Provence* (☎ 34 2347), 42 Ave Fkih Errafil and the *Hotel Bruxelles* (☎ 34 2072), 40 Rue Ibn Khaldoun; they are both one-star hotels and are at the junction of these two streets. Both are very clean and pleasant, have friendly staff and hot showers, but the Provence is definitely the better of the two. Indeed, I'd rate it the best hotel in El Jadida. Singles/doubles at the Bruxelles are Dr 58/70 with own shower but shared toilet and Dr 67/86 with own shower and toilet, plus taxes.

The Provence costs Dr 66/85 for singles/doubles with own shower and shared toilet and Dr 85/98 with own shower and toilet, plus taxes. The Provence has a popular licensed restaurant which serves delicious food and there's a choice of Moroccan, French and seafood specialities. Average costs are around Dr 60 to Dr 65 for a three-course meal. Visa cards are accepted and English is spoken (the owner, Geoffrey Hurdidge, is English).

If the above hotels are full, there's a choice of two other one-star hotels, the *Hotel Royal* (☎ 34 2839), 108 Ave Mohammed V and the *Hotel Suisse* (☎ 34 2816), 145 Rue Zerktouni. Both of them cost the same as the Provence but there are no hot showers at the Royal.

Places to Stay – top end

If you can afford a touch of exotic – even florid – luxury then the three-star *Hotel Palais Andalous* (☎ 34 3906), Rue Curie/Ave Pasteur, is the hotel of choice. Someone has attempted to recreate here the glories of Moorish Andalusia, and they've been largely successful. In this extremely spacious hotel, there are hectares of polished marble, stunning plaster work, comfortable salons and a bar and restaurant. The rooms are done in the same style and cost Dr 175/212 for singles/doubles plus tax. It's excellent value, though a little out of the way. A garage is available if you have your own transport.

Going up in price, the most expensive hotel in town is the *Hotel Doukkala* (☎ 34 3737), Rue de la Ligue Arabe. This hotel has all the amenities you would expect of a four-star hotel, including a swimming pool and tennis courts, and costs Dr 234/292 for singles/doubles plus taxes.

Places to Eat

There's a reasonable selection of restaurants lining the road between the Hotel Provence and the Place Hansali (which is now a pedestrian precinct), but check prices before ordering as they vary considerably. On the Place Hansali, check out the popular *Restaurant Chahrazad* which offers a variety of dishes (soup, salads, tajine, etc). A meal here will cost you around Dr 30. If it looks full, they have a mezzanine floor as well. Otherwise, try the *Café des Amis* at the southern end of Place Hansali.

Don't forget the restaurant at the Hotel Provence for a little splurge.

Entertainment

There are two bars which are popular in the evenings on Ave Fkih Errafil, between the restaurants mentioned above. Otherwise, try the one at the *Hotel de la Plage*, on Ave el Jamia al Arabia.

Getting There & Away

The bus terminal is at the northern end of town on Rue Abdelmoumen el Mouahidi, close to the junction with Ave Mohammed V. It's a 10-minute walk from here to the main hotel area, or 15 minutes to the fortress along Ave Mohammed V. There are regular departures to Casablanca and Safi.

AZEMMOUR

Whilst you're in El Jadida it's worth making a half-day excursion to this little-visited fortress town just 15 km to the north. Here you'll find yet another monument to those energetic seafaring and fortress-building people, the Portuguese. Though they only

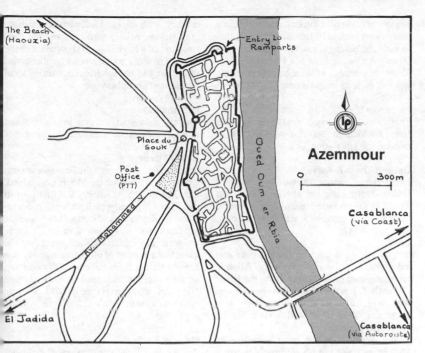

stayed a short while, from 1513 to 1541, it was sufficient time for them to construct this magnificent fortress alongside the banks of the wide Oum er Rbia, one of Morocco's largest rivers, which rises far away in the Middle Atlas and empties into the sea about one km down river from Azemmour. The best views of this fortress and its whitewashed, though crumbling, medina are from the bridge across the river. It reminded me somewhat of Varanasi (India) though, naturally, there are no bathing ghats here.

Azemmour once had a thriving Jewish community but, since their exodus to Israel, their houses have fallen into ruin, with only the façades remaining in many cases. There is still, however, a synagogue here in reasonable shape with lettering in Hebrew and English above the door saying 'Rabbi Abraham Moul Niss'.

The ramparts are open to visitors but

you'll first have to get the guardian to unlock the entrance door which is in the open square at the extreme north-eastern tip of the fort. Finding him is no problem: he'll find you, either in the Place du Souk or at the entrance to the ramparts. You'll know you have the right person since he'll proudly introduce himself as Azemmour's official – and only – guide, and show you his badge. Once introductions are over, you need to agree on a price for his services otherwise he's likely to ask for a king's ransom; Dr 10 should be sufficient. Once up on the ramparts, he rattles off a plethora of dates, facts and not a little fantasy and carefully steers you under a live, high-tension electricity wire which loops across the walls at waist height at one point. After that, he walks you through the medina and brings you back to where you entered.

There's nothing much of interest in the new part of town outside the ramparts but, if you get here early in the day, and aren't in a hurry to get back to El Jadida, you might like to visit the beach (Haouzia) which is about 30 minutes' walk from the Place du Souk. There are a number of basic cafés here where you can pick up refreshments or a meal.

Places to Stay
There's only one basic hotel in town – the *Hotel La Victoire*, 308 Ave Mohammed V, close to the bus station.

Getting There & Away
Local buses connect Azemmour with El Jadida. Petits taxis are also available and would be the preferred means of transport if there's a small group of you to share the cost.

SAFI
Safi is largely a modern fishing port and industrial centre, which sits on the Atlantic coast in a steep crevasse formed by the River Châabah. It has a lively walled medina and souk, with fortresses dating from the Portuguese era. Also, it is well known for its traditional potteries.

Safi may not be the most attractive of Moroccan towns but it's definitely worth a day of your time if you are in the area.

History
Safi's natural harbour was known to the Phoenicians and was probably used by the Romans later on. However, involvement with Europeans really came with the arrival of the Portuguese in 1508. They began construction of a fortress, using Essaouira as their base. Though what they constructed at Safi was of monumental proportions (as all Portuguese military installations tended to be in those days), their stay at Safi was of limited duration and the town was voluntarily evacuated in 1541.

This event didn't herald the end of European contact. In the 17th century the French established a consulate at the port and were responsible for signing many trading treaties with the indigenous rulers. By the 19th century, however, the port had faded into insignificance. Its revival came in the 20th

century, with the establishment of a fishing fleet (taking mainly sardines) and the construction of a huge industrial complex to the south. The latter manufactures fertilisers and sulphuric and phosphoric acids using local pyrites and phosphate ores.

Information
There's no tourist information centre and maps of the city are hard to track down.

Qasr el Bahr
In the walled city which the Portuguese constructed and to which the Moors later added, the Qasr el Bahr is usually the first port of call. This fortress was built by the Portuguese to protect the old port and to house the governor, and was restored in 1963. There are good views from the south-west bastion, as well as a number of old Spanish and Dutch cannon dating from the early 17th century, notably two manufactured in Rotterdam in 1619 and two in the Hague in 1621. Visiting hours are 9 am to noon and 3 to 7 pm. A guide is provided.

Medina & Around
Across the street from the Qasr el Bahr lies the walled medina. At the very top of the medina is the Kechla, a massive defensive structure with ramps, gunnery platforms, living quarters and a museum. The views over the medina and the Qasr el Bahr are magnificent.

Inside the medina is the palace constructed by the Moroccans in the 18th century to house the provincial governor; the gardens which surround it are beautifully laid out. Entry costs Dr 10 and you're allowed to walk around as long as you like without any supervision. Visiting hours are 9 am to noon and 3 to 7 pm.

The medina itself is very domestically oriented, and there's little in the way of crafts. There are, however, the remains of a Portuguese church (the Chapelle Portugaise) which was intended to be the cathedral had the Portuguese remained at Safi; as it turned out, they stayed only long enough to complete the choir. To get to it, head up Rue du

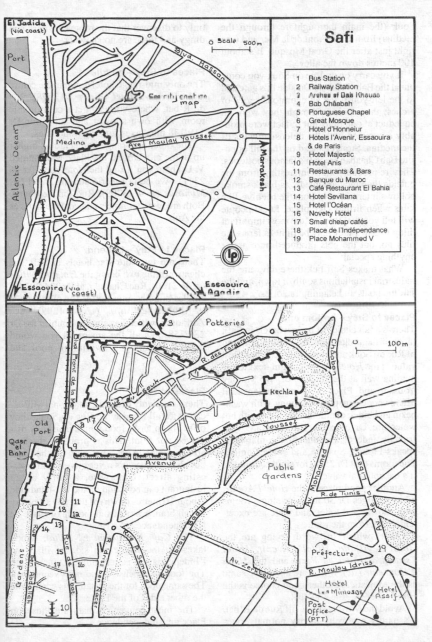

Safi

1. Bus Station
2. Railway Station
3. Arches of Bab Khouas
4. Bab Châabah
5. Portuguese Chapel
6. Great Mosque
7. Hotel d'Honneur
8. Hotels l'Avenir, Essaouira & de Paris
9. Hotel Majestic
10. Hotel Anis
11. Restaurants & Bars
12. Banque du Maroc
13. Café Restaurant El Bahia
14. Hotel Sevillana
15. Hotel l'Océan
16. Novelty Hotel
17. Small cheap cafés
18. Place de l'Indépendance
19. Place Mohammed V

Souk (the main thoroughfare through the medina) from Blvd Front de la Mer and turn right just after the Great Mosque. It's about 100 metres down the alley.

If you carry on up Rue du Souk you come out at the Bab Châabah. Outside this gate and to the left you'll see an enormous series of arches; they look as though they were an aqueduct at one time, but in fact were probably associated with the defensive walls of the medina. Straight ahead on the hill opposite Bab Châabah are Safi's famous potteries. They're probably more interesting from the outside than they are inside, as black smoke bellows intermittently from the beehive-like kilns when firings take place. Local people will tell you that they're 'the most important thing in Safi'; they may be right as far as the tiles go, but the pots produced here aren't anything special.

What makes Safi tick these days are the industrial installations south of town, and the sardine boats and canning factories.

Places to Stay – bottom end
There's a fair choice of budget hotels in Safi, most of them clustered around the port end of Rue du Souk and along Rue de R'bat. Best value is the *Hotel Majestic*, right next to the medina wall at the junction of Ave Moulay Youssef and Place de l'Indépendance. It offers very clean, pleasant rooms with washbasin and bidet; communal showers with hot water are Dr 5 extra. The staff are very friendly indeed, and one of the managers speaks French, Spanish and some English. The rooms cost Dr 25/40 for singles/doubles. It's exceptional value.

Another good place is the *Hotel l'Avenir*, which charges Dr 30 for large single rooms with shower and toilet, and there are excellent views from the roof.

Others which are worth trying are the *Hotel Sevillana*, *Hotel l'Avenir*, *Hotel Essaouira*, *Hotel de Paris* and the *Hotel d'Honneiur (sic)*. Prices are about the same as the Majestic. Another good choice is the *Hotel l'Océan*, Rue de R'bat.

Avoid the *Novelty Hotel*, off Rue de R'bat. It's hardly a novelty to pay normal prices only to discover that the rooms are dark and dingy and there are no showers.

Places to Stay – middle
The only mid-range hotel down in the centre is the two-star *Hotel Anis* (☎ 46 3078), Rue de R'bat, where you can get a comfortable room with own shower and toilet for Dr 119/138 plus taxes for singles/doubles.

The other mid-range hotels are all higher up in the city around the Place Mohammed V. Up here you'll find the *Hotel Assif* (☎ 46 2311), Ave de la Liberté and the *Hotel Les Mimosas* (☎ 46 3208), Rue ibn Zeidoune. Both are two-star hotels and cost the same as the Anis.

Places to Stay – top end
There are two four-star hotels in Safi, the cheaper of the two being the *Hotel Atlantide* (☎ 46 2160), Rue Chaouki, at Dr 234/292 for singles/doubles, plus taxes. Top of the range is the *Hotel Safir* (☎ 46 4299), Ave Zerktouni, which has singles/doubles for Dr 280/358 plus all the amenities you would expect including a swimming pool and tennis courts.

Places to Eat
There are plenty of small, traditional Moroccan cafés all the way up Rue du Souk; they offer cheap, tasty food which is usually displayed out front. This is probably the best area in which to eat – not only for the food, but also because it's a very lively and interesting street. Otherwise, a fairly cheap restaurant can be found on the left-hand side (about 10 metres down) of the only alleyway which branches off from the top of Place de l'Indépendance.

The *Café Restaurant El Bahia*, which takes up the whole top side of Place de l'Indépendance, is very much a tourist trap. The food is expensive and not exceptional. The same goes for the restaurants which line the other sides of the Place.

The most convenient bars are those on Place de l'Indépendance.

Getting There & Away

Most of the CTM buses stopping in Safi originate elsewhere so it's a good idea to book in advance. There are buses to Agadir/Tiznit at 10 am and Essaouira at 5 pm. The only CTM buses which originate from Safi are the ones to Casablanca, which depart daily at 4.30, 8.30 and 11 am and 2.30 and 4 pm.

Several other bus companies operate out of the same bus terminal including Transportes Chekkouri which has buses to Agadir (four times daily), Casablanca (10 times daily), Essaouira (5 am daily) and Marrakesh (five times daily).

There are two trains daily from Safi to Casablanca (Casa Voyageurs) at 5.45 and 8.05 am. Both involve a change at Benguerir. The later train is the faster of the two and takes four hours.

Getting Around

Both the bus terminal (Ave Président Kennedy) and the railway station (Rue de R'bat) are quite some way from the centre of town, so it would be a good idea to either take a bus or share a taxi from these places to the centre (Place de l'Indépendance). A bypass (Blvd Hassan II) circles the main part of town, so buses don't go through the centre.

The Middle Atlas

A visit to the Middle Atlas can take in such diverse activities as snow skiing at the exclusive mountain resort of Ifrane, a visit to Morocco's largest and best preserved Roman ruins at Volubilis, trekking or simply relaxing at Azrou in the mountains, a wander through the labyrinthine medina of Fès, and a visit to Moulay Idriss' huge palace complex at Meknès.

Fès

Fès is the oldest of the imperial cities of Morocco, having been founded shortly after the Arabs swept across North Africa following the death of the Prophet. It has been the capital of Morocco on a number of occasions and for long periods of time. Those periods of greatness and importance have left their mark not only on the city itself which, like Marrakesh and Meknès, is full of magnificent buildings reflecting the incomparable brilliance of Arab-Berber imagination and artistry, but also on the psychology of the inhabitants. Fassis (the name by which the people of Fès are known) justifiably look on their city as the cultural capital of Morocco and so consider themselves a cut above the rest of the inhabitants of the country. No sultan has fared well or even survived very long without taking the wishes of the Fassis into consideration.

The medina of Fès el-Bali (Old Fès) is one of the largest in the world and the most interesting in Morocco. That it has survived intact and essentially unchanged over the centuries is, in itself, unique. With the exception of Marrakesh and a few ancient cities in the Middle East, there is nothing remotely comparable with this city in the Arab world. One day it will surely be nominated as a World Heritage site. Its narrow winding alleys and covered bazaars are crammed with every conceivable sort of craft work-

shop, restaurants, meat, fruit and vegetable markets, mosques, medersas, and extensive dye pits and tanneries. What is more, the gates and walls which surround the whole are magnificent. But it's not just the sights that are going to draw you here. The exotic smells, the hammering of the metalworkers, the call of the *muezzin* (mosque official) and the need to jostle through crowded bazaars and past teams of uncooperative donkeys all add up to an experience you're never going to forget. You can easily spend a week wandering through this endless labyrinth and still not be ready to leave.

Though far from Persia, Fès is the living embodiment of the '1001 Nights', and tradition is what dictates the lives of its inhabitants. Much of the atmosphere of the medinas of Meknès and Marrakesh may have been lost in the scramble for the tourist dollar, but Fès has been able, so far, to absorb this influx, if only because of its sheer size. International credit card stickers, for instance, are still largely absent from the doors of shops in the souks and, if you've managed to shake off the touts at the Bab Bou Jeloud entrance, it's unlikely you'll be hassled once you're deep inside. Trading is still largely done in the style it always has been – slowly over mint tea with an exchange of news and stories.

Change is, nevertheless, on its way and is most obviously visible in the fashions, life styles and aspirations of its young people. As a visitor, you may not be aware that this is happening behind the high walls of the houses lining its narrow alleyways, but it is very obvious in the ville nouvelle. On the other hand, that this is happening should come as no surprise, as Fassis have always had their finger on the pulse of trade and business. Meanwhile, come here and enjoy what is still a unique experience – a city with deep roots in the past but a firm grip on the present.

History

Idriss I founded Fès on the right bank of the Oued Fès in 789 AD, in what is now the Andalous Quarter. His son, Idriss II, extended the city onto the left bank in 809; these two parts of the city are now known as Fès el-Bali

The earliest settlers were mainly refugees from Córdoba (Spain) and Kairouan (Tunisia), the former favouring the right bank of the oued, and the latter the left bank. Both groups were from well-established Islamic centres of brilliance. The skills which they brought with them were of inestimable value in laying the groundwork on which Fès would later draw, becoming one of the most important centres of Islamic intellectual and architectural development in the West.

These early days, however, were far from peaceful. As the Idrissid kingdom disintegrated, Morocco became the object of a tug-of-war between the Omayyads of Spain and the Aghlabids of Tunisia. Fès experienced several changes of ruler, though both sides were responsible for improving the fortifications which enclosed the city.

The score was finally settled when the Islamic fundamentalist Almoravids swept out of the deserts of Mauretania and took Fès in 1069, going on from there to conquer Spain. This was the age of religious fundamentalism *par excellence*, and this affected not only the Muslims but the Christians on the other side of the Mediterranean. Probably no other age witnessed the formation of so many ascetic religious sects bent on the strict observance of scriptural laws. Like all the rest, however, once the fervour of conquest and purification waned, the Almoravids gradually succumbed to the pleasures of luxury and urban living. They were overthrown by the Almohads in 1146.

In their conquest of Fès, the Almohads destroyed the walls of the city and only replaced them when they were assured of the loyalty of the inhabitants. Large sections of the walls of Fès date from this period. Not only that, both the Almoravids and the Almohads preferred Marrakesh as their

capital; consequently Fès remained a backwater for many years.

The city finally entered its period of brilliance under the Merenids. This dynasty took the city in 1250 (after gaining and losing it again two years earlier), and it remained the capital of Morocco throughout the duration of their rule. Never absolutely sure of the loyalty of his subjects, the second Merenid sultan, Abu Youssef Yacoub (1258-86), constructed a self-contained walled city outside the old one. This was known as Fès el-Jdid and was where the sultan stationed troops who could be relied upon to side with him in the event of a mutiny; foremost among these were Syrian and Christian mercenaries. Later on, in the 14th century, the Jewish community (itself originally descended from Spanish refugees during Idrissid times) was forcibly relocated from Fès el-Bali to the new city as an additional buffer. Though definitely regarded as second-class citizens and treated as such, the Jews were important economically in the life of the nation and were to become increasingly so. Because they enjoyed the protection of the sultan, they could be relied upon to side with the ruler in the event of an insurrection.

Few Jewish families remain in Fès these days. The great majority left for Israel during the 1950s and 1960s, and their synagogues have been converted into carpet warehouses and the like.

Following the rise to power of the Saadians in the 16th century, Marrakesh once again became the capital and Fès slipped into relative obscurity. However, the city enjoyed a revival under the Alaouite ruler Moulay Abdallah in the 19th century and, despite its period of decline, Fès remained one of the most important centres in the kingdom.

In 1916, following the establishment of the protectorate, the French began construction of the ville nouvelle on the plateau to the south-west of the two ancient cities. That Fès, in common with most Moroccan cities, did not experience the wholesale destruction and rebuilding which characterised colonial practice in Algeria, is largely due to the

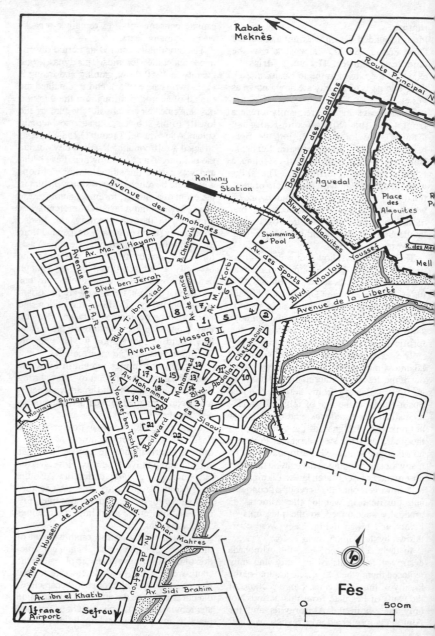

Fès

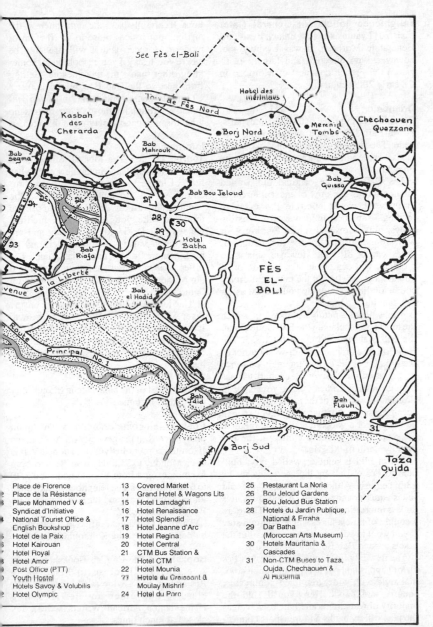

1	Place de Florence	13	Covered Market	25	Restaurant La Noria
2	Place de la Résistance	14	Grand Hotel & Wagons Lits	26	Bou Jeloud Gardens
3	Place Mohammed V &	15	Hotel Lamdaghri	27	Bou Jeloud Bus Station
	Syndicat d'Initiative	16	Hotel Renaissance	28	Hotels du Jardin Publique,
4	National Tourist Office &	17	Hotel Splendid		National & Frraha
	English Bookshop	18	Hotel Jeanne d'Arc	29	Dar Batha
5	Hotel de la Paix	19	Hotel Regina		(Moroccan Arts Museum)
6	Hotel Kairouan	20	Hotel Central	30	Hotels Mauritania &
7	Hotel Royal	21	CTM Bus Station &		Cascades
8	Hotel Amor		Hotel CTM	31	Non-CTM Buses to Taza,
9	Post Office (PTT)	22	Hotel Mounia		Oujda, Chechaouen &
10	Youth Hostel	23	Hotels du Croissant &		Al Hocemia
11	Hotels Savoy & Volubilis		Moulay Mishrif		
12	Hotel Olympic	24	Hotel du Parc		

enlightened policies of General (later Marshal) Lyautey, the first French Resident-General in Morocco. It was Lyautey too, however, who directed (and largely instigated) the French conquest of Morocco in the early 20th century.

Orientation

Fès today is comprised of three distinct parts: Fès el-Bali, Fès el-Jdid and the ville nouvelle. The first two form the medina, while the last is the administrative area built by the French.

Fès el-Bali is the original old walled medina and is the area of most interest to visitors. Its walls encircle the massive medina – an incredible maze of twisting alleys, blind turns and souks. Finding your way around, at least for the first couple of times, can be difficult. However, this is no problem: you can either take a guide or, if you get lost, pay one of the many children a couple of dirham to guide you at least as far as a familiar landmark.

The wall has a number of gates, of which the most spectacular are the Bab Bou Jeloud, the Bab Mahrouk and the Bab Guissa. The Bab Bou Jeloud, in the south-west corner of the old part of the city, is the main entrance to the medina. You will probably pass through it many times during your stay in Fès. This is also one of the areas where cheap accommodation popular with travellers can be found. For a good view over the medina, walk up to the Merenid tombs on the hill directly north of the Bab.

Fès el-Jdid is another walled city, built next to Fès el-Bali by the Merenids in the 13th century. Although it houses the old Jewish quarter and a couple of mosques, it is far less interesting than Fès el-Bali. There are a couple of hotels here, where you can stay if you want to be close to the medina but the hotels around Bab Bou Jeloud are full.

The new city lies to the south-west of Fès el-Jdid and is laid out in typical French colonial style with wide, tree-lined boulevards, squares and parks. Here you'll find the majority of restaurants and hotels, as well as the post office, banks and transport connec-

tions. It certainly lacks the atmosphere of the medina, but it does pulse to the rhythm of modern Morocco and it will probably be where you'll stay if you're looking for something other than a medina cheapie. Getting from here to the Bab Bou Jeloud is just a 10-minute bus ride and the buses run frequently throughout the day, so there's no great disadvantage to staying in this area.

Information

Tourist Offices The ONMT office is on Place de la Résistance in the new city. It has little of interest other than the printed brochures which are available all over the country, but you can get yourself an official guide to take you through the medina. Guides cost Dr 35 for half a day and are pretty good value – you may well end up paying more for an unofficial guide. The office is open from 8 am to noon and 2 to 6 pm Monday to Friday, and 8 am to noon on Saturday.

The local syndicat d'initiative is on the Place Mohammed V, also in the new town. It is open the same hours as the ONMT office and has the same range of maps and brochures. You can also arrange an official guide here.

Money Most of the banks are in the new city on Blvd Mohammed V.

Post & Telecommunications The main post office is in the new city on Ave Hassan II, on the corner of Blvd Mohammed V. It is open Monday to Saturday from 8 am to 2 pm in summer, and from 8 am to noon and 2.30 to 6 pm in winter. The telephone office (open longer hours) is around the side; entrance on Blvd Mohammed V.

There is also a post office in the medina, hidden away near the Kairaouine Mosque.

Bookshops The English Bookshop, at 68 Ave Hassan II, close to Place de la Résistance, has a wide range of textbooks, classics and other novels (including Heinemann's African Writers series). It's closed at lunch times.

The best place to find foreign newspapers and magazines (such as the Herald Tribune) is the newsagent/bookshop on Blvd Mohammed V, one block back from Place Mohammed V, towards Ave Hassan II.

Guides Official guides can be hired at the tourist office (ONMT) or the syndicat d'initiative for Dr 35 per half day, but there are also plenty of unofficial hopefuls hanging around Bab Bou Jeloud. The latter *can* be good and are usually cheap (as low as Dr 10 per half day) but there are a few things you need to settle before agreeing to go with one. Make sure that you know exactly which sites you will be seeing, and if you don't want to be shown one craft shop after another, make that clear at the beginning as well. If you don't, you'll end up being dragged around the carpet warehouse circuit in no uncertain manner.

Although not strictly necessary, it's probably a good idea to take a guide for your first two or three visits to Fès el-Bali, if only to get an idea of the layout of the streets and the location of the activities that most interest you. However, if you don't take a guide and get hopelessly lost (which you will), it's no problem: for a couple of dirham, there are any number of children who will lead you out of the maze to a familiar landmark.

If you do take a guide, beware of some things. The way that guides make their money (apart from the fee you pay them) is from commissions from shopkeepers into whose shops you are taken. There's nothing intrinsically wrong with this; after all, without your guide, you may not have been able to find particular places on your own. Guides also have to make a living, particularly with unemployment as high as it is in Morocco. Nevertheless, when you are taken into a shop under these circumstances, there's inevitably a feeling that you're under pressure from two angles to buy. On your own, you'd only have the shopkeepers (and their assistants) to contend with.

Some travellers maintain that you always pay more for something if you're in the company of a guide. Frankly, I think this is a contentious issue. Buying in Morocco involves bargaining and the price you get something for depends on your skill and tenacity at this game. So how much money are you going to 'save' by not having a guide with you, if you're no good at bargaining? Of course the guide's cut is built into anything you buy, but it's minimal.

One thing you should deal firmly with, however, if you're without a guide, are hangers-on who won't leave you and then follow you into a shop claiming they brought you there. Before going anywhere, sort this out.

The other important point with guides is to make sure that you have a common language. Many guides speak enough of a particular language to point out the obvious features of the things you're seeing, but not enough to be able to answer any questions.

Fès el-Bali

This is the original old walled medina and is the area of most interest to visitors. Its walls encircle the massive medina – an incredible maze of twisting alleys, blind turns, arches, mosques, medersas, shrines, fountains, workshops and every conceivable type of market. Because there are many cemeteries outside the walls, and also because of the enlightened policies of General Lyautey in siting the ville nouvelle well away from the old city, building activity has not taken place immediately outside the walls. Finding your way around, at least for the first couple of times, is very difficult, but a delightful way to get lost and found. Even if you do get the feeling that you're irrevocably lost, simply keep walking – you'll eventually arrive at one of the enormous gates, though it might not be the one you expected!

There are innumerable sights in this incredible city, and it will take you several days and a great deal of walking to get around just some of them. And while notable buildings – mosques, medersas and the like – are interesting, they're only part of the essence of Fès. Many of them, in any case, are closed to non-Muslims. You're much more likely to find the real Fès by letting

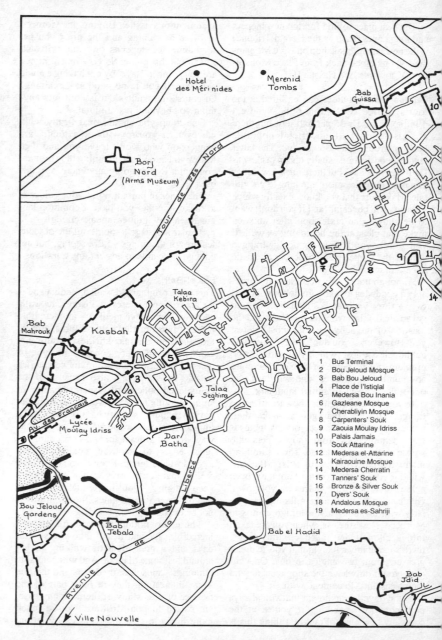

1 Bus Terminal
2 Bou Jeloud Mosque
3 Bab Bou Jeloud
4 Place de l'Istiqlal
5 Medersa Bou Inania
6 Gazleane Mosque
7 Cherabliyin Mosque
8 Carpenters' Souk
9 Zaouia Moulay Idriss
10 Palais Jamais
11 Souk Attarine
12 Medersa el-Attarine
13 Kairaouine Mosque
14 Medersa Cherratin
15 Tanners' Souk
16 Bronze & Silver Souk
17 Dyers' Souk
18 Andalous Mosque
19 Medersa es-Sahriji

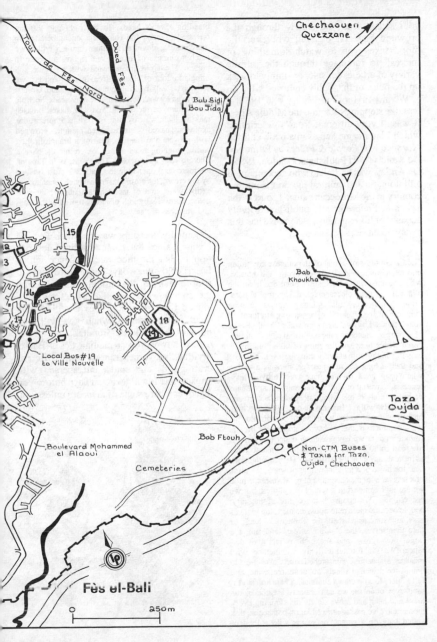

your senses lead you slowly through the crowded bazaars, pausing wherever the mood takes you to watch something of interest, to rummage through the infinite variety of articles for sale, or simply to soak up the pulse of this richly endowed city.

When I first visited Fès back in 1963, it was like stepping back into the Middle Ages. It wasn't very different from a description which I later came across in a book entitled *Morocco – Its People & Places* by Edmondo De Amicis (Darf Publishers, London, 1985). De Amicis was an Italian who accompanied a diplomatic and cultural mission from that country to the Moroccan sultan's court in the 1880s and subsequently published a lively account of his experiences there. He has this to say about Fès:

The first impression is that of an immense city fallen into decrepitude and slowly decaying. Tall houses, which seemed formed of houses piled one upon the other, all falling to pieces, cracked from roof to base, propped up on every side, with no opening save some loophole in the shape of a cross; long stretches of street, flanked by two high bare walls like the walls of a fortress; streets running uphill and down, encumbered with stones and the ruins of fallen buildings, twisting and turning at every thirty paces; every now and then a long covered passage, dark as a cellar, where you have to feel your way; blind alleys, recesses, dens full of bones, dead animals, and heaps of putrid matter; the whole steeped in a dim and melancholy twilight. In some places the ground is so broken, the dust so thick, the smell so horrible, the flies so numerous, that we have to stop to take breath. In half an hour we have made so many turns that if our road could be drawn it would form an arabesque as intricate as any in the Alhambra. Here and there we hear the noise of a mill, a murmur of water, the click of a weaver's loom, a chanting of nasal voices, which we are told come from a school of children, but we see nothing...We approach the centre of the city; people become more numerous; the men stop to let us pass, and stare astonished; the women turn back, or hide themselves; the children scream and run; the larger boys growl and shake their fists at a distance...We see fountains richly ornamented with mosaics, arabesque doors, arched courts...We come to one of the principal streets, about six feet wide, and full of people who crowd about us...There are a thousand eyes upon us; we can scarcely breathe in the press and heat, and move slowly on, stopping every moment to give passage to a Moor on horseback, or a veiled lady on a camel, or an ass with a load of

bleeding sheep's heads. To the right and left are crowded bazaars; inn courtyards encumbered with merchandise; doors of mosques through which we catch a glimpse of arcades and figures prostrate in prayer...The air is impregnated with an acute and mingled odour of aloes, spices, incense and kif; we seem to be walking in an immense drug-shop. Groups of boys go by with scarred and scabby heads; horrible old women, perfectly bald and with naked breasts, making their way by dint of furious imprecations against us; naked, or almost naked, madmen, crowned with flowers and feathers, bearing a branch in their hands, laughing and singing...We go into the bazaar. The crowd is everywhere. The shops, as in Tangier, are mere dens opened in the wall...We cross, jostled by the crowd, the cloth bazaar, that of slippers, that of earthenware, that of metal ornaments, which altogether form a labyrinth of alleys roofed with canes and branches of trees.

Essentially, the only way in which Fès has changed since that somewhat lurid description is that the moderate affluence which Fassis enjoy these days has enabled them to restore many of the buildings and clean up the streets. However, that hasn't radically altered the atmosphere; Fès is still worlds apart from anything which you will find north of the Straits of Gibraltar.

Like any Moroccan medina, Fès el-Bali is divided into areas representing different craft guilds and souks interspersed with houses, and it will take you days before you discover where some of them are unless you

employ a guide. Personally, I find that the process of discovering them is as enjoyable as the discoveries themselves, but if your time is limited, then you'd be wise to take a guide.

As one might expect from its long history, Fès el-Bali is replete with fascinating old buildings, most of them of a religious nature. However, the majority of them are unfortunately closed to non-Muslims and, because of the incredibly compact nature of this part of the city, little can be seen from the outside. No-one particularly minds if you discreetly peer through the doorways, but that's the limit. And that being the case, there's no point in giving you long and detailed descriptions of places you can't visit. The ones which you are allowed to go into can easily all be seen in a day or less.

Bab Bou Jeloud The Bab Bou Jeloud is the main entrance to Fès el-Bali. Although, as at the main entrances to most large Moroccan cities, you will encounter people offering to be guides, there's not that much hassle if you tell them you don't want their services. Should they be persistent, tell them you're staying at one of the cheap hotels just inside the gate. If they simply won't let go, sit down and have a mint tea at one of the numerous cafés just inside the gate and wait until they go away.

Medersa Bou Inania Not far from the Bab Bou Jeloud is the Medersa Bou Inania, built by the Merenid sultan Bou Inan between 1350 and 1357, and said to be the finest of the theological colleges built by the Merenids. It has been restored in recent years, and the skill which went into that restoration is proof that Moroccans have lost none of the talents for which they are justly famous. The carved woodwork here is simply magnificent. This is one of the few religious buildings which non-Muslims are allowed to enter, and there are excellent views over Fès from the roof. It's open between 8 am and 5 pm (except at prayer times); closed Friday mornings. Entry costs Dr 10.

Kairaouine Mosque Right down in the guts of the city is the Kairaouine Mosque. This is one of the largest mosques in Morocco and is said to be capable of holding 20,000 people. It was built between 859 and 862 by Fatma bint Mohammed ben Feheri for her fellow refugees from Tunisia; it was enlarged by the first Fatimid governor and brought to its present size by the Almoravid sultan Ali ben Youssef. The Almohads and Saadians also contributed to the detail. It contains one of the oldest universities in the world (with an average of 300 students in residence at any one time) and one of the finest libraries in the Muslim world. Unfortunately, non-Muslims are prohibited entry, and it's so hemmed in by other buildings that little can be seen of it from the outside.

Medersa el-Attarine The Medersa el-Attarine was built by Abu Said in 1325 and offers some particularly fine examples of Moroccan work. It's open from 9 am to noon and 2 to 6 pm; closed Friday mornings. Entry costs Dr 10. There are good views of the courtyard of the Kairaouine Mosque from the roof.

Andalous Quarter The only attractions here are the Andalous Mosque and the Medersa es-Sahriji. The latter was built in 1321. The basic structure of this college is very simple, but the inside is richly decorated and there are good views from the roof. Much of the structure lay in ruins until fairly recently, but restoration work is in progress.

Fès el-Jdid

Fès el-Jdid is the other walled city, built next to Fès el-Bali by the Merenids in the 13th century. Although it has the old Jewish quarter and a couple of mosques, it is far less interesting than Fès el-Bali. However, it does have some spectacular buildings and is much easier to get around. No-one will hassle you for guide services here.

The entrance to the Dar el-Makhzen (Royal Palace) on Place des Alaouites is a stunning example of modern restoration work. The grounds cover some 200 acres and consist of palaces, pavilions, medersas, mosques and pleasure gardens; the complex has been used to host an Arab League conference. It used to be possible to visit the palace with prior permission from the tourist office, but this is no longer possible unless you have political or cultural elbow.

At the northern end of the main street – Grande Rue de Fès el-Jdid – is the enormous Merenid gate of Bab Dekakene, which was formally the main entrance to the royal palace. Between this gate and Bab Bou Jeloud are the Bou Jeloud Gardens, which are very well maintained and a quiet place to relax, though the partially dried-up lake is used as a rubbish dump by litter louts. Through the gardens flows the Oued Fès, which is still the city's main source of water.

The Grande Rue de Fès el-Jdid, though lined with shops and a few hotels and cafés, lacks the atmosphere of the main street in Fès el-Bali, so it's unlikely you will spend too much time here.

Museum of Moroccan Arts

One place on the border of Fès el-Jdid and Fès el-Bali, which you should not miss, is the Dar Batha, now the Museum of Moroccan Arts. It is on Place de l'Istiqlal, about five minutes' walk from the Bab Bou Jeloud. Built as a palace about 100 years ago by Moulay el Hassan and Abd el Aziz, it houses historical and artistic artefacts from ruined or decaying medersas, fine Fassi embroidery, tribal carpets and ceramics dating from the 14th century to the present. It's open daily, except Tuesday, from 9 am to noon and 3 to 6 pm. Entry costs Dr 10.

Outskirts

For a spectacular overview of Fès, walk to the end of the Grande Rue de Fès el-Jdid and through the Bab Dekakene; then, instead of turning right towards the Bab Bou Jeloud, continue straight on through the old *mechouar* (royal assembly palace) and out through the Bab Segma, taking the road which follows the west wall of the Kasbah des Cherarda, to the junction with the Tour de Fès Nord. Turn right here and walk down

towards the Borj Nord. The whole of Fès lies before you in the valley below.

The Borj Nord itself was a former fortress, built in the late 16th century by the Saadian sultan el Mansour, who used Christian slaves for labour. It now houses the Arms Museum, which consists mainly of endless rows of muskets, rifles and cannon, many of them taken from Riffian rebels in 1958. Opening hours are the same as the Dar Batha and entry costs Dr 10.

Merenid Tombs

Further along from here, near the burnt-out Hotel des Mérinides, are the Merenid tombs. These date from the time when the Merenids abandoned Chellah in Rabat as their necropolis. Unfortunately, they're in an advanced state of ruin and little remains of the fine work with which they were originally decorated. There are, however, good views over Fès from here.

Places to Stay

Fès is a large city, so where you stay on arrival will depend largely on the time of day and the season. In summer, when many of the smaller hotels tend to fill up towards the end of the day, there's not much point in heading for the Fès el-Bali side of town if it's getting late. Take something close to where you are for the first night and have a look around the following morning. Also, in summer many of the cheapies in Fès el-Jdid and Fès el-Bali hike up their prices, and you end up paying the same as you would for far better accommodation in the ville nouvelle. At this time, too, single rooms in the cheapies are almost impossible to find – hoteliers make more money by letting them out to two or three people at correspondingly double and triple prices.

Places to Stay – bottom end

Fès el-Bali The most colourful and interesting places to stay are the bunch of cheapies clustered around the Bab Bou Jeloud at the entrance to Fès el-Bali. They're all pretty basic and most of them don't have showers (or not a functioning shower), but that's no problem as there's a good hammam very close by with separate times for men and women. The best of the bunch here is the *Hotel du Jardin Publique*, down a side lane (signposted) just outside the Bab. It's clean, quiet, friendly and good value at Dr 35/50 for singles/doubles. There are a couple of rooms on the 3rd floor with windows in the outside wall. These are preferable to the more claustrophobic lower rooms which face the internal courtyard, although the upper ones are hotter in summer. The hotel has cold showers.

If the Jardin Publique is full, try the nearby *Hotel Erraha* or the *Hotel National* (the latter is down an alley, on the left going uphill from the Erraha). Just inside the Bab, on the right, are another couple of hotels: the *Hotel Mauritania* and the *Hotel Cascades*. The latter is probably the better of the two, as the rooms at the Mauritania are very basic and very small. Both charge Dr 30/50 for singles/doubles. The Cascades even has a laundry service!

Fès el-Jdid If all the previously mentioned hotels are full (which they often are late in the day during summer), or if you don't like what's offered but prefer to be as close as possible to the medina, there are three other cheap hotels in Fès el-Jdid. All of them are along the Grande Rue de Fès el-Jdid (the main street), and prices are similar to those at Bab Bou Jeloud. The one closest to the Bab Bou Jeloud, up near the end of the street, is the *Hotel du Parc*, which is clean and good value for money. At the bottom of the street just inside the Bab Smarine (Semmarin) are the *Hotel du Croissant* and the *Hotel Moulay Mishrif*.

Ville Nouvelle The cheapest hotels here are the *Hotel Moghreb*, 25 Ave Mohammed es Slaoui, the *Hotel Regina*, 25 Rue Moulay Slimane, and the *Hotel Renaissance*. The Moghreb and the Regina are basic but clean and have no showers. They cost Dr 40 to Dr 50 for a single and Dr 70 a double. The Renaissance is an old, cavernous place with an entrance lobby resembling an art gallery.

It's friendly and clean, has no showers and costs the same as the two previous hotels.

Possibly slightly better value are the *Hotel Volubilis*, Blvd Abdallah Chefchaouni, and, just round the corner, the *Hotel Savoy*. At both you can get good, clean, airy rooms with washbasins and there are communal showers (cold water). Rooms cost Dr 40 to Dr 50 a single and Dr 60 to Dr 70 a double. Very similar is the *Hotel Jeanne d'Arc*, 36 Ave Mohammed es Slaoui.

Youth Hostel The cheapest place in the new city is the *Youth Hostel*, 18 Rue Mohammed el Hansali. It costs Dr 15 per person and there are cold showers. It's a fairly new building, and they will allow you to sleep on the roof if there are no beds left. The warden here is very strict about his ban on bringing alcohol into the hostel. If you're caught, he'll confiscate the grog and throw you out. The hostel is open from 8 to 9 am, noon to 3 pm and 6 to 10 pm.

Camping Camping isn't really feasible unless you have your own transport, as the nearest site is some six km out of town off the Ifrane road. It's known as *Camping Diamant Vert* and it sits at the bottom of a valley through which a clean stream passes. There's plenty of shade. Facilities include a swimming pool and disco with occasional live music. Camping costs Dr 25 per person (children Dr 5), Dr 10 for a car, Dr 15 for a caravan and there are tents for rent at Dr 10. Public bus No 218 will get you here from Fès.

Places to Stay – middle
The ville nouvelle has a good selection of one and two-star hotels to choose from. Cheapest is the *Hotel CTM* (☎ 62 2811) and the *Hotel Excelsior* (☎ 62 5602), both on Blvd Mohammed V. Rooms at both these places cost Dr 58/70 for singles/doubles with shower but shared toilet, and Dr 67/86 with own shower and toilet, plus taxes.

In this same area and slightly more expensive, but excellent value for money, is the *Hotel Central* (☎ 62 2333), 50 Rue du

Nador, at the junction with Blvd Mohammed V. It's friendly, very clean, secure and easy-going. Rooms with own shower (hot water in the mornings and evenings), bidet and handbasin cost Dr 66/85 for singles/doubles or Dr 85/98 with own shower and toilet, plus taxes. Baggage can safely be left in reception if you're catching a late bus or train. At the same price, but further afield nearer the railway station, is the *Hotel Kairouan* (☎ 62 3590), 84 Rue du Soudan. It's a good hotel to stay at, though 'guides' tend to hang about in the lobby in the mornings.

In the two-star range, the cheapest places to stay are the *Hotel Lamdaghri* (☎ 62 0310), 10 Kabbour el Mangad, the *Hotel Royal* (☎ 62 4656), 36 Rue d'Espagne and the *Hotel Amor* (☎ 62 3304), 31 Rue du Pakistan. Most convenient for the Blvd Mohammed V and CTM bus station is the Lamdaghri which has singles/doubles with own shower and toilet for Dr 92/112, plus taxes. It's a good choice. The Royal and Amor are across the other side of Ave Hassan II at Place de Florence. They're just as good as the Lamdaghri and room prices are the same. All three hotels have hot water.

Going up in price again but not such good value is the *Hotel Olympic* (☎ 62 4529), Blvd Mohammed V, adjacent to the covered market. Rooms here cost Dr 94/119 for singles/doubles with own shower and shared toilets or Dr 119/139 with own shower and toilet, plus taxes. There's hot water only in the evenings and mornings.

At the top end of this category are four three-star hotels to choose from. The newest of this bunch are the *Hotel Splendid* (☎ 62 2148), 9 Rue Abdelkrim el Khattabi and the *Hotel Mounia* (☎ 62 4838), 60 Rue Azilah, which both offer self-contained rooms with hot water at Dr 175/212 for singles/doubles, plus taxes. Somewhat older establishments are the *Grand Hotel* (☎ 62 5511), Blvd Abdallah Chefchaouni next to the Place Mohammed V and the *Hotel de la Paix* (☎ 62 5072), 44 Ave Hassan II, near the Place de la Résistance. Both cost the same as the previous two hotels. The Grand has a basement parking lot which is guarded 24 hours a day.

All these hotels have their own restaurants and bars.

Places to Stay – top end
At the lower end of this range, try either the *Hotel Sofia* (☎ 62 4260), 3 Rue du Pakistan, close to the Amor, or the *Hotel Volubilis* (☎ 62 1125), Ave Allal ben Abdallah (the latter not to be confused with the budget-priced hotel of the same name). Both have self-contained singles/doubles for Dr 280/358 plus taxes. Those who would like to stay within a stone's throw of the Bab Bou Jeloud should check out the brand new *Hotel Batha* (☎ 63 3773), Place Batha, at the end of Ave de la Liberté, which costs the same as the above two. All these hotels are four-star.

At the top end of this category are two five-star luxury hotels. They are the *Hotel Palais Jamais* (☎ 63 4383), Bab el Guissa and the *Hotel de Fès* (☎ 62 5002), Ave des FAR. If you hanker for authenticity and immersion in the medina then the Palais Jamais is rated as one of the best hotels in Morocco. It was built by the Jamai brothers in 1879 and is a fine example of Hispano-Mauresque architecture.

Places to Eat
The best places to find a cheap meal in Fès el-Bali are at the restaurants clustered around the Bab Bou Jeloud and the Bab Guissa; however, the ones around the former are pretty indifferent to quality these days, as they get to see a few too many tourists. The best of the bunch is probably the *Restaurant Bouayad*, next to the Hotel Cascades, which offers reasonable tajine and is open until late at night. The *Restaurant des Jeunes*, closer to the gate, also has good set meals, although they have two menus and give you the one they think you can afford – one has Dr 25, the other Dr 35 for the same set meal! Good tajines for Dr 18, soup Dr 4 (with bargaining). Also recommended just inside the Bab Bou Jeloud is the *Restaurant Typiquement*.

There are similar restaurants along the Grande Rue de Fès el-Jdid, close to the Bab Smarine. For something better check out *La Noria*, in the Bou Jeloud Gardens. This is popular with young Moroccans, but expect to pay considerably more for a meal here. They specialise in couscous.

In the ville nouvelle there's a good choice of relatively cheap restaurants along or just off the Blvd Mohammed V, with most of them clustered around the municipal market. Take your pick, but check out prices before ordering because if you eat a full meal of soup, barbecued meat, salad and bread it can cost you as much as what a modest splurge in a more expensive restaurant would set you back.

A slightly more expensive, but excellent, place to eat in this area is the *Restaurant Chamonix*, which has a good range of Moroccan and Western-style food as well as fixed-price lunches and dinners for Dr 42. The staff are friendly and it's a popular place to eat with travellers staying nearby. They also have the usual range of breakfast foods – omelettes, etc. Similar is the *Restaurant la Medaille*, on Blvd Mohammed V, which offers set lunches and dinners for Dr 60 plus a service charge, and à la carte dishes from Dr 20 to Dr 25, as well as pizzas.

The *Café Restaurant Mounia*, at 11 Blvd Mohammed Zerktouni, just around the corner from the Hotel Jeanne d'Arc, is a very stylish place (waiters with bow ties!), but the prices are reasonable and they have a decent wine list.

For an expensive splurge in Fès head for the *Hotel Palais Jamais*, close to the Bab Guissa, in Fès el-Bali, which has a terrace overlooking the medina. The food here is excellent and there's a choice of French or Moroccan cuisine, but you'll be up for a minimum of Dr 160 per person without wine for the sumptuous buffet spread.

Entertainment

Few of the bars in the ville nouvelle of Fès could be described as 'entertaining'. At most, it's the usual all-male company, some of it a little worse for wear. The same goes for the bars at most of the mid-range hotels, though I was told that the best bar for mixed company was that at the Hotel Mounia.

Drinks at the hotel bars are more expensive – Flag is Dr 12 and Heinneken Dr 15.

Getting There & Away

Air The airport serving Fès is 15 km to the south. There are four flights weekly to Casablanca, two per week to Marrakesh and one to Tangier. There are also three flights weekly to Paris and one to Marseilles.

Royal Air Maroc (**☎** 62 5516) is at 54 Ave Hassan II.

Bus The CTM station is in the ville nouvelle on Blvd Mohammed V. Tickets can be bought up to five days in advance, and you should buy them as early as possible as demand is high, especially on the Fès-Tangier and Fès-Marrakesh runs. There are departures to: Casablanca (six daily); Marrakesh (twice daily at 6.30 am and 9 pm, Dr 95); Meknès (six daily); Oujda (once daily at 12.30 pm, Dr 52); Tangier (once daily at 6 pm, Dr 67.50); and Tetouan (once daily at 8 am).

There are also international departures to Paris (three times per week) and Brussels (once per week). For details of these, see the Morocco Getting There & Away chapter in the introductory section.

Non-CTM buses use a couple of different stations, both near Fès el-Bali. Buses for Oujda, Chechaouen, Al Hoceima and Taza leave from the station at Bab Ftouh, the south-eastern gate.

Buses to all other destinations leave from the station at Place Baghdadi, just up from Bab Bou Jeloud. There is a booking office where you can make reservations for the most popular runs.

Train The railway station is in the ville nouvelle, 10 minutes' walk from the centre. Trains are the best bet if you are headed for Casablanca, Marrakesh, Meknès, Oujda, Rabat or Tangier.

The main direct departures are: Casablanca (eight daily at 1.03, 3.20, 7.22 and 10.10 am, 12.05, 2.25, 4.50 and 6.08 pm, five hours); Marrakesh (once daily at 7.22 am, eight hours); Oujda (five daily at 3.33 and

6.38 am, 1.20, 3.07 and 7 pm, between five and six hours); and Tangier (two daily at 5.51 am and 2.56 pm, six hours).

All other departures from Fès to Marrakesh (five in total) involve a change of trains at either Rabat or Casa-Voyageurs (Casablanca). All trains between Fès and Casablanca or Fès and Marrakesh stop at Meknès and Rabat.

Taxi Grands taxis leave from a couple of locations: Bab Ftouh for Taza and east, and the streets around the CTM station for Meknès (frequent, fast and convenient, Dr 15) and elsewhere.

Car Rental All the major companies have offices here, including: Avis (☎ 62 6746), 50 Blvd Abdallah Chefchaouni; Budget (☎ 62 0919), c/o Grand Hotel; Europcar/InterRent (☎ 62 6545), 41 Ave Hassan II; and Hertz (☎ 62 2812), c/o Hotel de Fès.

Getting Around

Bus Fès has a fairly good local bus service, although the buses are like sardine cans at certain times of the day. The bus number is displayed on the side of the bus, near the back door. Useful routes include: No 3 – Place de la Résistance to Bab Ftouh (for the Andalous Quarter); No 9 – Ave Hassan II to Place de l'Istiqlal (Dar Batha & Bab Bou Jeloud); No 10 – railway station to Place de l'Istiqlal; and No 19 – railway station to Place Baghdadi.

Taxi The red petits taxis are cheap and plentiful. The drivers use the meters without any fuss. Expect to pay about Dr 10 from the CTM station to Bab Bou Jeloud.

AROUND FÈS
Sefrou

As a contrast to the intensity and size of Fès, it's well worth paying a visit to this picturesque little Berber town set against jagged mountain bluffs and surrounded by rich farm lands and olive groves. Just 28 km from Fès and about the same size as Chechaouen, Sefrou once had one of the largest Jewish

communities of any Moroccan city and it was here, in a nearby *ksar* (fortified stronghold), that Moulay Idriss II lived whilst he planned the construction of Fès.

The small but interesting walled medina and mellah lie on either side of the garbage-strewn gorge of the Oued Aggaï across which there are a number of bridges. You can walk through this complex of narrow streets at your leisure without anyone hassling you. The best points of entry/exit are the Bab Taksebt, Bab Zemghila and the Bab Merba. The town walls which stand today were constructed in the 19th century.

Once you've visited the walled town, it's well worth walking up the gorge of the river to the waterfall about 1½ km from town. To get there, follow the Ave Moulay Hassan over the bridge which spans the river and turn left at the first turn-off (signposted 'Cascades'). Follow this road around to the left of El Kelâa (a sort of semi-walled ksar) and then simply follow the dirt road alongside the river until you get to the waterfall.

Information The main post office and a branch of the BMCC bank are along Blvd Mohammed V.

Places to Stay – bottom end There's only one unclassified hotel in the town itself – the *Hotel les Cerises*, Blvd Mohammed V. It's friendly, basic and clean and rooms with either a double bed or two single beds with handbasin and communal showers (cold water only) cost Dr 60. There are no singles.

The only other cheapie is the *Hotel Bar les Cascades*, which overlooks the waterfall. It has only six rooms which are all doubles and they cost Dr 60 with shared bathroom (cold water only). If you like the sound of falling water, it's a good place to stay and relax. As the name suggests, there's a bar here and meals can be provided, but the choice of food is limited and it would be a good idea to order in advance.

Camping There's a superb campsite here with plenty of shade, on the hill overlooking town, but it is a long, steep walk from the

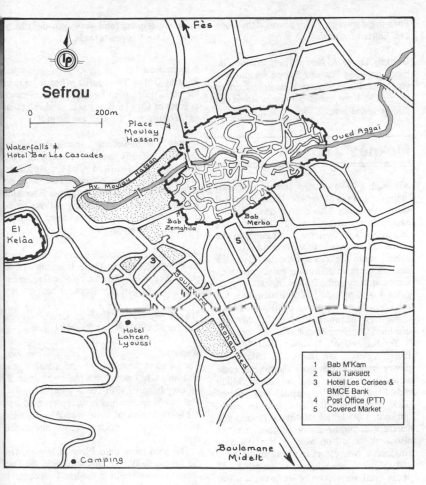

Sefrou

0   200m

Waterfalls &
Hotel Bar Les Cascades

Place Moulay
Hassan

Oued Aggaï

Av. Moulay Hassan

El
Kelâa

Bab
Zemghila

Bab
Merba

Hotel
Lahcen
Lyoussi

1 Bab M'Kam
2 Bab Taksebt
3 Hotel Les Cerises &
   BMCE Bank
4 Post Office (PTT)
5 Covered Market

Boulemane
Midelt

Camping

centre if you don't have your own transport. Facilities include showers (cold water only) and toilets. When I last visited, there was no-one around so I don't know the price, but it's probably in line with other campsites around the country.

Places to Stay – middle The only mid-range hotel in Sefrou is the *Hotel Sidi Lahcen Lyoussi* (☎ 66 0497), up on the hill in the ville nouvelle, on the same road which leads

to the campsite. It's a very pleasant place to stay and is surrounded by trees and gardens. Self-contained rooms at this two-star hotel cost Dr 119/138 for singles/doubles plus taxes. The hotel has its own restaurant and bar.

Places to Eat There's a good choice of small, cheap restaurants to eat at on either side of the covered market and at the entrance to the Bab Merba. Take your pick.

For a slight splurge, go for a meal at the *Hotel Sidi Lahcen Lyoussi*.

Getting There & Away There are regular buses between Fès and Sefrou which drop you at the Place Moulay Hassan in front of the Bab M'Kam and Bab Taksebt. Taxis can also be found here.

Meknès

Although a town of considerable size even in the days of the Merenids (13th century), it wasn't until the 17th century that Meknès experienced its heyday. In 1672, having fought for and won the succession to the throne, Moulay Ismail, the second Alaouite sultan, made Meknès his capital. Over the next 55 years an enormous palace complex surrounded by some 25 km of wall with 20 gates was completed by armies of slaves and workers, often whipped on by Moulay Ismail himself. By the time he died in 1727, Meknès had been transformed out of all recognition.

Yet this wasn't to last. After Moulay Ismail's death, the traditional balance of power between Fès and Marrakesh reasserted itself; two reigns later, under Sultan Sidi Mohammed, the capital was moved back to Marrakesh. The disastrous earthquake in 1755 which destroyed Lisbon and severely damaged many Moroccan cities also took its toll on Moulay Ismail's constructions. No restoration was undertaken and the city was allowed to crumble and decay until very recently when the tourism potential of this vast complex was realised and major restoration work began.

Orientation

The old medina and the French-built ville nouvelle are neatly divided by the small valley of the Oued Bou Fekrane. Train and CTM bus connections are in the new city, while the private buses, cheap hotels, campsite and sights are in the old city. It's a 20-minute walk between the two, although there are regular (and very crowded) local buses as well as petits taxis.

Information

Tourist Office The tourist office is next to the main post office facing Place de France in front of City Hall. It has a good selection of literature and the staff are helpful.

Money The banks are concentrated in the new city, mainly on Ave Hassan II, Ave Mohammed V and Blvd Allal ben Abdallah. The BMCE operates a *bureau de change* on Ave des FAR, opposite the Hotel Excelsior which is open daily including national holidays, Saturdays and Sundays from 10 am to 2 pm and 4 to 8 pm.

Post The main post office is in the new town on Place de France. There is another large post office in the Medina, on Rue Dar Smen, near the corner of Rue Rouamzine.

Travel Agencies Thomas Cook/Wagons Lits (☎ 52 1995) is at 1 Rue du Ghana.

Medina

The focus of the old city is the massive gate of Bab èl Mansour, the main entrance to Moulay Ismail's 17th-century Imperial City. The gate is exceptionally well preserved and is highly decorated, with (faded) zellij tiles and inscriptions which run right across the top.

The gate faces onto Place el Hedim. On the far north side of this square is the Dar Jamai, a palace built in the late 19th century which has recently been turned into a very good museum. As is often the case with museums housed in historic buildings, the building itself is as interesting as the exhibits. The domed reception room upstairs is fully furnished in the style of the time, complete with plush rugs and cushions. It is open daily, except Tuesday, from 9 am to noon and 3 to 6 pm. Entry costs Dr 10.

The medina proper stretches away to the north behind the Dar Jamai. The most convenient access is through the arch to the left of the Dar Jamai. Though nowhere near as extensive or as interesting as the medina at Fès, it is, nevertheless, worth a visit and it's unlikely you will be hassled by 'guides'. Most interesting, perhaps, are the carpet souks, which are just off to the left of the main medina street, about five minutes' walk from Dar Jamai. If you are looking for rugs to buy, Meknès is not a bad place, as the shopkeepers are a little more relaxed than elsewhere in Morocco. The Palais du Tresor d'Or, Rue Fékharine, Bab Moulay Idriss, and Lalambra, 13 Derb el Anboub, Hammam Jdid, in particular, have excellent collections of top-quality carpets and rugs.

Further along the covered main street is the Medersa Bou Inania. Like the one of the same name in Fès, it was built in the mid-14th century. It is not all that conspicuous apart from the dome over the street, which is easy to spot. It has the same layout and features as the Fès medersas. It's about the only one where you are allowed up on to the roof, as it has all been restored at one time or another. The Medersa Bou Inania is open daily from 9 am to noon and 3 to 6 pm. Entry costs Dr 10.

Imperial City

A visit to the Imperial City itself starts from the Bab el Mansour. The gate gives onto the mechouar, a parade ground where Moulay Ismail reviewed his famed Black regiments. From here, the road runs straight ahead and then round to the right. On the right there is an open grass area with a small white building with a green tiled roof, the Koubat al-Khayattine, which was once the reception hall where foreign ambassadors were received. It's now very plain and hardly worth visiting, but beside it is the entrance to an enormous underground granary complete with vents which open onto the surface of the lawn. If you have a guide with you, you'll probably be told this was the Christians' prison but this is just a figment of the imagination. Entry to the vaults and the reception hall costs Dr 10.

Continuing on through another recently restored gate, you come to the Mausoleum of Moulay Ismail – one of the few Islamic monuments in the country which is open to foreigners. Despite his extreme brutality, Ismail was and is held in very high esteem; hence the fact that his tomb is actually a shrine. Once inside, everything is fairly modestly decorated. Entry is free but it's customary to tip the guardian. The mausoleum is open from 9 am to noon and 3 to 6 pm. It's closed on Friday morning. On the opposite side of the road are a number of craft and carpet shops belonging to a cooperative of artisans. It's worth having a look in these shops because there's an excellent and very comprehensive selection of Meknassi specialities here and very little pressure to buy.

From the tomb, the road continues through another gateway and into a very long, double-walled corridor which flanks the Dar el-Makhzen, Moulay Ismail's palace complex and now one of King Hassan's official residences. The palace is not open to visitors.

It's a long 20-minute walk through this corridor to the southern corner but it's here that you come to the Aguedal Basin, an enormous, stone-lined lake some four metres deep which was once fed by the Oued Bou Fekrane (the river which divides the old and new parts of Meknès) and served as both a reservoir for the sultan's gardens and as a pleasure lake. Facing the lake are the spectacular Heri es-Souani granaries and stables. The storerooms themselves are impressive in size, and wells for drawing water can still be seen. The first few vaults have been restored but the stables, which once housed 12,000 horses, stand in partial ruin with no roof, yet they stretch seemingly for ever. Such is the atmosphere here that the place vies with Aït Benhaddou (near Ouarzazate) as one of the country's favourite film sets. It is open daily from 9 am to noon and 3 to 6 pm. Entry costs Dr 10.

Steps on the outside of the Heri es-Souani (towards the basin) lead up to a beautiful roof café and garden area which is an excellent place for a rest.

Just before you reach the Heri es-Souani,

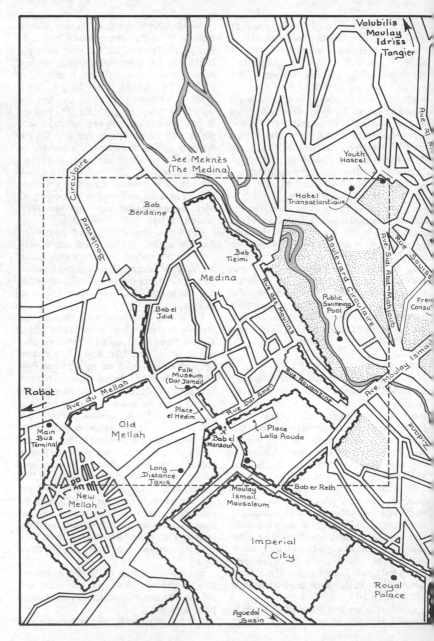

1 Post Office (PTT)
2 Hotel Palace
3 Hotel Touring
4 Hotel Moderne
5 Hotel Majestic
6 Abdelkader
  Railway Station
7 Hotel Central
8 CTM Bus Terminal &
  Hotel Volubilis
9 Hotel Excelsior &
  Hotel Toubkal
10 Hotel Continental
11 BMCE Late Bank
12 Hotel Panorama
13 Tourist Office
14 Rif Hotel
15 Wagons Lits
16 Hotel de Nice
17 Restaurant Metropole
   Annexe
18 Hotel du Marché

Meknès

500m

Azrou

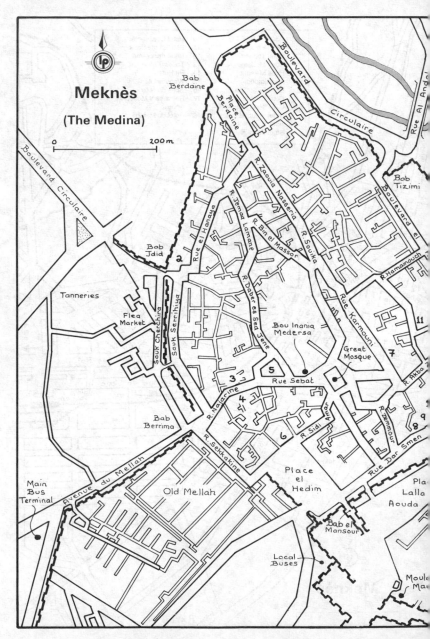

Meknès

(The Medina)

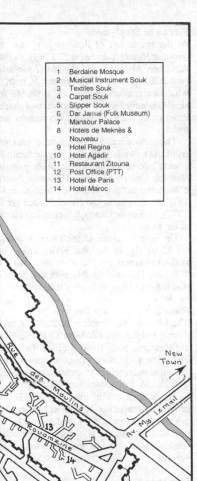

1 Berdaine Mosque
2 Musical Instrument Souk
3 Textiles Souk
4 Carpet Souk
5 Slipper Souk
6 Dar Jamaï (Folk Museum)
7 Mansour Palace
8 Hotels de Meknès & Nouveau
9 Hotel Regina
10 Hotel Agadir
11 Restaurant Zitouna
12 Post Office (PTT)
13 Hotel de Paris
14 Hotel Maroc

New Town

Bus Terminal (Chechaouen)

Rue des Moulins

Av. My Ismail

Rue Rouamzine

Rue Sidi Nedjar

Rue Sidi Amar

the shady and well-equipped campsite is through an arch to the left.

Places to Stay – bottom end

Most of the cheapest places are clustered together in the old city along Rue Dar Smen and Rue Rouamzine. The best of the lot and excellent value for money is the *Hotel Maroc*, on Rue Rouamzine. It's quiet, clean, pleasantly decorated and furnished, all the rooms have a handbasin, and most face onto a well-kept courtyard. The (cold) showers and toilets are also clean and well-maintained. It's a bargain at Dr 30/50 for singles/doubles. Not as good, but acceptable, is the *Hotel de Paris*, also on Rue Rouamzine. This is an older hotel with large airy rooms, table, chair and handbasin, with singles/doubles for Dr 25/40 or Dr 30 for a room with one large bed. There are no showers.

The rest of the cheapies are nothing special, and many don't have showers. The *Hotel Agadir*, Rue Dar Smen, is definitely clean but the rooms are tiny, there are no showers, and it's definitely overpriced at Dr 30/60 for singles/doubles. Slightly better is the *Hotel Regina*, Rue Dar Smen, which is a cavernous edifice with the air of a Dickensian workhouse about it. Rooms (singles or doubles) here vary from Dr 30 to Dr 40. Try to get a room on one of the top floors, as the ground-floor rooms are very gloomy. Again, there are no showers. The *Hotel de Meknès*, a few doors away from the Regina, is similar.

Over in the ville nouvelle, one of the cheapest places to stay is the *Hotel Central*, 35 Ave Mohammed V, close to the CTM bus station and Abdelkader railway station. Local people, however, warned me off this place saying it was one of the city's principal brothels and that the sheets were not always changed. A better choice would be the nearby *Hotel Toubkal* (☎ 52 2218), which costs Dr 52/85 for singles/doubles or Dr 104 for a room with two double beds. Bathrooms are shared but I was told there is hot water in the showers. Another reasonable cheapie is the *Hotel du Marché*, Ave Hassan II, which costs Dr 30/60/90 for singles/doubles/triples.

Going up in price, most travellers would find the one-star *Hotel Touring* (☎ 52 2351), 34 Blvd Allal ben Abdallah, quite adequate and reasonably good value though the 'hot' water in the showers is only ever lukewarm. It's secure, the rooms are a decent size, towels are provided and singles/doubles with own shower but shared toilet cost Dr 62/78. Similar, but more modern, is the *Hotel Panorama* (☎ 52 2737), just off the Ave des FAR, though the hotel has no singles. Most of the rooms here have their own shower but shared toilet and cost Dr 89 a double, but they also have four rooms with own shower and toilet for Dr 106.

Also in this category is the one-star *Hotel Excelsior* (☎ 52 1900), 57 Ave des FAR, which has singles/doubles with own shower and shared toilet for Dr 70/93 or Dr 89/106 with own shower and toilet.

Somewhat more expensive is the two-star *Hotel Continental* (☎ 52 0200), 42 Ave des FAR, which is an old-style hotel with singles/doubles for Dr 79/100 with own shower but shared toilet and Dr 96/120 with own shower and toilet. There's hot water in the showers.

Youth Hostel The *Youth Hostel* is very close to the large Hotel Transatlantique in the ville nouvelle, about one km from the centre. This is one of the best hostels in Morocco and is clean as a new pin. It's open from 8 to 10 am, noon to 3 pm, and 6 to 10.30 pm except on Sundays when it's open from 10 am to 6 pm. A dormitory bed costs Dr 20.

Camping There is an excellent campsite complete with shady, mature trees on the south side of the Imperial City right up against the walls, though it's quite a walk if you are on foot. A taxi from the railway station or the CTM bus station costs Dr 10. It costs Dr 12 per person, Dr 8 for a tent and Dr 8 for a hot shower. The toilets are well maintained, and there are washing facilities, a shop and a restaurant. The site is open 24 hours.

Places to Stay – middle
At the lower end of this category are the two-star *Hotel Moderne* (☎ 52 1743), 54 Ave Allal ben Abdallah, and the *Hotel Majestic* (☎ 52 2033), 14 Ave Mohammed V, both of which are reasonable value at Dr 98/118 for singles/doubles with own shower and shared toilet or Dr 123/146 with own shower and toilet.

Those looking for guaranteed creature comforts and a full range of private facilities couldn't do better than to stay at the popular *Hotel de Nice* (☎ 52 0318), 10 Zankat Accra, a three-star hotel with singles/doubles at Dr 151/198. Similar is the *Hotel Palace* (☎ 52 5777), 11 Rue du Ghana, which offers rooms at the same price.

Up in price again is the *Hotel Volubilis* (☎ 52 0102), 45 Ave des FAR, which has self-contained singles/doubles for Dr 179/220. The only trouble with this hotel is that it's on a busy and noisy intersection.

Places to Stay – top end
The four-star *Rif Hotel* (☎ 52 2591), Zankat Accra, and the *Hotel Zaki* (☎ 52 1140), Blvd al Massíra, both have similar facilities including swimming pool, restaurant, bar and air-conditioning throughout, and cost Dr 280/358 for singles/doubles plus taxes.

Top of the line is the five-star *Hotel Transatlantique* (☎ 52 0002), Rue el Mériniyine, which has 122 air-conditioned rooms, tennis courts, a swimming pool and all the other facilities you would expect of a hotel of this nature.

Places to Eat
If you are staying in the old town, there's a fair choice of simple restaurants doing standard fare along Rue Dar Smen between the Hotel Regina and Place el Hedim. One of the best is the *Restaurant Économique*, at No 123, one of the few with a sign. It's right opposite Bab Jama en Nouar, the gate which takes the traffic, just up from Bab el Mansour. There are a few others along Rue Rouamzine.

Similarly, in the ville nouvelle there are plenty of sandwich and hamburger bars as

well as roast chicken grills along Blvd Allal
ben Abdallah, Ave Mohammed V and the
road leading down to the Abdelkader railway
station from Ave Mohammed V. Take your
pick but you can eat well at most of these
places for between Dr 25 to Dr 30 or even
less.

One place which stands out is the *Rotisserie Karam*, at 2 Rue du Ghana, near the
corner of Ave Hassan II. They do some of the
best chips in the country, and the set meal of
salad, meat and dessert is superb value at Dr
24.

For a splurge, many travellers go to the
Restaurant Metropole Annexe, 11 Rue
Charif Idrissi, round the corner from the
junction of Ave Hassan II and Ave Mohammed V. A three-course, Moroccan-style meal
at this place costs Dr 70. The food is excellent, the service quick and beer and wine are
available.

For a major splurge in incomparably
beautiful traditional Moroccan surroundings, check out the *Restaurant Zitouna* (☎ 53
2083), 44 Jamaa Zitouna, in the medina. This
is a veritable palace of a restaurant which you
would go to as much for the atmosphere as
for the superb Moroccan specialities. The
restaurant doesn't sell alcoholic drinks and
it's quite expensive but it's probably the best
in Meknès. Another place to splurge, but
which is more formal, is the *Palais Terrab*
(☎ 52 1456), 18 Ave Zerktouni, in the ville
nouvelle, east of the Abdelkader railway
station. A full meal here would cost you
around Dr 300 per person. Naturally they
accept all the major credit cards.

Getting There & Away
Air Royal Air Maroc (☎ 52 0963) is at 7 Ave
Mohammed V.

Bus – CTM The CTM terminal is on Ave
Mohammed V near the junction with Ave des
FAR. There are seven departures daily to
Casablanca and Rabat (the first at 8 am and
the last at 12.30 am); two daily to Errachidia
(at 10 and 11.30 pm – the first continues on
to Rissani); five daily to Fès (the first at 11

am and the last at 11 pm); one daily to
Tangier (at 7 pm); one daily to Taza and
Oujda (at 5 pm); and one daily to Ifrane and
Azrou (at 4 pm)

CTM also operates international buses to
Paris and Brussels – for details see the
Morocco Getting There & Away chapter in
the introductory section.

Bus – non-CTM A new bus terminal has
been built for non-CTM buses on the north
side of the new mellah along Ave du Mellah.
There are regular departures to Fès and elsewhere.

Train The main train station is some way
from the centre of the new city, on Ave du
Sénégal. It's much more convenient,
however, to use the Abdelkader station, one
block down and parallel to Ave Mohammed
V, as all trains stop here. All trains to or from
Fès also stop in Meknès.

Taxi All the grands taxis leave from opposite
the old bus station in the old town, down
from Bab el Mansour. There are regular
departures to Fès (Dr 15) and Moulay Idriss
(for Volubilis, Dr 6).

Getting Around
Bus There are local buses which run
between the medina and the new city, but
they are invariably very crowded and hard to
get on at times.

Useful routes include: No 2 – Bab
Mansour to Blvd Allal ben Abdallah, returning to the medina along Ave Mohammed V;
and No 7 – Bab Mansour to the CTM bus
station.

Taxi A useful petit taxi route, which connects
the new and old cities, starts in the new city
from Rue du Ghana near the corner of Ave
Hassan II, right opposite the Rotisserie
Karam. The petits taxis are always silver
Mercedes with black roofs. The fare is Dr 5
per person.

AROUND MEKNÈS
Volubilis
About 33 km from Meknès is the site of the largest and best preserved Roman ruins in Morocco. Volubilis dates largely from the 2nd and 3rd centuries AD, though excavations have revealed that the site was originally settled by Carthaginian traders in the 3rd century BC.

Volubilis was one of the Roman Empire's most remote outposts, and capital of the province of Mauretania (as North Africa was then known). Direct Roman rule lasted for only 240 years after the area was annexed by Claudius in 45 AD. Its population of Berbers, Greeks, Jews and Syrians continued to speak Latin and practise Christianity right up until the coming of Islam. Unlike Lixus, to the north-west, which was abandoned shortly after the fall of the Roman Empire, Volubilis continued to be habited right up until the 18th century, when its marble was plundered for the building of Moulay Ismail's palaces in Meknès.

If you like ancient ruins, Volubilis is worth a visit. It is an easy day trip from Meknès, and you can also take in the nearby town of Moulay Idriss.

The whole site has been well excavated. Its most attractive feature are the stunning mosaics, made even more so by the fact that they have been left *in situ*. A few officious men in blue coats with whistles patrol the site, making sure you don't do what you shouldn't (ie walk on the mosaics); this is good to see, but they tend to take themselves a bit too seriously at times. The site is open daily from sunrise to sunset and entry is Dr 20.

The major points of interest are in the northern part of the site, although it's convenient to start at the south. Once over the Oued Fertassa, the path from the entrance takes you through an unremarkable residential quarter. The House of Orpheus, a little higher up and identifiable by the three pine trees growing in the corner, was a sumptuous mansion for one of the city's wealthiest residents. Its two mosaics, one representing the Orpheus myth and the other the chariot of Amphitrite, are still in place.

The basilica, capitol and forum are, typically, built on a high point. The capitol dates back to 217 AD; the basilica lies to the north of it.

On the left, just before the Triumphal Arch, are a couple of roped-off mosaics. One depicts an athlete being presented with a trophy for winning a *desultor* race, a competition in which the rider had to dismount and jump back on his horse as it raced along. Opposite these mosaics are the remains of an aqueduct and fountain.

The Triumphal Arch on the Decumanus Maximus, built in 217 AD in honour of the emperor Caracalla and his mother Julia Domna, used to be topped with a bronze chariot. Sadly, this is there no longer, and the arch looks very plain and ordinary these days.

The Decumanus Maximus stretches away up the slope to the north-east. The houses lining either side of the road contain the best mosaics on the site; these days they are usually named after the mosaics found in them. The first house on the far side of the arch is known as the House of the Ephebus and contains a fine mosaic of Bacchus in a chariot drawn by panthers. Next along is the House of Columns (so called because of its columned façade), and adjacent to this is the Knight's House, with its incomplete mosaic of Bacchus and Ariadne.

Behind these houses is the amazing sight of the old trolleys and tracks used to carry away the excavated material. The size of the pile of waste moved to uncover the site is also astonishing – there's a sizable artificial hill out there.

In the next couple of houses are excellent mosaics of the Labours of Hercules and of Nymphs Bathing. The best collection on the whole site, however, is in the House of the Cortege of Venus, one block further up and one block to the right. Although some of the house is roped off, there is a viewing platform built along the southern wall which gives you a good vantage point to see the two best mosaics – the Abduction of Hylas by the Nymphs and Diana Bathing.

The Decumanus Maximus continues up

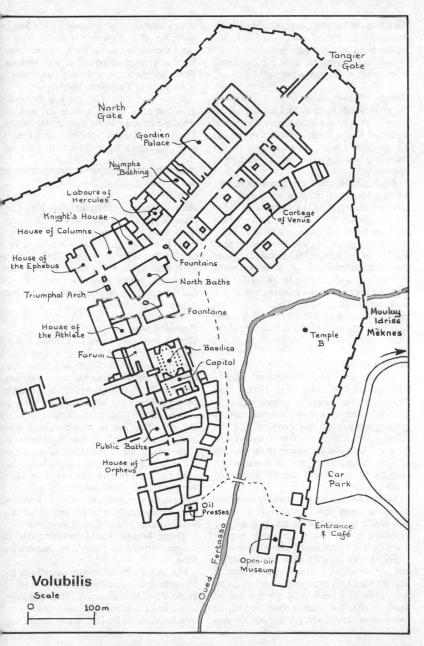

Tangier Gate

North Gate

Gordien Palace

Nymphs Bathing

Labours of Hercules

Knight's House

House of Columns

House of the Ephebus

Triumphal Arch

House of the Athlete

Forum

Public Baths

House of Orpheus

Fountains

North Baths

Fountains

Basilica

Capitol

Oil Presses

Cortege of Venus

Temple B

Moulay Idriss Meknès

Car Park

Entrance & Café

Open-air Museum

Oued Fertassa

Volubilis

Scale

0   100 m

the hill to the Tangier Gate, past the uninteresting Gordien Palace, which used to be the residence of the city's administrators.

Back at the entrance, there is a good café where you can rehydrate yourself.

Getting There & Away

To get to Volubilis from Meknès it's best to get a small group together and hire a taxi from just below Place el Hedim in the old city (about Dr 6 per person each way, not including waiting time, which you must negotiate).

Alternatively, there are buses to nearby Moulay Idriss which leave when full from the same place and cost Dr 4 each way. There are also grands taxis to Moulay Idriss, which are more frequent than the buses. If you take the bus or a grand taxi, ask the driver to drop you off at the turn-off (signposted), about two km from Moulay Idriss, at the bottom of the hill, and walk from there (a further 2½ km). As long as it's not stinking hot, it is a pleasant one-hour walk. There is a good chance of being able to hitch a lift back to Meknès with tourists from the carpark at the site.

Moulay Idriss

The other main place of interest outside Meknès is Moulay Idriss, about 4½ km from Volubilis. The town is named after its founder, Morocco's most revered saint, a great-grandson of the Prophet and the founder of the country's first Arab dynasty. Moulay Idriss fled Damascus in the late 8th century AD after the great civil war which split the Muslim world into the Shiite and Sunni sects.

Moulay Idriss is certainly a very attractive town when seen from a distance, as it nestles in a cradle of lush mountains. It is heavily promoted in the tourist literature, but the town itself is a profound disappointment.

For Moroccans it's a place of pilgrimage, and non-Muslims can well get the feeling that they are only grudgingly tolerated (it's been open to infidels only for the last 70 years or so). You cannot visit any of the mosques or shrines and you are not allowed

to stay overnight. This being so, it's hardly worth the effort. However, if you do want to check it out take a taxi or bus from just below Place el Hedim in the old city at Meknès. These are the same taxis and buses which you take from Meknès to Volubilis.

If you do decide to go, the best day to do so is Saturday; this is market day and the place is a lot more lively than at other times. There are also many more buses and grands taxis making the trip, in the morning at least.

AZROU

Azrou is a primarily Berber town. It's a very pleasant place in which to relax in the mountains surrounded by pine forests, when you've had enough of souks and handicraft hustlers down on the plains. There's not a great deal to do other than trek into the mountains, but the people are very friendly and there is absolutely no hassle. It's another dimension of Morocco.

Places to Stay – bottom end

Behind the main street is a small square around which you'll find four budget hotels – the *Ziz*, *Atlas*, *Beau Séjour* and *Salam*. The first three are all about the same standard, and cost Dr 20 a single and Dr 30 a double. None of them have hot water (and it's cold in the mornings at this altitude – 1250 metres). The Ziz is parsimonious with blankets, too, and it's a hassle to get more out of the management. The Hotel Salam, which is a little more modern, is slightly better and costs Dr 12 per person. The rooms are clean but the toilets stink and there's only cold water in the communal showers. In addition, there's only one blanket per bed which certainly wouldn't be sufficient in winter.

These hotels would be adequate in summer but in winter they'd be Desperation Row.

For only a little more you can stay at the far superior one-star *Hotel des Cèdres* (☎ 56 2326), Place Mohammed V, which has large, airy, comfortable and spotlessly clean rooms with hot showers for Dr 5 at any time of day.

The staff are very friendly, and singles/doubles cost Dr 70/93 with own shower but shared toilet and Dr 89/106 with own shower and toilet, including taxes. The hotel has its own restaurant though it's relatively expensive at Dr 54 for the 'tourist menu' or Dr 60 for the full menu. On the other hand, the food is tasty and there's plenty of it.

There's also the one-star *Hotel Azrou* (☎ 56 2116), Route de Khenifra, which costs the same as the Cèdres but is quite a way from the centre of town.

Places to Stay – top end

There are no middle range hotels in Azrou so, if you're looking for a touch of luxury, it's down to the three-star *Hotel Panorama* (☎ 56 2010) which has 36 rooms with heating and private bathrooms for Dr 151/186 plus taxes for singles/doubles. It's a pleasant, relaxing place with its own bar and restaurant and adequate parking facilities.

Places to Eat

The cheapest restaurants are those clustered on the street opposite the park below the main roundabout. You can get a good meal here for around Dr 15.

Things to Buy

A visit to the Co-opérative Artisanale on the right-hand side on the road to Khenifra (signposted) is well worthwhile. Here you can find work in cedar and iron, as well as Berber carpets typical of the Middle Atlas.

IFRANE

Just 17 km from Azrou on the road to Fès is Ifrane, a town the likes of which you will not see anywhere else in Morocco. Indeed, there's nothing Moroccan about it at all. With its tree-lined avenues, manicured lawns, landscaped gardens, conspicuously expensive detached villas and bored youth, it's a perfect replica of a French alpine weekend village. Most of the time, there's no-one around and nothing to do. The villas are obviously owned by the very affluent who come here in summer to escape the heat of the plains or to enjoy winter sports after the snow has fallen. Perhaps at those times it comes alive but, in between, it's as dead as a door nail. This is Morocco's premier ski resort so you can give it a miss unless you're flushed with cash.

Places to Stay & Eat

Given that this is a resort village for the rich, there's no such thing here as a budget hotel. The cheapest places to stay are the *Grand Hotel* (☎ 56 6407), Ave de la Marché Verte, and the *Hotel Perce Neige* (☎ 56 6404), Rue des Asphodelles, both of which are two-star hotels. Singles/doubles at either, with private bathroom and hot water, are Dr 119/138, plus taxes. Both hotels have their own bar and restaurant.

Top of the line is the *Hotel Michlifen* (☎ 56 6416), a resort hotel with swimming pool, bar, restaurant, nightclub and all the other amenities you would expect of a five-star hotel.

Getting There & Away

There are regular buses from both Fès and Azrou to Ifrane.

TAZA

Despite its tempestuous history, Taza is a relatively quiet city these days. Nevertheless, it is worth a visit if you are passing through the area going to or coming from Algeria, if only for the views and the crumbling fortifications. And, if you have your own transport, the drive around Mt Tazzeka with a visit to the Gouffre du Friouato – one of the most incredible open caverns in the world – is superb.

Since it was an important French military and administrative centre during the protectorate, Taza too has a ville nouvelle which, as usual, is separate from the old town. However, here the two are quite some distance from each other – three km in fact – though urbanisation is rapidly closing the gap.

History

The fortified citadel of Taza, built on the edge of an escarpment overlooking the only feasible pass between the Rif Mountains and the Middle Atlas, has been important throughout Morocco's history as a garrison town from which to exert control over the eastern extremities of the country. The Taza Gap, as it is known, has provided the traditional invasion route for armies moving west from Tunisia and Algeria. The Romans and the Arabs entered Morocco via this pass, and the town itself was the base from which the Almohads, Merenids and the Alaouites swept down onto Fès to conquer lowland Morocco and establish their respective dynasties.

All the various Moroccan sultans had a hand in fortifying Taza. Nevertheless, their control over the area was always tenuous, since the fiercely independent and rebellious local tribes were always willing to exploit any weakness in the central power in order to overrun the city.

Taza's most notable inhabitant, however, was Bou Hamara, who lived here at the end of the 19th century and who almost succeeded in usurping the Moroccan throne. Accused of intrigues by the Alaouite sultan, he was imprisoned and later went into exile in Algeria. Several years later he returned disguised as a devout traveller and quickly established a widespread reputation as a marabout (saint).

Taking advantage of the unpopularity of Sultan Abd el Aziz, who was accused of conspiring with the Christians, Bou Hamara had himself proclaimed sultan, raised the standard of revolt among the neighbouring tribes and for the next seven years fought a successful campaign against the central authorities. With final victory within his grasp, however, his followers were trounced by the army of Abd al-Hafid, who had succeeded his brother, Abd el Aziz, as sultan. Thousands of his followers were butchered and Bou Hamara himself was captured. He was brought to Fès in a cage and there, jeered at by the people, was thrown to the lions in the sultan's menagerie.

The French occupied Taza in 1914, after which it became the main French base from which they fought the prolonged rebellion against their rule by the tribes of the Rif and Middle Atlas.

Orientation
Arriving by bus or train, you'll find yourself on the main Fès-Oujda road which might appear to be the centre of town but in fact is quite some distance from the actual centre – the Place de l'Indépendance – on or near which are the banks, post office and most of

the hotels and restaurants. If you arrive by CTM bus, on the other hand, you're in luck because the terminal is right on this square. The old town is further away still. The easiest way to get from one part to another is by petit taxi.

City Walls
Most of the city walls, which have a circumference of about three km, date from the time of the Almohads (12th century). Since they have had to withstand many sieges, they are ruined in parts. There's also a solid bastion at one corner of the town, which was built by the Saadians in the 16th century.

The most interesting part of a trip around the walls is the Bab er Rih (Gate of Winds), from which there are incredible views over the surrounding countryside. On the extreme left you can see the wooded slopes of Mt Tazzeka and before that, across the Oued Taza, the terraced gardens and dry ravines of the foothills of the Rif. On the right, below the park, is the ville nouvelle, with the Rif Mountains in the distance.

Great Mosque
Not far from the Bab er Rih is the Great Mosque, which was begun by the Almohads in 1135 and added to by the Merenids in the 13th century. Non-Muslims are not allowed to enter. Stretching from here down to the far end of the old town is the main thoroughfare (Rue Kettanine/Rue Nejjarine/Rue Koubet/ Rue Sidi Ali Derrar). This is perhaps the most interesting part of town: there are many examples of richly decorated doorways and, occasionally, windows high up in the walls guarded by very old, carved cedar screens.

Souks
The souks are about halfway down the street, around the Mosquée du Marché. They are of minor interest unless you are searching for second-hand European clothing. However, there are a few shops which offer mats and carpets woven by the Beni Ouarain tribe in the surrounding mountains.

Most of the shops cater for household necessities and foodstuffs, as do the ones in

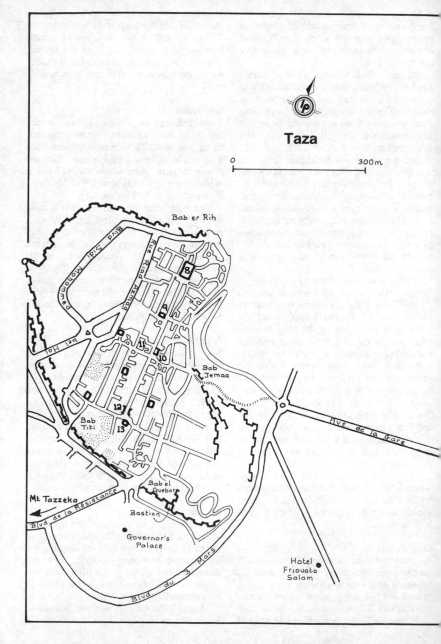

Taza

0   300m

Fès

Railway
Station

● Buses
& Taxis

Oujda

Place
de
l'Indépendance

● Mosque

● Camping

1	Hotel de la Gare
2	Grand Hotel du Dauphin
3	Hotel (no name)
4	BMCE Bank &
	Restaurant Majestic
5	Restaurant Le Fath
6	Post Office (PTT)
7	Hotel de la Poste &
	CTM Bus Terminal
8	Great Mosque
9	Sidi Azuoz Mosque
10	Mosquée du Marché
11	Souks
12	Mechouar
13	Andalous Mosque

the nearby *kissaria* (the commercial centre of the medina). Whilst in this part of the city don't miss the minaret of the Mosquée du Marché, which is perhaps unique in Morocco in that its upper part is wider than its base.

Andalous Mosque

Right at the end of the main street, close to the mechouar, is the Andalous Mosque, constructed in the 12th century. Nearby is the ruined house once occupied by Bou Hamara, and the Merenid Bou Abul Hassan Medersa. It may be possible to gain entry to the latter if you ask around and enlist the help of a guide.

Places to Stay – bottom end

The choice of accommodation in Taza is limited. What hotels there are, are all in the ville nouvelle.

If arriving by non-CTM bus or train, the nearest place is the *Hotel de la Gare*, more or less opposite the railway station. It's cheap and plain but adequate, and convenient if you want to be near the transport terminals. However, it is not convenient for the centre of town.

All the other hotels, except one, are around the Place de l'Indépendance. The cheapest is the one with an Arabic name only, which is basic but clean, costs Dr 52 a double with shared bathroom, and has cold showers only. Better is the *Hotel de la Poste*, which offers good, clean rooms with shared bathroom for Dr 50/60 for singles/doubles. It's a very friendly place and has hot water all day.

Camping For campers, there's a campsite uphill along the Ave de la Gare towards the old town. However, facilities are minimal and it can't seriously be recommended.

Places to Stay – middle

The *Grand Hotel du Dauphine* (☎ 67 3567) is a two-star hotel housed in an attractive colonial-style building and is the best place to stay if you have the money. It's comfortable, pleasant, friendly and very old fashioned, with period bathrooms and balco-

nies overlooking the square. Rooms with private bathroom (complete with stained glass) cost Dr 123/146 for singles/doubles. There's hot water in the evenings only. Downstairs is a lively bar and a very sedate dining hall with a very limited choice of food. Meals here are fairly expensive.

Places to Stay – top end

The only top-end hotel in Taza is the *Hotel Friouato Salam* (☎ 67 2593), set in its own well-maintained grounds about halfway between the Place de l'Indépendance and the old town (see map). It's a modern three-star hotel and has self-contained singles/doubles for Dr 175/212, plus taxes. There's a bar, restaurant, swimming pool and tennis courts. It also has its own very good restaurant and bar.

Places to Eat

There are very few restaurants in Taza and most of them are on the streets just off the Place de l'Indépendance. I'd recommend the very modern and clean *Restaurant Majestic*, which offers omelettes, kefta, kebabs, chops, soup and chips. It's excellent value and you can eat well for around Dr 10 – more if you take meat.

Getting There & Away

Bus & Taxi Buses and grands taxis leave for Fès and Oujda several times a day from the main bus station. The grands taxis arrive in Fès at the Bab Ftouh in Fès el-Bali, so you'll need to take a local taxi from there to the ville nouvelle or to the Bab Bou Jeloud.

Non-CTM buses to Nador and Al Hoceima on the Mediterranean coast leave twice a day but usually between 4.30 and 5 am.

The CTM terminal is on the Place de l'Indépendance so it's more convenient for the hotels.

Train There are daily trains to Fès and Meknès at 12.45 and 1.53 am, and 12.23, 1.10, 2.05, 3.21 and 10.11 pm. The 1.53 am and 12.23 pm trains to Fès continue on to Tangier; the others continue on to Casablanca via Rabat. To Oujda there are daily trains at 3.45, 5.46 and 8.43 am, and 3.16, 5.26 and 9.08 pm.

AROUND TAZA

If you have your own transport (hitching isn't really feasible), there's a fascinating day trip you can make around Mt Tazzeka, which takes in the Cascades de Ras el-Oued (waterfalls), the Gouffre du Friouato (cavern), Daïa Chiker (a lake) and the gorges of the Oued Zireg. There's a good tarmac road the whole way. If you don't have your own transport it would be worthwhile getting a small group together and hiring a taxi for the day.

Having negotiated the long, winding road up from Taza onto the plateau, you'll find yourself in a completely different world. It's almost eerie in its apparent emptiness, with small patches of farmland and a few scattered houses and, closer to Mt Tazzeka itself, dense coniferous forests. There are superb views from many points, but particularly from the semiderelict hamlet of Bab Bou Idir (this hamlet must have been a beautiful retreat at one time with its tiled alpine-style houses but it appears to have been completely abandoned).

The waterfalls and the lake are only really worth visiting after heavy rainfall in the winter months since, during the dry summer months, the falls are reduced to just a trickle and the lake is usually dry.

Daïa Chiker is a geological curiosity associated with fault lines in the calciferous rock structure. It is connected to a subterranean reservoir whose water is highly charged with carbon dioxide. Depending on the season and the state of affairs in the subterranean reservoir, the surface of the lake can change dramatically. The nearby Grottes du

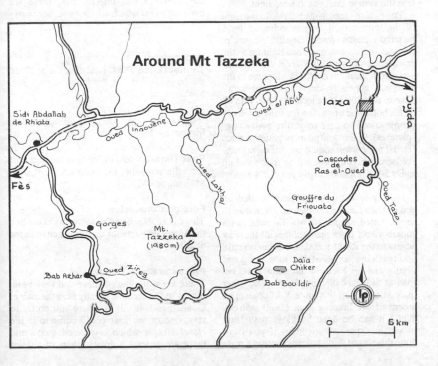

Around Mt Tazzeka

Chiker (caves) at the northern end of the lake have been explored and are said to give access to a five-km-long underground river, but they are not open to casual visitors.

The Gouffre du Friouato is the big draw here and an absolute must at any time of year. I don't think I've seen anything quite as spectacular as this cavern anywhere in the world except perhaps the Niah Caves in Sarawak, Borneo. This vast cavern is said to be the deepest and possibly the most extensive in the whole of North Africa and has only been partially explored to date. The main part plummets vertically some 200 metres to a floor below, where it snakes away to who knows where. Several flights of precipitous steps with handrails lead you to the floor of the main cavern, and since there's a large hole in the roof of the cavern which lets in light, you can get this far without a torch or flashlight. If you plan on going any further into the system then you'll need light.

The cavern is up on the hillside to the right of the tarmac road, and is indicated by a battered old sign saying 'Gouffre'. If you're driving, there's a tarmac road right up to the entrance; otherwise it's a good 20 minutes' walk from the main road. The entrance to the cavern is generally locked, but you won't have to wait long for a local youth to ride up on his horse and open it up for you (not many people come up here so you're pretty conspicuous). Before you go in, negotiate a price (Dr 10 per person should be sufficient) otherwise when you come out he'll demand up to Dr 50. Even at that silly price, it's almost worth it!

Further down the tarmac, past the dried-up bed of Daïa Chiker, the plateau gives way to the forested slopes of Mt Tazzeka, with superb views from many points all the way across to the Rif Mountains. Further on still, you reach the gorges of the Oued Zireg and finally end up back on the main Fès-Taza road at Sidi Abdallah de Rhiata. The other main attraction of this route is, of course, an ascent of Mt Tazzeka itself (1980 metres). While it can be done by those with little mountain experience, it helps if you have done this sort of thing before. There is a *piste*

(track) as far as a TV relay station, about nine km off to the right from the main road, where cars can be left. Unlike for Mt Toubkal south of Marrakesh, there are no guidebooks available to help you with information about this mountain.

OUJDA

This is the last town before the Algerian border and, if you have just come from Algeria, make the most of the very relaxed atmosphere – there is no hassling, apart from the occasional offers to change money.

The town itself has been transformed out of all recognition over the last few years and the ville nouvelle is reminiscent in many ways of Casablanca, though essentially of little interest. The old medina – still partially walled – is quite small and sells mainly clothing. If you arrive from Tlemcen during the day and are heading for Fès, there are evening trains which will get you there early the next morning.

Information
Tourist Office The tourist office is on Place du 16 Août 1953 at the junction with Ave Mohammed V.

Money The banks are concentrated on Ave Mohammed V.

Post The main post office is in the centre of the ville nouvelle, on the main street, Ave Mohammed V.

Foreign Consulates
There is an Algerian Consulate in Oujda. See the Morocco Facts for the Visitor chapter for details.

Places to Stay – bottom end
There are a number of cheap and very basic places in the medina, mostly near the Bab el Ouahab end. If this is where you prefer to stay, one of the first you'll come to is the *Hotel Afrique* which is quite adequate, and there are at least a dozen others of similar

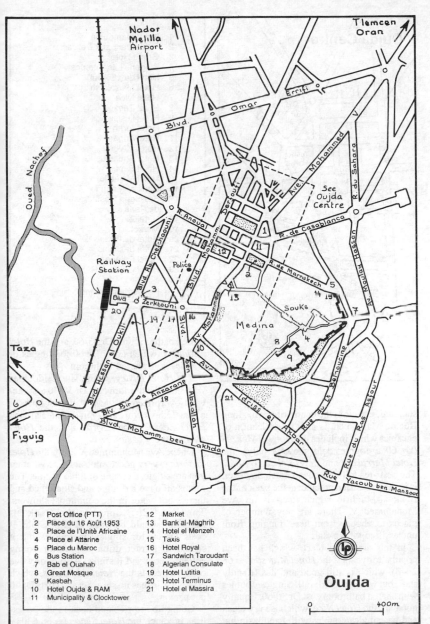

1	Post Office (PTT)	12	Market
2	Place du 16 Août 1953	13	Bank al-Maghrib
3	Place de l'Unitè Africaine	14	Hotel el Menzeh
4	Place el Attarine	15	Taxis
5	Place du Maroc	16	Hotel Royal
6	Bus Station	17	Sandwich Taroudant
7	Bab el Ouahab	18	Algerian Consulate
8	Great Mosque	19	Hotel Lutitia
9	Kasbah	20	Hotel Terminus
10	Hotel Oujda & RAM	21	Hotel el Massira
11	Municipality & Clocktower		

Oujda

0   400m

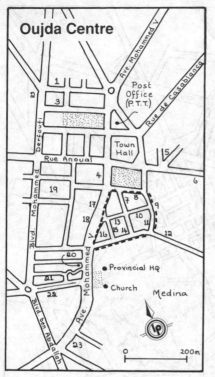

Oujda Centre

1 Hotel Mamounia
2 Restaurant aux Delices
3 Grand Hotel
4 Wagons Lits/Europcar
5 Hotel de 16 Août
6 Hotel Marrakesh
7 Hotel Nice
8 Hotel Zegzel
9 Hotel Disley
10 Hotel Afrah
11 Hotel Angad
12 Hotel d'Alger
13 Hotel Andalous
14 Hotel Simon
15 Hotel Majestic
16 Bank al-Maghrib
17 Brasserie Restaurant
   de Paris
18 Hotel Ziri
19 Market
20 Hotel de l'Oasis
21 Hotel des Lilas
22 Hotel Palace
23 Hotel Oujda & RAM

⌐⌐ Pedestrian Precinct

standard. Closer to the centre of town, along Rue de Marrakech, is another collection of cheapies which includes the *Hotel el Menzeh* (Dr 60 a double, cold showers only), the *Hotel Marrakesh* and the *Hotel de 16 Août*. The best area to find a cheap hotel, however, is in the pedestrian precinct at the back of the Bank al-Maghrib which itself is on Ave Mohammed V. There are any number of places to choose from here, ranging from unclassified to two-star.

In this area, one place which has been popular for years is the *Hotel Majestic* (☎ 68 2948), which is still good and has friendly staff, but which is often full. Singles/doubles with shared bathroom cost Dr 30/60. Equally good are the *Hotel Nice*, which is very clean and has singles/doubles with handbasin but

shared bathroom for Dr 35/60, and the *Hotel Andalous*, which costs Dr 60 for singles or doubles with shared bathroom.

The *Hotel Disley*, where singles/doubles with shared bathroom cost Dr 38/70 is somewhat overpriced in view of the facilities it offers. Others you can try in this area are the *Hotel Zegzel*, *Hotel Afrah* and the *Hotel d'Alger* (very basic).

On the Ave Mohammed V itself, the *Hotel Victoria* is very good value at Dr 75 whether you are single, a couple or three people. The rooms all have a double and single bed and there's hot water in the communal showers. The *Hotel Ziri*, opposite the Bank al-Maghrib, should be avoided if possible. It costs Dr 60 for singles or doubles but it seems to attract dubious-looking young entrepreneurs and it stinks. Also poor value on this street is the *Hotel de l'Oasis*, which is very basic, has no showers and costs Dr 40 per person.

Going up in price and back in the pedestrian precinct, the *Hotel Simon* (☎ 68 6303),

1 Rue Tarik ibn Ziad, is a one-star hotel and good value for Dr 70/93 for singles/doubles with own shower and shared toilet or Dr 89/106 with own shower and toilet.

Further afield, the one-star *Hotel Royal* (☎ 68 2284), 13 Blvd Zerktouni, is excellent value at Dr 70/93 for singles/doubles with own shower and shared toilet and Dr 89/106 with own shower and toilet. They also have cheaper rooms. There's hot water in the showers and the hotel has its own garage parking.

Closest to the railway station is the *Hotel Lutitia* (☎ 68 3365), 44 Blvd Hassan el Oukili, on the roundabout at the junction with Blvd Zerktouni. This two-star hotel has singles/doubles for Dr 79/100 with own shower and shared toilet and Dr 96/120 with own shower and toilet.

Places to Stay – middle
In the pedestrian precinct, one of the best places to stay is the brand-new, two-star *Hotel Angad* (☎ 69 1451), Blvd Ramdane el Gadi (formerly the Rue Isly). Self-contained rooms here with hot water cost Dr 123/146 for singles/doubles. The hotel has its own tea salon and accepts Visa and MasterCard. Further afield but not far from the main post office is the *Grand Hotel*, an older style, two-star hotel with self-contained doubles for Dr 120. There's hot water 24 hours a day. It's a large place and unlikely to be full.

Places to Stay – top end
One of the cheapest in this range is the new *Hotel des Lilas* (☎ 68 0840), Rue Jamal Eddine el Afghani, which is just off the bottom end of Blvd Mohammed Derfoufi near the junction with Blvd Zerktouni. The rooms are fairly small but comfortable and self-contained (hot water) and cost Dr 155/196 for singles/doubles. If it's a touch of luxury you're looking for you won't be disappointed here, but avoid the hotel's restaurant – both the food and the service are lousy.

Going up in price into the four-star range, there are the *Hotel Oujda* (☎ 68 4093), Ave Mohammed V, and the *Hotel Al Massira*

(☎ 68 5301), Blvd Maghreb el Arabi. Both of these have self-contained singles/doubles for Dr 234/292 plus taxes and have their own bar, restaurant and swimming pool.

Top of the line is the *Hotel Terminus* (☎ 68 3211), Place de l'Unité Africaine, right next to the railway station. Singles/doubles are Dr 280/358 plus taxes. The hotel has all the usual amenities.

Places to Eat
There's not an oversupply of cheap eating places in Oujda. One good one is *Sandwich Taroudant*, on Blvd ben Abdallah, just around the corner from the Hotel Royal. They serve excellent rabbit tajines for Dr 15, and also have good salads and other dishes. There are other cheap places on Ave Mohammed V between the public gardens and the Bank al-Maghrib. The *Restaurant Maghreb el Arabi*, in this area, has good sandwiches and tajines.

In the evenings, stalls are set up just inside Bab el Ouahab in the medina. These serve all sorts of things, mainly fried animal organs, but do have other more appetising things like fish, potato omelettes and chips.

A little further afield, the *Restaurant aux Delices*, close to the Grand and Mamounia hotels, offers hamburgers, brochettes (kebabs), salads and pizzas, all priced at between Dr 10 and Dr 15.

For a splurge in air-conditioned comfort, with black-suited waiters and starched white linen, try the *Brasserie Restaurant de Paris*, on Ave Mohammed V. The food here is excellent but you're looking at around Dr 100 per person, including beer and service charges.

Getting There & Away
Air The airport which serves Oujda is 15 km from the town centre. There are regular flights to Casablanca.

Bus The bus station for all buses is across the Oued Nachef on the south edge of town, about 15 minutes' walk from the railway station. It's well organised and advance booking is available on the major runs.

CTM has daily departures to Taza and Fès at 5 and 11 am, and to Taza and Nador at 7 and 10 am and 1 and 3.30 pm. Ligne du Sahara has departures to Figuig (via Bouarfa) at 6 am and 1.30 pm, (seven hours, Dr 61.60). Transportes des Hautes Plateaux has departures to Figuig at 10 am and 3 pm and to Bouarfa at 7 am. Ligne de Casablanca has departures to Fès at 2.30 pm and to Casablanca/Rabat at 6 am and 5, 6, 7.30 and 8.30 pm.

There are buses to the Algerian border (13 km) every half hour throughout the day from near the Place du Maroc (medina), and the cost is Dr 3. There are plenty of taxis at the border. Allow two hours for border formalities.

Train The railway station is fairly close to the centre, at the west end of Blvd Zerktouni. There are departures for the west of the country at 8.23, 10.44 and 11.56 am and 6.35, 9.24 and 10.18 pm. All these trains call at Taza (four hours), Fès (6½ hours) and Meknès (7½ hours). The 8.23 am and 10.18 pm trains continue on to Tangier. The others continue on to Rabat and Casablanca. First and 2nd-class sleepers are available on the 6.35, 9.24 and 10.18 pm trains.

Taxi Grands taxis to Nador leave from Place du Maroc and from outside the bus station.

The High Atlas

Few places inspire the imagination quite as much as Marrakesh, and a wander through the ancient alleys of its medina will not fail to provoke the senses.

Once your desire for bargaining in the souks is sated, a trek in the High Atlas could restore your sanity, or at least bring you in touch with another aspect of Morocco. Failing this, a few days relaxing on the magnificent and untouristed beaches near Essaouira should do the trick.

Agadir

Agadir was destroyed by an earthquake in 1960 and, although it's now been rebuilt, it's hardly a typical Moroccan city any longer. Most of the activity here centres around catering for the short-stay package tourists from Europe, who flock in by the plane-load daily in search of sun, sand and an acceptably sanitised version of the mysteries of the Barbary Coast.

The reek of Ambre Soleil and the rustle of *Paris Match, Der Spiegel* and the airmail *Sunday Times* fill the air. Not that it's unpleasant – it's just that it could be any resort town on the northern Mediterranean coast. Agadir is also one of the more expensive cities in Morocco. However, it's the take-off point for visits east and further south, so you'll probably have to stay here overnight at least.

The main market outside town is worth a look – take bus No 1 along Blvd Mohammed V to get there.

Information
Tourist Office The national tourist office (ONMT) (☎ 82 2894) is on Ave Prince Sidi Mohammed. There's also a syndicat d'initiative (☎ 84 0695) on Blvd Mohammed V at the junction with Ave du Général Kettani. Both places offer a free map of

Agadir but are otherwise not much help to budget travellers.

Money The American Express representative is Voyages Schwartz (☎ 82 0252), Place du Marché Municipal, Ave Hassan II.

Post Office The post office here is open daily from 8.30 am to 6.45 pm.

Foreign Consulates There are a number of foreign consulates in Agadir. See the Morocco Facts for the Visitor chapter for details.

Places to Stay – bottom end
Most of the budget hotels and a few of the mid-range hotels are clustered around the bus terminal area and along Rue Allal ben Abdallah. In the high seasons you must get into Agadir early in the day if you want to be sure of a room. If you arrive late you may have to sleep out or pay through the nose at an expensive hotel. Disappointed backpackers wandering around with nowhere to go are a common sight by 8 pm.

There are basically only three unclassified hotels to choose from in the bus terminal area and none of them are anything special. The best is probably the *Hotel Canaria*, which is friendly and has singles/doubles/triples with communal showers (cold water only) and toilets for Dr 30/40/62.

Next best is the *Hotel Select* (signposted as *Hotel Douche Select*), Rue Allal ben Abdallah, which has singles/ doubles with shared bathroom for Dr 40/52. Least desirable is the *Hotel Massa*, since the rooms are very small and dingy and the place seems to attract quite a few dubious characters. The manager will assure you that there's 'hot water all day' (a likely story!). Singles/ doubles/triples with communal bathroom cost Dr 30/40/60.

The *Hotel Amenou* (☎ 82 3026), at 1 Rue Yacoub el Mansour, is far better value. This

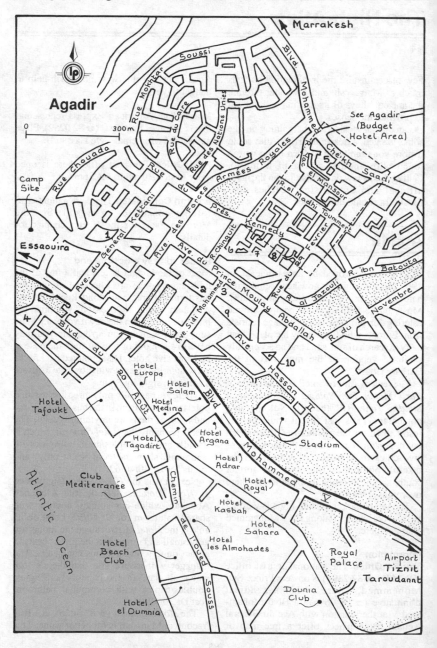

1 Royal Air Maroc
2 Tourist Office
3 Post Office (PTT)
4 Public Swimming Pool
5 Bus Station, Cheap Restaurants
& Budget Hotel Area
6 Hotel Talborjt
7 Hotel Itrane
8 Hotel Ayour
9 Hotel Atlantic
10 Voyages Schwartz (Amex)

one-star hotel is very comfortable and has singles/doubles for Dr 48/60 with shared bathroom for Dr 62/78, including taxes, with own shower and hot water. If it's full, try the *Hotel Ait Laayoune* (previously the *Hotel Tifawt*) (☎ 82 4375), Rue Yacoub el Mansour, which is clean and modern and has communal hot showers. Singles/doubles are Dr 52/75, including taxes.

Three others to try in this range are the *Hotel Excelsior* (☎ 82 1028), Rue Yacoub el Mansour, the *Hotel Diaf* (☎ 82 3179) and the *Hotel de la Baie* (☎ 82 3014). The latter two are both on Rue Allal ben Abdallah. All these have singles/doubles with communal bathroom for Dr 62/78, or Dr 71/94 with own shower and toilet.

Going up in price, try the *Hotel Bahia* (☎ 82 2724), Rue Yacoub el Mansour, another one-star hotel, with singles/doubles for Dr 70/93 with own shower but shared toilet and Dr 89/106 with own shower and toilet. Very similar and the same price is the *Hotel Itrane* (☎ 82 1407), Rue de l'Entraide.

Places to Stay – middle

The *Hotel de Paris* (☎ 82 2694), Rue du Président Kennedy, has been a popular place to stay for years and it's clean and comfortable but may not have hot water. It's a two-star hotel and costs Dr 98/118 for singles/doubles with own shower and shared toilet or Dr 123/146 with own shower and toilet. Breakfast is available. Similar and close by is the *Hotel Ayour* (☎ 82 4976), 4 Rue de l'Entraide.

If you're thinking of staying in Agadir for

a few days and want something closer to the centre of things as well as to the beach then you can't beat the *Hotel Atlantic* (☎ 82 3662), Ave Hassan II, for value. Another two-star hotel, it's very clean and comfortable and has boiling hot water 24 hours a day. The staff are friendly and singles/doubles with own shower and toilet cost Dr 123/148, including taxes. It attracts mainly a Dutch and German clientele. Breakfast is available in the pleasant, leafy courtyard.

Similar in price is the *Hotel Sindibad* (☎ 82 3477), facing the small square at the back of the bus offices, and the *Hotel Talborjt* (☎ 82 0671), Rue de l'Entraide.

Places to Stay – top end

Going up to three-star and beyond, there's a bewildering choice of hotels, many of them lining the ocean front along Blvd Mohammed V and Rue de la Plage/Blvd du 20 Août. Virtually all of them cater for package tourists. There are far too many to mention so, if you have the money and a yen for staying in one of them, it's suggested you book into a cheaper place first and check them out. The more expensive ones are, of course, resort

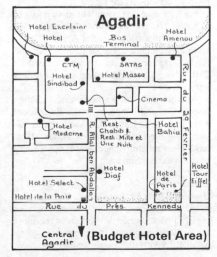

hotels with swimming pools, tennis courts, multiple bars and restaurants and nightclubs.

Places to Eat

There are a number of cheap restaurants and sandwich bars on the same street as the bus terminals and they're reasonable value. You can get almost anything from seafood to kebabs to sandwiches to yoghurt.

Just at the back of the bus terminal street is a small plaza where there are three restaurants next to each other. These are very popular with travellers and night strollers from the tourist district in search of a change. They are the *Restaurant Chabib*, the *Restaurant Mille et Une Nuits* and the *Café Restaurant Coq d'Or*. They might look expensive (judging from some of the clients) but they're not and the food is very good. All offer you a choice of sitting inside or at tables in the open air. Typical prices at these restaurants are: couscous or tajine (Dr 17 to Dr 20), omelette (Dr 9 to Dr 12) and salad (Dr 5 to Dr 9). They're good value.

The restaurant at the *Hotel Select* is also very good value – Dr 16 for a couscous or Dr 22 for a three-course meal. Also good value is the *Restaurant Tifaut* between the main mosque and Ave du Général Kettani. It offers three-course meals for Dr 30.

For a splurge that doesn't involve going to a hotel, try the *Restaurant Scampi*, Ave Hassan II opposite the Hotel Atlantic. They have an excellent range of dishes here and the food is superb. It isn't cheap at around Dr 250 for two people including wine, but it is very popular.

Another place for a splurge and a change from tajine and couscous is the *Restaurant Phi-Long*, Ave Hassan II, a Vietnamese restaurant at the northern end of Hassan II. It has a pleasant atmosphere and is open every evening except Sundays.

Bars

If you're looking for a cleansing ale or a bottle of Moroccan wine, the tourist palaces on Blvd Mohammed V are hardly the most lively places to go and the clientele is going to regard you with disdain unless you have just emerged from the laundromat. There are much livelier Moroccan-style bars if you take the trouble to wander around.

For takeaways go to one or other of the two supermarkets on the opposite side of the street from the Hotel Erfoud, Ave Hassan II. There's an excellent choice of local and imported beers, wines and spirits.

Getting There & Away

The bus terminals are all on Rue Yacoub el Mansour. CTM has daily buses to Beni Mellal (3 pm); Casablanca (10 pm); Dakhla (8 pm); El Jadida (7.30 am); Essaouira/Safi (7.30 am); Marrakesh (3 pm); Smara/Layoune (8.30 pm); Taroudannt (5.30 am); and Tiznit (6.30 am and 3.30 pm).

SATAS has buses to Casablanca (6.30 am via Essaouira and 9.30 and 10.30 pm via Marrakesh); Essaouira (6.30 am, and 12.30, 1.45 and 6 pm); Marrakesh (6.30, 8 and 10.45 am); Tafraoute (1.30 pm), Tantan (5.30 am and 2 pm via Goulimime); Taroudannt (6, 6.30 and 9.45 am, and 2.30 and 5.30 pm); Tata (6 am via Taroudannt); and Tiznit (5.30 am, and 1 and 2 pm).

AROUND AGADIR

If you're looking for less crowded beaches than those at Agadir, and for fellow independent travellers (most with their own transport), then head north of Agadir. There are beautiful sandy coves every few km.

Most of the beaches closer to Agadir have been colonised by Europeans who have built their winter villas here. Further north this gives way to a sea of campervans, but by the time you are 20 to 25 km north of Agadir you might find something resembling space and even peace and quiet.

The main villages along this part of the coast until you get to Cap Rhir are Tamrhakht, Tarhazoute and Amesnaz.

Taroudannt

Taroudannt, with its magnificent and extremely well-preserved red mud walls, has played an important part in the history of Morocco. As far back as 1056, it was overrun by the Almoravids at the beginning of their conquest of Morocco. It played only a peripheral role in the years which followed until, in the 16th century, it was made the capital of the Saadians. This dynasty was responsible for the construction of the old part of town and the kasbah; most of the rest dates from the 18th century.

The Saadians eventually moved on to Marrakesh, but not before the fertile Sous valley in which the city stands had been developed into the country's most important producer of sugar cane, cotton, rice and indigo – valuable items of trade along the trans-Saharan caravan routes.

The city narrowly escaped destruction in 1687 at the hands of Moulay Ismail, after it became the centre of a rebellion opposing his rule. Instead, Moulay Ismail contented himself with a massacre of its inhabitants. It regained some of its former prominence when Moulay Abdallah was proclaimed sultan here at the end of the following century. It was to remain a centre of intrigue and sedition against the central government throughout much of the 19th century though, by then, its importance in the overall scheme of things had begun to decline rapidly.

Unlike many Moroccan towns of its size and importance, Taroudannt was never chosen as a French administrative or military centre; consequently, there is no 'European' quarter of wide boulevards and modern buildings tacked onto the original city. It still has a very Moroccan feel to it but, because of its proximity to Agadir, it pulls in the package tourists by the bus-load. During the day they inundate the Place Assarag but, if you stick around until they go (none of them ever stay here), peace descends and it's a very pleasant place to stay.

Inevitably, due to the tourist influx, touts are everywhere, but the souk here is so small (about the size of a hotel complex) that this is just total overkill. By no stretch of the imagination does anyone need a 'guide'.

Information

Most of the city's hotels, banks and the bus terminals are grouped around the Place Assarag, though there are other hotels outside this area.

Ramparts

You can explore the ramparts of Taroudannt on foot, but it is better to hire a bicycle or engage one of the horse-and-cart drivers who hang out just inside the main entrance (see map). It's a long way round the walls!

Souk

The souk at Taroudannt is relatively small. However, the items for sale are of a high quality and feature limestone carvings and traditional Berber jewellery – the town is populated mainly by Chleuh Berbers. This jewellery has been influenced by the tribes of the Sahara as well as the Jews; the latter were a significant part of the community until the late 1960s.

Tanneries

There are tanneries here similar to the ones at Fès, though smaller. You get to them by following the main street out of Place Assarag (on the opposite side from the bank) and continuing down until you reach the ramparts. Turn left as you come out of the gate, continue for about 100 metres and then take the first right. Let your nose guide you from there.

Most of the skins (which you can buy) are from sheep and cattle, but the tanneries also cater for those who couldn't care less about the extermination of wildlife.

Places to Stay – bottom end

Most travellers like to stay as close to the centre of activity as possible, and in Taroudannt you can do this without paying a lot of money. There are many hotels around or close to Place Assarag.

One of the cheapest is the *Hotel de la Place*, which is pleasant and clean, though basic; the owner is friendly and eager to please. A rooftop double overlooking the square costs Dr 40. Hot showers are avail-

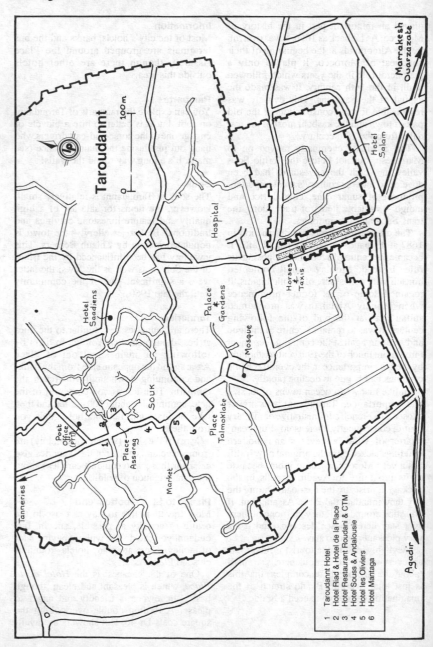

Taroudannt

100m

Marrakesh
Ouarzazate

Hotel Salam

Hospital

Horses
Taxis

Palace
Gardens

Mosque

Hotel Saadiens

Souk

Post
Office
(PTT)

Place
Assarag

Place
Talmoklate

Market

Tanneries

Agadir

1 Taroudant Hotel
2 Hotel Riad & Hotel de la Place
3 Hotel Restaurant Roudani & CTM
4 Hotel Souss & Andalousie
5 Hotel les Oliviers
6 Hotel Mantaga

able at certain times of day. Next door is the *Hotel Restaurant Roudani*. There are good views from the upper terrace but, unlike the rooms on the lower floor, the rooms up here don't have their own showers. This hotel is very clean and the staff are friendly. Doubles without own shower cost Dr 30 and singles/doubles with own shower cost Dr 30/60. Hot water is available in the evenings and mornings, but the tank is small so don't leave it too late.

Three other basic but clean places worth considering just off the Place Assarag are the *Hotel Souss* (which has its own restaurant), the *Hotel Andalousie* and the *Hotel les Oliviers*. There's not much to chose between them and you're looking at Dr 20/30 for singles/doubles with shared bathroom. Hot showers at the Souss cost Dr 4 extra. Even more primitive is the *Hotel Essabah*, just off the square in the opposite direction, which has rooms with two beds for Dr 30 without handbasin or table and chair, and communal cold showers and toilets. The *Hotel Liberté* is poor value at Dr 30/40 for singles/doubles since there are no showers whatsoever. Close by is the *Hotel Mantaga* which has singles/doubles for Dr 30/60 and hot showers in the evenings.

The best place of all to stay in this category is the *Taroudannt Hotel* (☎ 85 2416), Place Assarag. In atmosphere and appearance, it's almost as if this hostelry has been transplanted from some French medieval village and, in fact, it was owned and run until her recent death by an eccentric and garrulous French woman. The rooms here surround a quiet and leafy courtyard and are clean and homely. It's a one-star hotel so the rooms cost Dr 80/95/125 for singles/doubles/triples with own bathroom and very hot water in the evenings. The staff are friendly and eager to talk, there's a bar (normal prices) and you can get a four-course meal of some of the best food in Morocco in the restaurant for Dr 61.

Places to Stay – middle

The only mid-range hotel in Taroudannt is the two-star *Hotel Saadiens* (☎ 85 2589), Borj Annassim, which offers bed and breakfast for Dr 139/178 or dinner, bed and breakfast for Dr 200/300 for singles/doubles, plus taxes. The rooms, which have their own bathroom with hot water in the evenings (though usually none in the mornings), overlook an internal courtyard complete with swimming pool. There's a roof-top restaurant with reasonable food and slow service but there's no bar. Locked parking is available. The staff try hard and the rooms are comfortable, but it's hard to escape the feeling of being inside a concrete box.

Places to Stay – top end

The cheapest of the top-end hotels is the four-star *Hotel Salam* (☎ 85 2312), right on the ramparts near the town's main roundabout. It has its own gardens, swimming pool, tennis courts, bar and restaurant and guarded parking and costs Dr 280/358 for singles/doubles, plus taxes.

Top of the line is the *Hotel La Gazelle d'Or* (☎ 85 2039), which was originally a French nobleman's hunting lodge. It consists of 30 bungalows (each with their own open fireplace) set in extensive gardens and there are all the usual amenities you would expect of a five-star hotel including swimming pool, tennis courts and even horse riding. Advance booking is recommended.

Places to Eat

There are quite a few small cafés along the main street just before you get to Place Assarag where you can get traditional food like tajine, salads and soups. Included among these small cafés are several fish restaurants where you can get seafood at rock-bottom prices.

Also very good are the restaurants on the ground floors of the *Hotel de la Place* (couscous with chicken for Dr 20 or with mutton or beef for Dr 25) and the slightly more expensive *Hotel Restaurant Roudani*. If there are tour groups visiting Taroudannt, however, you can forget about the Roudani at lunch times as that's where they all go to sip tea or coffee and it's hard to get a table.

Don't forget the restaurant at the *Tar-*

oudannt Hotel for a minor splurge and excellent, tasty, French-Moroccan food.

Getting There & Away

All the bus companies have their terminals on the Place Assarag. CTM has only their buses to Paris posted up on the timetable. SATAS run to Agadir (5.30, 10 and 11 am, and 2 and 5.30 pm) and Marrakesh (4 am via Tizi-n-Test Pass and 5 am via Agadir). ATM (2nd-class) runs to Agadir and Casablanca at 5.20 pm. The fare to Agadir is Dr 13.75.

AROUND TAROUDANNT
Tizi-n-Test Pass

The road between Taroudannt and Marrakesh goes over the spectacular Tizi-n-Test Pass – one of the highest in Morocco. It's a good road all the way, though it twists and turns endlessly and, in some places, is hair-raising. The views from many points are magnificent. If you can't arrange a lift with tourists, SATAS has buses daily at 4 am which arrive in Marrakesh at around 2 pm. If you take this bus you'll start going up the pass around dawn. Towards the end of the journey the road passes Asni, which is the starting point for treks up Mt Toubkal, the highest mountain in North Africa.

Essaouira

Essaouira is the most popular of the coastal towns with independent travellers, and only rarely do you see package tourists here. The town has a magnificent beach which curves for miles to the south, and its atmosphere is in complete contrast to the souk cities of Marrakesh, Fès, Meknès and Tangier. It can be summed up in one word: relaxation.

Essaouira was founded in the 16th century by the Portuguese, who continued to occupy it until the mid-18th century, when the trans-Saharan trade routes fell apart. The present town dates from 1765, when Sultan Sidi Mohammed ben Abdallah re-established it to serve as a fortress town and base from which to suppress a revolt at Agadir. The fortifica-

tions are thus an interesting mixture of Portuguese and Berber military architecture, though the walls around the town date mainly from ben Abdallah's time. They're certainly very impressive and their massiveness lends a powerful mystique to the town; yet inside the walls it's all light and charm. You'll find narrow, freshly whitewashed streets, painted blinds, tranquil squares, artisans in tiny workshops beavering away at fragrant thuya wood, friendly cafés – and there's not a hustler in sight. It's one of the few places in Morocco where you feel that local people aren't thinking of you as a tourist, with everything that this normally implies elsewhere.

Information

There is a tourist office in the square between Place Prince Moulay Hassan and the fishing harbour, but I've never ever seen it open.

The banks are all clustered around the Place Prince Moulay Hassan.

Museum

This is on Rue Laalouj, and has displays of jewellery, costumes and weapons. Given the history of this town it could be better. It's open daily except Tuesday from 8.30 am to noon and 2 to 6 pm; entry is Dr 10.

Ramparts

You can walk along most of the ramparts on the seaward part of town and visit the two main forts *(skalas)* during daylight hours. The Skala du Port, however, is locked at lunch times plus there's an entry charge of Dr 10. The Skala de la Ville is particularly impressive, with its collection of 18th and 19th-century brass cannon from various European countries. There's no entry charge to this part.

Just off the coast to the south-west is the Ile de Mogador, on which there's another massive fortification. It's actually two islets; they were known as far back as Phoenician and Roman times, when they served as an entrepôt for Mediterranean merchants and were known as the Isles Purpuraires on account of the purple dye, much favoured by

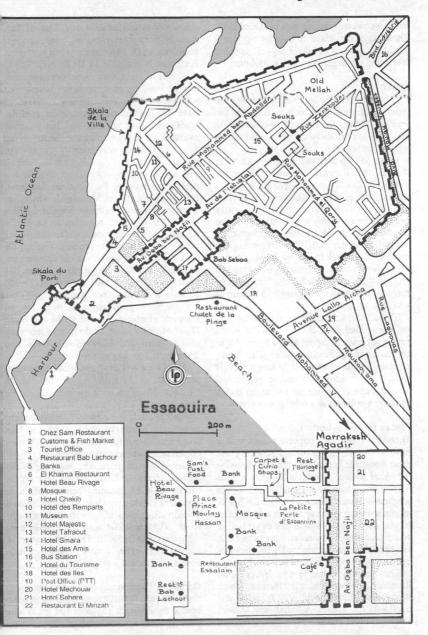

Essaouira

0   200 m

1   Chez Sam Restaurant
2   Customs & Fish Market
3   Tourist Office
4   Restaurant Bab Lachour
5   Banks
6   El Khaima Restaurant
7   Hotel Beau Rivage
8   Mosque
9   Hotel Chakib
10   Hotel des Remparts
11   Museum
12   Hotel Majestic
13   Hotel Tafraout
14   Hotel Smara
15   Hotel des Amis
16   Bus Station
17   Hotel du Tourisme
18   Hotel des Iles
19   Post Office (PTT)
20   Hotel Mechouar
21   Hotel Sahara
22   Restaurant El Minzah

Roman emperors, which was obtained here. These days the island is a sanctuary for a particular species of falcon as well as other birds, and visits are normally prohibited.

Beach

The beach stretches some 10 km down the coast to the sand dunes of Cap Sim. On the way you'll pass the ruins of an old fortress and pavilion partially covered in sand, as well as the wreck of a ship.

Close to Cap Sim and inland about a km through sand dunes and scrub is the Berber village of Diabat, which became a legend among hippies in the 1960s as the result of a visit by Jimi Hendrix. It subsequently became a freak colony similar to those on the beaches of Goa in India, but was cleared by the police in the mid-1970s following the murder of several freaks by local junkies. These days it has returned to its own tranquil self and there's a simple hotel where you can stay for Dr 75 – as many people to a room as you like.

There's still a campsite some three km past the village and parallel to the sea but you'd need your own transport to get there. Adjacent to the campsite is the *Auberge Tangaro*, a small but attractive place to stay which is usually empty during the week. If you intend staying there take your own food, as meals are only available, as a rule, at weekends.

Places to Stay – bottom end

There are three very popular places where travellers stay. The first, and probably the most attractive because of the sea views, is the *Hotel Smara*, Rue de la Skala, which is very quiet, clean and friendly and offers singles/doubles/triples for Dr 39/52/62. The rooms with sea views are much sought after so you may have to wait a day or so before you can get one. Showers cost an extra Dr 2, and breakfast is available for Dr 10. Bicycles can also be hired at the hotel.

The second place is the *Hotel Beau Rivage*, Place Prince Moulay Hassan, which is excellent value, clean, very friendly, and overlooks the square. A brand new shower and toilet block has just been completed and

hot water is available at any time of day. Rooms here cost Dr 39/52 for singles/doubles plus Dr 28 for an extra bed in a room. Breakfast is available for Dr 8.

The third place is the *Hotel des Remparts*, a huge building on three floors with a vast roof terrace. Unfortunately, few of the rooms have sea views. Singles/doubles cost Dr 50/60 with own shower, and hot water is available from 4 pm to 11 am the following day. The staff are very friendly and keen to please.

Another place where you can find a reasonable room is the *Hotel du Tourisme*, Rue Mohammed ben Massaoud, which has a range of rooms available. Singles/doubles cost Dr 20/40, there are triples for Dr 40, Dr 45 and Dr 50, and rooms which sleep four people and five people are available for Dr 65 and Dr 80 respectively. Cold showers are available. The *Hotel des Amis*, likewise, has a whole range of rooms from singles (Dr 30) to those which sleep five people (Dr 50) but it's not such good value as there are no showers available. The very old and basic *Hotel Majestic*, Rue Laalouj, also has very cheap rooms and, although it's clean and friendly, it, too, has no showers.

Also cheap and clean and with large rooms for Dr 40 is the *Hotel Agadir* on Ave de l'Istiqlal. Hot showers are available here for Dr 3 extra.

Further afield is the *Hotel Chakib*, a fairly pleasant modern hotel, which has singles/doubles/triples for Dr 30/50/70 with communal bathroom (cold water only).

Going up in price, the one-star *Hotel Tafraout* (☎ 47 2120), 7 Rue de Marrakech, off the Rue Mohammed ben Abdallah, is excellent value, very clean, comfortable and friendly. Singles/doubles without own bathroom cost Dr 45/64 and those with own bathroom cost Dr 58/70. There's hot water in the showers. The 'double' rooms contain both a double and a single bed.

Camping The best campsite is the one about three km past the village of Diabat and adjacent to the Auberge Tangaro. You get to it by driving about six km south of Essaouira on the Agadir road and then turning off to the right. It should be signposted (if the sign hasn't disappeared). You will need your own transport to get there.

Otherwise there is the *Camping Municipal*, just off the Blvd Mohammed V, but it's nothing but a patch of dirt with no shade whatsoever. You'd have to be desperate to stay here.

Places to Stay – middle

A good place in this category is the two-star *Hotel Sahara* (☎ 47 2292), Ave Oqba ben Nafii, which has large, airy, self-contained rooms (including hot water) for Dr 96/120 for singles/doubles. Many of the rooms contain two double beds or a double and a single bed. It's a very quiet place and breakfast is available. There's no bar and the restaurant functions only in the high season. Next door is the *Hotel Mechouar*, something of a strange place where few people seem to stay. It has doubles with own shower for Dr 80 but there's only cold water. If you want a hot shower, you have to use communal facilities.

Going up in price, there's the three-star *Hotel Tafoukt* (☎ 47 2504), 98 Blvd Mohammed V, which has self-contained singles/doubles for Dr 179/220 but which is much too far from the centre of things to be an attractive proposition, unless the only thing you're interested in is the beach itself. There's a restaurant but no bar.

Places to Stay – top end

The four-star *Hotel des Iles* (☎ 47 2329) on Blvd Mohammed V is currently the only top-end hotel in town, though another is under construction next to the Provincial headquarters and will be known as the *Mogador Palace Hotel*. Rooms at the Hotel des Iles cost Dr 280/358 plus taxes for singles/doubles, and there's a restaurant, bar and nightclub.

Places to Eat

There are quite a few small Moroccan-style restaurants which offer good, tasty food and where you can eat well for around Dr 15. For this you get bread, a salad, tajine or kefta and chips. All these little places display what they have for sale in the front window. There's a cluster of them about three-quarters of the way up Rue Mohammed ben Abdallah, walking away from Place Prince Moulay Hassan, where the road begins to narrow. There are others in the narrow street and small square between the mosque on Place Prince Moulay Hassan and the ramparts which flank Ave Oqba ben Nafii. They include the *Restaurant de la Place* and the *Restaurant l'Horloge*. The latter is a popular hang-out with travellers.

Also popular is the *Restaurant Essalam*, on Place Prince Moulay Hassan where you can pick up an excellent four-course meal for around Dr 35. Right opposite is a small café which is run by very friendly, English-speaking people.

For a splurge, there's a choice of five restaurants. *La Petite Perle d'Essaouira* is a fairly new restaurant and has a superbly intimate Berber atmosphere, but you need to check your bill carefully as their imagination sometimes runs away with them. Examples of prices here include salads (Dr 15), couscous/tajine (Dr 25 to Dr 30) and omelettes (Dr 12 to Dr 15). They take most major credit cards.

Also good, but with more formal atmospheres, are the *El Khaima Restaurant*, Rue Laalouj, a large new place where you can get four-course meals for Dr 60, grilled fish for Dr 35 to Dr 40 and other à la carte dishes, and the *Restaurant El Minzah*, Ave Oqba ben Nafii. The Minzah offers seafood, couscous, steaks and spaghetti as well as three-course meals for Dr 42, and four-course meals for Dr 52.

Popular for years, and famous throughout Morocco, is *Chez Sam Restaurant*, at the far end of the port area past the boat builders. The building which houses the restaurant looks like it's been transported from some windswept cove on the coast of Cornwall or Brittany and it has a delightfully eccentric atmosphere. It specialises in seafood and the cuisine is excellent. You can either eat à la carte or take one of the set menus, of which there are two – Dr 62 or Dr 140. It's open daily from 11 am to 3 pm and 7.30 to 11 pm. The restaurant is licensed (beer and wine) and takes most major credit cards. Don't leave Essaouira without having a meal here.

Back on the Place Prince Moulay Hassan is the *Restaurant Bab Lachour*, which also specialises in seafood. It's probably as good as Chez Sam plus the salads are excellent. A four-course meal here costs Dr 61, and wine is available (but not beer). However, you need to think twice before ordering wine as they charge Dr 70 for a bottle which would cost around Dr 30 in a store.

Finally, there's the *Restaurant Chalet de la Plage*, right on the beach, just outside the city walls. It offers four-course meals for Dr 70 (extra for cheese, tea and coffee) but it seems to cater mostly for package tour buses.

Entertainment

The Hotel Beau Rivage, with its outdoor tables and chairs, is a very popular place to sit and have coffee or mint tea. You can watch the world go by at any time but particularly in the evening. It's frequented by both visitors and local people.

If you're looking for a bar, there's not much choice. There's one at the Chalet de la Plage, but they may not be keen on you drinking there unless you buy a meal. Otherwise, there's the bar at the Hotel des Iles, and you don't have to be a resident to drink there.

The only nightclub in town is at the Hotel des Iles.

Things to Buy

Essaouira is a centre for thuya carving, and the quality of the work is superb. Most of the carvers have workshops under the Skala de la Ville and they're very laid back, so you can walk around and look at what they are doing without any pressure to buy. It's unlikely that you won't want to buy something but, because there's no pressure, don't expect to be able to reduce their stated prices by anything but a small fraction. Nevertheless, you won't find this sort of craftwork cheaper anywhere else in Morocco.

There are also quite a few craft shops with an equally impressive range of goods in the immediate vicinity. Interesting chess pieces are the only thing you won't find here; although they are made in Essaouira, most are very plain indeed.

Carpet and rug shops, as well as bric-a-brac, jewellery and brassware shops, are clustered together in the narrow street and the small square between Place Prince Moulay Hassan and the ramparts which flank the Ave Oqba ben Nafii.

Getting There & Away

The bus terminal is just outside the city walls at the north-eastern end of town and is a good 10 minutes' walk from the Place Prince Moulay Hassan. There are regular departures to Agadir, Marrakesh and Safi with CTM and other private companies.

Marrakesh

There can be few travellers who have not heard of Marrakesh. During the 1960s and 1970s it was the travellers' mecca, along with Istanbul, Kabul and Kathmandu – and rightly so! This turn in the fame and fortunes of Marrakesh is only the most recent of the Scheherazadian sagas which this city has experienced.

Sitting against a backdrop of Morocco's highest mountains which are snowcapped for much of the year, the city has a scenic setting that is hard to surpass.

History

Once one of the most important artistic and cultural centres in the Islamic world, Marrakesh was founded in 1062 AD by the Almoravid sultan Youssef Ibn Tachfin. It experienced its heyday under Youssef's son, Ali, who was born to a Christian slave mother. It was Ali who was responsible for constructing the extensive underground irrigation canals (the *khettara*), which still supply the city's gardens with water. Later, as a result of the Almoravid conquest of Spain, Fès became more prominent; yet

Marrakesh remained the southern capital, and much of the wealth which flowed to the kingdom was lavished on extending and beautifying the city.

The city was razed by the Almohads in 1147, though the walls and the gateway to Ali's huge palace were spared. It was rebuilt shortly afterwards in the Omayyad style and became the capital of the Almohad Empire until its collapse in 1269. For the next 300 years the focus of Moroccan brilliance in the arts was Fès, but, following the rise to power of the Saadians in the 16th century, Marrakesh once again became the capital of the empire after a brief period during which Taroudannt enjoyed that honour. The Saadian takeover of the city had been preceded by hard times. Even the Portuguese had made a vain attempt to capture Marrakesh in 1515, and in the following years there had been famines which reduced activity in the city and surrounding countryside to a low level.

Saadian control brought prosperity once again. During their reign the Portuguese were forced to abandon all their coastal enclaves with the sole exception of El Jadida. The mellah, the huge mosque of el-Mouassine and the mosque of Ben Youssef with its adjacent medersa were all built in these times. The Saadians also set up a customs house for the Christian colony which had been established in Marrakesh. The el-Badi Palace, constructed using Muslim-Spanish designs and techniques, was also a creation of the later Saadian sultans.

In time, decadence set in and Morocco was taken over by the Alaouites, who made Meknès their capital. Marrakesh could not be ignored, however. Although Moulay Ismail was responsible for tearing apart the el-Badi Palace for building materials, his successor, Sidi Mohammed ben Abdallah, poured resources into rebuilding or restoring the walls, the kasbah, the palaces, mosques and mechouars of the city as well as creating new gardens (such as the Menara Gardens).

By the 19th century, Marrakesh was again on the decline, though it did regain some of its former prestige when Moulay Hassan was crowned there in 1873. Its most recent return to fame and fortune is largely the result of French activities during the protectorate period, when the ville nouvelle was built, the medina was revitalised and resettled, and the Place Foucauld was created below the Djemaa el Fna. Increasing tourism in Marrakesh since then has ensured it's continued prosperity.

Its days as a magnet for hippies in the 1960s and early 1970s have long since passed, though a few survivors of this endangered species still find their way here. The focus now is on more affluent travellers and package tourists and this has had a major impact on the atmosphere and the attitude of local people to visitors. Not all these changes have been beneficial as far as travellers are concerned, but it's unlikely that the craft guilds in the souks are complaining. Business is booming as never before.

Orientation

As in Fès and Meknès, the old city and the ville nouvelle of Marrakesh are about the same size; you'll find it convenient to use public transport to get from one to the other.

The main thoroughfare connecting the two is Ave Mohammed V. Along this road in the ville nouvelle is the main post office, the tourist office and, on or just off it, many of the mid-range and top-end hotels. The railway station lies to the west of Ave Mohammed V along Ave Hassan II, which joins the former at Place du 16 Novembre.

The heart of the old city is the Djemaa el Fna, a large, irregularly shaped square overlooked by the city's most prominent landmark, the Koutoubia. Most of the budget hotels are clustered in the narrow streets branching off the eastern and south-eastern sides of the square. The souks lie to the north of the Djemaa el Fna and the palaces to the south. The main bus station lies just outside the old city walls and is within 10 to 15 minutes' walk north-west of the Djemaa el Fna.

Information

Tourist Office This is at the junction of Ave

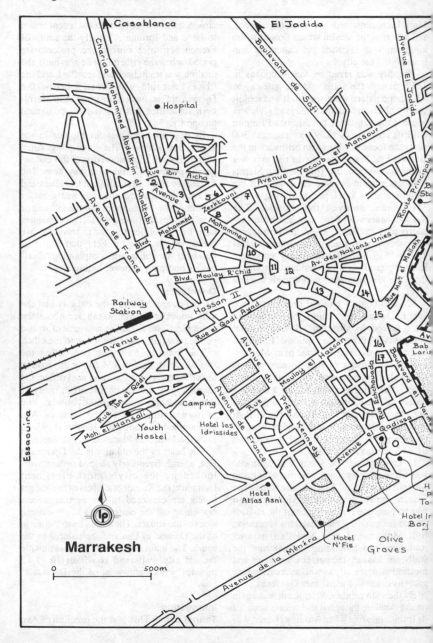

1	Hotel Agdal
2	Hotel Oasis
3	Hotel Mouatamid
4	Hotel Renaissance
5	Hotel Franco-Belge
6	Hotel al Bustan
7	Hotel Smara
8	Thomas Cook/Wagons Lits
9	Tourist Office
10	Voyages Schwarz (Amex)
11	Post Office (PTT)
12	Place du 16 Novembre
13	Hotel ibn Batouta
14	Hotel le Marrakech
15	Place de la Liberté
16	Hotel de la Menara
17	Hotel Imilchil
18	Hotel des Almoravides
19	Club Méditerranée
20	Djemaa el Fna
21	Koutoubia
22	Hotel Foucauld
23	Grand Hotel du Tazi
24	Hotel Chems
25	Hotel Mamounia
26	Kasbah Mosque & Saadian Tombs
27	Public Swimming Pool

Post Office The main post office is on Place du 16 Novembre in the ville nouvelle. There is a branch office on the Djemaa el Fna.

Foreign Consulates The French Consulate (☎ 44 1748) is at Dar Moulay Ali next to the Koutoubia.

Djemaa el Fna
The focal point of Marrakesh is the Djemaa el Fna, a huge square in the old part of town where many of the budget hotels are located. Other than the souks, this is where everything happens; visitors are destined to spend a lot of time here. Although it's a lively place at any time of day, it really comes into its own in the late afternoon and evening. There's no place quite like it anywhere else in Morocco.

Almost without warning, the curtain goes up on one of the world's most fascinating and bizarre spectacles. Rows and rows of open-air food stalls are set up and mouth-watering aromas quickly fill the square. Jugglers, storytellers, snake charmers, magicians, acrobats and benign lunatics quickly take

Mohammed V and Ave du Président Kennedy. They have the usual range of glossy leaflets and a list (without prices) of the classified hotels in Marrakesh, but precious little else. This is pretty pathetic in view of the city's position as a prime tourist destination.

Money The Banque du Maroc on the south side of the Djemaa el Fna next to the post office will not change travellers' cheques and will direct you elsewhere. The main banks are in the ville nouvelle.

The BMCE bank, opposite the tourist office, has a money exchange facility which is open daily, including Saturday, Sunday and public holidays, from 10 am to 2 pm and 4 to 8 pm.

American Express is represented by Voyages Schwartz (☎ 43 3321), Immeuble Moutaouakil, 1 Rue Mauritania. Thomas Cook/Wagons Lits (☎ 43 1687) is at 122 Ave Mohammed V.

Snake charmer

over the rest of the space, each of them surrounded by an audience of jostling spectators who listen or watch intently and then fall about laughing. In the meantime, assistants hassle them for contributions. In between the groups weave hustlers, thieves, knick-knack sellers and bewildered tourists. And, on the outer edges, kerosene lanterns ablaze, are the fruit and juice stalls.

Overlooking one end of the square are the huge, eerily-lit Berber tents on the terrace of the Club Med hotel; you will occasionally hear snatches of folk music being played for the well-heeled up there. Down below the medieval pageant presents its nightly cornucopia of delights; Brueghel would have had a field day here!

Souks

Just as the Djemaa el Fna is justifiably famous for its energy and life, the souks of Marrakesh are some of the best in Morocco, producing a wide variety of high quality crafts as well as trash (for the unwary or just plain stupid). The streets here are just as labyrinthine as those in Fès and every bit as busy. There is a difference, however: it's a long time since *Marrakesh Express* was written but it sure as hell put the place in the limelight.

There is no way you can get within even sniffing distance of any of the entrances to the medina these days without being besieged by 'guides'. And there is no way you can shake them off – they'll pursue you every inch of the way. Not only that, shake one off, and there will be another there within seconds.

Until your face gets familiar, attempting to go to the medina without a 'guide' is a total waste of time and extremely frustrating. Forget trying and take a guide. Just remember that the only thing they are basically interested in is the commission they make by getting you to buy things in the shops. Some are better than others, of course, but that's the bottom line.

The tourist blurb raves benignly to the effect that 'merchants sit cross-legged on heaps of merchandise, a fan waving indo-

lently in the hand'. Nothing could be further from the truth. You are about to confront high-pressure sales tactics, high prices and contempt bordering on abuse if you refuse to buy anything or baulk at the quoted prices. Never spend a lot of time in any one shop unless you are seriously interested in the merchandise, otherwise you may well be in for a traumatic experience. Almost every one of the shops in the souks here have stickers displaying the fact that they will accept American Express, Diners Club, Visa, MasterCard and many other more obscure credit cards. This is *not* Fès! It's more like Barter Town in *Mad Max Beyond Thunderdome*!

Never believe a word you are told about anything relating to silver, gold or amber. The gold and silver are always plated, never solid, and the amber is plastic (put a lighted match to it and smell it). Anything claimed to be 'authentic', 'tribal' or 'antique' is generally nothing of the sort. Techniques for ageing anything whatsoever are well known here. Thousands, perhaps hundreds of thousands, of tourists are conned here every year and waste their money on trash.

Having said that, there are, of course, some things which can't be faked such as brass plates, leatherwork, woodwork and, up to a point, carpets. There are, also, some merchants who do offer genuine jewellery, though they take some finding.

So why has it got to this state of affairs? The simple answer is package tourism. When you see the tightly knit groups of well-heeled tourists from the Club Med and other top-end hotels being escorted around the souks by official guides spouting a running commentary, then it's easy to understand why shopkeepers are only interested in the size of their wallets. Why treat you differently? Unless you spend some time there and visit a particular shop two or three times without buying anything, then the way they'll see things is that your first visit is the last so that's their only opportunity to sell you something.

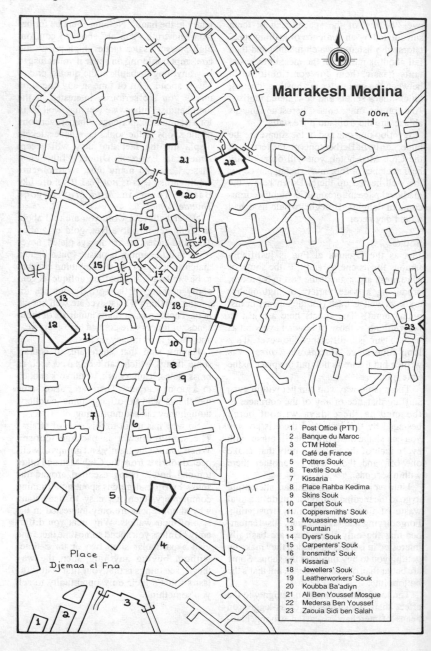

Marrakesh Medina

0   100m

1   Post Office (PTT)
2   Banque du Maroc
3   CTM Hotel
4   Café de France
5   Potters Souk
6   Textile Souk
7   Kissaria
8   Place Rahba Kedima
9   Skins Souk
10   Carpet Souk
11   Coppersmiths' Souk
12   Mouassine Mosque
13   Fountain
14   Dyers' Souk
15   Carpenters' Souk
16   Ironsmiths' Souk
17   Kissaria
18   Jewellers' Souk
19   Leatherworkers' Souk
20   Koubba Ba'adiyn
21   Ali Ben Youssef Mosque
22   Medersa Ben Youssef
23   Zaouia Sidi ben Salah

Place
Djemaa el Fna

Mosques & Medersas

Like their counterparts elsewhere in Morocco, the mosques and medersas in Marrakesh are generally closed to non-Muslims; this being so, a detailed description of them is largely pointless. And, as in Fès, the ones inside the medina are generally so hemmed in by other buildings that little can be seen from the outside.

Ali ben Youssef Mosque The largest of the mosques inside the medina is the Ali ben Youssef Mosque, first built in the second half of the 12th century by the Almoravid sultan of the same name. It's the oldest surviving mosque in Marrakesh. However, the building itself is of fairly recent date, as it was almost completely rebuilt in the 19th century in the Merenid style in response to popular demand. When first constructed it was about twice its present size but it was severely damaged when the Almoravids were overthrown by the Almohads. The Almohads restored it later on; the Saadians, too, had a hand in the restoration work. The mosque is closed to non-Muslims.

Medersa ben Youssef Adjacent to the Ali ben Youssef Mosque is the Medersa ben Youssef, the largest theological college in the Maghreb, built by the Saadians in 1565. There is accommodation here for more than 100 students and teachers. Of the annexes to the Ali ben Youssef Mosque only the Koubba Ba'adiyn survives, the fountain having disappeared during the last century when the kissaria was constructed. The koubba is said to be one of the finest examples of Maghrebi work in existence but was only rediscovered in 1947. This is one of the few religious buildings which foreigners are allowed to visit. Entry costs Dr 10.

Mouassine Mosque The other large mosque in the medina is the Mouassine Mosque, built in the 16th century by the Saadians on land formerly occupied by the Jewish community. Its most notable features are the three huge doorways and the intricately carved cedar ceilings. The fountain

Moroccan Koran holder

attached to this mosque still survives and is quite elaborate, with three sections – two for animals and one for humans. The mosque is closed to non-Muslims.

Ben Salah Mosque Of the other mosques in the medina, the Ben Salah Mosque (also known as the Zaouia ben Salah) is the most prominent; its brilliant green-tiled minaret can be seen from many places. It was built by the Merenid sultan, Abu Said Uthman, between 1318 and 1321. Again, it's closed to non-Muslims.

Koutoubia The only mosque whose perspective you can really get an idea of is the Koutoubia, across the other side of Place Foucauld from the Djemaa el Fna. It is also the tallest and most famous landmark in Marrakesh, being visible for miles in any direction. If any building characterises Marrakesh, this is it. It was constructed by the Almohads in the late 12th century and is the oldest and best preserved of their three most famous minarets – the other two being the Tour Hassan in Rabat and the Giralda in Seville (Spain). The Koutoubia minaret set the standard for future Moroccan architecture; its features are mirrored in many other minarets throughout the country, though nowhere else is there an attempt to reproduce its sheer size.

When first built, the Koutoubia was covered with painted plaster and brilliantly coloured tiles, but this has all now disappeared. What can still be seen, however, are the decorative panels, which are different on each face and which practically constitute a textbook of contemporary design. The views from the summit would be incredible, were it possible for non-Muslims to climb up there.

Palaces
Palais el-Badi The most famous of the palaces of Marrakesh was the el-Badi Palace, built by Ahmed el Mansour between 1578 and 1602. At the time of its construction it was reputed to be one of the most beautiful in the world; it included marble from Italy and other precious building materials from as far away as India. The enormous cost of building the palace came largely from the ransom which the Portuguese were forced to pay out following their disastrous defeat at the hands of the Saadians in 1578 in the Battle of the Three Kings (26,000 Portuguese, including the flower of the nobility, were killed or taken prisoner). Unfortunately, the palace is now largely a ruin, having been torn apart by Moulay Ismail in 1696 for materials with which to build his new capital at Meknès.

What remains today is essentially just a huge square surrounded by devastated mud walls enclosing a sunken orange grove and a number of modern concrete pools. If you're a dreamer or like ruins then the historical hyperbole which the tourist literature indulges in might strike a chord, and you'll feel your time and effort have been well spent. If not, you may well wonder why you bothered since there are far more interesting

and considerably more intact ruins elsewhere in Morocco. Judge for yourself. It's open to the public daily, except on certain religious holidays, between 8.30 am and noon and 2.30 to 6 pm. Entry costs Dr 10. You're free to wander around on your own though guides will initially hassle you to engage their services. The palace is also the venue for the annual Folklore Festival, usually held in May.

The easiest way to get to the el-Badi Palace is to take Ave Houmane el Fetouaki down from the Koutoubia to where the ramparts begin and where there's a large gateway. Go through this and turn to the right. There's usually a number of tour buses parked outside.

Palais de la Bahia The Palais de la Bahia dates from the reign of Sidi Mohammed II, when it was built as the residence of the Grand Vizier, Si'Musa. It was added to in the late 19th century by Moulay Hassan and Abd el Aziz. It's a rambling structure with fountains, living quarters, pleasure gardens and numerous secluded, shady courtyards, but it lacks architectural cohesiveness. The palace was ransacked by the sultan in 1900 and left to rot, but has been partially restored in recent years. It's open daily, except on certain religious holidays, from 9.30 am to 1 pm (11.45 am in winter) and 4 to 7 pm (2.30 to 6 pm in winter). Entry costs Dr 10, and you must take a guide, who will expect a tip at the end.

Dar Si Said The other palace which is definitely worth a visit is the Dar Si Said, which these days is the Museum of Moroccan Arts. It was built towards the end of the 19th century by Sidi Said, Moulay Hassan's Grand Vizier, as his town house. The museum houses one of the finest collections in the country, including jewellery from the High Atlas, the Anti-Atlas and the extreme south; carpets from the Haouz and the High Atlas; oil lamps from Taroudannt; blue pottery from Safi and green pottery from Tamegroute; leatherwork from Marrakesh; and many other art objects from various epochs. It also has an extensive display of Berber muskets, pistols and daggers. It's open from 9 am to noon and 4 to 7 pm (2.30 to 6 pm in winter); closed Tuesday. Entry costs Dr 10.

Saadian Tombs

Adjacent to the Kasbah Mosque is the necropolis begun by the Saadian sultan Ahmed el Mansour, who also built the el-Badi Palace. Unlike the palace, however, the tombs escaped Moulay Ismail's depredations – possibly because he was superstitious about plundering the dead. Instead, he sealed the tombs and, as a result, even though they are partially in ruins, they convey some of the opulence and superb artistry which must have been lavished on the palace. Sixty-six of the Saadians, including el Mansour, his successors and their closest family members, lie buried under the two main structures, and over 100 more outside them. The tombs – particularly the so-called 'Chamber of the Twelve Columns' – display a fine balance between brilliantly coloured and plain surfaces which is hard to match anywhere else (though the style was obviously influenced by that of the Alhambra in Spain).

Though the mad sultan, Moulay Yazid, was also laid to rest here in 1792, the tombs essentially remained sealed following Moulay Ismail's reign. They were not 'rediscovered' until 1917, when General Lyautey, his curiosity awakened by an aerial survey undertaken of the area, ordered the construction of a passageway to them. Since then they have been restored and are now open to the public every day, except Friday morning, from 8 am to noon and 2 to 7 pm (6 pm in winter). Entry costs Dr 10 and you're allowed to wander around at will, though, if you prefer, a guardian will accompany you and explain what you are looking at. You will be expected to offer a tip at the end.

To get to the tombs, take Rue de Bab Agnaou to the Bab Agnaou itself (the only surviving Almohad gateway in Marrakesh), which is on the left and almost adjacent to the Bab er Rob (outside which there is a dirt patch which serves as the terminus for local buses and taxis to Ourika and other nearby destinations). Go through the Bab Agnaou and walk straight on past a row of shops until you come to the Kasbah Mosque. Turn right here down Rue de la Kasbah and, when you get to the end of the mosque, you'll see a narrow alleyway on the left. Go down it, and the entrance to the tombs is at the end.

Festivals

If you're in Marrakesh in June, enquire about the Festival of Folklore which is held in the Palais el-Badi at that time. It's essentially a festival of folk dancing and singing, which is performed by some of the best troupes in Morocco. In July, there's the famous Fantasia, pictures of which you'll often see in the tourist literature. This is the charge of the Berber horsemen, which takes place outside the ramparts.

Places to Stay – bottom end

The cheapest deals in accommodation are found in the area immediately south of the Djemaa el Fna and east of the Rue de Bab where there are scores of reasonably priced hotels. There's not a lot to choose between most of them, other than whether they offer hot showers or not (not important in summer but definitely so in winter) and the effort which is made to create atmosphere and keep the place clean. Most of the cheapies will charge extra for hot showers (usually Dr 5) and some even charge for cold showers (Dr 2). Prices vary little and are usually Dr 30 a single, Dr 50 a double and Dr 70 to Dr 75 a triple. In summer, most of them hike up their prices according to demand, which means that you could end up paying more in these places than you would for a better room in a classified (and, therefore, price-controlled) hotel.

Personally, I think most of these hotels are cashing in on a fading legend, especially in the high seasons, and that their prices don't adequately reflect the facilities which they offer. This applies to the rooms at the *Hotel de France* (☎ 44 3067) which is right on the Djemaa el Fna and has an excellent roof

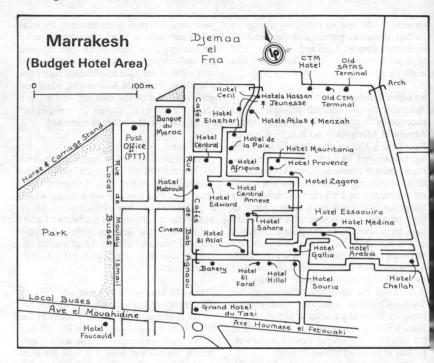

Marrakesh
(Budget Hotel Area)

0   100 m

Djemaa el Fna

Horse & Carriage Stand

Rue de Moulay Ismail

Local Buses

Park

Post Office (PTT)

Banque du Maroc

Hotel Mabrouk

Rue de Bab Agnaou

Cinema

Cafés

Cafés

Hotel Cecil

Hotels Hassan & Jeunesse

Hotel Elazhar

Hotel Central

Hotel de la Paix

Hotels Atlas & Menzah

Hotel Afriquia

Hotel Mauritania

Hotel Provence

Hotel Zagora

Hotel Central Annexe

Hotel Edward

Hotel Sahara

Hotel El Atlal

Hotel Essaouira

Hotel Medina

Hotel Gallia

Hotel Arabia

Bakery

Hotel El Faral

Hotel Hillal

Hotel Souria

Hotel Chellah

Grand Hotel du Tazi

Ave el Mouahidine

Ave. Houmane el Fetouaki

Hotel Foucauld

CTM Hotel

Old SATAS Terminal

Old CTM Terminal

Arch

Local Buses

terrace. But legends die hard and who doesn't want to stay within a stone's throw of the Djemaa el Fna?

Most of these budget hotels are marked on the detailed map of this area. Take your pick.

While researching this second edition I checked out almost all of these hotels and not one of them was offering hot showers, but other travellers have written in to say that some of them were offering hot showers for an extra Dr 5.

It's perhaps unfair to single out individual hotels for a recommendation, but some of them were better than others. In this category I'd put the Hotels *Central, Atlas, Cecil, Afriquia, Addekhla* and *Sahara* and I'd definitely avoid the *Hotel de Jeunesse* (which stank). Other people are bound to disagree.

If you don't mind paying a little extra in this same area then try the popular *CTM Hotel* (☎ 44 2325) right on the Djemaa el Fna. This one-star hotel has a range of rooms but, essentially, it costs Dr 50/65 for singles/doubles without own shower and Dr 93/109 for doubles/triples with own shower. There's hot water in the mornings. There's a large roof-top area, which is a great place to watch the activity below in the late afternoon. Get here early if you want a room as it fills up rapidly.

In the same area but not overlooking the Djemaa el Fna there are the two-star *Hotel Gallia* (☎ 44 5913), 90 Rue la Recette, and the *Grand Hotel du Tazi* (☎ 44 2152), on the corner of Ave el Mouahidine and Rue du Bab Agnaou. The Gallia is a small hotel and excellent value. It's spotlessly clean, has a quiet courtyard, a TV lounge and hot showers. Rooms here cost Dr 79/100 for singles/doubles with own shower but shared toilet, and Dr 96/120 with own shower and toilet. The Grand Hotel du Tazi is a much larger hotel but, perhaps, less desirable. Prices are the same as for the Gallia but it does have its own bar and restaurant.

In the same category is the *Hotel Foucauld* (☎ 44 5499), Ave el Mouahidine, diagonally opposite the Grand Hotel du Tazi, but I'd be reluctant to stay here because it's an extremely busy intersection and the traffic noise and fumes would deter even a 'greenie-basher'.

There are very few cheap hotels in the ville nouvelle. The cheapest is the one-star *Hotel Franco-Belge* (☎ 44 8472), 62 Blvd Zerktouni, close to the tourist office. Rooms cost Dr 62/78 for singles/doubles with shower but shared toilet and Dr 71/94 with shower and toilet. Another is the *Hotel Oasis* (☎ 44 7179), 50 Ave Mohammed V, which has singles/doubles with own shower and shared toilet for Dr 70/93 and Dr 89/106 with own shower and toilet.

At the two-star *Hotel Ali*, just behind the main post office, it's possible to sleep on the sheltered sun terrace for just Dr 25 including breakfast, and there's a room where you can lock up your gear.

Youth Hostel For the obsessed, there's a *Youth Hostel*, close to the railway station, which costs Dr 20 a night for a dormitory bed and, although it's clean and pleasant, it's much too far away from the action to be of much interest. Youth hostel hours are strictly maintained here.

Camping The campsite is close to the Youth Hostel, just off the Ave de France and so of little interest. The ground is stony and, although there's some shade, there's not that much of it. Camping costs Dr 10 per person (Dr 7.50 for children) plus Dr 8 for a car or Dr 22 for a bus/truck. Tents can be rented for Dr 11 and an electricity line for Dr 14.

Places to Stay – middle
Other than the two-star hotels mentioned previously, most of the mid-range and top-end hotels are to be found in the ville nouvelle. There are a lot of them, especially in the three and four-star category.

Close to the tourist office is the two-star *Hotel al Mouatimid* (☎ 44 8855), 94 Ave Mohammed V, which has singles/doubles with own shower and shared toilet for Dr 98/118 and Dr 123/146 with own shower and toilet. Cheaper, but further afield, is the *Hotel el Hamra*, 31 Ave Abdelkrim el Khattabi, which has singles/doubles with own shower but shared toilet for Dr 79/100 and Dr 96/120 with own shower and toilet.

Going up in price to the three-star range, but also close to the tourist office, are three hotels. Closest is the *Hotel Renaissance* (☎ 44 7998), 89 Ave Mohammed V, facing the roundabout, which has self-contained singles/doubles for Dr 155/194. The hotel also has its own (very popular) ground-floor and roof-top bar/restaurants. Close by along Blvd Mohammed Zerktouni going north-east are the *Hotel Smara* (☎ 43 4150) and *Hotel Boustare* (☎ 44 6810). Both have rooms for the same price as the Renaissance.

Almost next door to the Renaissance are two other, more expensive, three-star hotels, the *Hotel Tachfine* (☎ 44 7188), and the *Hotel Amalay* (☎ 43 1367). Both these hotels have self-contained singles/doubles for Dr 179/220. The Amalay has its own bar and restaurant but the Tachfine has neither.

Back on Ave Mohammed V, at No 279, is the two-star *Islane Hotel*. The rooms are spacious, and are centrally heated in winter. The charge is Dr 167 for a double with bath, and a good breakfast.

Also in this area but in the opposite direction is the *Hotel ibn Batouta* (☎ 47 4051), Ave Yacoub al Marini, which costs the same as the Amalay and Tachfine but has its own bar, restaurant and swimming pool.

Further afield and closer to the old city, an excellent place to stay is the *Hotel de la Menara* (☎ 44 7354), Ave des Remparts overlooking Place de la Liberté. The self-contained rooms are huge and they all have a balcony plus the hotel has its own bar, restaurant and swimming pool (though the prices in the bar and restaurant are definitely close to the bone). On the next corner is the *Hotel Imilchil* (☎ 43 4150), Ave Echouhada, which has similar facilities and the same prices. Both cost the same as the Amalay and Tachfine.

Places to Stay – top end

There are some 20 top-end hotels in Marrakesh, with more being built. Most of them are in the ville nouvelle but, if you'd prefer to be within striking distance of the Djemaa el Fna then stay either at the *Hotel Chems* (☎ 44 4813), Ave Houmane el Fetouaki, or the *Hotel des Almoravides* (☎ 44 5142), Arset Djnane Lkhdar. The former is a four-star B hotel with singles/doubles for Dr 234/292 plus taxes and the latter is a four-star A with singles/doubles for Dr 280/358 plus taxes. Both have all the amenities you would expect of such hotels, including swimming pool, tennis courts, bars and restaurants.

Most of the other top-range hotels are along the Ave de France and are all four or five-star hotels.

Places to Eat

There are cheap restaurants all around the Djemaa el Fna and along the Rue de Bab Agnaou which offer a mixture of Moroccan and European-style food. Many of them do their cooking on the pavement outside the café, so you can see what they have on offer. Some of the cooks and waiters can be very entertaining in at least five or six languages. Take your pick. There's not a lot to choose between them, though, naturally, you get what you pay for. The average cost of a meal is around Dr 15 to Dr 20.

In the evenings, between 5 and 9 pm, you can't beat eating at the food stalls in the Djemaa el Fna. There's an incredible range of food to choose from – tajine, kebabs, soup, fish and even chips – and you're looking at around Dr 10 for a meal. Just about half the city eats here in the evening.

If you'd prefer a normal sit-down meal in semicivilised surroundings in this area, then try a meal at either the *Grand Hotel du Tazi* (Dr 61 for the fixed menu) or the *Hotel Foucauld* (Dr 65 for the fixed menu). Also in this area is the *Hotel Islane*, on Ave Mohammed V opposite the Koutoubia, but expect to pay around double what you would at the Tazi or Foucauld.

In the ville nouvelle, there are many places where you can eat either cheaply (for not much more than in the old city), or expensively. Two places where you can pick up a reasonably cheap meal either at lunch or dinner times are the *Café Agdal* (Dr 38 for the set menu) or the *Hotel Oasis* (Dr 50 for the set menu). Both are on Ave Mohammed V just beyond the tourist office.

For an expensive meal, choose one of the restaurants attached to the multistar hotels in the area.

Entertainment

One of the most popular bars in the ville nouvelle is the roof-top Hotel Renaissance (which you have to take a lift up to). There's often a good crowd up here and you may well find yourself part of a group which subsequently goes off to a disco. The bar closes around 11 pm. Don't mistake this bar for the one on the ground floor.

If you want to party on, then many of the hotels in the ville nouvelle have nightclubs. As elsewhere in Morocco, the usual entry fee varies between Dr 50 and Dr 100 including the first drink. Most offer the predictable standard fare of Western disco music and cliques who appear to avoid eye contact like the plague, but there are a few exceptions. One of them is a nightclub in the street at the back of the Hotel Renaissance which caters to Moroccans. It kicks off around 11 pm with some of the best folk music you'll hear, which lasts for some two hours after which it's contemporary Moroccan pop music (largely ballads) mixed with normal disco music.

As far as normal discos go, two of the most popular are the Diamant Noir in the Hotel le Marrakech, on Place de la Liberté, and the Temple de la Musique in the Hotel N'Fis, at the junction of Ave de France and Ave de la Ménéra.

There are plenty of other distractions involving local tribal singing and dancing put on by various hotels and up-market restaurants which usually involve a meal, but they are far from cheap – you're looking at Dr 250 to Dr 300 per person. If you're interested, enquire at the tourist office – it's just about the only thing they know about.

Getting There & Away

Air There are five flights per week to Ouarzazate. The fare is Dr 185.

Bus Although CTM and SATAS still have garages on the Djemaa el Fna, the main bus station from which all buses (regardless of the company) leave is just outside the city walls at Bab Doukkala. This is a 20-minute walk or a Dr 8 taxi ride from the Djemaa el Fna.

Train The railway station is on Ave Hassan II and is a long way from the Djemaa el Fna. Take a taxi or bus into the centre.

The main departures from Marrakesh to Fès (via Casablanca, Rabat and Meknès) are: 1 am (change at Casa-Voyageurs), 7.38 am (change at Casa-Voyageurs), 9.08 am (change at Rabat), 2.15 pm (direct) and 5.10 and 6.41 pm (change at Casa-Voyageurs); it's 8¼ hours on the direct train.

Trains to Tangier (via Casablanca and Rabat) depart at: 1 am (change at Casa-Port), 7.38 am (change at Casa-Voyageurs & Sidi Kacem), and 7.41 pm (direct); the journey takes 10½ hours on the direct train.

Most of the changes that have to be made above involve very little waiting – an hour at most and, in some cases, much less.

Car Rental The addresses of the main companies are as follows:

Budget
    583 Blvd Mohammed V (☎ 43 4604)
Europcar/InterRent
    63 Blvd Zerktouni (☎ 43 1228)
Hertz
    154 Blvd Mohammed V (☎ 43 4680)
Nomade Car
    112 Blvd Mohammed V (☎ 43 1873)

Getting Around

To/From the Airport A petit taxi from Mar-
rakesh to the airport should be Dr 30 but you'll rarely get it for that price.

Bus & Taxi Local buses and grands taxis to the villages on the north side of Mt Toubkal, including Asni, leave when full from the Bab er Rob, a dirt patch on the north-east side of the medina. Petits taxis around town cost around Dr 8 per journey, but if you give them a Dr 10 note don't expect any change. From the railway station to the Djemaa el Fna the official fare is Dr 10 but you'll rarely get away with less than Dr 15.

Horse-Drawn Carriages Horse-drawn carriages are a feature of Marrakesh which you won't find in the other cities, but they're definitely a tourist attraction with prices to suit. I was frequently quoted Dr 100 to Dr 120 for a ride round the city – two hours, say. The cheapest I ever got was a one-way ride from Djemaa el Fna to the Place de la Liberté for Dr 20. If you're interested, they're based at the south-west side of the Djemaa el Fna.

AROUND MARRAKESH
Cascades d'Ouzoud

It's well worth a day trip to these waterfalls off the Marrakesh-Beni Mellal road. If you're driving, the waterfalls are signposted. Else take a bus to Beni Mellal and then another to Bin-el-Ouidane (where there's a dam and lake) or to Azilal a little further south. From here you'll have to hire a taxi. The road is paved all the way to the falls.

Near the falls there's a campsite and a hotel, though the hotel has no bedding, electricity or water (get water from the river or bottled from the stores). A room at the hotel costs Dr 30 a double and meals are available for Dr 20 to Dr 25. To get to the waterfall from the hotel, take the dirt road past the hotel on the right-hand side and keep going.

High Atlas Trekking

If you have good shoes/boots, plenty of warm clothes and a sleeping bag, it's well

worth trekking to the summit of Mt Toubkal (4165 metres), Morocco's highest mountain. It's a spectacularly beautiful area and, on clear days, there are incredible views in all directions, but especially south into the Sahara.

You don't need mountaineering skills to get to the top so long as you're going up the normal route from Imlil and staying at the Neltner Hut for the night, though there are one or two semidangerous patches of loose scree along the trail. You can do this trek in two days – up to the Neltner Hut the first day, then up to the summit and back down again the second.

The best time to go is during the months of April and May after most of the snow has melted and before it gets unbearably hot. In October the weather can be very unpredictable, even if there is no snow. You will not get to the summit of Toubkal after snow has fallen *unless you have full alpine gear*. Of course, unofficial guides will agree to take you, knowing full well that it's impossible.

The usual starting point for the trek is the village of Imlil, 17 km south of Asni on the Tizi-n-Test road from Marrakesh to Agadir. Other possible starting points are the villages of Setti Fatma and Oukaïmeden in the Ourika Valley, but you're looking at a longer trek starting from these places.

Trekkers intending to go to the summit of Mt Toubkal should be familiar with the symptoms of altitude sickness (AMS) and hypothermia. Both are dangers at this altitude.

Getting to Imlil

There are frequent buses to Asni from Marrakesh which leave from the Bab er Rob when full. They take two hours and cost Dr 8. Alternatively, you can take a shared taxi to Asni from the same place. These cost Dr 20 per person and take about one hour. From Asni there are fairly frequent trucks to Imlil and you can easily get a lift with them for around Dr 15. The journey takes about an hour and the road is fairly rough for much of the way, though, by the time you read this, it may be much improved as dozers and graders were working on it recently.

There are also taxis from Asni to Imlil but you'll have to negotiate a price as they could be stuck up there for hours waiting for a return fare.

Asni

There's not a great deal to do in Asni itself except on Saturdays when there's an excellent market here. It attracts coach loads of package tourists these days, but this has its advantages as you don't get hassled by touts.

If you want to stay the night at Asni there is a *Youth Hostel* which is basic but clean and friendly and costs Dr 20 per night. The only other place to stay is the *Grand Hotel du Toubkal* (☎ 3) which is a three-star hotel with singles/doubles for Dr 175/212 plus taxes. The hotel has its own bar, restaurant, swimming pool and guarded parking.

Imlil

Most trekkers give Asni a miss and stay here for the first night. A good place to stay is the *CAF (Club Alpin Français) Refuge* on the village square. It offers dormitory-style accommodation for Dr 10 (members), Dr 15 (YHA members) and Dr 20 (nonmembers), plus there's a common room with an open fireplace, cooking facilities (Dr 5 for use of gas), cutlery and crockery. The warden is a friendly man and does a good job looking after the place. You need a sleeping bag to stay here. If you're trekking in summer, this is where you should make bookings for the *gîtes* (huts) further up the mountain, otherwise you may find them full. Bookings can also be made through the Club Alpin Français (☎ 27 00 90), 1 Rue 6ème Henri, BP 6178, Casablanca-Bourgoune, or through CAF, BP 888, Marrakesh.

Another popular place to stay is the *Café Soleil* across the other side of the village square. It offers simple rooms without showers for Dr 30 to Dr 50. Meals can be bought here for around Dr 15 (tajine and bread) and you can store excess baggage for free. There's also a small shop where you can arrange basic equipment hire.

The other place to stay is the newly constructed *Hotel Etoile du Toubkal* which is very clean and offers rooms with own shower and hot water for Dr 100 (whether single or double). Meals are available for about twice the normal price – tajine/couscous for Dr 70 to Dr 80 and salads for Dr 15. They also do a full range of equipment hire and they *may* have detailed maps of the area for sale, but don't count on this.

There's a wide range of foodstuffs available in the shops in Imlil, including canned and packaged goods, mineral water, soft drinks, cigarettes, etc, but no beer. There's also a bakery. Stock up here before starting the trek as there's nothing for sale further up the mountain, though the warden at the Neltner Hut can usually cook up a tajine for you if given advance notice.

Guides

You don't need a guide if you're just doing the normal two-day trek, but if you're going further afield or for a longer period, then you're going to need one. You may also need a mule to cart your gear – make sure it's a mule you hire and not a donkey – there's a big difference. All this should be arranged in Imlil: enquire at the CAF refuge or the other two hotels. Prices are negotiable to a degree, but the government-controlled rate for a

trained guide is Dr 150 per day and Dr 60 per day for a mule. The guide's food is extra.

Check the guide's credentials – all official guides have them. Unofficial guides are usually alright on the most popular treks but if you are climbing, trekking over snow or in winter, trekking to a remote place, or trekking without mules, then take an official guide and be prepared to pay more. Official guides are trained to deal with accidents and emergencies. Unofficial guides may have no idea what to do in those circumstances.

Those starting off from the Ourika Valley should ask for either Houssein or Lacem Izahan at the Café Azagya, about two km before the village of Setti Fatma. These two young guides know the Atlas like their pockets. They can take you for half-hour walks or treks lasting three to 10 days (or more), and they're reliable.

Guide Books Those intending to do more than the normal two-day trek would be advised to get hold of the guide *La Grande Traversée de l'Atlas Morocain* by Michel Peyron, which is published in English by West Col Productions, UK. Volume I (Moussa Gorges to Ait ben Wgemmez) covers the Toubkal massif. West Col's other guide, *Atlas Mountains* by Robin G Collomb, is nowhere near as useful or detailed, and some of the general comments in the book might leave you wondering how much time the author spent in lowland Morocco as opposed to gazing at snowcapped peaks. Remarks such as 'All Berbers are beggars by nature' and, '...couscous – a sort of Lancashire hot pot cooked in a basin of semolina' stretch the bounds of credibility.

Karl Smith's book, *The Atlas Mountains – A Walker's Guide* (Cicerone Press, 1989), does not actually have the scope implied by the title, though it's quite sound on the Toubkal region.

Another excellent guide, in French, is *Le Haut Atlas Central* by André Fougerollesi (Guide Alpin). This is intended for serious alpinists, not trekkers. It may be available in the better bookshops of Morocco.

The Two-Day Trek

On the first day of the trek you walk from Imlil to the Neltner Hut (3207 metres) via the villages of Aroumd and Sidi Chamharouch. This takes about five hours. Bottled drinks are usually available at both these villages. The Neltner Hut is a stone cottage built in 1938 and has beds for 29 people in two dormitories, though you have to provide your own sheets and blankets or a sleeping bag. There's also a kitchen with a gas stove, and a range of cooking utensils and hot water are available. The charge is Dr 30 per person for non-CAF members, plus an extra charge if you use the cooking facilities or need hot water. There's a resident warden, who'll let you in. You must bring all your own food with you – there's none for sale here – though the warden may, if you give him plenty of notice, prepare meals for you. Don't turn up at this hut without a booking in the high season or you may find it full.

The ascent from the Neltner Hut to the summit should take you about four hours and the descent about two hours. It's best to take water with you in summer, but this isn't generally necessary in winter. Any water you take out of the streams on the mountainside should be boiled, otherwise there's a fair chance you'll pick up giardia. It can be bitterly cold at the top even in summer, so bring plenty of warm clothing with you.

Other Treks If you prefer a longer trek (about five hours) then that to Tacheddirt from Imlil is recommended. The walk takes you over a pass at 3000 metres above the snow line, then down the other side and up again. There's a good CAF refuge here with panoramic views where you can stay for Dr 20 plus Dr 5 if you want to use the gas for cooking. The warden is helpful and can supply bread and eggs. He may also be willing to cook you a meal in his own home for around Dr 30. It's a beautiful place and very relaxing. Many other treks are possible from Tacheddirt including a seven-hour trek at military pace back down to Asni.

There's another CAF refuge at Tazaraght and the key for it can be found at Tizi Oussem village. All CAF refuges are open year round.

Those starting out from the Ourika Valley should head first for the village of Setti Fatma. There are buses to this village from Marrakesh which go when full from the Bab er Rob and cost Dr 8. Alternatively, you can take a shared taxi which costs Dr 30 per person and takes about one hour. The road is partially washed-out in some places as a result of floods in 1987.

In Setti Fatma there are two places to stay. The *Hotel Azrou* overlooks the river and is cold and gloomy but probably the best place to stay. It costs Dr 40 a double, and meals, such as tajine, and drinks are available for Dr 15. The *Hotel Restaurant la Chaumière* is the other place but it's run down, desolate and squalid. Rooms cost Dr 35 a double.

An old English friend, Rick Crust, who spends a lot of time trekking in the High Atlas, suggests the following treks for those with three to seven days to spare:

1. From Imlil, take mules over the Tizi Mzic to the village of Tizi Oussem. Stay the night at the guesthouse run by Si Mohammed ou Omar. This place is much more relaxed than the CAF refuges at Imlil or Neltner. Prices are not fixed, but expect to pay about the same as at the CAF refuges. If you're happy with your muleteers keep them; if not, ask Si Mohammed ou Omar if he can provide you with mules for the next stage. The following day, ascend the Azzaden Valley to the Lépiney Refuge (Tazaraght), which is very peaceful. Options for the following day are:

• A scramble on foot up to Tizi Melloul or the Tazaraght Plateau. Be sure to leave early in the day to be able to get back to Lépiney before dark. You will need a guide for this.

• Cross over to Neltner via the Tizi-n-Taddate – hard going but worth it. Again, a guide is essential. The track is too steep for mules but they can be sent back the long way round via Imlil and will probably arrive at about the same time.

After the above, you can climb Toubkal itself but it won't be as good as what you've already done.

2. Find transport to Oukaïmeden. Outside the ski season, there are no buses or regular taxis, but it should be possible to persuade a grand taxi to go there. The price will take into account that the driver will have no passengers on the return journey. Alternatively, get a bus or taxi to Aghbalou and then hitch up to Oukaïmeden (be prepared for long waits and hard bargaining). In spring or early summer, Oukaïmeden is marvellous – almost deserted, but the CAF refuge will be open and so will *Chez Ju Ju* (except during Ramadan). There are no mules to be hired here but it should be possible to arrange mules for a couple of days ahead – ask at the CAF refuge. You will need to bring all your own supplies with you from Marrakesh as there are no food shops at Oukaïmeden. The CAF refuge makes a good base and there are

some tremendous walks in the area – enough to keep you occupied for two to three days.

When your mules arrive you have two possibilities:

• Descend to Imlil via Tacheddirt (one day).

• Descend the upper Ourika Valley either directly or via Tacheddirt stopping at Timichchi and ending at Setti Fatma (two to three days).

Organised Treks

Group treks can be organised for you before you arrive in Morocco by writing (in French) to the brothers Imar and Mohamed Imzilen, Guides de Montagne, Imlil, BP 8, Asni, Région de Marrakech, Maroc, and asking for their leaflet. You can also contact them via the Hotel Etoile du Toubkal in Imlil. Treks ranging from seven to 14 days from May to October are available on many circuits, including Mt Toubkal, Mt M'Goun, Mt Saghrou, Mt Siroua and the Plateau de Yagour. The price is approximately Dr 250 per person per day which includes guides, donkeys, food and accommodation either in tents, refuges or with local people.

Ouarzazate

Ouarzazate was created by the French as a garrison and regional administrative centre. The town did not exist prior to this, though the Glaoui kasbah of Taourirt at the far end of town on the road to Tinerhir has been here for a long time. It's become a sort of boom town in recent years and has doubled in size over the past four years. The population is now well over 600,000.

Except for the kasbah, it's a pretty nondescript town with little of interest in itself, though the recent build-up has been sympathetically done in traditional style. Club Méditerranée has also seen fit to build a huge hotel/resort on the hill overlooking the town. The best thing about Ouarzazate, in fact, is getting here from Marrakesh over the Tizi-n-

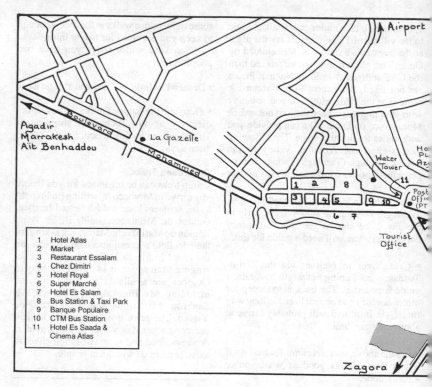

1 Hotel Atlas
2 Market
3 Restaurant Essalam
4 Chez Dimitri
5 Hotel Royal
6 Super Marché
7 Hotel Es Salam
8 Bus Station & Taxi Park
9 Banque Populaire
10 CTM Bus Station
11 Hotel Es Saada &
  Cinema Atlas

Tichka Pass. There are superb views over the mountains and down into the valleys below from many points on this journey. Ouarzazate's other drawcard is the famous kasbah of Aït Benhaddou, off the Marrakesh road – a popular location for film makers, and well worth a visit.

Most travellers spend the night in Ouarzazate en route to or from Zagora in the Drâa Valley or the Todra and Dadès Gorges. If you're here in winter make sure you have plenty of warm clothes. Bitterly cold winds whip down off the snow-covered High Atlas Mountains at this time of year.

Information

Tourist Office The tourist office is in the centre of town, opposite the post office. The staff are helpful and, unlike elsewhere in Morocco, keen. Which other tourist office in Morocco has several noticeboards full of information of use to travellers? Top marks for the guy who runs this place.

Money The Banque Populaire on Blvd Mohammed V is open for changing money Monday to Thursday from 8 to 11.30 am and 2 to 4.30 pm. On Fridays it's open from 8.15 to 11.45 am and 2.45 to 4.45 pm. On Saturdays and Sundays it's open from 3 to 6 pm and 9 am to 1 pm respectively.

Supermarket The Supermarket on Blvd Mohammed V carries an excellent range of goods, including alcoholic drinks (beer and wine) and even nappies (diapers).

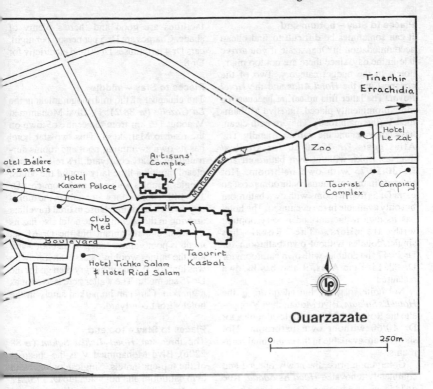

Ouarzazate

0 _____ 250m

Kasbah & Around

The only place worth visiting in Ouarzazate itself is the kasbah at the eastern end of town. In the heyday of the Glaoui chiefs during the 1930s this was one of the largest kasbahs in the area. In those days it housed numerous members of the Glaoui dynasty, along with hundreds of their servants and workers. It appears to have been largely abandoned, however, after the government took it over at independence.

Wandering through the narrow streets of this kasbah, you'll be struck by how deserted it all feels and how derelict it has become. Indeed, part of the outer walls facing the River Drâa appear to be ready to collapse. The actual 'palace' which the Glaouis occupied consists of courtyards, living quarters,

reception rooms and the like, and is open from 9 am to noon and 3 to 6 pm; closed Sunday. A guide is provided and entry costs Dr 10. It's worth a visit, but you'll only be shown a part of the complex. The rest of the kasbah can be visited at any time.

Opposite the entrance to the kasbah is another building in the same style, which today houses an artisans' centre. Here you can find stone carvings, pottery and woollen carpets woven by the region's Ouzguita Berbers. It's open Monday to Friday from 8.30 am to noon and 1 to 6 pm, and on Saturdays from 8.30 am to noon. Don't expect too many bargains – Club Med is virtually next door and there are direct flights to Paris from Ouarzazate!

Places to Stay – bottom end

It can sometimes be difficult to find cheap accommodation in Ouarzazate if you arrive late in the day, since there are not too many hotels in the budget category. Two of the cheapest are the *Hotel Atlas* and the *Hotel Royal*. The latter fills up earlier because it's more prominently placed, on Blvd Mohammed V (the main road). They're both clean, have hot water and the staff are friendly. The Atlas costs Dr 25/40/60 for singles/doubles/triples without own bathroom and Dr 30/50/75 with own bathroom. Hot showers in the communal bathrooms cost an extra Dr 5 (free in rooms with own bathroom but only available in the evenings). The hotel has its own restaurant and is very popular with travellers. The Royal has singles/doubles without own bathroom for Dr 25/47 and doubles with own bathroom for Dr 82. Like the Atlas, it also has its own restaurant.

Not quite so good, but adequate, is the *Hotel Es Salaam*, Blvd Mohammed V, opposite the Royal, which has singles/doubles for Dr 40/60 without own bathroom. Hot showers are available in the communal bathrooms.

Going up in price, the newly opened and completely renovated *Hotel Es Saada*, Rue de la Poste, is a bargain. This one-star hotel is spotlessly clean, has a very friendly manager who speaks English and French fluently, and the rooms are very comfortable. Singles/doubles with own bathroom and hot water cost Dr 85.50/105 including taxes. It's much better value than the two-star Gazelle.

About two km out of town on the Zagora road is another very good cheap hotel. The *Hotel de la Vallée* is right beside the road and is a very friendly place. There are no singles but a double room with one large bed and a small bed costs Dr 70. Hot showers are available on request and they can also do you a three-course meal for Dr 45.

Camping A new campsite (signposted) has opened next to the Tourist Complex off the main road out of town towards Tinerhir about two km from the bus station. The facilities are good and there's plenty of shade. Charges are Dr 5 per person per night, cars Dr 4, minibuses Dr 20 and electricity for Dr 8.

Places to Stay – middle

The cheapest of the mid-range hotels is the *La Gazelle* (☎ 88 2151), Blvd Mohammed V, about 1½ km from the centre of town on the road to Marrakesh. This two-star hotel has its own swimming pool and rooms surrounding a leafy courtyard. It's relaxing and clean, though a little tatty around the edges. Singles/doubles with own bathroom cost Dr 123/148. There's hot water only in the mornings, which is not much use to tired travellers arriving in the evening. The hotel also has its own bar and restaurant but the Dr 61 set menu is poor value – 'soup' is just hot water and the tajines wouldn't satisfy anyone who was hungry. If you are hungry then go for the Dr 75 set menu. The waiter here is as sour as a gherkin. Cars can be parked safely in the hotel's front courtyard.

Places to Stay – top end

The three-star *Hotel Tichka Salam* (☎ 88 2206), Blvd Mohammed V, is the cheapest of the top-end hotels. Singles/doubles with own bathroom and hot water are Dr 175/212 plus taxes. There's heating in the rooms and the hotel has its own bar, restaurant, tennis courts and swimming pool.

In the four-star bracket there are a total of four hotels. They are the *Hotel PLM Azghar* (☎ 88 2058), Blvd Prince Moulay Rachid; the *Hotel Bélère* (☎ 88 2803), Blvd Prince Moulay Rachid; the *Hotel Le Zat* (☎ 88 2521), Aït Gief; and the *Hotel Riad Salam* (☎ 88 2206), Rue Mohammed Diouri, just off Blvd Mohammed V. The best of them is probably the Bélère but they all have swimming pools and their own bar and restaurant. Singles/doubles at all of them cost Dr 280/358 plus taxes.

Places to Eat

Most travellers eat at either the *Hotel Atlas* or the *Hotel Royal*. Both these places offer reasonably priced couscous, tajine, soups and omelettes, though the Royal often has nothing left in the evenings except omelettes. The *Restaurant Essalam* on the corner below the Atlas is also good value.

For a minor splurge, or if you're looking for good Moroccan food, you can't beat *Chez Dimitri*, Blvd Mohammed V, a block west of the Royal. The owner is an ex-legionnaire and quite a character. The food is excellent – it's a very popular place to eat, and the only restaurant (apart from the Gazelle and large hotels) where you can buy beer, wine and spirits. A meal here costs Dr 50 to Dr 60. It's definitely the only place to go on a winter's evening, as they have a pot-belly stove from which you can soak up enough heat to keep you warm all night. Get there early if you don't want to wait for a table.

Getting There & Away
Air Royal Air Maroc flies to Agadir (twice weekly, Dr 410), Casablanca (three times weekly, Dr 360) and Marrakesh (four times weekly, Dr 185).

Bus & Taxi CTM and the private bus companies have their terminals on the main street (Blvd Mohammed V), close to the post office. The taxi and truck park is in a small square behind the main street, below the water tower.

CTM has buses to: Casablanca ('Mountaz' at 9 pm, Dr 95); Errachidia (via Boumalne du Dadès) (10.15 am, nine hours, Dr 55); Marrakesh ('Mountaz' at 8.30 am and 9 pm, Dr 45, and 1st-class at 11 am and noon, Dr 37, five hours) and Zagora/ M'Hamid (12.15 pm, Dr 23 to Zagora and Dr 43.50 to M'Hamid, four hours to Zagora).

There are private buses to Agadir (4, 8 and 10 am, and 10 pm, Dr 58) and to Taroudannt (4, 8 and 10 am, Dr 48).

Shared grands taxis to Zagora cost Dr 40 and go when full.

Car Rental Since the Drâa Valley down to Zagora and beyond to M'Hamid is such a spectacular and interesting journey, it's worth considering car rental before you leave Ouarzazate. With your own vehicle,

you'll be able to stop wherever you like to explore the *ksour* (fortified strongholds) or take photographs. In a bus or shared taxi you'll simply speed through all these places and catch only fleeting glimpses. This way, you'll probably arrive in Zagora feeling very disappointed. It's far better to get a group together and hire a vehicle in Ouarzazate – there are no car rental places in Zagora.

Europcar/InterRent (☎ 88 2035) has an office on the Place du 3 Mars on Blvd Mohammed V, though there may be cheaper agencies if you hunt around.

AROUND OUARZAZATE
Tifoultoutte
From any vantage point in Ouarzazate you can look out south-west across the valley of the Drâa and see another magnificent mud-brick fortress. This is the kasbah of Tifoultoutte which, like the one in Ouarzazate, formerly belonged to the Glaoui.

It certainly looks romantic from a distance. However, in the 1960s, it was converted into a hotel for use by the cast of *Lawrence of Arabia* and has since become somewhat kitsch. Package-tour groups are ferried in here regularly for dinner along with supposedly authentic tribal music and dance evenings. The restaurant here would be a nice splurge one evening if there are no package groups but, without your own transport, you'd have to take a taxi and have the driver wait for you. A three-course meal here costs Dr 75, or Dr 120 for the special menu (Moroccan specialities).

The best way to get there is to take the road to Marrakesh and turn off at the sign for Tifoultoutte. It's about nine km from Ouarzazate to Tifoultoutte.

Aït Benhaddou
In the same direction, again off the road to Marrakesh some 31 km from Ouarzazate, is the village of Aït Benhaddou. Here is one of the most exotic and best-preserved kasbahs in the whole Atlas region. This is hardly surprising, since it has had money poured into it as a result of being used for various film sets, notably *Lawrence of Arabia* and

Jesus of Nazareth. Much of the village was rebuilt for the filming of the latter. Its fame lives on, but the population has dwindled. One of the locals may hassle you to engage him as a guide but this is totally unnecessary.

Places to Stay & Eat If you want to stay here for the night there's a choice of two places, both of them alongside the tarmac road. The *Auberge Restaurant al Baraka* offers rooms with a double beds for Dr 60 or rooms with two double beds for Dr 80. Bathroom are shared and hot water is available (gas heated). The rooms are nothing special, but quite adequate, and there's a roof terrace.

The restaurant at the Auberge offers Moroccan-style, three-course, set-menu dinners for Dr 45 which are good value.

Next door is the *Café Restaurant la Kasbah* which offers similar facilities but also has dormitory beds.

Getting There & Away To get there, take the main road to Marrakesh and turn off after 22 km when you see the signpost for the village; Aït Benhaddou is another nine km down a good bitumen track. Occasionally local buses travel to Aït Benhaddou from Ouarzazate, but it's a lot easier to get there by sharing a taxi. Otherwise, ask around among tourists in the restaurants or at the Gazelle. Hitching is difficult.

Skoura

There are also some very impressive kasbahs in the oasis town of Skoura, some 38 km east of Ouarzazate on the road to Tinerhir. CTM has buses there from Ouarzazate daily at 10 am and 3 pm; cost is Dr 9.

The Gorges

BOUMALNE DU DADÈS & THE DADÈS GORGE

The first of the gorges you come to on the road from Ouarzazate to Errachidia, the Dadès is a complete contrast to the Todra Gorge, which is near Tinerhir. Like the Todra, it's peppered with an endless number of magnificent ruined and lived-in ksour but the valley is much longer, the soil a deep red, and there are some of the most monumental and incredible rock formations you're ever likely to see. The only way I can describe them is as a weathered conglomerate of fused Olmec sculptures. The valley, too, is much wider on the whole than Todra and, instead of date palms and small, irrigated fields of cereal filling the valley bottom, here it's figs and other trees. There are endless photographic opportunities. A visit to this valley is a must; it's one of Morocco's top sights.

A good macadam road runs through this fantasia for about 23 km from the main Ouarzazate-Boumalne road, after which it reverts to a poorly maintained, pebble dirt track. It's possible to drive along this pebble dirt track in a normal car but it's agonisingly slow and definitely puncture country but by then, in any case, you've seen most of what there is to see. You'd have no problems going further with a 4WD vehicle.

Places to Stay & Eat

In the Gorge The choice of places to stay in the gorge is very limited. At Km 15 is the *Hotel Restaurant Kasbah* which overlooks the fantastic rock formations on the other side of the valley. It's an interesting little place with small balconies, and is constructed in a style which is a mixture of modern and traditional. Expect to pay Dr 40 a double.

At Km 24 is the village of Aït Oudinar where there's the *Auberge Gorge du Dadès*. This has 12 rooms with communal hot showers and electricity for part of the evening. It's a friendly place and costs Dr 40 a double, plus they'll cook you up a very tasty meal for Dr 25. You can organise trips further up the valley from here.

Even further up the valley at Km 27 is the *Hotel Restaurant Camping de Peuplier*, owned by Mohammed Echaouiche. He's very hospitable and rooms are a bargain at Dr 20; you can get a meal here for Dr 15.

Boumalne du Dadès Unless you stay up the

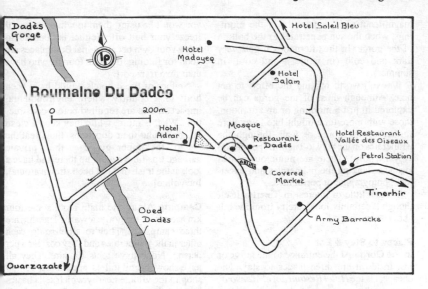

Dadès
Gorge

Boumalne Du Dadès

0   200m

Hotel Soleil Bleu

Hotel
Madayeq

Hotel
Salam

Hotel
Adrar

Mosque

Restaurant
Dadès

Hotel Restaurant
Vallée des Oiseaux

Petrol Station

Covered
Market

Tinerhir

Oued
Dadès

Army Barracks

Ouarzazate

gorge, this town on the main Ouarzazate-Errachidia road is probably where you'll spend the night. The best place to stay here, though quite a walk from the centre of town (where the buses stop), is the *Hotel Restaurant Vallée des Oiseaux* which is very friendly, spotlessly clean and comfortable. Singles/doubles with shared bathroom (constant hot water) cost Dr 40/60. The hotel has a good restaurant and prices are very reasonable. Up the side track from here – and an even further walk from town – is the *Hotel Salam*, which has doubles with own shower and hot water for Dr 60, and the *Hotel Soleil Bleu*. Both of these places have their own restaurants.

Back down the hill in the centre of town, there is the *Hotel Adrar* which has adequate singles/doubles for Dr 40/60. The hotel has its own restaurant.

The most expensive hotel in town is the four-star *Hotel Madayeq*, right on top of the hill overlooking the town and the start of the gorge. Rooms cost Dr 234/292 plus taxes for singles/doubles. The hotel has its own bar, restaurant and swimming pool.

If you're not eating at your own hotel then the *Restaurant Dadès* next to the covered market is a good place to eat.

Getting There & Away

I was told there are buses from Boumalne to Aït Oudinar, but I never saw one and the budget travellers I passed were all walking. Perhaps they wanted to walk, but there can't be many buses along this road each day. This means that if you don't have transport, you'll have to hire a taxi in Boumalne. The one-way price to Aït Oudinar should be Dr 10 sharing, but it's unlikely you'll get it for that price so, if you don't plan on staying in the gorge for the night, negotiate a price for a round trip or hire a taxi by the hour.

TINERHIR & THE TODRA GORGE

Some 14 km from Tinerhir (Tineghir on some maps), at the end of a lush valley full of *palmeraies* (oasis-like areas) and mud-brick villages hemmed in by barren, craggy mountains, is one of Morocco's most magnificent natural sights. This is the Todra Gorge: some 300 metres high but only 10 metres wide at its narrowest, and with a crystal clear river running through it. It's a magnificent sight, especially in the mornings, when the sun penetrates to the bottom of the gorge. In the afternoons it gets very dark and cold (in winter), and cool (in summer).

It's well worth making the effort to get here. Although most of the gorge can be explored in just a morning or an afternoon, those with more time might like to explore further up the gorge or walk through the palmeraies on the way to Tinerhir (people are very friendly). There are numerous ruined kasbahs flanking the palmeraies and excellent photographic opportunities.

There's little of interest in Tinerhir itself though it certainly looks pretty from the hill above town.

Places to Stay & Eat

In the Gorge At the entrance to the gorge or just inside it are three places to stay. The cheapest is the *Hotel Restaurant el Mansour*, right at the entrance to the gorge. It's a friendly place, has sun for most of the day, a good selection of Western music and costs Dr 40 a double for a clean, basic concrete box. The toilets are clean but primitive and there's neither hot water nor electricity – kerosene lamps light the night's activities. The hotel has its own restaurant, and although the food is a little expensive, it's very good. Tajine and salad costs Dr 25 to Dr 30, salad Dr 10, omelette Dr 8. The staff try hard to make you welcome.

Right inside the gorge itself are two other places, the *Hotel Yasmina* and the *Hotel Les Roches* which is where the package tourists are brought for a midday meal but don't stay, so you'll have the place to yourself in the evenings. Both places have hot water and wood fires at night in winter (demand permitting). Despite catering for package tourists, they charge only Dr 40 a double in winter (more in summer) and offer a good set menu for Dr 45 (soup or salad, tajine and dessert). The best rooms are those which face onto the river – the others are pretty dark. Both places have Berber tents in the grounds with tables, chairs and divans, which makes them an excellent place to eat in the summer;

you won't be using them in winter or you'll freeze your butt off. Neither is licensed so bring your own beer or wine. Both places are good for finding lifts with tourists who have their own transport.

Neither of these hotels would have been built in a country where environmental impact studies are required before construction. What is more, while they keep a clean image around their doorsteps, they treat the rest of the upper gorge as their private garbage tip. Take a walk up there and have a look at the trash that has been strewn around. Incredible!

Camping Along the main road, some four km back from the gorge towards Tinerhir, are three campsites. They're all next to each other in the palmeraies and they cost Dr 5 per person. None have tents for hire. They all have showers and toilets, and there's a small shop in the village nearby which sells basics (but no cigarettes – get these from Le Lac). The sites are *Camping Le Lac*, *Camping Atlas* and *Camping Auberge*. Take your pick.

Tinerhir If you decide not to stay at the gorge itself or need somewhere to stay in Tinerhir, there are three hotels, all of them around the main square. The cheapest is the *Hotel Salam* which is basic but quite adequate for a night and costs Dr 40 a double with shared bathroom. The hotel has its own internal compound so, if you have your own vehicle, safe parking is available. The hotel restaurant is good value.

If you have the money, the best place to stay is the *Hotel Bar Restaurant du Todra*, 37 Ave Hassan II, on the bottom side of the main square. It's a two-star hotel and offers singles/doubles with shared bathroom for Dr 54/64 and Dr 92/112 with own shower and toilet plus taxes. Quite a lot of travellers stay here, although the restaurant should be avoided.

Top of the line is the four-star *Hotel Sargho*, which is up on top of the hill overlooking town. The views are superb and the hotel has an enormous swimming pool as well as a bar and restaurant, but the rooms are small and tatty, the 'tourist menu' is outrageously expensive at Dr 100 and there are always hustlers up here. Singles/doubles cost Dr 234/292 plus taxes. Visa cards are accepted.

If you're not eating at your hotel or at the *Restaurant la Gazelle*, next door to the Hotel Salam, go for a meal at the *Kasbah Restaurant* on the main street. This has a very comfortable and relaxing Berber setting with three-course meals for Dr 50. The tajines and salads are excellent though the omelettes are somewhat greasy and overcooked. It's a friendly place but not licensed.

Getting There & Away

There are no buses from Tinerhir to the gorge but there are frequent shared taxis from the main square for Dr 10 per person which will take you right to the entrance to the gorge. Make it clear you want to share the taxi otherwise you will sometimes be quoted ridiculous figures. It is possible to hitch if you can't afford a taxi. Simply walk out of Tinerhir in the direction of Errachidia until you get to the bridge across the river. Turn left here and wait for a lift. Unless tourists come along you may have to pay for a lift in any case.

Southern Morocco

Southern Morocco is remarkable as much for its stunning landscapes and geological wonders as for its numerous Berber kasbahs.

From the abandoned mud-brick villages around Tafraoute, the strange Spanish-Moroccan hybrid that constitutes Sidi Ifni, and the palmeraies and oases of the Drâa and Ziz Valleys, a trip to Southern Morocco offers the traveller a unique and rewarding experience.

Southern Morocco is also where you catch your first glimpse of the vast Sahara Desert.

Anti-Atlas Mountains

TIZNIT

In an arid corner of the Sous Valley at the very end of the Anti-Atlas range, Tiznit has the appearance of being a very old town, with its six km of encircling red mud walls, yet it is a fairly recent creation.

The best time to be in Tiznit is when the package-tour buses from Agadir have all departed (mid to late afternoon). It then reverts to normality and is a pleasant place to hang around and explore. This is also the best time to have a look at the silver jewellery which is reputedly some of the best in the south.

History

Though there was a settlement of sorts here previously, the town dates substantially from 1881. In that year it was chosen by Sultan Moulay Hassan as a base from which to assert his authority over the semi-autonomous and rebellious tribes of the Sous and Anti-Atlas, as well as the nomadic Touareg further to the south. He was only partially successful in this quest; it wasn't until the 1930s – 20 years after Spain and France had partitioned Morocco between themselves – that the tribes were finally 'pacified'.

In the first decade of the 20th century, Tiznit became a focal point of resistance against foreign incursions. The resistance was led by El Hiba, an Idrissid chief from Mauritania who was regarded as a saint and credited with performing miracles. In 1912 he had himself proclaimed sultan at the mosque in Tiznit, and he succeeded in uniting the tribes of the Anti-Atlas and the Touareg in a fanatical effort to repel the French invaders.

Places to Stay – bottom end

The best hotels are on Place Almachouar, the main square within the city walls. Many have rooftop terraces where you can escape the tourist hordes during the middle of the day. They're all much the same price and offer similar facilities. Where you stay will largely depend on what you take a fancy to and which hotel has room.

Most travellers stay at the *Hotel Atlas*, which has one of the best and liveliest restaurants. It's clean and costs Dr 30 for a room with one large and one small bed and Dr 40 for a room with two large beds. Showers and toilets are communal and, although the manager showed me an electric plug which he claimed was for 'hot water', it would be prudent to assume there's only cold water available. Similar are the *Hotel des Amis, Hotel de la Jeunesse, Hotel Café al-Massira, Hotel Touriste* and the *Hotel Voyageur*. The latter costs Dr 25/35 for singles/doubles with shared bathroom (cold water only).

Off Place Almachouar is Rue Bain Maure, along which there are several other cheapies. Perhaps the best of them is the *Hotel Al Mourabitine*; this is clean and costs Dr 40 a double, but has only one handbasin and toilet for the whole hotel. It's adequate and secure, but poor value on the whole. There's a tea room on the 1st floor. Just as good is the *Hotel Zohour*, which has a friendly manager and costs Dr 20/30 without own bathroom.

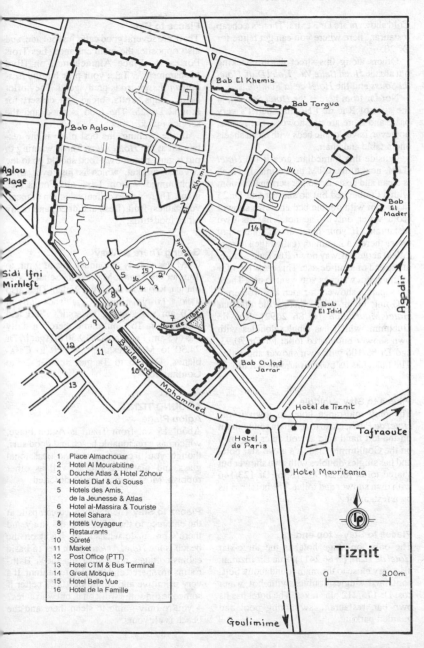

Bab El Khemis

Bab Targua

Bab Aglou

Aglou
Plage

Bab
El
Mader

Sidi Ifni
Mirhleft

Agadir

Rue du Souk

Rue Khemis

Bab
El Jdid

Rue de l'Hôpital

Boulevard Mohammed V

Bab Oulad
Jarrar

Hotel de Tiznit

Tafraoute

Hotel
de Paris

Hotel Mauritania

Goulimime

Tiznit

0   200m

1   Place Almachouar
2   Hotel Al Mourabitine
3   Douche Atlas & Hotel Zohour
4   Hotels Diaf & du Souss
5   Hotels des Amis,
    de la Jeunesse & Atlas
6   Hotel al-Massira & Touriste
7   Hotel Sahara
8   Hotels Voyageur
9   Restaurants
10 Sûreté
11 Market
12 Post Office (PTT)
13 Hotel CTM & Bus Terminal
14 Great Mosque
15 Hotel Belle Vue
16 Hotel de la Famille

Cold showers are Dr 3 extra. There's a cheap restaurant here where you can get tajine for Dr 20.

Others along this street worth checking out are the *Hotel Belle Vue*, *Hotel Diaf*, *Hotel du Souss* and the *Hotel de la Famille*.

Nor far from here is the *Hotel Sahara*, at the start of Rue de l'Hôpital, but it's very basic and there are no showers. The rooms, however, have double beds with clean sheets and a table and chair.

Outside this immediate area is the *Hotel CTM*, next to the CTM bus terminal, which is clean and costs Dr 15 per person in a room with a double bed but no shower and Dr 25 in a room with double bed and own shower (cold water only). The hotel has its own restaurant. If your hotel doesn't have hot water there's a hammam (called the Douche Atlas) about halfway down Rue Bain Maure, at the end of a cul-de-sac. This costs Dr 4 for as much hot water as you want to use. There are separate showers for men and women.

Going up in price, there's the one-star *Hotel Mauritania* (☎ 86 2092), Rue de Guelmim, which has singles/doubles with own shower but shared toilet for Dr 70/93, and Dr 89/106 with own shower and toilet. The hotel has its own bar and restaurant.

Places to Stay – middle

The only mid-range hotel in town is the *Hotel de Paris*, close to the main roundabout on the left hand side as you enter the town on the Goulimime road. It's a two-star hotel and has singles/doubles with own shower but shared toilet for Dr 98/118, or Dr 123/146 with own shower and toilet. The hotel has its own restaurant.

Places to Stay – top end

The only top-range hotel is the three-star *Hotel de Tiznit* (☎ 86 2411), Rue Bir Inzaran, also very close to the main roundabout. Self-contained singles/doubles with hot water cost Dr 175/212 plus taxes. The hotel has its own bar, restaurant, swimming pool and guarded parking.

Places to Eat

There are several good cafés just outside, and also opposite, the main entrance (Les Trois Portes) to Place Almachouar, on Blvd Mohammed V. Take your pick but the *Restaurant Essahara* is pretty good. They offer salad, chips, kefta, bread and dessert for around Dr 25. The food is good and the service quick.

In the evening, the best place is the restaurant at the *Hotel Atlas*. Those wanting to put together their own food should go to the covered market, which is just over Blvd Mohammed V from Les Trois Portes (see map). There's an excellent selection of meat, vegetables, fruit (fresh and dried) and many other foodstuffs.

Getting There & Away

CTM has a daily 'Mountaz' bus at 9 pm to Tangier via Agadir, Marrakesh, Settat, Casablanca, Rabat, Larache and Asilah. They also have a 1st-class bus to Casablanca daily at 5.30 am via Agadir, Essaouira, Safi and Azemmour. To Goulimime there's a daily bus at 5 am. Fares are Dr 19.50 to Agadir, Dr 74.50 to Marrakesh, Dr 125.50 to Casablanca, Dr 205 to Tangier and Dr 24 to Goulimime.

AROUND TIZNIT
Aglou Plage

About 15 km from Tiznit is Aglou Plage, which has a reasonable beach and good surf, though you'll come across the occasional glass and plastic bottle as well as other rubbish. Most of the time it's deserted.

Places to Stay There's a walled campsite at the entrance to the village but it's stony and there's no shade whatsoever. Right on the beach is the *Hotel Aglou* which has 15 basic cabins/cottages all with a sea view. Bathrooms are shared and there's a restaurant. It's very primitive and would be 100% better if someone did some work on it, but who cares? – you're only going to sleep there and the beach is all yours.

TAFRAOUTE

The attraction of Tafraoute, like a number of places in southern Morocco, is not so much in the town itself but in its setting and the journey there. Its setting is spectacular. Hemmed in on all sides by massive boulder-strewn mountains, its nearest equivalent is Hampi in India, except that here the prevailing colour is pink instead of grey. The boulders are smooth and well-weathered – quite a contrast to the craggy *jebels* (hills) elsewhere in Morocco.

Palmeraies and small cultivated areas hog the river courses. There are plenty of pisé (mud-brick) villages nearby, and the economy is based on the almond trees. It's good walking country, and the town itself is very laid back. Stay here a few days, go on a few hikes around the countryside and you'll find it hard to leave.

The road between here and Agadir is spectacular, and there are excellent photographic possibilities – abandoned Berber mud-brick villages and kasbahs perched on hair-raising precipices, others, inhabited, built on the summits of conical rock outcrops and, of course, the vistas from the summits of mountain passes. Some of the roads are rough in parts, but there's nothing which an ordinary car can't handle. The road south to Tiznit is also spectacular, though much more forbidding and barren, particularly towards the end; you may get the feeling that you've taken the wrong turning and won't see another village until you get to Timbuktu.

Market day is Wednesday.

The Painted Rocks

Tafraoute is famous for its painted rocks – the work of the Belgian artist Jean Veran. To get to them, take the tarmac road leading away from Agadir until you reach a sign indicating a fork (about two km). The sign indicating straight on is in Arabic but the one pointing right is in Roman script. Take the latter and go straight through the village to the square where there's a mosque. From here, turn right and then left to get around the mosque and then head out into the country-side for a further two to three km. You'll

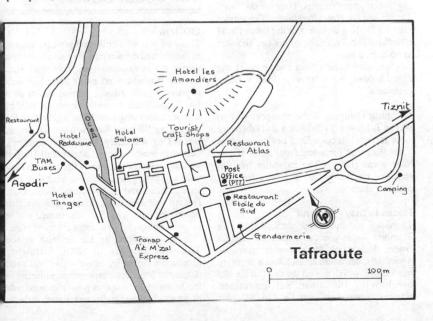

Hotel les Amandiers

Restaurant

Oued

Hotel Reddwane

TAM Buses

Agadir

Hotel Tanger

Hotel Salama

Tourist/ Craft Shops

Restaurant Atlas

Post Office (PTT)

Restaurant Etoile du Sud

Tiznit

Camping

Gendarmerie

Transp Ait M'zal Express

Tafraoute

0   100 m

come to some pale blue rocks on the left-hand side but keep going, following the track bearing left to another set which includes a large blue boulder with a purple rock on top. Go around this and to your right and you'll come to the best display of painted rocks. The walk is worthwhile even without the painted rocks.

The Carved Gazelle

To get to this beautiful and supposedly very old carving, take the road over the crest of the hill on top of which stands the Hotel les Amandiers, and head for the village on your right. The road climbs up a hill from here and you need to get in behind this hill, leaving it to your left. You'll see a crude drawing of an animal on a rock on the hill. Walk up to it. The carving is on the top side of a fallen rock right in front of this one. The walk from Tafraoute takes about 20 minutes.

Places to Stay – bottom end

There are two budget hotels in the centre which offer much the same facilities, including their own restaurants. They are the *Hotel Tanger* and the *Hotel Redduane*. The former charges Dr 30 a double and the latter Dr 35 a double. The Redduane offers hot showers at no extra cost.

There used to be a third budget hotel, the *Hotel Salama*, but it 'blew up' and is being renovated.

Camping Camping is the cheapest way to stay in Tafraoute *if* you have a tent (there are none for hire). It costs Dr 5 per person plus a small charge for a tent, and extra if you have a car (Dr 5). The campsite has hot showers, electricity and is a very friendly, pleasant place to stay.

Places to Stay – top end

There are no mid-range places to stay in Tafraoute so, if you can't hack the budget hotels, there's only the four-star *Hotel les Amandiers*, an amateur architect's travesty of a kasbah, which sits on the crest of the hill overlooking the town. Self-contained singles/doubles here cost Dr 234/292 plus

taxes. The hotel has its own bar, restaurant, swimming pool and guarded parking.

Places to Eat

Both budget hotels have their own reasonably priced restaurants, though the *Hotel Tanger* definitely appears to be the most popular.

For a splurge, try the *Restaurant Etoile du Sud* opposite the post office. The *Restaurant Atlas*, further up the square, purports to be of the same standard but the meal (salad and a mediocre tajine), which I ate last time I was there, was poor value.

Getting There & Away

Tafraoute isn't the easiest of places to get to without your own transport and hitching isn't really feasible. SATAS has a daily bus from Agadir to Tafraoute at 1.30 pm daily and there *may* be buses from Tiznit depending on demand.

The South Coast

SIDI IFNI

Those of you who collected postage stamps in the dim and distant past may recall coming across the occasional one from Sidi Ifni. Finding out where on earth this place was required a good atlas. It turned out to be a tiny Spanish colony on the southern coast of Morocco. But why here? The motivation for colonising Western Sahara (then known as Río de Oro) was fairly obvious (phosphates), but what was so special about Sidi Ifni? It was this which drew me to the place, along with a lingering fascination to visit tiny esoteric colonies and ex-colonies (Macau, Goa, Daman and Diu, East Timor and Pitcairn Island, for instance). Sidi Ifni turned out to be quite delightful in a strange sort of way.

It was acquired by the Spanish at the Treaty of Tetouan in 1860, following Morocco's defeat by Spain – the first such defeat the Moroccan armies had suffered at the hands of a European power in hundreds of years. It was finally evacuated only in

Top: Market scene, Fès, Morocco (IIΓ)
Left: Carpet shop, Agdz, Morocco (HF)
Right: Unusual building materials, Moulay Idriss, Morocco (HF)

Top: Souvenir stall, Ait Benhaddou, Morocco (HF)
Bottom: High Atlas Mountains, Morocco (HF)

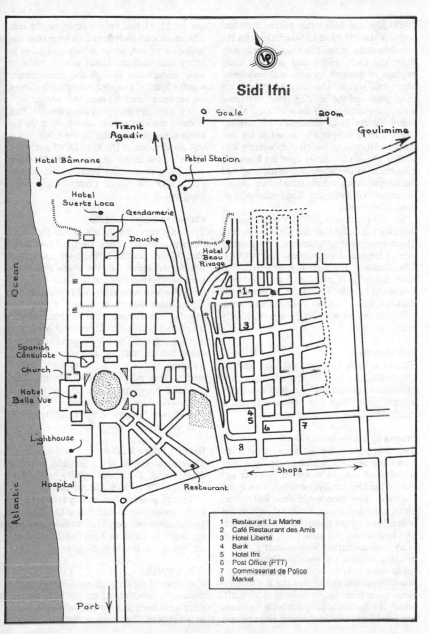

Sidi Ifni

0 | Scale | 200m

1 Restaurant La Marine
2 Café Restaurant des Amis
3 Hotel Liberté
4 Bank
5 Hotel Ifni
6 Post Office (PTT)
7 Commissariat de Police
8 Market

Tiznit
Agadir

Goulimime

Hotel Bâmrane

Petrol Station

Hotel
Suerte Loca

Gendarmerie

Douche

Hotel Beau
Rivage

Ocean

Spanish
Consulate

Church

Hotel
Belle Vue

Lighthouse

Hospital

Restaurant

Shops

Atlantic

Port

1969, after the Moroccan government had sealed all land borders into the colony for the previous three years. The town dates largely from the early 1930s and is an eclectic mixture of Spanish art deco and traditional Moroccan styles. The church just off the main plaza and the building (built to imitate a ship) on the edge of the cliff next to the Hotel Suerte Loca shouldn't be missed! There's even a Spanish Consulate on one corner of the plaza, which is apparently still staffed, though it's rarely open for business. Elsewhere in the Spanish quarter, many of the houses are locked and boarded up and are in various states of decay. The former port no longer functions.

So why come here? If decay can be described as delightful, that's it in a nutshell. The prevailing atmosphere is a very relaxing one of enigma, abandonment and lethargy. The beaches are virtually deserted, but they're not up to much and are used as a rubbish tip unless you get well away from the town. I didn't expect to see more than one or two travellers here, yet there was a steady stream of them.

Information
There's a bank (fast and efficient and no commission on travellers' cheques), a post office and a gendarmerie, as well as a lively market (fish, fruit and vegetables) and a number of fairly well-stocked shops.

Places to Stay – bottom end
The most popular budget hotel by far is the Hotel Suerte Loca, which is run by a very friendly old man (who speaks Spanish and French) and his family (two of the sons speak English). The rooms are excellent value, clean, quiet and secure, though there's no hot water. Most of the rooms have a handbasin. The roof terrace is a great place on which to relax and sunbathe. Rooms cost Dr 25 a double; singles are also available. Good meals are available in the restaurant downstairs (breakfast and dinner but not lunch – siesta lasts from about noon to 4.30 pm!), which is a favourite hang-out with travellers and local youths in the evening. Hot showers

can be found just up the street on the left. This is quite an experience – a huge concrete tank full of hot water which you have to scoop into buckets. Local women bathe in their underwear, though the management won't object if you strip completely. There are separate times for men and women.

If it's full, try the Hotel Beau Rivage. This is more modern and doesn't have quite the same atmosphere as the Suerte Loca, but is still good value at Dr 30 to Dr 45 a double. There's a restaurant and bar on the 1st floor, with tasty meals and beers at the normal price. Like the Suerte Loca, it's a popular hang-out.

Places to Stay – middle
There are two other hotels in Sidi Ifni, both of them one-star. They are the Hotel Belle Vue, 9 Place Hassan II (the main plaza), and the Hotel Bâmrane, on the beach. Both have their own restaurants and bars, but service at the Belle Vue runs at a snail's pace – it took 40 minutes for them to get a mint tea together! The Bâmrane has the air of a 1960s' Yugoslav state-government hotel, but service is good. The bar is open to non-residents, but the beer has an uncanny habit of 'running out' if you go there for a session with a few people in the evening. This doesn't happen at the Beau Rivage. Singles/doubles at either cost Dr 70/93 with own shower but shared toilet and Dr 89/106 with own shower and toilet.

Getting There & Away
The easiest way to get to Sidi Ifni is by bus from Tiznit. There are usually two a day. They cost Dr 10 and take two hours.

There's also one bus per day at about 2 pm from Goulimime to Sidi Ifni; it also costs Dr 10 and takes two hours. From Sidi Ifni there are buses to Tiznit at 7 am and 2 pm. The 7 am bus continues on to Agadir.

GOULIMIME
The myth of the Goulimime Saturday camel market persists, despite the fact that for years there have been more tourists than camels to be seen here. The camels that are brought

here are purely for the benefit of the package tourists, who arrive by the bus-load from Agadir. It's really just a tourist trap and one you can afford to miss.

The town itself is featureless, boring and remarkable only for its lack of interest.

Camel Market

If you feel you must contribute to the myth of the camel market, it takes place outside town (take a taxi) on Saturday mornings. Get there just after sunrise, otherwise you won't be able to see the camels for the tourists.

Places to Stay – bottom end

The *Hotel Place Bir Inzarane* is one of the cheapest places, at Dr 35 a double, but it's poor value and there are cold water showers only. However, it's better than the *Hotel Oued Eddahab*, which is very primitive. Many of the rooms here are dark and dingy, the locks on the doors are a joke and there are cold showers only; still, the sheets, at least, are clean. It costs Dr 30 a double. Both hotels are on the main roundabout in the centre of town.

Camping There is a campsite at Fort Bou Jerf, 40 km from Goulimime. It is an oasis of civilisation in the desert, meals are available and it's well worth the effort to get to.

Places to Stay – middle

The only hotel in this range is the two-star *Hotel Salam*, which has its own bar and restaurant and costs Dr 79/100 for singles/doubles with own shower but shared toilet and Dr 96/120 with own shower and toilet.

Places to Eat

For a cheap but basic meal of fried fish, chilli sauce and bread, go to the café a few doors up from the Hotel Place Bir Inzarane as you walk away from the roundabout. A meal here costs less than Dr 10.

The only two decent restaurants in town are the *Café de la Poste* and the *Café Jour et Nuit*, opposite the post office where the main road from Tiznit and the road from the bus terminal meet. Here you are looking at about Dr 45 for a three-course meal.

Getting There & Away

The bus terminal is about one km from the centre of town, which you get to by turning right after coming out of the terminal.

CTM operates one bus daily between Tiznit and Goulimime (at 5 am from Tiznit, Dr 24). SATAS operates two buses daily between Agadir and Goulimime via Tiznit (at 5.30 am and 2 pm from Agadir). There's also one local bus per day from Goulimime to Sidi Ifni at around 2 pm. The cost is Dr 10, and the journey, which takes approximately two hours, passes through some interesting countryside.

Drâa Valley

ZAGORA

The journey down through the Drâa Valley, with its innumerable crumbling red-mud kasbahs and lush green palmeraies, hemmed in by its forbidding, barren and craggy cliffs on either side, has to be one of the world's most colourful and exotic experiences. It's pure magic from what feels like another world. All the more reason to expect something special of Zagora.

Unfortunately, Zagora, like Ouarzazate, is by and large a fairly recent creation, dating from French colonial times when it was set up as an administrative centre. Nevertheless, there are plenty of interesting places to explore in the vicinity and the town does have its moments, particularly when a dust storm blows up out of the desert in the late afternoon and the lighting becomes totally surreal. Zagora is also where you'll see that somewhat battered sign saying 'Tombuktoo 52 jours', which just about everyone has to be photographed against.

It's still a fairly small town (population around 12,600) but the developers have started moving in. Over the last few years a new four-star hotel-resort complex has gone up, as well as another two-star hotel, and the entry into town has been converted from a two-lane highway into what amounts to an airport runway. Just why such a vast amount of tarmac should have been laid at the entrance to such a small town is a mystery. It would have been better used to resurface the rough patches of road further south.

Information

Market days are Wednesday and Sunday. Fruit and vegetables, herbs, hardware, handicrafts, sheep, goats and donkeys are brought in to be bought and sold.

Things to See

The spectacular jebel (hill) which rises up across the other side of the river is worth climbing for the views – if you have the stamina and you set off early in the morning.

Places to Stay – bottom end

There are two unclassified budget hotels to choose from in town which stand next to each other on the main street, Blvd Mohammed V. Possibly the best, if you can get a front room, is the *Hotel Vallée du Drâa*. This costs Dr 40/55 for singles/doubles with shared bathroom and Dr 65/84 with own shower and bathroom. It's clean, friendly and has its own restaurant, though this doesn't function in the low season. The other is the *Hotel des Amis*, which is very similar

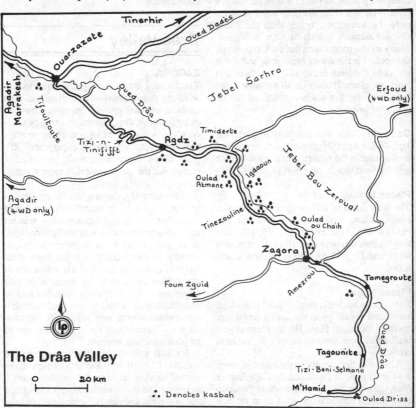

The Drâa Valley

0   20 km

∴ Denotes kasbah

and offers rooms with and without own bathroom. Prices are the same as at the Vallée du Drâa. Both are very popular with travellers but neither has hot water.

Going up in price, there's the very popular one-star *Hotel de la Palmeraie*, also on Blvd Mohammed V, where the staff are very friendly. The rooms – most with their own balcony – cost Dr 42/59/83 for singles/doubles/triples with own shower but shared toilet and Dr 68/92 for doubles/triples with own shower and toilet. There's hot water in the showers. If you have your own bedding they'll also let you sleep on the roof for Dr 10 per person. The hotel has a lively bar and its own excellent restaurant where you can get a three-course meal for just Dr 40. Camel treks can also be arranged here.

Camping Campers have a choice of three sites. The most convenient is *Camping*

d'Amezrou, about 200 metres past La Fibule Hotel along the dirt track which runs alongside the irrigation channel. There are toilets and plenty of shade. Also over this side of town is *Camping Montagne*, which is at the foot of the jebel that you get to by crossing the bridge over the irrigation channel immediately past La Fibule Hotel, and then following the signpost. It's about two km down the dirt track from here. There's plenty of shade and toilets, and cold drinks are available, but you're advised to bring your own food.

The third site is *Camping Sindibad*, where there are toilets, hot showers and a café.

Places to Stay – middle

If you can afford it, the most relaxing place to stay in Zagora is *La Fibule Hotel*, on the south side of the Oued Drâa, about one km from the centre. The Hotel is set in the pal-

1	Hotel de la Palmeraie	7	AGIP Station
2	Restaurant Timbouctou	8	Bicycle Shop & Hire
3	Market	9	La Fibule Hotel & Restaurant
4	Hotel Vallée du Drâa	10	Camping d'Amezrou
5	Hotel des Amis	11	Hammam
6	Bank	12	Hotel Kasbah Asma

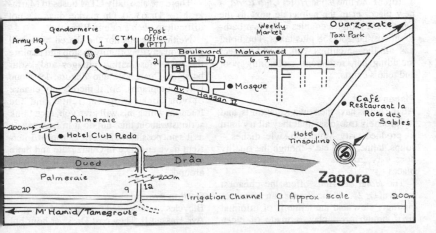

meraie, with its own shady garden, restaurant and swimming pool, and the rooms have been built and furnished in traditional Berber style, with the addition of showers (hot water from 7 to 11 am daily) and toilets. It's been expanded since first built so it isn't likely to be full. Singles/doubles cost Dr 98/118 with own shower but shared toilet (very few of these) and Dr 123/146 with own shower and toilet. Excellent meals are available in the restaurant for Dr 60 (three-course) or Dr 81 (four-course) and they stock wine (but no beer). There's guarded parking at the rear. Camel treks can be arranged at this hotel, but they're fairly expensive at Dr 250 per person overnight, including food.

If La Fibule is full, there's the *Hotel Kasbah Asma*, just down the road. This is another two-star hotel which has been built to resemble a Berber ksar. Singles/doubles with own shower and toilet cost Dr 96/120. We've had good reports from people who have stayed here. The hotel has its own bar and restaurant, and guarded parking.

Places to Stay – top end

The cheapest place to stay in this category is the *Hotel Tinsouline*, which has 90 rooms and its own bar, restaurant and swimming pool. Singles/doubles with own bathroom cost Dr 234/292 plus taxes.

Top of the line is the *Hotel Club Reda*, a new place set in the palmeraie next to the Oued Drâa. Singles/doubles with own bathroom cost Dr 280/358 plus taxes. The hotel has all the amenities you would expect including bar, restaurant, swimming pool and tennis courts.

Places to Eat

All the hotels have their own restaurants, and it's probably true to say that they all try hard to produce tasty Moroccan-style dishes – soups, tajine, salad etc – though the quality does vary from day to day at the cheaper places.

The *Hotel des Amis* offers the cheapest meals at Dr 25, but the service can be excruciatingly slow and the tajine is of minimal size, though great play is made of clean plates for each course. It's often better to eat at either the *Hotel Vallée du Drâa* for Dr 35 or the *Hotel de la Palmeraie* for Dr 40, since the service is quicker and the servings more substantial. Both these two stock beer and wine.

For a change from the hotels try a meal at the *Restaurant Timbouctou*, which offers excellent food and is popular with local people. The complete menu costs Dr 25, or you can buy items separately – soup (Dr 3), salad (Dr 5), tajine (Dr 15). There's also the *Café Restaurant la Rose des Sables*, just up the street from the Hotel Tinsouline, and the *Café Restaurant Essahara*, in the market square, which offers soup, tajine and salad for Dr 20.

Even if you are not staying at *La Fibule* you should try to make it there for a meal one day. The food is excellent and the surroundings very relaxing.

Getting There & Away

There's a CTM bus once daily in either direction between Zagora and Ouarzazate at 7 am. This bus starts out at M'Hamid and comes past La Fibule at about 6.30 am so, if you're staying there, you can flag it down right outside the door. The fare to Ouarzazate is Dr 23. Grands taxis are also available at Dr 20 per person and they leave when full.

There are also daily CTM buses to Marrakesh for Dr 63.50. On market days it's not difficult to hitch a ride to Rissani.

Neither the bus nor the shared taxis will give you any opportunity to stop and explore the many fascinating villages and ksour between Ouarzazate and Zagora, let alone take photographs. So, if there's any chance of you considering car rental and the freedom which this will give you, then think seriously about this, but do it in Ouarzazate as it's not possible in Zagora. Europcar/InterRent have an office in Ouarzazate and there may be other, cheaper, agencies if you hunt around.

Getting Around

Bicycles can be rented from a repair shop on Ave Hassan II. They cost Dr 5 per hour but the price is negotiable. They're ideal for visiting Amezrou and Tamegroute to the south, or Tinezouline to the north, without going to the expense of hiring a taxi.

SOUTH OF ZAGORA
Amezrou
Across the other side of the River Drâa, about three km south of Zagora, is the village of Amezrou. It has an interesting old Jewish mellah, which is still a centre for the casting of silver jewellery. Jews lived here for centuries and formerly controlled the silver trade, but they all took off for Israel in 1948 leaving the Berbers to carry on the tradition. If you look like you might buy something, the locals will be willing to show you the whole process. Because the village is so close to Zagora local children will leap on you offering to be guides, but it's fairly low-key hassle.

Elsewhere in the palmeraie life goes on much as it always has. It's well worth spending a morning or an afternoon or even a whole day wandering through the shady groves along the many tracks which dissect it. The dates which are grown here are reputed to be the best in Morocco, but times have been getting harder over the last few years as the result of a disease which is attacking and killing the palms.

Tamegroute
Further south, about 18 km from Zagora, is Tamegroute. For many centuries, right up until recent times, it was an important religious and educational centre whose influence was felt far and wide. The town consists of a series of interconnected ksour, at the centre of which is the zaouia and its famous library.

The library (which is signposted on the main road as 'Librarie Coranique') houses a magnificent collection of illustrated religious texts, dictionaries and astrological works, some of them on gazelle hides. The oldest texts date back to around the 13th century. Most of them are kept on shelves behind glass doors but others are displayed in glass cases of the type used in museums.

They're beautifully illustrated but perhaps of limited interest to anyone other than an Arabic scholar. Visitors are allowed into the outer sanctuary and the library in the morning and late afternoon (it's generally closed from noon to 3 pm). You'll be expected to leave a donation for the upkeep of the place – Dr 5 to Dr 10 should suffice. There is no shortage of local people willing to act as guides but you don't need one. Also in Tamegroute is a small potters' souk.

If you'd like to eat in Tamegroute, there's the tourist-oriented *Riad Nacin Restaurant* on the left hand side as you enter town from Zagora.

The Dunes
About five km south of Tamegroute you can get your first glimpse of the Sahara Desert. Off the road to the left are a number of isolated sand dunes which, if you've never seen the desert proper or are not intending to go there, might be worth a visit. Otherwise, it's hardly worth the effort. There are the inevitable craft tents selling everything from silverware to carpets, but the guys who own them are very pleasant and will invite you in for mint tea. Sales pressure is at a minimum.

Places to Stay
By the road side before you turn off for the dunes is the *Auberge Repos du Sable*, a beautiful, traditional-style hostelry with a very friendly owner. It's well worth considering staying here if you'd like to experience the desert at first hand. The rooms are cosy, warm and rustic and there are shared bathrooms. Singles/doubles/triples cost Dr 40/60/70. There's a large comfortable Moroccan-style dining area and even a swimming pool! Camel treks can also be organised from here. This place offers total peace, apart from the occasional tourist buses going to the dunes.

M'Hamid
Most people who come to Zagora try to make it to the end of the road at M'Hamid, about 95 km to the south. M'Hamid in itself is nothing special, though people here are very

friendly and you'll end up with half the village following you around. The attraction of this trip is the journey itself. The valley of the Drâa widens dramatically after Zagora and there are magnificent vistas; vast tracks of stony desert, oases and two passes are waiting for you, as well as the beginning of the Sahara Desert as you get close to M'Hamid (though this is nothing like a *grand erg* (large sand sea). There's also the very interesting village of Oulad Driss, with its traditional mud-brick mosque and kasbah, which offers excellent photographic possibilities.

Places to Stay & Eat The *Hotel Restaurant Sahara* has simple but adequate facilities, and charges Dr 20 per person. The food is likewise simple and somewhat overpriced, so it might be an idea to bring some with you. The hotel can also arrange donkey trips to some huge dunes about 10 km away, for Dr 30.

Getting There & Away There's a daily CTM bus from Zagora to M'Hamid around 4 pm, and it returns the next day between 4 and 5 am. If you're lucky you may be able to get a lift with other tourists.

If you just want to take a day trip from Zagora, it comes down to hiring a taxi. The usual charge is Dr 350 for the day, though this is negotiable to a degree. Taxis take up to six people, so you'll need to get a group together to share the cost. This is the best way to see the area as the driver will stop wherever you like.

Ziz Valley

ERRACHIDIA

Formerly known as Ksar es Souk, Errachidia is a large town and an important crossroad south of the High Atlas Mountains. However, it's a modern town and holds little of interest for the traveller; it usually serves as an overnight stop to and from the Ziz Valley.

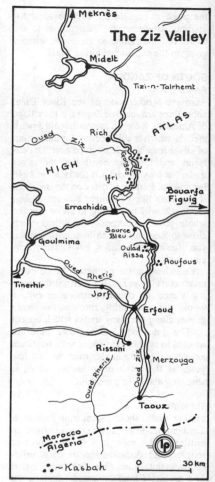

The best part of Errachidia is getting there or leaving via the Gorge du Ziz, between Errachidia and the town of Rich, on the way to Midelt and Fès/Meknès. This spectacular gorge, through which the main road runs, deserves to be regarded as the Grand Canyon of Morocco. It twists for miles upon miles until finally reaching the dam just outside Errachidia. If you take this road, make sure you get a daytime bus or grand taxi.

Information
Tourist Office There is a local syndicat d'initiative in the square opposite the covered market on Ave Moulay Ali Cherif, the main road through town. It's rarely open.

Places to Stay – bottom end
The *Hotel Royal* and the *Hotel les Oliviers*, both on Rue Mohammed Zerktouni, close to the taxi park, are the cheapest places in town. They're basic but clean and singles/doubles with shared bathroom (cold water only) cost Dr 20/40. The friendly woman who runs the Royal speaks only Arabic but you shouldn't have any problems communicating.

Better, and considerably more comfort-able, is the *Hotel Restaurant Renaissance*, Rue Moulay Youssef, where singles/doubles with shared bathroom cost Dr 50 a double or Dr 40/58 for singles/doubles with own shower and shared toilet. Hot water is available in the showers between 1 pm and late evening. The staff are friendly and both French and English are spoken.

Camping The closest campsite is *Camping Source de Bleu Meski*, 16 km out along the Erfoud road. It is a pleasant place with a swimming pool and natural spring.

Places to Stay – middle
If you have the money it's worth thinking

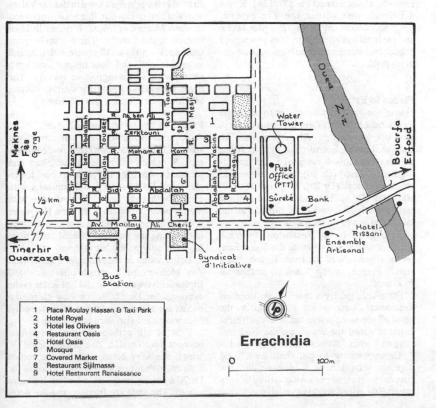

1	Place Moulay Hassan & Taxi Park
2	Hotel Royal
3	Hotel les Oliviers
4	Restaurant Oasis
5	Hotel Oasis
6	Mosque
7	Covered Market
8	Restaurant Sijilmassa
9	Hotel Restaurant Renaissance

Errachidia

0   100m

about staying at the two-star *Hotel Oasis* (☎ 57 2519), Rue Sidi Bou Abdallah, which offers very attractive, warm, carpeted rooms with their own shower and toilet and hot water. It costs Dr 123/146 for singles/ doubles, and the hotel has its own bar and restaurant.

Somewhat cheaper is the *Hotel Meski* (☎ 57 2065), Ave Moulay Ali Cherif (the main street), where singles/doubles with own shower but shared toilet cost Dr 79/100 and Dr 96/120 with own shower and toilet. The hotel has its own restaurant.

Places to Stay – top end

The only top-end hotel in Errachidia is the four-star *Hotel Rissani* (☎ 57 2136), Route d'Erfoud, just across the Ziz bridge. Singles/doubles cost Dr 234/292 plus taxes, and the hotel has all the amenities you would expect including bar, restaurant and swimming pool.

Places to Eat

One of the most popular places to eat is the *Restaurant Sijilmassa*, on the main street – look out for the sign 'All food is here' in English, French, Spanish and Italian! It has a limited but sensible range of dishes including harira (soup) (Dr 10), tajine, barbecued chicken or steak (Dr 20), omelettes (Dr 10) and salad (Dr 8). The food is good and the staff friendly. Eat inside, or outside at the tables and chairs on the sidewalk.

Also good is the *Restaurant Imilchil*, which is diagonally opposite the Sijilmassa, on the other side of the road. It, too, has a sign in French, saying 'Look no further, all food here'.

For a splurge, try a meal at the licensed *Restaurant Oasis*, which is attached to the hotel of the same name but has a different entrance round the corner on the dual carriageway where the post office is situated.

Those wishing to put their own food together should have a look around the covered market, where a wide variety of very reasonably priced food is available.

Getting There & Away

All buses operate out of the central bus station (see map).

CTM has daily departures to Casablanca (7.30 pm), Marrakesh (5.45 am), Meknès (10 pm), Ouarzazate (5.45 and 11.30 am), Rissani (via Erfoud, 5 am) and Tinerhir (5.45 am).

Other bus lines have departures to Erfoud several times throughout the day.

A grand taxi between Errachidia and Erfoud should cost Dr 13.50 but that's the locals' price and you'll be very lucky to get it for that. Most drivers will quote you silly prices.

ERFOUD

Erfoud is the principal town in the Ziz Valley south of Errachidia but, like many small and modern Moroccan towns, it offers little of interest to the traveller. There is no labyrinthine souk – just a small square with fruit and vegetable stalls and three or four handicraft shops with super-aggressive owners. The town is the take-off point for visits to Rissani and Merzouga further into the desert.

Places to Stay – bottom end

A popular place to stay, but somewhat spartan, is the *Hotel Bar Ziz*, 3 Ave Mohammed V, which offers basic but clean and pleasant rooms for Dr 30 a double downstairs and Dr 40 for a double upstairs with shared bathroom, and Dr 70 a double with own shower. There are no singles. Hot water is available in the evenings. It's overpriced considering the facilities offered but it does have the only public bar in town.

Better value is the *Hotel les Palmeraies*, Ave Mohammed V, which offers doubles/ triples with own shower and hot water in the evenings for Dr 52/73. It's very clean, the rooms are pleasant and the staff are friendly. Meals here are also very good value.

Best of all, perhaps, is the *Hotel Restaurant La Gazelle*, Ave Mohammed V, which has very clean, comfortable rooms with own shower (hot water) and toilet for Dr 70 a double (negotiable for less if you're alone). The staff are friendly and the hotel has one of the best – if not *the* best – restaurant in town.

It may also be possible to find a very basic room at the *Restaurant de la Jeunesse*, Ave Mohammed V. Local students find semi-permanent lodgings here. The people are very friendly indeed but the restaurant isn't open all day.

Camping There is a campsite next to the river, which charges Dr 5 per person for a very basic concrete block room with bunks or for pitching a tent, and Dr 5 per vehicle. There are supposed to be hot showers, but

it's a dump of a place with no character or life whatsoever, and no shade. Give it a miss unless you're determined to camp just on principle.

Places to Stay – middle

The only place to stay in this category is the one-star *Hotel Restaurant Sable d'Or*, Ave Mohammed V, a brand-new place and excellent value for money. It's clean, very comfortable, all the rooms have their own shower, toilet, table and chair, and there's hot water 24 hours a day. The management are friendly and eager to please, and there's a

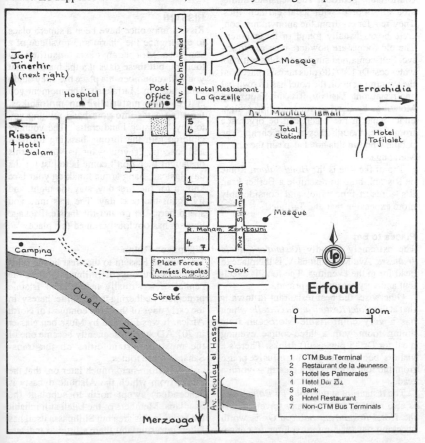

1	CTM Bus Terminal
2	Restaurant de la Jeunesse
3	Hotel les Palmeraies
4	Hotel Dar Ziz
5	Bank
6	Hotel Restaurant
7	Non-CTM Bus Terminals

Erfoud

0   100 m

roof-top terrace with great views over town. There are no singles, and doubles/triples including taxes cost Dr 112/156. The hotel has its own restaurant.

Places to Stay – top end

The cheapest place to stay in this category is the three-star *Hotel Tafilalet*, Ave Moulay Ismail. A whole new building programme has been under way here for some time and is due to be completed soon. The new rooms on the far side of the swimming pool are superb and consist of a large sunny balcony, comfortable bedroom and separate dining area all floored with local earthen tiles. They're a far cry from the anonymous, concrete boxes usually found in these hotels. The old rooms are nowhere near as attractive. Self-contained singles/doubles with hot water cost Dr 151/186 plus taxes. Apart from the swimming pool, the hotel has its own bar and restaurant. Visits to Rissani, Taouz and Merzouga by Land Rover including a night under tents in the desert can be organised from here, though they're not cheap. The people who run this hotel also run the one in Merzouga.

Top of the line is the *Hotel Salam*, Route de Rissani, built to resemble a Berber ksar. It's a resort-type hotel and considerably more expensive than the Tafilalet.

Places to Eat

The extremely friendly *Restaurant de la Jeunesse*, Ave Mohammed V, is the place to head for in the evenings. The food is excellent and very reasonably priced.

Otherwise, the best restaurant in town is that at the *Hotel Restaurant la Gazelle* which has a very comfortable Moroccan-style dining room with a three-course evening meal for Dr 35 plus (soft) drinks. There's a visitors' book here containing effusive praise from the four corners of the earth – worth a read.

The restaurant at the *Hotel les Palmeraies* is also rated highly by many travellers and the *Hotel Restaurant Sable d'Or* is worth checking out for a minor splurge in conge-

nial surroundings (Dr 45 for a three-course meal or à la carte for Dr 30 to Dr 45).

Getting There & Away

CTM has one bus daily between Erfoud and Errachidia at 8.30 pm, for Dr 12. This bus continues on to Rabat and Casablanca. Other private buses, which have their offices on the Place FAR, connect Erfoud with Errachidia and Rissani.

Alternatively, grands taxis are available between Erfoud, Errachidia and Rissani. To Rissani should cost Dr 10 and the journey will take about half an hour.

RISSANI

Rissani may once have been a superb place to experience the charm and mystique of a southern Moroccan oasis unsullied by tourism, but these days it's the hustlers that you will remember this place by. They outdo even those in Marrakesh. The moment you arrive, they materialise on motorbikes, thrusting cards into your hand inviting you to buy 'Touareg handicrafts'. The younger children join the throng, hassling for pens and sweets. If you want to survive this onslaught then don't come here just for the day. Instead, hang around making your face known for the first day, stay the night, and try again the next day. The less time you spend here, the greater the hassle. Package tourism has obviously ruined this place.

Sijilmassa Ruins

Just outside Rissani to the west lie the ruins of the fabled city of Sijilmassa, once the capital of a virtually independent Islamic principality adhering to the Shiite 'heresy' in the early days of the Arab conquest of North Africa. It was founded by Musa ben Nasser in 707 AD and subsequently became one of the most important cities on the trans-Saharan trade routes.

It was from here, much later on, that the Filali (from which the Alaouite dynasty is descended) swept north to supplant the Saadians. Members of the Filali still inhabit the ksour in this area but Sijilmassa itself has fallen into ruin and there's little to indicate

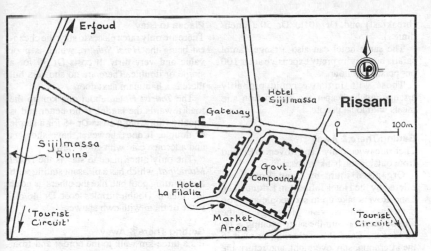

its past glories except two decorated gateways and a few other structures. It's really only of interest to archaeologists these days, but you're free to wander around the ruins if the whim takes you. You can find it off to the right-hand side of the 'Tourist Circuit' as you enter Rissani from the north.

'Tourist Circuit'

A so called 'Tourist Circuit' (signposted) has been established which makes a 21 km loop around the palmeraies south of Rissani. It takes you through most of the villages in the palmeraies but is really of mild interest only, the exceptions being the beautiful gateway at Oulad Abdelhalim, built by sultan's elder brother in 1900, and the zaouia of Moulay Ali Cherif, founder of the Alaouite dynasty (though this is closed to non-Muslims).

The road is extremely dusty (or muddy when wet) and is only really feasible with your own transport or by hired taxi. As in Rissani, if you stop anywhere, the local children will besiege you, demanding pens and sweets.

Places to Stay & Eat

The cheapest place to stay is the *Hotel La Filalia*, which is basic but adequate. This hotel is where the buses drop off and pick up passengers.

Better is the new *Hotel Sijilmassa*, which is clean, comfortable and offers spacious rooms with own shower and toilet for Dr 130 (there are no singles). The management is eager to please and there's a restaurant on the ground floor.

If you're not staying at the Sijilmassa, there are a number of simple restaurants fronting the market where you can eat well and cheaply.

Getting There & Away

There are many buses and grands taxis between Erfoud and Rissani.

MERZOUGA

Merzouga is famous for being about the only place in Morocco where you can see a genuine Saharan erg – those huge, drifting expanses of sand dunes which typify much of the Algerian Sahara.

Places to Stay

If you stay overnight, there's the *Hotel Merzouga* (owned by the Hotel Tafilalet) which costs Dr 100 a double with shared bathroom. Meals are available for Dr 15 (breakfast) and Dr 40 to Dr 50 (lunch/dinner).

The same hotel can also arrange camel safaris but they're pretty expensive at Dr 100 per person per hour.

Those with initiative could probably arrange much cheaper accommodation and meals with local people.

Getting There & Away

There are twice-daily Land Rovers to Erfoud from outside the bank in Rissani.

Organised tours by Land Rover are offered by the Hotel Tafilalet in Erfoud. The Land Rovers take up to six people and you have two options: visit Merzouga in the afternoon and return the same evening – Dr 500 for the Land Rover sharing; or visit in the afternoon, stay overnight, and return the next day – Dr 1200 for the Land Rover and accommodation.

The East

BOUARFA

This town is situated between Oujda and Figuig, but is of little interest.

Places to Stay & Eat

There's only one hotel in the town: *Hotel des Hauts Plateau* on the main street. It's very basic and is way overpriced at Dr 60 a double – filthy bed linen, no showers and sporadic water.

The *Café Chorria*, at the opposite end of the main street, is pretty good and very cheap.

FIGUIG

This is a beautiful old Berber village and the last Moroccan town before you get to the Algerian border. Palm trees blanket the ruins of the old city.

There's no black market here for Algerian dinar and you cannot reconvert excess dirham into hard currency.

Places to Stay

There are only three places to stay, the cheapest being the *Hotel Sahara*, which is poor value and very dirty. It costs Dr 30 for a single or double. There are no showers but there is a hammam next door.

The *Tourist Hotel*, about one km up the road towards the border, is no better and is equally filthy, but it costs Dr 45 for a single or double. It does, however, have showers and a terrace café with good views.

The only other place to stay is the *Hotel Municipal*, which has a pleasant setting with a swimming pool but, like the others, is none too clean. Doubles/triples cost Dr 48/60, some of them with own shower.

Getting There & Away

It's a three-km walk to the border and from there it's another one km to Beni Ounif. Don't forget to visit the police for an exit stamp before walking off to the border. Be prepared for heavy searches on the Algerian side, although this seems to happen less frequently these days.

Western Sahara

Few countries have recognised Morocco's occupation of Western Sahara, and the war of attrition between Rabat and the Polisario front has continued, until recently, with both sides making conflicting claims. It has been generally acknowledged, however, that the Moroccans have had the upper hand and that Polisario's activities have been drastically restricted. This is due for the most part to the 1600-km-long sand wall which the Moroccans constructed, from their previous border west of Tindouf (Algeria) to the coast south of Dakhla, and which has been protected by some 100,000 Moroccan regular soldiers. However, the latest news to date is that a UN-supervised ceasefire is now in force in the disputed region. Encouraging reports suggest that this is the first stage of a peace plan designed to give inhabitants the choice between independence and Moroccan rule.

Prior to the ceasefire, as a measure of Moroccan confidence, it was no longer necessary to obtain military permits to visit the area as far south as Dakhla. There are daily scheduled CTM buses from most large Moroccan cities to Smara, Layoune and Dakhla.

TARFAYA

Tarfaya has been described by travellers as 'a real hole and very noisy when the desert wind is blowing; a quiet desert town with only one hotel'.

The same travellers described the beach as very good if the wind isn't too strong, and mentioned that it was well worth walking to one or other of the four shipwrecks which lie within seven km of the town.

Places to Stay & Eat

The hotel doesn't even have a sign but it's only Dr 30 a double. There are no restaurants as such but there are a couple of simple cafés which sell soup, omelettes and salads. The best of them is the one opposite the hotel to the left. It sells harira and bread, which is very filling, for Dr 1, but make sure you are there around 5.30 pm – otherwise they'll have sold out.

LAYOUNE

Layoune is another quiet desert town, where you can walk along the streets without the usual beggars, guides and dealers hassling you. It's a modern town with some attractive buildings and a bird sanctuary.

Places to Stay & Eat

The best budget hotel is the *Hotel Marhaba*, Ave Hassan II, which is very clean and offers large rooms for Dr 60 a double. On the roof there are good washing facilities and excel-

lent views of the town and the surrounding sand dunes.

The *Hotel Liberte*, on Rue Oued ek Hanchi close to the four-star Hotel Parador, is cheap but has cold showers only.

There are numerous places to eat along the Ave Hassan II, especially around the place where the bus from Tarfaya stops.

Getting There & Away

CTM operates daily buses at 8 am to Dakhla (Dr 121). Book in advance to ensure a seat, or take a shared taxi for Dr 150 per person.

There are flights direct from Layoune to the Canary Islands for Dr 831, from where there are connections to Mauritania (43,200 Ptas to Nouakchott). In the tourist season there are also flights from the Canaries to Banjul (The Gambia) for 35,000 Ptas.

DAKHLA

Dakhla is on the end of a sandy peninsula stretching out 30 km from the main coastline. The scenery between here and Layoune is fantastic.

Due to the proximity to Dakhla of the war with Polisario, the town is consequently full of soldiers. For this reason it can be difficult to find accommodation.

Places to Stay

There are many cheap hotels but these are almost always full of soldiers, so just keep looking. The average price for a single room is around Dr 22.

If you are in a vehicle it is OK to camp overlooking the sea on the landward side of the peninsula.

Getting There & Away

There's a daily CTM bus to Layoune for Dr 121. It's not possible to continue south from Dakhla into Mauritania.

ALGERIA

Facts about the Country

HISTORY SINCE 1830

The French presence in North Africa started in earnest in 1830, when they blockaded and attacked Algiers, supposedly because the *dey* (governor of the janissaries) of Algiers insulted the French consul. The real motive, however, was the need at home for a military success to revive the flagging fortunes of Charles X.

Within three weeks of the French landing on July 5, the government of the dey had capitulated. A couple of weeks later, Charles X himself had been overthrown; his successor, Louis Philippe, favoured colonisation.

By 1845, General Bugeaud had conquered the greater part of the country and had been proclaimed governor general of Algeria. However, it wasn't until 1847 that the west of the country, which had been under the control of the famous Abdelkader, finally came under French control.

Abdelkader was a *sherif* (descendant of the prophet), who had been elected locally as the leader in the conflict with the invading European Christians. He had been recognised by the French by the Desmichels

Abdelkader

Treaty of 1834, which effectively gave him control of western and inland central Algeria. His position was further strengthened by the Treaty of Tafna in 1837. Such was his charisma and ability to rally people around him that, by late 1838, the area under his control stretched from Biskra to the Moroccan border in the south, and from the Kabylie to Oran in the north. This area virtually constituted a separate state, with its own judicial and administrative system.

After a six-year struggle against the French following their breaking of the treaty in 1839, Abdelkader was forced into Morocco, where he called on the sultan, Abd er Rahman, for support. This was provided, but the army was trounced by the French at Isly (near Oujda) in 1844. Abdelkader finally surrendered to the French in 1846 on condition that he be allowed to live in the Middle East. Despite this, he was imprisoned in Toulon, Pau and Amboise until 1852; he was finally allowed to settle in Damascus, where he died in 1883 after 36 years of exile. He was by far the greatest figure in Algeria's nationalist movement and is a national hero today, with many streets named after him and a major statue commemorating him in central Algiers.

French domination of the entire country was complete in 1871, when the people of the mountains of the Kabylie (to the east of Algiers) were finally subdued.

During the next 50 years of French occupation land was appropriated and European settlers – mainly of French, Italian, Maltese and Spanish origin – established their domination of the local inhabitants. Local culture was actively eliminated, and the Arab *medinas* (cities) were replaced with streets laid out in grids.

Many Algerians worked in France, particularly in the factories supporting the war effort from 1914 to 1918, and it was among these expatriate workers that some of the first stirrings of nationalism occurred. This led to the formation of the Parti du Peuple Algérien, which was followed by the establishment of the Association of Algerian Ulama, a largely religious body, in Algeria itself.

After WW II the French president, Charles de Gaulle, offered citizenship to certain categories of Muslims. This was considered inadequate, and an uprising near Sétif saw the massacre of more than 80 Europeans. By 1947, however, all Muslims had been given full French citizenship rights and the right to live and work in France.

The Algerian war of independence really began on 31 October 1954 with an outbreak of violence in Batna. This was led by young men who had formed the new National Liberation Front (FLN) – a body whose stated aim was the bringing down of the French administration by military means at home and diplomacy abroad. The bitter and bloody fight, which was to continue for the next seven years, cost at least a million Algerian lives.

By 1956, the fight for Algerian independence was being actively supported by the country's neighbours, both former French protectorates. This led to the construction by the French of a series of massive barbed-wire fences and observation posts which separated Algeria from both Morocco and Tunisia. The fence along the Moroccan border was over 1000 km long, and the remnants can still be seen today. The fences were actually some distance in from the border, and the buffer zones were patrolled day and night by Algerian forces. The idea (successful, as it turned out) was to cut off the revolutionaries from Tunisian and Moroccan support.

As Algeria was in fact a part of metropolitan France, there were over three million French settlers living there. They were obviously unwilling to see the country lose touch with France and, in an uprising in early 1958, thousands of these settlers called for continued integration with France; it was largely these people (colons) who voted de Gaulle back into power, using the slogan Algérie Française.

These same settlers became increasingly troubled when it became obvious that de Gaulle was thinking about granting Algerian independence. In 1961 some of them even went to the extent of forming what amounted to a settler terrorist organisation, the Organisation de l'Armée Secrète (OAS). De Gaulle was unmoved and, on 18 March 1962, agreement was reached for a referendum in Algeria which, if the vote went the right way, would grant the country independence. In the event, the vote was six million in favour and only 16,000 against. The trickle of French settlers returning to France turned into a flood, with only some 40,000 staying on after independence.

The cost of the war to Algeria had been tremendous – over a million Algerians had lost their lives, and a further two million had been displaced in an effort by the colonial authorities to disrupt all attempts to organise an effective nationalist movement.

Ahmed Ben Bella was the first elected premier; he pledged a 'revolutionary Arab-Islamic state based on the principles of socialism and collective leadership at home and anti-imperialism abroad'. Although popular, his leadership style did not foster orderly administration and he was overthrown in 1965 by the defence minister and FLN Chief of Staff, Colonel Houari Boumedienne. Ben Bella spent many years in exile in Switzerland, but in 1990 he returned to lead his party, the Movement for Democracy in Algeria (MDA).

Boumedienne was a cautious pragmatist. He set about rebuilding the country's economy, which had come unstuck at the time of independence with the departure of the majority of the country's administrators and technical experts, all of whom were Europeans. Unemployment and underemployment remained serious problems and many Algerians were forced to work in France, despite the ill feeling which existed there towards them.

Large gas and oil reserves in the Sahara were developed and, despite the fact that over 70% of the workforce were employed on the land, agriculture was neglected in favour of industry in the 1970s. As a result, agricultural production fell below levels achieved under the French.

Colonel Boumedienne died in December 1978 and, at a meeting of the FLN in Algiers, Colonel Chadli Benjedid was elected president, a post he has held ever since. He was re-elected in 1984.

There has been very little political change in Algeria since independence. The FLN continues to be the sole political party and it pursues socialist policies. Bad planning by the lumbering centralised bureaucracy is largely responsible for the poor state of the agricultural sector. The last few years have seen President Chadli undertaking a certain amount of cautious reform with the aim of reducing Algeria's dependence on imported food, clothes and medical supplies.

The most radical reform since independence came in late 1987 when Chadli abolished the central planning authority, the bastion of socialist economic control. The new legislation removed most public companies from direct government control and freed up the banking system. Such reform is encouraging private-sector participation, but Chadli has been careful not to move too fast for fear of opposition within the ruling FLN, where the old-timers regard any moves away from central control of the economy with deep suspicion.

Algeria is often seen as being anti-Western in its foreign policy, but it is an active member of the Non-Aligned Movement, and in fields such as gas exports it is in direct competition with the Soviet Union.

The country has become well respected on the world stage for its strong stand on a better deal for the Third World and in its support of liberation struggles. It is a staunch supporter of the Polisario struggle against the Moroccan occupation of Western Sahara and the Polisario base is in fact at Tindouf. The two countries have come close to war over the issue on a couple of occasions, and the border situation does change from time to time. In 1988 there was a rapprochement between the two countries so hopefully now the position will remain more stable.

Until 1988 there was little real opposition to the government, although there were a number of minor incidents. In 1985, a group

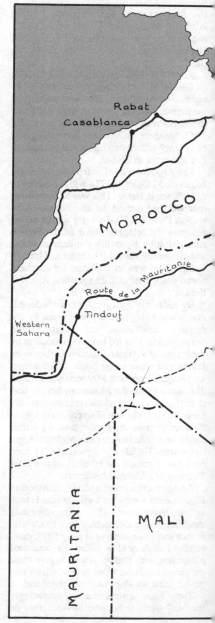

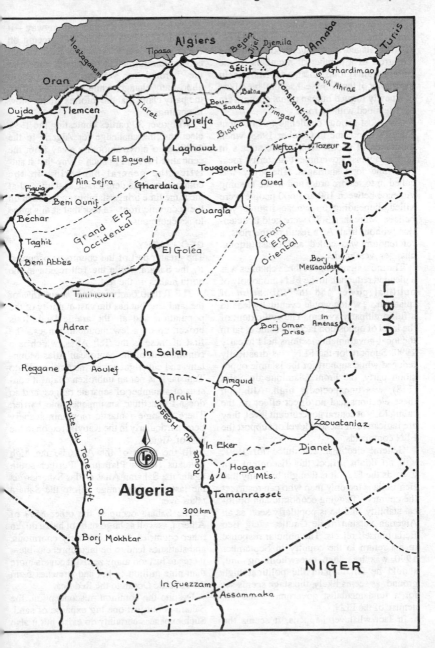

of Muslim extremists attacked a police barracks, and in the Kabylie region, Berber activists staged a 24-hour strike following the arrest of a number of members of the cultural rights group, Enfants des Martyrs. In December of the same year several members of a newly formed human rights group were also detained without trial.

The most serious challenge to President Chadli's rule came in October 1988, when thousands of people took to the streets in protest against government austerity measures and food shortages. The army was called in to restore order and in the ensuing violence between 160 and 600 people were killed, depending on whose figures you believe. More than 3000 were held in detention without trial. As a result of the riots, a referendum was called and constitutional changes were made.

The most significant of these changes was a pledged reduction in the FLN monopoly of political power and the formation of 'platforms', which would eventually lead to a full multiparty system. The full extent of the level of opposition faced became clear in the local-government elections held in early 1990. Support for the FLN was drastically reduced while support for the Islamic opposition party, the Front Islamique du Salut (FIS), was unexpectedly high. Although these elections had no direct effect on the ruling FLN at central government level, they are indicative of the low level of support the FLN commands.

General elections, scheduled for 1991, will no doubt reflect the discontent felt towards the FLN. It is thought by many that Ben Bella is the only man who can resurrect the country's flagging economic and political stability, and he is popularly seen as an Algerian version of de Gaulle, a tag Ben Bella himself rejects. The popular response to his return to the country in September 1990 was less than overwhelming and, should he fail to gain the political high ground, as seems likely, the stage seems set for a fundamentalist government and the demise of the FLN.

In fact whatever happens, it seems the days of the FLN are numbered anyway – it is in turmoil, with factions disagreeing on major policy issues, especially political and economic reform. The old guard, known as the 'barons', are vehemently opposed to almost any change, while moderates within the party claim that the reforms are too slow in coming.

With over 30 parties contesting the 1991 elections, the challenge for Algeria in the 1990s is to move smoothly away from the centralised system in such a way that it satisfies the general hankering in the community for a democratic system, and at the same time brings stability and growth on the economic front – a task that at this stage looks enormous.

GEOGRAPHY

The greater part of the country is occupied by the Sahara, while the Tell region in the north makes up the rest.

The Tell accounts for only about 15% of the land area but has the vast majority of the population and all the arable land. It is broken up by a few mountain ranges. The first of these is the Tell Atlas, which is a continuation of the Moroccan Atlas Mountains and cuts right across the north and into Tunisia. It is not an unbroken chain: it consists of a number of separate ranges, and so doesn't constitute an impenetrable barrier. There is some fantastic mountain scenery here, particularly in the Kabylie region to the east of Algiers.

To the south of the Atlas lie the high plateaus (Hauts Plateaux). Further south again, the Saharan Atlas (Atlas Saharien) is the last mountain range before the Sahara takes over.

The Sahara occupies the other 85% of Algeria, as well as large slabs of half a dozen other countries. It is absolutely enormous, and statistics tend to be incomprehensible – there are just too many zeros! It covers more than nine million sq km and stretches from the Atlantic Ocean to the Red Sea.

Despite the common misconception, the Sahara is not just one big expanse of sand. Such expanses certainly do exist, but it also has mountain ranges (such as the Hoggar, which peak at around 3000 metres), dead-flat plains (where the most prominent feature for miles around is a rock the size of a tennis ball) and numerous oases, which support small numbers of people and produce the most delicately flavoured dates in the world.

The vegetation of the desert varies from esparto-grass plains in the M'Zab to areas the size of England where not a thing grows. Absolutely nothing.

As might be expected, the only major river systems are in the north of the country, and even many of these are only seasonal. The main reservoirs for irrigation are in the mountains to the west of Algiers, while those in the north-east produce the 5% of the country's power which is generated by hydroelectricity.

Distances

With an area of some 2.4 million sq km (about the size of Western Australia, or five times the size of California or France), Algeria is the second-largest country in Africa, smaller only than Sudan.

Distances are great: from Algiers to Tamanrasset, for example, is more than 2000 km – greater than the distance from Algiers to Paris.

CLIMATE

Algeria's geography, vegetation and, therefore, its settlement pattern are dominated by climate rather than relief.

Rainfall ranges from 1000 mm annually in the Kabylie region to virtually nil in some places in the Sahara; in fact, some Saharan towns go for up to 20 years without any rainfall at all! Summer in the north is generally hot (around 32°C), with high humidity along the coast. In the Sahara the temperature is regularly 45°C, and it's not that uncommon for the mercury to climb to 50°C and above.

Winter in the north is wet and cold, with snow common on the peaks south of Algiers; in the Sahara it never really cools down that much, and daytime temperatures are about 25°C.

Tamanrasset, in the Hoggar Mountains, has a milder summer and a colder winter, as it has an elevation of over 1500 metres, and at nearby Assekrem the temperatures drop to below freezing at night.

The following table gives the average daily minimum and maximum temperatures in °C.

Average Temperatures			
	Algiers	Ghardaia	Tamanrasset
Jan	7-15	6-19	4-19
April	13-20	18-31	13-30
July	21-29	25-37	21-35
Oct	17-25	19-31	15-30

GOVERNMENT

Officially known as the Democratic and Popular Republic of Algeria, the country is governed by the FLN. Executive power is in the hands of the president, as laid down in the original National Charter of 1976. President Chadli had a new Charter approved by referendum in 1986. Revised versions of the constitution were passed in late 1988 and early 1989. These political reforms of the late 1980s should bring about major changes in the political make-up of the country in the 1990s.

Legislative power in Algeria is vested in the 281-member National Assembly which is elected to a five-year term by universal adult suffrage.

Directly below the central government is the *wilaya* (province). There are 48 wilayas, each of which is headed by an elected executive council and a member of the central government, known as the *wali*. A majority of these positions are now held by members of the fundamentalist FIS party following their unexpected successes in the 1990 local government elections.

On the bottom of the administrative ladder are the local collectives. These are financed predominantly by local taxes, although the state does intervene with funds to meet the commune's needs.

ECONOMY

Since independence the emphasis has been on industry rather than agriculture (it was the other way round during the French colonial days).

The country relies almost exclusively on oil and gas for exports (98%) and was hit hard by the slump of 1986. Until this time the Algerian economy recorded a yearly trade surplus. Although the hydrocarbons industry still receives the major portion of annual government expenditure, increasing importance is being placed on agriculture (15% of spending) and associated medium and light industry such as farm equipment and fertilisers.

In an effort to streamline the public sector, 60 of the country's national companies were broken up into 400 smaller, more manageable, decentralised new companies in 1985.

At present, only about 5% of the land is under cultivation, and the local produce supplies only about 40% of the country's food needs (as against 95% at independence). The amount of cultivated land could increase to as much as 30% when the numerous dams which are under construction come on line.

Many of the reforms of the last few years have targeted the agricultural sector as the area in greatest need of streamlining. Much has been done to boost production and allow greater initiative on the part of the small farmers. State-owned farms are now offered for lease, and eventual purchase, to cooperatives and individuals who can raise loans; they can manage the farms as they want.

The forests in the north were devastated during the war of independence, but large areas have been replanted in an effort to generate some more income; the country is already one of the world's major suppliers of cork. Other exports include wine, tobacco and foodstuffs.

A tight control is kept over imports, the result being that there is very little for sale in the shops which is not produced in Algeria. There are often shortages of certain items so the demand for foreign goods is high.

Radical economic reforms planned by the FLN look certain to bring about the advent of a full free-market economy in the near future, *if* the country does not slide into political chaos in the meantime.

Social Conditions

With a staggering 50% of the population aged 18 or less, great strain is placed on the social services. Education is particularly affected and the younger children have to go to school in shifts, as there are insufficient numbers of both schools and teachers.

Health care is available free to those under 16 and over 60, and income earners pay according to what they can afford. The state provides pensions for the old, the disabled and war veterans.

Housing is a major problem, particularly with the movement of people out of rural areas and into the larger cities in recent years. To alleviate the problems and to encourage people to stay in the country, row upon row of massive apartment blocks have been built on the outskirts of many towns in the interior; these are available for low rent or subsidised purchase from the government.

POPULATION & PEOPLE

The population of Algeria is about 25 million and it is increasing at the alarming rate of more than 3% per year. More than 50% of Algerians are under the age of 18. Life expectancy is low, at 54 years for men and 56 for women. The average population density is around two people per sq km, but, obviously, this figure is affected by the massive unpopulated areas of the Sahara – 90% of the people live in 5% of the land area.

The majority of people are Berbers, with the main minority group being Arabs; however, there has been so much intermingling over the centuries that there is no clear ethnic boundary between the two.

There are places where the Berber language and life style have been preserved, mainly in the Kabylie region of the north.

Touareg

The Touareg people in the south are also Berber and often speak the Berber dialect

Tamahaq. They live in southern Algeria, Libya, Niger and Mali.

The two main Touareg groups in Algeria are the Kel Ahaggar from the Hoggar region and the Kel Ajjer from the Djanet area, although within each group there are various subgroups which have slightly different languages and customs. Traditional Touareg society is rapidly breaking down, mainly due to the agrarian reform policies of the government, the influx of large numbers of Arabs from the north and a series of crippling droughts which have forced many people into the towns to search for work.

Touareg women play a much more active role in the organisation of the society than do their Islamic counterparts. The fact that they generally go unveiled has led to some misunderstandings about their morals.

The men often wear a blue or white head cloth *(tagelmoust)*, tied in such a way that it covers most of the face; in the past this cloth was usually dyed with indigo – these days it is imported and synthetically dyed.

RELIGION

Islam is the predominant religion and is one of the few things which unites a variety of fairly disparate groups. There are also small Christian and Jewish communities.

Algeria is by far the most conservative of the three Maghreb countries. Apart from those in Algiers, a high proportion of women wear veils. These vary from the white, lacy, handkerchief-type ones worn in the north which cover just the lower half of the face, to the robes worn by the women of the M'Zab (the area around Ghardaia) which are held together in such a way that only one eye is visible – a bizarre sight.

For a full rundown on Islam, see the Religion section in the Facts about the Region chapter.

Facts for the Visitor

VISAS & EMBASSIES

The Algerian visa situation is pretty straight-forward for nationals of most countries. People from the following countries do not require a visa for a stay of up to three months: Denmark, Finland, Italy, Norway, Sweden and Switzerland. All other nationals require visas and these must be obtained before you show up at a border, as they are not issued on the spot.

Visas generally cost the equivalent of AD 50 (at the official rate, around US$2.50), although Brits are in for a wallet-thinning exercise with the cost currently set at UK£35 for a one-month, single-entry visa. Also note, Brits *must* apply for a visa *in the UK only*. Don't arrive in Morocco in the hope of getting one there.

Currently the Algerian Embassy in Tunis is not issuing visas to anyone other than residents of Tunisia, so you need to make provision for this. Similarly the consulate in Oujda (Morocco) is unreliable and often knocks back applications – apply in Rabat or elsewhere.

As a result of Algeria's support for Iraq in the Gulf War (or, at least, its opposition to Western involvement in Saddam Hussein's invasion of Kuwait), nationals of Australia and the UK were being refused visas to Algeria in early 1991. Strangely, despite their countries' more than obvious presence in the Gulf War, no such bans were imposed on French and American citizens! This situation should have changed by now, but check in advance before heading off in the hope of travelling through Algeria. There was a bottleneck of disappointed and frustrated travellers stuck in Morocco in late 1990 because of the frightful mess in the Gulf.

Nationals of South Africa and Israel are banned from entering.

All tourists entering Algeria are required to declare all their foreign currency (cash and cheques) on a declaration form, and change the equivalent of AD 1000). These forms are important and *must* be kept in order if you want to avoid hassles when leaving. The idea is that you change your money at the official rate and don't use the black market, which pays something over three times the official rate. For the full story on how to play the black market for fun and profit, see the Money section.

Algerian Embassies

Visas can be obtained from the following Algerian embassies and consulates:

Benin
    Les Cocotiers Lot H 27 (PO Box 1809), Cotonou (☎ 30 0454)
France
    50 Rue de Lisbonne, Paris 75016 (☎ 4225 7070)
Germany
    Rheinalee 32, 5300 Bonn, Bad Godesberg (☎ 35 6054)
Greece
    Vassileos Constantinou 14, Athens 78 (☎ 751 8625)
Italy
    Via Barnaba Oriani, 2600197 Rome (☎ 87 8680)
Jordan
    3rd Circle, Jebel Amman, Amman (☎ 41 271)
Morocco
    10-12 Rue d'Azrou (PO Box 448), Rabat (☎ 76 5474)
    1 Blvd Bir Anzarane, Oujda (☎ 68 3740; unreliable)
Niger
    Rue du Sahel (PO Box 142), Niamey (☎ 72 3164)
Nigeria
    26 Maitama Sule St, SW Ikoyi (PO Box 7288), Lagos (☎ 68 3153)
Senegal
    5 Rue Mermoz (PO Box 3233), Dakar (☎ 22 3509)
Sierra Leone
    Premier Blvd opposite Armed Forces Building (PO Box 1004), Conakry (☎ 41 503)
Spain
    12 Calle General Oraa, Madrid (☎ 411 6065)
Switzerland
    74 Wallading, WEG 3006 Berne (☎ 44 6961)
Tanzania
    35 Upanga Rd (PO Box 2963), Dar es Salaam (☎ 20 846)

UK
    6 Hyde Park Gate, London NW8 (☎ (071) 221-7800)
USA
    2118 Kalorama Rd NW, Washington SCN 20008 (☎ 32 8530)

Visa Extensions

Tourist visas are valid for one month and are easily extendable for a further two months in Algiers at the Département des Étrangers, Blvd Zeroud Youssef 19A. To get the extension, however, you need to show bank receipts to prove that you have been changing money legally and not playing the black market. If you have changed the equivalent of the AD 1000, the receipts which prove this are sufficient.

Visas can supposedly be extended at the capital of any wilaya, but in practice it seems you may be sent to Algiers for it, so be prepared for this. We've had reports from a couple of travellers who tried for an extension in Ghardaïa and were knocked back. Extensions cost AD 60 (payable only in fiscal stamps available from the post office), require two photos and take 24 hours to issue.

You may also be asked for a certificate from the hotel you are staying at. Often a receipt is sufficient; if not, bear in mind that it may take a couple of days to get the hotel manager to sign a declaration stating that you are staying at that hotel. The whole thing is a bit of a farce, but hopefully you won't have to go through it.

The staff at the foreigners' office in Algiers do not speak English but are very helpful and polite. As usual, the forms are all in French.

Foreign Embassies & Consulates in Algeria

Algiers is not a bad place for picking up visas, but as Mali and Niger both have embassies in Tamanrasset, it is easier to pick those ones up on your way south.

The visa situation often changes here, and, as the embassies are mostly out in the suburb of Hydra, it pays to make a phone call first.

The best way to get out to Hydra is to catch a No 31 bus from Place Audin, get out at the big marketplace just before the end, and from there catch a No 44 bus to Hydra.

Burkina Faso The embassy (☎ 61 3897) is at 12 Rue Mouloud Belhouchat. Visas are issued without fuss.

Cameroun The embassy (☎ 78 8195) is at 35 Rue J Apremont, Bouzèreah. It usually refers applications to Douala, so a visa can take up to four weeks.

Central African Republic Contact the French Embassy here (☎ 60 4488); it's at 6 Ave Larbi Alik, Hydra. It issues only 48-hour transit visas.

Chad The embassy (☎ 60 6637) is at 18 Chemin Ahmed Kara, Cité des DNC. With a letter of recommendation, visas cost AD 107 and take 24 hours to issue.

Mali The embassy (☎ 60 6118) is at Cité DNC Villa 15, Chemin Ahmed Kara, Hydra. They will probably tell you to get your visa in Tamanrasset (Ave Emir Abdelkader; ☎ (09) 74 4115)

Niger The embassy (☎ 78 8921) is way out in the suburbs, at 54 Rue du Vercos, Rostomia, Al-Hamadya, Bouzaréah. A taxi there costs at least AD 40, or else take a No 59 bus from Place des Martyrs. Telephone ahead to make sure it is open.

Visas take up to three days to issue, cost AD 40, and you need a yellow fever vaccination certificate and sometimes your Algerian currency form.

It is easier to get visas from the consulate in Tamanrasset (Ave Emir Abdelkader), where you need to have three passport photos and AD 80. Visas there take from one to three days to issue.

Nigeria The embassy (☎ 59 3298) is at 77 Cité des PTT, Hydra. Visas cost from nothing (Irish) up to AD 256 (UK), depending on your nationality, and are usually issued the same day if you're patient. You also need a letter of recommendation from your own embassy.

Tunisia The embassy is at 11 Rue du Bois de Boulogne, Algiers (☎ 78 1480). There are also Tunisian embassies in Annaba (☎ (08) 82 4447/8) and Tébessa; however, they are not recommended, as visas take at least three weeks to be issued.

Other countries with diplomatic representation in Algeria include:

Australia
  12 Djenane Malik, Hydra, Algiers (☎ 60 1965)
Austria
  Les Vergers, Rue No 2 Lot 9, Bir Mourad Rais, Algiers (☎ 56 2699)
Benin
  16 Lot du Stade, Birkhadem, Algiers (☎ 56 6271)
Burundi
  22 Lot du Carrefour, El-Biar, Algiers (☎ 79 4729)
Canada
  27b Rue Ali Messaoudi, Hydra, Algiers (☎ 60 6190)
Congo
  179 Lot Cadat, Djenane, Ben Omar, Kouba, Algiers (☎ 58 3888)
Denmark
  29 Blvd Zighout Youssef, Algiers (☎ 62 8871)
Egypt
  Chemin Abdelkader Gadouche, Ben Aknoun, Algiers (☎ 60 1807)
France
  6 Ave Larbi Alik, Hydra, Algiers (☎ 60 4488)
  Rue Gouta Sebti, Annaba (☎ (08) 82 6391)
  28 Blvd M Belouizdad, Constantine (☎ (04) 93 7602)
  3 Square Émile Cayla, Oran (☎ (06) 33 5300)
Gabon
  80 Rue Ali Al-Hamadya, Bouzaréah, Algiers (☎ 78 0264)
Ghana
  62 Rue des Frères Benali Abdallah, Hydra, Algiers (☎ 60 6444)
Guinea
  43 Blvd Said Hamdine, Hydra, Algiers (☎ 60 0059)
Guinea Bissau
  Cité DNC Villa 17, Chemin Ahmed Kara, Hydra, Algiers (☎ 60 0151)
Italy
  8 Rue Mohammed Tahar Rkhaya (☎ (08) 70 9707)

Japan
  1 Chemin Al-Bakri, El-Biar, Algiers (☎ 78 6200)
Mauritania
  107 Lot Baranès Al-Hamadya, Bouzaréah, Algiers (☎ 79 2044)
Morocco
  8 Rue des Cèdres, Algiers (☎ 60 7408)
  26 Rue Cheikh Larbi Tebessi, Oran (☎ (06) 33 1784)
  5 Ave de l'ANP, Sidi-Bel-Abbès, (☎ 24 3470)
Rwanda
  30 Rue Doukdouk Abdelkader, Rostomia, Algiers (☎ 78 7769)
Senegal
  1 Rue Mahieddine Bacha, El Mouradia, Algiers (☎ 56 9043)
Spain
  10 Rue Ali Azil, Algiers (☎ 61 7062)
  7 Rue Mohammed Benabdeslem
UK
  7 Chemin Capt Hocine Sliman, Algiers (☎ 60 5038)
USA
  4 Chemin Cheikh Bachir El Ibrahimi, El-Biar, Algiers (☎ 60 1186)
Zaire
  104 Lot Cadat, Djenane Ben Omar, Kouba, Algiers (☎ 58 0679)

MONEY
Currency
The local currency is the Algerian dinar, which is divided into 100 centimes. Coins in use are 5, 10, 20 and 50 centimes, and 1, 5 and 10 dinars. The coins have only Arabic writing and numbers. The 10 dinar coin is very distinctive, as it is 10 sided and the colour of brass. Notes in circulation are 5 (rare), 10, 20, 50, 100 and 200. Again, they have only Arabic writing but, unlike the coins, they have familiar numerals, so are a bit easier to identify. There used to be a AD 500 note, but this has been taken out of circulation in order to make it harder to smuggle large amounts of cash in or out of the country. If you buy dinar in Morocco or elsewhere don't accept any AD 500 notes, as some people will try to off-load these onto unsuspecting foreigners.

The fact that prices are sometimes expressed in French can be confusing. For instance, AD 20 is *deux milles* (2000 centimes).

Exchange Rates

US$1 = AD 21.43
UK£1 = AD37.08
FFr1 = AD3.74
Dm1 = AD12.70
Y100 = AD16.53
A$1 = AD17.06
NZ$1 = AD12.19
C$1 = AD19.06

The above rates reflect the recent devaluation of the Algerian dinar.

The AD 1000 Catch

The catch when entering Algeria is that all foreigners must change the equivalent of AD 1000 on arrival. There are no exceptions to the rule and, if it makes you feel any better, even Algerians themselves have to change AD 700 if they have been away.

Not only must you change AD 1000, you must do so at the official rate. It is quite possible that on arrival you will not be compelled to change on the spot, but will just be told to change at the first bank. In this case there is then nothing to make you change the money and you could use the black market the whole time. However, if you haven't changed the right amount you can expect hassles when you leave, particularly if you cross from In Guezzam into Niger.

The likely penalty is that you will have to change AD 1000 and then hand it straight over to the officials. This is not always the case; some people have got away with changing only half that amount, but it's most unlikely that you will get out without having to hand over some money. You might just as well change it officially to start with and get something for your money, rather than see it go to a customs official who then does who-knows-what with it. Not only that but for a country with a legitimate government and limited reserves of foreign currency, your contribution to the pool can only help.

It is supposed to be possible to re-exchange dinar back to hard currency if you have receipts, but in practice it is extremely difficult and can only be done at the international ports and airports, not on the land borders. If you have Algerian currency when leaving the country, you can hand it in and

get an official receipt for it. It is then supposedly possible to get the money back if you return within 12 months.

Currency Declaration Form

Everyone entering the country has to fill in one of these forms. On it you must list all your foreign currency in both cash and cheques, and the officials may demand to see and count it. All official transactions are then recorded on the form during your stay. On departure, the money you are carrying must tally with what you brought in, minus exchanges recorded on the form. It is important to keep this form in order and get bank receipts to back up any official transactions.

If you lose the form you are in deep shit, and can expect to spend a week or so learning the ins and outs of Algerian bureaucracy. It is possible you may even get sent back to the point of entry at which the form was issued, so look after it.

If you can't show the right amount on leaving, expect a 'fine' which might be as much as (or more than) your shortfall.

It's also a good idea to declare any valuables, particularly cameras, and get them put on the form. It has happened in the past that travellers have had such items confiscated when leaving because they were not listed on the form. The same thing applies if you are bringing in a vehicle and are carrying lots of big spare parts.

Exactly how thoroughly you and your form get scrutinised on leaving varies from day to day and border to border, but as long as you keep a cool head and adopt a non-confrontationist approach things should be OK.

It is also necessary to prove that you have changed the compulsory AD 1000 if you need to get a visa extension, buy an internal plane ticket or an international plane or ferry ticket.

Black Market

There is a thriving black market in hard currencies and goods which are hard to obtain in Algeria. By far the best currency is French francs, as most people are familiar

with them. You can also use US dollars and pounds sterling, but in many places people are reluctant to take anything other than francs.

At the time this book was researched, the black market rate was triple (or more) what you could get officially; however, due to the recent devaluation of the Algerian dinar, this may not be the case by the time you reach Algeria. It is still worth investigating the black market rate when you arrive.

Obviously, if you want to change money on the black market, it must be with money that is over and above the official amount listed on your form. It is easy enough to smuggle it in (and out), but as searches at some borders are thorough (particularly Figuig-Beni Ounif), make sure it is very well hidden. Any extra money which is found will be confiscated.

The black market is usually not that hard to find, especially in places which are on the tourist route, such as it is. Algiers is one place where it is not that easy to change money unofficially.

The best people to deal with are the owners of souvenir shops, as they are used to dealing with foreigners and are the most ready to change money. The most discreet way of bringing up the subject is to express interest in an item and then ask if they take dollars or francs. If you get no response, try another shop. It is really very straightforward and the risks are minimal, but tact and common sense are necessary. Hotel owners are also often willing to change. The bottom line is that the risk is greater for the locals than for you.

The people not to change with are the ones who approach you in the street. Some may be OK, but others definitely are not.

The government keeps tight control on imports, and with the recent severe austerity measures they were one of the first things to suffer. Items in demand are jeans, T-shirts, sunglasses (Ray-Bans), running shoes, instant coffee, cameras (as long as they are not on your currency form), car parts and jerry cans (metal or plastic). At the official rate it will appear that you are being offered outrageously high prices for things, but keep in mind that it is the black-market rate which reflects the true value of the dinar; the official rate is there only to get more out of you (and the locals) when entering the country.

If you are only going to be in the country for a week or 10 days the chances are that the black market will be of little use to you until you have spent your AD 1000, although it is often possible to exchange goods for handicrafts or for services (such as a mechanic).

If you are coming from Morocco, it is well worth considering buying Algerian dinar in Ceuta, Melilla or Oujda. The rate is usually better than what you would get on the black market inside Algeria. There are plenty of moneychangers doing the rounds in Oujda and Melilla.

Credit Cards

The only places in Algeria which accept credit cards are some of the expensive hotels in Algiers and the head-office branch of Air Algérie. Everywhere else you'll need to have cash or travellers' cheques.

A couple of travellers have reported that they managed to get cash advances with a Visa card at the Banque Crédit Populaire d'Algérie on Rue Didouche Mourad in Algiers. They deserve medals.

The Banque Extérieure d'Algérie in Algiers may accept American Express cards, but don't count on it.

Costs

Prices given in this guide were effective at the time the book was researched; however, given the recent inflation in Algeria, it is possible that you may find prices have changed when you arrive.

Even if you are staying just a short time and are using up your AD 1000, costs are very reasonable. The longer you stay in the country and take advantage of the black market, the less it costs comparatively.

At the official rate, a double room in an average hotel is going to cost about US$12, but this will be much less unofficially. Internal flights, which must be paid for at the official rate, are very cheap by international

standards: US$60 from Algiers to Tamanrasset, for example.

Generally speaking, your AD 1000 should last you about a week, or more if you stay in the cheapest hotels and hitch a lot.

If you have your own vehicle and are not paying for accommodation it is possible that you will have trouble spending all of your AD 1000, especially if you pay for fuel with second-hand clothes or other items.

Bargaining

Bargaining is an integral part of the buying process; don't just pay the asking price, as this is usually inflated. Basically, the more time you are prepared to spend, the more likely you are to get a realistic price.

It is often possible to trade goods you are carrying when buying souvenirs. Things such as jeans, running shoes and cameras are good items for barter.

WHEN TO GO

The ideal time for a visit is in the spring. Autumn is the next choice, but the only hassle is that for most of the time the skies are very hazy due to a heat and dust haze that builds up over the summer.

If you are only going to be in the north, summer is also a possibility, although the high humidity of the coastal areas can be very tiring.

Travellers intending to take in the Sahara shouldn't even consider heading off in summer. It can be done, but you need to spend quite a few hours of each day indoors, out of the heat, and the rest of the time trying to keep up your intake of fluid to match what is being lost through perspiration. For the rest of the year, and especially in winter, the temperatures are pleasant and make for comfortable travelling.

TOURIST OFFICES
Local Tourist Offices

With less than 300,000 foreign tourists annually, Algeria does not have much of a tourist industry and this is reflected in the amount of tourist information available.

Inside the country, the national tourist

body, Office National Algérien du Tourisme (ONAT), has offices in just about every major town. However, they are more like travel agencies for Algerians travelling overseas than offices for foreign tourists looking for info. Of more use are the local tourist offices run by the wilayas. The ones at El Oued, Oran and Tamanrasset are all reasonably helpful.

Overseas Reps

You can try writing to the following addresses before you go if you really want some information, but don't hold your breath waiting for a reply:

France
    ONAT, 28 Ave de l'Opéra, Paris 75002
Germany
    Algerisches Verkehrsburo, Taunustrasse 20, 6 Frankfurt (☎ 230 7641)

BUSINESS HOURS

To a certain extent, business hours are dictated by the climate. In summer, shops tend to close up for most of the afternoon, and a lot of businesses are closed altogether after about 2 pm.

The working week is from Saturday to Thursday morning. During the month of Ramadan businesses are open for only a few hours in the mornings; shops open up again late in the evening.

Government Offices & Businesses

These are open Saturday to Wednesday from 8 am to noon and 2 to 5.30 pm. On Thursdays, they're only open in the morning.

Banks

Most banks are open from Saturday to Thursday from 9 am to 3 pm, although some banks are shut on Saturday as well as Friday.

Shops

Shops are open from approximately 8.30 am to noon and 2.30 to 6 pm, but these hours are quite flexible.

HOLIDAYS

Most public holidays are connected with important events in the Islamic year. For a list of these, see the section in the Facts about the Region chapter.

There are also a number of holidays which are related to events and people important in the formation of the modern state.

New Year's Day
    1 January
Labour Day
    1 May
Anniversary of the Overthrow of Ben Bella
    19 June
Independence Day
    5 July
Anniversary of the Revolution
    1 November

CULTURAL EVENTS

There are numerous fêtes and festivals held throughout the year, the principal function of which is to attract tourists. The main ones are:

March-April
    Spring Festivals in Biskra, Djanet, Ghardaia and Timimoun
March-May
    Tomato Festival, Adrar
    Cherry Festival, Tlemcen
    Carpet Festival, El Oued
    Old Ksar Festival, El Goléa
May
    International Fair, Algiers
December-January
    Folklore Festival, Tamanrasset

POST & TELECOMMUNICATIONS
Post

The Algerian postal system is slow but, in the end, the mail gets through. Allow at least three weeks for letters posted from Algeria to reach their destination, and about the same for letters to arrive in Algeria from overseas.

It is far better to hang onto letters and send them from a major town, rather than from a smaller centre, where it's likely to take a week or more for the letter to reach even Algiers.

There are yellow post boxes all over the

Top: Old apartment block, Algiers (HF)
Left: Martyrs' Monument, Algiers (HF)
Right: The main square, Constantine, Algeria (HF)

country but, although I have never actually had anything go astray, letters posted at them take even longer than from a post office. Post offices can be distinguished by the 'PTT' symbol.

Parcel Post Sending a parcel is simple enough, but is best done at one of the bigger post offices such as in Algiers, Constantine or Tlemcen.

Take your parcel to the post office for inspection before you wrap it. Parcels posted by surface mail to Australia usually take up to four months to arrive; they take a bit less to get to Europe.

Receiving Mail All post offices in the larger towns operate a poste restante service where you can have mail sent. Make it clear to people writing to you that it is important that they write your surname clearly in block letters, preferably putting only the initial for the given name to avoid confusion.

Mail is held for a period of one month before being returned to the sender (or chucked out, I suspect), except at Tamanrasset, where it is held for 15 days only.

American Express is not represented in

Algeria, so there are no card-holder services available.

Telephones
The Algerian telephone system is badly overloaded but manages to cope most of the time. There are public phones all over the country and they are heavily used.

In theory, it is possible to make international calls from public phones. In the north of the country it is usually possible to get through after a dozen or so attempts; in the south you may have to try for an hour or more and so it's often easier to go through an operator at a post office or large hotel. Payphones take AD 1, AD 5 and AD 10 coins. To make a direct international call, get the dial tone, dial 00 and wait for a second dial tone, then dial the country and number you want.

Local and internal long-distance calls suffer similar problems.

All post offices have a telephone office, easily recognised by the yellow-and-red PTT symbol. These offices are often open longer hours than the regular post office. The Algiers and Constantine offices are open 24 hours a day.

To give you an idea of the cost, a call to Australia costs AD 90 for three minutes.

The area dialling codes for the main towns in Algeria are:

Algiers	02	Batna	04
Biskra	04	Constantine	04
El Oued	04	Bejaia	05
Jijel	05	Sétif	05
Oran	06	Adrar	07
Béchar	07	Tlemcen	07
Annaba	08	Ghardaia	09
Ouargla	09	Tamanrasset	09

TIME
Time in Algeria is the same as GMT from November to April; GMT plus one hour from May to October.

ELECTRICITY
Algeria uses both the 240 and 120-volt systems, so check before using any appliances.

BOOKS & MAPS
People & Society

In 1846 Alexandre Dumas was asked by the Ministry of Public Instruction in France to travel in Algeria and write a book on it, so that French people could learn a bit about the new acquisition. The result is *Adventures in Algeria* (or *Tangier to Tunis)*, and it provides a good insight into the life of both the colonists and the locals in the early days.

Early this century Isabelle Eberhardt went to North Africa, became a Muslim and spent years travelling in Algeria on horseback, dressed most of the time as a man, before she drowned in a flash flood in Ain Sefra in 1904. She was the illegitimate daughter of a French woman and an ex-pope of the Russian Orthodox Church. The diaries she kept have been translated into English and are published as *The Passionate Nomad* (Virago, London, 1987). This book is interesting reading, as she had a deep understanding of Arab culture and politics.

Travel Guides

For a complete coverage of the African continent, *Africa on a shoestring* is the definitive guide. It's written by Geoff Crowther and published by Lonely Planet.

If you are taking your own vehicle across the Sahara, there are several excellent books available. One of the best is the *Sahara Handbook* by Simon and Jan Glen (Lascelles, London, 1987, UK£17.95). Despite the hefty price tag this book is worth carrying, as it has detailed descriptions of all the navigable routes in the Sahara.

Other good books are the Hachette guide (French) and the Polyglott book (German). Both are similar to the Sahara Handbook, so if you are fluent in French or German they may be worth having as well.

The best overall guide to the country's attractions is the French *Algérie* (Hachette Guides Bleus, Paris, 1986). It is expensive, but compact and well worth carrying if your French is up to it.

None of these guidebooks are available in Algeria itself; get the ones you want before setting off.

Periodicals

The *Africa Review* and *Middle East Review* are published annually by World of Information (21 Gold St, Saffron Waldon, Essex CB10 1EJ, UK) and are a useful source for recent developments within the individual countries of the region. They include a business guide and directory for each country with some useful addresses, so it may be worth consulting one before setting off.

Maps

The most detailed map available is the Michelin map No 172 of Algeria and Tunisia. It has excellent, detailed coverage of the north of the country but doesn't include the bulk of the Saharan region. For this you have to go to the Michelin map No 153, which covers the whole of West and North Africa and so doesn't have the depth of detail which some people may require.

Another quite good map which covers the same region is the Baedeker's map of North and West Africa.

Unfortunately, there is no decent map of Algeria alone. The state oil company, SONATRACH, published an excellent map of the country in the 1970s, but there are very few copies floating around now.

There is a National Mapping Office on Rue Abane Ramdane, Algiers, not far from the Touring Club d'Algérie office. They have topographic maps covering large areas of the country, but you need to give 24 hours notice and fill in a form to get hold of any of these. They also have some good city maps, such as Oran, and these are readily available.

Finding your way around cities can present problems, as a lot of the bilingual street signs have had the French writing painted over, leaving only the Arabic – very handy.

MEDIA
Newspapers & Magazines

There are no English-language newspapers or magazines published in the country, nor can you find any of the international current affairs magazines such as *Time* and *Newsweek*.

The closest you can come to some news in English is the inside back page of Monday's edition of the daily *Horizons* newspaper; this is printed in English, but one page once a week doesn't exactly keep you well informed.

The major French-language daily is the *El Moudjahid*, with a circulation of over 350,000 copies daily.

Papers printed in Arabic include *El Massaa*, *Al Chaab*, *An Nasr* and *Al Joumbouria*.

Radio broadcasts are predominantly in French and Arabic, with some transmissions in Berber and English. TV transmissions are exclusively Arabic and French.

FILM & PHOTOGRAPHY

Agfa and Fuji film is sold everywhere and prices are reasonable, although the expiry date should be checked – some of it looks like it has been lying around for years.

There are facilities for getting film developed in all the major towns of the north, but this is not especially cheap and takes a couple of days.

With the variety of scenery and people within the country, there are some fantastic photographic possibilities. Use a bit of discretion when photographing people – particularly women, who usually object to having a camera pointed at them. Ask first,

HEALTH

For a full rundown of health precautions you need to be aware of for the whole of the Maghreb, see the Facts for the Visitor chapter.

If you are arriving from a yellow fever zone (West Africa) you will need to show a vaccination certificate.

Make sure that you have an up-to-date International Health Certificate with a valid cholera stamp. Despite the fact that the vaccination is less than 100% effective, officials will not allow anyone to enter the country from the south without a cholera jab; they may even demand that you have one on the spot.

Malaria

There is a small risk of catching malaria, but it is so minimal, it is not worth worrying about.

If you are heading for West Africa you will have to start taking anti-malarials at some stage, so you may as well do it sooner and so protect yourself in Algeria as well.

Water

Tap water throughout the country is safe to drink, although at times it tastes pretty awful.

The water in the southern oases comes from underground and varies from sweet (El Goléa) to hard and saline (In Salah).

Bottled water is sporadically available for those with troublesome guts. Don't bother buying it in El Goléa, however, because it is the ground water here which goes into the 1½ litre plastic bottles anyway! When buying bottled water, check the plastic seal to make sure it is intact; otherwise you may be paying for plain old tap water.

Mineral water is also available, mainly in Algiers where it is known by the generic name of Vichy.

ACCOMMODATION
Camping

There are a number of campsites in the country, particularly in the Sahara where there are relatively large numbers of tourists with vehicles and camping gear. In the north the sites are limited to a few low-key resorts along the coast.

In the south it is possible to sleep under the stars for much of the year, so if you have a sleeping mat or groundsheet this is the way to go. It's the cheapest way to travel and, if you are hitching, the campsites are the best places to hunt around for lifts with other travellers.

Camping facilities range from primitive (Tlemcen and In Salah) to above average (Ghardaia), and the cost is about AD 15 to AD 25 per person and a similar amount for a vehicle.

In the south of the country the best campsites are in the middle of nowhere but, obviously, these are an option only if you have your own vehicle.

If you have your own campervan and are looking for a place to stay in towns in the north, it is usually possible to park in the corner of a Naftal service station for the night. Always ask permission and give the manager a packet of cigarettes or other small gift.

Youth Hostels

There is a system of youth hostels throughout the country and these can often be good, cheap places to stay if you don't mind dormitory accommodation. The charge is generally AD 15 to AD 20. The major drawback is that they are often inconveniently located.

There are youth hostels in the following towns: Annaba, Batna, Bejaia, Biskra, Constantine, El Kala, El Oued, Ghardaia, Ouargla, Tamanrasset, Touggourt and Zeralda

Hotels

In most towns there is a fair selection of hotels, particularly in the budget range. A room in a basic hotel costs about AD 50 to AD 80 for a double.

In the north, most of the hotel buildings date back to the colonial days and still have the original fittings and furnishings: window shutters, washbasin, bidet, wardrobe and a bed which is so old it wouldn't be out of place in a museum. Occasionally, breakfast is added to the price and, although it is tacked on as an extra, it will usually be compulsory: no breakfast – no room.

Even in the cheapest hotels the rooms are often cleaned daily, and the general standard of cleanliness is good.

For men the option at the very bottom of the range is the *hammam* (Turkish-style bathhouse) *(bain maure* in French). Although hammams are not spectacularly appointed and are usually hot and damp, they are an option when everything else is full. They are certainly not a realistic choice for very long, as you always have to vacate early in the morning and then find somewhere to put your gear all day. Just ask around in the centre of any town.

Top-end accommodation is in fairly short supply, but there is always at least one hotel in each town which offers above-average accommodation. These hotels are often government run and suffer from indifferent service and the couldn't-give-a-stuff attitude (from both management and staff) that frequently goes with state-run hotels. It often happens that these places check your currency form. The usual charge is around AD 120/185 for a one-star hotel, up to AD 250/300 for three-star rating.

Places fill up early in the day in summer and it's not uncommon to find a couple of places full before you strike it lucky.

THINGS TO BUY

As usual, carpets make an excellent souvenir but, unless it's possible to buy and post in the same place, their sheer bulk make them an impractical purchase.

Ghardaia is the main centre for carpets, and there are a dozen or so shops selling them. Designs vary from region to region and many of the rugs you see displayed are actually from another region.

In Algiers there are a couple of large shops in the centre which sell nothing but carpets and, although prices are high, they have some good stuff. One of these shops is on Rue Ali Boumendjel near Square Port Said, just up from the Grand Hotel des Étrangers.

Tamanrasset also has a lot of stuff in the way of souvenirs, most of it of Touareg origin. At the market across the *oued* (river)

there are always Touareg from the whole region selling jewellery, bags and other knick-knacks. Much is made purely for the tourist market but there is still some genuine stuff for sale. Unfortunately, the reason why a lot of these people are selling this stuff is that the drought conditions have deprived them of their traditional income.

El Oued is another big centre for handi-craft buying but, again, most items are made with the tourist industry in mind and the prices asked are often ridiculous.

STOP PRESS

The first round of Algeria's first free multiparty elections held on 26 December 1991 resulted in a landslide lead to the Muslim fundamentalist Islamic Salvation Front (FIS).

The FIS are dedicated to setting up an Islamic fundamentalist state – the first in north Africa. This would have major implications for Algeria's population, and in particular, for women, who could lose the right to vote or to work outside the home.

President Chadli Benjedid, who maintained that the democratic process should be adhered to, and who thus sanctioned the second round of elections scheduled for 16 January 1992, was encouraged to resign by military leaders who feared that the election would confirm an Islamic victory.

The military-dominated Higher Security Council stepped into the breach casued by Mr Chadli's departure, and have appointed a five-person presidency with a mandate to rule under a state of emergency until December 1993. The titular head of the new ruling committee is Mr Mohammed Doudiaf.

Since the installation of Mr Boudiaf, the FIS has issued statements denouncing the military takeover; however, Islamic leaders in Algeria have reportedly rejected violence as a means of establishing an Islamic state. ∎

Getting There & Away

You can enter Algeria by air from Europe, the Middle East and West Africa, by sea from France or Spain, or overland from Morocco, Tunisia, Niger and, if the border has been reopened, Mali.

Regardless of where and how you enter the country, it is compulsory to declare your foreign currency on a declaration form and to change the equivalent of AD 1000. Read the Money section in the Facts for the Visitor chapter before entering Algeria.

AIR

The main international airport is at Algiers, but there are others at Oran, Tlemcen, Constantine, Ghardaia and Annaba as well. Most of the flights from these other towns go only to places in France.

Airlines serving Algiers include Air Algérie (the national flag carrier), Aeroflot, Air France, Alitalia, Egyptair, Iberia, Libyan Arab Airlines, Royal Air Maroc, Sabena, and Tunis Air.

Air Algérie flies from Algiers to the following cities:

Athens, Greece	weekly
Bamako, Nigeria	twice weekly
Barcelona, Spain	twice weekly
Berlin, Germany	weekly
Cairo, Egypt	twice weekly
Casablanca, Morocco	daily
Dakar, Senegal	weekly
Frankfurt, Germany	three times weekly
London	four times weekly
Lyons, France	daily
Madrid, Spain	twice weekly
Marseilles, France	twice daily
Moscow, USSR	twice weekly
Niamey, Niger	weekly
Nouakchott, Mauritania	weekly
Ouagadougou, Burkina Faso	weekly
Paris	twice daily
Tunis	daily

To/From Europe

There are frequent connections with all the major cities in Europe but, as there is not a great volume of traffic, you will be up for the full economy fare.

To/From North America

There are no direct flights. The best way would be a flight to London or Paris and then another flight from there.

To/From Australia

Again, there are no direct flights and the best way is probably via London or Athens. If you want to fly straight from Australia you will have to go via Athens and pay the full fare of at least A$1800 return (low season). This doesn't include the fare to North Africa.

LAND

To most people a trip to Algeria means a trip across or into the Sahara. However, there are many places in the north of the country which are well worth a visit, particularly if you are interested in Roman history.

Whether you are going south from Tunisia or Morocco to West Africa, or are doing a trans-Maghreb trip across the top of North Africa, it is easy to spend at least a month exploring Algeria. Remember that once you have changed the mandatory AD 1000 at the official rate you can start to make use of the black-market rates and travelling becomes much, much cheaper.

The following itineraries are suggestions which make the most of what Algeria has to offer.

Overland through Algeria

Tunisia to Niger Most people enter Algeria at El Oued, but the more interesting crossing is up in the north between Tabarka or Ain Draham and Annaba. From here you can then go along the coast and the Corniche Kabyle, and then cut south to Sétif and the Roman ruins at Djemila.

From Sétif you can head east again to Constantine, Batna and the exceptionally well-preserved Roman city at Timgad, going

on to the El Abiod Gorges and Biskra, and then through the desert to El Oued, Ghardaia, In Salah and south to Tamanrasset and the Hoggar Mountains.

Morocco to Niger The best bet here is to cross up in the north from Oujda, in Morocco, to Tlemcen, in north-west Algeria, then head south for Béchar and loop around the southern edge of the Great Western Erg, which should take in Taghit, Beni Abbès and Timimoun.

Many people use the crossing further south, between Figuig and Beni Ounif, but this way you miss the fascinating city of Tlemcen in northern Algeria, and you also have to walk from Figuig to the border, and then from there to Beni Ounif (about 4 km).

From Timimoun you have the choice of heading south for Adrar and then across to the main N1 route south at In Salah, or continuing around the erg to El Goléa and possibly nipping up to Ghardaia (highly recommended) before heading south again from there. Both routes are served by public transport, but the latter is the more reliable if you are hitching, although even then you will probably end up on the bus between In Salah and Tamanrasset.

Morocco-Tunisia These routes can be done easily in either direction on public transport or by hitching. My ideal route would be from Tlemcen, south to Béchar, and around the Great Western Erg up to Ghardaia and then Algiers. From Algiers head east through the mountains of the Kabylie region to Dejaia,

from there go south to Sétif and Djemila through the Kherrata Gorge (although you now don't see a lot of the best scenery in the gorge because of a new tunnel) and then to Constantine.

If you want to see more of the desert, head south from Constantine through Batna (and Roman Timgad) and Biskra to El Oued, from where there are good connections to Tozeur in Tunisia. Alternatively, take the northern route from Constantine through Annaba to Tabarka on the north coast of Tunisia, or Ain Draham up in the mountains behind the coast.

To/From Morocco
There are two crossing points between the two countries: between Oujda and Tlemcen not far from the coast in the north, and between Figuig and Beni Ounif 300 km to the south.

Although relations between Morocco and Algeria have been strained at times, things have been fairly stable in the last few years. However, if the ceasefire in Western Sahara fails, and the war continues with Algeria supporting the Polisario movement, the border situation could change.

Oujda-Tlemcen From Tlemcen there are four buses to the border between 7.40 am and 2.10 pm. The trip takes about an hour and costs AD 15. The buses stop in Maghnia, so you could jump on there.

The two border posts are right on either side of the fence, so there is no enormous tract of neutral territory to cross.

From the Moroccan side there are regular buses and taxis to Oujda, 13 km away.

People with vehicles should be aware of the fact that before you can import a vehicle into Morocco you must have a letter or telex from your embassy in Rabat confirming that you will indeed re-export the vehicle. This can take a week or so to come through, so contact your embassy in good time or be prepared to hang around in Oujda until it does come through.

People with vehicles have been known to get through the border here with just a carnet or a green card, but there is no guarantee of this. There are banks on both sides of the border.

Trains also run between Oujda and Tlemcen, continuing on to Oran. There is one train in each direction daily, leaving Oujda at 9.30 am heading east, and from Oran at 2 pm heading west. It is much quicker to go by bus and cross on your own, rather than wait while hundreds of people get processed at the border.

Figuig-Beni Ounif This border crossing is straightforward enough, although you will have to walk a total of about four km. In summer make sure you have some water and a hat, as this is an extremely hot place at that time of year.

This crossing is renowned for the thoroughness of the Algerian officials who search your baggage for Algerian dinar and undeclared foreign currency. Hide any excess cash very well.

Don't bother setting off from Figuig late in the afternoon, as the formalities and walking take up to three hours.

To/From Tunisia
There are several crossing points between Algeria and Tunisia, not all of them always open. The most popular crossing points are between El Oued and Nefta, and up in the north between Souk Ahras and Ghardimao.

All the crossings are generally straightforward and the officials bored and amiable.

Bus There is a daily air-conditioned bus from Tunis to Annaba run by the Tunisian national bus company, SNTRI. It is a popular run and you need to book 24 hours in advance at the Tunis south bus station or the Annaba bus station. The trip takes about eight hours (depending on the border crossing) and costs TD 11.250.

This bus is by far the easiest way to cross between the two countries; the drawback is that you have to get on at the point of origin, as they don't stop en route to pick up passengers.

Train There is a daily train, the Trans-Maghreb Express, which connects Tunis, Annaba, Constantine, Algiers, Oran, Oujda and Casablanca. It's not a straight through run, however, as you have to change trains in Annaba, Algiers and possibly Oran, with an overnight stop in Algiers on the journey from Tunis to Morocco.

Heading west the departures are: Tunis noon, Annaba 22.15 pm, Constantine 1.06 am, Algiers 7.30 am, Oran 2 pm, arriving in Casablanca at 8 am the following day. In the opposite direction the departures are as follows: Casablanca 9.50 pm, Oujda 9.30 am, Oran 4.20 pm, Algiers 9 pm, Constantine 2.45 am, Annaba 9.30 am, arriving in Tunis at 6 pm.

Taxi From El Oued there are infrequent taxis to and from the border (AD 50). There's a four-km walk between the two posts and from the Tunisian side there are *louages* (Peugeot 404 taxis which seat four or five passengers) and a daily bus to Nefta.

The Algerian post is called Bou Aroua, and there is a small bank here, although it's not always open. If that's the case it's possible to change small amounts of US dollars cash with the custom's at the border. The officials here are generally friendly and reasonably helpful.

To/From Niger
The border post between the two countries is between In Guezzam (Algeria) and Assammaka (Niger), a bit over 400 km south of Tamanrasset.

When leaving Algeria it is not necessary to clear immigration in Tamanrasset, as this is taken care of in In Guezzam. You must still, however, check with customs when leaving Tamanrasset.

There is a weekly truck/bus from Tam to In Guezzam on Mondays, returning from there the next day. Although it does get you 400 km further along the way it is next to useless, as you still have to wait around in In Guezzam for a lift further on. As any vehicle leaving Tam will be going through In Guezzam anyway, you may as well wait in relative comfort at Tam and try and get a lift right through.

Hitching south from Tam is relatively easy, although you may have to wait for a few days before you find a lift. The campsite is the best place to try.

To/From Mali

At the time of writing the Algeria/Mali border was closed, but this should have changed by now. Check with the Mali Consulate in Tam or Algiers, or ask other travellers for the latest.

There is a crossing on the Route du Tanezrouft between Algeria and Mali at a place called Borj Mokhtar. This isolated outpost is 660 lonely km south of Reggane.

There are twice-weekly buses from Adrar to Borj Mokhtar, but you are better off trying to hitch out of Adrar than catching the bus down to the border and then having to wait a week for a lift going further. If coming north, Gao is the place to wait for a lift, not Bourem.

There are trucks doing the run from Adrar to Gao, a further 800 km south of the border, but it may take a few days to get a lift. The trip takes up to a week, so stock up with supplies before setting off.

It is necessary to clear customs at Adrar, check in with the police at Reggane, and just for good measure you will be checked again in Borj Mokhtar. There are no banking facilities between Adrar and Gao, so make sure you have what you need. When heading south (with a vehicle) there is a charge of CFA 1000 payable at the border, while coming north you'll be up for Algerian insurance (AD 250 per month for large 4WDs, AD 130 for cars and AD 60 for motorcycles) so make sure you are carrying some French Francs.

If you are driving, the road south is surfaced as far as Reggane; from there on it is *piste* (tracks, often a couple of miles wide), although 4WD is not necessary and the route is in fact easier on vehicles than the Route du Hoggar from Tamanrasset. You need to carry enough fuel to get from Reggane to Gao; although there is a station at Borj Mokhtar,

you might have to wait for a few days for some fuel to arrive. Borj Mokhtar is also the only watering point between Reggane and Gao.

From Borj Mokhtar there is a piste direct to Tamanrasset. It is a long, lonely stretch of road.

SEA
To/From France

The government-owned Compagnie Nationale Algérienne de Navigation (CNAN) operates regular ferry services between Marseilles and Oran, Algiers, Bejaia, Skikda and Annaba, and between Sète and Oran.

In summer these services are very heavily subscribed; if you intend bringing a vehicle across, make a reservation as far in advance as possible.

These are the most expensive of the Mediterranean ferries. Those to Morocco and Tunisia are cheaper.

Annaba-Marseilles Four ferries sail per month in summer, and there are two sailings per month in winter. Fares are as for Algiers.

Algiers-Marseilles This is the most popular (and therefore most crowded) route. In summer there are departures almost daily but this drops to three or four per week in winter. Fares from Algiers are AD 409/748 one way/return per person, and about AD 1500 one way for the average 4WD vehicle.

From Marseilles the fares are UK£66 in economy-class and UK£110 in 'basic'. *Couchettes* (sleeping berths) cost UK£8.20 to UK£10.90 per person extra and cabins UK£2.80 to UK£26.70 per person extra. Cars/caravans cost UK£171.80 to UK£207.30.

Bejaia-Marseilles There are seven per month in summer, and one per week or less in winter. Fares as for Marseilles-Algiers.

Oran-Marseilles There are 20 sailings per month in summer, dropping to two or three weekly in winter. Fares are AD 461/832 one

way/return for passengers and AD 1250 for
a vehicle.

Skikda-Marseilles There are one or two
departures per month. Journey time is 24
hours and fares are the same as for Algiers.

Oran-Sète There are three sailings per
month in summer.

To/From Spain

There are regular sailings from the Spanish
port of Alicante to Oran and Algiers. The port
of Palma on the Balearic island of Majorca
is also served by ferries from Algiers.

Oran-Alicante There are eight sailings per
month in summer, three in winter. The
economy-class fare is AD 270/474 one
way/return per person. For a vehicle you are
up for AD 942 one way.

Algiers-Alicante There are only two sailings per month in summer, nothing in winter;
AD 325/596 one way/return; AD 1058 for a
vehicle.

Algiers-Palma This is another popular
route. The boats stop in Palma and continue
on to Marseilles. There are four per month in
summer, one per month in winter; fares as
between Oran and Alicante.

Addresses
CNAN has the following offices in France
and Spain:

Marseilles
    29 Blvd des Dames, Marseilles 13002 (☎ 9190
    6470)
Paris
    25 Rue St Augustin, Metro Opéra, Paris (☎ 4927
    9120)
Lyons
    37 Rue Servient, Lyons 69003 (☎ 60 1387)
Palma
    Agencia Schembri, Plaza Lonja 2 to 4 (PO Box
    71) (☎ 22 1417)
Alicante
    Agencia Romeu Jorge, Plaza 18 Julio 2, Alicante
    (☎ 20 8333)
Madrid
    Romeu Y. Cia SA Cristobal Bordiu 19 to 21
    (☎ 234 7407)

In Algeria there are offices in all the major
towns and cities along the coast; these are
listed in the appropriate sections on each city.

LEAVING ALGERIA

One thing to be aware of if you are buying a
ferry or plane ticket (local or international)
is that you have to change money specially
(at the official rate) to do it. Even if you have
receipts to prove that you have already
changed AD 1000, these are not sufficient.
When changing money for an international
ticket, ask for a paper called 'Attestation de
Cession de Devises', which the bank fills out
in triplicate. You then give one copy to the
office where you buy the ticket and you keep
another to show when leaving the country, if
asked. The issue of the form is also noted on
your currency declaration form.

Getting Around

AIR

Algeria has a well-developed internal air network, and there are regular connections between Algiers and other major centres. One of the main problems is that most of the flights radiate from Algiers, so although two towns might have good connections with Algiers there will be no direct flight between them.

Airfares are heavily subsidised by the government, so the locals look on the internal flights rather like a bus service. Don't expect any in-flight comforts such as food or drinks; this is basic, no-frills people transport, and you'll be lucky if you even have a safety belt which works.

Things such as seat allocation are also unheard of so, with overbooking a common event, boarding a flight can be a real circus – this was the scenario at Algiers' Houari Boumedienne Airport for an *international* flight: find the correct check-in desk (unmarked), thrust arm holding passport and ticket in with the tangle of other passports and tickets all trying to get the clerk's attention, receive boarding card (without seat number) and proceed to departure lounge. Jostle for a place on the shuttle bus to plane, jump out of bus, identify baggage (now placed on tarmac – wet or dry) and stow it in hold of aircraft. Race round or under plane to stairs on other side, jump on and hopefully (if you haven't been dragging your heels), there'll be a spare seat – good luck!

Local Air Services

Even at the official rate of exchange, internal flights are very cheap by international standards. All flights are usually heavily booked (and often overbooked), so you need to make a reservation as far in advance as possible. Air Algérie, which has a computerised booking system and offices in most towns, operates the following flights.

The fares quoted are one way and include a tax of AD 40; all flights also operate in the opposite direction.

Algiers to	Frequency	Fare
Adrar	four times weekly	AD 397
Annaba	three times daily	AD 331
Béchar,	daily	AD 445
Bejaia	daily	AD 157
Biskra	daily	AD 260
Constantine	three times daily	AD 258
Djanet	six times weekly	AD 558
El Goléa	twice weekly	AD 407
El Oued	daily	AD 298
Ghardaia	twice daily	AD 300
Hassi Messaoud	four times weekly	AD 374
Illizi	three times weekly	AD 462
In Amenas	three times weekly	AD 409
In Salah	three times weekly	AD 430
Jijel	twice daily	AD 209
Oran	three times daily	AD 298
Ouargla	twice daily	AD 345
Tamanrasset	twice daily	AD 576
Tébessa	daily	AD 368
Tindouf	four times weekly	AD 544
Tlemcen	daily	AD 366
Touggourt	daily	AD 299

Adrar to	Frequency	Fare
Béchar	twice weekly	AD 202
Biskra	twice weekly	AD 291
Borj Mokhtar	twice weekly	AD 291
Ghardaia	twice weekly	AD 259
In Salah	weekly	AD 135
Oran	four times weekly	AD 339
Tamanrasset	weekly	AD 314

Annaba to	Frequency	Fare
Béchar	weekly	AD 625
El Oued	three times weekly	AD 244
Ghardaia	twice weekly	AD 370
Oran	twice weekly	AD 594
Ouargla	twice weekly	AD 355

Béchar to	Frequency	Fare
Ghardaia	weekly	AD 350
Oran	three times weekly	AD 292
Tindouf	twice weekly	AD 288

Biskra to	Frequency	Fare
Ghardaia	weekly	***
Tamanrasset	weekly	AD 210

Constantine to	Frequency	Fare
Ghardaia	weekly	AD 311
Oran	four times weekly	AD 504
Tamanrasset	weekly	AD 557

Djanet to	Frequency	Fare
Ghardaia	weekly	AD 404
Illizi	four times weekly	AD 135
In Amena	weekly	AD 185
Ouargla	daily	AD 363
Tamanrasset	weekly	AD 191

El Goléa to	Frequency	Fare
Tamanrasset	twice weekly	AD 346

Ghardaia to	Frequency	Fare
Borj Mokhtar	twice weekly	***
Constantine	weekly	AD 311
Djanet	weekly	AD 404
In Salah	twice weekly	AD 241
Oran	twice weekly	AD 333
Tamanrasset	five times weekly	AD 410

In Amenas to	Frequency	Fare
Oran	weekly	AD 481

In Salah to	Frequency	Fare
Borj Mokhtar	weekly	AD 273
Ouargla	weekly	AD 244
Tamanrasset	three times weekly	AD 238

Oran to	Frequency	Fare
Ouargla	weekly	AD 412
Tamanrasset	weekly	AD 571
Tindouf	twice weekly	AD 430

Ouargla to	Frequency	Fare
Illizi	daily	AD 269
In Amenas	twice weekly	AD 244
Tamanrasset	three times weekly	AD 389

Tamanrasset to	Frequency	Fare
In Guezzam	weekly	AD 240

*** Price on application

BUS

Virtually all buses in the country are operated by the national bus company. This is known

by various initials, most commonly TVE, but also SNTV and TVSE. The buses are usually bright orange, although the newer ones are white.

The larger towns have a purpose-built bus station while the smaller towns have, at the very least, an office where you can make reservations and from which the buses leave.

Bus travel is fast and comfortable throughout the north, with frequent departures connecting all the towns. In the south things are much the same on the good roads, except that there are fewer services. Points as far south as Adrar, El Goléa and Hassi Messaoud are all served daily by regular buses.

There are public buses even on the bad roads, although they are buses with a difference – they are usually Mercedes trucks, with a passenger cabin with seats for about 20 people built on to the chassis. As you can well imagine, these are real bone shakers: 18 hours on one of them along roads which defy description leaves you feeling totally zonked, although mercifully the roads are gradually being improved and the really long, arduous stretches are becoming fewer by the year.

These truck/buses operate on the route south from In Salah to Tamanrasset and In Guezzam, and from Adrar to Borj Mokhtar and across to In Salah. The incredibly tough conditions that they have to endure day after day mean that they are prone to breakdowns. The main routes are usually kept serviced, but services on the less frequented ones, such as from In Salah to Adrar, may be suspended if there aren't enough buses in one piece at any one time.

From Tamanrasset there are no buses out to the Hoggar Mountains or to Djanet, nor are there any services south of In Amenas on the route to Djanet from Touggourt.

Booking in advance is advisable, particularly in the summer. It is only possible to book 24 or sometimes just 12 hours in advance; this varies from one place to the next. Bus fares are reasonably priced – AD 90 from Algiers to Constantine, AD 118 to Ghardaia and AD 87 to Oran; there is an AD 10 to AD 20 charge made for any bag which goes in the luggage compartment.

In summer especially, it's worth trying to work out which side the sun is going to be beating down, as tinted windows and air-conditioning are nonexistent, and curtains are rare.

TRAIN

There is a rail network in the north of the country and the trains are reasonably fast and efficient. The greatest advantage of travelling by train is that, on the main lines at least, they have air-conditioning (and heating). This is something of a mixed blessing, however, as there is consequently little ventilation and on long journeys the pungent cigarette smoke can become stifling. Second-class is much worse than 1st-class in this respect. On the night journeys between Constantine and Algiers, and Oran and Algiers, there are couchettes and these must be booked in advance; seven days is the maximum.

The main line goes clear across the north of the country connecting Souk Ahras in the east with Tlemcen in the west. There are small feeder lines heading south from Constantine to Touggourt, Annaba to Tébessa and from Mohammadia (near Oran) south to Béchar.

Trains are generally fairly uncrowded, and there are buffet cars on the main routes. The main services are as follows:

Algiers to Oran
    five daily, six hours
Algiers to Constantine
    two daily, eight hours
Algiers to Annaba
    three daily (via Constantine), 11 hours

Constantine to Touggourt
    two daily, eight hours
Tlemcen to Moroccan border
    three daily
Mohammadia to Béchar
    one daily, 10 hours

TAXI

Louages (large shared taxis) operate only in the northern part of the country. They go as far south as Adrar on the Route du Tanezrouft, El Goléa in the centre and Hassi Messaoud in the east.

They don't run to any schedule but just leave when full. For this reason they can be more convenient than the buses, but they are considerably more expensive. Count on about AD 40 per 100 km.

All taxis are yellow Peugeot station wagons, either the old 404, or the newer 504 or 505.

CAR
Car Rental

It is possible to rent cars, but the tariffs are astronomically high, especially as you have to show that you have changed money officially. The main rental company is Algérie Auto Tourisme, which has offices in Algiers, Annaba, Oran, Constantine and El Oued.

The tariff for the smallest category (Peugeot 205) is AD 490 per day, plus AD 4.6 per km, and AD 96.50 per day insurance, plus fuel – not cheap.

Fuel

Fuel is fairly cheap in Algeria, particularly in comparison with neighbouring Tunisia and Morocco.

The hydrocarbons industry is wholly owned and run by the state company SONATRACH. Naftal is the brand name given to the state's petrol and to service stations.

Particularly in the south it is sometimes possible to pay for your fuel with goods which you don't want, especially vehicle spare parts and jerry cans.

The price of fuel is cheap by world standards – even at the official rates. Petrol *(essence)* is set at AD 3.75 per litre for super, AD 3.10 per litre for regular. Diesel ('Gasoil') is much cheaper at only AD 0.95 per litre. On the black market the prices are downright crazy – 30 litres of diesel for US$1!

It is obviously much more economical to be driving a diesel-powered vehicle, and an added advantage is that diesel is more widely available than petrol.

When buying petrol check whether you are getting super or regular, as there is often a shortage of super.

Vehicle Insurance

When you are bringing your own vehicle into Algeria, insurance has to be purchased at the port or border post.

The cost of insurance varies for different vehicles and is shown in the table called Vehicle Insurance. There is also a vague tax of about AD 40 that has to be paid on top of the insurance.

LOCAL TRANSPORT
Bus

Most cities and towns have a local bus network but, other than in Algiers, usually only the route number is intelligible to non-Arabic speakers.

In Algiers the system is well organised and there are route maps at all the main stops. In other places it is less easy to get a grasp of the system and you need local advice on which bus to catch. Local people will generally go out of their way to help.

Taxi

Local taxis are yellow, just the same as the long-distance ones. Fares should be negoti-ated in advance, although in Algiers drivers will use the meter.

Metro

There is a metro system under construction in Algiers but it is unlikely to be open in the near future.

HITCHING

This is one of the joys of Algeria. In the north it is really a dream come true. No sooner have you got your pack off and the thumb out than a car stops, and you can even be choosy about which cars you pick. Lifts are always free and often lead to an invitation to someone's house for a meal or even over-night, especially if you can converse in French. It is not, however, recommended for women to hitch without a male companion.

The only real problem with hitching is that you need to get yourself to the outskirts of the town before you start, as most traffic is only local and it's a waste of time trying to get a ride in the centre of town. The best plan in the bigger towns is to catch a local bus to the first small town along your route. Other-wise, a taxi to the edge of town can save an hour's hard slog and usually only costs a few dinar.

In the south it's a different story. Yes, you can still hitch all the way to Tamanrasset for free, but it is becoming increasingly difficult. A lot of the vehicles on the roads are trucks, many of which belong to the state-owned transport company (SNTR) and have a large 'D' on top of the cabin. Drivers of these trucks are forbidden to carry passengers and risk losing their jobs if they are caught with someone else in the cab. Some drivers will pick people up if they know there is no police checkpoint along the road they will be using.

Hitching south from Ghardaia to Taman-

Vehicle Insurance				
Type	*10 Days*	*20 Days*	*1 Month*	*2 Months*
motorcycle	AD 40	AD 50	AD 60	AD 110
car	AD 70	AD 90	AD 130	AD 250
truck, 4WD	AD 120	AD 190	AD 250	AD 450

rasset is generally a lot easier than hitching in the opposite direction, mainly because there are a fair number of foreigners in vehicles heading south, but very few going north. They will usually give lifts where possible, but most are so loaded to the eyeballs with gear that there is just no room for an extra body or two. Nevertheless, people still do get to Tam (and beyond) for free, although waits of two or three days to get out of places like In Salah are not unheard of.

Registration Plates The last two numbers of the licence plates of Algerian vehicles identify the wilaya (province) that the vehicle is from. It can sometimes be useful, especially when hitching, to know whether the vehicle is local or from somewhere else and therefore likely to be travelling further. It could also help to pass the time ...

The main wilaya numbers are:

Adrar	01
Batna	05
Bejaia	06
Biskra	07
Béchar	08
Tamanrasset	11
Tlemcen	13
Algiers	16
Annaba	23
Constantine	25
Ouargla	30
Oran	31
Illizi	33
Tindouf	37
El Oued	39
Ghardaia	47

Algiers

Known as Alger in French and El Djazair in Arabic, Algiers is the capital of Algeria; with a population of three million, it is also far and away the largest city in the country.

As a city it is not all that fantastic, but it's still a pleasant enough place to spend a few days in. It's especially good if you need to pick up visas, as just about every African country has diplomatic representation here.

As is the case in most countries in the developing world, what you find in the capital is hardly typical of the whole country – in Algiers the pace is faster, the hemlines higher and veils are few and far between. Most of the buildings in the medina (and indeed in the rest of the city) date back only to the time of the French occupation – nearly all the local buildings were pulled down to make way for the French buildings. There are a few magnificent mansions and palaces built by the Turks but, with a couple of exceptions, you can look at these from the outside only.

History

Known as Icosium in Phoenician and Roman times, Algiers was definitely overshadowed by the main North African capital, Cesare (Cherchell), about 100 km to the west.

It fell to the Vandals in the 5th century, but its fortunes revived under the Byzantines. Icosium remained a commercial outpost until the 10th century, when the town was revived by a Berber dynasty of the Sanhaja federation under the name of El Djazair.

Piracy became a major occupation on the Barbary coast and, in the 16th century, the famous pirate Barbarossa (from whose name Barbary is derived) occupied the city. After he defended it against Spanish invasion the title of beylerbey was conferred on him by the sultan of Constantinople.

During the years of Ottoman occupation the city prospered, and the large kasbah built on the hill overlooking the bay became the beylical residence (a *bey* was a provincial governor in the Ottoman Empire).

On 14 June 1830 the French landed at Sidi Fredj, and by 5 July the last governor of Algiers capitulated to them. Algiers became the administrative and military capital of the French colony.

During WW II the city became the headquarters of the Allied forces in North Africa. During the late 1950s and early 1960s it was the focal point in the nationalist struggle against the French. In 1962 Algiers became the capital of independent Algeria.

Orientation

The city centre is hemmed in against the bay by the mountains which rise steeply from the coast. The skyline of the city is dominated by two structures, both impossible to miss. To the south of the centre is the Martyrs' Monument (Makam ech Chahid), a 92-metre-high concrete memorial in the shape of three highly stylised palm fronds. Closer to the city centre, the box shape of the four-star Hotel Aurassi is dominant.

The commercial and business centre is the area directly south of the medina. Here you'll find all the major shops, banks, hotels and the post office. The railway station and ferry terminal are only five minutes' walk from this area, and the bus station is 15 minutes away.

Everything in the centre is within walking distance, and nothing is far from the main street, Rue Larbi Ben M'Hidi. This is a tree-lined pedestrian precinct running north from Place Grande Poste to the medina. Place Grande Poste is a major square, where you'll find the post office and local bus terminal; at present, with the new metro under construction, it is also a building site.

The medina itself is fairly run down and has become something of a slum area, although there has been a concerted effort in the last few years to clean up the place a bit.

In the centre, the buildings along the waterfront road, Blvd Zighout Youssef, provide a grand architectural sweep as they look out over the docks and the bay; the boulevard itself is popular with evening promenaders. Below this road, almost at water level, is another road running parallel to the waterfront; on this reclaimed strip of land is the railway station and ferry terminal.

Out in front of Place Port Said, a small square on Blvd Zighout Youssef, there is what looks like a water tower. It is in fact an *ascenseur* (passenger lift), which for 50 centimes will take you from one level to another – handy if you have just got off the train and have a heavy pack to lug up the ramps which connect the two road levels. On the lower level the lift is right by the railway station entrance.

The embassies are nearly all out in the suburb of Hydra, five km south of the centre, or in the suburbs of El Biar and Bouzaréah. All these places are easily reached by taxi. Otherwise take bus No 31 from Place Audin to a large marketplace, and a bus No 44 from there to Hydra; to get to Bouzaréah, take bus No 59 from Place des Martyrs (Martyrs' Square).

Just to make life easier for foreigners, all the bilingual Arabic-French street-name signs have had the French painted over leaving only the Arabic, which is of very little use to the average visitor. This is a practice which has been pursued throughout the north.

Information

Tourist Offices For what it's worth, there are branches of ONAT (Office National Algérien du Tourisme; ☎ 64 1550), behind the Hotel Safir, and at 2 Rue Didouche Mourad (☎ 63 1066). Neither of these offices has any information, but the staff do try to help.

The Touring Club d'Algérie (☎ 66 0887) has an office at 21 Rue Abane Ramdane, which runs off Place Port Said. The people staffing this office are helpful and can sometimes supply maps of the country. If you have

a vehicle and need assistance, these are the people to see.

A good map of Algiers is available from the bookshops along Rue Larbi Ben M'Hidi for AD 10.

Also extremely helpful are the city maps on signboards which can be found on the footpaths at various places around town. Two handy ones are at Place Port Said and behind the town hall, right near the entrance to the Safir Hotel.

Money There are banks all over the central part of town. If you have to get an Attestation de Cession de Devises (for a plane or boat ticket), the Banque Centrale d'Algérie at 8 Blvd Zighout Youssef on the waterfront issues them without too much fuss.

If you are stuck for cash outside bank hours, any of the expensive hotels should be able to help. The most convenient is the Hotel Safir, Blvd Zighout Youssef; the entrance is on the inland side of the building.

Post & Telecommunications The main post office is on Place Grande Poste, at the southern end of the main street, Rue Larbi Ben M'Hidi. It's an imposing neo-Moorish building complete with arches and mosaics, and is worth a look inside even if you have no business to do there.

The well-organised poste restante counter is in the telex office, which is at the end of the small alley on the left of the main entrance to the post office. The doorway is at the top of a short flight of steps. There is a charge of AD 1 for every letter collected.

The parcel-post counter is in the main hall of the post office, as is the philatelic section.

The post office is open Saturday to Wednesday from 8 am to 7 pm, Thursday 8 am to 1 pm; closed on Fridays.

The international telephone office is by Place Grande Poste on the corner of Rue Asselah Hocine. It is open 24 hours a day and you can dial direct to most larger countries.

The Algiers telephone area code is 02.

Foreign Embassies Algiers is an important African capital, and most African countries

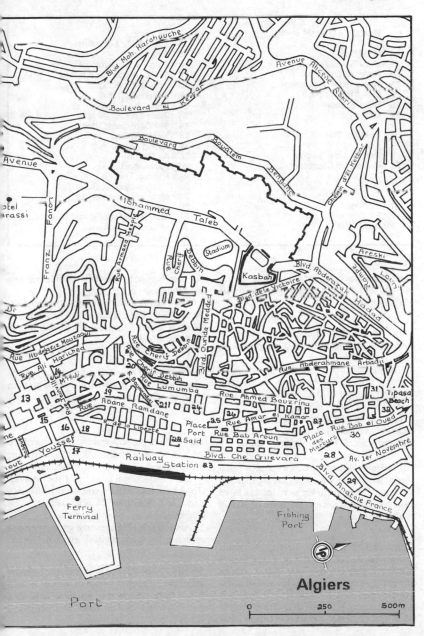

Algiers

0   250   500m

PLACES TO STAY			4	Air France
16	Hotel Safir		5	Place Audin Local Buses
19	Hotel Grand Touring		6	Air Algérie
20	National Hotel		8	Palais du Government
21	Grand Hotel des Étrangers		9	Grande Poste Local Buses
22	Grand Hotel Tipaza		10	Post Office (PTT)
26	Hotel El Badr		11	Telephone Office
27	Grand Hotel		12	Office des Étrangers
			13	Place Emir Abdelkader
PLACES TO EAT			14	501 Department Store
			15	Tourist Office
7	Restaurant le Saigon		17	Airport Buses
25	Restaurant Couscous		18	Air Algérie
			23	Passenger Lift
OTHER			24	National Theatre
			28	Mosque Djemaa el Jedid
1	Cathedral		29	Mosque Djemaa el Kebir
2	Footbridge		30	Local Buses
3	Bus Station		31	Museum of Popular Arts & Traditions
			32	Mosque Ali Bichnine

have embassies here. For a complete list see the visa section in the Algeria Facts for the Visitor chapter.

Visa Extensions The Office des Étrangers for visa extensions is on the corniche at 19A Blvd Zighout Youssef.

The office is open Saturday, Monday and Tuesday from 8.30 to 11.30 am, Sunday and Wednesday from 8.30 to 11.30 am and 1.30 to 3.30 pm; closed Thursday and Friday.

Extensions take 24 hours to issue, and you need to have receipts to prove that you have changed your AD 1000. Without these you will have a hard time getting the extension. Also required are two passport photos and a signed letter from your hotel saying that you are staying there or, at the very least, a hotel receipt with your name on it. A fee of AD 60 is also payable.

Cultural Centres The British Council Library (☎ 60 5682) is at 6 Ave Boudjemaa Souidani, just above Place Addis Ababa above the Palais du Peuple. It has live satellite TV from the UK, as well as newspapers and magazines. It is open daily from 9 am to noon and 2 to 5 pm, and while officially it is

for members only, they will often let visitors in if things are not too busy.

The French Cultural Centre (☎ 63 6183) is at 7 Rue Capt Hassani Issad, while the German Goethe Institute (☎ 63 4683) is at 165 Rue Sfindja.

Bookshops There are a number of shops along Rue Larbi Ben M'Hidi which have an excellent range of French and Arabic books, but not a thing in English.

Maps There is a government mapping office on Rue Abane Ramdane, almost opposite the Hotel Grand Touring, and they have topographic maps of all regions of the country. To get copies of them you need to fill in a form and then wait 24 hours for it to be approved.

Also on sale here are some good city maps – such as Oran, and regional maps of Algeria.

Photo Shops If you need passport photos there are a couple of small shops around Place Emir Abdelkader on Rue Larbi Ben M'Hidi which can do them in a couple of hours.

Left Luggage There is a left-luggage office (*consigne*) at both the bus station and the railway station. The one at the railway station is more convenient, but is expensive at AD 10 per item for the first 12 hours, AD 20 for each 12-hour period after that. At the bus station it is cheaper at AD 10 per item for each 24-hour period.

Vaccinations It is possible to get vaccinations from the Pasteur Institute, not far from the Museum of Fine Arts.

Medina
The best place to start a wander around the medina is Place des Martyrs, at the northern end of the corniche (which is called Blvd Ché Guevara at this end). The large open square is a terminus for local buses and is busy throughout the day. The square was created in the 1860s when the government knocked down a large number of old houses.

The medina is largely a tangle of narrow streets, which still follow the ancient plan but which are lined with French buildings; many of these have decayed badly in the last 25 years and look like they may not last another 25. The area is definitely seedy, but is not dangerous.

Mosques Near the waterfront side is the Djemaa el Jedid mosque, also known as the Mosquée de la Pêcherie. As the name suggests (*jedid* means new), it is a relatively new mosque, built in 1660 for the Hanefite Turks. Two blocks further along, past the Chamber of Commerce, is the Great Mosque, the Djemaa el Kebir. This one dates back to the 11th century and was built by the founder of Tlemcen, the Almoravid Youssef Ibn Tachfin, on the site of a Christian church from Icosium. Both these mosques are closed to non-Muslims.

Just a short way along Rue Bab el Oued lies the Mosque of Ali Bichnine, built in 1623 by an Italian pirate.

Rue Omar Hadj opens out at Place Cheikh Ben Badis and the Ketchaoua Mosque. Dating originally from 1162, the mosque was completely rebuilt in 1794 by Hassan Pacha (dey of Algiers). It was converted to a church in July 1930, and then back to a mosque after independence. No entry to non-Muslims.

Museum of Popular Arts & Traditions Cunningly concealed in the tangle of streets up behind the Ali Bichnine Mosque is the Museum of Popular Arts & Traditions. It is housed in one of the finest Turkish palaces in the city, construction of which was started in 1570. After the French took Algiers in 1830 this building became the city's first town hall. To find it, follow the large orange signs from the Ketchaoua Mosque. Alternatively, take the first left up the hill beyond the Ali Bichnine Mosque (alongside the high iron fence blocking off a building site), then take the first left again at a café (Rue Hadj Omar), and then turn right up the stairs of Rue Mohammed Akli Malek. The museum is 30 metres up on the right at No 9.

Today the museum houses excellent displays of rugs, jewellery, costumes and pottery. The palace itself is still in good condition – the reception room on the 3rd floor has a beautiful stucco ceiling and parquet floor (the latter is in fact a French addition). It is open daily, except Saturday, from 10 am to noon and 1 to 5 pm; closed Friday morning and Saturday; entry is AD 4.

Turkish Mansions Back towards the centre along Rue Hadj Omar there are some more fine Turkish mansions, easily recognisable by the small windows and the way the upper floors hang over the street. At No 10 is the building (known as Dar Ahmed) which houses the administration headquarters of the Algerian National Theatre. It was occupied by the dey Ahmed from 1805 to 1808.

Two other mansions are found at No 12 and 17 in the same street. The relatively plain exteriors of these places belie the opulence within: faïence tiles from Europe, marble columns and doorways, stucco ceilings and mirrors.

Next door to the Ketchaoua Mosque is another Turkish palace, Dar Hassan Pacha; this was built in 1790 and now houses the ministry responsible for religious matters. Up the small side street, Rue Cheikh el Kinai, is yet another mansion (at No 5); this one is now home to the Wilaya Committee, and they may let you wander around. Also on this street is the Hammam Sidna, the oldest hammam still in use in the city. It was built in the 16th century and, for men at least, it's worth a stroll inside.

Right opposite the Ketchaoua Mosque is yet another fine building, the Dar Aziza Bent el Bey – the Princesses' Palace. It now houses the Ministry of Tourism and it's quite OK to take a wander around. In fact there's usually an old bloke to show you around. He's a real mine of information and will utter enlightenments such as 'très ancien' at every stop. There are excellent views from the roof, so make sure he takes you up there.

Ville Nouvelle

From Place Cheikh Ben Badis, Rue Ahmed Bouzrina leads to the market up behind the National Theatre on Place Port Said, and eventually to the main street of the ville nouvelle (new city), Rue Larbi Ben M'Hidi. This street is now a pedestrian precinct and is crowded at any time of day.

About a third of the way along is Place Emir Abdelkader, which has an enormous statue of Abdelkader on horseback. There is an expensive pavement café here. The street is lined with some fancy shops, one of the most amazing being the cavernous '501' department store, one block back towards the medina.

On the other side of the metro excavations at Place Grande Poste, Rue M Addoun leads up to Rue Didouche Mourad and Place Audin – a busy intersection and another local bus terminal.

Rue Didouche Mourad – one of the main shopping streets – which heads up the hill to the south, also has several airline offices and some fancy restaurants. About 500 metres along, it changes name to Rue Franklin Roosevelt and starts to twist and curve up the hill. Soon you will come to an absolutely dreadful concrete church, the Sacred Heart Cathedral. Continuing up the hill along Rue Franklin

Roosevelt, before long you come to another pocket of Turkish palaces, all three of which house museums. To save your legs, take bus Nos 31, 32 or 33 from Place Audin, or 35 or 40 from the Grande Poste, and get off at the Palais du Peuple stop.

Bardo Museum The first museum you come to along Rue Franklin Roosevelt is the Bardo Museum, which has a collection that's a strange combination of prehistory and ethnography. The prehistory section has literally thousands of stone hand tools and arrow heads, and seemingly every piece of ancient bone and stone ever dug up in the country. Pride of place goes to a 20-cm-long elephant tooth and the two-metre horn of a long-extinct type of buffalo.

Upstairs, the ethnography museum has a very peaceful courtyard. The rooms around it have displays of costumes and handicrafts of the various Algerian ethnic groups, including the Touareg and the Kabylie. One of the most impressive displays is the collection of coral-studded jewellery.

The museum is open in summer from 9 am to noon and 2.30 to 5.30 pm, and in winter from 9 am to noon and 2 to 5 pm; closed on Friday morning and all day Saturday; entry is AD 4.

National Museum of Antiquities Further up the hill, on the right, is the National Museum of Antiquities; it's actually in the small Parc de la Liberté, on the corner of Ave Franklin Roosevelt and Blvd Salah Bouakouir (right by the Palais du Peuple bus stop). It houses a collection of various bits and pieces from all over the country. The display of coins must be among the best anywhere, and the 5th-century Vandal manuscripts on wooden tablets are priceless. Both these displays are in the antiquities room, to the left inside the entrance. Other rooms contain Roman statuary and Islamic art. The museum is open the same hours as the Bardo, and entry is free on Friday afternoon.

Palais du Peuple Another 100 metres up Ave Franklin Roosevelt, on the left, are the vast luxuriant grounds of the Palais du Peuple. This is the former residence of the Algerian head of state and, before him, of the French governor.

In 1987 the palace did finally become a 'people's palace', as the whole place is now open to the public. There are a few museums on the site. The History Museum is in an incredibly ornate and luxurious Turkish palace, with gold leaf everywhere, mosaics on the floors and walls, monstrous chandeliers and carved wood – a classic example of Turkish opulence. In any other place the exhibits would stand out; here they are totally outclassed by the building itself. There is a fantastic collection of old jewel-encrusted swords, but unfortunately all the exhibits are labelled only in Arabic.

The Flora & Fauna Museum has three floors of plants, trees, insects, and stuffed birds and animals from all over the world – a good display if that's your interest.

At the top of the site is a house full of 19th-century photos, which give a good insight into the country as it was in the 1850s – well worth the visit.

Entrance to the palace is from either down the bottom near the Museum of Antiquities or up at the top at Place Addis Ababa. To get there catch bus Nos 35 or 40 from Grande Poste or Nos 31, 32 or 33 from Place Audin to either of the two stops. The palace grounds are open from Monday to Saturday from 9 am to 9 pm, and the museums are open from 9 am to noon and 2 to 6 pm; closed Friday. Entry to the grounds is AD 10, and this pays for entrance to all the museums.

Musée National du Jihad Beneath the Martyrs' Monument is the Musée National du Jihad, which covers the 'holy war' – the struggle for independence from 1955 to 1962. The museum is exceptionally well set out and has excellent displays of equipment used in the war. A major drawback is that because this place is the centre of nationalistic pride, everything is labelled in Arabic. This makes it hard for most foreigners to gain a full understanding of the Algerian viewpoint, although many of the displays need no

interpretation. The museum is open from 9 am to 6 pm Monday to Friday; Sunday from 2 to 6 pm; closed Saturday. Entry is AD 5.

Army Museum At the opposite end of Riad El Fet'h from the Martyrs' Monument is the Army Museum. Looking more like a five-star hotel, it is another expensive reminder of the war for independence. The interior too would do justice to an international hotel – piped classical music, chandeliers, fountains, white marble floors, polished granite stairways – the works. The displays are all of a military nature and are quite interesting, although the building is so large that they tend to get lost in the open spaces. It is open the same hours as the Jihad Museum.

Museum of Fine Arts At the foot of the hill below the Martyrs' Monument is the Museum of Fine Arts (Musée des Beaux Arts). It has a small collection of sculpture, and one floor of paintings with some minor works by some major artists of the 19th century – Renoir, Monet, Courbet and Degas, to name a few. You may have to wake the attendants to get the lights switched on.

The museum is open Monday to Thursday from 10.30 am to 12.30 pm and 1.30 to 5.30 pm, and Friday and Sunday from 2.30 to 5.30 pm; closed Saturday. To get there from the centre, catch a No 9 bus from Place des Martyrs; the trip takes about 20 minutes. Get out directly below the Martyrs' Monument, or ask the conductor for the Musée des Beaux Arts.

Jardin d'Essai Across the road from the Museum of Fine Arts is the entrance to the somewhat overgrown botanical gardens. They must have been amazing at one stage but are sadly neglected now. At the far side, towards the sea, is a small zoo with a motley collection of animals, most of them kept in depressingly small cages. The gardens are open from 10.30 am to 6.30 pm Sunday to Friday; closed Saturday. To get there, follow the directions for the Museum of Fine Arts.

Martyrs' Monument From Place Audin (or

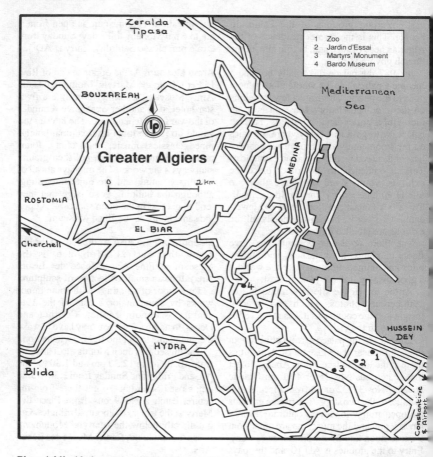

1	Zoo
2	Jardin d'Essai
3	Martyrs' Monument
4	Bardo Museum

Greater Algiers

Place Addis Ababa on the hill directly above the Palais du Peuple), a No 32 bus passes within a few hundred metres of the Martyrs' Monument, which is on top of the hill to the south of town. Get off at the stop where the bus goes under the overpass, right on the top of the hill.

This is a concrete monstrosity of truly gargantuan proportions, but somehow it works. It was built as a memorial to all those who died in the struggle for independence, and was opened in 1982, to mark the 20th anniversary of Algerian independence. It is now seen as the true heart of this developing country and represents everything the Algerian people have struggled for. It all sounds like good propaganda but it really is hard not to be impressed by the monument, although one wonders whether the millions of dinar couldn't have been spent in a way which would directly benefit a lot more people.

In the area beneath the three stylised palm fronds is an eternal flame guarded night and day by two armed soldiers. The views out over the city from the edge of this area are the best you'll get.

Riad El Fet'h Stretching away from the

monument is a massive concrete concourse known as Riad El Fet'h (Victory Park). This is a major gathering point for people, especially on weekends. In the centre is a round sunken courtyard with three levels of fancy shops, boutiques and restaurants. This place, known as the Bois des Arcades, has been a resounding success and is always packed with people. In the centre of the courtyard is the Théâtre du Verdure – an open-air theatre given over to various performances.

Places to Stay – bottom end
The centre of things as far as accommodation is concerned is Place Port Said. The square itself is the hang-out of some of Algiers' homeless and is a fairly seedy place, but the hotels in the area are quite OK. There are a few cheap places close by, as well as up near the medina and along the main street, Rue Larbi Ben M'Hidi.

The best cheap hotel in the city is the enormous *Hotel El Badr* (☎ 62 7102), at 31 Rue Amar el Kamar. It is just off Place Port Said and, with over 80 rooms, it is rarely full. Rooms are cleaned daily and cost AD 55/79 for a double with breakfast; hot showers are AD 12. The staff are extremely friendly and helpful, and all in all it's one of the best hotels in the country. Rue Amar el Kamar is a narrow street running off the north-west corner of the square. The hotel has no sign in English, but is about 50 metres along on the left and has a green-and-black tiled doorway.

A little further back towards Place Port Said and on the other side of the road is the *Hotel Tunis* (☎ 71 4882), at 38 Rue Amar el Kamar. It's not as good as the El Badr and has no showers, although there is a hammam close by. It too has no English sign and, because it is much smaller, it fills up early. The room rate at this place is AD 50/70 with breakfast.

Right in the thick of things, off Rue Larbi Ben M'Hidi, are a couple of places on Rue des Tanneurs, but these should only be tried if all else fails. The street runs west off the main street, not far from Place Port Said. The *Hotel Club* (☎ 64 9987) and the *Hotel es*

Saada (☎ 63 6505) are at Nos 2 and 1 respectively. The es Saada is the cheaper at AD 50/80 for a single/double, while the Club has the nerve to charge AD 60/85 and AD 10 for a cold shower! As mentioned, leave these until last.

At the other end of the main street, about five minutes' walk past the Grande Poste, is the *Hotel du Soleil*, at 15 Rue Ferroukhi Mustapha, the street which runs from the Air France building diagonally up the hill to Rue Didouche Mourad. Rooms cost AD 44 for a large single, and AD 55 for a double. No charge for the grumpy abuse you may encounter.

Also on Rue Ferroukhi Mustapha, at No 23, is the *Hotel Britanic* (☎ 63 8175), a good place in a good location which charges AD 75/94 for single/double rooms, plus AD 12 per person for breakfast.

Youth Hostel & Camping
The closest hostel and campsite are at Zeralda, 40 km west of Algiers, on the coast. Zeralda is easily reached by bus, which takes about an hour, although you then have to walk roughly three km. It is probably the best bet for people with their own vehicles who don't want to pay for a hotel. Buses run from the central bus station throughout the day, until about 6 pm. Any bus going to Cherchell or Tipasa will take you through Zeralda.

Places to Stay – middle
There is a wide choice in this category and, again, Place Port Said is a good place to start looking. Right on the south side of the square is the one-star *Grand Hotel Tipaza* (☎ 63 0040). Rooms cost AD 115/155 for a single/double with bath and breakfast. The green fluorescent sign has only 'Hotel' written in English; all the rest of the script is in Arabic.

Also on the square and of a similar standard to the Tipaza is the *Grand Hotel des Étrangers* (☎ 63 3245); this is a couple of doors along from the National Theatre, at 1 Rue Ali Boumandjel, the street which connects Place Port Said with Rue Larbi Ben

M'Hidi. Single/double rooms here cost AD 89/122 with breakfast and shower.

Also well located is the one-star *Grand Hotel National* (☎ 63 4173) at 1 Rue Patrice Lumumba, a street which is actually the northern continuation of Rue Larbi Ben M'Hidi. It's a friendly, well-kept place which charges AD 87/118 for rooms with bath and breakfast.

Moving up the price scale a bit, these next few places charge more but don't really give you much extra. The best of the bunch is the *Hotel du Palais* (☎ 61 4087), at 18 Rue Abane Ramdane, a street off Place Port Said to the south. Here rooms cost AD 119/159 with bath and breakfast.

Parallel to Rue Larbi Ben M'Hidi, and one block towards the waterfront, is Rue Ben Boulaid, which has two two-star hotels, the *Grand Hotel Regina* (☎ 64 9900) at No 27 and the *Hotel d'Angleterre* (☎ 63 6540) at No 11; both hotels are quite good. The Angleterre is the cheaper of the two, with rooms at AD 125/170, while rooms at the Regina are AD 170/227, all with bath and breakfast.

Just a shade better is the *Hotel Grand Touring*, opposite the Hotel du Palais. This place is good value at AD 104/134, but it does fill up early.

Places to Stay – top end

At all of the top-end places listed here it is possible to pay with Visa or American Express credit cards. Apart from the head office of Air Algérie, these are about the only places in the country that do take plastic.

Right on the corniche, the four-star *Hotel Safir* (☎ 73 5040) actually has its entrance around the back in Rue Asselah Hocine. It is the most central of the deluxe places and charges AD 280/380 for singles/doubles.

Another over-the-top place is the modern *Hotel Aurassi* (☎ 74 8252), on Ave Dr Franz Fanon; it's that great blot on the landscape which towers over the city. The Aurassi is the only real 'international standard' hotel in Algiers, and this is reflected in the prices: AD 780/970 for singles/doubles at the back of the building; AD 850/1050 for a room

with the spectacular view of the whole city and harbour. You'll need to take a taxi from the centre of town, as it's a long, hard slog up the hill on foot.

Less pretentious than both these two is the three-star *Hotel Albert I* (☎ 63 0020), at 5 Ave Pasteur, just 100 metres uphill from the main post office. Rooms cost AD 185/265 with bath and breakfast.

The only other top-of-the-range establishment in Algiers is the *Hotel el Djazair* (☎ 59 1000), on Ave Boudjemaa Souidani, just above Place Addis Ababa. It's actually an old palace which has been converted, although it's hardly palatial these days. Rooms cost AD 700/850.

Places to Eat

Local Food For local Algerian food, there is a stack of places in the web of streets between Rue Larbi Ben M'Hidi and Rue Abane Ramdane, between Place Emir Abdelkader and Place Port Said. They all sell the usual stuff – soup, brochettes (kebabs), chicken, chips and salads.

One place that stands out is the tiny restaurant at 7 Rue du Coq, a small street running to the right off the northern end of Rue Larbi Ben M'Hidi. Here AD 20 gets you a good omelette and plate of excellent salade variée, which makes a decent meal with a bit of bread. The restaurant is popular with locals and is right opposite a driving school.

In the north-west corner of Place Port Said, near the beginning of Rue Amar el Kamar, the *Restaurant Le Grande Maghreb* does the usual couscous (a semolina dish), chicken, rice, salad and chips fairly cheaply, although things run out by early evening. Right next door is a good stand-up snack place which sells various seafood cassecroûtes (stuffed French bread), and of course chips.

For good local food of the filling-and-unexciting kind there are a few popular restaurants in the street directly behind the Grand Hotel Tipaza at Place Port Said. These include the *Restaurant Le Tlemcen, El Bahdja* and the *Restaurant de la Poste*. All offer standard food at standard prices.

Fast Food The fast-food fad has finally hit Algiers, which now boasts a couple of burger places in the American mould. At 23 Rue Larbi Ben M'Hidi is the *Royal Burger*, which is definitely not cheap but if you are really hanging out...Prices range from AD 30 to AD 45 for various burgers. There's also the *Fast Burger* up at Riad El Fet'h.

Speciality Restaurants There is an excellent place for Chinese food: *Restaurant Le Saigon* (☎ 64 0623), near Place Audin. It serves all sorts of dishes, priced between AD 30 and AD 60, and is so popular with expatriates living in Algiers that you need to make a reservation by phone or get there at 7 pm to get a seat without waiting. The restaurant closes early at 9.45 pm. It is at 10 Rue Valentin, the street which runs uphill along the left-hand side of the Air Algérie head office at Place Audin.

There's another Chinese place, *Le Chinois*, at 5 Rue Ahane Ramdane, but this is expensive and the food is very mediocre. Close by on the same street are a few other restaurants, including the *Pizzeria* at No 17 and the *Restaurant Europe*; all these places sell alcohol.

For a minor splurge, the air-conditioned *Restaurant Marivaux*, at 5 Rue du Coq, does a four-course set menu for AD 60; it also has fish dishes for AD 70 and meat ones for AD 60.

Up at the Martyrs' Monument on the top of the hill is a whole bunch of restaurants in the Bois des Arcades; however, none of them are particularly cheap. They have everything from Western-style fast food (*Fast Burger*) to the local cuisine offered by top-class Algerian speciality restaurants (*El-Boustane, Dar Hizia*). Other cuisines featured at restaurants here include Italian (*La Gondole*), Japanese (*Fujiyama*), seafood (*La Pêcherie, Soltan Ibrahim*) and Continental (*Le Grill Room, La Soummam*).

Seafood There's a curious little pocket of restaurants almost beneath Martyrs' Square which specialise in seafood. To get to them, go down the stairs next to the Djemaa el Jedid mosque on Martyrs' Square. The entrance to the stairs is through two arches which have been incorporated into the façade of the mosque and is known as the Rampe de la Pêcherie.

There are half a dozen or so restaurants here and the atmosphere is good, although the prices are high. Cheapest of the lot is the first restaurant on the right, *La Porte de la Mer*, where you can get a plate of prawns for AD 24 and the usual chicken and chips.

Further along the prices start to rise. *Restaurant Le Sindbad* is the best known seafood restaurant in Algiers, and this is reflected in the prices; expect to pay around AD 250 *per kg* for any seafood. The produce is all laid out on a table and after you have made your selection it is weighed and then cooked.

Just down from the Sindbad, the *Sirène de la Mer* is marginally cheaper at AD 200 per kg.

All the restaurants here have a reasonable selection of local wines but, again, the prices are high.

In the Bois des Arcades, up at the Martyrs' Monument, there is the excellent *Soltan Ibrahim Restaurant*; here too the prices are way up.

Getting There & Away

Air Air Algérie has a number of agencies around town. The head office (☎ 64 5788) is at 1 Place Audin, near the university, about 10 minutes' walk from the post office.

There is another agency at 29 Blvd Zighout Youssef (☎ 63 3847), but it handles only international bookings. There is an agency on Rue de la Liberté (around the back of this office) which handles only internal flights and is open seven days a week.

The following international airlines also have offices in Algiers:

Aeroflot
    7 Rue Malki Nassiba (☎ 60 5661)
Air France
    Mauritania Building, Blvd Colonel Amirouche (☎ 64 9010)
Alitalia
    7 Rue Hamani Arezki (☎ 64 6850)

Egyptair
    4 Rue Didouche Mourad (☎ 63 0505)
Iberia
    11 Rue Hamani Arezki (☎ 63 3712)
Lufthansa
    49 Rue Didouche Mourad (☎ 64 2736)
Royal Air Maroc
    64 Rue Didouche Mourad (☎ 63 0458)
Sabena
    61 Rue Larbi Ben M'Hidi (☎ 63 3214)
Swissair
    19 Rue Didouche Mourad (☎ 63 3367)
Tunis Air
    6 Rue Emir El-Khettabi (☎ 63 2573)

Air Algérie flies to just about every major city in the north and all the far-flung oases in the Sahara. Even at the official rate, fares are relatively cheap (US$60 to Tamanrasset, for example).

For full details of flights and fares, see the Algeria Getting There & Away and Getting Around chapters.

Bus The main bus station is down at the waterfront, south of the centre, about 15 minutes' walk from the Grande Poste. Take the road heading towards the water from Place de Perou and then go down the road ramp to the right. There is a small bus station at the bottom but ignore this, as the main station is another 300 metres further on.

There are buses to just about every major town in the country as far south as Béchar, Ghardaia and El Oued. The station is well organised and all the ticket windows have the destination and departure time displayed. There is an information booth in the centre of the hall.

For most of the year there are enough departures to satisfy demand but things get a bit hectic in the summer months. Buy tickets the day before you plan to travel for all trips.

From Place des Martyrs the blue-and-white city buses Nos 72, 77 and 05 go past the bus station.

The left-luggage office is on the left inside the entrance and is open from 1 am to 10 pm. It costs a hefty AD 10 per article per day.

Train Although the main railway station is also close to the centre, on the lower street level directly below Place Port Said, most departures are from the Algiers Agha station, just near Place de Perou.

The main departures are as follows:

Destination	Departures	2nd-Class Fare
Annaba	7.05 am, 9 pm	AD 126
Bejaia	6 am, 3 pm	AD 52
Constantine	2 pm, 9 pm	AD 93
Oran	7.30, 11.30 am, 5.15 pm	AD 85
Tunis	9 pm	AD 503

Taxi The long-distance taxis leave from the ramps which connect the upper and lower street levels in front of Place Port Said. At any one time there are up to 100 taxis in the queues, and it's easy to find the one you want – just ask the drivers.

There are departures at all hours to Batna, Bejaia, Biskra, Constantine, Oran, Tizi-Ouzou, Sétif, Tébessa and many other places.

Car Rental Algérie Auto Tourisme has offices at 5 Rue Professeur Curtillet (☎ 74 4855), at the Hotel Aurassi (☎ 64 8252) and at the airport (☎ 75 1209).

Sea The Compagnie Nationale Algérienne de Navigation (CNAN) sells tickets for the ferries to France and has offices at 6 Blvd Mohammed Khemisti (☎ 64 0420) and at 7 Blvd Colonel Amirouche (☎ 63 8932). There is also an office at the ferry terminal, at Quai 9, Nouvelle Gare Maritime (☎ 57 9312) and at Riad El Fet'h (☎ 66 4232).

The passenger terminal is at the Nouvelle Gare Maritime, right in the centre of town in front of the Hotel Safir. You can enter from either the upper or lower street levels.

CNAN operates ferries from Algiers to Marseilles and Sète in France. For details of departures, see the Algeria Getting There & Away chapter.

Getting Around
To/From the Airport Blue-and-white buses leave for the 45-minute run out to the Houari Boumedienne Airport from Blvd Zighout

Youssef, right across the road from the Air Algérie office near the Hotel Safir.

At the terminal building, the buses leave from an area to the right of the exit approximately every half hour from 5 am to 11.30 pm; the fare is AD 10.

Bus There are buses which serve all parts of the city. The four major stations for these buses are Place des Martyrs, Place Grande Poste, Place Audin and Place 1 Mai.

At each of the platforms (and at major stops en route) there are signboards giving the destination and the route taken. Entry is through the back door, where you pay the conductor.

From Place des Martyrs take bus Nos 5, 72 or 77 for the main bus station. For the embassies in Bouzaréah, Hydra, El Biar, Bir-Mouad-Rais and El Mouradia, see the table below.

From Place Grande Poste take bus Nos 35 or 40 for the Bardo and other museums. From Place Audin take No 31, 32 or 33 for the museums; the No 32 goes on to the Martyrs' Monument.

Local Bus Routes		
To	*From*	*Route No*
Bir-Mourad-Rais	Place Audin	33
Bouzaréah	Place des Martyrs	51
El Biar	Grande Poste	41
El Mouradia	Place Audin	54
Fine Arts Museum	Place 1 Mai	89
Hydra	Place Audin	31
Museums	Grande Poste	35, 40
Museums	Place Audin	31, 32, 33
Place 1 Mai	Grande Poste	15

Taxi There are taxis everywhere, and you just flag them down – there are no taxi stations. All taxis have a meter, and you should ensure that the driver uses it.

Around Algiers

ZERALDA

Zeralda is situated some 40 km along the coast to the west of Algiers, and has a reasonable beach. It's about the closest you can get to the capital if you want to camp; there is a youth hostel here as well.

Places to Stay

The *Youth Hostel* (☎ 81 2112), where you can also camp, is down by the beach, right behind the Complexe Touristique – just follow the signs to the latter. It's inconvenient, as it is about 20 minutes' walk from Zeralda itself; also, there are no restaurants in the immediate vicinity. The hostel is on the right just before the entrance to the resort. There is no sign in English, but the driveway is right beside an electrical substation with the letters 'EGA' on it.

During the summer months the youth hostel has tents set up on frames. In winter the frames are still there, but the tents are gone. However, at this time the hostel is usually empty and you can sleep inside. If you stay here you need to bring all your own supplies.

Getting There & Away

Buses leave from the main bus station in Algiers throughout the day, until about 6 pm. Any of the buses going to Tipasa, Bou Ismail and Cherchell go through Zeralda.

TIPASA

Further around the coast is the village of Tipasa. The ruins of this Phoenician and Roman trading post are right on the edge of the sea. These days they are accompanied by two modern vacation villages, but fortunately these don't intrude too much.

The site itself does not really compare with Djemila or Timgad, south-east of Algiers, but it is unusual in that it is right on the coast and is set in quite thick bush. If you can't make it to either of the other sites or feel like a day trip out of Algiers, this is the place to come.

The new village of Tipasa is right by the ruins, so access is easy. Being only 70 km from Algiers, Tipasa can easily be seen in a day trip from the capital; alternatively, there are a few accommodation possibilities in the

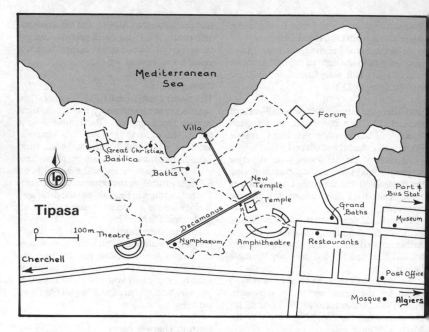

Tipasa

immediate vicinity. The streets right by the entrance to the Parc Archéologique have been made into pedestrian malls, and are lined with shady peppercorn trees and a few up-market restaurants.

History

The ancient town prospered until the time of the Vandal invasion in 430. The majority of the inhabitants were Christian; when the invaders brought with them the heresy of Arianism, townspeople who refused to give up their orthodox Christian faith were persecuted and fled to Spain.

The town revived briefly during the Byzantine occupation in the 6th century, but by the time the Arabs arrived, the town was derelict; hence the Arabic name, Tefassed, which translates roughly as 'badly damaged'.

The Ruins

The entrance to the ruins is one block from the main road, towards the water. They are open from 9 am to noon and 2 to 5.30 pm daily, except Saturday; entry is AD 1.

On the right as you enter is the amphitheatre, and beyond that are two temples. The first is known as the Anonymous Temple and the second, on the other side of the Decumanus Maximus, as the New Temple.

The Decumanus Maximus here is actually the old Cherchell to Icosium (Algiers) road. It is more than 14 metres wide, and there is a stretch of about 200 metres which is not in bad condition.

From the New Temple the road continues through a residential area to the Villa of Frescoes, on the water's edge. This villa, which must have belonged to one of the town's wealthiest residents, was named after the finds which were made in it during the course of excavations.

Up on a small rise to the right are the ruins of the Judicial Basilica, which dates from the 2nd century AD. Above the basilica is the well-preserved forum and, towards the lighthouse, you'll find a small Christian chapel.

Along the waterfront to the left of the Villa of Frescoes, the path leads past the ruins of a *garum* factory (garum was a spicy, fish-based sauce), a bath complex and a cavalry station; it eventually comes to a hemispherical well-cover, on which the rope marks can be clearly seen.

From the well, the track heads steeply up the small cliff to what is left of the Great Christian Basilica; you can reach this more easily by backtracking a bit until you come to a sandy path leading up to the right. The nine-nave basilica measures more than 40 by 50 metres and dates back to the 4th century.

Back near the entrance, the Decumanus Maximus leads past the Nymphaeum, complete with marble fountain, to the theatre.

Other Attractions

Outside the entrance to the ruins, the street leads past the ruins of another baths complex to the museum (on the left-hand side of the road). Although very small, the museum does have some excellent pieces, including some particularly fine glass exhibits. It is open the same hours as the ruins and costs AD 1.

Further along the same street is the old Punic port, which is now a small fishing harbour, and a Phoenician tomb.

Places to Stay

The only hotel in Tipasa is the *Hotel Sindbad*, on the main road near the start of town as you arrive from Algiers. There is no sign, but it is on the left and is the only building that looks remotely like a hotel. Rooms here cost AD 145 for a double with breakfast.

The only alternative (apart from camping) is one of the expensive resort hotels. In summer these are completely booked out by holidaying Algerians, but the rest of the time there should be no problem. The *Tipasa Plage* resort (☎ (02) 46 1820) is 1½ km west of town, and the enormous *Tipasa Village* (☎ (02) 46 1761) with its 600 bungalows is three km to the east along the Algiers road.

Camping At the village of Chenoua, a couple of km along the beach to the west (or about four km by road), is a campsite with permanent tents for hire. It costs a pricey AD 85 for a four-bed tent, but is not a bad place if you have your own tent. The beach here is not bad at all either. To walk to the campsite from Tipasa, get to the beach through the tourist complex and walk around from there. A taxi between the two places costs about AD 15, or else you can hitch.

Getting There & Away

There are buses to Cherchell and Algiers. They leave regularly from the open space down by the fishing harbour.

CHRÉA & BLIDA

The ski resort of Chréa lies 1510 metres above sea level, in the mountains 70 km south of Algiers. The resort is not that well developed by European standards, but there are a few runs. In summer too it is a popular vacation spot, and there are numerous walking trails in the area.

The ascent to the resort starts at the the town of Blida, 20 km back towards Algiers, and the views are spectacular as you climb up the Atlas from the fertile Mitidja plains.

Blida, the capital of a wilaya of one million inhabitants, is the centre of an important agricultural region that grows oranges, lemons and olives. The town's connection with agriculture and irrigation goes back to the 16th century, when Andalusian immigrants settled there and began using the water from the Oued el Kebir.

Today the town is of little interest to the traveller, although the Grand Mosque is impressive with its turquoise dome and four tiled minarets.

Places to Stay

Chréa The only hotel in Chréa is the small, one-star *Hotel Des Cèdres* (☎ (02) 13), which is likely to be fully booked in summer. Rooms cost AD 145 for a double with breakfast

Blida It is unlikely that you would want to stay in Blida but, should the need arise, there are a couple of possibilities. The cheapest of these is the well-appointed *Youth Hostel* (☎ (02) 49 9601), at 39 Ave Kritli Mokhtar, about two km from the bus station. The other alternative is the *Hotel Royal* (☎ (02) 49 2801), which is on the main square, Place 1 Novembre.

Getting There & Away
Bus The main bus station for buses to Algiers, Ghardaia and towns to the west is about 1½ km from the centre of Blida. Local buses run from outside the gate into the centre.

Buses for Chréa leave from south of the main street in Blida; ask to be shown where the departure point is.

Train The railway station is near the bus station. There are departures for Algiers and Oran.

North-East Algeria

The north-east region of the country is sadly neglected by visitors to Algeria. It stands out as a tourist destination in its own right but most people pass it by, as it is the Sahara that they have come to conquer.

The mountains of the Kabylie region, in the area directly to the east of Algiers, are spectacular and the stretch of coastline between Bejaia and Jijel, known as the Corniche Kabyle, is one of the most rugged and scenic in North Africa.

Inland lie the ruins of the Roman city of Cuicul, present-day Djemila, with its beautiful setting in the mountains. A little further on is Constantine, seat of the ancient kings of Numidia, built right on the edge of the deep and precipitous gorges of the Rhumel – not to be missed.

Further east lies Annaba, Algeria's third city, site of the ruins of the Roman city of Hippo Regius and seat of the great Christian reformer St Augustine. Today it is largely an industrial town, but it is the main northern gateway to Tunisia, as there are good transport connections all the way to Tunis.

South of Constantine are the Aurès Mountains, part of the Saharan Atlas, which run from Morocco in the west right through into Tunisia. The range roughly marks the boundary between inhabited, arable land in the north and desert in the south. The Aurès Mountains are quite barren and spectacular, but the real draw card is the fantastically preserved Roman city of Thamugadi (present-day Timgad). For once the ruins are well served by public transport, and there is accommodation close by. It's a place well worth visiting if you are passing through the area.

The Kabylie

The range of mountains known as the Grande Kabyle run from south of Algiers across to Bejaia in the west. The region is home to the country's largest Berber minority, the Kabylie. These people speak Berber first, French second and Arabic third. Over the years the government has not been at all sympathetic to their demands for a separate cultural identity, and this led to serious disturbances in the area in the early 1980s.

Because of the mountainous terrain, it may be difficult to use many of the high roads for about six months of the year over winter. In spring and summer the region is cool and colourful – a blessed relief from the heat and humidity of the coast.

There is a reasonable beach at Tigzirt, which has the only accommodation along this stretch of coast.

The area around Tikjda, south of Tizi-Ouzou and in the centre of the forests of the Djurdura Mountains, is now a ski resort. During the war for independence the forests were decimated by French napalm bombs (these days the French play with their bombs in the Pacific arena instead, but that's another kettle of radioactive fish altogether)

TIZI-OUZOU

With a population of about 300,000, the city of Tizi-Ouzou is the capital of the wilaya of the same name. It is not a particularly riveting place but is the best base for any explorations in the area, and the setting is pleasant.

Places to Stay & Eat

The only budget choice is the relatively new *Hotel Olympia*, up a side street one block north of the main street, Rue Larbi Ben M'Hidi, and about 10 minutes' walk from the bus station. Rooms are cleaned daily and cost AD 60/105 for a single/double with washbasin. There are no showers in the place but this is not a problem as there is a public hammam right across the street. To find the hotel from the bus station, walk uphill along the main street, turn left at the roundabout (Place

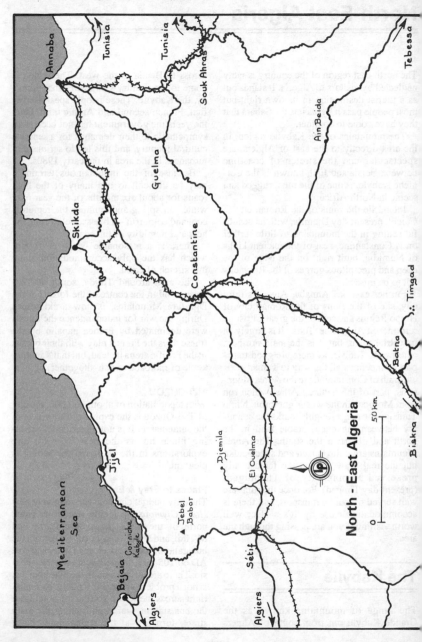

Lamari Meziane) and then take the first street on the right. The hotel is on a corner about two blocks along on the left. It is above a pharmacy and has only the word 'Hotel' painted on the building. Ask the locals – they all know it.

Next up is the two-star *Hotel Beloua* (☎ (03) 40 4612), which is at 16 Rue Larbi Ben M'Hidi, only 100 metres or so from the roundabout and five minutes from the bus station. Rooms cost AD 145/190 for singles/doubles with breakfast.

There are a couple of restaurants in the same street as the Hotel Olympia. Almost directly opposite is the *Restaurant Mediterranean*, which caters more for drinkers; beer is AD 12 for a small bottle and local wine is AD 50. The food is not bad, but it's cheaper and just as good elsewhere. There are also a few cheap restaurants in Rue Larbi Ben M'Hidi.

Getting There & Away
Bus The bus station is on Rue Larbi Ben M'Hidi (the Algiers road), 300 metres down the hill from the main roundabout at Place Lamari Meziane. It is a large blue building; the ticket offices are upstairs and the buses downstairs, where there is also a helpful information office.

This is about the only area in the country where private buses augment the government services.

There are buses for Algiers almost every hour, and less frequently to other towns in the region such as Tizgirt, Azazga, Beni Yenni (great name!), Dellys and Bouira.

There is no direct connection to Bejaia; you have to catch a bus to Azazga, then a taxi to Hammam Keria, and then another bus from there. This is a spectacular trip and well worth the effort involved. It can easily be done in a day, but there are hotels at Hammam Keria, Adekar and Azazga should you decide to linger.

Train There are regular departures for Algiers; the 2nd-class fare is AD 22.

Taxi Taxis also run from the bus station and

there are always a few in the parking area. There are regular departures for Algiers and Bouira from here.

For towns to the east of Tizi-Ouzou and places up in the mountains, the taxi station is on the main road, 500 metres in the opposite direction from the main roundabout.

TIGZIRT
This is a small town on the coast. Although it sees a few tourists in summer, it is very much off the track and is likely to remain that way. The town never seems to get out of first gear; it just rolls slowly along, and nothing much disturbs the sleepy atmosphere that pervades the whole place.

Surprisingly, it is a town with a history, as is testified by the ruined Christian basilica (5th or 6th century), which is right in the middle of the town. The town site was in fact inhabited in prehistoric times and eventually became the important Roman trading port of Iomnium.

The beach is only average, as it is quite stony; however, it is sheltered as the town is tucked right in under the hills which separate it from Tizi-Ouzou.

There is a local tourist office on the main street but this is open only during the summer months.

Places to Stay & Eat
The only place which is halfway reasonable is the *Hotel el Awres* (☎ (03) 42 8094), on the main street. The staff are extremely indifferent, not giving a stuff whether you stay or not. Rooms cost AD 95 for a double; those at the front have views of the water and catch what breeze there is.

The up-market alternative is the two-star *Hotel Mizrana* (☎ (03) 42 8085), a couple of km above the town to the east.

Getting There & Away
Buses terminate at a small square just near the waterfront. There is no office but there are always people hanging around. There are several departures daily for the short trip to Tizi-Ouzou (AD 6.50, one hour).

The trip over the mountains from Tizi-

Ouzou is quite spectacular in itself, with the road winding up and over the range.

There are also infrequent departures to Dellys, further along the coast to the west, from where there are buses back to Tizi-Ouzou.

BENI YENNI

The town of Beni Yenni is 760 metres above sea level, up in the mountains 50 km south of Tizi-Ouzou.

Places to Stay

The only hotel is the two-star *Hotel Le Bracelet D'Argent* (☎ (03) 59), which charges AD 145/190 for singles/doubles with breakfast.

In summer it should be possible to camp in the area, although you would need to be pretty well self-sufficient as there is no equipment available locally.

Getting There & Away

In summer there are regular buses between Beni Yenni and Tizi-Ouzou.

Bejaia & the Corniche Kabyle

BEJAIA

Bejaia is a port town with a population of 150,000. It is built in a beautiful spot: it's on the flank of Jebel Gouraya, at the eastern end of the Gulf of Bejaia. (A *jebel* is a mountain.)

The city itself is very pleasant, although things have been spoiled to a great extent by the construction of a petrochemical complex on the edge of the town, which has resulted in pollution of both the air and water.

The centre of the town is a congested mess of very narrow streets which wind up the hillside. The view out over the harbour, the bay and the mountains from Place 1 Novembre is really something (when the pollution is not too bad, that is).

Despite its long history, there is really very little to see in the town itself. However, the

beach at Tichi (17 km to the east) is one of the best in the country, and there is some good walking out to Cap Carbon and around.

History

In Roman times the town was called Saldae. When it became a major town of the Hammadid chief Emir En Nasser it really prospered and was renamed En Nassria.

En Nasser's son, el Mansour, built a beautiful palace within the fortifications built by his father. The last Hammadid ruler, Yahia, ruled over a town which flourished on the trade in goods across the Sahara and grew to over 100,000 inhabitants.

The downfall of the Hammadid Empire came in 1152, when the Almohad ruler Abd el Moumen invaded from Morocco. In the 13th century the town became part of the Hafsid Empire, when that dynasty came to power in Tunis.

Piracy was a major occupation along the Barbary coast in the years up to the beginning of the 16th century. About this time the activities of the pirates in Bejaia brought the town to the attention of the Spanish, who besieged it in 1509. The Spaniards were followed by the Turks in 1555 and the French in 1833, by which time the population had dwindled to a meagre 2000.

Orientation

The centre of the town is actually up on the side of the hill but, because of the terrain, the transport connections are all at the bottom, about 20 minutes' walk from the centre.

Suburban buses run up as far as the impossibly small and busy square, Place Chérif Medjahed, which has an unusual sculpture in the centre. Around the square you'll find the post office, shipping office, Air Algérie and banks. The hotels too are close by.

Place 1 Novembre is a beautiful open terrace 100 metres towards the water along Rue Ben M'Hidi, a small pedestrian street. It is flanked by two old colonial buildings – the Banque Centrale d'Algérie and the Hotel de l'Étoile (the place to stay if money permits). The view from here is excellent, and a stairway near the hotel entrance leads down to the museum below.

To help you get your bearings, there is a map of the town on the wall of the cinema, on the right at the entrance to Place Chérif Medjahed as you come up from the bus station.

Information

Tourist Office The ONAT office (☎ (05) 92 0261) on Place Chérif Medjahed is staffed by helpful people but, as usual, they have very little in the way of information. This office is also the CNAN booking office (☎ (05) 92 0360) for the ferries to France.

Money The main bank is on Place 1 Novembre.

Post & Telecommunications The post office is also on Place Chérif Medjahed. The telephone office is through the door to the left of the main entrance. The post office steps are a gathering point for local youth.

Museum

The museum is one of the town's more peculiar sights. The entrance itself is strange enough: you can go down the stairs from Place 1 Novembre but, as these have been used as a *pissoir* about a thousand times too often, it is preferable to walk around to the bottom street entrance and go in there. The museum is on the 1st floor, and there is no sign on the various doors at street level – ask for help if you can't find the stairs.

Once inside things get stranger: the museum has an enormously varied collection, ranging from paintings by local artists to hundreds of stuffed birds in various stages of decay – a real mishmash of exhibits. Entry costs AD 1 and the museum is closed from noon to 2 pm.

Other Attractions

There are a few remnants from the past but they are all either run down, closed or both. The kasbah (closed) is down near the waterfront, straight down from Place Chérif Medjahed, and dates from the time of the Spanish occupation.

About 10 minutes' walk up the hill behind the square along Rue Fatima is the small 16th-century Sidi Soufi Mosque with its square minaret. Further on up the hill is the marketplace. Higher still is Fort Moussa, which also dates from the 16th century; it was built by the Spaniard Pedro Navarro, possibly on the site of the palace built by the Hafsids. This building too is closed.

The walk out to Cap Carbon takes a solid couple of hours, as it is over seven km from the centre. From the end of the road it is a further 30 minutes on foot to the lighthouse, which is near the tip of the cape.

If you are really keen, there is a road up to the Spanish fort on top of Jebel Gouraya, behind the town. To get to this, follow Rue Fatima up to Fort Moussa and then take Rue Gouraya; this goes past an Islamic institute, which was opened in 1972 and was built on the site of an Islamic university established by the saint Sidi Touati.

Places to Stay

The best cheapie you'll find is the friendly *Hotel Touring* (☎ (05) 92 0383), at 6 Rue Hocine Hihat, the street which slopes gently uphill directly opposite the post office. Rooms cost AD 72 for a double and those at the back are quieter than the ones on the street. Cold showers only.

Similarly priced but not as good is the *Hotel Saada*, on the pedestrian street, Rue Ben M'Hidi, which connects the two squares.

The best place for the money is the one-star *Hotel l'Étoile* (☎ (05) 92 9895), on Place 1 Novembre. Some of the large rooms have great views from the balconies out over the bay and the coast to the east. It's not all that expensive at AD 105/145 for a single/double with breakfast.

Places to Eat

The cavernous *Restaurant de la Soummam* is right next to the Hotel Touring, at 4 Rue Hocine Hihat. It sells all the usual stuff and does a good-value, two-course lunch for AD 27.

There is another restaurant almost opposite, but this place serves alcohol as well and the atmosphere is just a shade seedy.

There are a couple more places on Rue Ben M'Hidi near the Hotel Saada.

Getting There & Away

Air The airport is three km south of town, off to the left of the road to Tichi and Jijel. Air Algérie has an office (☎ (05) 92 5731) on the west side of Place Chérif Medjahed.

There are daily flights to Algiers; the trip takes 50 minutes and costs AD 157.

Bus The bus station is at the bottom of the hill, south of the city centre. It is about 20 minutes away on foot; all the local buses from the terminal halfway down the hill go past it. There is a booking office where a reasonably up-to-date timetable is on display.

There are regular departures to Algiers, Bouira, Constantine, Jijel, and Sétif. There are no direct buses to Tizi-Ouzou. The best you can get is a bus to Hammam Keria and then local transport on to Azazga and Tizi-Ouzou.

Taxi The taxis depart from the intersection of the Algiers and Jijel roads, about two km past the bus station.

Hitching This intersection is also where you will have to get yourself to for hitching, either to Algiers or Tizi-Ouzou in the west, or to Jijel and Sétif to the east. There is plenty of traffic in both directions and hitching is easy.

TICHI

The beach at Tichi, 17 km east of Bejaia, is not too bad at all. The beach right in the town itself gets quite crowded, but you only have to walk a few hundred metres back towards Bejaia and the crowds thin out.

The only problem here is that the pollution from the oil refinery at Bejaia is sometimes so bad that the water line is dotted with dirty great globs of tar. It makes life mighty unpleasant to have your feet stained black while walking along the beach. This may have been an isolated incident, but I have my doubts.

Places to Stay

There are a couple of places, but neither represents fantastic value. In fact the *Hotel du Golfe* (☎ (05) 92 6806) must be someone's idea of a joke. The rooms here are incredibly small and dingy, and the bar/restaurant, although right on the edge of the beach, is completely caged in, either to keep stray people from the beach out, or to keep the drunks in. Either way it's a dump which is best avoided.

Up on the rise towards the eastern edge of the town is the *Hotel Bar Restaurant Les Hammadites* (☎ (05) 92 6680). This has quite a good terrace bar with views around the bay to Bejaia. Pity the rest of the place isn't up to much. Rooms cost AD 145 for a double with breakfast.

Camping It is possible to camp on the five km or so of beach stretching back towards Bejaia. This area is extremely flat and exposed with no protection from either the sun or the wind. There is one campsite, run by the Touring Club d'Algérie, which is open in summer only.

Getting There & Away

Buses to and from Bejaia and Jijel stop on the road through Tichi. It's just a matter of flagging them down in the centre of the town.

CORNICHE KABYLE

Fifteen km east of Tichi is Souk et Tnine, and from here the roads east along the coast and south through the Kherrata Gorge to Sétif pass through some amazingly rugged country. There is quite a bit of traffic along both roads, so hitching is not too bad.

Between Souk et Tnine and the fishing village of Ziama Mansouria, the mountains of the Petite Kabylie come down almost sheer to the water, and at times the road is carved out of the rock face. It twists and winds around and is usually only one lane wide; the way some of these people drive makes life pretty interesting.

There are a few sheltered bays with sandy beaches along the coast near Grotte Merveilleuse, and it should be possible to camp here if you have your own vehicle.

Towards Jijel the mountains recede, but there is still surprisingly little development.

JIJEL

The town of Jijel is really off the tourist track but, if you spend any time on the Corniche Kabyle, you will probably end up here for at least a night. It's an easy-going place but has no specific attractions.

Information

The post office is on Rue 1 Novembre 1954 (the date of the start of the revolution), about 300 metres along from the town hall, the building with the clocktower at the main intersection, Place de la République.

Rue 1 Novembre 1954 is the main street, and on it you'll also find the Air Algérie office and the banks.

Places to Stay

There are only two cheapies. The better by far is the *Hotel du Littoral*, on Rue 1 Novembre 1954, not far from Place de la République and only about five minutes' walk from the bus station. It is old and somewhat cavernous but clean enough, and rooms cost AD 55/66 for singles/doubles. There are no showers in the place but there are public ones right next door.

The other cheapie is the *Hotel En Nassre*, a couple of blocks back and inland from the Littoral. This is a bit of a dive but would do in a pinch.

The only other place in town is the two-star *Hotel Tindouf* (☎ (05) 96 2071), at 14 Rue Larbi Ben M'Hidi. The rooms are nothing flash and are arranged around a courtyard, so the windows open in. Rooms cost AD 90/115 for singles/doubles with washbasin. In one corner of the courtyard is the shower room, which is in fact a public

douche – even hotel guests have to pay the AD 7 for a hot shower.

Places to Eat

Slim pickings here. The restaurant attached to the *Hotel En Nassre* is not too bad, although women and couples have to sit in the adjoining 'salon'. There are a couple of other places in the main street.

Getting There & Away

Air The Air Algérie office (☎ (05) 96 5894), is on the main street, Rue 1 Novembre 1954.

Bus The bus station is about 100 metres from the town hall, in the opposite direction from Rue 1 Novembre 1954.

There are local buses and TVE departures for Algiers (six daily), Annaba (two daily), Bejaia (frequent) and Constantine (four daily).

KHERRATA GORGE

The narrow road which connects the coast with Sétif crosses the Petite Kabylie range of mountains through this narrow gorge. It is a pity, however, that the most spectacular (and dangerous) part of the gorge has been bypassed (underpassed?) by a new tunnel which cuts right through the guts of the mountain range.

It may still be possible to use the old road but this seems unlikely, as it was chronically prone to rock falls. It would make an excellent walk but you would need to carry all your gear, as there is no accommodation between Sétif and Tichi.

The tunnel, built by an Italian company, is an impressive piece of engineering and the approach to the northern end of it is even more so. The tunnel entrance is some 50 metres up the side of the mountain, so a bridge 1½-km long has had to be built to gain access. It is being touted as the longest bridge in Africa.

The village of Kherrata, on the inland side of the gorge, is huddled beneath Jebel Babor, which at 2004 metres is up there amongst the highest in the country. It is possible to hire guides in the village who will take you up some of the peaks in the surrounding area – it is not technical climbing, just bloody hard slogging.

The waters of the Oued Agrioun have been dammed here by the Ighil Emda Dam to form a small lake, which is used to generate hydro-electricity.

Sétif & Djemila

It's not the town of Sétif itself which is the attraction in this area inland from the Corniche Kabyle and west of Constantine, but the surrounding region. This is because the ruins of Roman Cuicul, present-day Djemila, are tucked away in the hills to the east.

SÉTIF

The town of Sétif is largely a product of the French colonial era. Until the French occupation in 1838 nothing much had happened in the town, other than the establishment of a veterans' colony by the Roman emperor Nerva; the ruins of this are still visible.

In 1945, however, the town became the focus of the emerging nationalist feeling. The raising of nationalist flags led to a uncontrolled riot in which 84 Europeans were massacred. French reprisals were both quick and indiscriminate; by French estimates at least 2000 Muslims lost their lives, so you can be fairly well assured that the figure was a good deal higher. Similar events were reported in nearby Kherrata and Guelma; Algerian estimates go to the opposite extreme and put the total number of deaths at 45,000.

Today the town has a population of about 200,000 and, at 1096 metres above sea level, is the second-highest wilaya capital in the country. Now how's *that* for trivia!

This town, with it's tree-lined streets, fountain and theatre, still has a very French feel to it.

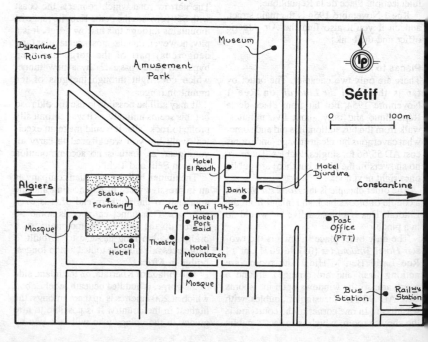

Information

The main street, Ave 8 Mai 1945 (the date of the massacres), runs east-west through the centre of town. On it you'll find the banks, the post office and airline offices.

Everything is within walking distance.

Things to See

The town's pride and joy is the huge amusement park (Parc d'Attraction), a couple of blocks north of the main street. Here there are rides of all sorts, giant slides and dodgem cars, and the whole thing seems to be just a tad out of place. The park itself is enormous: it has an artificial lake and fountains, and a small zoo with animals in tiny cages. There is even a coffee shop set up in a traditional Bedouin tent. It is a popular place in the evenings, but people come here to stroll rather than to actually use the rides.

On the western edge of the park are the ruins of a Byzantine fortress, while at the eastern end is the modern museum, accessible only from Blvd de la Palestine (outside the park). It has a collection of bits and pieces from prehistoric to Islamic times, including a couple of good mosaics. The museum is open from 9 am to noon and 2 to 6 pm; closed Friday morning and all day Saturday.

Places to Stay – bottom end

The best place is the relatively clean and friendly *Hotel Port Said* (☎ (05) 90 7183), at 6 Ave Ben Boulaid. Large rooms with shower cost AD 55/66 for singles/doubles and come complete with resident cockroaches (nothing unusual), although they are only small ones! As is often the case, there is no sign in English, and the unmarked entrance is in between two restaurants.

The *Hotel Djurdura* (☎ (05) 90 4655) is on Rue des Frères Habbèchc, the side street next to the Banque Centrale d'Algérie. Rooms cost AD 60 for a double but they are not very private.

There is also a local hotel on Place de l'Indépendance. This is a place for males only; expect to pay about AD 35 for a bed.

Places to Stay – middle & top end

The *Hotel El Readh* (☎ (05) 90 4778), on Rue Frères Meslem, is a one-star hotel that charges AD 145 for a double with breakfast.

Just a couple of doors up from the Hotel Port Said is the featureless two-star *Hotel Mountazeh* (☎ (05) 90 4828), at 12 Ave Ben Boulaid. Prices are the usual AD 145/190 for singles/doubles.

The town's top-end place is the three-star *Hotel El Hidhah* (☎ (05) 90 4043) in the north-eastern corner of the park, north of the museum.

Places to Eat

There's a restaurant on either side of the entrance to the Hotel Port Said; both are quite good, but the one on the south side is marginally better.

There are the usual patisseries all over the place, with the standard array of cakes and coffee.

The restaurant at the *Hotel Readh* does a four-course set menu for AD 50.

Getting There & Away

Air The Air Algérie office (☎ (05) 85 1818) and the Air France office (☎ (05) 85 2230) are on Ave 8 Mai 1945.

Bus The bus station is south of Ave 1 Novembre 1954, 50 metres along the street which runs down beside the post office. There are daily connections to Algiers, Batna, Bejaia, Constantine and Ghardaia.

Buses for El Ouelma, which is 17 km east and is the turn-off for Djemila, leave regularly from outside the railway station.

Train The railway station is another 150 metres from the bus station. Turn left past the bus station and then take the second street on the right.

There are at least three trains daily to Algiers and Constantine.

Hitching The road to the north coast runs alongside the Byzantine ruins. It's about a two-km walk to the edge of the town along this road.

For Constantine, the best bet is to take a local bus from the railway station to El Ouelma (AD 3.50) and then hitch from there.

DJEMILA

Ho hum, another Roman site? Well, yes, but this one is really something. The setting is superb and the major buildings are remarkably well preserved.

Although there is no accommodation here, the transport connections are good and it is easy enough to visit the ruins in a leisurely day using Sétif as a base. There are a few spartan restaurants where you can get a bite to eat and a cold drink.

As well as the ruins themselves, Djemila has an incredible museum which is absolutely chocker with mosaics found on the site. The 10-metre-high walls are covered in them, and the effect is a bit overpowering.

The site is open daily from 7 am to 6 pm in summer, 5 pm in winter. The museum is open only from 9 am to noon and 2 to 5 pm; closed Saturday.

History

Ancient Cuicul was built as a military garrison on a narrow triangular plateau in amongst some fairly rugged country at the confluence of two rivers. The site was chosen largely because of the rich arable land surrounding it.

The town was built to the standard pattern of a forum at the centre with two main streets, the Cardo Maximus and the Decumanus Maximus, forming the major axes. During the reign of Caracalla in the 3rd century, however, the town's administrators pulled down some of the old ramparts and built a new forum, surrounding it with even bigger and more grandiose edifices than graced the old one.

The building and expansion pattern was

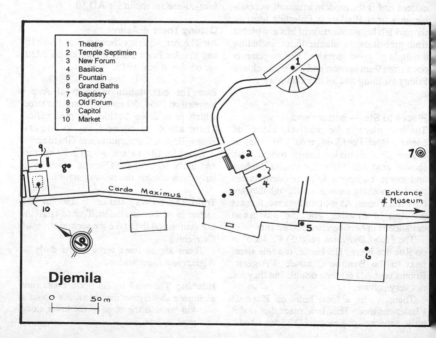

1 Theatre
2 Temple Septimien
3 New Forum
4 Basilica
5 Fountain
6 Grand Baths
7 Baptistry
8 Old Forum
9 Capitol
10 Market

Cardo Maximus

Entrance
& Museum

Djemila

0   50 m

so limited by the terrain that the theatre had to be built *outside* the town walls – a very unorthodox move.

When Christianity became all the rage in the 4th century, a basilica and baptistry were built on the slope to the south of the town; they are among the major attractions of the ruins today.

The Ruins

The museum is right by the entrance to the ruins. Inside, among other things, is a good model of the site; one of the attendants can point out the major features. The mosaics here are just superb, particularly the one showing gladiators doing battle with wild animals in an amphitheatre. There is also a very impressive collection of everyday items found during excavations; these simple things such as surgical instruments, door locks, glass and jewellery give a much better insight into the life of these people than a hundred mosaics or marble statues ever could – fascinating stuff.

From the museum the path leads down the slope; along here you will no doubt be hounded by unofficial guides and people selling bits of carved marble and other bits and pieces. Some of this stuff is obviously genuine, and some is just as obviously not.

The new dome of the baptistry is visible up to the right. The building is kept locked to ensure that the mosaics inside don't come to any harm. It's a bit of a scramble down to the enormous Grand Baths, which cover an area of over 2500 sq metres. The walls of some rooms are still standing, and in places it is still possible to see the channels and pipes which used to carry the water and direct the steam.

The road continues past a marble fountain on the left to the new forum, officially called Place Serverus after the emperor Septimus Serverus, who was from Africa. The road to the west spanned by the highly decorative Triumphal Arch (built in 216 AD and dedicated to the emperor Caracalla) was the road to Sétif. The Decumanus Maximus, to the north, was the road to Jijel; to the east, the

road led to Constantine, while the southern route was to Timgad.

The Temple Septimien stands on the south-eastern corner of the forum; in it were found statues of Septimus Serverus and his Syrian wife, Julia Domna.

The road leads downhill, past the town brothel on the right (easily identifiable by the phallic symbol carved in the stone by the entrance), to the old forum. There is a 3rd-century altar in the centre; on the western side, the bas reliefs of the sacrificial animals and a man with a mace are still amazingly clear.

The market backs onto the forum and is entered through an arch on the Cardo Maximus. This market is one of the delights of Djemila. The tables for vendors around the walls are still in position and, at about shoulder height in the wall which backs onto the forum, there are six holes which used to hold the poles for measuring scales. In front of these is a small stone table with three cavities with holes in the bottom. These were standard measures for produce: when you bought your oil or grain, a cavity was filled and you placed your receptacle underneath. The market was named after its donator, Cosinius Primus.

Next to the market entrance on the Cardo Maximus, under the civil basilica, is the old town prison.

The theatre is actually outside the original city walls and is set in the side of the valley, which is quite steep at this point.

Places to Stay & Eat

There is a hotel right outside the entrance to the site. It is not a bad place, although there is water only in the mornings. Showers, when they are running, are hot. The charge is AD 125 for a double.

The township of Djemila has a few standard basic restaurants.

Getting There & Away

Buses do run to Djemila but very infrequently, so you are much better off catching a taxi from El Ouelma on the main Sétif-Constantine road. They operate frequently and cost AD 15 per person. Be warned that Friday is not a good day to see the ruins as there is very little traffic, especially in the afternoons. It is still possible, just a bit more difficult.

There is usually enough traffic to make hitching an option, at least on the stretch from Sétif to El Ouelma.

From El Ouelma, the taxis gather in a parking lot near the multistorey apartment blocks, 300 metres along the signposted road to Arbaoun and Djemila, just on the edge of town towards Sétif. The bus station is in a spare block on the other side of the apartment buildings, five minutes' walk away.

Constantine

'An eagle's nest perched on the summit of a crag' was how Alexandre Dumas described Constantine when he travelled through here in the 19th century. A fit enough description.

The main part of the town is built on a neck of land with precipitous drops on one side to the plains below. On two other sides the cliffs drop down into the Rhumel Gorge and rise equally sheer on the other side, only 100 metres away.

The setting is stunning, especially with the four bridges across the gorge, all of different types. Closer inspection of the gorge, however, reveals a national disgrace – it has become little more than a massive rubbish dump. It is all too easy for residents of the medina to just chuck their rubbish over the edge; at one point there is a Naftal service station which has its waste outlet at the edge of the cliff, so there is a dirty black stain right down one side at this point. In summer at least, the Oued Rhumel at the bottom is little more than a trickle of black water; with the higher rainfall in winter it's not so bad.

Pollution aside, this city of 600,000 inhabitants is well worth a visit, although there is little to see other than the gorge itself.

History

The Punic town of Cirta Regia became the capital of Numidia. The Numidian king Massinissa, who reigned in the 2nd century BC, allied himself with the Romans in their battles against the Carthaginians.

Jugurtha, the grandson of the famous Massinissa, ended up doing battle with the Romans soon after the fall of Carthage and came off second best.

In the early years of the Christian era, the colonial Cirta became the capital of a confederation of cities in the region and then, in the 2nd century, became a colony of Cuicul (Djemila) to the west. In this era it became one of the richest cities in Africa.

After an uprising in the town in 311 AD, it was destroyed by Maxence. Its fortunes were revived under the emperor Constantine and the city took on the name Constantina.

From the 8th century on, the city fell to various regional Islamic dynasties – the Fatimids, Zirids, Hammadids, Almohads and the Hafsids. It was conquered again in the 16th century, by the Ottoman Turks (who were already based in Algiers), and became the important *beylik* of Qacentina.

The city finally fell to the French in 1837, on their second attempt to take it. They had been successfully repelled in an initial attack on the town the year before.

Orientation

The city has two squares, Place des Martyrs and Place 1 Novembre. The latter is the main focus, and around it is the post office, theatre and banks; the hotel and restaurant area is right behind it. The square is always busy during the day but takes on a slightly aggressive atmosphere at night, when all the university students hang out with nothing to do and there is an air of expectancy around, as though something is about to happen.

The streets of the medina are narrow and congested and, due to the terrain, the transport services are all some distance from the centre. The railway station is across the gorge (within easy walking distance) while the bus station is a few km south of the city, by the river.

Getting around on foot is no problem and in fact is the most interesting way to go.

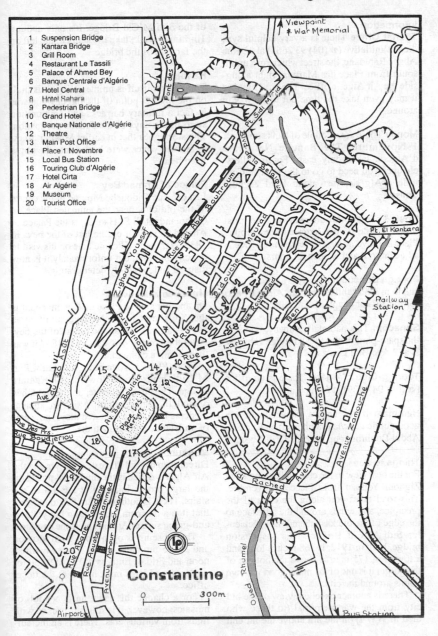

1	Suspension Bridge
2	Kantara Bridge
3	Grill Room
4	Restaurant Le Tassili
5	Palace of Ahmed Bey
6	Banque Centrale d'Algérie
7	Hotel Central
8	Hotel Sahara
9	Pedestrian Bridge
10	Grand Hotel
11	Banque Nationale d'Algérie
12	Theatre
13	Main Post Office
14	Place 1 Novembre
15	Local Bus Station
16	Touring Club d'Algérie
17	Hotel Cirta
18	Air Algérie
19	Museum
20	Tourist Office

Constantine

0   300m

Information

Tourist Office There is a very helpful syndicat d'initiative (☎ (04) 93 2661) at 32 Rue Abane Ramdane, the street which runs uphill south from Place des Martyrs, right alongside the Air Algérie office. The guys running it may even take the time out to show you around.

Money There are a couple of banks on Place 1 Novembre. The Banque Nationale d'Algérie takes only cash. For travellers' cheques you need to go to the Banque Centrale d'Algérie, just along Blvd Zighout Youssef.

Post & Telecommunications The post office is one of the large edifices around Place 1 Novembre. The telephone office is adjacent to it and is open 24 hours.

Foreign Consulates There is a French Consulate in Constantine. See the Algeria Facts for the Visitor chapter for details.

Sonacom This national company, which is the spare-parts dealer for all foreign vehicles, is at 2 Ave Bidi Louiza.

Touring Club d'Algérie There is an office (☎ (04) 94 6129) at 6 Rue Zabaane.

Hammam If you need a shower there is a good public *douche* (bathhouse) on Rue Sidi Abdul Bouhroum up near the Grill Room.

Things to See

For the best view of the city, walk along Blvd Zighout Youssef from Place 1 Novembre. This road takes you along the edge of the precipice, and winds around the cliff face to the edge of the old kasbah and the spectacular Sidi M'Cid Bridge. This suspension bridge, built in 1912, is 168 metres long and a towering 175 metres above the bottom of the gorge; it is one of the many good vantage points around the city.

There is another excellent view of the old city from the war memorial (to those who died in WW I) on the hill above the far end of the Sidi M'Cid Bridge. It's only about a 10-minute walk; take the stairs to the left on the far side of the bridge.

Kasbah

The kasbah itself is uninteresting. It is built on the highest point of the old city and was in fact a military barracks and ammunition store in the days of the French occupation. The story goes that in earlier Muslim times, unfaithful wives were hurled into the abyss from here.

Palace of Ahmed Bey

Just off Rue Didouche Mourad in the centre of the old city, near the animated Place du Commandant Si El Haouès, is the Palace of Ahmed Bey, built by the last of the beys in 1835. Napoleon III came here on his visit to the city in 1865, but unfortunately it is now disused and is rapidly deteriorating.

Mosques & Medersa

On another side of Place du Commandant is the Souk el Ghazal Mosque, built by a Moroccan in 1730 on the orders of the bey. After the French took the city in 1837 it was turned into a cathedral.

From Place 1 Novembre, Rue Larbi Ben M'Hidi leads down towards El Kantara bridge. The Great Mosque, on the right, has a modern façade. Further on, an ancient medersa faced with coloured tiles is now part of an Islamic studies institute.

Museum

Directly up behind Place des Martyrs and the Air Algérie office is the municipal museum, the large brown building at the top of the stairs. There is nothing in English to indicate that it is a museum, but it has a big yellow-and-green sign in Arabic above the entrance.

The museum is open from 8 am to noon and 2 to 5 pm daily except Thursday afternoon and Friday. Entry is AD 1, AD 0.50 for students, and bags must be left at the ticket office.

For a change this museum is not full of mosaics; however, it is still jam-packed with finds from various eras. There is an incredible variety of stuff – there are even snail shells which had holes drilled in them by Neolithics so that they could suck out the innards! The collection of African coins is vast and includes some unusual gold coins dating back to the Byzantine times.

Bridge
Just past the medersa is the passenger lift and stairs, which take you down the 30 or so metres to the start of the pedestrian bridge across the Rhumel, although at the time of writing the lift was unserviceable so you had to slog it up or down on foot; maybe it's working again now. Crossing this bridge can be a little disconcerting at times because it sways quite alarmingly if there are any number of people on it.

Places to Stay – bottom end
The street for cheap hotels is the narrow, cobbled Rue Hamloui, one block up from Place 1 Novembre. It's a slightly seedy area, particularly in the evenings, but is not in the least bit threatening.

There is a shortage of water in Constantine, and all the hotels are without it for at least a few hours each day.

I found the best place to be the *Hotel Central* (☎ (04) 94 3309), at 19 Rue Hamloui. It is clean, secure and friendly and rooms cost AD 50/70 for singles/doubles. Couples can usually just take a single room, as the beds are doubles. There are hot showers but these are obviously limited to the times when the water is running. It is right above a café, which is convenient for early morning croissants and coffee.

The *Hotel National* (☎ (04) 94 9437), a bit further up the street at No 12, is similar, but there are no showers.

Another good bet is the friendly *Hotel Sahara* (☎ (04) 94 3274) on Place Adjali Abderachidi, a small square leading off Rue Larbi Ben M'Hidi at No 23; the hotel is in the far left corner of the square. This clean little hotel has no singles, and doubles cost AD 70.

Youth Hostel There is a *Youth Hostel*

(☎ (04) 69 5461) in the Quartier Filali, some distance from the centre of town. If you are really keen, take a bus from the centre to the mosque in Quartier Filali, and ask for directions from there.

Places to Stay – middle
A good place in this category is the one-star *Grand Hotel* (☎ (04) 94 3092) at 2 Rue Larbi Ben M'Hidi, right by Place 1 Novembre. It's a typically French hotel and none of the furniture or fittings look like they have been changed since independence. It's quite good value at AD 87/117 for a single/double with bath and 'breakfast' – a pathetic offering of a stale croissant and a cup of tepid coffee.

Places to Stay – top end
If you can afford it, the place to stay is the grand old *Hotel Cirta* (☎ (04) 94 3033), at 1 Ave Achour Rachmani, right on the edge of Place des Martyrs. It is another remnant of the colonial era, with a grand entrance and typically overstated decor. Room rates are AD 141/242 for singles/doubles with bath and breakfast.

Places to Eat
Again, Rue Hamloui is a good place to start. The *Restaurant el Baraka* at No 23 is not bad and does all the standard stuff – rice and meat, or couscous, for AD 25, salads for AD 8. Further down the street at No 29 is a similar place, the *Restaurant Dounyazed*, complete with tacky fish pond, fountain and fluted columns.

Right at the very bottom of Rue Hamloui is a small network of narrow streets, and here you'll find a dozen or so snack eateries, all with their food on display. Just take a wander around and choose what you like. In Rue Sidi Abdallah Bouhroum is the *Grill Room*, which has fast food of a reasonable standard.

For something a bit more flash, the *Cirta Hotel* has a good, although expensive, restaurant, and a bar.

Getting There & Away
Air Air Algérie has an enormous office (☎ (04) 93 9211) at Place des Martyrs, right

in the centre of town. Air France (☎ (04) 93 6662) is at 8 Rue Abane Ramdane. Constantine's Ain-el-Bey Airport is seven km south of the city.

There are flights to Algiers (at least twice daily, AD 258), Ghardaia (weekly, AD 311), Oran (four times weekly, AD 504), Tamanrasset (weekly, AD 557) and Tindouf (weekly, AD 620).

Bus The bus station is a few km south of the centre, right by the river at the bottom of the ravine, which widens out considerably not far from the centre of town. It is known locally as *sontavay*, after the SNTV initials of the national bus company. The quickest way from the centre is a shared taxi from the bottom of the stairway between the Hotel Cirta and the Touring Club d'Algérie (AD 5), or on a bus from the local bus station (AD 3).

Because it is a major city, there are buses to just about anywhere, but the timetables are poorly displayed and the whole place is a bit of a shambles. Bookings should be made 24 hours in advance.

Destinations include Algiers, Annaba, El Oued, Ghardaia, Jijel, Oran, Sétif and Tébessa.

Train It is about a 15-minute walk from the centre to the railway station, which is on the other side of the gorge. The most direct access is via the footbridge.

Night-train couchettes can (and should) be booked in advance; for other trains just show up half an hour before departure.

There are five trains to Algiers every day, two to Skikda, two to Touggourt and one to Tunis (via Annaba).

Taxi Taxis also leave from the main bus station. There are departures for Algiers (AD 170), Annaba, Sétif and Souk Ahras.

Getting Around
Bus The city bus system has its main terminus just off to one side between Place des Martyrs and Place 1 Novembre.

The only buses you are likely to need are those to the bus station or the youth hostel.

Taxi Yellow taxis are everywhere and can be flagged down. Fare is by negotiation and should be established before you take off. To the bus station from the centre should cost AD 10 for the cab, not per person.

AROUND CONSTANTINE
Tiddis
Spectacularly situated some 30 km north of Constantine, Tiddis (meaning 'red' in Arabic) is another Roman site and one well worth visiting. The only problem is that it's relatively inaccessible – you need your own vehicle, or you could charter a taxi for a half day.

Named after the amazing red soil of the surrounding countryside, the ancient city of Tiddis is unusual in that it is located on the side of a fairly steep slope, so the Romans' usual penchant for dead straight roads had to give way to practicality and the Cardo snakes up the side of the hill.

The ruins are quite extensive, the major features being the cisterns and water channels. It seems that ancient Tiddis relied totally on rain water, so almost every house and building had its own cistern for storing water.

From the carpark, where a caretaker will miraculously appear and sell you a ticket, the entrance to the site is through the north gate on the Cardo, and almost immediately on the right you come to one of the more unusual sights in Tiddis, the Temple of Mithra complete with the much-photographed carving of a large winged phallus.

It's worth taking the time to wander right through the ruins as the unusual setting, and the red colouring of the soil, set them quite apart from anything else you'll see in north Africa. There's usually an old man hanging around who, for a small fee, will show you around the site. He's fairly knowledgeable about the ruins and will show you things which are otherwise easily missed, such as the cleft in the rock above the site which is like a walk-in sauna – hot, damp air comes up from the depths. He went way down in my estimations, however, when he tried to fondle my bum.

Getting There & Away

The turn-off to Tiddis is signposted off to the left, 27 km north of Constantine along the Skikda road. From the main road it is seven km along a narrow bitumen road to the site. Access is not a problem at any time of year. If you don't have a vehicle a taxi will cost AD 250 return from Constantine, including an hour or so spent at the ruins.

Annaba

Set on one of the few coastal plains in the country, the city of Annaba is one that has been booming, as is attested by the massive steel works south of the city.

With almost 500,000 inhabitants, it is now the fourth-largest city in the country; it boasts a university and Algeria's third-largest port.

The heart of the city is the wide main street, Cours de la Révolution, and this broad avenue, with its central shady strip, is just so French it's ridiculous. It is also the focus of activity in the evenings, when the dozen or so pavement cafés and ice-cream kiosks which line the central strip come to life.

The city is ringed by hills. The skyline to the south-west is dominated by the incredibly ugly Basilica of St Augustine, while the opposite direction boasts a full complement of even uglier apartment blocks.

The city is a pleasant enough place in which to pass a day or two on the way to or from Tunisia.

History

The site of the Roman town of Hippo Regius is just to the south of town, and it was here that St Augustine was a bishop for 34 years.

Augustine was very influential in Christianity in Africa and was one of the main opponents of the Donatist movement in the latter half of the 2nd century. He also developed a theory which gave orthodox Christian rulers the right to move forcefully against heretics; this eventually led to the crushing of the Donatist schism. His main work was *De Civitate Dei* (The City of God), and he is now regarded as one of the major writers and thinkers of Christianity.

The town later took the name Bona el Hadida, and in French times this was shortened to Bône.

In the 16th century the city was conquered by the corsair Khair Ed Din (Barbarossa) and was briefly occupied by the Spanish in the same century.

French troops moved into the town in 1832. During WW I the town was heavily bombed by the Germans and in WW II it was an operational base for the allied armies of the UK and the USA. It was bombed heavily again during the winter of 1942-43.

Information

Tourist Office As the city is virtually devoid of both tourist attractions and tourists, there's even less motivation to visit the tourist office here than in other cities. If you can't help yourself, the office is behind the Grand Hotel d'Orient on Rue Tarik Ibn Zaid and is open from 8 am to noon and 2 to 6 pm.

Money There are banks on Cours de la Révolution and around the corner on Place 1 Mai.

Post The main post office is on Ave Zighout Youssef, the extension of Cours de la Révolution.

Foreign Consulates The following countries have diplomatic representation in Annaba: France, Tunisia and Italy.

Don't arrive here expecting to get a Tunisian visa in a hurry – they take at least three weeks to come through.

Touring Club d'Algérie The office of the national motoring organisation (☎ (08) 82 6461) is at 1 Blvd Zighout Youssef, right next to the post office.

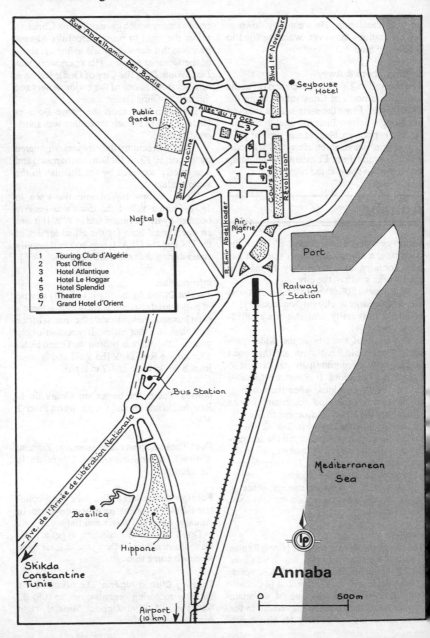

1	Touring Club d'Algérie
2	Post Office
3	Hotel Atlantique
4	Hotel Le Hoggar
5	Hotel Splendid
6	Theatre
7	Grand Hotel d'Orient

Rue Abdelhamid ben Badis

Blvd 1er Novembre

Seybouse Hotel

Public Garden

Allée du 17 Oct

Cours de la Révolution

Blvd .B. Hocine

Naftal

Air Algérie

R. Emir Abdelkader

Port

Railway Station

Bus Station

Ave. de l'Armée de Libération Nationale

Basilica

Hippone

Mediterranean Sea

Skikda
Constantine
Tunis

Annaba

0   500m

Airport
(10 km)

Things to See

There's very little to see, really. The Basilica of St Augustine is a 30-minute walk to the south, out past the bus station. It is really no thing of beauty and is on a par with the one at Carthage in Tunisia. It was built at the turn of the century, and is open from 8.30 to 11.30 am and 2.30 to 4.30 pm.

To find your way up, take the street to the left of the factory on the far side of the roundabout by the bus station. At the far end of the factory is a street to the right and this takes you up to the top. The best part about the walk up to the basilica is not the basilica itself but the view from out the front of the town, with the port and lovely apartment blocks in the distance.

The ruins of Hippo Regius (also called Hippone) are at the foot of the hill beneath the basilica. The entrance is 300 metres along from the roundabout by the bus station. The site is only open on Wednesday, Thursday and Friday, and there's not really all that much to see. The museum is the white building on the small hill.

Places to Stay – bottom end

The cheapest place, but a male-only option, is the local hotel in the side street behind the theatre. It's AD 35 for a bed, nothing more.

The *Hotel du Théâtre* is just around the corner from the Hotel Atlantique. Rooms here cost AD 70, and are clean and quite adequate.

Further up the scale, and good value, is the one-star *Hotel Atlantique* on Allée du 17 Octobre, 50 metres off the main street. Breakfast is included in the price of AD 145 for a double.

Places to Stay – middle

There are a couple of two-star places around a small square just off Cours de la Révolution. The one to avoid is the *Hotel Le Hoggar*, which can really only be described as a filthy rip-off. The rooms are absolutely infested with cockroaches and look as though they haven't been cleaned in ages, the water rarely works and the whole place is a bad joke.

The hotel further up towards Allée du 17 Octobre on the same side is a better bet.

Places to Stay – top end

In the main street is the *Grand Hotel d'Orient* (☎ (08) 82 2051), which is left over from colonial days and still has all the period touches like chandeliers and a grand piano in the café. It is right next to the theatre. Double rooms cost a hefty AD 240 including breakfast and douche.

Top of the range is the *Hotel Seybouse International* (☎ (08) 82 2409), on Rue 24 Février 1966 (the date of the foundation of the UGTA trade union), where you'll pay a mere AD 600 for a double for the night. The main reason you are likely to want to come here is to change money outside banking hours.

Places to Eat

There's nothing very special here, and in fact, good meals are hard to find in Annaba.

In the middle of the Cours de la Révolution there are cafés and ice-cream kiosks which open up in the evenings.

Getting There & Away

Air Air Algérie has an office (☎ (08) 82 0020) at 2 Cours de la Révolution. The Air France office (☎ (08) 82 6666) is at 8 Rue Prosper-Dubourg. The airport is 12 km from the centre of town.

There are regular flights to Algiers (twice daily, AD 331), Béchar (once weekly, AD 625), El Oued (three times weekly, AD 244), Ghardaia (twice weekly, AD 470), Oran (twice weekly, AD 594) and Ouargla (twice weekly, AD 355).

Air Algérie also operates international flights from Annaba to Lyons, Marseilles and Paris, while Air France flies to Marseilles and Paris.

Bus The bus station is one km along Ave de l'Armée Libération Nationale from the centre – it's about a 20-minute walk. From the outside the station looks very modern and efficient but inside it is pretty dirty and gloomy. The ticket windows are upstairs, and a timetable of arrivals and departures is displayed.

Most long-distance trips can be booked in advance, but trying to find out when the ticket window is open can be an exercise in persistence.

There is a daily departure to Tunis at 5 am for the eight-hour journey. Tickets for this service definitely have to be bought in advance, particularly in summer.

Other destinations include: Algiers (three daily), Constantine (six daily), El Oued (daily), Ghardaia (two daily), Ouargla, Tébessa (two daily), and Souk Ahras (five daily).

Train The railway station is right in the centre on Place 1 Mai. It is in fact closed most of the time and only opens up when there is a train arriving or departing. If you need information, there are offices around the left-hand side of the station.

Departures are at 10.50 am and 10.15 pm for Algiers (10½ hours) and Constantine (three hours), 4.40 pm to Tébessa (five hours) and 9.30 am to Tunis (8½ hours).

Taxi There are long-distance taxis to Constantine for AD 70 from a couple of blocks west of the hotel area – just ask around.

Sea Tickets for the ferries to Marseilles can be bought at the CNAN office (☎ (08) 82 5555) on Cours de la Révolution, in the next block up from the theatre. The ferry port is right in the centre of town.

There are sailings about four times a month in summer to Marseilles, dropping to two per month in winter. The journey takes about 23 hours.

EL KALA

From Annaba the road heads inland before joining the coast again at El Kala, a beautiful small town hemmed in against the sea by the forested mountains of the Kala National Park.

The beach here is fairly reasonable and the town is a minor summer resort for holidaying Algerians.

It is possible to hitch from El Kala to Tabarka, the first town on the Tunisian Mediterranean coast. There is less traffic along the road which heads up through the mountains and across the Tunisian border at Babouch. The best way to get along this road is to catch the daily Annaba-Tunis bus. It is not possible to pick the bus up en route.

Places to Stay & Eat

The town has the two-star *Hotel El Morjane* (☎ (08) 82 0242), which is not especially cheap at AD 180 for a double with breakfast. The *Hotel de Post* has also been recommended.

Other than that, it may be possible to camp on the beach in the summer months at Plage de la Messida, 10 km to the east.

For an excellent meal, take the street on the left corner of the main square (as you face the port), and go to the second restaurant.

Getting There & Away

There are regular buses and taxis for Annaba. A shared taxi to the Tunisian border costs AD 6.

SOUK AHRAS

This town is built in rugged country and is the last large town before the Tunisian border. There is really no reason to stop here, but if you get stuck there is the one-star *Hotel d'Orient*.

The bus station is at the top of the hill, on the road to Annaba, about 15 minutes' walk from the centre.

The only train through here each day is the Trans-Maghreb Express from Tunis to Algiers, which passes through at 6 pm on the journey west, and 11.50 am heading for Tunis.

Aurès Mountains

These mountains are part of the Algerian Saharan Atlas range, which is an extension of the Moroccan Atlas. The entire Atlas range runs south-west to north-east clear across Algeria into Tunisia.

The ruins of Roman Thamugadi, or Timgad, some 40 km east of the unexciting provincial capital of Batna, are the area's main attraction.

Between Batna on the north side of the mountains and Biskra on the south, two roads wind through some spectacular country. The northern route is the faster of the two and has more transport, while the southern one is the more interesting, due mainly to the spectacular gorges of the Oued El-Abiod and the local mud-brick villages.

Biskra is an important regional centre and is really the gateway to the desert in this part of the country.

The people of the Aurès are Chaouias, a Berber tribe who have retained their original language and culture much as the Kabylies have further north.

BATNA

There is not really much of interest in Batna. However, the setting in the wide valley is pleasant, and the altitude of over 1000 metres keeps the air clear and the temperatures bearable. Batna also boasts one of the biggest collections of the ugly apartment blocks which blot the skyline in most Algerian towns.

When visiting Timgad you really need to use Batna as a base, as the two hotels at Timgad are currently closed.

Information

There is a somewhat disorganised tourist office here on Ave de l'Indépendance, the main street. They have little in the way of information.

The banks and the post office are in the compact central area, about five minutes' walk from the bus station.

There are public showers for men and women just around the corner from the Hotel Laverdure, towards the bus station: AD 9 for a shower only or AD 15 complete with soap, towel and shampoo.

Places to Stay – bottom end

There are a couple of cheapies here. The *Hotel Laverdure* (☎ (04) 55 1163) is at 3 Ave de l'Indépendance, only a couple of minutes' walk from the bus station. It doesn't win any prizes for friendliness or value for money, but is reasonably clean and not too bad. Rooms cost AD 80 for a tiny double. From the bus station, go straight on past the fountain roundabout and take the first street left; the hotel is on the right above a café.

Also near the bus station is another hotel, without a name, although it does have 'Hotel' on it. It costs AD 40 for a bed in a shared room or AD 100 for the whole room, as there are no doubles and you have to pay for the three beds regardless of how many you use. From the bus station, turn right at the roundabout and the hotel is on the right after 100 metres.

Another good bottom-end place is the friendly *Hotel Es-Salaam* (☎ (04) 55 6847) at 10 Ave de l'Indépendance. It has no sign in English but has a distinctive black-tiled entrance. Rooms cost AD 80/100, but there are no showers.

Places to Stay – middle

A good place in this category is the *Hotel el Hayat* (☎ (04) 55 2601), at 18 Rue Mohammed Salah Benabbes, about five minutes' walk from the bus station. The rooms are well appointed, if a bit small, and are centrally heated in winter. The charge is AD 120/160 with bath, and this includes breakfast in the patisserie on the ground floor. To find the hotel, head down the hill along Ave de la République from the Air Algérie office and post office, and the hotel is on the edge of the small square which you come across after a couple of blocks.

Further along Ave de la République, at No 10, is the *Hotel Karim* (☎ (04) 55 8981) which has good rooms for AD 105/140 with breakfast, or AD 115/155 with bath and breakfast.

Places to Eat

For a standard local meal there's a number of places near the Hotel el Hayat and the market. For something a bit better the *Restaurant Kimel*, on Ave de l'Indépendance where it crosses the small oued in the centre of town, charges around AD 60 for an excellent two-course meal.

Getting There & Away
Air The Air Algérie office (☎ (04) 55 2665), is near the post office, about five minutes' walk from the bus station.

Bus The enormous bus station is right in the centre of town in a spot where one would normally expect to find the town hall or some other public building. There is a big government supermarket opposite the station, and next to it is a large roundabout, complete with fountain.

Timetables are displayed inside the station, and tickets can be bought in advance for longer journeys. There are daily departures to Algiers, Annaba, Constantine and Biskra.

For Timgad, there are four regional buses daily which drop you off right at the entrance to the ruins. The first bus is supposedly at 9 am, the last at 5 pm, but the schedule seems to be very flexible. The Timgad buses leave from the small yard behind the supermarket directly opposite the bus station. The trip takes 40 minutes and costs AD 5.

Train The railway station is on the edge of town, a 15-minute walk from the centre along Ave de la République. There are two trains daily to both Constantine and Biskra (with connections on to Touggourt).

Taxi The taxi station is a couple of blocks from the bus station, in the opposite direction to the fountain. There are departures to all surrounding towns (including Timgad) and to Algiers.

Hitching Batna is a difficult place to hitch out of because there is a ring road around the city and the through-traffic doesn't come anywhere near the centre of town.

From the centre, it's about a 30-minute walk to the outskirts in the direction of Con-

stantine, and a similar distance to the south for Biskra.

TIMGAD
The old Roman town of Thamugadi is 40 km east of Batna in rolling countryside. Even in mid-summer the temperature here is mild and walking around is a pleasure rather than an endurance test.

The ruins are unusual in that the desert sands have perfectly preserved everything up to a height of about half a metre. From there up there is little left, but the result is that the layout of the town and the buildings is exceptionally clear. Well worth a day trip from Batna.

The entrance to the site is just one block from the main road. If you come on the bus it drops you close to the gate. The site is open every day from 9 am to 5 pm; the museum only from 9 am to noon and 2 to 5 pm; both are closed Saturday and Wednesday morning; entry is AD 4.

History
The town was founded during the reign of Trajan in the 1st century AD as a place where retired legionnaires were given land.

The town prospered during the Roman era but was destroyed by Berbers during a revolt in the 6th century. It was rebuilt in part by the Byzantines, only to be destroyed again during the Arab invasion.

The Ruins
The museum is just inside the entrance, on the left. For once the display of mosaics is not too overpowering; however, the other exhibits, although good, are poorly labelled.

These other exhibits include an extraordinary array of bits and pieces from everyday life, which give a very vivid idea of how the people used to live. There are items such as jewellery, geometry and surgery instruments, coins, locks and keys, bone clothes pins and fibulas, and a amazing glob of barely recognisable gold coins which were fused in a fire.

The town itself was small, covering an area of only about 12 hectares. On the right,

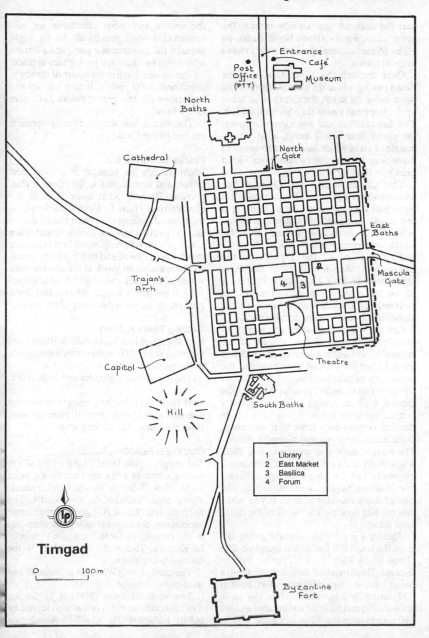

Timgad

0 _____ 100 m

Post Office (PTT)

Entrance

Café

Museum

North Baths

Cathedral

North Gate

East Baths

East Market

Trajan's Arch

Mascula Gate

Capitol

Theatre

Hill

South Baths

1 Library
2 East Market
3 Basilica
4 Forum

Byzantine Fort

past the museum and actually outside the town limits, are the Grand North Baths, an 80 by 66 metre complex which used to have over 30 rooms.

Once through the North Gate with its rutted paving where the chariot wheels have worn away the stone, the Cardo Nord leads up the slope and passes the library on the left. This has columns and a semicircular room; the paved floor is still intact, apart from a couple of slabs which have been removed to make way for lighting (which looks like it hasn't worked for years).

The Cardo meets the Decumanus Maximus at a T-junction. If you turn left it leads past the east market on the right (up a few stairs). At the end of the street, on the left before the Mascula Gate, are the east baths, which were erected in 146 AD.

To the right of the T-junction the Decumanus Maximus leads to the main monument, Trajan's Arch. It was built early in the 3rd century and marks the western extremity of Trajan's town. Once again the stones in the roadway are deeply rutted.

Outside the gate, on the right, is a small temple (dedicated to the 'genius of the colony'); the Market of Sertius on the left is named after the official who provided the money for its construction.

Further up to the left past the market is the capitol, built on a high point and actually outside the town limits. It was built late in the 2nd century on a large platform, along the front of which is a row of small columns. The temple itself was enormous and there was a flight of 28 steps up to the entrance. It originally had six 14-metre-high columns, two of which have been reconstructed. The size of these columns really hits you when you see just how big the pieces of the fallen ones are.

There's a good view over the entire site from the small hill just near the capitol. The Grand South Baths lie a bit further over to the east. Three hundred metres south along a rough track is a large Byzantine fort, built in 539 during the reign of Justinian. The walls are over 2½ metres thick and enclose an area 110 metres long and 70 metres wide. Inside,

the rooms and other structures are still remarkably well preserved. To the right through the entrance is a pool, and a terrace which still has the brick paving tiles in place.

The theatre, back in the centre of the town, could seat 3500 people. It now has modern accretions for the performances held here every May.

The forum lies almost directly opposite the end of the Cardo.

Places to Stay & Eat

Right outside the entrance is a small post office, and next to this is the *Hotel & Restaurant Timgad*. Next door to it is the characterless *Hotel El Kahina*. However, at the time of writing both were closed due to lack of patrons and it's unclear if and when either or both will reopen. It's best to assume they're both closed and day trip from Batna.

There's a small kiosk at the site entrance which does snack meals and drinks. Otherwise there are a couple of standard local restaurants on the main street of the town.

Getting There & Away

Bus There are four buses daily to Batna from the main street, 100 metres from the entrance to the ruins.

The trip takes 40 minutes and costs AD 5.

Taxi Taxis run more frequently from near the entrance to the town, about 10 minutes' walk from the ruins; AD 12 for a seat.

OUED EL-ABIOD

The gorges of the Oued El-Abiod are worth seeing, either as a day trip from Batna, or en route from Batna to Biskra or vice versa. Three roads connect the two towns. The northern one (Route N3) goes through some spectacular country, including the steep gap in the ranges, the Défilé, near the village of El Kantara. This is the route taken by the Batna-Biskra buses.

The central one (W54) is a minor road and has little of interest.

The southern route (N31) is by far the most spectacular but is not as well served by public transport. The Oued El-Abiod runs north-east to south-west alongside the road, and there are a few viewing points along the way. The best scenery is between Arris and M'Chouneche and the village of Rhoufi is in the middle of this stretch, just off the road 90 km from Batna. The view into the gorge from here is magnificent, with the palm trees in the bottom and the old village of Rhoufi. Take the signposted 'Circuit Touristique' which takes you right out to the edge of the cliffs to the Balcon de Rhoufi – it's a couple of km walk or drive.

It's possible to visit Rhoufi in a day trip from Biskra as there are infrequent buses and shared taxis. It's not possible from Batna, however, as the buses stop at Arris, and the route winds precariously up over an 1800-metre pass, and so takes quite a while. When coming from Batna, however, the change in the scenery and vegetation is quite dramatic – from quite heavily treed hills in marginal agricultural land you pass through a narrow cleft and suddenly you're amongst completely barren hills and, if you're heading further south, you won't see many more trees (apart from date palms) until the other side of the Sahara.

Walking the Gorges

For the more adventurous types, the Oued El-Abiod Gorges lend themselves perfectly to exploration on foot. If you are self-sufficient with food and sleeping gear, it is possible to trek along the gorge from Rhoufi to Biskra in four days. The following is a traveller's account of a recent trek in the area:

We set off south from Rhoufi late one afternoon, having hitched up from Biskra the same day. The gorge is beautiful, with steep red walls, clinging to which are the ruins of old mud-brick villages which run for around 15 km. It is worth setting out around noon so you can sleep the first night in one of these villages.

We stopped in a village at dusk. It was completely deserted so we chose a house to stay in, making sure it wasn't about to collapse. We built a fire upstairs on the terrace overlooking the valley – what a view!

The next morning we walked along a path halfway up the gorge wall. The gorge itself got deeper and deeper, much like the Grand Canyon in appearance, and there were no signs of life. After around four

hours walking there was a gully which we scrambled down, and this got us to the river at the bottom. After another three hours the gorge opened out into the beautiful oasis of Baniane. There were a few more ruins at the northern end of the oasis, but the southern end is better for camping. After a night sleeping out in the oasis, we headed south again, following the riverbed, although there is also a track along the side. There are fantastic views over the plains to the south from here, and after about five hours you find yourself looking over another beautiful oasis – M'Chouneche. We lashed out on the Hotel El Kahina here after our two nights of roughing it.

On the fourth day we set out on the last part of the gorge to the artificial lake on the edge of the Sahara. Again, it was a matter of walking (and wading) along the riverbed, or taking a track along the side of the gorge. After three hours the gorge ended at a small oasis, and after another hour we reached the lake shore. We hitched back to Biskra with no problems.

The walk was a highlight of my time in Algeria, and was well worth the effort. Logistically, there are supplies available in Rhoufi, Baniane and M'Chouneche; otherwise bring everything from Biskra. We drank the water from the oued after treating it. It gets cold at night but it's still possible to sleep out with just a sleeping bag. The best time to walk the gorge is September/October – in winter and spring there would be too much water in the river; in summer it's just too damned hot.

Chris Barton, UK

Places to Stay

There is no accommodation in either Arris or Rhoufi, the two towns on the routes, although there is the *Hotel El Kahina* at M'Chouneche, 37 km north of Biskra on the southern route. A double room here costs AD 200 with breakfast, and this place also has a restaurant.

Getting There & Away

There is only one bus between Batna and Biskra along the southern road, and it leaves Biskra at 5 am! Buses from Batna go as far as Arris, but there are then buses and taxis to Biskra and the villages en route.

Traffic along this road is fairly light but hitching shouldn't be too much of a problem.

BISKRA

This is the beginning of the desert and is the first of the real oasis towns, although those further south are much more interesting.

There is really no reason to stop here but if you want to stay the night there are a few choices. The town's most 'famous' attraction is the thermal baths, Hamma Salihine, a couple of km from the centre. This is a vast complex with baths and other activities. It's hardly worth the effort – a bath in very sulphurous hot water costs AD 20.

The small local tourist office (☎ (04) 71 3712, 71 2336) at 37 Ave de la République has a good information booklet and map for sale for AD 5.

Places to Stay – bottom end

Biskra has a couple of good bottom-end choices, and a good youth hostel. The best bet is the *Hotel Chaoui*, just off the main street, Ave Emir Abdelkader, close to the fancy Hotel Guendouz. The rooms are large, airy and clean, and go for AD 55/75. There are no showers on the place but there are two public douches very close by. There are a couple of other cheapies in the same street.

Youth Hostel The Biskra *Youth Hostel* (☎ (04) 71 3222) has an excellent location, right in the centre at 12 Ave Emir Abdelkader. The only drawback is that it is closed on Fridays. A bed in a dormitory costs AD 20.

Camping The Touring Club d'Algérie runs a site (☎ (04) 71 2864) south of the *pal-*

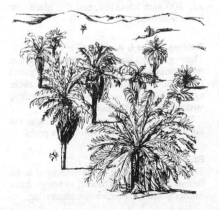

meraie (an oasis-like area) near the small village of Bab Ed Darb.

Places to Stay – middle

The *Hotel du Palmier* is at 23 Ave Hakim Saadane, the main street which crosses Ave Emir Abdelkader near the post office. It's good value at AD 119/159 with bath and breakfast.

Places to Stay – top end

At the top of the range is the *Hotel Guendouz* (☎ (04) 71 5769) in the centre at 39 Ave Emir Abdelkader. A room here will set you back AD 143/196 with breakfast.

Places to Eat

There are plenty of local restaurants in the small streets around the Hotel Chaoui; a good one is the *Delices du Minaret*. The more expensive hotels also have more expensive restaurants.

Getting There & Away

Air The Air Algérie office (☎ (04) 71 2371) is on Ave Ben Badis. There is a daily flight at 3.30 pm connecting Biskra with the capital. The one-way fare is AD 260. There are also flights to Adrar (twice weekly, AD 291), Ghardaia (weekly) and Tamanrasset (weekly, AD 210)

Bus The bus station is in the north of the town, about 300 metres' walk north along the main street. It is a modern complex, complete with hotel, restaurant and separate waiting rooms for men and women.

There is a timetable displayed above the ticket windows and there are regular departures for Algiers (three daily), Batna (6 daily, one via Arris at 5 am), Constantine (four daily), El Oued (four daily), Ghardaia (two daily), In Amenas (once weekly), Ouargla (four daily) and Touggourt (three daily).

Train There are twice daily trains to Constantine (four hours) and Touggourt (4½ hours).

Taxis The large shared-taxi depot is right by

the bus station. There are departures for Batna, Constantine, Touggourt, El Oued, Algiers and Bou Saada.

For taxis to Rhoufi and Arris along the Oued El-Abiod road, the depot is at the southern end of Emir Abdelkader, about 200 metres from the post office and 100 metres before it crosses the very wide oued.

High Plateau

The central High Plateau lies to the west of the Aurès Mountains and also forms part of the Saharan Atlas Range. It's a fairly barren area as it is right on the fringe of the Sahara itself. The main towns of the region are Laghouat (pronounced 'Larouat') and Bou-Saada. The former lies on the main N1 route, about 400 km from Algiers, and is the first Saharan town you come across on the route south, while Bou-Saada is set among barren hills and during colonial times was something of a weekend getaway from Algiers.

Laghouat

As mentioned, this is the first real desert town you come across on the route south. It has few attractions but there are good views of the town and surrounding oasis from the small Marabout of Sidi Mohammed ben Abdelkader and from the Great Mosque; both are on the ridge of a small hill which bisects the town.

There is a bank and post office on the main street, Ave de l'Indépendance.

The main N1 highway actually skirts the town to the west.

Places to Stay The choices here are strictly limited. The only cheapie is the *Hotel Sayah* (☎ (09) 72 3063), close to the Hotel Marhaba. Rooms go for AD 75/90, and although there are no showers there is a hammam on the ground floor.

Perhaps the best cheap option is the *Youth Hostel* (☎ (09) 72 3980), which is signposted about 500 metres south of the bus station. A

bed costs AD 20, plus AD 5 for a sheet; breakfast costs AD 5.

The only other hotel is the three-star *Hotel Marhaba* (☎ (09) 72 4667), at the northern end of the main street. It is well set out and all rooms have a balcony overlooking the swimming pool. Room charges are AD 185/225 with bath, air-conditioning, fridge and breakfast, and the charge will be written on your currency form.

Places to Eat Laghouat has surprisingly few restaurants. Just a short way along from the Hotel Marhaba is the *Restaurant du Soleil Rouge* which does very mediocre food – soup and côtelettes (chops) for AD 45. This place is closed in the evening, so you are limited to a couple of greasy chicken & chip joints on the main street, or a splash-out meal at the Hotel Marhaba.

Getting There & Away
Air The Air Algérie office (☎ (09) 72 2090) is on Ave de l'Indépendance.

Bus & Taxi The bus and taxi station is right on the western edge of the town, close to the ring road. It's about one km from the centre, so you can catch a No 3 local bus from the roundabout at the bus station, or from opposite the Hotel Marhaba in the town centre.

There are direct buses to Ghardaia, Algiers, Oran and Aflou, and many others which call in en route to places such as Constantine.

Shared taxis run to Algiers, Djelfa, Ghardaia and Tiaret.

Bou-Saada

Although it's not worth a special detour, the oasis town of Bou-Saada has a spectacular setting in amongst barren hills on the edge of the Sahara. The Oued Bou Saada flows south to north along the eastern edge of the town in a deep gorge, lined along the bottom and sides with small terraces which form the basis of the oasis.

The town had its heyday during the French days when it became popular as a weekend getaway, the attraction being the mineral springs of Moulin Ferrero, about two km south of town along the oued. All that remains of the spa centre are the ruins of the building, by a small waterfall. It's worth the wander from the town.

The focus of the town centre is the shady Place des Martyrs, and close by you'll find a bank, post office and the town's restaurants.

Places to Stay The cheapest place is the *Youth Hostel* (☎ (05) 54 4945), about 500 metres from the centre of town near the bus station; AD 20 for a bed.

Next up the scale is the amazing *Hotel Transat*. This place has to be seen to be believed – at one stage it must have been quite a comfortable hotel; these days it's a wreck. Nothing has been spent on maintenance in years and to look at the outside you'd never know the place was still functioning. The map in the lobby is a 1942 War Office publication. Rooms still cost AD 80/120 for rooms with bath but there's cold water only and plumbing which floods the room. The toilets in the place are utterly disgusting; they're totally unusable – the worst I've seen in years of travelling on three

continents. Add to this the fact that the nearby mosque gives an amazingly loud call at the usual early hour in the morning and you have the ideal place to stay!

The only other place is the *Hotel le Caid* (☎ (05) 54 4394), also near the bus station. This is a good three-star hotel complete with bar, swimming pool and restaurant. Rooms cost AD 250/300 with breakfast.

Places to Eat The best restaurants are right on Place des Martyrs. The *Restaurant El Feth* is pleasant and clean, and has a set two-course menu for AD 35.

Getting There & Away The bus station is 15 minutes' walk from the centre. There are regular departures for Algiers (nine daily), Biskra (three daily), Constantine (two daily), El Oued (one daily), Ghardaia (three daily), Oran (one daily) and Sétif (two daily), although many of these just pass through en route and there's no guarantee of a seat.

Shared taxis leave from just up the hill from the Place des Martyrs. There are departures for Biskra, Djelfa and M'Sila.

North-West Algeria

Apart from the city of Tlemcen (the capital of the central Maghreb for three centuries from the 12th century), the area to the west of Algiers holds little of interest to the visitor.

The coast has some beaches but there is little accommodation, while the interior is just a collection of nondescript industrial and dormitory towns.

Oran is worth a brief visit but don't lose any sleep if you can't get there. Tlemcen, on the other hand, should not be bypassed.

If you do want to take your time crossing the region, there are hotels of one-star standard (AD 145 double) or cheaper in Sidi-Bel-Abbès, Oran, Mostaganem, Relizane, Tiaret, Ténès and Cherchell.

Tlemcen

More than other cities in northern Algeria, Tlemcen is a curious blend of Islamic and French-colonial architecture. The mosques of the city are the country's finest, while the main tree-lined square with the town hall on one side is very European.

It's unfortunate that most people bypass this city and cross to or from Morocco at Beni Ounif. The small amount of extra time it takes to come via Tlemcen is well worth the effort, and the amount of walking you have to do to get across the border near Tlemcen is virtually nil, compared with about four km at Beni Ounif. If you are coming up from the Sahara and heading for Morocco consider going via Tlemcen, as it is not a much longer route but is vastly more interesting.

With a population of only 150,000, Tlemcen is a manageable size. The town has a very easy-going atmosphere, and its altitude of 830 metres makes it just that little bit cooler than the plains of the coast.

History

Although the area around Tlemcen was occupied from prehistoric times, it is only after the Arab invasion that things start to get interesting. Idriss I established a town here (called Agadir) late in the 8th century.

It wasn't until the 11th century that Tlemcen itself was founded by the Almoravid Youssef Ibn Tachfin, who named it Tagrart ('the camp'); it was under Almoravid rule that the Great Mosque was built.

The town became the capital of the central Maghreb and reached its peak under the Berber Abd el Wadids, or Zianids, whose leader, Yaghmoracen, founded a dynasty here in 1236. The city thrived on the trans-Saharan trade and became an important link between Black Africa and Europe.

The Zianids' Berber cousins, the Merenids, ruled in Morocco and the rivalry between the two was the only threat to Tlemcen's prosperity. The Merenids fought for control of the city three times and each time occupied it briefly.

The first siege came at the end of the 13th century. It was during this siege that the Merenids built the walled city of Mansourah on the western outskirts of the city, under the leadership of Abou Yacoub. The second and third sieges took place in 1337 and 1353.

The decline in power of the Zianids in the 15th century saw the control of the city oscillate between the Merenids in the west and the Hafsids of Tunis in the east. The Spanish had settled in Oran and they too were an interested party, but it was the Turks from Algiers who, in 1555, were finally able to overrun Tlemcen.

The city went into a long decline over the next three centuries, and at the time of the French occupation of Algiers in 1830 Tlemcen was divided once again. This time the Turks and Kouloughlis (an important ethnic minority descended from Turkish men and local women) sided with the French,

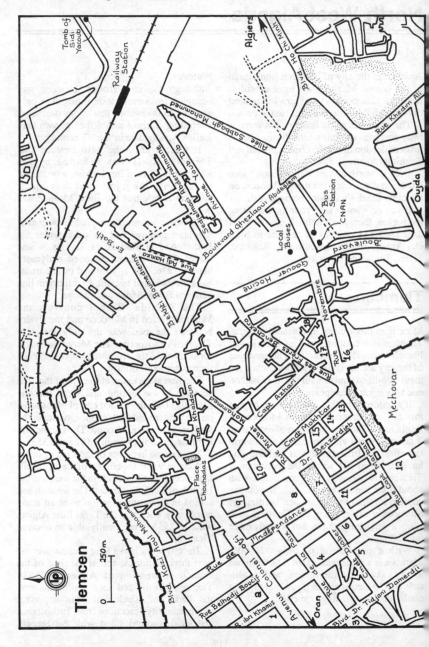

Tlemcen

Railway Station

Tomb of Sidi Yacoub

Algiers

Oujda

Allée Sabbagh Mohamed

Blvd Ho Chi Minh

Rue Khedim Ali

Avenue Yous Dib

Sebdamoci Abderrahmane

Bus Station

Local Buses

CNAN

Boulevard Ghezlaoui Abdeslem

Boulevard

Gaouar Hocine

Rue Adil Hamza

Er'Batih

Blvd Boumediene

Rue les Frères Benchera

Rue 1 Novembre

18

17

16

Ibn Khaldoun

Blvd Mohammed

Mechouar

Capt. Aznari

Rue Mader Mohammed

Rue Cmdr Mokhtar

15

14

13

Dr. Benzerdieb

Rue Nador

Rue Cot

12

Place Chouhadas

10

7

11

9

8

6

Blvd Kazi Aoul Mohammed

Rue de l'Indépendance

Rue de la Paix

Rue Loti

1g

1

4

5

Rue Cap 3

Avenue Colonel Lotfi

Rue Belhadji Boucif

R. Ibn Khamis

Oran

Blvd. Dr. Tidjani Damerdji

250m

0

1	Post Office (PTT)
2	Banque Centrale d'Algérie
3	Air Algérie
4	Public Douche (Showerhouse)
5	Air France
6	Mosque Sidi Bel Hassan
7	Place Emir Abdelkader
8	Great Mosque
9	Snack Shop
10	Market
11	Banque Nationale d'Algérie
12	Tourist Office
13	Hotel Maghreb
14	Hotel Majestic
15	Restaurant
16	Restaurant du Coupole
17	Hotel Moderne
18	Hammam

while the Moors and Berbers favoured union with the Alaouite sultans of Morocco. The French won out, and in 1842 Tlemcen officially became part of French Algeria.

Tlemcen was an important centre in the nationalist movement. Before the French takeover, Emir Abdelkader was very active in the area; and in 1924 the city saw the foundation by Ahmed Messali Hadj of the MTLD (Mouvement pour le Triomphe des Libertés Démocratiques), the fororunner of the FLN.

Information

Tourist Office There is a local tourist office (☎ (07) 20 3456) on Ave Commandant Faradj, just near the entrance to the *mechouar* (royal assembly place). A good hand-out map is available here, and the people staffing the office are helpful.

Money There are banks all over the centre, the main one being the Banque Centrale d'Algérie next to the post office.

Outside banking hours it is possible to change money at the four-star Hotel Les Zianides.

Post & Telecommunications The post office is in the main street, the tree-lined Ave Colonel Lotfi. It is open Saturday to Wednes-

day from 8 am to 6.30 pm, Thursday from 8 am to 4 pm, and Friday (for stamps only) from 8 to 11 am.

The parcel-post counter is in the room to the left of the entrance, and the telephone office is at the rear of the building – entry is through the carpark.

Market Tlemcen has an excellent produce market just off the central Place Emir Abdelkader.

Hammams The cheap hotels here have no bathing facilities, so the hammams are the answer.

For men only, there is a public shower-house on Rue Ibn Khamis, not far from Place Emir Abdelkader. It is open from 7.30 am to 5.30 pm.

For more traditional hammams, the most convenient is the one just off Rue 1 Novembre, which is open for women from 9.30 am to 4.30 pm, and for men from 5.30 to 9 am and 5 to 9 pm; AD 15 for a wash, which includes towel and soap.

Place Emir Abdelkader

The best place to start is Place Emir Abdelkader. This is very much the centre of the city and is very pleasant with its fountain and cafés. It's a popular place in the early evenings, and this is the best time to sit at one of the cafés and sip on a mint tea or a coffee. On summer evenings you can also witness the local phenomenon of literally thousands of small birds screeching in the trees overhead. For obvious reasons, it is best not to sit at a table directly under one of the branches. The eastern half of the square is actually called Place Khemisti.

On the south side of the square is the town hall, which dates back to 1843.

Great Mosque

The Great Mosque backs onto the square. This is one of the few important mosques in the whole of the Maghreb where visitors are allowed to wander around inside the prayer hall. The entrance is down the side alley on the right; the mosque is open to non-

Muslims from 8 to 11 am daily, except Friday.

The mosque was built by the Almoravid Ali ben Youssef in 1135 and was later added to by the Zianid sultan Abou Ibrahim ben Yahia Yaghmoracen, who was responsible for the polychrome-tiled minaret. The entrance leads straight into the prayer hall, which has 13 naves and six rows.

The dome above the *mihrab* (prayer niche facing Mecca) has some excellent stalactite decoration and the mihrab itself, although heavily restored, is covered with delicate stucco work. The wooden *minbar* (pulpit) slides on tracks into a niche next to the mihrab.

The monstrous wooden and brass chandelier which holds literally dozens of candles is a relatively modern piece and replaces a much older one, remnants of which are in the museum. Also of interest is the collection of grandfather clocks around the walls, and the ablutions fountain out in the small courtyard.

Tradition has it that Yaghmoracen is buried in the mosque, beneath the first nave to the right of the mihrab. All the other Zianid sultans are buried in the domed *koubba* (sanctuary) in the south-west corner of the mosque, which is visible from the square.

Mosque Sidi Bel Hassan/Museum of Antiquities

At the western end of Place Emir Abdelkader is the small Mosque Sidi Bel Hassan, which has been turned into the Museum of Antiquities. The mosque itself was built in honour of Yaghmoracen at the end of the 13th century. It is named after a famous theologian who taught here in the early 14th century.

The arch of the mihrab, which is supported by onyx pillars, and the surrounding stucco decoration represent the peak of Zianid art. Amongst the museum pieces themselves are some beautiful carved wooden panels (12th to 14th century) and faïence mosaic tiles (14th century).

The museum is open Sunday to Thursday from 9 am to noon and 2.30 to 6 pm; closed Friday am and all day Saturday. Entry is free.

Mansourah

Further out of town, about a km to the west, are the ruins of ancient Mansourah. It is about a 20-minute walk from the centre. The four km of walls date from around the end of the 13th century and mark the perimeter of the walled Merenid town, which covered an area of about 100 hectares. The only ruins left inside the walls are the minaret and the mosque. Of the minaret, only three sides are left standing and even these were restored in the late 19th century. On the inside you can see where the stairs used to lead up to the top.

Mansourah was only used during the Merenid invasions; after that time it was deserted and became a handy source of building materials for structures in Tlemcen.

Mosque & Tomb of Sidi Bou Mediène

Out in the opposite direction from Mansourah, two km east of the centre, is the mosque and tomb of Sidi Bou Mediène, also known as El Eubbad. This is an important example of Merenid architecture.

Sidi Bou Mediène, a mystic born in Spain who taught in Seville, Fès and Bejaia, died here on his way from Bejaia to Marrakesh. His real name was Ibn Hussein El Andalousi, but his surname was Bou Mediène El Ghouts and from this came his popular name. It is no coincidence that the name is remarkably similar to that of the former president of Algeria: in 1956, Mohammed Boukharouba took on the name Houari Boumedienne in honour of the famous teacher.

The present koubba was built in 1339, but the original decoration suffered during restorations in the 18th century. With its bronze-clad cedar doors and cupola with stalactites, the monumental porch to the mosque is as fine a monument as you'll see anywhere in the Maghreb.

There is an adjoining medersa dating from 1347, which was visited by the great Islamic historian, Ibn Khaldoun, in the 14th century.

To get there, walk out along the road to the left above the Hotel Les Zianides.

Other Attractions

Back in town, Rue Mrabet Mohammed has

Top: Beni Abbès, Algeria (HF)
Left: Craft shop, Timimoun, Algeria (HF)
Right: Kabylie Mountains, Algeria (HF)

Top: Music store, Beni Abbès, Algeria (HF)
Left: Kids in old town, Timimoun, Algeria (HF)
Right: Oasis swimming pool, Beni Abbès, Algeria (HF)

been turned into a pedestrian mall and is now one of the main shopping streets. It's a good place to go looking if you want to buy a *burnous*, the brown full-length robes worn by the men in winter. These are of varying quality, and prices range from about AD 150 for a rough cheapie up to about AD 800 for a good camel-hair one. This area to the east and north of the square is the old Andalusian part of town and is known as the Hadar Quarter.

One block south-east of the main square is the mechouar, the site of the residence of the palace of the early Almohad governors. The present walls date only from the time of the French occupation; as the buildings inside are occupied by a cadet school, it is off limits to visitors.

To the north of Ave Colonel Lotfi are the old city ramparts, and from these there is a good view of the industrial area of town!

Places to Stay – bottom end

For such a large town, the accommodation is surprisingly limited. Pick of the very small bunch here is the *Hotel Majestic* (☎ (07) 26 0766), on the shady Place Cheikh Bahir Ibrahimi, one block south-east of Place Emir Abdelkader. It is the grey building on the corner. There is no English sign, only a small red-and-white one in Arabic above the entrance, which is in the side street. Rooms cost AD 80/120 for singles/doubles, but couples pay only for a single. The beds are almost museum pieces and there are no showers.

The *Hotel Moderne* (☎ (07) 20 8796), at 20 Rue 1 Novembre is a good deal cheaper at AD 70 for a single (no doubles), but it is a bit gloomy and none too friendly.

Camping The *Camping Municipale* is amongst the olive groves at Mansourah. It is a solid 20-minute walk from the centre and more from the bus or railway station.

The facilities are extremely basic to say the least but the security is good, as the place is guarded by two large and noisy German shepherd dogs. It costs AD 10 per person,

AD 15 for a tent and the same again for a vehicle.

If you are coming from the border by car or bus, the camping is on the right just after you pass the large ruined minaret at Mansourah. From the centre of town, follow the signs for Maghnia; just after the arch over the road by the hospital the road forks, and the campsite is 100 metres along the right-hand fork.

Places to Stay – middle

The *Hotel Maghreb* (☎ (07) 26 3571) is on Place Commandant Faradj, just along from the Hotel Majestic. It is expensive at AD 150/210 for singles/doubles with breakfast and bath. It is possible to change money here out of banking hours.

Places to Stay – top end

If you have the money and the inclination, the *Hotel Les Zianides* (☎ (07) 26 7118) will relieve you of AD 210/290 for a single/double with breakfast. The building is a charmless monolith in an inconvenient location, 10 minutes' walk from the centre.

Places to Eat

As with the accommodation, there is no oversupply of restaurants. One good little place is on the next corner up from the Hotel Majestic (although it is often closed on Friday and Saturday). Here a good meal of half a chicken, chips and salad will set you back AD 35.

For snacks such as Spanish omelette (tortilla) and chips, there is a tiny place on a small square just to the north of the market.

On Rue 1 Novembre, the *Restaurant du Coupole* has a reasonable set menu for AD 60, while across the road the *Restaurant Moderne*, attached to the hotel of the same name, charges AD 45 for soup, salad, côtelette and chips.

For a splurge, the restaurant of the *Hotel Maghreb* is not bad. The spaghetti entree is big enough for a main course and with a salad you have a decent meal for AD 60. Bottles of a cheeky local red wine cost AD 80.

Getting There & Away

Air The Air Algérie office (☎ (07) 20 4518) is on Blvd Dr Tidjani Damerdji. Air France (☎ (07) 20 4300) has an office on the corner of Rue Commandant Djaber and Rue Ibn Khamis. Tlemcen's Zenata Airport is 24 km from the centre of town, and there are buses and taxis into the centre.

There is at least one flight daily to Algiers (AD 366). Air Algérie also operates direct flights to Marseilles and Paris.

Air France has weekly flights to Paris.

Bus The main bus station is on the basement level of the building on the corner of Rue 1 Novembre and Blvd Gaouar Hocine, about 10 minutes' walk from the centre. There are stairs down from both streets.

There is a timetable on display, and tickets are sold from numbered windows. Any of the uniformed staff who seem to drift aimlessly around the whole time can usually help.

The main departures are: Algiers (three daily); Moroccan border (four daily); Oran (seven daily from 5 am to 4.30 pm); Sebdou (three daily) and Tiaret (daily).

If you are staying at the campsite and are heading for the border, you can flag down the buses from the stop outside the hospital, just by the arch on the main street, 100 metres back towards town from the campsite.

Train The railway station is a grand white building, about 15 minutes' walk east of the town centre.

There is a daily train from Oran to Casablanca and this passes through Tlemcen at 4.30 pm, arriving in Oujda at 6.55 pm and Casablanca at 8 am the next day. On the return journey, it passes through Oujda at 9.30 am and Tlemcen at 1.40 pm.

There are at least three other departures for Oran (three hours) and two to the Moroccan border.

Hitching For the route south, the best plan is to take a bus to Sebdou, 30 km to the south, as most of the traffic heading south from Tlemcen is just local traffic coming here anyway.

Oran

Not the most fascinating city in the country and certainly not worth a special detour, but if you are passing through, there are enough things to see in Oran to keep you occupied for a day or so. It's also a possible entry point to the country, as there are direct ferries from Alicante (Spain) and Sète (France).

With a population of 700,000, Oran is the second-largest city in the country. It is situated on a crescent bay, which is dominated to the west by Jebel Mudjadjo, with the 16th-century fort of Santa Cruz and the basilica clearly visible on its flanks. For a view from here, take the cable car to the top (reached by a bus No 25 from the centre).

History

Oran is one of the more recent towns in the country, having been founded only in the 10th century by Andalusian Arab sailors. It was relatively prosperous during the Almohad and Zianid dynasties, and maintained good relations with Spain and other Mediterranean countries.

The Spanish occupied the city from early in the 15th century until 1792, when they left following a massive earthquake in 1790. It was occupied by the Turks until 1831, when the French moved in.

Development of the city suffered a major setback following a cholera outbreak in

1	Banque Centrale d'Algérie
2	Air Algérie
3	Post Office (PTT)
4	Tourist Office
5	Cathedral
6	Pizzeria Hamburger
7	Hotel de l'Ouest
8	Hotel Meliani
9	Market
10	Hotel Riad
11	Bus Station (for Tlemcen)
12	Bus Booking Office
13	Douches Ghislane

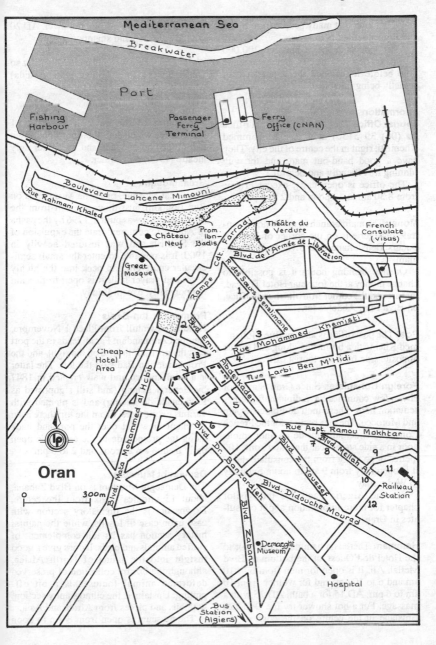

Oran

0   300m

1849, but after that many people from Spain and France settled here.

After independence, a massive 200,000 Europeans deserted the city, and it was some time before it regained the appearance of actually being inhabited.

Information

Tourist Office There is a local tourist office (☎ (06) 39 5130) at 4 Rue Mohammed Khemisti, right in the centre of the city. They have a good hand-out map, and the guy running it is friendly and helpful.

The office is open daily, except Friday, from 8.30 am to 12 noon and 2 to 5 pm.

Money The main branch of the Banque Centrale d'Algérie is on the corner of Rue des Soeurs Benslimane and Blvd de la Soummam.

Outside banking hours it is possible to change money at the four-star Hotel Timgad, just around the corner from the tourist office, on Blvd Emir Abdelkader.

Post The post office is also on Rue Mohammed Khemisti, a bit further along and on the opposite side from the tourist office.

Foreign Consulates Since Oran is a major city, a few countries have diplomatic representation here. These include France, Spain and Morocco. The visa section for the French Consulate is actually inside an anonymous door in a side street near the waterfront, 100 metres or so away from the consulate itself. It is open only from 9 am to noon, Saturday to Wednesday.

See the Algeria Facts for the Visitor chapter for more information about consulates in Oran.

Hammam There is a hammam next door to the Hotel de l'Ouest, at the bottom of Blvd Mellah Ali. It is open for men from 6 to 10 am and 6 to 10 pm, and for women from 10 am to 6 pm; AD 15 for a bath, AD 25 with a massage. For a hot shower try the Douches Ghislane in the centre on the edge of the cheap hotel area; AD 13 for a shower, AD 20 with towel, soap and shampoo.

Water Oran's tap water is incredibly salty so you'll have to buy bottled water (Saida) which is in short supply at times.

Place 1 Novembre

The centre of the new city is Place 1 Novembre, which has the enormous town hall (1888) on one side and the rather ugly theatre (1906) on another.

Great Mosque

The Great Mosque, or Pasha Mosque, is on Rue Boutkhil, just down the hill from the main square. It was built in 1796 by the pasha of Algiers to commemorate the expulsion of the Spanish and was restored heavily in 1900. It is possible to enter the small semicircular courtyard and peek into the highly decorated prayer hall. It is open from 8 am to noon daily, except Friday.

Promenade Ibn-Badis

Heading downhill from Place 1 Novembre, Rampe Commandant Faradj leads to the port past the open-air theatre on the right, and the Promenade Ibn-Badis on the left. The latter is a small garden and walk created in 1847 by General Létang (and still signposted as Promenade de Létang) and is planted with various exotic trees. From the top there is an excellent view out over the port and back along the promenade to the east. It is open daily from 8 am to noon and 2 to 5 pm.

Demaeght Museum

The Demaeght Museum is on Blvd Zabana, about 15 minutes' walk from the centre. Downstairs is the prehistory section with case upon case of fossils, while the natural history section has its full complement of stuffed animals and birds. It does give a good insight into the fauna of North Africa, although the bizarre collection of preserved deformed animal foetuses is a bit off-putting. Upstairs is the ethnography section, with bits and pieces from Africa and Asia.

The museum is open from 8 am to noon

and 1.30 to 5 pm Sunday to Thursday; closed Friday afternoon and all day Saturday. Entry is AD 4.

Other Attractions

The old Sacré Coeur Cathedral in the centre of town has been deconsecrated and turned into the city library. It is grotesquely decorated on the outside. At one time, churches outnumbered mosques in Oran.

Places to Stay – bottom end

The best place is the *Hotel Riad* (☎ (06) 36 3846), at 46 Blvd Mellah Ali, right opposite the railway station and one of the bus stations. There is no sign in English, but it is next door to a driving school. Rooms cost AD 75/100 with bath, and clean sheets every day. It's a friendly place in a good location.

Further down the street is the *Hotel Meliani* (☎ (06) 34 3845) at No 14. Single/double rooms cost AD 80/125 including breakfast, but there are no showers.

There is a whole stack of cheaper places down closer to the centre in an area just off Blvd Emir Abdelkader, but none are fantastic value. Rue Ozanam has plenty of hotels and is easy to find, as it is the street which runs down off Blvd Hamou Boultélis directly in front of the cathedral.

The *Hotel Takadoum* (☎ (06) 39 4102) at 5 Rue Ozanam is friendly and the rooms are OK at AD 50/100 for a single/double, or AD 75 for a couple in a single room. Again, there are no showers. There is no sign in English but there's a large yellow one in Arabic above the footpath.

Opposite the Takadoum, at No 6, is the *Hotel Baalabek* (☎ (06) 39 2324), which is unspectacular at AD 95/125 for a single/double with breakfast.

If all these places are full (unlikely), there are plenty of others in the vicinity.

Places to Stay – middle

At the bottom of Blvd Mellah Ali is the *Hotel de l'Ouest* (☎ (06) 36 4698) at No 6. It charges AD 110/150 for a single/double with breakfast, but the rooms have their own bathrooms, heating and air-conditioning.

Places to Stay – top end

Top of the range is the *Hotel Timgad* (☎ (06) 39 4797), right in the thick of things at 22 Blvd Emir Abdelkader. It's a four-star hotel, so you can expect to pay in the range of AD 360/460 for singles/doubles.

Places to Eat

For cheap local food, there's a good little restaurant at 14A Blvd Mellah Ali, right next to the Hotel Meliani. In the street behind the Hotel Riad, the *Rotisserie Grillade Le Chalet* is not too bad, although the service is erratic.

On Rue Ozanam in the cheap hotel area is a similar but larger place, on the first corner on the right as you face downhill.

Other than that you have a choice of any number of three-star restaurants on Blvd Emir Abdelkader and Rue Mohammed Khemisti.

Getting There & Away

Air The Air Algérie office (☎ (06) 39 8146) is right in the centre at 2 Blvd Emir Abdelkader. Air France (☎ (06) 33 5944) is at 5 Place Abdelmalek Ramdane. Oran's Es-Senia Airport is at Tafraoui, 18 km south-east of Oran. There are local buses from Place 1 Novembre.

There are flights with Air Algérie to: Adrar (four times weekly, AD 339); Algiers (at least twice daily, AD 298); Annaba (twice weekly, AD 584); Béchar (four times weekly, AD 292); Constantine (three times weekly, AD 504); Ghardaia (twice weekly, AD 333); Ouargla (weekly, AD 412); Tamanrasset (weekly, AD 571); and Tindouf (twice weekly, AD 430).

International destinations served by Air Algérie include: Casablanca, Geneva, Lyons, Marseilles, Paris, Toulouse and Zürich. Air France has flights to Lyons, Marseilles, Paris and Toulouse, and Royal Air Maroc connects Oran with Casablanca and Fès.

Bus There are two bus stations. The one right outside the railway station is for regional buses and destinations to the west, including Tlemcen. The booking office is on Rue Tenazet, 100 metres from the station.

The other bus station is a solid 10-minute walk south of the museum. This one is much larger (and more crowded) and handles destinations to all parts of the country not served by the smaller station.

Train The railway station is on Blvd Mellah Ali at the top of the hill. It is the large white building with the clock tower.

There are departures to: Algiers (five daily, six hours); Mohammadia (for Béchar, once daily); and Tlemcen (four daily). There is one train daily to Oujda and Casablanca in Morocco, leaving Oran at 2 pm, arriving in Oujda at 6.55 pm and Casablanca at 8 am. In the other direction it leaves Casa at 9.50 pm and Oujda at 9.30 am, arriving in Oran at 4.20 pm and Algiers at 8.25 pm.

Sea There is a CNAN office (☎ (06) 33 2767)) at 13 Blvd Abane Ramdane, near the French Consulate, where you can buy tickets for ferries to Alicante and Marseilles. The ferry terminal is directly in front of the centre of town at the bottom of Rampe Commandant Faradj. There are departures for Alicante eight times per month in summer, falling to three per month in winter. The fare per person is AD 270 one way and AD 942 for an average 4WD; the trip takes 12 hours.

There are also 20 departures per month to Marseilles in summer, fewer in winter. The one-way fare is AD 461 per person and AD 1250 for a 4WD; the trip takes 24 hours.

The French town of Sète is also served by ferries from Oran, although there are only three per month in summer. Fares are the same as between Oran and Marseilles and the crossing takes 29 hours.

The Algerian Sahara

The Sahara Desert, the greatest desert on earth, stretches right across the countries of northern Africa, but the lion's share lies in Algeria. A full 85% of the country is occupied by it, and yet this area accounts for only 10% of the country's population.

The Sahara offers the traveller the ultimate challenge. To get out there and cross it is one of the last great adventures left in a world which is rapidly shrinking. It is definitely not a trip for those who love their creature comforts, as transport is usually uncomfortable, conditions often primitive, the climate extreme and the range of food limited.

In Algeria the Saharan road network is fairly well developed, and there is public transport to the southern border with both Mali and Niger. It is still possible to hitch across the Sahara for free, but this is the exception rather than the rule these days.

Basically, without a vehicle you can take any of the routes normally followed by the overland crowd by using a combination of public transport and hitching. However, on some of the routes transport is infrequent, so you need to be prepared to take a plane to get you out or else sit around for a week or more waiting for a lift. This applies mainly to the eastern route from Hassi Messaoud down through In Amenas and Djanet to Tamanrasset. The Route du Hoggar presents no such problems, although you may end up on a bus between In Salah and Tamanrasset.

It is essential that you are prepared for this sort of travelling, particularly if you hitch and end up for three days on the top of a truck, exposed to the elements. The two essential items to have are a decent hat with a brim, and a water bottle that will hold at least a couple of litres. Travellers do set out without these things and do survive, but why make things more uncomfortable than need be?

History

The prehistoric rock paintings in the Hoggar and Tassili N'Ajjer clearly show that at that time, the Sahara was a much more hospitable place than it is today. The paintings depict mainly men hunting and women and children playing. They suggest that the Sahara of 6000 years ago must have been much like the savanna lands of East Africa today.

Before the 5th century BC, the area was inhabited by hunter-gatherers. From the 4th to the 2nd century BC the people began herding animals and took up a more settled existence.

The horse was first seen in the desert around 1000 BC; an indication that the area was getting drier was the introduction of the camel in the early years of the Christian era.

Trans-Saharan trade became well established, and it was due to this that many of the Punic and Roman towns in the north flourished. The Berbers were the ones who controlled this trade, however, as they were the ones who knew the desert and were able to make the trips across it.

With the Arab invasions in the north in the

7th century, the indigenous Berbers, keen not to be assimilated, retreated to the desert as well as the mountains of the north.

Today the towns and villages of the Algerian Sahara are populated largely by Touareg, who are themselves Berber. However, there have been large numbers of Arabs coming down from the north, in search of work or as civil servants who have been sent here to fill administrative posts.

The towns are relatively prosperous. Nevertheless, with the crippling droughts that have hit the Sahel (the semidesert area directly south of the true desert) they are being increasingly surrounded by slums (bidonvilles) inhabited by destitute nomadic Touareg, who have gravitated to the population centres in the hope of something better. At Tamanrasset in the market you'll see Touareg men selling jewellery; some of it is obviously made for tourists, but other pieces are genuine tribal jewellery which they hope will make them a few dinar.

Grand Erg Occidental

One of the two great sand seas (ergs in Arabic), the Grand Erg Occidental (Great Western Erg) occupies an enormous area south of the Saharan Atlas Mountains in the west of Algeria. Anywhere else this would constitute a sizable desert in its own right, but in the Sahara things are a bit different.

On the fringes of the erg are some of the most beautiful oases in the country; these are all relatively accessible, as the erg is flanked on two sides by good, tar-sealed roads. The N6 is the main road from Oran on the north coast to Adrar and this skirts around the western edge of the erg, passing through Ain Sefra, Beni Ounif (for the Moroccan border), Béchar and Beni Abbès. North of Adrar the N51 forks off to the north-east and follows the edge of the dunes to El Goléa, which is on the eastern edge. El Goléa is also on the main N1 road, which connects Algiers and Tamanrasset, a distance of over 2000 km.

If you are coming from Morocco and Beni Ounif, the places to stop are Taghit and Beni Abbès; then head for Timimoun and El Goléa if you want to hitch south. It's easy enough to get to Adrar, but the traffic from there across to the main road at In Salah is negligible. There is supposed to be a weekly bus across this route but it always seems to be the first route to be axed when there is a shortage of buses due to breakdowns, and that happens quite often because of the pounding the desert bus/trucks take on the pistes of the south.

The best sand dunes are at Taghit, Beni Abbès and Kerzaz, so make sure you see at least one of these places. Timimoun is a beautiful town in itself, while El Goléa has some good dunes but not much else.

AIN SEFRA

This town in the Saharan Atlas Mountains is the gateway to the desert from the north-west.

This is about as far north as you will find sand dunes on this side of the country, and they are quite a sight blown up against the foot of the mountains.

There is little of interest in the town itself and, with the only accommodation being a flash three-star place with air-con and pool, it's best to move on. The trouble is that all along the Western Erg the accommodation is not that cheap. Sleeping out in the campsites is the best option; these are only found in Taghit, Timimoun and El Goléa. Perhaps the most famous thing about the town is that it was here that the young writer and adventurer Isabelle Eberhardt was drowned in a flood in 1904. She was a Russian born in Switzerland who spent most of her adult life in the Algerian Sahara. She became a Muslim, dressed as a man and spent most of her time travelling on horseback. She had a particularly good understanding of Arab culture and politics, and her diaries make interesting reading (The Passionate Nomad, Virago, 1987). She is buried in the town's Muslim cemetery.

As you come into the town from the north, the most striking feature is the modern architecture by the side of the road. These multicoloured apartment blocks must rate as some of the worst eyesores in the country.

The town has a Cultural Week from the 13th to the 19th of May.

Places to Stay

There's no choice here. The only place is the *Hotel el Mekhter* (☎ (07) 31 1417). Rooms cost AD 175/225 for singles/doubles with breakfast and, since the hotel is more than 1½ km out of town, you have to pay AD 110 for dinner as well.

The hotel is signposted past the military barracks, which you are advised not to photograph unless you want to take a closer look at the inside of a cell.

Getting There & Away

Bus There are buses north to Tlemcen, Algiers and Oran, and south to Béchar.

Hitching The town lies a couple of km to the east of the main road, and there is still enough traffic as far south as Béchar to make hitching fairly easy.

BENI OUNIF

Still in the Saharan Atlas, this is a totally unremarkable little town; however, for many travellers it is their first taste of Algeria. Don't worry, things get a lot more interesting before very long.

The town is small and is only about half a km from one end to the other, so there is no difficulty in finding anything.

There is a bank here but it is not authorised to exchange travellers' cheques; you are unlikely to want to use it, as you will probably have just been made to change the equivalent of AD 1000 at the border anyway.

The road between here and Béchar still has some of the few remaining signs of the battle for Algerian independence. Right along this border, some distance in from the actual line, the French built a continuous barrier of barbed wire some five metres wide. The whole section was patrolled by soldiers stationed at forts, each built in sight of the next, and the line was over 1000 km long on this side of the country. The idea,

largely successful, was to isolate the Algerian nationalists from any support from Morocco. Most of the forts are still there today; so is much of the barbed wire, although most of it has been rolled up into large bundles, which you see every few hundred metres.

Places to Stay & Eat

The only hotel in town is the *Hotel Afrique*, on the main road near the turn-off for Figuig. Rooms cost AD 60/100 for a single/double.

If you miss out here it's a fairly easy hitch or bus ride to Béchar, 114 km to the south.

The *Restaurant el Feth*, on the corner of the main road at the main intersection has spaghetti and salad for AD 30, or omelette and chips for AD 20.

Getting There & Away

Bus There is no bus station here; all the buses just stop outside the Hotel Afrique. You have to be lucky to get a seat at times as these buses are all going through Beni Ounif in transit, and are often full.

Train The railway station is just near the shops in the centre of the town. There is one train daily in either direction: at 8.30 am for Béchar, and at 6.05 pm to Mohammadia for Oran, Tlemcen and Algiers.

Hitching There is enough traffic here to make hitching an option. Just walk to the edge of town and stick out the thumb.

To/From Morocco The road to Morocco leaves the main road in the south of town, just near the customs house – you can't miss it. You can see the Algerian border post, about 1½ km distant in the gap in the mountains. A taxi from the town will cost around AD 40.

From here it's another few hundred metres to the Moroccan side, from where it's a further few km to Figuig.

The whole crossing takes about half a day, and the heavy searches and hostile officials once encountered at this border seem be a thing of the past – these days it's a very straightforward crossing.

BÉCHAR

This is a modern, sprawling administrative town and capital of the Saoura region (as this corner of the Sahara is known). It has nothing at all to recommend it, but you will probably find yourself stopping for a night here on the way through.

There are a couple of banks here, and it is the last major town in which you can stock up on things for the road south. The Air Algérie office (☎ (07) 23 9469) and the tourist office are on the Ain Sefra side of Place de la République. Right next to the mosque with the large minaret on Ave Colonel Lotfi in the centre is a good market with a fair selection of fruit, vegetables and meat.

From Béchar the road heads south-west for 100 km before curving around the western corner of the Great Western Erg. Here the N50 heads straight on for the 800 km journey to Tindouf in the far west of the country. This route into Mauritania has been closed, due to the war in Western Sahara. Tindouf is the main base for the Polisario fighters, who are actively supported by Algeria. It is possible, however, in light of the recent UN-supervised ceasefire in the disputed region, that the route may re-open.

Places to Stay

The Béchar *Youth Hostel*, signposted off the Taghit road, looks fine from the outside but is disappointing on the inside. The charge is AD 25 for a dorm bed.

The best place is the friendly *Grand Hotel de la Saoura* (☎ (07) 23 8007), at 24 Rue Kada Belahrech, just around the corner from the post office near the main square, Place de la République. It's a clean place but not all that cheap at AD 80/120 for singles/doubles without breakfast.

The other choice is the *Hotel de la Paix* (or *Hotel Salaam*) in the same area. Although it looks locked, just knock on the side door. It's none too friendly a place, and rooms cost AD 120 for a double.

For men only there is also a cheaper local hotel close by, but it has no signs of any sort and is rough as guts. Ask around.

As there are only the two cheapish hotels, they tend to fill up by about noon.

Béchar also has a three-star place, the *Hotel Antar* (☎ (07) 23 7161), signposted just off the main road one km towards Beni Abbès. Rooms cost AD 140/180 with breakfast and it's quite likely that your currency form will be checked.

Getting There & Away

Air The airport is seven km north of town and local buses make the trip out there.

There are flights to: Adrar (twice weekly, AD 202); Algiers (daily, AD 445); Annaba (twice weekly, AD 625); Ghardaia (weekly, AD 350); Oran (five weekly, AD 292); and Tindouf (twice weekly, AD 288).

Bus The busy bus station is in the street next to the market, on the opposite side to the mosque. Timetables are displayed, and tickets should be bought in advance whenever possible. Most of the buses heading north travel in the late afternoon and evening, as this is one of the hottest areas in the country.

The main destinations are: Adrar, Algiers, Beni Abbès, Taghit, Timimoun, Tindouf and Tlemcen.

Train There is a daily train to Mohammadia, departing at 3.40 pm and taking something over 16½ hours to cover the 650 km – an average of a lightning-fast 40 km/h.

Taxi Taxis to Adrar leave from outside the bus station. Taxis to Beni Ounif leave from a corner of Place de la République.

Hitching Béchar is the sort of town which hitchers could easily get to hate. It is extremely spread out, so getting to the edge of town is a pain. If you're heading towards Beni Abbès there are local buses which run along the main drag the few km to the edge of town. If you're heading towards Ain Sefra you have to walk.

TAGHIT

Pronounced 'Ta-rit', this small oasis village 90 km south of Béchar has some of the most spectacular dunes in the Western Erg. The dunes tower over the eastern edge of the town, and the view as you come over the hill is really something.

The old mud-brick part of the village is dominated by the old *ksar* (fortified stronghold), which is still occupied by the military. This section of the village is a real maze of winding lanes, and the architecture is typical of this part of the Sahara.

There is no bank here, but there is a post office, a fuel station and a few general stores.

A climb up the dunes is a must, as the view from the top is magnificent: the sand sea stretches endlessly to the east, while the oasis and the Oued Zousfana are spread out before you to the west. Take a lead from the local kids and have a slide down a dune on a piece of tin or cardboard.

Because of the limited transport and accommodation, if you are coming from Beni Abbès the best idea is to take the morning bus from there to Taghit, and then the afternoon bus on to Béchar.

Places to Stay & Eat

The only hotel is the expensive *Hotel Taghit*. You can't miss it, as it's the only big place in the village. As far as such places go, this one is not bad; it has a nice garden and swimming pool (probably empty). Air-conditioned rooms cost AD 160/200 for singles/doubles with breakfast.

There is a campsite on the road heading south of town, out past the shops, on the edge of the palmeraie. There are basic toilets and showers, and the nightly charge is AD 25.

Apart from the AD 80 set menu at the hotel, there is only a small restaurant near the entrance of the old village. Otherwise it's a case of buying tinned food and bread from the bakery (near the bus stop) and putting your own food together.

Getting There & Away

There is one bus daily to Beni Abbès and another to Béchar. It should be possible to

hitch in either direction, although the traffic is very thin. The road to both Béchar and Beni Abbès has been surfaced, so the amount of traffic using the road has increased.

Taxis go to Béchar a couple of times a day and there may be one to Beni Abbès if the demand warrants it.

BENI ABBÈS

Another beautiful oasis town, Benni Abbès is built on the edge of an escarpment, so it looks down on the palmeraie and the oued. The town is backed by high dunes, and the favourite occupation of the local kids is sliding down these on pieces of tin and plastic. Give it a whirl – it's great fun.

From the top of the dune, there is nothing but sand out to the east. If you are taking a camera up here, make sure it is well protected, as the wind really whips the sand up and it wouldn't take much to ruin the mechanism. On a really windy day, leave cameras behind.

Information & Orientation

On entering the town across the oued, the track to the right just before the shops leads to the palmeraie, which has an ancient ksar and an excellent swimming pool.

To the left the road leads to the good little museum and zoo run by the Centre National de Recherches sur les Zones Arides.

The road straight ahead leads up the escarpment past a small row of shops, and then forks. Up to the right lies the market, bus station, post office and defunct Hotel Grand Erg, while to the left is the Hotel Rym, the bank and the dunes.

There are two bakeries in town, one at the market and one along the road to the museum. Neither is open on Fridays, so stock up the day before.

Also up by the market is the town supermarket in the large blue building. Don't get your hopes up at the idea of a supermarket – this one has the usual collection of about six different products, but hundreds of each!

Things to See

The track into the palmeraie leads past the

old abandoned mud-brick ksar off to the right. This dates from the last century and is now gradually returning to the earth.

Beyond the ksar and beneath the stone water tower on the edge of the escarpment is a small swimming pool, known as La Source. It is a cool, green retreat from the blinding desert all around. A few trees give shade to the pool which is filled by beautifully clear spring water and is in a paved enclosure. The pool is maintained by a caretaker and is open during daylight hours.

The other obvious sight is the dunes. Take a scramble up them in the late afternoon when the light is at its best.

The museum is about 100 metres along the track to the left along the oued, and then up the first street on the right. It has an interesting selection of desert fauna and flora. Someone has spent a lot of time and effort putting together the display that has samples and descriptions of more than 70 different types of dates!

The zoo is in the same compound and, although the birds and animals displayed are interesting, once again the cages are depressingly small.

Both are open from 7 am to noon and 2 to 5 pm daily, except Friday; entry is AD 4.

Places to Stay

The *Hotel Grand Erg* used to be a reasonable two-star hotel and you could camp in the gardens. At the time of writing it had closed, although some travellers have reported that the caretaker still lets people camp occasionally – check it out.

Next to La Source there is a small campsite on an old tennis court. There is a guard at night so the place is secure. Charge per person is AD 30.

The only other hotel is the *Hotel Rym* (☎ (07) 23 3203), at the foot of the large dune. It was built with tour groups in mind, and they charge AD 170/215 for singles/doubles with bath and breakfast.

Places to Eat

Meagre pickings indeed: there are only two restaurants in town. The one up by the bus station has a menu which is limited to meat, omelettes and chips.

Down on the corner of the main road and the track to the museum is another small place, which does much the same stuff but also has occasional vegetables. Other than that it's a case of putting your own food together or paying out at the *Hotel Rym* – AD 95 for a four-course set menu.

Getting There & Away

The bus station is up by the market. There are twice-daily departures to Béchar, and buses leave once a day for Adrar and Timimoun. All these buses pass through en route from somewhere else, so seats are not guaranteed.

There is also a bus to Taghit every morning.

ADRAR

Adrar is a major regional capital 120 km south of the road which rings the Great Western Erg. Where this road branches off to the south is a café, where you can wait for a lift to Adrar if necessary.

The town has very little in the way of formal attractions but its uniform brick-red colour is interesting. The centre of town is an absolutely enormous main square (Place des Martyrs) – you could just about land a plane on it! Around it are the main buildings: the banks, post office, Air Algérie (☎ (07) 25 9365) and the main hotel. Because the square is so big the midday sun here is blinding, and you need to follow the local example and retreat somewhere cooler – the town seems to be virtually deserted in the afternoons, as everything is closed up in tight.

On the way into the town from the north, keep your eyes out for the *fouggaras* or underground water channels, identifiable above ground by the lines of small wells on the surface. This system of channels, now superseded by more modern methods, once stretched for over 2000 km in this area.

If you are heading for Mali along the Route du Tanezrouft (if the border is open), make sure you check in at the customs post when leaving the town to the south. It may

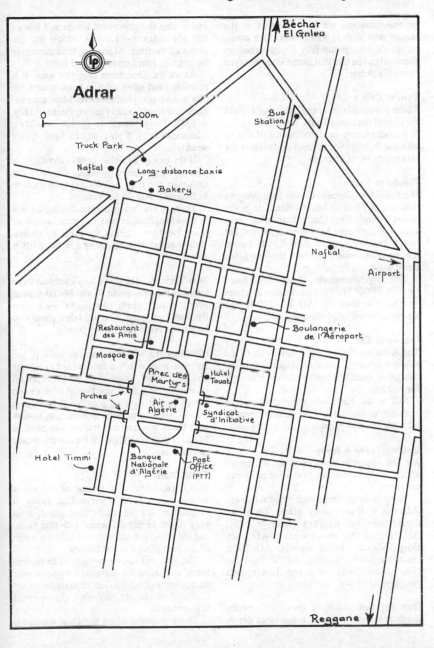

be that customs are now handled at the border post at Borj Mokhtar 800 km away, but you'd look pretty silly if you turned up there only to be told that formalities are taken care of in Adrar!

Tourist Office

There is a small syndicat d'initiative around the side of the Hotel Touat, through the arch. It has absolutely no information of use to tourists, but the local handicraft items for sale might be of interest.

Places to Stay

With only two places to choose from, the one that comes close to being affordable is the *Hotel Timmi*, one block from the main square. Rooms cost AD 105 with shower, but treat with scepticism the claim that the rooms are air-conditioned, as half the machines don't work.

The only other choice is the *Hotel Touat* (☎ (07) 25 9933) on the main square, where you have to shell out AD 170/220 for an air-conditioned single/double room.

Places to Eat

The *Restaurant des Amis* is down one of the streets leading off the main square. Here you can get an excellent chicken and potato stew for AD 22.

Out at the bus station there is quite a reasonable restaurant – the best in town in fact. It's just a pity that it is such a long walk.

Getting There & Away

Air The airport is three km from the centre and, other than walking, taxi is the only way out there.

Being a fairly important regional town, Adrar is well served by plane. There are departures to: Algiers (four weekly, AD 397); Béchar (twice weekly, AD 202); Borj Mokhtar (twice weekly, AD 291); Ghardaia (twice weekly, AD 259); Oran (four weekly, AD 339); and Tamanrasset (weekly, AD 314).

Bus The bus station is about 500 metres north of the main square. It is a large depot,

and is also the graveyard for quite a few of the Mercedes truck/buses which use the pistes all the time. At any one time there may be three or four being repaired here.

As all the departures originate here, it is possible (and advisable) to book tickets the day before you plan to leave. Main destinations include: Aoulef (daily); Béchar (daily, 6 pm); Borj Mokhtar (twice weekly); Ghardaia (daily, 5 pm); and In Salah (twice weekly).

If the bus to In Salah is not running, it is possible to get there by taking the daily bus to Aoulef and then a 4WD taxi from there to In Salah for AD 70 per person.

There is not much point catching the bus to Borj Mokhtar, as you may then have to sit there for days waiting for a lift into Mali. You're better off organising a through lift in Adrar.

Taxi Taxis run regularly to Timimoun from beneath the tree close to the Naftal station near the truck park, 10 minutes' walk from the centre of town. The trip takes about two hours and costs AD 80 per person.

Hitching It's about a one-km walk to the northern edge of town for the road to Béchar and Timimoun. There is an SNTR depot up by the Naftal station north-west of the town centre, and it may be possible to arrange a lift in a truck from here. However, as always with these government trucks, you need to be discreet as it's illegal for the drivers to take passengers.

TIMIMOUN

If you can stop at only one of the oases around the Great Western Erg, make it Timimoun. It's an enchanting place, built very much in the Sudanese red-mud style, and the residents are very friendly – it's one of the best places in the Sahara.

The town is built on the edge of an escarpment, and there are fantastic views out over an ancient salt lake to the sand dunes in the distance; on a bright, moonlit night the effect is just magic.

The population of the town and the area is

a real mix: the Haratine (non-Negroid Blacks), the Zénète Berbers, the Chaamba Arabs (originally from the east) and the Black Africans (descendants of Malian slaves). The predominant language of the region is Zénète, a Berber dialect similar to those spoken in the Kabylie and the M'Zab.

Information

Tourist Office
The tourist office is in the municipality building, near the roundabout on the main street. Here you can see a copy of the Gourara Circuit map.

Money
There is a branch of the Banque Nationale d'Algérie by the market square, about halfway along the main street.

Post
The post office is also close to the roundabout, on the road that connects the main street with the main Adrar-El Goléa road.

Gourara Circuit
If you have access to a vehicle the Gourara Circuit is an absolute must. This is a 70-km loop through a few oasis villages to the north of Timimoun and takes in the finest of the desert scenery. The ideal way to see this area would be to hire a camel and guide for a few days and do it at a leisurely pace. The guy at the tourist office may be able to fix you up, or a more likely bet might be the sharp young lads who run the campsite. They seem to have good contacts, but women alone may have to set them straight about exactly where they stand. There is a map of the circuit in the tourist office.

Other Attractions
The town lends itself well to photography; just walking up and down the main street you'll see plenty of possibilities, with the red buildings and the koubba in the middle of the road. The Hotel Rouge de l'Oasis is a fine old building and, although it is now only partially open, it is worth a wander around

inside to see the walls, which are decorated with traditional designs.

The administrative buildings of the town are also built to a similar design but are hidden behind a high wall.

Down towards the palmeraie, along the road to the campsite, the old section of town is a maze of dusty alleys and red-mud houses. The palmeraie itself is cool and shady, and the individual plots are divided by mud-brick walls. Enter by the road which leads from the main roundabout down past the high school to the campsite and Hotel Gourara.

Places to Stay – bottom end
The cheapest place is the *Hotel Ighzer* on the southern end of the main street. Spartan rooms cost AD 80 and these are adequate. It is also possible to camp in the backyard for AD 15 per person, but there is no shade.

Camping Although you can camp in the grounds of the Hotel Ighzer, a much better alternative is the *Camping la Palmeraie* on the edge of the escarpment. It is more expensive at AD 25 per person and AD 20 per vehicle, but there is plenty of shade, hot showers and the guys running it are eager to help.

Places to Stay – middle & top end
The *Hotel Rouge de l'Oasis* (☎ (07) 23 4417) may or may not be open. It suffered a minor collapse a few years ago and, although the bar is still open, there is some doubt as to whether the hotel will remain open. At the time of writing, rooms were AD 120 for a double. It will be a real crime if this place is allowed to fall into ruin, as it is one of the most colourful hotels in the whole country.

The alternative is the government-run *Hotel Gourara* (☎ (07) 23 4451) right on the edge of the escarpment, just past the campsite. It has fantastic views over the salt lake and dunes, but rooms are not cheap at AD 170/220 for singles/doubles with breakfast. Even if you are not staying here it's not a bad place to come for a beer on the terrace at sunset.

Places to Eat

The choices are strictly limited here. Other than putting your own food together with bread and whatever you can find in the market, there is only one restaurant. It's just off the main street, in the street between the Hotel Rouge de l'Oasis and the gardens opposite the municipality building. It's the place to come if you want to try camel stew, although this is nothing special.

The *Café November 1* on the main square is the main hang-out, and you can get a coffee here, but they don't serve meals.

There is a bakery in the street which runs off the main street, alongside the gardens.

Things to Buy

For souvenirs, the Artisanat du Grand Erg shop is on the road down to the campsite and has a small selection of locally made goods.

Getting There & Away

Air The Air Algérie office (☎ (07) 23 4555) is also on the main square. The airport is eight km to the south-east of town.

There are flights to: Algiers (twice weekly, AD 340); Béchar (twice weekly, AD 165); and Ghardaia (three times weekly, AD 208).

Bus The TVE station is on the main street, almost opposite the mosque. It is possible to book in advance on only some of the services, as most are just passing through and don't originate in Timimoun.

There are daily services from Timimoun to Adrar, Béchar and Ghardaia.

Taxi Taxis leave from just next to the bus station. The main destination is Adrar. The trip takes two hours and costs AD 80 per person.

Hitching The town itself is only a five-minute walk from the main highway connecting El Goléa and Adrar, so getting out onto the road for hitching in either direction is easy enough.

EL GOLÉA

The most easterly oasis of the Great Western Erg, El Goléa is a major stop on the route south. With over 180,000 palm trees, it is one of the biggest oases of the south.

The town is dominated by the old ksar, El Menia, built on a rocky knoll in the east of town. It was built by the Zénète Berbers in the 10th century and is now in a sad state. It's worth the scramble up to it for the views of the town and surrounding oasis.

The water here is some of the sweetest in the whole Sahara; fill up your tanks if you're driving, especially if you are heading south, as the water at In Salah is absolutely foul. It is possible to buy bottled water in the supermarket here but this seems a bit pointless, as all you are getting is exactly the same as what's in the tap.

El Goléa has a bank, post office and Air Algérie office. Accommodation is limited to a fancy three-star hotel, an inconveniently located budget-priced hotel and one of the best campsites in the country.

Right opposite the campsite is a supermarket, which is not at all well stocked.

The oasis itself is very lush and, apart from palms, supports a large variety of fruit trees including plum, peach, apricot, cherry, orange and fig. The market here has the last decent produce (apart from potatoes and onions) on the southward route, so stock up.

Just near the ksar is a cemetery, where Charles de Foucauld (who was responsible for the hermitage in the Hoggar) was buried in 1929.

Places to Stay – bottom end

The only reasonably priced place is the *Hotel Vieux Ksar* on the road to the south, 30 minutes' walk from the centre. It's good value at AD 110 for a double with breakfast, but it's location is really against it. There are some air-conditioned rooms.

Camping There are two choices here. The better place is the private campsite on the road north out of town, a couple of hundred metres from the centre. The outside wall just has a high corrugated iron gate with 'Camping' written on it. It is an old garden which has been turned into a campsite, so you can sleep out under the palm and citrus trees and there's plenty of shade; it does, however, attract a few mosquitoes. Facilities are good and it costs AD 25 per person, AD 15 for a tent and AD 20 for a car. The site is locked up at night, but late arrivals can bash on the gate to be let in.

The other campsite is run by the Touring Club d'Algérie and is three km south of the centre. It is not as shady or private as the first one, and it costs AD 20 per person.

Places to Stay – top end
The *Hotel el Boustan* is east of the centre, on the road to the ksar. It is not a bad place and is one of the few where the swimming pool is actually serviceable. Rooms cost AD 145/170 for a single/double.

Places to Eat
There's a little restaurant, almost opposite the Naftal station on the road out to the north,

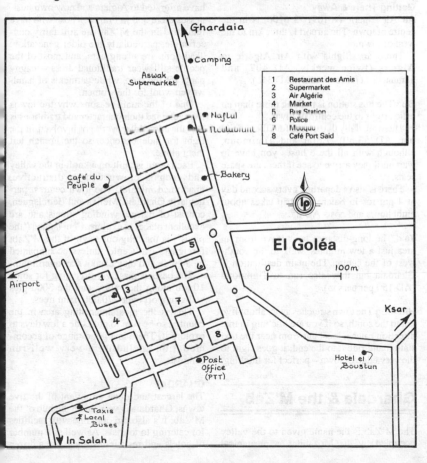

1	Restaurant des Amis
2	Supermarket
3	Air Algérie
4	Market
5	Bus Station
6	Police
7	Mosque
8	Café Port Said

El Goléa

0   100m

and this place has good chicken, chips and salad.

Other than that, the *Restaurant des Amis* in the centre has very mediocre food but is open late, as it caters to the bus passengers who stop here for a meal break on the Ghardaia-Adrar run.

On the southern side of the block with Air Algérie in it is a very good sandwich and juice bar run by a friendly guy who speaks German. Inside the market is a good café for a breakfast of omelettes and coffee.

Getting There & Away

Air Air Algérie (☎ (09) 73 6100) is in the centre of town. The airport is three km to the west of town.

There are flights with Air Algérie to Algiers (twice weekly, AD 407) and Tamanrasset (twice weekly, AD 346).

Bus The bus station is nothing more than an office right in the centre of town.

There are daily departures for Ghardaia (3 pm, AD 53.50), Adrar and Timimoun, although with all these buses you have to wait until they arrive to see if there are spare seats.

There is also a departure every second day at 4 pm for In Salah. The trip takes about eight hours and costs AD 85.

Taxi The long-distance taxis leave from an area just a few minutes' walk to the south-west of the centre. The main destination is Ghardaia but they also run to Timimoun (AD 150 per person).

Hitching The town stretches away about five km to the south, so if you are hitching in that direction catch a local bus from near the taxi station and ride it to the end; it goes right to the very edge of town – perfect for hitching.

Ghardaia & the M'Zab

The M'Zab is the name given to the valley occupied by the Mozabites, a puritanical Islamic sect that broke away from the mainstream in the 11th century. They are a Berber people who speak a dialect similar to that spoken by the people of the Kabylie in the north.

The 100,000 inhabitants of this deep narrow valley live in a pentapolis – five villages which have developed independently of the rest of the country. Ghardaia is the main town and the others, which surround it, are Melika, Beni Isguen, Bou Noura and El Ateuf. The Mozabites are well known for being astute merchants; many of them have migrated to Algiers and now own businesses there and in France. Those who have remained in the M'Zab are still fairly conservative, particularly the older generation. Traditions are strong here, and most of the people still wear traditional dress – baggy pants for the men, white garments of hand-woven wool for the women.

One of the main reasons why the towns have retained their character and traditions is that the Mozabites were not involved in the fight for independence, so the French left them alone.

Each town is built on a knoll in the valley and each is crowned by a distinctive, unadorned minaret. The town centres, particularly Ghardaia, Melika and Beni Isguen, consist of narrow winding streets and are excellent places to explore. Beni Isguen ('the pious') is the religious town of the M'Zab; foreigners can't enter unless accompanied by a guide and they cannot stay overnight.

The oasis is massive, stretching for some 10 km along the valley, and the 3000-plus wells support over 270,000 palm trees.

This is the most interesting area in the country, so be sure to put aside a few days to explore it. There is a good range of accommodation including a very well-run campsite.

GHARDAIA

The largest and most important of the five towns, Ghardaia is very much the hub of the M'Zab; it's also the only one with facilities for catering to tourists. As well as a number of hotels and restaurants, there are a dozen

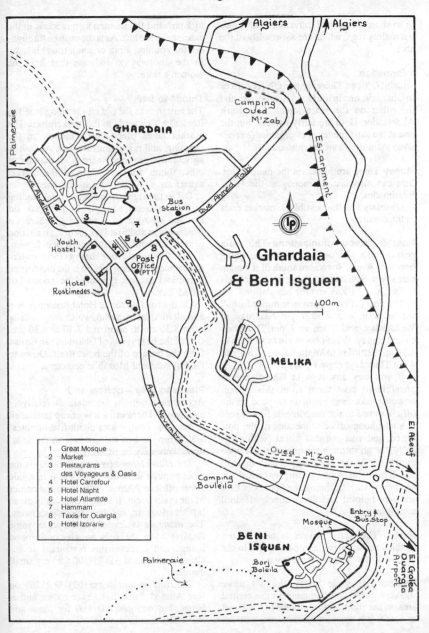

Ghardaïa
& Beni Isguen

0   400m

1   Great Mosque
2   Market
3   Restaurants
    des Voyageurs & Oasis
4   Hotel Carrefour
5   Hotel Napht
6   Hotel Atlantide
7   Hammam
8   Taxis for Ouargla
9   Hotel Izorane

or so shops which sell souvenirs of all kinds but mainly rugs, which are a speciality of the area.

Information

Tourist Offices There are two ONAT offices in Ghardaia, one in the Hotel Rostimedes and the other on the main street, Rue Emir Abdelkader. Both are fairly useless, but the one at the Rostimedes does organise (expensive) tours if you are interested.

Money There are banks on the main street. You can also change money at the Hotel Rostimedes.

Ghardaia has the best black market rates in the country.

Post & Telecommunications The main post office is also on the main street, which becomes Ave 1 Novembre south of the main side street, Rue Ahmed Talbi; the latter leads to the Oued M'Zab and the bus station.

The post office is open in summer from 7 am to noon and 4 to 7 pm Saturday to Wednesday, and 7 am to 1 pm Thursday; closed Friday. Winter hours are from 8 am to 6.30 pm Saturday to Wednesday and 8 am to 4 pm Thursday; closed Friday.

If you buy any rugs in Ghardaia it is possible to post them from this office; however, take them along unwrapped, as the officials need to see the contents first. There is a telephone office at the side of the post office, and you can dial direct (with difficulty), or go through the operator; it's open until 9 pm. As this is a busy place it's quicker to call from the Hotel Rostimedes (you don't need to be staying there); the operators here are very helpful and don't knock off until midnight.

Market The daily market is held in the cobbled marketplace, an open square in the middle of the old part of the town.

Hammam If your hotel doesn't have showers, there is a hammam in the central area, to the right of the entrance to the Hotel es Saada. It is open for women from 8.30 am to 1 pm, and the women's entrance is in the side lane to the left. As is the custom throughout the country, a rag or small towel is hung in the doorway to indicate that it is the women's time.

Things to See

The entrance to the old city is along Rue Ibn Rosten, which leads to the marketplace. The market takes place daily, mainly in the morning, and is a colourful affair. As well as agricultural produce, there is all manner of other things for sale. Around the market square are a number of souvenir shops.

Off to the right of the square and leading up to the Great Mosque is the Souk Ed Dellada (a *souk* is a market), where on Wednesdays and Sundays there is an auction of stuff; it's similar to the one at Beni Isguen.

The Great Mosque has a fortress-like appearance; its main feature is the unadorned pyramidal minaret, typical of the mosques of the M'Zab.

On the road up to the Hotel Rostimedes is a small folklore museum, which is open daily from 8.30 am to noon and 3.30 to 6.30 pm. One of the best views of Ghardaia can be had from the terrace of the hotel itself. Down to the left is an old Mozabite cemetery.

Places to Stay – bottom end

Accommodation in Ghardaia is relatively expensive. There are a few cheap hotels, all in the same central area about five minutes' walk from the bus station. Late in the afternoon there may be little choice.

The *Hotel Napht* (☎ (09) 89 0009) is the most popular with travellers and is in a side street off Rue Ahmed Talbi, near the corner of the main street. It's not fantastically clean but it's adequate, and there are cold showers. The manager is friendly and speaks some English, and there is an air-conditioned lounge and a reasonable restaurant downstairs. Rooms cost AD 75/100 for very small doubles.

The *Hotel Atlantide* (☎ (09) 89 2536), on Rue Ahmed Talbi, has larger rooms and is better, but charges AD 100 for them and AD 10 for a cold shower.

In the same area is the *Hotel 1001 Nuits* which is poor value at AD 60/100, and there are no showers.

Youth Hostel There is a *Youth Hostel* (☎ (09) 89 4403) on the corner of the main street and the road that leads up to the Hotel Rostimedes. It is open in the morning and late afternoon, and costs AD 20 for a bed. There is a three-day limit.

Camping Ghardaia boasts one of the best campsites in Algeria. The *Camping Bouleila* is about one km south of the town centre on the El Goléa road. It is well shaded and the security is good. It costs AD 20 per person, AD 15 for a tent and AD 10 for a vehicle. There are places to eat close by.

There is a second campsite, *Camping Oued M'Zab*, on the route out of town to the north. It's OK if you have a car, but it's location is inconvenient otherwise, especially as there are no restaurants close by. Prices are similar to the Boulella.

Places to Stay – middle
The *Hotel Carrefour* (☎ (09) 89 3179) is on Rue Emir Abdelkader, almost on the corner with Rue Ahmed Talbi. The rooms are not bad; they have fans and cost AD 145 a double.

Up a notch is the *Hotel Izorane* (☎ (09) 89 1560), a good place on Ave 1 Novembre, not far from the post office. There are no singles here; doubles cost AD 160 with bath and breakfast.

Places to Stay – top end
The three-star *Hotel Rostimedes* (☎ (09) 89 2999) is on the hill to the west overlooking town, just a couple of minutes' walk from the centre. It has been designed to blend in with the landscape, but the result is that parts of the interior are very gloomy and dungeon-like. There is a good swimming pool, which it is sometimes possible to use if you are not staying here – but you have to sneak in. All the rooms are air-conditioned and cost AD 183/246 for singles/doubles, including breakfast.

Places to Eat
There is a good choice of restaurants in Ghardaia. One of the best is the *Restaurant M'Zab*, next to the Hotel 1001 Nights on Rue Ahmed Talbi. The food is all the usual stuff – couscous, chicken, chips and shakshuka (vegetable stew) – and the staff are friendly. It closes by about 9 pm and things start to run out before that.

Up near the entrance to the old city is the *Restaurant Oasis*, upstairs on the corner with the main street. Here you can get decent chicken and chips for AD 25. Opposite is the *Restaurant des Voyageurs*, which is also not bad but is not as popular with the locals.

The restaurant at the *Hotel Napht* does quite decent food but, almost directly opposite, the *Restaurant Zahia* does possibly the worst couscous in North Africa. The other meat dishes are not so bad, and it's pleasant sitting outside. Behind it there is a tiny snack shop which does very good shakshuka.

The restaurant of the *Hotel Atlantide* offers very unexciting fare and has a four-course set menu for AD 40.

If you are staying at the Camping Bouleila, there's no need to walk all the way into town to get a meal as there are a couple of restaurants just up the road. The *Restaurant Carrefour* is on the same road, towards the town centre, while the *Restaurant 5 Novembre* is on Ave 1 Novembre.

Things to Buy
If you are interested in buying any of the beautifully colourful rugs here check the quality closely, as they vary enormously. The better quality ones have more knots per sq cm. The greatest concentration of shops is around the market square.

You need to haggle over the prices, which may seem outrageously expensive, but when you think in real (black market) terms, are actually very reasonable. It is also possible to do a bit of bartering with some of the shopkeepers, using any surplus goods or undeclared hard currency which you may have.

As an example of prices, a 1½ by 2½ metre rug will cost around AD 2500; officially that's US$120, but you can expect to pay less than this on the the black market. If you are paying in undeclared foreign currency you can get a better price again, but be discreet.

Getting There & Away
Air The Air Algérie office (☎ (09) 89 3592) is on Ave 1 Novembre. The airport is 10 km south of town on the road to El Goléa.

As this is a major centre, it is well served by Air Algérie. There is a weekly flight direct to Paris. The internal flights are to: Adrar (weekly, AD 259); Algiers (twice daily, AD 300); Annaba (twice weekly, AD 370); Béchar (weekly, AD 350); Constantine (weekly, AD 311); Djanet (weekly, AD 404); In Salah (twice weekly, AD 241); Oran (twice weekly, AD 333); and Tamanrasset (five times weekly, AD 410).

Bus The main station is on Rue Ahmed Talbi, just across the Oued M'Zab, only five minutes' walk from the centre. The ticket office can be a bit of a shambles, and demand for tickets is often high, so make reservations in advance. A timetable is displayed.

The main destinations are: Adrar (daily); Algiers (three times daily); Biskra (daily), Constantine (twice daily); El Goléa (daily, AD 53.50); El Oued (every second day); In Salah (every second day); Laghouat (daily); Oran (three times daily); Ouargla (daily); and Timimoun (daily).

Taxi Taxis for Algiers, El Goléa and Ouargla leave from over the oued, opposite the bus station. For Laghouat they leave by the bridge at the bus station. As with everything in Ghardaia, there is very little activity in the afternoons.

Hitching For hitching south out of town, catch a local bus heading for El Ateuf and get off at the main roundabout near Beni Isguen. The El Goléa road heads off south up the escarpment from here.

Getting Around
To/From the Airport There is a bus which goes to and from the airport to meet incoming flights. There is a timetable of departure times in the Air Algérie office, and in some of the hotels.

Bus The station for the local buses is just opposite the entrance to the old city. There are buses for Beni Isguen, El Ateuf and Bou Noura.

AROUND GHARDAIA
Beni Isguen
This is the most important religious town in the M'Zab. The people here hang on very firmly to their traditional ways, and the amount of outside influence is kept to an absolute minimum. One of the major restrictions in this direction is that the residents must marry within the town.

The town itself is built on the slope of the hill, 2½ km south of Ghardaia. The best time for a visit is in the late afternoon, when the market square comes alive with the daily auction. Here locals sell hand-made cloth, rugs and other general items. It is interesting to watch: there are no cafés in the town, so this becomes the social event of the day, and all the men sit out around the square. The auction takes place every day except Friday.

The narrow streets are entered from the main Ghardaia road, and, as it is compulsory for all non-Muslims entering the town to have a guide, you can pick one up here. This will cost you AD 10 per person. There are plenty of guides, so try to get one with whom you have a common language; many of the older men speak no English. Photography and smoking are forbidden in the town, and modest dress is compulsory (no shorts or singlets) and there are signs up at the entrance to remind you.

The guide will show you all the interesting bits and pieces in Beni Isguen. The highlight is the Turkish tower, Borj Cheikh el Hadj (also known as Borj Boleila), in the eastern corner of the town. The view from the top of the tower is excellent and you are allowed to take photos. Your guide will probably leave you at the marketplace, around which there are a few shops selling the colourful local rugs; the prices here are a bit more negotiable than in Ghardaia.

The palmeraie at Beni Isguen is probably the best in the M'Zab. It stretches for a couple of km behind the town. Just continue on the road, past the entrance to Beni Isguen, where it winds around to the back of the palmeraie. The gardens here are green havens, veritable Gardens of Eden. They are difficult to see properly, however, as they are mostly behind high walls. It is usually not long before someone invites you in to sit in the shade of their fruit trees. Once behind the wall, the contrast is vivid – fruit trees of all kinds battling each other for room. You'll find every kind of fruit here, from grapes and figs to bananas and dates.

Getting There & Away Local buses leave Ghardaia from outside the entrance to the old city. They drop you outside the gates to Beni Isguen (AD 2); alternatively, it's a half-hour walk

Melika

It is from Melika that you get the best overall views of the Oued M'Zab and Ghardaia itself. The town is about a km to the south-east, high above the oued.

The main point of interest is the curious cemetery on the northern side, although the town itself is interesting to wander around.

Getting There & Away The easiest way up to Melika is on foot. It takes about 30 minutes to make the climb, and the best route is the road which leads south opposite the bus station. It is also possible to cross the oued anywhere and just scramble up the side of the hill.

Guerara

This small oasis is 73 km east of the main road at Berriane, which in turn is 69 km north of Ghardaia. It is a good spot to rest up if you have your own transport. Seek out Baba Hamdi who runs the Restaurant Sindbad and the campsite in the palmeraie. There's a hot spring close by which is great for swimming

– there are specified times for segregated swimming.

Grand Erg Oriental

The Great Eastern Erg is much larger than its western counterpart. From central-eastern Algeria it stretches north and east into Tunisia.

Close to its northern edge is the oasis of El Oued, in the centre of the Souf region. This is a series of oases dotted throughout a small triangular area. For many people El Oued is their first Algerian town, as there is a good road connecting it with Nefta and the towns of the Chott el Jerid in Tunisia. It is worth spending a couple of days here before moving on.

In the Souf region an ingenious method of agriculture has been developed, which allows for the growing of dates and fruits in one of the hottest areas of the Sahara. Great depressions are excavated with hand tools and the sand piled up on all sides; palm fronds are then stuck along the ridges to stop the sand blowing back into the dip. Palms and other plants are grown in the bottom, from where their roots can reach the subterranean water. It is not uncommon to see just the tip of a palm tree sticking out of the top of an excavated pit.

Touggourt is another oasis town, right on the western edge of the erg, south of El Oued. The road that connects the two towns passes through some magnificent sand-dune country. At times the dunes are actually creeping across the road and it is a constant struggle to keep it clear.

Further south again is oil country, from where the majority of Algeria's exports come. Hassi Messaoud is the heart of the oil industry, although Ouargla on the edge of the erg is as close as most people will need to go, unless they are heading for Djanet.

EL OUED

El Oued has been dubbed 'The Village of a Thousand Domes' and it doesn't take long to

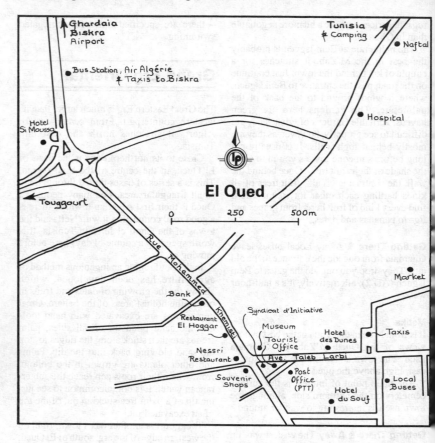

El Oued

work out why: virtually all the buildings use vaults and domes in an effort to alleviate the incredible summer heat. Temperatures as high as 60°C are not unknown here and for days on end it will hit 45° or more with monotonous regularity, so be prepared for it if you are here then. It gets so bloody hot in this place that everything is hot to touch – even the handrails inside the buses and the door handles of the hotel rooms!

The town is also famous for its carpets, many of which bear the brown Cross of the Souf motif on a white background. There are simpler designs on the rough black rugs with red and white lines through them. Many of the carpets sold in Ghardaia are actually made in El Oued and, obviously, the prices at the source are better.

The dozen or so villages around El Oued are worth a poke around, particularly Nakhla, 15 km to the south-east, and Guemar, 18 km along the Biskra road.

In the entire Souf region the women wear a single robe/veil which covers everything except for one eye. This makes them a truly bizarre sight; if ever a garment has had a dehumanising effect, it has to be this one.

Information
Tourist Offices There are two tourist

offices, virtually next door to one another, on Ave Taleb Larbi near the corner of Rue Mohammed Khemisti. The local syndicat d'initiative (☎ (04) 72 8248) is the more helpful of the two and has a reasonable hand-out map of the town and Souf area.

Because of the heat everything shuts up tight by noon, and throughout the afternoon nothing stirs until about 4 pm.

Money There are two banks on Ave Taleb Larbi which are open for exchange. It is also possible to change money at the Hotel du Souf, and there is a bank at the Tunisian border, although it is not always open.

Post & Telecommunications The post office is just behind the tourist offices, in a small pedestrian precinct. There are direct-dial phone boxes outside.

Water The town's tap water tastes pretty dreadful but is safe to drink. Bottled water is not widely available.

Things to See

The daily market in the old part of the town is a colourful and animated affair. It is at its busiest on Fridays. Most of the stuff for sale is food and everyday items, but there are a few stalls which cater to the tourist trade.

The museum opposite the tourist offices consists of just one room. However, it has some good displays including old aerial photos of the area, a collection of the various insects and animals of the region, some good sand roses and other geological curiosities. There are also a couple of traditional rugs, and the boots with wool-and-camel-hair soles which are used to walk on the burning hot sand. The whole thing is a bit dusty and moth-eaten but is worth a quick look. It is open daily from 9 am to noon and 3 to 6 pm; closed Monday; entry is AD 1.

Places to Stay – bottom end

The most central place is the *Hotel des Dunes*, on Ave Taleb Larbi. It is in a tra-ditional domed building and has the feel of a caravanserai. The facilities are basic and

barely adequate, and rooms are overpriced at AD 70 for a double. Showers are AD 5 but the water is on for only an hour in the morning and an hour in the afternoon.

Much more modern, more comfortable and far better value is the *Hotel Si Moussa* (☎ (04) 72 8381), on Rue Mohammed Khemisti near the fancy roundabout com-plete with pavilion which is at the intersection of the Touggourt road. It is a 15-minute walk from the centre but is very handy to the bus station for early morning departures. There are also local buses which shuttle back and forth to the centre, so the location is not too bad. Rooms cost AD 60/90 for a single/double with washba-sin; AD 80/130 with air-conditioning, and there are free showers. It is also possible to sleep on the roof here.

Another place in the centre, next to the Hotel des Dunes, is the new *Hotel Central* (☎ (04) 72 8825). It too is good value at AD 60/110, but there are no showers.

Youth Hostel & Camping There is a *Youth Hostel* at Nakhla, 15 km to the south-east, where you can stay or camp.

The *Camping de Crepuscule* is a few km north of town on the Tunis road, next to the Naftal station. Facilities are limited and there is not a scrap of shade, but it's the only place.

Places to Stay – top end

The only other place is the *Hotel du Souf* (☎ (04) 72 8170), a couple of blocks south of the tourist office, complete with swim-ming pool and tower. Rooms here cost a mere AD 250/300 for a single/double with breakfast.

Places to Eat

Food is expensive in El Oued. Halfway along the main street, the *Restaurant El Hoggar* is about the best place in town. It is one of the few places which doesn't close up in the afternoons and is a cool retreat from the heat outside. The food is good, but a bit expensive at AD 70 for a set meal. The place diagonally opposite the tourist office is similar.

Getting There & Away

Air The Air Algérie office (☎ (04) 72 8666) is at the bus station, 20 minutes' walk north of the centre on the Biskra road. The airport is at Guemar, 18 km to the north, and can be reached by local bus.

There are flights to Algiers (six times weekly, AD 298) and Annaba (four times weekly, AD 244).

Bus The main bus station is about two km north of the town centre – a 20-minute walk, or there are local minibuses which take you to or from the centre.

There are departures to: Algiers (nightly, 7 pm); Annaba (daily, 6 am); Constantine (daily, 4.30 am); Ghardaia (every other night, 10 pm); and Ouargla (daily, 6 am);

Taxi Yellow long distance taxis leave when full from just next door to the Hotel des Dunes for Touggourt (two hours, AD 80 per person), the Tunisian border (AD 50), Ouargla and towns in the Souf area.

Taxis for Biskra leave from next to the bus station.

Getting Around

Local bus services for the surrounding towns leave from opposite the taxi station. Not much happens after 7 pm.

Indian Tata minibuses also leave from here, and run back and forth to the bus station.

TOUGGOURT

A totally unremarkable oasis town, Touggourt is perhaps most famous as the starting point of the first motorised crossing of the Sahara. The Citroen half-track vehicles of the Haardt and Audouin-Debreuil expedition set off from here in 1922 for Timbuktu via Tamanrasset. The event is marked by a simple pillar in the town square.

Today the town is a regional administrative centre, with a large palmeraie and a couple of vaguely interesting old mud-brick villages to the south. There are a couple of banks, a post office and an Air Algérie office.

Market day is Friday; in winter especially, the town is full of itinerant merchants who have come for the market. The marketplace is just off the road to El Oued, near the taxi station.

From the main square, the road to the right curves around past the cinema to the bus stop for buses to Temacine. The road straight ahead leads past the old hotel on the left to the Hotel Oasis and Temacine.

If you have a day to spare you could do worse than spend it here, but don't lose any sleep if you miss it.

Places to Stay – bottom end

The *Hotel Marhaba* is right by the taxi station and costs AD 80 for a double, although this is negotiable. The best idea is to follow the local custom and sleep on the roof in summer, as the rooms become intolerably hot. The showers and toilets are cockroach infested but that's nothing new. In summer you'll be lucky if you can stand under the shower, as the water pipes are above ground and get incredibly hot.

Between the market and the main street is the *Hotel de la Paix*, but it is no different from the Marhaba.

Youth Hostel There is a *Youth Hostel* well signposted right in the centre of town – very well located. A bed is AD 20.

Places to Stay – top end

The only improvement on these places is the expensive *Hotel Oasis*, one km south of town on the road to Temacine, although even this place seems to suffer from the general malaise that grips the rest of the town. Rooms cost AD 230 for a double with breakfast. The swimming pool is only just usable as the water is a sickly shade of green. The most useful thing in the hotel is the map of the town on the wall in the lobby.

Places to Eat

Between the taxi station and the market are a couple of ultra-basic restaurants. The one closest to the Hotel Marhaba serves food that doesn't exactly make the mouth water but is at least edible.

The *Restaurant de la Liberté* has good meals for AD 30.

Getting There & Away

Air There is an Air Algérie office (☎ (09) 72 6096) in the town centre. The airport is five km east of town along the El Oued road. There are daily flights to Algiers (AD 299).

Bus The new bus station is right on the western edge of town, a couple of km from the centre; you'll need a taxi if you can't face the walk.

There are daily buses to: Algiers, Biskra, Constantine, El Oued, Ghardaia, Hassi Messaoud and Ouargla.

Train The railway station is close to the centre of town. There are two trains to and from Constantine and Biskra. Departure times are 12.45 am and 12.30 pm, and the trip takes 4½ hours to Biskra, eight hours to Constantine.

Taxi The taxi station is just off the main El Oued road, five minutes' walk from the centre, past the marketplace.

There are departures for Biskra, El Oued and Ouargla, but very little happens after about 1 pm.

Getting Around

Bus Local buses for Tamelhat and Temacine leave from a stop along the road that curves around to the right at the end of the main street – just ask around.

AROUND TOUGGOURT

Tamelhat

On the edge of the palmeraie 12 km south of Touggourt is Tamelhat, a traditional mud-brick village which, although inhabited, has the air of a place that has been abandoned. There are large open spaces where buildings have collapsed completely.

The narrow lanes wind between high walls, and in places the houses actually span the lanes. The occasional open door reveals a small courtyard where the family donkey is kept and where the women work spreading chillies out to dry.

In the centre of the town is the mosque and mausoleum of Sidi El Hadj Ali; the cupola above the latter is decorated with some coloured tiles and stucco.

Chances are one of the local kids will latch onto you as a guide, although what they can actually show you is limited. One thing they will try and drag you along to is the 'sea'. This is a small brackish lake between Tamelhat and Temacine – forget it.

Getting There & Away There are local buses from close to the centre of Touggourt and these drop you at an intersection a couple of km from the main road. Tamelhat is directly on the right; Temacine a few km to the left. Taxis run back to Touggourt via Temacine and the Hotel Oasis.

Temacine

Temacine is much the same as Tamelhat. However, it is more picturesque, as the houses are built around a ksar on top of a small hill. Palm tree trunks have been used extensively in the construction of the fortifications. The mosque here dates from 1431; all the building materials used in its construction were imported from Tunisia.

OUARGLA

The town of Ouargla has even less attractions than Touggourt, although if you find yourself stuck here there are a couple of hotels (neither of them cheap), a youth hostel and a campsite.

Ouargla is very much a modern oil town; if you are driving in the area at night the horizon is bright orange with the glow of the oil burn-off flames.

Places to Stay

The *Hotel de Tassili* (☎ (09) 70 0154) and the *Hotel El Mehri* (☎ (09) 70 2066) are both two-star and cost AD 145/180 for a single/double with breakfast.

Camping The campsite is called the *Kamel Camping Rouissat* (☎ (09) 70 5776); it's signposted 4½ km from the town centre on the Touggourt road.

Getting There & Away

Bus The new bus station is at the eastern end of town, on the Ghardaia road, about 1½ km from the centre. There are buses to Algiers, Annaba, Constantine, El Oued, Hassi Messaoud, In Amenas and Oran.

Taxi The taxis congregate about 300 metres before the bus station on the Ghardaia road. They leave regularly for Biskra, Ghardaia (AD 70, two hours), Touggourt and El Oued (at least 2½ hours).

HASSI MESSAOUD

This is purely an oil boom town, 85 km south-east of Ouargla. There is absolutely nothing of interest, but you will find yourself coming through on the way south on the Route du Tassili N'Ajjer.

Places to Stay

The only hotel is three km from the town centre at the northern end of town, and it's expensive at AD 150 for a single, plus AD 22 for a very good breakfast.

Getting There & Away

There are regular buses between here and Ouargla, and a daily service to In Amenas, although you'd be lucky to get a seat on it as it comes from Ouargla and is likely to be full.

Route du Tassili N'Ajjer

This route heads south from Hassi Messaoud along the Gassi Touil, a large oued between two sections of the Great Eastern Erg, to In Amenas, 730 km to the south-east and very close to the Libyan border.

The road is bitumen as far as In Amenas but turns to piste between there and Djanet and Tamanrasset.

There is a weekly bus along here between Biskra and In Amenas but very little other traffic – just the occasional truck. If you are

heading for Tamanrasset, the easiest and quickest way is to hitch to Ghardaia and then head down the N1. If you have the time and don't mind running the risk of getting stuck for a few days in some tiny backwater it is possible to get to Djanet and then on to Tamanrasset this way, but it's not a trip which should be undertaken lightly. In winter there is a trickle of tourist vehicles but there's no guarantee that they'll be able to pick you up.

If you get really stuck there are flights from In Amenas and Illizi to Ouargla and Djanet.

IN AMENAS

This is a modern, characterless town built to service the oil industry. There is a post office, petrol station and SNTR truck depot, where it may be possible to get lifts.

On arrival you must check in at the *daira* (municipal headquarters) and give them the details of your trip to Djanet.

Places to Stay

The only formal accommodation is the *Hotel Cash*, which charges AD 145 for a double. Other than that it is possible to camp outside the police station.

Getting There & Away

Air The airport is 14 km south-east of town. There are flights to: Algiers (twice weekly, AD 409); Djanet (weekly, AD 185); Oran (weekly, AD 481); and Ouargla (twice weekly, AD 244).

Bus The bus station is south-west of the centre of the town. There is just the one bus per week to Biskra. There used to be a weekly bus to Illizi, but we haven't heard about this for some time.

ILLIZI

Nearly 300 km south of In Amenas, Illizi is the main settlement between there and Djanet.

The town boasts a fuel station, hospital, basic shop, customs post (where you have to check in) and a hotel (of sorts).

If you really get stranded here there are

flights to: Algiers (three times weekly, AD 463); Djanet (four times weekly, AD 135); and Ouargla (daily, AD 269). The 'airport' is five km north of town and there's not a building at the place – just a graded runway.

DJANET

The main town of the Tassili, Djanet is a pretty place built on the edge of a palmeraie. Here you'll find all the facilities, including post office, bank, basic restaurants and shops.

The main attraction is the rock paintings in the Tassili National Park, around Tamrit. Without a vehicle the only way to get out to these places is on a tour (expensive) or by hitching with other tourists. Even if you do have a vehicle, it is not possible to go into the park unless accompanied by an official guide.

Places to Stay

The only place to stay is the *Camping Zeribas* in the centre of town. The zeribas (grass huts) cost AD 60 per person. There is a restaurant attached.

It is prohibited to camp in the palmeraie.

Getting There & Away

Air There is an Air Algérie office (☎ (09) 73 5032) in the town centre. The airstrip is at Ilasadadi, 40 km from town.

There are flights to: Algiers (six times weekly, AD 558); Ghardaia (weekly, AD 404); Illizi (four times weekly, AD 135); In Amenas (weekly, AD 185); Ouargla (daily, AD 363); and Tamanrasset (weekly, AD 191).

Hitching There is no public transport into Djanet other than plane. It's a matter of hitching with trucks or tourists. There are a fair number of vehicles running between here and Tamanrasset, so hitching shouldn't be a great problem.

Route du Hoggar

From El Goléa, Route N1 continues south across the amazingly flat Tademait plateau, where in places the largest thing in sight is a rock the size of a tennis ball. After 410 km of good bitumen road you hit In Salah, the last town of any size before Tamanrasset. The latter is another 710 km further south, along a road which is now bitumen for all but the last 100 km into Tam. Tamanrasset is a good place to rest up for a while and a base from which to explore the Hoggar Mountains, which shouldn't be missed.

From Tam the piste continues for another 410 km to In Guezzam, 10 km before the Algerian border crossing with Niger. The road is fairly punishing on vehicles but 4WD is not necessary. At the time of writing the army was in the process of surfacing this road, but how far they've got is anybody's guess.

Right along this route there's a fair amount of traffic, mostly trucks and travellers in vehicles, and hitching is possible; however, it is a lucky traveller who can get all the way to Tamanrasset without having to catch a bus.

IN SALAH

Built in the red Sudanese style, In Salah is really a very pleasant, friendly town but one overlooked by most travellers, who spend so little time here as possible. The name means 'salty source' and refers to the terrible water. Bring as much water with you as you can from Tamanrasset or El Goléa, as the water here really is foul. Even the local soft drinks are made from it and bottled water is only sporadically available.

The most interesting feature of the town is the creeping sand dunes on the western edge by the Aoulef road. Behind the mosque you can see how the dune is gradually encroaching on the town. From the top of the dune it becomes apparent that In Salah has actually been cut in two.

The dunes move at the rate of about one

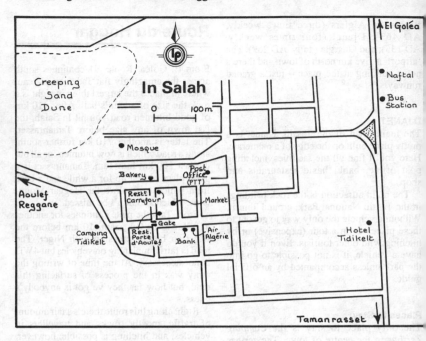

metre every five years. The amount of sand on the move actually remains fairly constant, so while it is swallowing up a building on its leading edge it is uncovering one behind it which may have been under the sand for a generation or two.

Once the ruins of a house have been uncovered, it is established who it used to belong to and then that person's relatives rebuild the place and move in.

The view from the top of this dune is great at sunset, although you will no doubt be pestered by the local kids with *'Donnez-moi stylo!'*.

To the west of town along the Aoulef road is the palmeraie, with its 225,000 trees. Date-growing has become the major occupation of the people of In Salah, a town which used to be important as a place of barter between European goods from the north, and gold, ivory and slaves from the south.

Information

There is a bank in the main street, and the post office is one block to the north.

The market is in the centre and has very little – just a few spuds and onions, and the occasional tomato or chilli.

The sole bakery in town is just up from the Restaurant Carrefour. It bakes only in the morning and competition for its wares can be strong, so be there early.

There is a big new hospital out in the east of town near the Hotel Tidikelt.

Places to Stay

The only hotel is the three-star *Hotel Tidikelt* (☎ (09) 73 0393) on the outskirts of town, 30 minutes' walk from the centre. The staff will tell you that it has a swimming pool but will neglect to say that it's empty most of the time. Rooms are air-conditioned and cost AD 230 for a double with breakfast.

It is possible to crash out in the sand

behind the bus station and stash your gear in the station during the day, but this is not really recommended for women (although chances are you'd be quite safe).

Camping The *Camping Tidikelt* at the end of the main street in the centre of town is the better of the two camping alternatives. There is a reasonable amount of shade and you can sleep in the tiny zeribas if you want some privacy. By now the new facilities should be complete, so at least it should be possible to get a decent shower – a far cry from a couple of years ago. It costs AD 25 per person to sleep here.

The other campsite is three km south of town on the Tamanrasset road. It is very desolate and has no shade, so there is really no incentive to stay here.

Places to Eat

The *Restaurant Porte d'Aoulef* is just by the arched gate over the street. It does very average food, which is, however, as good as you'll find anywhere.

Just along the street behind the gate, on the left where the footpath is raised, is another small place which does a fair ragoût (stew) and chips.

The *Restaurant Carrefour* used to be the place to eat but now, sadly, the standards have reached rock bottom. Most of the food comes straight out of tins.

The *Hotel Tidikelt* has a fancy restaurant where AD 55 gets you a four-course meal, and upstairs at the bus station there's a café which stays open late.

Getting There & Away

Air The Air Algérie office (☎ (09) 73 0239) is on the main street, next to a bank. The airport is 10 km to the north, to the right of the El Goléa road.

There are flights to: Adrar (weekly, AD 135); Algiers (three times weekly, AD 430); Borj Mokhtar (weekly, AD 273); Ghardaia (weekly, AD 241); Ouargla (weekly, AD 244); and Tamanrasset (four times weekly, AD 238).

Bus The bus station is out in the east on the main Tamanrasset-El Goléa road, about 20 minutes' walk from the centre. It is actually just a new shopping centre (most of it unoccupied), and the bus office is inside towards the back.

There are buses to Adrar, Ghardaia and Tamanrasset. The Ghardaia buses leave at 4 pm every second day and it is essential that you book at 9 am on the day you plan to travel.

For Tamanrasset, there are departures in Mercedes truck/buses on Tuesday, Thursday and Sunday at 4 am. Tickets are sold in the afternoon the day before and, again, booking in advance is crucial. On these buses there are no numbered seats, and it is important to get there at least half an hour before departure if you don't want to end up in a seat behind the rear wheels (or, worse, in the aisle with no seat at all), as the ride is incredibly rough. The trip takes about 19 hours and costs AD 130 and AD 20 for a rucksack. There are stops made along the way (including a meal at Arak), but basically you need to be prepared with a bit of food and water.

The buses to Adrar are scheduled to run twice weekly but they are often suspended. Ask (persistently) at the bus station to try and track them down. They usually leave not from the bus station but from the street to the right of the gate in the centre of town.

Taxi Taxis run regularly from In Salah to Aoulef (AD 60 per person), 170 km west along the road to Adrar, and from there you can catch a daily bus to Adrar. This In Salah-Adrar road is surfaced, except for about 90 km of piste between In Salah and Aoulef.

Hitching From the main road you can hitch north from just by the Naftal station, or south from past the Hotel Tidikelt. I met two guys who sat by the road for three days trying to get to Tamanrasset before they ended up catching a bus.

There is very little traffic to Adrar, but you can stand on the road down near the Camping Tidikelt and try your luck.

There is an SNTR depot not far from the

Hotel Tidikelt and it may be possible to organise a lift with one of the drivers. They sometimes park overnight by the side of the road which runs from the centre of town to the bus station.

ARAK

Although the gorges around Arak are quite spectacular, the little settlement itself is very humble. It doesn't have the altitude that Tamanrasset has and subsequently is as hot as all hell.

There is a campsite with zeribas, a restaurant where you can get a reasonable meal, and a fuel station.

If you are on the bus it will stop here for a meal break.

TAMANRASSET

Despite the increase in tourism over the years, Tamanrasset (known locally as Tamenghest) is still quite an appealing Touareg town. It now has a population approaching 30,000, although many people have been driven here by the droughts in the Sahel and now live in the bidonville on the far side of the oued.

With an altitude of nearly 1400 metres, it has a climate which stays relatively moderate all year round. Even in mid-summer the temperature rarely gets above 35°C.

The town is the centre of the Hoggar region and, despite the number of Arabs from the north, the Kel Ahaggar Touareg men can be seen all over the place, often riding a camel down the main street.

Tamanrasset is also the place from which to arrange trips up into the Hoggar Mountains to the east, something which should not be missed on any account. If you can't hook up with other travellers with vehicles in the campsite, it is possible to get a group together and hire a vehicle and driver from one of the travel agencies around town.

The town is one of those places where virtually all trans-Saharan travellers stop for a few days to rest up and make repairs to equipment, so at any time there may be a dozen vehicles coming and going each day from the campsite. With such a high turnover

you rarely have to wait longer than a few days for a lift.

If you are heading south, make sure you clear customs on the southern edge of town when you leave. They will scrutinise your currency form (which is handed in at In Guezzam) and check over your gear. Passport control is handled at the border post, 10 km south of In Guezzam.

If you have just arrived from Niger, check with the authorities at the daira (in the military fort), even though you have already been checked at the border.

Information

Tourist Office There is a small syndicat d'initiative in one of the main streets, Ave Emir Abdelkader. It is of little use, but the staff may be able to help if you have a specific enquiry.

Money The only bank which will take travellers' cheques is the Banque Centrale d'Algérie, close to the post office. To change cheques you need to have the original receipt as proof of purchase. It is open from 8.30 am to 1 pm and 4 to 5 pm daily except Friday.

Post & Telecommunications The post office is in between the two main streets. It has a telephone office where it's possible to make international calls, although you may have to wait a while. It's worth noting that in the past the poste restante counter (open all day, in the telephone office) has only held mail for 15 days before returning it.

Market There is a daily market in the late afternoon held on the far side of the oued. As well as limited fruit and vegetables, there are usually a few Touareg from Algeria, Niger and Mali selling jewellery and other traditional items. Much of it is made specifically for the tourist trade but other stuff is genuine.

Foreign Consulates Both Mali and Niger have consulates here. They are next door to each other on the main road out to the campsite, about 500 metres from the centre. See

Top: Main street, Tamanrasset, Algeria (HF)
Bottom: Dunes encroaching on In Salah, Algeria (HF)

Top: Bus in the Algerian Sahara (HF)
Left: Municipality buildings, Timimoun, Algeria (HF)
Right: Ghardaia medina, the M'Zab, Algeria (HF)

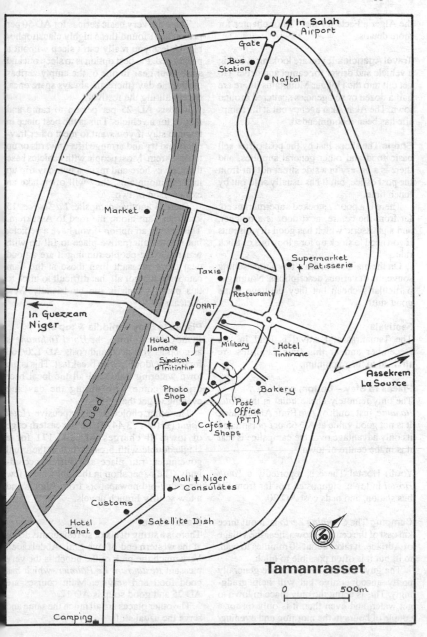

In Salah
Airport

Gate

Bus
Station

Naftal

Market

Supermarket
& Patisserie

Taxis

Restaurants

ONAT

In Guezzam
Niger

Hotel
Ilamane

Military

Hotel
Tinhinane

Syndicat
d'Initintive

Assekrem
La Source

Photo
Shop

Bakery

Post
Office
(PTT)

Cafés &
Shops

Oued

Mali & Niger
Consulates

Customs

Hotel
Tahat

Satellite Dish

Tamanrasset

0   500m

the Algeria Facts for the Visitor chapter for more details.

Travel Agencies If you are looking at hiring a vehicle and driver (or camel and driver) to get out into the Hoggar Mountains, there are half a dozen or so agencies scattered around town. The Akar Akar agency out at the campsite has been recommended.

Shops The shops just by the post office sell basic food and other general supplies, and there is a bakery in a side street not far from the post office, but it has usually sold out by lunch time.

There is a poorly stocked supermarket not far from the centre; next door is a butcher, and a patisserie which has good dry biscuits if you need to stock up for a long bus or truck ride.

On the main street are a few shops selling souvenirs of various descriptions. Nothing is particularly cheap but they do have some good stuff.

Festivals
The Tamanrasset Festival is held in late December and at this time facilities are strained to the maximum.

Places to Stay – bottom end
The only remotely cheap hotel is the *Hotel Ilamane*, just south of Ave Emir Abdelkader. It is not good value at AD 65 per person and its only advantage over the campsites is that it is in the centre of town.

Youth Hostel There is reportedly a *Youth Hostel* in town, signposted not far from the bus station, and beds cost AD 20.

Camping The *Camping Zerib* is about three km east of the centre of town, near the village of Adriane. It takes about 40 minutes to walk to it, but it is often possible to hitch.

The guys running the place are generally pretty uncooperative but will help grudgingly. This is about the only place in town to get water, and even then it is only on for a couple of hours in the morning and evening.

There are very basic zeribas for AD 50 per person but I found these highly claustrophobic. Unless you really can't sleep without a proper bed, the best option is to sleep out and stash your gear in one of the empty zeribas during the day (there are always spare ones, except during the festival).

It costs AD 25 per person to camp and AD 15 for a vehicle. This is the best place in town to stay if you want to meet other travellers and try and arrange lifts onwards or up to Assekrem. Most people with vehicles base themselves here and make a two-day trip up into the mountains; they will often take an extra person or two.

There is another campsite, *La Source*, 15 km from Tam along the road to Assekrem. This is only an option if you have a vehicle, but it is an alternative place to fill up with water and the people running it are a good deal more pleasant than those at the Tam campsite. It's not all that difficult to hitch to this place, which is run by friendly West Africans.

Places to Stay – middle & top end
In the centre of town, the *Hotel Tinhinane* is as good as you need and costs AD 120/160 for a single/double with breakfast. This is the town watering hole, and all the local beer drinkers come here during the day and evening to get their fill.

The other choice is the expensive *Hotel Tahat* (☎ (09) 73 4474), on the eastern edge of town. It charges AD 145/171 for a single/double with breakfast. It is the usual government-run place and suffers accordingly. The paper shop in the lobby has a few three-day-old newspapers from Algiers and a few scruffy French novels.

Places to Eat
There is a string of six or so restaurants down at the western end of Ave Emir Abdelkader. Very much the pick of the bunch is the very pleasant *Restaurant Le Palmier*, which has good food and service. Main courses are AD 25 and good soup is AD 12.

The other places are all much the same and serve the usual stuff.

There is another small place on the north side of the group of shops near the post office. It is just around the back of the Air Algérie office and has a couple of umbrellas outside, where you can sit.

The restaurant of the *Hotel Tinhinane* has a three-course set menu for AD 70 per person.

Getting There & Away

Air The Air Algérie office (☎ (09) 73 4174) is in the group of shops by the post office. The airport is 12 km north of town, off to the left of the main road. Yellow taxis meet all incoming flights and seats cost AD 15 per person for the trip into town. You may have to abandon your bags and grab hold of a door handle when a taxi rolls up, as demand for seats can be high.

There are flights from here to: Adrar (twice weekly, AD 314); Algiers (at least one daily, AD 576); Constantine (weekly, AD 557); Djanet (weekly, AD 191); El Goléa (twice weekly, AD 346); Ghardaia (five times weekly, AD 410); In Guezzam (weekly, AD 240); In Salah (four times weekly, AD 238); Oran (weekly, AD 571); and Ouargla (three times weekly, AD 389).

Bus The bus station is in the northern part of town. It is a 20-minute walk from the centre of town and a solid hour from the campsite. If you arrive late at night, or are heading out early in the morning, it is standard practice to doss down at the station, which is quite safe. It is a modern building but gets very little use. The bus schedule (which differs slightly from time to time) is displayed on a board inside the building.

Make sure you reserve your ticket the day before departure. They usually go on sale at 4 pm but it is worth checking earlier in the day, as things vary and demand is sometimes high.

The main destination is In Salah. There are three departures weekly, on Monday, Wednesday and Saturday at 4 am (5 am in winter). The trip takes a gruelling 19 hours (barring breakdowns) and, for the privilege of having yourself tossed around inside a tin box on a truck chassis, you pay AD 130 and AD 20 for your bag – what a travel bargain!

There is also a weekly departure to In Guezzam (Monday morning) but there is little point in catching this bus, as you still have to get across the border to Agadez. It's better to arrange a lift all the way from Tam.

Locally there are weekly buses to Idelès (Thursday, 9 am) and Silet (Thursday, 11 am).

AROUND TAMANRASSET

Assekrem

Without your own transport, getting out into the Hoggar can be difficult. However, it's worth making the effort to get to Assekrem, 73 km north-east of Tamanrasset by the shorter of the two routes.

The scenery around here is absolutely incredible and a sunrise in the these mountains is an experience you're likely never to forget. Words can't even come close to doing the place justice – get up there and see it for yourself.

Charles de Foucauld, a dedicated Christian who came to the Hoggar early this century, built a hermitage up here in 1910; this is still lived in and maintained by a religious order. The hermitage is on top of the Assekrem plateau and can only be reached on foot. It takes about 30 minutes to walk up from below and it is the place to come for the sunrise.

Places to Stay & Eat It is possible to stay at the refuge below the hermitage but you need to bring all your own food.

Getting There & Away The only way to get up to Assekrem is to get a lift. If you can't strike it lucky at the campsite in Tam, the only other alternative is to hire a 4WD and driver from one of the agencies in Tam. It is not possible to hire a vehicle without a driver.

This is only an option if you have five or six people, as it costs around AD 1500 per day for vehicle and driver. There are sometimes enough backpackers at the campsite to arrange a trip like this, but it may take a few days to organise. If you want extras such as food the agency will charge an additional fee for this – typically about AD 150 per person per day.

If you want to keep the expense to a minimum, it is best to hire a vehicle from about 2 pm for a 24-hour period. The drive up there takes about three hours, so this arrangement makes best use of the time and means you get to see the sunrise.

If you do manage to get out to Assekrem with someone who is going on to Djanet and you want to go back to Tam, you will probably have to spend anything up to a few days in Assekrem waiting for a lift back. You definitely can't walk there, although the agencies will organise trips with camels from Tamanrasset if you want to do it this way.

If you are driving up and have some spare room, you can do the restaurant owner a favour and take him up some water, as he has no regular supply.

IN GUEZZAM

What was a collection of half a dozen huts a few years ago has grown into a tent settlement of about 3000 people today. Unfortunately, most of the people aren't here by choice but, because of the droughts in the Sahel, have gravitated to the nearest place where they are likely to get food.

The town is 416 km south of Tamanrasset and is the last place in Algeria before you cross into Niger. The Algerian border post is 10 km south of In Guezzam, so there is really no need to stop here for long.

This border post used to be the worst in the country, with drunken guards and the like, but these days things are considerably more manageable. This doesn't mean that you won't be searched thoroughly or have your currency form scrutinised closely, but at least you're not likely to get harassed. The morning is the best time to go through. The guards are generally gruff and indifferent, but as long as you are polite, firm and friendly (no need to grovel) there should be no problem. Don't arrive there between noon and 4 pm, as the border is closed and you have to sit it out in the heat without a scrap of shade. They don't even let you go back to In Guezzam.

Places to Stay & Eat

Really the only place is *Le Restaurant des Dunes chez Omar*. Apart from a good collection of Western music, you can get OK food and can stay overnight.

Getting There & Away

Air There is a weekly flight between In Guezzam and Tamanrasset but I can think of no reason to take it.

Bus The same goes for the bus. It leaves Tam on Monday morning and In Guezzam on Tuesday morning for the return journey, but you are far better off arranging a through lift at least as far as Arlit or Agadez from Tamanrasset.

TUNISIA

Facts about the Country

HISTORY SINCE 1830

In Tunisia, the struggle for independence didn't take the violent course that it did in Algeria. The Huseinid ruler Ahmed Bey, who governed from 1837 to 1855, encouraged Westernisation and brought in military and other advisors to this end. In 1861, during the reign of Mohammed Sadiq, a constitution – the first in the Arab world – was proclaimed.

These Western reforms, however, exacted a heavy toll on the country's limited finances, and there was heavy borrowing in the form of high-interest loans from European banks. Proposed higher taxes led to internal revolt, and by 1869 the country was in such a financial shambles that control of its finances was given to an international commission.

The last attempt to hold off European control came in a short-lived effort from 1873 to 1877 by the reformer Khaireddin, but he was forced from office and his plans were scuttled. At the Congress of Berlin in 1878, the major European powers divided up the southern Mediterranean region, and the only challenge to French dominance in Tunisia came from the Italians.

In order to consolidate their position, the French announced in 1881 that Tunisian tribespeople had made incursions into Algeria and that they, the French, would retaliate. Some 30,000 troops were sent into Tunisia, and before long they had occupied Tunis. In 1883 the *bey* (provincial governor) signed the Convention of La Marsa, which gave the French control over Tunisian affairs. The bey was answerable to a French Resident who presided over both domestic and foreign affairs.

Until WW I the protectorate prospered under French rule, although it was at the expense of local interests. Unlike in Algeria, land was not sequestered on any scale, but the best of the fertile land (in the Medjerda Valley and Cap Bon peninsula) passed into European hands. Mineral and phosphate reserves were tapped and a railway network was constructed to service them. Tunisians were totally denied any say in Tunisian affairs, and agitation and resistance wasn't long in coming.

In 1920, the first nationalist political party, the Destour Party, was formed (*destour* means constitution in Arabic; the party was named after the constitution of 1861). Its demands for democratic government, despite being supported by the bey, were ignored by the French, and the nationalist movement lost its way for some years.

In the early 1930s, a young Tunisian lawyer, Habib Bourguiba, led a breakaway movement from the Destour Party. In 1934 he founded the Neo-Destour, which soon totally replaced the old guard of the Destour. Thanks to the tireless efforts and popular appeal of Bourguiba, the party was quick to gain popular support. The French, keen to put down any potential threat, outlawed the party and jailed Bourguiba.

With the fall of France during WW II, the Neo-Destour leaders, who had been imprisoned there, were handed over to the Italians by the Germans. Although they were well treated in Rome, they refused to support Italy.

In 1942 the Germans landed in Tunis in the hope that they could turn back the Allied advances from east and west; the Americans were on the way from Algeria, and the British forces, led by Field Marshal Montgomery, were driving back Rommel's Afrika Korps in Egypt. The campaign in Tunisia raged for six months; only after the loss of over 15,000 men were the allies able to take Bizerte on 7 May 1943.

In the same year the Neo-Destour leaders were finally allowed to return to Tunisia, where a government with Neo-Destour sympathies was formed by Moncef Bey.

When the French resumed control after the war, they were as uncompromising as

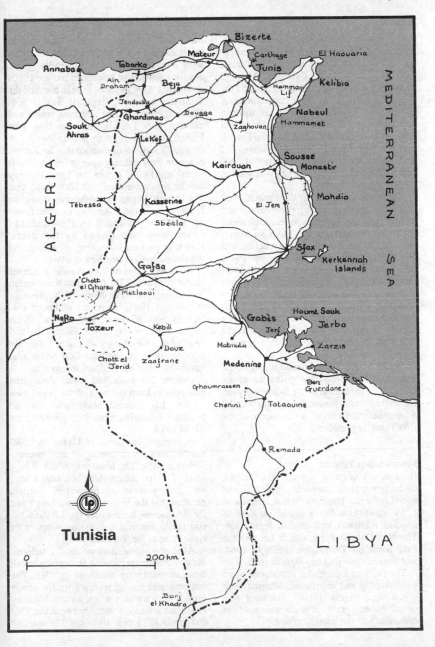

Tunisia

0 _____ 200 km.

ever; the bey was deposed and Bourguiba was forced to flee to Cairo to avoid capture. In the next few years he organised a propaganda campaign aimed at bringing Tunisia into the international limelight. He was extremely successful in this, and by 1951 the French were ready to make concessions. A nationalist government was set up and Bourguiba was allowed to return. No sooner had this been accomplished than the French had a change of mind – Bourguiba was exiled and most of the ministers were arrested. Violence followed, and the country was soon in a state of total disarray.

There was little left for the French to do other than grant complete independence, and in July 1954 the French president announced plans for negotiations for Tunisian autonomy. In 1955 an agreement was reached, and Bourguiba returned to the country and a hero's welcome. The agreement reached was restrictive in the fields of foreign policy and finance, and was condemned by Salah Ben Youssef, former secretary of the Neo-Destour, as a sellout. He attempted to lead an armed insurrection, but Bourguiba was the one with popular support and Ben Youssef soon fled the country.

On 20 March 1956 Tunisia was granted independence, with Bourguiba as prime minister. In the course of the following year, the last bey was deposed, the country became a republic and Bourguiba was declared the first Tunisian president.

Independent Tunisia

Bourguiba was quick to undertake the task of bringing about sweeping political and social reforms. The constitution, passed in 1959, gave him fairly broad powers to appoint ministers and initiate legislation. The Neo-Destour Party, which became the Parti Socialiste Destourien (PSD) in 1964, was the only party of any significance.

The reforms Bourguiba introduced were wide-ranging and impressive. Women were given equal rights, family planning was introduced and great advances were made in education and the legal structure.

In the field of foreign policy, Bourguiba has looked very much to the West, and in particular to France and the USA. Relations with France have been generally good, despite a few major hiccups in the late 1950s and early 1960s. In 1958, France bombed the Tunisian border village of Sakiet Sidi Youssef, claiming that Algerian rebels had crossed into Tunisia and that they (the French) had the right to pursue them. The enraged Tunisians demanded that the French evacuate their military base in Bizerte, but it wasn't until 1961 (when the Tunisian army saw its first action and lost 1000 men), that the French began to withdraw, doing so finally only in 1963. Another incident flared up in 1964, when Tunisia suddenly nationalised land owned by foreigners. France responded by cutting off all aid, but the situation was remedied in 1966.

At home, Ahmed Ben Salah, a former leader of the UGTT (the first trade union federation), had taken charge of the planning ministry in 1961; his policy of forced collectivisation of farms was typical of his radical reforms. By 1969, Bourguiba had decided that the country should be following a more moderate course; Ben Salah was imprisoned and his policies revoked.

Despite his autocratic style, Bourguiba managed to keep the bulk of the population on side; his ill health notwithstanding, the National Assembly made him president for life in 1974.

A curious incident in Gafsa in 1980 resulted in a strengthening of the Tunisian-American link. The town was attacked by a band of armed commandos but, after a brief siege, they were overpowered. Tunisia claimed that the men came from Libya and the Americans, keen to see the Libyans discouraged, became the major supplier of equipment to the Tunisian army.

After promising more political freedoms, the government persuaded Bourguiba to call the first multiparty elections in 1981. The outcome was a total letdown for the newly formed opposition parties, as the National Front (the alliance formed between the TSD and the UGTT) took all of the 136 seats on offer. There were in fact cries of foul play from the opposition.

The bread riots of 1984 were a spontaneous backlash to the announcement that the bread subsidy was being withdrawn. They died out only after about six days, when Bourguiba resumed the subsidy.

As the 1980s progressed, Bourguiba was seen to be more and more out of touch with both the people at home and with Tunisia's position in the Arab world. At home he would build up the career of a possible successor, only to later cut the ground out from under his feet. An example was Prime Minister Rachid Sfar, appointed in July 1986 to replace Mohammed Mzali (who was the scapegoat for the economic crisis in 1986) and deposed only 12 months later. Sfar was replaced by the tough minister for the interior and former general in the armed forces, Zine el-Abidine Ben Ali, who eventually orchestrated the ousting of Bourguiba.

On November 7 1987, a group of doctors assembled by Ben Ali were asked to examine the 83-year-old president, who was, predictably, declared unfit to carry out his duties. It seems that, despite a heart condition, his physical health was not too bad for a man of his age; it was his mental health that was causing the concern.

In ousting Bourguiba, Ben Ali acted on two things: firstly, he had heard that Bourguiba intended to get rid of him; and, more importantly, the appeal of five Muslim radicals, members of the outlawed MTI (Islamic Tendency Movement) who had been sentenced in September, was coming up on November 9. One of these radicals had been given the death sentence and the others heavy jail terms. It is known that Bourguiba was unhappy with this and wanted heavier terms, which went totally against popular opinion within the country. He was in fact becoming less and less the people's leader. As it turned out, the jailed radicals' appeal was upheld and they were retried.

Bourguiba was held for some time in detention in his palace in Carthage before being shunted off to 'retirement' in another palace outside Sfax.

All in all it was a popular coup within the country, and one which many people felt was long overdue, although many also felt that it could have been done with a little more decorum. At any rate it removed the uncertainty which had surrounded Bourguiba's succession for the previous five or so years.

On taking power Ben Ali appointed some new ministers but, significantly, retained the defence minister, indicating that he had made sure the army was on side before he moved against Bourguiba and had kept them informed as to what he was doing.

The downfall of Bourguiba saw the demise of one of the world's great rulers and the longest-serving Third-World leader. Undoubtedly his greatest achievements were the fostering of a strong national identity and the development of a standard of living which puts the country at the top of the pile in the developing world.

In his first few years in office Ben Ali has built on the popularity of his overthrow of Bourguiba by introducing political and economic reforms. The ruling PSD party was renamed the Rassemblement Constitutionel Democratique (RCD) and much 'new blood' was brought in. Political pluralism was legalised, political prisoners released, the State Security Court abolished and police powers of detention limited. Political exiles were invited to return, and many decided that it was now safe to return to Tunisia.

Ben Ali's personal popularity was highlighted in the results of the 1989 presidential elections which saw him re-elected with 99.27% of the vote. Although there was no credible opposition, if there was any amount of bad feeling towards him this would have been reflected in a high protest vote, which wasn't the case.

On the economic front, reforms have mainly involved the lifting of heavy subsidisation of food prices. This has resulted in hefty rises in the price of many foods, and in order to avoid a repetition of the 1984 bread riots, the price of bread remained the same but the loaf size was decreased by 20%. Other reforms in the pipeline include changes in the levels of tax and labour laws, and it's even suggested that the dinar may become a convertible currency.

Tunisia occupies an important position in the Arab world. Since 1979, when Egypt signed a peace treaty with Israel, Tunisia has been home to the Arab League. The PLO has its headquarters just outside Tunis, although these were badly damaged by an Israeli bombing raid in 1985 in retaliation for the killing of three Israelis in Cyprus. In a deplorable incident in 1988 an Israeli hit squad was sent in to assassinate the PLO second-in-command, Khalil Al-Wazir (also known as Abu Jihad), at his home in Sidi Bou Said, as an act of retaliation against the Palestinian uprising in the Occupied Territories.

GEOGRAPHY

The main topographical feature in the north of the country is the Tunisian Dorsale, a range of mountains which runs south-west to north-east and tapers off towards the Gulf of Tunis. These mountains are actually a continuation of both the Algerian Saharan Atlas and the High Atlas mountains of Morocco. The highest mountain (*jebel*) in the country, Jebel Chambi (1544 metres), rises in this range just west of Kasserine, near the Algerian border.

North of this range is the Medjerda Valley, the principal river system in the country, which drains into the Gulf of Tunis. This was the granary of ancient Rome and is still the major grain growing area in the country. The waters of the river are used for irrigation and the generation of hydroelectricity.

Directly south of the range is a 200 to 400-metre-high treeless plain, which drops down to a series of *chott* (salt lakes) before the country gives out completely to desert in the south. Although this is only the very edge of the Sahara, it attracts up to two million tourists to the country each year. Abundant artesian water makes cultivation possible in places, and from these green oases come some of the finest dates in the world.

The sand sea (*erg*) which completely covers the southern tip of Tunisia is the eastern extremity of the Great Eastern Erg

(Grand Erg Oriental), which covers a large area of Algeria.

The country borders on Algeria to the west and Libya to the south-east. The ragged and irregular 1400-km coastline forms the eastern and northern boundaries.

Distances

With an area of 164,000 sq km, Tunisia is by far the smallest of the Maghreb countries; it's about half as big as Italy, or about the same size as Washington State in the USA or Victoria in Australia.

Its long narrow shape means that it measures 750 km from north to south but only 150 km from east to west.

FLORA & FAUNA

The climate largely dictates which plants and animals can exist in any region. With the mild conditions in the north, cork forests flourish, and these are home to many wild boar.

The semi-arid Sahel region in the east-central part of the country is where olives are grown; when you are driving through, the rows upon rows of olive trees seem to stretch on forever. If you fly between Jerba and Tunis in daylight you can see the lines of trees covering enormous areas.

The treeless plains of the south support large areas of esparto grass, which is gathered for use in the production of high-quality paper. It is also woven into donkey-harness straps and reed mats by the local inhabitants.

Further south the vegetation gives way altogether to desert, and, apart from at the occasional oasis, there is barely a single bush or even a blade of grass to be seen. There was widespread hunting for gazelle in the past but fortunately this has been banned – only just in time, as the animals were in danger of extinction.

GOVERNMENT

The 1959 constitution of the Republic of Tunisia gives legislative power to the chamber of deputies, which consists of 141 members elected directly by universal suffrage to a five-year term.

The president has executive power and is the head of both the state and the government. The constitution states that the president must be a Muslim and can serve for no more than three consecutive terms; however, the first president of independent Tunisia, Habib Bourguiba, was elected president for life in 1974 before being ousted in 1987.

Political reforms since the ousting of Bourguiba have seen the legalisation of opposition parties. The ruling party, which holds all 141 seats despite gaining only 80% of the vote in the 1989 elections, is the Rassemblement Constitutionel Democratique (RCD). The main opposition comes from the Islamist organisation known by the Arabic *Hizb Nahda* (Renaissance Party), and the secular party, the Mouvement des Democratiques Socialistes (MDS). The Nahda movement is as yet an unrecognised political party, mainly because many of its leaders served prison sentences during the Bourguiba years, but it fielded many independent candidates in the 1989 elections and they gained 13% of the vote.

Other legalised opposition parties include the previously mentioned Mouvement des Democrates Socialistes (MDS), the Communist Party, the Mouvement de l'Unite Populaire, the Parti Social pour le Progres (PSP) and the Rassemblement Socialiste Progressiste (RSP).

ECONOMY

The mixed Tunisian economy, in which both the public and private sectors participate, relies heavily on tourism and, up until the Gulf crisis in 1990, remittances from nationals working in the Gulf states.

Petrol and petroleum products account for about 25% of exports, but the lack of refining capacity within Tunisia means that most of the country's heavy petroleum needs have to be met with imports. Other important exports include textiles and leather (30%), fertilisers and chemicals, with the main destinations being France, the USA, Italy and Germany. Imports are chiefly food, raw materials and capital goods.

The agricultural sector has become smaller in the last 20 years and now provides work for less than 30% of the workforce; almost 40% of food required has to be imported. Despite the fact that large areas of the south of the country are desert, over 55% of the land is cultivated. The main crops are wheat, barley, maize, sorghum, olives and dates.

Major industries are concentrated in the fields of processing agricultural produce and minerals, including textiles, foodstuffs, cement, steel and phosphate.

The mining industry is also important to the economy and Tunisia is the world's sixth-largest producer of phosphate.

Unemployment is widespread and the situation is exacerbated by the fact that most manufacturing is small scale and most businesses employ no more than five people.

Social Conditions

Living standards are generally good and are considered high by developing-world standards. Per capita GDP is around US$1300.

Education is free and, thanks to the high government spending (typically 25% of total expenditure), the number of schools has increased rapidly since independence. Literacy is fairly high, at about 60% in males and 40% in females. School attendance is not compulsory, but the primary schools especially are well attended. It seems that, no matter which town you are in, at any time during daylight hours there are hundreds of young kids in their school tunics on their way to or from school.

Health care is also free, and low income earners are eligible for extra benefits such as free milk for newborn babies and free school lunches. Although there are still shortages of trained personnel and modern facilities, general health conditions have improved dramatically in the last 20 years. This has led to infectious diseases such as typhoid and diphtheria being brought under control.

The social security system also provides old age and disability pensions, and compensation for sickness and injury.

POPULATION & PEOPLE

The people of Tunisia, who number around eight million, are basically Arab Berber. The vast majority are Muslims, and in fact the non-Muslim population numbers less than 40,000 (down from over 300,000 in the 1950s).

The country has a fairly high growth rate of about 2.5%. Almost half the population is under the age of 15, which places a great strain on social services. Another problem is the population distribution, which varies from over 2000 per sq km in Tunis to less than 10 per sq km in the south.

The Berbers were the original inhabitants of the area, but waves of immigration over the centuries have brought Phoenicians, Jews, Romans, Vandals and Arabs. There was a major influx of Spanish Moors in the 17th century, while over the last 300 years the Ottoman Turks have added their bit to the great ethnic mix.

RELIGION

Islam is the state religion in Tunisia and, with the amount of Westernisation and reform, it is not surprising that it takes a fairly liberal form.

Bourguiba was very keen on liberalisation and it is largely because of this that religious observance has decreased markedly in the last 20 years.

Recently there has been a definite resurgence of religious adherence, particularly among the young and unemployed, in the form of the outlawed Islamic Tendency Movement (MTI). It was partly Bourguiba's firm opposition to *any* activity in this direction which was the catalyst for his ousting in 1987. Since that time the MTI has changed its name to the *Harakat* (Movement) and, more recently, *Hizb Nahda* (Renaissance Party). Although it is no longer outlawed, it was not granted political legitimacy and was unable to contest the 1989 elections.

Ramadan

Ramadan is the ninth month of the Muslim calendar when all Muslims must abstain from eating, drinking, smoking and sex from dawn to dusk. It commemorates the month when Mohammed had the Koran revealed to him; the purpose of the physical deprivation is to strengthen the will and forfeit the body to the spirit.

For the traveller it can be an interesting, although at times frustrating, time to travel. During the day it's often difficult to find a restaurant that's open, although the big hotels which cater to tourists usually function as normal. You should also be discreet about where you drink and smoke – don't do it openly during the day. Probably the biggest advantage during the daytime is that the trains and buses are smoke free!

When the sun goes down things get really busy, and people seem to make up for the daytime inactivity. Restaurants and shops open, and many stay open until well into the night. In all, it's a great contrast to the normal routine when very little happens in towns after about 9 pm.

Minority religious groups include Christians and Jews, and account for about 40,000 people.

Facts for the Visitor

VISAS & EMBASSIES

Nationals of European countries, the USA, Canada and Japan need no visa for a stay of up to three months: you just roll up and get a small stamp in your passport – simple.

Australians and New Zealanders (and anyone else not covered above) do need one-month tourist visas, and these can be obtained wherever Tunisia has diplomatic representation overseas. Even though you can obtain a one-week extendable visa on arrival at any airport (Tunis, Monastir, Jerba), it is strongly recommended that you get a tourist visa before arriving. The extension process is complicated beyond belief and can take anything up to 10 days, during which time you have to remain in Tunis.

If you are entering overland from Algeria you need to be in possession of a visa in advance, although some travellers have obtained them at the land borders, albeit with some difficulty. It's also worth noting that the Tunisian Embassy in Algiers and the consulates in Annaba and Tébessa take *three weeks* to issue tourist visas, so either allow plenty of time or get the visa in Morocco or elsewhere.

Standard one-month tourist visas cost the equivalent of TD 6, while one-week transit visas are TD 3.

Nationals of Israel and South Africa are not allowed to enter the country.

Tunisian Embassies

Visas can be obtained from the following Tunisian diplomatic representatives abroad.

Algeria
11 Rue du Bois de Boulogne, Algiers (☎ 78 1480)
Blvd du 1 Novembre 1954, Annaba (☎ 82 4447/8)
Post Box 280, Tébessa (☎ 97 4480)
Austria
Chegastr 3, 1030 Vienna (☎ 78 6552)

Belgium
278 Ave de Tervuesen, 1150 Brussels (☎ 762 1448)
Canada
515 Oscannor St, Ottawa (☎ 237 0330)
Egypt
26 Rue El Jazirah, Zamalek, Cairo (☎ 69 8940)
France
17 Rue de Lubeck, Paris
3 Blvd d'Athènes, 13001 Marseilles
Germany
Godesberger Allee 103, 53, Bonn 2 (☎ 37 6981)
Italy
7 Via Asmara, Rome (☎ 839 0748)
Piazza Ignazio Florio 24, Palermo (☎ 32 8996)
Jordan
Ave el Aksa, 4th Circle, Amman (☎ 67 4307)
Libya
Rue Bechar El-Ibrahimi, Tripoli (☎ 30 331)
Mauritania
BP 681, Nouakchott (☎ 52 871)
Morocco
6 Ave de Fas, Rabat (☎ 73 0636)
Senegal
Rue el Hadj Seydou, Nourou Tall-Dakar (☎ 31 261)
Spain
Plaza Alonzo Martinez 3, Madrid (☎ 447 3508)
Syria
6 Jaddet Al Chaffi, Damascus (☎ 66 0356)
UK
29 Prince's Gate, London SW7 (☎ (071) 584 8117)
USA
2408 Massachusetts Ave NW, Washington DC 20008 (☎ 234 6644)

Transit Visas

These are available on arrival at Tunis port, the international airports and at the land border posts for TD 3. The visas are valid for one week only, but can be extended (with difficulty).

Visa Extensions

If you are one of the poor unfortunates who has to go through this convoluted process, here's how you go about it.

First of all, wait until about the fourth day

of your one-week visa before even bothering to apply for the extension; they won't entertain your request before that.

Arm yourself with two passport photos, bank receipts showing that you have changed enough money to support yourself during your stay, and a *certificat d'aubergement* from your hotel. This certificate is simply a declaration from the hotel owner stating that you are in fact staying in that hotel. It's a totally meaningless document but without it you cannot get the extension. You need to let the hotel know a couple of days before you need one, as hotel employees won't usually do it and the owner is more often than not somewhere else. If for some reason you can't get one, a simple receipt should be adequate. It's also a good idea to photocopy the bank receipts, so that if you want to exchange dinar back to hard currency when you leave you have some proof of exchange.

The next step is to take all these goodies along to the appropriate office of the Ministry of the Interior, in the main MOI building on Ave Habib Bourguiba, Tunis. The entrance is around the side on Rue Abderrazak. Here you'll be given a form to complete which you hand in along with your passport, upon which you will be told to come along in a couple of days to collect it. These couple of days can turn into a week, as every day when you go back to the office, you will be told 'perhaps tomorrow'. When you go to collect, make sure you buy fiscal stamps to the value of TD 3 in advance. These are available from the Recette des Finances, at 22 Ave de la République, a nondescript office near the beginning of the flyover.

If you are lucky, you will have your extension within three days; mine took 12 and involved an interview (interrogation might be a better word) at the Ministry of the Interior, so be prepared for a wait.

Foreign Embassies in Tunisia

Countries which have diplomatic representation in Tunis include:

Algeria
    136 Rue de la Liberté (☎ 28 3166)
    The Algerian Consulate is currently only issuing tourist visas for residents of Tunisia only.
Australia
    Australian affairs are handled by the Canadian Embassy in Tunis.
Canada
    Rue du Sénégal (☎ 28 6577)
Côte d'Ivoire
    84 Ave Hedi Chaker (☎ 28 3878)
Egypt
    16 Rue Essayouti, El Menzeh (☎ 23 0004)
France
    Place de l'Indépendance, Ave Habib Bourguiba (☎ 24 5700)
Gabon
    29 Ave Charles Nicolte (☎ 78 5720)
Germany
    Ave Jugurtha (☎ 28 1246)
Jordan
    84 Ave Jugurtha (☎ 78 5829)
Libya
    48 Rue du 1 Juin (☎ 78 0866)
Mauritania
    17 Rue Fatima Ennachi (☎ 23 4935)
Morocco
    39 Rue du 1 Juin (☎ 78 0257)
Senegal
    122 Ave de la Liberté (☎ 28 2393)
UK
    5 Place de la Victoire (☎ 24 5100)
USA
    144 Ave de la Liberté (☎ 28 2744)

MONEY

The Tunisian dinar is a nonconvertible currency, and import or export thereof is prohibited. Most major currencies are readily exchanged inside the country, although Australian travellers should be aware that Australian dollars are not accepted.

There is no black market and it is not necessary to declare your foreign currency on arrival.

When leaving the country you can reconvert only up to 30% of the amount you have changed to dinar (up to a limit of TD 100), so hang on to exchange receipts and don't change too much towards the end of your stay. If you don't have any receipts to show you won't be able to reconvert *any* dinar.

Currency

The Tunisian currency is the dinar, which is divided into 1000 millimes. Coins in circulation are 5, 10, 20, 50, 100, 500 millimes and one dinar. Notes in use are 1 (rare), 5, 10 and 20 dinars. The 20 dinar note is too big for everyday use, and even the 10 can be difficult to change.

Exchange Rates

Exchange rates are regulated and so you get the same rate everywhere. Banks charge a standard 351 millimes commission per travellers' cheque, while the larger hotels take slightly more.

US$1	=	TD 0.9584
UK£1	=	TD 1.6585
FFr1	=	TD 0.1671
DM 1	=	TD 0.5681
Y100	=	TD 0.7394
A$1	=	TD 0.7629
NZ$1	=	TD 0.5453
C$1	=	TD 0.8524

Foreign currency is exchangeable only at banks and flash hotels.

Credit Cards

Major credit cards such as Visa, Amex and MasterCard are accepted widely throughout the country at large shops, tourist hotels, car-rental agencies and banks. If you want to get a cash advance you can get only local currency.

Costs

Tunisia is not all that cheap to travel in. Its generally high standard of living and the fact that it is certainly not a Third World country are reflected in the cost of everyday items.

Accommodation costs for an average presentable hotel are around US$10 for a double and US$7 for a single. By the time you add food and transport costs, you are looking at around US$20 to US$25 per day all up.

Obviously you could spend a lot more than this; you could also spend quite a bit less if you are prepared to rough it a bit, staying

in hotels with cold showers (or no shower at all) or youth hostels, and hitching or taking buses rather than trains or louages (shared taxis).

CLIMATE & WHEN TO GO
Climate
Tunisia basically has a Mediterranean climate, which features mild wet winters and hot dry summers. Winds are generally mild and from the west, but at times in summer the sirocco wind can blow in hot and strong from the Sahara for days on end, and the temperature can hover around 40°C in Tunis and even higher in the south.

Rainfall is extremely variable, but the averages range from 1500 mm annually in the north right down to 150 mm (and less) in the south.

When to Go
Summer is the most popular time for visiting Tunisia, mainly because that is the European holiday season, but it is far from being the ideal time to see the country. Even in Tunis the mercury regularly hits 40°C and more, and in the south and interior it is usually hotter. You really have to have a masochistic streak to be able to enjoy trudging around a ruined Roman city getting your brains baked in weather like this.

At this time of year it is sheer madness to try and do anything between about 1 and 4 in the afternoon. Despite the heat, summer is the high season, so it is also the time when transport is stretched to the limit and hotel rooms can be hard to find after noon. Archaeological sites can also be crowded, and, all in all, it's a good time to avoid if at all possible.

The best time of all to visit is in spring, when the north is still green, the south is pleasantly warm and the summer hordes have yet to arrive. Autumn is the next choice, the only drawback being the fact that throughout most of the country the skies can be very hazy, due to the heat and dust build-up over the summer.

Winter can be downright cold and unpleasant in the north. Tunis becomes a cold, rainy and somewhat dreary place, while places up in the hills, such as Ain Draham and Le Kef, often get snow.

The Celsius temperatures in the table called Average Temperatures – Tunisia are annual averages, and in no way indicate how fierce the summer can be (and usually is), especially in the south, nor how cold the winter.

TOURIST OFFICES
The government doesn't put out a great deal of printed information, but does issue some glossy hand-out stuff in various languages.

Local Tourist Offices
The government-run Office National du Tourisme Tunisien has the following offices dotted around the country. The staff are generally helpful but speak little or no English.

Bizerte
    1 Rue de Constantine (☎ (02) 32 897)
Douz
    Rue Farhat Hached (☎ (05) 90 930)
Gabès
    Ave Hedi Chaker (☎ (05) 70 254)
Gafsa
    Place des Piscines Romaines (☎ (06) 21 664)
Hammamet
    Ave Habib Bourguiba (☎ (02) 80 423)
Jerba
    Houmt Souk (☎ (05) 50 016)

Average Temperatures – Tunisia						
	Tunis	*Bizerte*	*Hammamet*	*Sousse*	*Tozeur*	*Jerba*
January	11.1	11.3	11.0	11.2	11.7	12.1
April	15.8	15.4	16.0	16.1	20.1	18.5
July	26.0	25.2	25.5	25.7	32.3	26.5
October	20.4	20.5	20.9	21.3	22.4	23.1
December	12.2	12.4	12.6	12.6	11.5	13.6

Kairouan
    Ave Habib Bourguiba (☎ (07) 21 797)
Monastir
    Rue de l'Independance (☎ (03) 61 960)
Nabeul
    Ave Taieb M'Hiri (☎ (02) 86 737)
Sousse
    1 Ave Habib Bourguiba (☎ (03) 25 157)
Tabarka
    32 Ave Habib Bourguiba (☎ (08) 44 491)
Tozeur
    Ave Abdulkacem Chebbi (☎ (06) 50 503)

There are also quite a few local tourist offices, usually called *syndicats d'initiative*, which have a limited amount of information on a particular area.

Overseas Reps

Overseas offices include:

Austria
    Tunesisches Fremdenverkehrsamt, Landes-gerichstr 22, 1010 Vienna (☎ 52 0208)
France
    Office National du Tourisme Tunisien, 32 Ave de l'Opéra, 75002 Paris (☎ 4742 7267)
Germany
    Fremdenverkehrsamt Tunisien, Am Haupt-bahnhof 6, 6000 Frankfurt (☎ 23 1891)
Holland
    Tunesisch National Verkeersbureau, Leidsestraat 61, 1017 Amsterdam (☎ 22 4971)
Italy
    Ente Nazionale Tunisino Per il Turismo, 10 Via Baracchini, 20123 Milan (☎ 87 1214)
UK
    Tunisian National Tourist Office, 77A Wigmore St, London W1H GLJ (☎ (071) 224 5561)

BUSINESS HOURS & HOLIDAYS
Business Hours
Government Offices & Businesses These are open Monday to Thursday from 8.30 am to 1 pm and 3 to 5.45 pm, and Friday and Saturday from 8.30 am to 1.30 pm. In summer offices do not open in the afternoon at all.

Banks Banking hours are from 8 to 11 am and 2 to 4 pm Monday to Thursday, and 8 to 11 am and 1 to 3 pm Friday. As with the government offices, banks are not open in the afternoons in summer.

In Tunis there are banks which are open outside these hours.

Shops Generally, shops are open Monday to Friday from 8 am to 12.30 pm and 2.30 to 6 pm, and from 8 am to noon on Saturdays. Summer hours are usually 7.30 am to 1 pm. These hours vary slightly from place to place, especially in the south where the weather is more extreme in summer.

Holidays
Public holidays and festivals are primarily religious celebrations, or festivities which mark the anniversary of various events in the creation of the modern state.

As the Gregorian (Western) and Islamic calendars are of different lengths, the Islamic holidays fall 10 days earlier every Western calendar year. For the Islamic holidays see the section in the chapter on Facts about the Region. Ramadan is the main one to watch out for, as for an entire month the opening hours of everything are disrupted.

Other public holidays in Tunisia are:

New Year's Day
    1 January
Independence Day
    20 March
Youth Day
    21 March
Martyrs' Day
    9 April
Labour Day
    1 May
Republic Day
    25 July
Public Holiday
    3 August
Women's Day
    13 August
Evacuation Day
    15 October
Anniversary of Ben Ali's Takeover
    7 November

Some of these holidays, such as Women's Day and Evacuation Day, pass without notice. On others everything comes to a halt, and there is absolutely nothing happening (although transport still runs). On some long weekends such as the Eid al Fitr (celebrating the end of Ramadan) transport is strained, as people return home for the festival.

CULTURAL EVENTS
Local Festivals
There are a number of festivals held at various times throughout the year. Most of them are fairly touristy and the 'folkloric' events are tacky, but they are worth a look if you are in the area. The main ones are:

December/January
>Sahara Festival, Douz. Everything from camel races to traditional marriages.
>Sahara Festival, Tozeur. The Douz festival all over again.

April
>Nefta Festival. Parades and folkloric events.

May
>Monastir Festival

June
>Dougga Festival. Classical performances at the Roman theatre.

July-August
>Carthage Festival. Main cultural event of the year; performances at the Roman theatre.
>El Jem Festival
>Siren Festival, Kerkennah Islands.
>Hammamet Festival. Musical and cultural events.
>Tabarka Festival. Music and theatre, and a coral exhibition.
>Ulysses Festival, Jerba. Strictly for the tourists this one, right down to the Miss Ulysses competition.

August
>Baba Aoussou Festival, Sousse.

October
>Carthage Film Festival (biennial; every other year it is held in Ougadougou!).

POST & TELECOMMUNICATIONS
Post
The Tunisian postal service is a little slow, but you will find that your things do arrive eventually.

Letters from overseas generally arrive in good time (up to a week), but mail can take much longer when going from Tunisia to other countries. Allow up to three weeks for letters to the USA and Australia, somewhat less to Europe. Post Offices in Tunisia can be distinguished by the 'PTT' symbol.

Postal Rates
Airmail letters to Australia and the USA cost 430 mills; slightly less to Europe. Postcards cost 350 mills.

Parcels are not particularly cheap; the rate for a 10-kg parcel to Australia is TD 28.

As well as at post offices, stamps are available from some general stores, major hotels and some newsstands.

Sending Mail
Post office hours are different in summer and winter, and can also vary a bit from town to town. Generally, they are open in summer from 7.30 am to 1.30 pm Monday to Thursday, and 7.30 am to 12.30 pm Friday. In winter the hours are 8 am to 6 pm Monday to Saturday. Summer hours are kept from 1 July until 30 September.

During Ramadan the hours are 8 am to 3 pm Monday to Saturday. The main post office in Tunis is open seven days a week.

Parcel Post
The best place to send parcels from is the parcel post office in Tunis on Ave de la République. You have to take the parcel there

unwrapped so that it can be inspected; if you want to send something surface mail make sure you stress the fact or you may find yourself getting charged for airmail.

There is a separate parcel post office at Bizerte too.

Receiving Mail
Mail can be received at any post office in the country. It should be addressed clearly and, if the clerks will cooperate, get them to check under your given name as well if you think you are missing mail.

Telephones
The phone system is quite sophisticated and functions smoothly. The international telephone office in Tunis is open 24 hours and you can dial direct to most countries. Making an international call from any other city is equally simple. The newer digital payphones are easier to use for international calls as they accept TD 1 coins; the older ones only take half dinar. Calls can also be made from major hotels but these are considerably more expensive.

Local calls cost 100 mills and there are public phones in most hotels and some cafés. The area codes are:

Tunis region	01
Bizerte, Hammamet	02
Nabeul	02
Sousse & Monastir	03
Sfax	04
Gabès & Jerba	05
Tozeur & Gafsa	06
Kairouan	07
Tabarka & Le Kef	08

TIME
Tunisia is one hour ahead of GMT from October to April, and two hours ahead of GMT from May to September.

ELECTRICITY
Most of the country is on 220 volts, but the occasional hotel in Tunis and some of the smaller towns in the south are still on 110 volts. Check before plugging in any appliance. The supply is reliable and uninter-

rupted. Wall plugs are of the two-round-pin variety, as in Europe.

BOOKS
The following are a few books which may help give you a better understanding of the country and its people. If you can read French, you'll find that there is a much greater range of material available in that language than there is in English.

People & Society
The Arabs by Peter Mansfield (Penguin, Harmondsworth) offers an excellent insight into the Arab psyche and is the most accessible text for the newcomer to the topic.

The Koran may seem like a strange recommendation, but it makes interesting reading for those who want to know more about the foundations on which Islam is based.

History
Africa in History by Basil Davidson (Paladin, 1974) is a very readable account of the history of the whole continent by one of the most knowledgeable Africa hands.

General
Salammbô by Gustave Flaubert (Penguin Classics) is really a pretty dreadful book, but this 19th-century novel is set in 3rd-century Carthage. It has a more than adequate quota of sex and violence.

Fountains in the Sand by Norman Douglas (OUP, 1986). This is an entertaining account of Douglas' trip through southwestern Tunisia early this century, so long as you ignore his intolerance of Arabs and everything Tunisian.

Middle East Review, published by World of Information, is a yearly digest of events in the Middle East and North Africa. It goes into a fair amount of detail on the economies and politics of each country, and has some basic tourist information as well.

Bookshops
Unless you want your literary diet to consist of nothing but expensive English newspa-

pers, bring enough books to keep yourself busy. Bookshops, although common, do not stock anything in English.

Maps

The Michelin map *Algeria & Tunisia* (No 172) is the best map of the region and is quite adequate. The Hildebrand's *Travel Map of Tunisia* (No 1-19-1) is much bigger than the Michelin map and gives more detail, but it is weak on place names.

Neither of these maps are available inside the country, but the tourist office in Tunis sometimes has a reasonable map which it gives out free of charge.

MEDIA

Understandably, the media in Tunisia are dominated by the French and Arabic languages. There are no English-language newspapers or broadcasts. However, in the main centres you can buy two-day-old English newspapers. International current affairs magazines such as *Time* and *Newsweek* are readily available from the kiosks in the dividing strip of Ave Habib Bourguiba in Tunis. French newspapers such as *Le Monde* are also widely available.

The French-language papers *La Presse*, *Le Temps* and *Le Renouveau* are the local offerings. Inside its back page *La Presse* has lists of exchange rates, aircraft departures and arrivals, useful phone numbers and air-conditioned bus and train departures.

Arabic daily newspapers include *Es Sabah* and *Al Houria*.

FILM & PHOTOGRAPHY

Name-brand film such as Kodak and Fuji is widely available but don't expect any bargains: it will cost you at least as much as it does at home. There are quick processing labs which can develop any type of print film in all the main towns.

People are often a bit touchy about having their picture taken. Always ask before taking photos of people and respect their decision if they say no.

Islam and photos of women don't go together and, although Tunisia is a relatively liberal country, photographing women is still a no-no in parts of the country. On the other hand, you may well find some people who are more than happy to have their 'mug shot' taken.

ACCOMMODATION

Tunisia is well geared for tourism, and the accommodation available runs the whole gamut from basic Tunisian hotels to five-star luxury resorts. Such resorts are totally isolated from the local communities; they cater to tourists who want to spend time on the beach and not trouble themselves with what the local culture might have to offer.

Camping

At the bottom of the scale there are a few official campsites around the country. Most of them have only basic facilities and charge about TD 2 per person. Campsites apart, it should be possible to camp anywhere as long as you get the permission of the landowner.

On the beaches in the north at Raf Raf and Ghar el Melh, sleeping out on the beach or renting one of the grass huts is the accepted thing. The same applies to the remote beaches of the north coast, although you won't find any grass huts there. In the resort areas of the Cap Bon peninsula and Sousse this would definitely be frowned on.

The official sites are at Nabeul, Hammamet, Hammam Lif, Tozeur and Degache (near Tozeur); the youth hostel just outside Bizerte is also a popular place to camp.

Youth Hostels

There are hostels in just about every major town, but they are almost without exception characterless concrete structures (usually near the local stadium) which have the spartan feel of an army barracks. Three notable exceptions are the hostels at Tunis, Bizerte and Houmt Souk (Jerba).

The usual cost is TD 4 for a bed and the hostels are open all year. For the most part, you can do just as well at one of the local hotels, where you won't have the inconvenience of being out of the town centre.

There are hostels at Ain Draham, Beja,

Bizerte, Gafsa, Houmt Souk, Kelibia, Matmata, Monastir, Nabeul, Tunis, Sfax, Sousse, Tozeur and Zaghouan.

Hotels

Tunisian hotels are generally clean, if a little shabby. Most come under the government's rating system and so have a maximum price that they can charge.

These hotels, rated from one-star through to four-star luxe, must display the tariff by the reception desk, so you can always see what the top price should be. Most hotels stick to these, and in fact, out of season, they often knock the prices down a bit. Often the ratings seem to make no sense at all, as you can find a well-kept one-star place that is far more comfortable than a run-down two-star.

The approximate highest high-season charges for each classification (and they do vary a bit from town to town) are: one-star TD 10/14 for singles/doubles including breakfast (often compulsory); two-star TD 13/20; three-star TD 18/26; four-star TD 30/44; four-star luxe TD 38/56. In the cheaper places, showers often cost about 500 mills extra.

Looking at these prices you may think it's going to be impossible to find a cheap bed, but below the one-star rating there are many unclassified hotels which are more than adequate and often better value than the rated places.

Medina (city) hotels are usually unclassified; they are basic, often with no showers, and you pay for a bed in a shared room. These cost around TD 3 per person and vary from quite good cheap hotels to filthy flophouses. On average you can find a good, clean double room for around TD 8, although in summer, places tend to fill up early and you may have little choice.

In many places, usually two-star and above, breakfast, consisting of French bread, butter, jam and coffee, will be included. Although it will be listed as an optional extra, it is usually incorporated in the cost for the room.

Hammams

Hammams are the modern equivalent of the old Turkish bath and are a great way to relax for an hour or two. Every town has at least one, and the bigger towns have separate ones for men and women, or else there are separate times for each sex. It is usually possible to have a massage as well.

Hammams can also be used for a cheap place to stay, but this is a men-only option. Also, as you can well imagine, they are damp and hot. An added inconvenience is that you have to be out by about 6.30 am, which is when they open.

THINGS TO BUY
Rugs & Carpets

These are amongst the most readily available souvenirs and, although they are not cheap, there are some really beautiful ones for sale. The main carpet-selling centres are Tunis, Kairouan, Tozeur and Jerba.

There are two basic types: knotted carpets and *mergoums* (Berber rugs). The former follow traditional designs and are highly decorative, while the latter are much more functional, more geometric in design and use brighter colours.

The ONAT (Office National de l'Artisanat Tunisien) office inspects all carpets for sale, classifies them by quality and affixes a label and seal on the back of each one.

The different qualities are Ordinary *(Deuxième Choix)*, Fine *(Première Choix)* and Superfine *(Qualité Supérieure)*, and they have up to 40,000, 90,000 and 250,000 knots per sq metre respectively.

Of course there are many carpets for sale which have not been inspected and classified by ONAT, and in these cases you are on your own as far as what you are getting for your money is concerned. The prices will be cheaper but the quality may be suspect – the only safeguard is to know your product.

Pottery

Tunisia has a long connection with the art of pottery, as the Romans were making the stuff here nearly 2000 years ago. The main centre is Nabeul, partly because of the number of tourists that pass through there; Guellala (on Jerba) is another.

Leather

There is plenty of leatherwork for sale in the *souk* (market) in Tunis, and some of it is really fine work. Much of it comes from Morocco, however, and is not all that cheap.

Leatherwork that originates in Tunisia often comes from Kairouan. Articles for sale include traditional pieces such as camel and donkey saddles, waterskins and cartridge pouches, as well as more mundane objects like wallets and belts.

Copper & Brass

Beaten copper and brass items are also popular and are widely available. Beaten plates, ranging in size from saucer to coffee table, make good souvenirs, although transporting the larger ones can be a problem.

A lot of the stuff is mass produced by the shopowners in the souk in Tunis and quality varies enormously.

Jewellery

Arabic jewellery (and particularly gold jewellery) is often too gaudy and ornate for Western tastes, but there are some styles which are attractive.

The Hand of Fatima (daughter of the Prophet) is a traditional Arabic design; it can be found in varying sizes, from small earrings to large neck pendants, and is usually made of silver. In pre-Islamic times this same design represented Baal, the protector of the Carthaginians, and is also known today as the *khomsa*.

Other traditional pieces of jewellery include:

Hedeyed These are finely engraved wide bracelets made of gold or silver.
Kholkal Similar to the hedeyed but worn around the ankle. In Carthaginian times they were a sign of chastity; today they are still a symbol of fidelity and are often part of a bride's dowry.

The quality of pure silver and gold jewellery can be established by the official stamps used

to grade all work. The quality of unstamped items is immediately suspect.

The stamps in use are:

Horse's Head Used to mark all 18-carat gold jewellery; the horse's head is the Carthaginian symbol for money.
Scorpion This is used on all 9-carat gold jewellery.
Grape clusters Used on silver graded at 900 mills per gram.
Negro Head Used on the poorer quality silver graded at 800 mills per gram.

Miscellaneous

Chechias *Chechias* are the small red felt hats worn by Tunisian men, although it is unusual to see young men wearing them these days.

The chechia souk in Tunis is the obvious place to look; you can see the poor blokes making them in sweat-shop conditions.

Quality varies, but an average price is around TD 3.

Straw Goods The rectangular woven straw baskets with patterns on them are practical and cheap. Some are pretty awful, with pictures of camels and 'typical desert scenes' woven into them, but there are plenty of other more simple designs.

Hats and fans are other popular goods. Most of the straw items come from Gabès and Jerba in the south of the country.

Perfume Cheap oil scents are sold everywhere. Bottle sizes range from a tiny five ml for TD 1 up to whopping half litres.

Sand Roses You'll find these for sale all over the country, and in fact all over the entire Maghreb. They are formed of gypsum, which is present in the sand and has been dissolved and then dehydrated many times. When it crystalises, some beautiful patterns are formed.

They are most prominent in the area from Ghardaia in Algeria right through into southern Tunisia, and range in size from about five-cm in diameter up to the size of a large watermelon.

They do make good souvenirs, but unless

you have a vehicle I can't imagine that you would be prepared to cart around a great load of gypsum for days or weeks on end.

Stuffed Camels Well, much as I hate them I have to mention them. It seems that in Arabic desert countries you can tell how well developed the tourist industry is by the number of stuffed camels for sale – Tunisia is way out in front in this field. Every souvenir shop has a selection, ranging from pocket size right up to about one-third full size!

Markets

Town and village life often revolves around the weekly markets. Market day is a good day to be in a town, as it will be far more lively than usual and, apart from the itinerant merchants selling fairly mundane household goods, there will be other local people who have travelled in from the outlying districts.

Some markets have become real tourist traps, and for that reason are crowded and worth avoiding; nevertheless, it is on market days that there is the best selection of stuff for sale. Nabeul is one that fits into this category.

Market days throughout the country are as follows:

Monday	Ain Draham, Houmt Souk, Kairouan and Tataouine
Tuesday	Beja, Ghardimao and Kasserine
Wednesday	Jendouba, Nefta and Sbeitla
Thursday	Douz, Gafsa and Tebersouk
Friday	Mahdia, Mateur, Midoun, Nabeul, Sfax, Tabarka, Zaghouan and Zarzis
Saturday	Ben Guerdane, El Fahs and Monastir
Sunday	El Jem, Hammam Lif and Sousse

Getting There & Away

AIR

To/From Europe

With up to two million tourists arriving every year, Tunisia has three international airports to cater for them: Tunis, Jerba and Monastir.

A large percentage of the flights using the Jerba and Monastir airports are charter flights from Europe. These can be incredibly cheap if you don't mind the restrictions on the tickets, which are usually to do with the minimum and maximum permitted length of stay. The tickets must be bought well in advance, although you can often buy them heavily discounted at the last minute.

The best sources of information are the overseas branches of the Tunisian National Tourist Office, which have lists of all holiday operators.

If you want to fly back to Europe it's going to cost you, as you will have to take a regular scheduled flight. If money is your main consideration, take the ferry to Italy and go overland from there.

One of the cheapest scheduled airlines out of the country is Tunisavia, which flies regularly to Malta. They have agencies in the larger cities in Tunisia. GB Airways has advance purchase tickets to London for

TD 225 return, or from London for UK£180, although these must be purchased 14 days in advance.

Other airlines which serve Tunis include: Aeroflot, Air Algérie, Air France, Egypt Air, GB Airways, Iberia, KLM, Lufthansa, Royal Air Maroc, Royal Jordanian, Sabena, Swissair and Tunis Air.

To/From North America

There are no direct flights between Tunisia and the USA or Canada. The cheapest option is a cheap fare to London and then a charter flight or bucket-shop deal from there.

To/From Australia

As with North America, there are no direct flights to or from Australia, so London is a good transit point.

The most direct route from Tunisia is to fly with Royal Jordanian to Singapore (via Amman) and then fly from there to Australia. A return flight from the Australian east coast to Tunis costs around A$1800, but you may get stuck in Amman for a few days as the connections are not that frequent. Buying the same ticket in Tunisia costs considerably more than buying it in Australia.

To/From Morocco

Royal Air Maroc and Tunis Air fly regularly between the two countries. The standard economy fare is about US$500 return.

LAND

To/From Algeria

There are numerous crossing points between Algeria and Tunisia, not all of them always open. The most popular points are at Babouch (connecting Annaba and Ain Draham), Ghardimao (Jendouba and Souk Ahras), Sakiet Sidi Youssef (Le Kef and Souk Ahras), Bou Chebka (Kasserine and Tébessa) and the desert post between Nefta and El Oued.

الخطوط الجوّيّة التونسيّة

TUNIS AIR

It is quite possible that if you have only travellers' cheques you won't be compelled to change the mandatory AD 1000 when entering Algeria. Instead they will tell you that you have to do it at the first town you get to. Although you could then travel through Algeria without changing at the bank, you run the risk on departure of being forced to change the money, only to have it confiscated straight away. See the Money section in the Algeria Facts for the Visitor chapter for more details.

Bus There is a direct air-conditioned SNTRI bus daily at 6 am from Tunis to Annaba which goes via the border at Babouch. The officials on the Algerian side are polite, you are not compelled to change money (but see the warning in the Algeria Money section) and there is only the most cursory baggage search. The return bus leaves Annaba at 6 am also. You need to book 24 hours in advance at the south bus station in Tunis or at the Annaba bus station. The fare is TD 11.250. This is the easiest way to cross between the two countries. The only drawback is that you have to get on at the point of origin as they don't stop en route to collect passengers.

Train The advantage of crossing by train is that, unlike crossing by bus, you can board en route (in Ghardimao in Tunisia, or Souk Ahras in Algeria) instead of at the point of origin. In summer it can be hellishly hot on the train and it takes a good deal of time to process everyone through customs. Women get preferential treatment.

The daily train is the Trans-Maghreb Express. After years of tense relations between Algeria and Morocco, the recent rapprochement means that it is once again possible to travel all the way from Tunis to Casablanca in Morocco, although changes of train are required in Annaba, Algiers and Oran.

The best bet is to take the train from Jendouba to Annaba (or vice versa), as there is not much in between. It leaves from Tunis daily at noon and from Annaba at 10.15 pm.

See the Morocco Getting There & Away chapter for the full timetable.

The fares (in Tunisian dinar) from Tunis are:

Destination	1st Class	2nd Class
Annaba	12.510	9.280
Constantine	17.960	13.190
Algiers	33.350	24.080
Oran	46.610	33.550
Rabat	74.710	53.670
Casablanca	77.630	55.770

Taxi There are frequent Algerian *louages* (shared taxis) which run between Tunis and various towns in eastern Algeria, including Constantine (TD 25), Annaba, Algiers (TD 40) and Sétif.

Of the local crossing points, the one in the desert between Nefta and El Oued is the most popular. There are a few louages daily from Nefta to the border at Hazoua; alternatively there's a daily bus at 10 am. Hazoua has a café/restaurant where you can stay for TD 2 for the night.

From Hazoua it's a four-km walk to the Algerian post known as Bou Aroua, although there are occasional Algerian louages shuttling back and forth between the two posts. It's an easy border crossing; both posts are staffed by friendly, not unhelpful officials and you should not encounter any hassles crossing in either direction.

From the Algerian side there are irregular louages to El Oued, 90 km away; a seat costs AD 50 or TD 5. If you are coming from Tunisia it is possible to off-load any excess Tunisian dinar with black market moneychangers in El Oued. There is quite a bit of tourist traffic on this road outside the summer months, so hitching shouldn't be too difficult. From Le Kef there are regular louages to the border at Sakiet Sidi Youssef.

To/From Libya
The border crossing between the two countries on the coast at Ras Ajdir is once again open. The only obstacle to entering that country now is getting a tourist visa – virtually impossible.

Libyans have been quick to seize the

opportunity to travel and this south-east corner is now a very busy part of the country. Smuggling is a profitable activity and many things for sale in the market in Sfax and places further south have come from Libya.

SEA
To/From Italy
There are frequent crossings throughout the year between Tunis and the Italian port of Trapani in Sicily. Some boats go on to (or start from) Cagliari in Sardinia and Genoa on the Italian riviera.

In summer the boats are heavily booked, and if you are taking a vehicle it is essential that you book well in advance. If you are on foot you may get on without a booking, but it can be torrid.

The Sicilian and Sardinian services are operated by the Tirrenia Line (see Addresses).

Trapani-Tunis The service from Trapani is weekly. Officially, the boat departs at 9 am on Tuesday, but you'll be lucky if it goes before noon. It arrives in Tunis at 4.30 pm, and the trip costs about US$65. In the other direction, the boat leaves Tunis at 8 pm on Tuesday and arrives in Trapani at 6.30 am on Wednesday.

Cagliari-Tunis This run is actually a continuation of the Trapani to Tunis service. It leaves Cagliari (Sardinia) at 7 pm on Monday, and arrives in Trapani at 6 am on Tuesday, departs Trapani at 9 am Tuesday and arrives in Tunis at 4.30 pm the same day. In the other direction it leaves Tunis at 8 pm on Tuesday, arrives in Trapani at 6.30 am the next day, departs again at 9 pm on Wednesday and arrives in Cagliari at 8.30 am on Thursday.

One-way fares from Cagliari to Tunis are about US$65 to US$140, and from Trapani to Tunis, US$55 to US$125. Cars from Trapani to Tunis cost US$110 to US$155.

Genoa-Tunis The Compagnie Tunisienne de Navigation (CTN) regularly operates a boat between Tunis and Genoa. Service varies between four per month in winter to 11 per month at the height of summer. The one-way fare is TD 56 and the trip takes about 24 hours.

Catania-Tunis From Catania on the southern coast of Sicily CTN operates a weekly car-ferry service. This leaves Catania at 9 pm on Saturday, arriving in Tunis at 3 pm on Sunday.

Departure from Tunis is at 6 pm on Thursday, arriving back in Catania at 6 am on Saturday. This service goes via Valletta in Malta on the way back to Italy.

Trapani-Kelibia From June until September, there is a ferry service three times weekly between Trapani and Kelibia.

To/From France
Marseilles-Tunis This service is also operated by CTN, and is packed in summer; vehicle owners will need to book ahead. There are five services per week in summer, and two in winter. The trip takes 22 hours and the fare is FFr 725 one way, and FFr 1040 return for an adult. For those with vehicles there are often off-season promotional fares available, so for two people and one vehicle it will cost around FFr 4300 return.

Addresses
There are CTN offices in:

Tunisia
> Navitour, 8 Rue d'Alger, Tunis (☎ (02) 24 9500)

Italy
> Tirrenia Line, Ufficio Passeggeri, Ponte Colombo, Genoa 16100 (☎ 25 8041)
> Molo Angiono, 80100 Naples, (☎ 31 2181)

France
> SNCM, 61 Blvd des Dames, 13002 Marseilles (☎ 9156 3200)

Germany
> Karl Geuther GmbH, Heinrichstr 9, Frankfurt 6000 (☎ 730 4711)

UK
> Continental Shipping, 179 Piccadilly, London W1V 9DB (☎ (071) 491 4968)

There are Tirrenia Line offices in:

Tunisia
122 Rue de Yougoslavie, Tunis (☎ 24 2775)

Italy
Via Roma 385, Palermo (☎ 58 5733)
Corso Italia 52, Trapani
Stazione Marittima, Molo Angiono, Naples (☎ 31 2181)
Agenave, Via Campidano 1, Cagliari, Sardinia (☎ 66 6065)

France
SNCM, 12 Rue Godot de Mauroy, Paris 75009 (☎ 4266 6019)

Germany
Karl Geuther GmbH, Heinrichstr 9, Frankfurt 6000 (☎ 730 4711)

Switzerland
Voyages Melia, 17 Rue de Chantepoulet, Geneva 1201 (☎ 31 7174)

Getting Around

The transport network is fairly well developed and, with the short distances, just about every town in the country has daily connections of some sort with Tunis.

For most of the year there is ample public transport to meet the demand. However, in the summer months, particularly August and September, and during public holidays, there are many more people travelling, both locals and tourists, and competition for seats is high. At these times booking in advance where possible is highly recommended.

AIR
Being such a small country there is very little call for a domestic air network, but Tunis Air does operate the following services: Tunis to Jerba (at least one per day; TD 22 one way); Tunis to Tozeur (Thursday and Friday); Tunis to Monastir (Monday and Thursday), Monastir to Jerba (Tuesday, Friday and Saturday); and Tozeur to Jerba (Monday and Tuesday).

BUS
SNTRI Bus
The national bus company operates daily air-conditioned buses to just about every town in the country. To the smaller places there is only one departure per day, while to major places there are three or four. The green-and-yellow buses run pretty much to schedule, are fast, comfortable and are not too expensive. For long-distance travel, they are the way to go.

In summer many of the departures are at night to avoid the heat of the day, so if you want to see something of the country you are travelling through, you will either have to hitch, or go by train, louage, or local bus.

Booking in advance, especially when leaving from Tunis, is advisable, particularly in the summer months.

All buses originating or terminating in Tunis stop en route to pick up and set down passengers, so you don't have to be going all the way to or from Tunis to use them. If you want to pick one up en route, however, there is no guarantee that seats will be available.

For intercity bus timetables, see the Getting There & Away sections for individual towns and cities in Tunisia.

Regional Buses
In addition to the national company, there are regional bus companies which operate services in a particular region, to other nearby cities just outside the region and often to Tunis as well.

The buses are reliable enough but are often getting on a bit, are slow and are never air-conditioned. Coverage of routes is good and is enough to meet demand most of the time. Booking in advance is not necessary and, in fact, just finding out when buses actually leave can be a major exercise in persistence, as you'll often get conflicting answers. The best you can hope for is that you will be able to confirm that there will be at least one bus sometime that day. Most depots do not have timetables displayed. Louages are usually a better bet but are a good deal more expensive.

TRAIN
The rail network is not all that well developed, and the services are often slow and inconvenient. The exception is the coastal route from Tunis to Sfax and Gabès, where there are frequent air-conditioned express services going via Sousse. To the south-west, a line goes to Tozeur, but passenger services have been discontinued and now go only as far as Metlaoui.

Passenger services run from Tunis to Gabès, Ghardimao, Le Kef, Sfax, Sousse (Monastir and Mahdia) and Tozeur. There are quite a few other lines in the country but they are either obsolete or carry freight services only.

Train fares are generally slightly more than what you would pay for a bus, and on the air-conditioned services you pay a supplement which hikes up the cost. Demand for seats is high during the summer, so book in advance if possible.

Train schedules are listed under the Getting There & Away sections for individual towns.

TAXI

Louages are long-distance taxis, many of them old, white Peugeot 404 station wagons with an extra seat in the back. The newer ones are Peugeot 504 or 505 wagons, usually with a distinctive red stripe. They all take five passengers and leave when full. They are the fastest way to get around, as it never takes long for one to fill up, and they are generally quite comfortable as the five-person limit is always adhered to.

The louage 'station' in most towns is usually just a convenient gathering point – a vacant lot or other open space – close to the town centre. In Tunis there are two main ones, both opposite the respective bus stations. If you are asking locals for directions to the louage station (or anywhere else for that matter) always get a second (and even third) opinion, as it's quite possible you'll inadvertently be led astray.

The louages themselves are instantly recognisable by their roof racks with white identification signs on the front and back. These have a town name on them – in Arabic or English or both – but, unfortunately, they do not tell you where the vehicle is going – just where it's licensed.

At certain times, particularly during the summer, public transport is in high demand and competition for seats on louages can be fierce. You may find it necessary to be fairly ruthless when it comes to the battle for a seat or you will simply not get on. Fortunately, this situation does not arise that often.

BOAT

There are two regular scheduled ferry services in the country. The first connects Sfax with the Kerkennah Islands, which lie about 25 km off the coast. In summer there are five crossings daily, dropping to four in winter. The trip takes 1½ hours and is free for passengers without vehicles. If you have a car it will cost TD 4.500. If you are taking a vehicle across you need to get in the queue well before the first departure at 7.30 am to be assured of getting across that morning.

The second service runs from Jorf on the mainland to Ajim on the island of Jerba. The crossing takes only a few minutes and the ferries run throughout the day and night.

CAR

Tunisia's roads are mostly excellent and are tar surfaced. The minor roads in the north are usually just a single narrow strip of bitumen.

In the south there are more unsurfaced roads but these are usually easily negotiated. The worst road you are likely to encounter is the one from Matmata direct to Medenine; though people will tell you it's for 4WDs only, it can be negotiated with caution in even the small Fiats and Citroens that the car rental companies have. Everywhere else the roads are surfaced.

Tunisian drivers are generally well behaved, and drive fairly safely and predictably. For someone used to driving in Europe the worst thing is not the cars but the thousands of moped riders who weave suicidally in and out of the traffic, and the pedestrians who think that it is their inalienable right to walk on the road regardless of traffic conditions. Don't expect them to move, even when it is blindingly obvious that they are a hazard to everyone, especially themselves.

Car Rental

Hire cars can be a great way to see the country in a bit more detail, but unless you have a fat wallet or are part of a small group they're not a realistic option in Tunisia. All the major international operators have offices in the larger towns. Rental conditions are fairly straightforward. If you are paying by cash, a deposit of roughly the equivalent of the rental is required. Credit cards don't have the same restriction.

Typical rental charges for the smallest cars

(Renault 4) are about TD 15 per day plus 170 mills per km. It is cheaper to take an unlimited-km deal, which works out to around TD 300 per week and includes insurance and the mandatory government tax of 17%. With the price of fuel being set at 490 mills per litre the costs mount up.

In summer, particularly in Jerba and Tunis, it's almost impossible to get a car straight away. You may have to wait up to a week unless you are prepared to take a larger and more expensive model. Book as early as possible and check with the company every day to make sure that they don't forget your booking, as this does happen. Out of season, when things are much quieter, you can easily get a small car and it is even sometimes possible to bargain a bit on the rates, especially if you are paying cash.

When you hire the car make sure there is an accident report form with the car's papers. If you have an accident while driving a hire car, both parties involved must complete the form. If the form is not completed, you may be liable for the costs, regardless of whether you have paid for insurance or not.

There are military checkpoints all over the country; although officials are not too bothered with checking foreigners, make sure you have your passport handy at all times.

MOTORCYCLE

The short distances and fair road conditions make motorcycling an ideal way of making the most of Tunisia. Unfortunately, unless you bring your own motorbike you won't be enjoying it, as there is no motorcycle rental in the country.

It is possible, however, to rent mopeds, but only on Jerba. This is by far the best way to see the island, and is affordable at TD 10 for a half day (six hours) or TD 15 for a full day. There is no insurance or licensing of any sort so you have to ride to survive.

If you are bringing your own motorbike make sure you are carrying some basic spare parts. These are virtually impossible to find within the country, as people just don't own motorbikes in Tunisia.

BICYCLE

Cycling is also an excellent way to see the country. In the height of summer it would be uncomfortably hot and winter is bleak, especially in the north, but for the rest of the year conditions are ideal. It's also possible to put a bike on the train if you want to skip a long stretch or get yourself back to Tunis.

There are a few places where bicycle rental is possible and you pay about TD 4 per day. A lot of the bikes are horrible old rattlers that leave you tired and sore at the end of the day. Where possible, check the bikes available for the best one and make sure that the brakes work. The locals are only really concerned that the bike goes and aren't too bothered about how to stop it. Maintenance is done on a very casual basis – when something stuffs up it gets patched up, but nothing is done that might prevent the thing from failing in the first place.

Where there is no setup for renting bikes, it is worth asking at one of the many local bike repair shops in each town to see if they will rent you one for a few hours – they often will.

HITCHING

Hitching is a definite possibility for one person but is more difficult (though not impossible) for two. Women attempting to hitch without a male companion may encounter harassment.

Conditions for hitching vary throughout

the country. The south is easiest as there is a great deal more tourist traffic – either people who hire cars in Jerba or overlanders heading for Tozeur and the Sahara. You shouldn't have to wait more than a couple of hours for a lift. In the north people seem less inclined to pick up hitchers, particularly in the summer when there are so many tourists in the country.

Between small towns, Peugeot 404 pickups are the usual means of transport and hitching on these is standard practice, although you may well be asked to pay something. If in doubt, check before you get in as to whether the driver expects payment or not, and try to establish what the locals are paying if you think you are being ripped off.

Tunis

Despite the claims made in the tourist literature, Tunis is not a wildly exciting city. The medina is only mildly interesting, and the French *ville nouvelle* (new city) is plain and functional in the extreme with few redeeming features. It is the places surrounding the city, rather than Tunis itself, which are interesting. As far as capital cities go, however, Tunis has an easy-going, unhurried air about it. It is quite easy to spend a few pleasant days here wandering in the medina, exploring the nearby ruins of Carthage and sitting on the beaches.

Tunis is many people's first introduction to Africa and the Arabs, and in this respect it is an easy place to make the adjustment from West to East. In fact, wandering around the new city, it is hard to tell that you are in a Muslim country, let alone in Africa. Islam takes a fairly liberal form in Tunisia, and the capital leads the way as far as Western trends are concerned.

History

With Carthage as a neighbour, Tunis remained in the background for centuries. In fact it wasn't until the Aghlabid ruler Ibrahim Ahmed I made Tunis his residence and built the Great Mosque there that it took on any significance.

Its glory was shortlived, for the Fatimids chose Mahdia as their capital in the 10th century. However, the ravages of the Beni Hilal invasion in the 11th century left Tunis untouched and saw it once again become the capital.

The period of Hafsid rule and the following two centuries were the golden age of Tunis: souks and *medersas* (theological colleges) were built, trade with Europe flourished and one of the great Islamic universities, the Zitouna Mosque, was established in the heart of the medina.

Until the time of the French protectorate, the medina remained very much the centre of things. However, when the French arrived they wasted no time in stamping their influence on the place by building a ville nouvelle directly to the east of the medina.

This new city, laid out on a grid, is today very much the heart of Tunis; it has a distinctly European feel with its wide main boulevard, street cafés and buildings complete with cast-iron balconies and wooden shutters.

Orientation

The city lies at the western end of the shallow and often smelly Lake of Tunis, which opens to the sea at La Goulette (the gullet). This is the first of a string of beach suburbs which stretch away to the north and it's here that the city's port is located. This coast area includes the ruins of Carthage and the picturesque coastal suburb of Sidi Bou Said (both dealt with in the Around Tunis section).

The lake itself is certainly not a thing of beauty and pollution is an increasing problem. However, in November there are often small flocks of pink flamingos on the edge of the causeway. This causeway carries both motor vehicles and the light-rail TGM line, and runs clear across the centre of the lake. It connects the beach suburbs, Carthage and the port with the centre of the ville nouvelle, the focus of which is the wide, tree-lined Ave Habib Bourguiba with its shady central paved strip.

The ville nouvelle contains all the major banks, department stores and administrative services. Virtually all the mid-range hotels are concentrated in the streets to the south of Ave Habib Bourguiba, and it's here also that you'll find the railway station, south bus station and the main louage station. Most of these streets are one way only, and it can be very frustrating getting to where you want to be if you are driving.

At the western end of Ave Habib Bourguiba is the Place de la Victoire and the entrance to the medina, where you'll find the cheap hotels, souvenir shops and points of interest. The airport is only eight km to the north-east.

Information

Tourist Office The tourist office (☎ 34 1077) is on Ave Habib Bourguiba, at Place 7 Novembre with its large roundabout and clocktower. This is the head office of the tourist authority, but the staff have only a limited amount of printed information, are none too clued up about things in Tunis and do not speak English. Getting information out of them can be like pulling teeth. The printed information in English is all of the glossy brochure type, full of flowery descriptions of places of interest. They do, however, have a good hand-out map of Tunis.

The office is open from 8 am to 1.30 pm Monday to Saturday in summer, and 8 am to noon and 3 to 6 pm in winter. It's closed Sundays and public holidays.

There is another branch of the tourist office at the railway station, which hands out train timetables among other things; yet another branch can be found on the mezzanine level at the airport.

Money There are branches of the major banks along Ave Habib Bourguiba, most of which are open longer than normal hours. The branch of the STB next to the Africa Hotel is one such bank.

There is another branch of the STB at the airport inside the arrivals hall, before you clear customs, which is open to meet incoming flights; however, if you arrive late at night you will probably have to wait for someone to come and open it up.

American Express is represented by Carthage Tours (☎ 25 4605) at 59 Ave Habib Bourguiba. Thomas Cook is represented by Tunisienne de Tourisme (☎ 34 2710), 45 Ave Habib Bourguiba.

Post & Telecommunications The main post office is the cavernous old building on Rue Charles de Gaulle, between Rue d'Espagne and Rue d'Angleterre. The poste restante counter is efficient and well organised. Postage stamps can often be bought from the small booths just inside the doors, which saves queuing with the mobs.

The post office is open in summer from 7.30 am to 12.30 pm and 5 to 7 pm Monday to Thursday, 7.30 am to 1.30 pm Friday and Saturday, and 9 to 11 am on Sunday.

The telecommunications office is in the same building as the post office, but the entrance is around the other side on Rue Jamel Abdelnasser.

It is open 24 hours and, although it can be crowded at times, making international calls is straightforward. You can dial direct to most countries.

The telephone area code for Tunis is 01.

Foreign Embassies & Consulates Tunis is a good place to pick up visas, as most countries in West Africa are represented here. The embassy area is up around the northern end of Ave de la Liberté. Buses No 5 and 35 go along the parallel Rue de Palestine, or a taxi costs about 500 mills from Ave Habib Bourguiba.

The Algerian Consulate is currently issuing tourist visas for residents of Tunisia only. This is a major pain in the area and means you'll have to plan ahead and get a visa before arriving in Tunisia. The consulate is open from 8.30 to 11.30 am Monday to Saturday. For a full list of countries which have diplomatic representation here see the Facts for the Visitor chapter for Tunisia.

Bookshops There are very few books available in English. The small shop in the lobby of the Africa Hotel has a selection of glossy coffee-table books on the country. If that's what you are interested in, check the stalls in the centre of Ave Habib Bourguiba, as they often have the same books for much less. These stalls also stock day-old English daily newspapers (the *Times*, the *Guardian*, the *Sun* and the *Sunday Times* to name a few) as well as *Time* and *Newsweek*. They also sell Italian, German and French newspapers.

For French books and some English classics, there are a couple of shops on the north

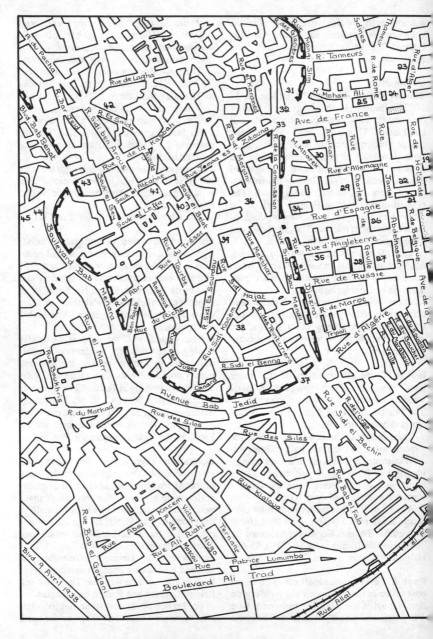

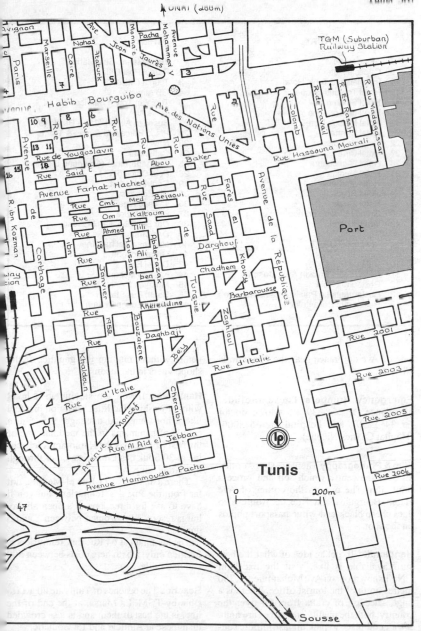

TGM (Suburban) Railway Station

Port

Tunis

0   200m

Sousse

UNAT (280m)

PLACES TO STAY		OTHER	
8	Africa Hotel	1	Tunis Marine Bus Station
9	Capitole Hotel	2	Parcel Post Office
14	International Tunis Hotel	3	Tourist Office
15	Hotel Transatlantique	4	GB Airways
16	Hotel Salammbô	5	Tunisian Travel Services
17	Hotel de Bretagne	6	Tunis Air
19	Hotel Maison Doree	7	Buses to Airport (35) & Bardo (3)
21	Hotel Central	20	Place Barcelona Buses & Trams
22	Hotel de Suisse	23	Navitour
27	Hotel Cirta	24	Cathedral
28	Hotel l'Agriculture	25	Carthage Tours (American Express)
31	Hotel Medina	26	Post Office (PTT)
33	Hotel Marhaba	29	Central Market
34	Hotel Royal	32	UK Embassy
35	Hotel Zarzis	36	Taxis to Algeria
30	Grand Hotel de France	37	Bab Al Jazira
42	Youth Hostel	38	Dar Ben Abdallah Museum
		39	Dar Othman
	PLACES TO EAT	40	Hamman Kachachine
		41	Great Mosque
10	Café de Paris	43	Dar el Bey
11	Restaurants Erriadh & Le Cosmos	44	Kasbah Mosque
12	Restaurant Abid	45	Museum 9 April
13	Restaurants Le Palais & Carcassonne	46	South Bus Station
18	Restaurant Bella Italiana	47	Main Louage Station

side of Ave de France near the Place de la Victoire.

Emergency Numbers These include: ambulance (☎ 24 5339, 25 6467); doctor (☎ 34 1250); and hospital (☎ 66 3000) (Hôpital Charles Nicolle).

Film & Photography There are shops dotted all over the centre which sell and process print film. The one on the corner of Ave Habib Bourguiba and Rue de Rome also does cheap black-and-white passport photos on the spot.

Handicrafts To get an idea of what the best stuff available is like, visit the excellent ONAT showroom on Ave Mohammed V, 200 metres north of the tourist office. There is a huge selection of crafts from all over the country; both the quality and prices are high. It's a good place to pick up last-minute sou-venirs without running the gauntlet of the shopowners in the medina.

Hammams If you are staying in a hotel without washing facilities, or if you just feel like a hot sauna and massage, there are a couple of hammams in the medina. One of the best (for men) is the Hammam Kachachine at 30 Souk des Librairies; enter through the barber shop.

There's another at 11 Rue el-Methira, not far from the Rue des Teinturiers, but you'll have to ask for directions. It's open all day but is reserved for women between 1 and 3 pm.

The hammam at 64 Rue des Teinturiers is for men only; a bath here costs between 500 and 650 mills.

Beaches The beaches of Tunis are all accessible by TGM. La Marsa, at the end of the line, is the best of them and is less crowded than those at Amilcar and La Goulette.

Medina

The medina in Tunis certainly doesn't compare with those in Cairo or Fès, but then again it is a whole lot more manageable and hassle free. If you have just come from Europe it is the ideal place to get a feel for the way of life, as medinas, with their mosques, cafés and hammams, are the focal points of any Arab city.

With the building of the ville nouvelle by the French on reclaimed land by the east gate early this century, the medina lost its importance as the centre of the city. A lot of what remains would also go, if it weren't for the thousands of tourists who pour through here each summer.

The most usual entry is through (or around) the old Porte de France gate at the end of Ave de France. In this paved square, Place de la Victoire, is a small signboard with a detailed map of the medina, and this has a 'Circuit Touristique' walk marked on it. The walk is also marked on the streets in the medina itself – just keep an eye out for the small orange signs.

Place de la Victoire is also something of an assembly point in the evenings; there are two roads which lead off in a 'V' to the heart of the medina and the Great Mosque. The one to the right, Rue de la Kasbah, is of little interest but is lined fairly solidly with shops catering to all tourist tastes. The street to the left, Rue Jemaa es Zitouna, is the one along which most tourists get led into the medina, and so contains the bulk of the souvenir shops and the most aggressive storekeepers (although really it's fairly low-key). If you just want to get an idea of prices, or have to do a bit of last-minute shopping, this is the place to do it. If you are going to other parts of the country you can buy the same stuff for quite a bit less elsewhere.

When visiting the places of interest within the medina, it's possible to buy a multiple ticket for TD 1 at either the Great Mosque or the Dar Ben Abdallah Museum. This ticket gives entry to these two sites as well as Dar Othman (an old palace in the process of restoration and slated to become another museum) and the Medersa Soulimanya (an old Islamic college in the medina which you can wander into).

Great Mosque Rue Jemaa es Zitouna eventually comes out at the entrance to the Great Mosque. Built by the Aghlabids in the 9th century, it was an important centre of theological study right up to the 1950s. Today it is just an ordinary mosque, and non-Muslims are allowed in as far as the courtyard between 8 am and noon daily, except Friday; modest dress is compulsory.

Souks The street to the left of the Great Mosque, the Souk des Librairies, has several medersas (old Islamic colleges). Through the barber shop at No 30 is the fairly clean and spacious Hammam Kachachine (men only).

To the right of the Great Mosque are more souks named after the main business activity which used to be carried on there. To a certain extent these names are still appropriate, but the medina is gradually decreasing in importance as the commercial area.

One of the most interesting souks is the Souk des Chechias, where you can see the traditional red felt hats being made. They are now being produced in various other lairy colours for the tourist trade. This souk runs between Rue Sidi ben Arous and Souk el Bey, just to the right and behind the Great Mosque.

Dar el Bey & Kasbah Mosque The prime minister's office is now housed in the Dar el Bey, a former palace guesthouse on Souk el Bey. The guards are a real sight in their fancy red uniforms.

The Dar el Bey is on the western edge of the medina at the Place de la Kasbah, and on the rise above this stood the kasbah; this is now an enormous open square, beautifully paved with local granite. The Kasbah Mosque here dates from the 13th century. The call to prayer is signalled by a white flag hung from the pole on the minaret. You have to be quick to spot it as they hang it out for only a minute or two.

Museum 9 April Just beyond the Kasbah Mosque is the Museum 9 April, which is housed in an old prison where Bourguiba was once interned for a while. It is full of photos and other memorabilia related to the fight for independence. Unfortunately, what could be an interesting display is rendered virtually meaningless to non-Arabic speaking (and reading) people, although the tiny cells speak for themselves.

Rue des Teinturiers & Dar Ben Abdallah Museum Back at the bottom of the medina the Rue des Teinturiers, one of the main thoroughfares, is off to the left of Rue Jemaa es Zitouna; it takes you to the southern gate, Bab Al Jazira. Along its length are a few points of interest. The street itself is named after the dyers who used to carry on their business here. There are a few still left in a couple of small alleys leading off to the right of the street about halfway along.

Close by, and signposted through an archway off Rue des Teinturiers, is the old deylical palace, Dar Othman. (*Dey* was the title given to the commanders of Turkish janissaries.) Built by Othman Dey at the beginning of the 17th century, the palace is an excellent example of period architecture. It is currently undergoing restoration but no-one seems to mind if you wander in and have a mosey around.

One of the finest sights in the old city, the Dar Ben Abdallah Museum, is signposted off the Rue des Teinturiers along Rue Sidi Kacem. Once an old palace, it now houses a collection of traditional costumes and everyday items. The building itself is probably of more interest: it has the usual highly ornate entrance way leading to the marble courtyard complete with fountains and sculptures. In one room is a very detailed map of the medina with all the hammams shown on it. Exactly why it is there I don't know, but it can be handy to know the location of the hammam nearest to your hotel if you are staying in a medina cheapie without showers. The museum is open Monday to Saturday from 9.30 am to 4.30 pm; entry is TD 1.

At Bab Jedid the street opens out onto the busy Place Bab Al Jazira. This section of the old city has a more Arab feel to it than most, probably because it is just left to get on with things and doesn't have a constant parade of tourists through it.

Ville Nouvelle

There are very few points of interest in the ville nouvelle. The only unusual building is the cathedral on Ave Habib Bourguiba, and that is remarkable only for its ugliness. It was built by the French in 1882.

The streets are lined with French buildings complete with louvre windows and balconies with wrought-iron railings. This gives the whole place a very European air, which is heightened by the numerous patisseries selling all manner of both sweet and savoury pastries, and the pavement cafés.

Bardo Museum

The best museum in the country, the Bardo is in an outer suburb to the west of the medina and is housed in an old palace set in a large garden. Even if you are normally bored shitless by museums, you'll be missing out badly if you don't pay at least a brief visit to the Bardo. It is organised in sections which cover the Carthaginian, Roman, Palaeo-Christian and Arab-Islamic eras.

The most interesting and by far the most impressive display is that of mosaics from the Roman era. It is no exaggeration to say that the Bardo has one of the finest collections anywhere in the world, and just when you think you have seen the best, another room reveals something bigger and better. There are so many mosaics, in fact, that they are overwhelming, and excellent pieces that would stand out on their own elsewhere get lost in the floor-to-ceiling displays. It is worth making a couple of half-day trips here if you are keen, rather than trying to do it all in one hit and becoming so saturated that it is hard to appreciate yet another mosaic.

The best mosaics include the one of the poet Virgil flanked by the muses of literature and drama (room 15) and that of the monumental Triumph of Neptune (room 10). The statues in room 6 from Bulla Regia are also worth a look.

Not to be missed is the haul from the wreck of a boat which came to grief off the coast at Mahdia in the 1st century BC. It was carrying a load of marble and bronze statuary, and this adds some welcome variety to the museum. The exhibits are displayed in rooms 17 to 22.

The Islamic section would be more interesting were it not for the fact that it is totally overshadowed and outclassed by the other exhibits.

The Bardo is open from 9.30 am to 4.30 pm Tuesday to Saturday; the only public holiday on which it is not open is the Eid festival at the end of Ramadan. Entry is TD 1 and there is a further charge of TD 1 if you want to take photos. To get there, take a No 3 bus from opposite the Africa Hotel, or a No 4 *metro leger* (tram). Both terminate right opposite the museum grounds, but the entrance is a couple of hundred metres further on and around the corner to the right.

Places to Stay

All hotels display a chart, both at reception and on the back of the door in the rooms, listing the maximum price they can charge. In the off season the prices are definitely negotiable, but in summer, just finding an empty room can be a major job if you are searching late in the day.

Places to Stay – bottom end

The real cheapies are either in the medina or very close to it. Most are extremely basic and often have no shower. This isn't really a problem, as there are a number of hammams dotted around.

On Rue de la Kasbah, which enters the medina near the UK Embassy at Place de la Victoire, there are a couple of hotels on the left after about 50 metres. They are both typical, basic Tunisian hostelries and are not recommended for women alone. Expect to pay about TD 2.500 for a bed in a shared room. The first is the *Hotel le Soleil* (☎ 25 4706) at No 32, and the other is the *Hotel*

Baghdad, a couple of doors away. The Soleil is marginally the better of the two.

In the new city, just on the edge of the medina, is the *Hotel Royal* (☎ 24 2780), at 19 Rue d'Espagne. One street to the south, the *Hotel Zarzis* (☎ 24 8031) is at 30 Rue d'Angleterre. The Zarzis charges TD 5 for a double room and there are (free) cold showers; the Royal is the same at TD 3/5, plus 500 mills for a hot shower.

The *Hotel Medina* (☎ 25 5056) is on Place de la Victoire at the entrance to the medina. It is basic but clean enough and doubles cost TD 7.500; hot showers are 500 mills. Unlike a lot of the cheapies, it has a few windows and doesn't get quite as stuffy in summer, although it is fairly noisy. The *Hotel Marhaba* (☎ 34 3118) is on the opposite side of the square at 5 Rue de la Commission. It has similar prices to the Hotel Medina.

In the new city, not far from the railway station, is the *Hotel de Bretagne* (☎ 24 2146), at 7 Rue de Grèce. It is quite OK; rooms have a washbasin and cost TD 5.500/6.500 for a single/double; showers are 600 mills.

One of the best places is the *Hotel Cirta* (☎ 24 1582) at 42 Rue Charles de Gaulle, five minutes' walk from the railway station and post office, and 15 minutes' walk from the bus station. It has over 30 rooms, so takes a little longer to fill up in summer. Rooms cost TD 5 for a single, TD 7 for a double, and have a bidet and washbasin. The whole place is cleaned daily and is spotless, although shabby. The only drawback is that not only do you pay 500 mills for a hot shower, they also charge the same for a cold one. The traffic noise from the street can be high at times, but this is common to virtually all the hotels. The *Hotel de l'Agriculture* (☎ 24 6394), right across the road, is similar to the Cirta, although it's a little less friendly.

Two of the few quiet hotels are both on a small lane (Rue de Suisse) which runs between Rue de Hollande and Rue Jamel Abdelnasser, one block north of Place de Barcelone. The *Hotel de Suisse* (☎ 24 3281) is run by a friendly guy and rooms cost TD 6.500/9.500 for a single/double with washbasin, TD 1 more for a double with bath. The other place is the *Hotel Central* (☎ 24 0433), which costs TD 6.500/9, and a hefty TD 1 for a shower.

If you really get stuck and even the youth hostel is full, you can crash out on the grass in the small park next to the railway station at the end of Rue de Russie. It's neither private nor comfortable nor highly recommended (women shouldn't even consider it), but it might do at a pinch.

Youth Hostel For once the *Youth Hostel* (☎ 56 7850) is a good place to stay. It is right in the heart of the medina on Rue Es Saida Ajoula, north-west of the Great Mosque. The dorms are quite good, if a little crowded, but you can't beat the price of TD 2.500 for a bed. The only drawback is that there's a three-day limit if the demand for places is high. Hot showers cost 500 mills, and breakfast is available at 700 mills.

Camping The nearest site is over 20 km to the south at Hammam Plage near Hammam Lif.

Places to Stay – middle
The *Hotel Bristol* (☎ 24 4836) is in the small cobbled alley (Rue Lt Mohammed Aziz Tedj) one block back from Ave Habib Bourguiba, behind the Café de Paris. It doesn't offer anything more than the cheaper places, but is conveniently located. Basic rooms cost TD 10.

A bit more comfortable is the *Hotel Salammbô* (☎ 24 4252) at 6 Rue de Grèce. Despite its kitschy foyer decor and pink rooms, it is quite good value at TD 8/10 for a single/double with bath; breakfast is included in the price. The *Hotel Transatlantique*, at 106 Rue de Yougoslavie, is similar, although showers have to be paid for separately. Both are good value.

Another very good place is the *Grand Hotel de France* (☎ 24 5876) at 8 Rue Mustapha Mbarek, not far from Place de la Victoire. It is an older style place which is reasonably priced. Rooms cost TD 9.900/ 13.200 with bath and breakfast, although

there are a few cheaper rooms without attached bath.

Probably the best in this category is the *Hotel Maison Doree* (☎ 24 0632), another old style place, at 6 Rue de Hollande, just north of the railway station. It is immaculately clean and well kept, the staff are friendly, and it even has a lift. Rooms cost TD 12/14 with washbasin, TD 14.800/ 16.400 with shower and TD 19/21 with bath. There's hot water available in the evenings and all prices include breakfast.

If you want to be right in the thick of things on Ave Habib Bourguiba, there's the noisy *Capitole Hotel* (☎ 24 4997) at No 60, right by the cinema of the same name. Room rates are TD 12.800/19.300 for singles/doubles, which includes a good breakfast.

Places to Stay – top end
For those people with the money and the inclination, Tunis has a full quota of expensive places, some of them real architectural disasters. Take a look at the *Hotel du Lac*, at the end of Ave Habib Bourguiba, behind the tourist office, and you'll see what I mean.

The *Africa Hotel* (☎ 34 7477), on Ave Habib Bourguiba, is also a bloody great blot on the landscape, especially as it's the only high-rise building in the whole street and practically the whole city. However, even if you are not staying here, the air-conditioned lobby with its luxurious armchairs is a welcome place to catch your breath for a few minutes on a hot and humid day. Expect to pay TD 57/70 for singles/doubles with breakfast.

Also on Ave Habib Bourguiba, at No 49, the *International Tunis Hotel* (☎ 25 4855) charges a mere TD 47.500/60 for singles/ doubles with bath and breakfast.

Hilton hoppers will be happy to find their favourite here too, on Ave Salammbô in the northern suburb of Mutuelleville, 10 minutes by taxi from the centre and the airport.

Places to Eat
Tunis has plenty of cheap and moderately priced restaurants but, although at first glance there appears to be plenty of variety,

they have remarkably similar menus with about a dozen standard dishes. Service, prices and decor are the biggest variables.

Markets For fresh fruit, the stalls around the Place de Barcelone by the railway station have a good selection of melons, peaches, grapes, figs and apples. Street vendors in and around the same area sell various things including halva, bread, nuts, cigarettes and pretzel sticks, all very cheaply.

The central market on Rue Charles de Gaulle is always a busy place and there's a good variety of produce available, as well as some excellent local cheeses and yoghurt.

Patisseries & Rotisseries These are at the bottom of the cheap-eats scale and are found all over the new city.

The patisseries stock all manner of sweet cakes and croissants. They usually do other things like small pizzas, savoury pâtés and crepes, which are generally excellent and all you need for breakfast or lunch. At the back of these places there is nearly always a café, where you can stand while eating your croissant with a coffee. Some of the best are on Rue Charles de Gaulle, between Ave Habib Bourguiba and Rue d'Espagne.

The rotisseries cook mostly roast (or fried) chicken and chips, but also have salads and, of course, bread. They are mostly stand-up joints where your food is served in a piece of paper; you either stand around and eat it with everyone else or take it away. You can find these places all over the ville nouvelle; they can usually be identified by the chicken-roasting ovens out the front.

Tunisian Restaurants There are a couple of local places, with local prices, which are popular and serve cheap and appetising food.

The best of these is the *Restaurant Carcassonne*, at 8 Ave de Carthage just off Ave Habib Bourguiba, near the Café de Paris. Although it is popular with both locals and foreigners, it is a basic place with welcome ceiling fans. The best value is the repas, a set menu of four courses for TD 2.200 which is

a real bargain – a four-course meal big enough to feed two people, especially when supplemented with the unlimited bread that is served here and in every other restaurant in the country. Individual dishes such as couscous (a semolina dish) and brochettes (kebabs) are also available for around TD 1.500 to TD 2 per plate – a very good place.

Another similar place is the *Restaurant Abid*, on Rue de Yougoslavie, near the corner with Rue Ibn Khaldoun. The menu is limited pretty much to chicken, haricot beans, couscous and brochettes, but the portions are more than adequate and it's a friendly place. This is the place to go if you want to sample half a sheep's head (demi tete d'agneau), good eating – even if you and the sheep don't see eye to eye. The *Restaurant Erriadh* around the corner on Rue Ibn Khaldoun is similar, although the service can be erratic.

On Rue Charles de Gaulle next to the Hotel Cirta is the *Restaurant Saidouna* which has good local food.

In the medina, on Rue Jemaa es Zitouna right at the end near the Great Mosque, there is a good place to sit and watch the world go by, as it has tables outside; the food is not bad either.

Other Restaurants There is a fair scattering of restaurants in which, for between TD 7 and TD 12 per person, you can get a decent meal with local wine. The best of these is the *Restaurant Le Cosmos* (☎ 24 1610), at 7 Rue Ibn Khaldoun. Despite the pretty awful paint job of the universe on the ceiling, this air-conditioned restaurant serves great food at quite reasonable prices. The white-coated waiters, however, are not overly friendly. The fish soup and the fresh fish (brought round on a tray for you to choose from) are both excellent. Expect to pay around TD 15 for two, and get here early (it opens at 7.30 pm), as it's popular in summer.

The *Restaurant l'Etoile* (☎ 24 0514), at 3 Rue Ibn Khaldoun, is similar to and slightly cheaper than Le Cosmos, and is one of the best in town for the money.

Another place in the same area is the *Restaurant Savarin* (☎ 24 4002), in the same small street as the Hotel Bristol, Rue Lt Mohammed Aziz Tedj, at No 29. It is next to the *Restaurant Poisson d'Or* (avoid this place), which has a large illuminated yellow sign. The Savarin has a good set menu of four courses for TD 2.800 – you get an enormous amount of food. The place has a bit of a men's-club atmosphere, but is friendly and popular with locals. Also good value is the *Restaurant de la Petite Hutte*, at 102 Rue de Yougoslavie.

Despite the name, the *Restaurant Bella Italiana*, on Rue de Yougoslavie, does nothing especially Italian; still, it has reasonable food for about TD 5 per head for a full meal.

The *Restaurant Le Palais*, just behind the Café de Paris on Ave de Carthage, is a slightly more up-market place with live entertainment on many summer evenings. The food, however, is only mediocre and not particularly good value, although the TD 3.500 repas at lunch times is OK.

At all these restaurants you need to arrive by about 8.30 pm at the latest or you miss out. They all serve alcohol – mostly local beer and red wine. Also, surprisingly, many are closed for their annual holidays for at least a couple of weeks right at the height of the season.

Cafés & Bars Café life is well established in Tunis, and there are numerous places with tables and chairs out on the footpath. The *Café de Paris* on the corner of Ave Habib Bourguiba and Ave de Carthage is very popular. It can be a good place to pass some time, although you pay a little over the odds for coffee, the croissants are very mediocre and the service is, at best, surly.

The bars in Tunis are real drinking dens. They have a thick, smoky atmosphere in which many women might not feel terribly comfortable. One exception, perhaps, is the *Bar Coquille* next to the Restaurant Carcassonne on Ave de Carthage.

Friday is a 'dry' day in Tunis.

Getting There & Away

Air Tunis Air flies daily to Jerba and less frequently to Tozeur, Sfax and Monastir. It can be difficult to get a flight in the middle of summer.

Air The main airline offices in Tunis include:

Aeroflot
    24 Ave Habib Thameur (☎ 34 0845)
Air Algérie
    26 Ave de Paris (☎ 34 1590)
Air France
    1 Rue d'Athènes (☎ 34 1577)
Egypt Air
    International Tunis Hotel, 49 Ave Habib Bourguiba (☎ 34 1182)
GB Airways
    17 Ave Habib Bourguiba
Lufthansa
    Ave Habib Thameur (☎ 34 1049)
Royal Air Maroc
    45 Ave Habib Bourguiba (☎ 24 9016)
Tunis Air
    48 Ave Habib Bourguiba (☎ 25 9189)
    113 Ave de la Liberté (☎ 28 8100)

Bus Tunis has two bus stations, one for departures to the north (Gare Routière Nord de Bab Saadoun) and the other for buses south and to Algeria (Gare Routière Sud de Bab el Alleoua). The north station is a fairly new building, 200 metres past Bab Saadoun, in the north-west of the city. To get there take a No 3 bus from Tunis Marine bus station or Ave Habib Bourguiba opposite the Africa Hotel, and get off at the first stop after Bab Saadoun (which you can't miss, as it's a massive triple-arched gate in the middle of a roundabout); the bus station is 100 metres over to the right.

This northern station is for departures to Bizerte and other places in the north of the country. There are SNTRI departures to: Ain Draham, Beja, Bizerte, Bourguiba, Jendouba, Mateur, Menzel and Tabarka. From the south station there are departures for all points in the country other than those already mentioned. As well as the SNTRI air-conditioned buses, which can be booked in advance at ticket windows No 1 and 2, some of the regional authorities also run buses to and from Tunis and have their own ticket windows at the station. It can be a bit of a battle to find out about buses and make a booking, especially as the SNTRI timetable is in Arabic. The staff in the booking office will grudgingly help you.

This station is also where you catch the international buses to Annaba (daily, 7 am, eight hours) in Algeria; these must definitely be booked the day before departure.

SNTRI departures from Tunis south bus station are to:

Destination	Frequency	Time
Douz	two daily	10 hours
Gabès	four daily	6 hours
Gafsa	three daily	7½ hours
Jerba	one daily	11 hours
Kairouan	eight daily	2½ hours
Kasserine	three daily	6 hours
Le Kef	three daily	4 hours
Medenine	three daily	8 hours
Nefta	one daily	8 hours
Sfax	six daily	5 hours
Sousse	two daily	2½ hours
Tataouine	one daily	9 hours
Tozeur	two daily	7 hours

Train The railway station is close to the centre of town and is the most convenient place to arrive, as there are plenty of hotels within five minutes' walk. It's a modern and efficient station, with all scheduled departures and arrivals displayed on an electronic board in the terminal building. There is a small information kiosk in the foyer which is staffed irregularly.

Although the services are crowded in summer, there is no need to reserve a seat, although you can do this the day before on the air-conditioned services to Sfax.

There are services from Tunis to: Bizerte (four daily, 1½ hours); El Jem (four daily, three hours); Gabès (two daily, five to six hours); Ghardimao (five daily, one continuing on to Algeria, three hours); Mahdia (three daily, 3½ hours); Metlaoui (one daily via Sfax, 9½ hours); Nabeul (nine daily, two direct and the others involve a change at Bir Bou Rebka, 1½ hours); Sfax (four daily,

3½ hours); and Sousse (seven daily, two hours).

Fares from Tunis are as follows:

Destination	Confort	1st-Class	2nd-Class
Bizerte	2.920	2.560	1.840
El Jem	7.270	6.370	4.580
Gabès	13.060	11.350	8.010
Hammamet	2.640	2.320	1.660
Jendouba	5.570	4.870	3.460
Nabeul	2.640	2.320	1.660
Sfax	8.740	7.630	5.420
Sousse	5.320	4.660	3.320

Taxi Louages are a good alternative to the buses. Although they are more expensive, services are also more flexible: if there are heaps of people trying to travel the louages keep running. They operate mainly in the mornings, so if you are planning on catching one you will have a shorter wait then. Things slow down considerably in the afternoon and you may have to wait awhile for one to fill up.

Tunis has two main louage stations, and these are right opposite the northern and southern bus stations. From the south station there are louages to Gabès, Gafsa, Jerba, Kairouan, Medenine, Nabeul, Sfax, Sousse, and Tozeur. From the northern station they run to Bizerte, Jendouba, Le Kef and Tabarka.

Car Rental All the major companies have offices at the airport and in town:

Avis
    In the lobby of the Africa Hotel (☎ 34 1249)
Budget
    14 Ave de Carthage (☎ 25 6806)
Carthage Tours
    59 Ave Habib Bourguiba (☎ 25 4605)
Europcar
    17 Ave Habib Bourguiba (☎ 34 0308)
Hertz
    29 Ave Habib Bourguiba (☎ 24 8559)
Topcar
    7 Rue de Mahdia (☎ 28 5003)

Sea The ferries from Europe arrive at the port, which is at La Goulette, at the end of the causeway across the Lake of Tunis. To get there take a TGM train to La Goulette

Vieille, and walk back alongside the line towards Tunis until you get to the railway crossing; turn left and walk for 200 metres, past the kasbah, and there is a sign to the port off to the right. The whole walk takes about 20 minutes.

When arriving at Tunis, come straight out of the port, turn left at the first main intersection (by the kasbah) and walk to the railway crossing; the station is away to the right. A taxi from the port to Ave Habib Bourguiba shouldn't cost more than TD 1.500.

Getting a booking on a ferry out of Tunis at the height of summer can take days – they are often booked out for up to 10 days in advance. This is especially so if you are taking a vehicle. Make your reservations as early as possible.

The Tirrenia Line office (☎ 24 2775) is at 122 Rue de Yougoslavie; it can be a real bun fight here, with people doing battle for tickets. Turn up first thing in the morning when things are marginally less frantic.

There are regular departures to France (Marseilles) and Italy (Cagliari, Genoa, Palermo and Trapani). See the Tunisia Getting There & Away chapter for full details of services.

Getting Around

To/From the Airport The Tunis-Carthage Airport is eight km north-east of the city. Yellow city bus No 35 runs there from the Tunis Marine terminus every 20 minutes or so between about 6 am and 9 pm. You can pick it up at the stop opposite the Africa Hotel. The trip takes about 20 minutes and costs 430 mills. A taxi to the Africa Hotel from the airport costs around TD 2.

From the airport the bus leaves from just outside the terminal building, to the right of the exit.

Bus The yellow city buses operate to all parts of the city but, apart from getting to the airport, the Bardo Museum or the north bus station you should have little cause to use them. The destination, point of origin and route number are displayed on a board by the entry door near the back. The number is also displayed in the front window. The set fare for a ride is 120 mills on most routes; 430 mills to the airport.

There are three main terminuses for the buses: Tunis Marine, which is right by the TGM station at the causeway end of Ave Habib Bourguiba; Place de Barcelone, in front of the railway station; and Jardin Thameur, 500 metres north of Ave de France. The No 3 bus to the Bardo and the No 35 to the airport both leave from Tunis Marine.

TGM This is the light-rail system that connects central Tunis with the beachside suburbs of La Goulette, Carthage, Sidi Bou Said and La Marsa.

It is fast, cheap and convenient, although a little crowded at times. Trains run 24 hours a day, with departures ranging from every 12 minutes during the day to every hour or so in the middle of the night. There are 1st and 2nd-class compartments. There seems to be little point in forking out the extra for 1st-class, although it is less crowded.

The 2nd-class fare from Tunis to La Goulette is 200 mills; to Carthage, Sidi Bou Said and La Marsa, it's 370 mills.

Tram The relatively new fancy tram service (Métro Léger) has four routes running to various parts of the city. The hand-out map from the tourist office has the lines, but not the route numbers, marked. The lines of most interest are the No 4, which runs past the Bardo Museum, and the No 3 which takes you past the north bus station. Unfortunately, these services terminate at a station inconveniently located about 500 metres north of Ave Habib Bourguiba, along Ave de Paris. You can get there on a No 2 service from Place de Barcelone, outside the railway station.

Taxi Taxis are a fairly cheap way of getting around. They're especially good if you are visiting embassies, as the drivers always know where these are and can save you a good deal of foot slogging. They always use the meter and a trip costs about 500 mills per km.

The only problem with the taxis is that there aren't enough of them. During peak hours this is a real problem; you just have to be patient and lucky. One of the best places to pick one up is by the railway station on Ave de la Gare, while Ave Habib Bourguiba is one of the worst places.

Around Tunis

There are quite a few places within day-trip distance of Tunis. Strictly speaking, the beach suburbs of Carthage, Sidi Bou Said and La Marsa are part of Tunis, but it takes a day trip to visit any or all of them.

Further away to the south are the excellent ruins of the Roman town of Thuburbo Majus. A visit to these ruins can be combined with the nearby town of Zaghouan to make a good day trip.

CARTHAGE

Despite its fascinating history and the position of dominance which Carthage held in the ancient world, the Romans did such a thorough demolition job on it that the ruins today are a major disappointment. For a full account of the city's history, see the Facts about the Region chapter.

Most of what there is to see is of Roman origin and there's not that much of it. However, as Carthage is so accessible, it's worth wandering around for a couple of hours. This can be combined with a visit to Sidi Bou Said or the beach at La Marsa.

If you have only a few hours, the best bet is to limit yourself to the museum and the ruins of Byrsa right outside it. With half a day you could also see the Antonine Baths, the Punic ports and the theatre, and in a whole day you would be able to see the lot.

The real hassle is that the sites are quite spread out. Although you can overcome this to a certain extent by making use of the TGM line which runs bang through the middle of the area, seeing everything requires a good deal of walking. In the heat and humidity of summer, this is more hassle than it's worth.

If you are intent on seeing the whole lot, the best way to tackle it is as follows: take the TGM to Carthage Salammbô and walk down to Tophet, the Punic ports and the Oceanographic Museum. From there take the TGM from Carthage Byrsa to Carthage Hannibal and head for the sea again to see the Magon Quarter. From here go back up the hill to the museum and Byrsa, and continue down the other side to the amphitheatre and cisterns; then go along the back road to the US war cemetery, from which you can cut across country to the basilica. From there, walk to the sea and the Antonine Baths via the theatre and Roman villas. Then take the street just back behind the sea to the Magon Quarter, from where it's a short walk to the Carthage Hannibal TGM station. Covering this whole route would take the best part of a day.

As is the case with the sites in the Tunis medina, it is possible to get a multiple ticket for the sites at Carthage. The only hassle is that it is only available at the museum, the Antonine Baths and the Roman villas. All sites are open daily from 8.30 am to 5.30 pm.

Hellenistic-style jug

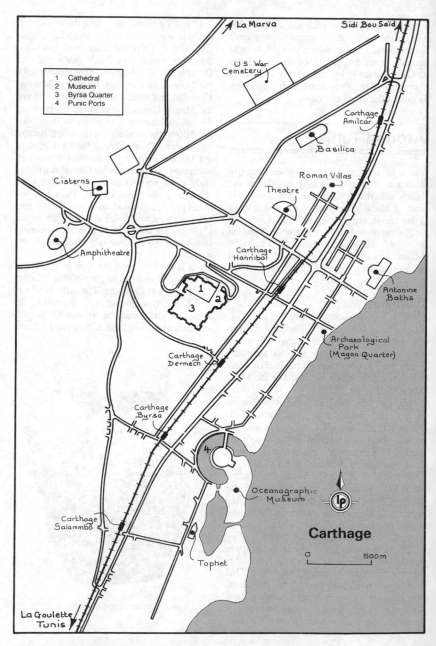

Carthage

1 Cathedral
2 Museum
3 Byrsa Quarter
4 Punic Ports

Tophet

When it was first excavated in 1921 this site created a good deal of excitement, as it revealed the first evidence of child sacrifice. The area contained urns, each marked with a stele and full of burnt child remains. However, just how these children died is still open to debate. The Romans were keen to condemn anything Carthaginian and got plenty of mileage out of the child sacrifice issue. Just how widely it was carried on is not known, although it certainly did exist and probably only died out after contacts with the Greeks and Romans. Animal sacrifice played a far bigger part in the local religion.

The word 'tophet' is in fact Hebrew and refers to a place near Jerusalem where human sacrifice was carried out. The other name for Tophet in Carthage is the Sanctuary of Tanit.

Today the small site, which covers half an acre or so, is basically a patch of overgrown weeds with a few excavated pits. There are also some vaults here, which are the remains of 4th-century Roman warehouses. If you don't have a ticket, you can still see almost as much from outside.

Punic Ports

Although they don't look too impressive today, these two basins were where the Carthaginians set sail from when they set off to challenge Rome. The northern one was the navy base and was originally circular with a diameter of about 300 metres. The island in the centre held the naval headquarters and the whole harbour was surrounded by a high wall on the landward sides. It is said that it could hold as many as 220 warships. The southern harbour was the centre of the commercial shipping.

Oceanographic Museum

This sorry display of fish and things nautical is a total waste of time. Entry is only 200 mills, however, so it won't break you if you feel like a wander around. It is open from 4.30 to 7.30 pm Tuesday to Sunday, and on Sunday mornings as well from 10 am to noon; it's closed Monday.

Byrsa Hill

This hill dominates the area. To get to the top, head uphill from Carthage Hannibal through the area of plush diplomats' residences, and then go up the stairs to the left at the top of the hill, just near the sign for the Reine Didon (a fancy hotel). Although the museum building is on the left here, the entrance is around to the right on the other side of the cathedral.

The cathedral on top of the hill is visible for miles around. Built in 1890, and an eyesore of truly massive proportions, it was dedicated to the 13th-century French king St Louis. It has now been deconsecrated and is no longer in use.

The National Museum is the large white building at the back of the cathedral. The displays here have recently been revamped, with Canadian and American assistance, and are well worth a look. The Punic displays upstairs are especially good.

The Byrsa Quarter (in the museum grounds) has really the only Carthaginian ruins left. The Romans levelled off the top of the hill, burying the Carthaginian houses under the rubble. The area has been well excavated and the finds are described in full (in French) in the museum.

Amphitheatre

The amphitheatre is down the other side of the hill, about 15 minutes' walk from the cathedral. It was here that many Christians were thrown into the ring unarmed and left to defend themselves against sword-wielding gladiators or wild animals.

The limited excavations and reconstructions date from 1919. The outer circle is hard to distinguish. The caretaker will latch on to you and babble away continuously in German or English (of sorts) if you don't speak French and then ask for TD 1.500 at the end.

Across the road from the amphitheatre are some old cisterns, which used to hold the water supply but are now ruined and not worth the scramble through the prickly pear bushes to see.

US War Cemetery & Basilica

The detour out to the war cemetery and basilica is only for the dedicated. The cemetery is extremely well kept, but the basilica across the field amounts to nothing much more than a few piles of stones.

Theatre & Villas

The theatre has been completely covered in concrete, and obscured with lighting towers and equipment for the annual Carthage Festival. It really has very little going for it.

The same applies to the Roman Villas Archaeological Park (called the Villa la Voliere on the ticket) just downhill from the theatre – it is a largely decorative site which has been over-restored.

Antonine Baths

The Antonine Baths are right down on the waterfront and are impressive more for their size and location than anything else. At the top of the steps just inland from the baths is a marble slab with a diagram of the baths, which helps to give some idea of just how big they used to be.

The entrance is about 100 metres before the sea. From Carthage Hannibal, take the main road (Ave Habib Bourguiba) and turn right, where the enormous capital from the baths sits in the middle of the intersection.

Magon Quarter

The Magon Quarter is another archaeological park, this time down by the water, one block south of the Antonine Baths. It has recently been excavated by a team of German archaeologists whose work has revealed a residential area. It is mildly interesting and the multiple ticket gets you in. If you don't have this ticket, don't bother.

SIDI BOU SAID

Sidi Bou Said is a small, whitewashed village set high on a cliff above the Mediterranean just north of Tunis, and it's on every tour-group itinerary. Despite this it is still a remarkably laid-back town, especially outside the main tourist season.

The centre of activity is the small cobbled square with its outdoor cafés and sweet stalls, which can be an agreeable place to sit for a while with a cold drink. In fact, other than this, there is very little to see in Sidi Bou Said; after a half-hour wander you will have exhausted the possibilities.

Just past the sweet stalls on the right is a steep path and stairway which lead down to a small and relatively uncrowded beach, where there are a few fairly up-market restaurants. From here it is possible to follow the road around and back up the hill to bring you out at Carthage Amilcar TGM station. The whole walk from Sidi Bou Said takes about an hour.

Places to Stay & Eat

The *Hotel Dar Said* (☎ 27 0792) is about 100 metres past the main square and is a beautiful old French villa. If you can afford the TD 19 for a double with breakfast it's a great place to stay, although it is closed in winter.

For a quick meal, the *Restaurant Le Chergui* has a pleasant open-air courtyard and reasonable prices. The *Restaurant Dar Zarouk*, on the opposite corner to the Dar Said, is also worth a visit, especially at lunch time when they have specials. You need to get there around noon, as it's only a small place and the food runs out early. Expect to pay around TD 5 per person for a two-course meal. It too is closed outside the main tourist season.

Getting There & Away

Sidi Bou Said is on the TGM line and it takes about 30 minutes to get there from Tunis. From the station it's about a 15-minute walk up to the top of the hill and the centre of the old part of the village.

LA MARSA

La Marsa is another of the beachside suburbs and is at the end of the TGM line from Tunis. Because of this, it is one of the least crowded on hot summer days, although weekends are a bad time on any beach.

Along with the area around the Byrsa Hill, La Marsa is one of the most exclusive residential suburbs of Tunis. There are a couple of good cafés and restaurants around the TGM station.

THUBURBO MAJUS

This old provincial Roman city, some 55 km south-west of Tunis, is easily accessible by both bus and louage from Tunis and, along with the nearby town of Zaghouan, makes an interesting day trip. If time is short, you could easily miss these places without losing any sleep.

If you are travelling from Tunis to Kairouan or vice versa it would also be possible to fit in Thuburbo Majus on the way. If

you are making a day trip from Tunis to Thuburbo Majus and Zaghouan, it is easiest to go first to Thuburbo Majus and then head for Zaghouan, as the transport connections are better this way.

Thuburbo Majus thrived as a town serving an agricultural hinterland from well before Roman times, but it wasn't until the 2nd century when the emperor Hadrian visited and declared it a municipality, that the town really prospered.

The Ruins

Ruins of the major monuments and various

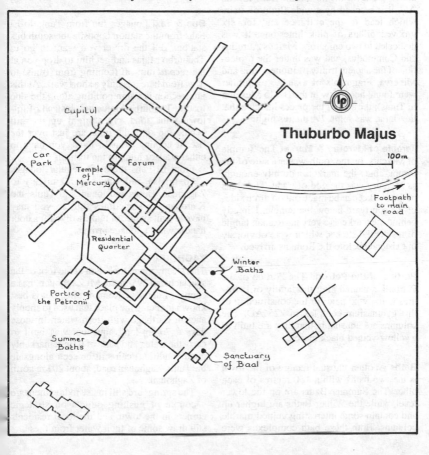

Thuburbo Majus

other monuments are scattered around the edge of this site.

Forum As usual, the forum was the public focus of the city, and was where its political and economic affairs were carried out. It is colonnaded on three sides; the columns were erected in 182 BC.

Capitol On the north-western side of the forum lies the capitol. It's in the required position of dominance, having been built on an artificial platform raised some two metres above the level of the forum. Built in 168 AD, it is reached by a wide flight of stairs which lead to the entrance and the six grooved pillars of pink limestone. It was dedicated to two emperors, Marcus Aurelius and Commodus, and was under the protection of the ancient trinity of Jupiter, Juno and Minerva. Fragments of a statue of Jupiter were found here (now in the Bardo Museum in Tunis); the size of the pieces indicate that the statue was some 7½ metres high.

Temple of Mercury & Market The Temple of Mercury, on the south-western side of the forum, abuts the market, naturally enough, as Mercury was the god of trade. The stalls of the market can be made out on three sides of the courtyard below the temple. Directly behind the market is a very un-Roman tangle of residential streets, which were obviously in existence before the Romans arrived.

Portico of the Petronii The Portico of the Petronii is named after the family of Petronius Felix, who paid for the construction of this gymnasium complex in 225 AD. The columns are unusual in that they are built of a yellow-veined black marble.

Baths Another unusual feature of the town is the two baths within 150 metres of each other. The Summer Baths are on the lower level, while the Winter Baths are higher up and contain some interesting veined marble columns. Both these bath complexes were full of mosaics, which are now exhibited in the Bardo Museum. The most plausible explanation which has been put forward for having two baths so close to each other is that the well supplying the winter baths with water dried up in summer, necessitating the construction of the other baths lower down the hill.

Getting There & Away
The totally dreary rural town of El Fahs is the closest settlement to Thuburbo Majus. At over three km away it can be a stinking hot walk in summer.

Bus & Taxi Louages run from Tunis to El Fahs from the station opposite the south bus station. Tell the driver you want to go to Thuburbo Majus and get him to drop you at the *second* turn-off (coming from Tunis) to it, as from here it is only a short walk. At this intersection is a sign pointing along the side road to Thuburbo Majus but, instead of following the road, cut straight up the hill behind the sign; the ruins are just over the rise. If coming from El Fahs, you have to either walk or hitch to the turn-off.

From El Fahs there are regular louages (750 mills) and buses (550 mills) to Zaghouan. Buses and louages to Tunis and Kairouan are sometimes full, so you may have to wait awhile or make a dive for a door handle when a louage arrives.

ZAGHOUAN
This sleepy town, tucked in at the foot of the spectacular 1295-metre Mt Zaghouan, has a couple of derisory Roman ruins, but is best known for being the place that used to supply ancient Carthage with fresh water. In those days a 70-km-long aqueduct was built to carry the water, and parts of it (in remarkably good condition) can still be seen alongside the Tunis-Zaghouan road, about 20 km north of Zaghouan.

The springs are still in use today; there are a couple of gushing outlets on strategic corners in the town, and the local residents still draw some of their water from these.

Places to Stay

There is a *Youth Hostel* here on the next hill over. The two-star *Hotel Les Nymphes* (☎ (01) 75 094) is up behind the town, and charges TD 14.800/19 for singles/doubles with breakfast.

Getting There & Away

There are regular louages and buses to both El Fahs and Tunis. Louages take 40 minutes to cover the 55 km to Tunis, and cost TD 1.750 per person. To El Fahs a bus costs 550 mills and a louage 750 mills.

The Cap Bon Peninsula

This is the tourist playground of Tunisia and consequently contains the majority of the country's resort hotels. Fortunately, the vast majority of these are centred around the Hammamet-Nabeul region on the south-east coast of the peninsula, leaving the rest of the area virtually untouched.

Even where the resort development has taken place, the size of the hotels has been kept to a relatively modest level and they are not too intrusive.

In summer the beaches are packed; both towns, which are gradually expanding and merging to form one, are crawling with scantily clad package tourists and the prices hike up. Despite this, it is still possible to find reasonable accommodation, and Nabeul has one of the best campsites in the country.

Kelibia to the north offers a more relaxed atmosphere; it has a decent beach a few km away at Mansourah. The area around the small town of El Haouaria right on the northern tip is also worth exploring.

The west coast is far more rugged, so has developed little. Transport connections and accommodation are limited, but if you have your own transport there are plenty of beaches without the crowds of Hammamet or Nabeul.

NABEUL

This is where it all happens in summer. A walk down the main street will probably turn up 10 tourists to one local. The town used to be important as a service centre for the agricultural interior of the peninsula, but these days it has turned its back on the land and opened its arms to the visitors, mostly from sun-starved northern Europe, who flock here in droves. Even in the off season there are probably more tourists per sq metre than in any other part of the country.

The beaches here are quite disgraceful – littered with all sorts of detritus (mainly plastic bottles) – and are just kept clean in front of the resort hotels. Unless you have a burning desire to be amongst other foreigners, you'd do well to bypass Nabeul in favour of more isolated spots such as Kelibia, 60 km to the north.

The Friday market in Nabeul has become one of the major tourist events in the country. Although it is basically for the tourists, it is here that you'll find the widest range of pottery in Tunisia, as Nabeul has long been associated with the craft. Many of the pieces on sale bear little relation to anything remotely Tunisian and owe more to the questionable tastes of the town's visitors. Because of the large number of tourists and the fact that most of them are only on short package tours, prices in Nabeul are high and bargaining is difficult. You stand a better chance on any day other than Friday, but even then it is difficult.

Information
Tourist Office The office of the ONTT (☎ (02) 86 800), the national tourist body, is on Ave Taieb M'Hiri between the beach and the centre of town. Even when it's closed they have bus, train and accommodation information posted outside the office.

Money As might be expected, there are plenty of banks ready to take your money, mostly along Ave Farhat Hached and Ave Habib Bourguiba.

Post The main post office is on Ave Habib Bourguiba, north of the main intersection with Ave Farhat Hached.

Market
The market is on Fridays, mainly in the morning. Things have pretty much died down by 2 pm. When it's on, Ave Farhat Hached is closed to vehicular traffic between Ave Habib Bourguiba and Ave Habib

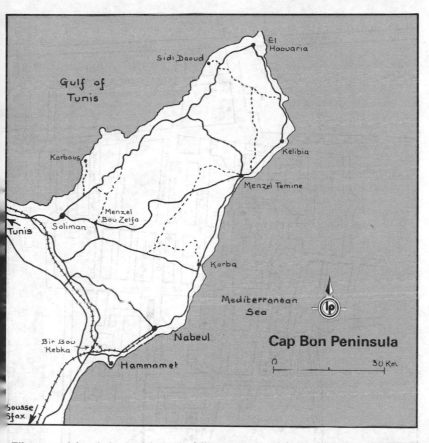

Cap Bon Peninsula

Elkarma, and the whole stretch becomes full of tourists and traders.

Museum

There is a small archaeological museum on Ave Habib Bourguiba near the railway station. It has a few pieces on display, but it's hardly worth it.

Places to Stay – bottom end

There are a couple of good choices here. Right in the middle of town is the *Pension les Roses* (☎ (02) 85 570), on Ave Farhat Hached. It is a friendly and comfortable place, although its proximity to one of the

mosques might give light sleepers a hard time. Charges are TD 6.500/10 for singles/doubles in the high season, dropping to TD 4.500/7 in the off season. Cold showers are free and hot showers cost 500 mills. It is right on the corner of the small open square where Ave Farhat Hached makes a dogleg in the centre of the town.

Out towards the beach is the *Pension les Oliviers* (☎ (02) 86 865). Another family-run place, it charges TD 8 per person, including a filling breakfast.

Another cheap possibility here is the *Pension les Hafsides* (☎ (02) 85 823); it's a bit out of the way on Rue Sidi Maaouia but

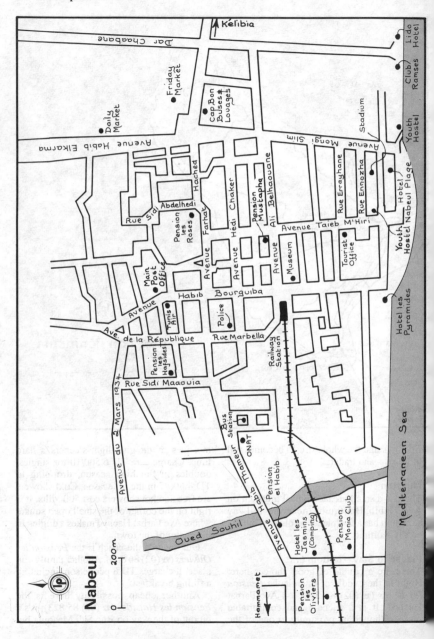

Nabeul

0   200m

Mediterranean Sea

is easy to find, as it's signposted off Ave Habib Thameur. It is a characterless place which charges TD 8/10 for singles/doubles.

The *Pension el Habib* (☎ (02) 87 190), on the noisy Ave Habib Thameur just over the Oued Souhil, is slightly better and charges the same.

Another good place is the *Pension Mustapha* (☎ (02) 22 262), on the corner of Ave Taieb M'Hiri and Ave Ali Belhaouane, not far from the railway station. It charges TD 7/11 for bed and breakfast, rising to TD 9.500/14 in the high season.

Youth Hostel Nabeul has two youth hostels, although both are likely to be full in midsummer. The better of the two is right on the beach at the end of Ave Mongi Slim. It is quite good value at TD 4.500 for a bed, dinner and breakfast. The other hostel (☎ (02) 85 547) is by the stadium. It is much newer, has little character and is comparatively poor value at TD 4 per person for bed only.

Camping The *Hotel Les Jasmins* (☎ (02) 85 343), signposted off to the left one km along the road towards Hammamet, has a congenial campsite in the shady olive garden attached to the hotel. It is private and secure, and costs TD 1 per person and a further 800 mills for a tent.

The hotel is well situated – it's only five minutes' walk to the beach; the extra bit of distance between it and Nabeul means that the beach is relatively uncrowded. On the beach is a small café, which has some welcome shade umbrellas and serves tea, cold drinks and sandwiches.

The best way to get here is to take a bus or taxi running between Hammamet and Nabeul; get out at the Slovegnia Grill Restaurant or just ask the driver for the campsite.

Places to Stay – middle
Close to the Pension les Oliviers is the *Hotel Les Jasmins* (☎ (02) 85 343), which was once a beautiful villa in an orchard. It's now a beautiful hotel in an orchard, and has a swimming pool and good restaurant. It is

likely to be fully booked in summer, but if you chance on a room it will cost TD 11 per person for bed and breakfast.

Places to Stay – top end
The half dozen or so resorts here are almost all fully booked throughout the summer by tour and charter groups from Europe. They all have swimming pools and other sporting facilities, and it's often possible to sit on their patch of beach with the shade umbrellas, or by the pool. If you want to stay at one, expect to pay upwards of TD 20 per person. You will be lucky to find a vacancy in midsummer; in winter prices drop and finding a room is less of a problem.

The *Hotel Les Pyramides* (☎ (02) 85 444) is typical and is in about the best location if you are on foot. Its beach is ridiculously crowded and claustrophobic, and such is its isolation from the real Tunisia that topless bathing is common. They charge TD 39/54 for bed and breakfast. It's no problem for nonresidents to use the facilities here if a little discretion is exercised.

Other places close to the centre of Nabeul are the *Club Ramses* (☎ (02 86 363) (TD 24/39 for singles/doubles with breakfast) and the *Lido Hotel* (☎ (02) 85 104) (TD 29/50). They're both on the beach, not far from the end of Ave Taieb M'Hiri.

Places to Eat
There are a few restaurants around the square on Ave Farhat Hached. The two on either side of the entrance to the Pension les Roses are both reasonable.

Things to Buy
There is an ONAT emporium on Ave Habib Thameur not far from the bus station. It has the same good quality stuff as the other branches in the country and gives you an idea of the maximum prices you should be paying for things.

Getting There & Away
Air The Tunis Air office (☎ (02) 85 193) is at 145 Ave Habib Bourguiba.

Bus & Taxi The station for buses and louages to Tunis and Hammamet is close to the centre of town on Ave Habib Thameur.

The regional bus service No 40 runs regularly from the Tunis south bus station. Buses to Hammamet run every half hour from 5.30 am to 7 pm. There are also small yellow taxis which buzz back and forth, in which you pay for just a seat (500 mills), although on seeing a tourist, the drivers often ask for more. Louages to Tunis cost TD 2 per person.

There are bus departures for Zaghouan (three daily), Kairouan (one daily at 6 am) and Sousse (one daily, 6.45 am) as well.

For transport north, vehicles leave from a dusty lot just to the east of the intersection of Ave Farhat Hached and Ave Habib Elkarma. From here there are regular louage departures to Kelibia as well as 12 buses daily between 5 am and 6.30 pm.

Train The station is close to the centre of town, two blocks south of Ave Habib Thameur.

There are up to nine trains daily to Tunis, but only one of these goes direct; the others go to Bir Bou Rebka on the main line down to Sfax, and you have to pick up another train from there. Connections are generally good, although at odd times you may have to wait for up to three hours. The direct trains leave Tunis at 2.17 pm, and Nabeul at 5.35 am; the journey takes 1½ hours.

Car Rental The major agencies are mostly represented in nearby Hammamet. Hertz (☎ (02) 85 027) has an office in Nabeul on Ave Habib Bourguiba.

Getting Around
Taxi Nabeul is reasonably spread out, and in summer it's a major effort to walk the km or so from the main street to the beach. Taxis cost only a few hundred mills and can be a life-saver; otherwise you can take one of the many *calèches* (horse carriages), but bargain hard and agree on a price before setting off.

HAMMAMET
This is Nabeul all over again, only more so. The kasbah here has been totally over-restored, and what was once a small fishing village has now become another tourist service centre.

The reason for Hammamet's popularity is its long stretch of beach, which is one of the better ones along this coastline.

Information
Tourist Office The tourist office (☎ (02) 80 423) is in the centre of town on Ave Habib Bourguiba. They have a good hand-out map of Hammamet and Nabeul.

Post The main post office is on the Nabeul road, Ave de la République, close to the centre.

Kasbah
There are good views from the ramparts of the kasbah, and the café on the top is a pleasant place at sunset, otherwise there is little to see. The kasbah is open from 8 am to 9 pm daily; entry is TD 1.

Cultural Centre
Hammamet has a cultural centre, about two km south of the town on the beach road. Unless there's a special performance on (check with the tourist office), it's not worth the walk.

Places to Stay – bottom end
Accommodation in Hammamet is not cheap. Best value for money is the *Pension Alya* (☎ (02) 80 218). All the rooms are pleasant and have balcony and bath attached, and the rooms away from the road have good views of the kasbah. The price is TD 12/18 in the low season, and this includes breakfast.

The *Hotel Sahbi* (☎ (02) 80 807) is on the main street. Backpackers are treated with disdain here, and the staff are surly. The tariff is TD 9.500/15 for rooms with breakfast.

Camping The *Ideal Camping* (☎ (02) 80 302) doesn't really live up to its name, but is passable. There is very little shade and the facilities are minimal. It is close to the centre on Ave de la République and charges TD 1.500 per person, 800 mills for a tent, and TD 1.500 for a vehicle. Cold showers are free; hot showers cost 800 mills.

Places to Stay – middle & top end

All the rest of the accommodation in Hammamet is of the resort-hotel type. These are all located on the beach to the north or south of town. Cheaper places include the *Venus* (☎ (02) 80 422), *Yasmina* (☎ (02) 80 222), *Kerkouane* (☎ (02) 80 841) and the *Chames* (☎ (02) 81 968).

Places to Eat

The best of the cheap places is the *Café de la Poste*, which is to the left of the parking lot outside the kasbah.

Getting There & Away

Bus All road transport leaves from a small vacant lot about 100 metres uphill from the kasbah. There are regular departures for Tunis and Nabeul.

Train The railway station is about one km from the centre, 15 minutes' walk past the tourist office. Train details are the same as for Nabeul. The direct departure for Tunis is at 5.53 am.

Taxi Small yellow taxis do the quick run to Nabeul for 500 mills per person. They leave outside the kasbah. If you don't want to hire the whole cab, make sure that the driver understands you're only paying for one seat (*une place*).

Car Rental The agencies with offices here include: Avis (☎ (02) 80 303), Rue de la Gare; Europcar (☎ (02) 80 146), Ave des Hôtels; Hertz (☎ (02) 80 187), Ave des Hôtels; and Topcar (☎ (02) 80 767), Ave de Koweit.

KELIBIA

Suddenly you've left all the commercialism behind, and what you have is a small dusty town which survives mainly on its fishing fleet. The town itself is not of great interest, but down by the small beach, two km away, are a couple of very low-key resort hotels. The port is dominated by a picturesque fort.

Despite the backwater feeling, Kelibia has international hydrofoil connections with Trapani in Italy from June to September.

Information

All the services such as banks and post office are in the town. If you don't take your meals at the hotels or are staying at the youth hostel, you'll need to stock up with food before heading for the beach.

Fort

The Romans were the first to occupy this area but the Byzantines built the first fort here. Today the fort has been largely restored and dates from the Spanish invasions of the 16th century.

A dirt track leads up to it on the far side from opposite the youth hostel on the Mansourah road, just past the port, and it's only a short hike up to the top.

The fort is open at very irregular hours and getting in is a matter of pot luck. Once inside, it's a surprise to find a few families living here; the whole area is something of a farmyard, with chickens and cows. It's still a restricted area of some sort, so it's advisable to ask permission before taking photos and to heed the *accès interdit* signs. The views over the coastline from the ramparts are magnificent to both the north and south.

Beaches

The best beach is at Mansourah, two km to the north and 500 mills by regular shuttle taxi. The beach at Kelibia itself is very small and not that flash.

Places to Stay & Eat

There's only a limited choice of places and they are all out at the beach by the harbour. The better of the two hotels is the fading *Hotel Florida* (☎ (02) 96 248), which has a nice shaded terrace by the water's edge. Room rates are TD 11/18 for singles/doubles including breakfast and TD 16/28 for pension complète.

Next door to the Florida is the *Hotel Ennassim* (☎ (02) 96 245), which looks as though it would be more at home on the moon. The staff can be incredibly surly and uncooperative, and it's not the best value at TD 9.500/14 including breakfast; other meals are available at additional cost. It is invariably full in summer, but your chances of getting a room are good if you arrive before noon.

Youth Hostel The *Youth Hostel* (☎ (02) 96 105) is a third choice but is not very attractive. It is down past the harbour on the Mansourah road, and is the usual masterpiece of architectural innovation and excellence. If you have a tent or vehicle, they usually let people camp in the grounds.

Getting There & Away
Bus & Taxi The bus station is a fair three km from the harbour and beach. There are regular louages doing the run between the two for 500 mills per person.

There are 10 bus departures daily along the coast to El Haouaria between 6 am and 2.45 pm. Louages leave regularly from the bus station for the 30-minute, 850 mill journey.

Hydrofoil As unlikely as it may seem, from June to September Kelibia becomes an international port, with hydrofoil departures three times a week to Trapani in Sicily, Italy. The trip takes only two hours. The agency that handles the operation is Tourafric (☎ (01) 34 1481) at 52 Ave Habib Bourguiba in Tunis.

EL HAOUARIA
This small town is tucked right in under the mountainous tip of Cap Bon. There are some interesting Roman caves just along from the

tip of the cape, three km beyond the village. As there is no accommodation, you have to visit El Haouaria in a day trip. The easiest way to manage this is from either Kelibia or Nabeul, or en route between Tunis and Kelibia.

The caves are a 45-minute walk out along the road straight through town; don't be surprised if a couple of locals latch onto you to guide you (unnecessary). The road curves around to the left, and although you can take a short cut straight ahead, this cuts right through the middle of the town garbage heap – a bloody unsavoury smelling place it is too.

The road ends at the small Café les Grottes, and the caves are to the right of the road. In some you can see where the Romans cut out and removed building blocks for their projects in Carthage. The official guide, complete with brass nameplate, is keen to show people around.

Places to Stay
The two-star *Hotel L'Epervier* (French for sparrowhawk; the hotel is so named because the village has been the centre of falconry in Tunisia) has been under construction for many years now. Maybe it will be finished by the time you get there. If not, the nearest possibilities are Kelibia or the expensive thermal resort hotel at Korbous, on the west coast of the peninsula.

Getting There & Away
Bus & Taxi Buses and taxis leave irregularly for Tunis, the former from the square, and the latter a further 100 metres down past the Hotel L'Epervier. The bus to Tunis crawls along the north coast of Cap Bon, calling at every little village along the way, and so takes 2½ hours; the trip costs TD 2.900. Louages are a good deal faster.

There are also regular departures for Kelibia.

Northern Tunisia

Since most tourists in Tunisia head for the Sahara and the beach resorts south of Tunis, the areas to the north of Tunis are far less crowded.

The beaches at Raf Raf and Sidi Ali el Mekki, between Tunis and Bizerte, are some of the best in the country and foreign tourists are relatively rare. The town of Bizerte itself is worth a quick look, and from there the road stretches west to Tabarka. The coastline along here is isolated and, if you have your own transport, there are some excellent beaches and small settlements to explore.

Tabarka is an attractive town, popular with holidaying Tunisians, and inland from here, up in the mountains and the cork forests, the town of Ain Draham is high enough to be pleasantly cool in summer while the rest of the country swelters.

The two ruined Roman cities in the north, Bulla Regia just south of Ain Draham, and Dougga, are arguably the two best sites in the country.

Bizerte

Bizerte is probably best known for being the place that the French hung on to after granting independence to Tunisia, which led to the loss of more than 1000 Tunisian lives in the attempt to oust them. The French finally withdrew on 15 October 1963 and the day has become a public holiday.

Located just a few km south of Cap Blanc (the northernmost tip of the African continent) Bizerte has some quite reasonable town beaches away to the north, and it is the best place for getting to the even better beaches of Raf Raf and Sidi Ali el Mekki to the south-east.

The French ville nouvelle follows the usual unimaginative grid; the medina is also true to form – a tangle of lanes and narrow streets. The two meet around the old port.

The shipping canal, first built by the Carthaginians, connects the large Lac de Bizerta (Lake Bizerte) with the Mediterranean. It has formed a natural buffer that allows the town centre to breathe without getting hemmed in by housing and development. The canal is spanned by a new bridge complete with a central span, which can be raised to allow larger ships to pass through.

Information

Tourist Offices The office of the national tourist body (☎ (02) 32 897) is on the corner of Quai Tarak ibn Ziad and Ave Taieb Mehiri. They have a reasonable hand-out map if you ask, and a useful sheet detailing the current accommodation prices for selected places in the whole northern region. It is not an exhaustive list but does give an idea of current prices.

The regional tourist office is clearly signposted on the corner of Ave Habib Bourguiba and Blvd Hassen en Nouri, right next to the service station. The office is open Monday to Saturday from 9 am to 1 pm and 4 to 7 pm, and on Sunday from 9 am to noon, and 4 to 7 pm.

Money The banks are mostly grouped around the square with the gardens and tennis club. Normal hours are 9 am to noon and 4 to 7 pm in summer, but one bank is always rostered to be open late; to find out which one, check the window of the regional tourist office on Ave Habib Bourguiba.

Post & Telecommunications The main post office is on Ave d'Algérie. There is a parcel post office *(colis posteaux)* in the same building further towards Ave Habib Bourguiba; around the back is the telecommunications office, which is open late.

Beaches

The beaches to the north of town towards Cap Blanc are not too bad at all. The strip of

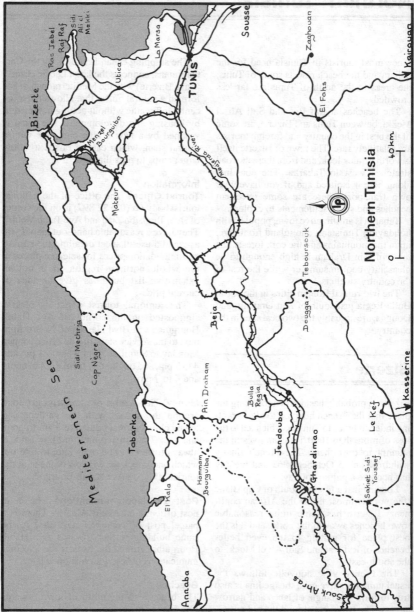

hotels has a monopoly on the first few km, but it's not too difficult to slip in and use the beach and facilities.

Further on, the beach backs directly onto the road and is very narrow – not that great. Further on still, around the first cape and along a few more km, the Les Grottes beach right at the foot of Cap Blanc is the best of the lot. Access can be a bit tedious without a car, however, as you have to rely on hitching or walking the last couple of km.

In the other direction, back towards Tunis, Remel Plage has a good strip of white sand and is a little easier to get to on your own. Buses from the main bus station heading for Raf Raf or Ras Jebel will drop you off at the turn-off, from where it's a one-km walk.

Places to Stay – bottom end

The cheapest place in the city is the *Hotel Zitouna*, which is noisy and somewhat claustrophobic, but is also undeniably cheap at TD 2.500 for a bed, and TD 3/5 for a single/double room. There is cold water only and showers are free.

The best of the cheapies, however, is the *Hotel Continental* (☎ (02) 31 436), on Rue d'Espagne, but even this is not great. It is somewhere approaching clean and rooms cost TD 5/8 for a single/double. There are cold showers only.

Youth Hostel & Camping There are two youth hostels. The first is up by the top end of the medina and is, as usual, more like a prison block.

The second hostel (☎ (02) 40 804) is a much better alternative. It is three km back towards Tunis, signposted down a dirt track at the turn-off to Remel Plage. Camping is possible at this one and it is a popular place with people who have their own vehicle. The hostel facilities are pretty basic, but adequate, and the relaxed atmosphere and location by the beach make it a good place. The cost is TD 4 for a bed, and meals can be ordered. To get there take a bus going to Ghar el Melh, Raf Raf or Ras Jebel and get off at the Remel Plage turn-off.

Places to Stay – middle & top end

The rest of the places are out along the beach strip to the north of the town. They all tend towards the top end of the scale and are usually booked out (in summer at least) with package tourists from Europe.

The cheapest of the resort-type places is the *Hotel Nador* (☎ (02) 31 846), which has a good stretch of beach, a swimming pool, tennis, poolside restaurant and all the other trappings. Charges are TD 14.400/21.250 for singles/doubles with breakfast in the low season and TD 20/31.500 in the summer.

Further out along the beach, the *Hotel el Khayem* (☎ (02) 32 120) is reasonable at TD 6.900/8.750 but it is a fair way out. Also, the beach here is very narrow and the road separates it from the hotel. The indescribably ugly Restaurant Zoubaida next door has to be seen to be believed.

If you can afford it, the best place for atmosphere is the *Hotel Petit Mousse* (☎ (02) 32 185), also out along the beach, although it too is separated from the beach by the road. It was built in the colonial days and good rooms cost TD 13.750/18.700 for singles/doubles with breakfast. Even if you don't stay here it's nice to have a drink at the bar or a meal in the garden in the evening.

Places to Eat

Bizerte is not overendowed with restaurants, but there are a few choices. The small, nameless local restaurant just along from the Hotel Continental does reasonable meals.

Just off Ave Habib Bourguiba, the *Restaurant du Bonheur* and the *Restaurant l'Aviation*, diagonally opposite the Tunis Air office, are both typical Tunisian eateries and there's not much to choose between them – both are basic and moderately clean.

For just coffee, cakes and ice creams the *Patisserie de la Paix*, right opposite the Hotel Continental, is something of a local hang-out; it's open long hours and has good products.

Out along the beach, past the major hotels, are a couple more choices. The *Hotel Petit Mousse* has a very pleasant well-run outdoor

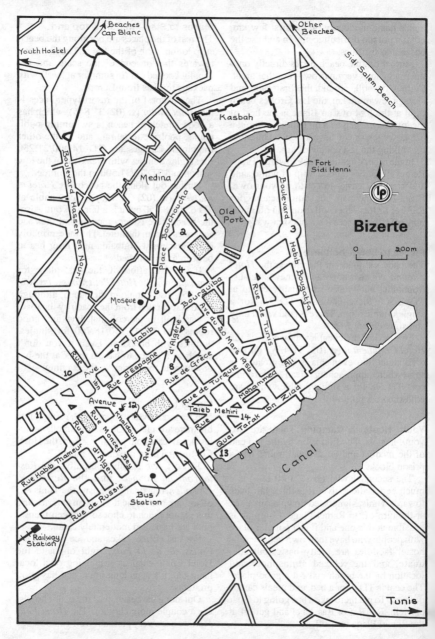

Bizerte

0   200m

1	Artisanat
2	Market
3	Buses to Northern Beaches
4	Louages (North Coast)
5	Local Restaurant
6	Hotel Zitouna
7	Hotel Continental
8	Main Post Office
9	Regional Tourist Office
10	Tunis Air
11	Restaurants du Bonheur & l'Aviation
12	Banks
13	Louages (Tunis, Raf Raf)
14	National Tourist Office

restaurant where a meal, including beer, costs around TD 15 for two.

Getting There & Away
Air The Tunis Air office (☎ (02) 32 201) is at 76 Ave Habib Bourguiba.

Bus The bus station is down near the canal at the end of Ave d'Algérie, less than 10 minutes' walk from the cheap hotels. There are SNTRI departures as well as more frequent regional services with SETGC.

Departures include Ain Draham (three daily), Raf Raf (five daily), Tabarka and Tunis. All the departures for Raf Raf and Ras Jebel will get you to the Remel Plage turn-off for the youth hostel and campsite.

Train The modern railway station is down by the port, near the end of Rue de Belgique.

There are four departures daily between 4.55 am and 6.20 pm for the 1½ hour trip to Tunis.

Taxi Louages for Tunis, Raf Raf, Ras Jebel and Ghar el Melh leave from close to the bridge. For Menzel Bourguiba and Tabarka they depart from a small square near the northern end of Ave d'Algérie.

Car Rental The following major agencies have offices in Bizerte: Avis (☎ (02) 33 076), 7 Rue d'Alger; Budget (☎ (02) 32 174); Hertz (☎ (02) 33 679), Place des Martyrs;

and Europcar (☎ (02) 31 455), 19 Rue Rejiba;

Sea The Compagnie Tunisienne de Navigation office (☎ (02) 32 440), where you can arrange ferry bookings for departures from Tunis, is at 29 Ave d'Algérie.

Getting Around
There are local buses out to the beaches towards Cap Blanc. The No 29 runs out along Blvd Hassen en Nouri. No 2 also heads out this way, and if you want to get to the beaches right by Cap Blanc it can drop you at the T-junction where the road leads off to the right to the beach. From there it's a two-km walk to Les Grottes beach, but hitching is usually possible.

AROUND BIZERTE
Ras Jebel
This is the only real town on this large promontory south of Bizerte, which ends in Raf Raf beach and Cap Farina. It is actually just a service town for the surrounding productive farming land and there's not much in the way of facilities.

The beach here is signposted from the main street but it is a three-km walk. The beaches at Raf Raf and Sidi Ali el Mekki are a better bet.

Places to Stay & Eat The only place to stay in town is the *Hotel Okba*, signposted down towards the market from the bus stop. From there the signs peter out, but all the locals know the hotel and can direct you.

This hotel is very disorganised and it would appear that visitors are a rare breed here. However, it is a reasonable place to stay and charges TD 10 for a double with bath.

There are no restaurants to speak of in the town. There is a small sandwich shop with casse-croûtes (stuffed French bread) and chips on the road out of town towards the Lee Cooper factory and Raf Raf.

Getting There & Away Buses leave Bizerte fairly regularly for Ras Jebel and they go on to Raf Raf. The stop in Ras Jebel is at the main intersection.

There are also louages running infrequently to both Raf Raf and Bizerte.

Raf Raf

Not only is Raf Raf one of the best beaches in the country, with long stretches of white sand and relatively few people if you don't mind walking a bit, it is also easily accessible.

Raf Raf beach is sheltered in a small bay, and the approach from Bizerte is spectacular: as you come over the hill from Raf Raf town (itself of no interest) the beach and bay are spread out below.

The scarred pine-clad ridge at the far end of the beach is Cap Farina, and it's usually deserted here because it is a km or so along from the main part of the beach. You can walk to Cap Farina along the beach or, if you have a car, you can follow the tracks around behind the town, past the mosque, to the carpark (complete with parking attendant on weekends!) at the end of the track. From there a footpath leads down to the beach.

Although foreigners are rare in Raf Raf, it is a favourite spot with holidaying Tunisians, so there are numerous up-market restaurants, grass beach huts and a hotel to cater for visitors. Raf Raf is very popular in summer, particularly on weekends. As most people come on day trips only, things really calm down in the evenings.

Places to Stay & Eat The cheapest way to stay here is to bring your own food from Bizerte and rent one of the grass huts on the beach. These are primarily built for daytime use and privacy but it's quite OK to stay the night in one. They cost TD 4 per day and have nothing in them (apart from sand), so you need to have something to sleep on. The only formal place to stay is the *Hotel Dalia* (☎ (02) 47 668) at the end of the road. It's quite a good place if you can afford the TD 16 for a double with breakfast. The restaurant on the ground floor does OK food, although because it is at a tourist place the prices are a bit inflated for what you get.

The unbelievably kitsch *Café Restaurant Andalous*, closer towards the water, has better prices and does excellent fish.

There are quite a few other restaurants, all signposted, but these are costly and cater to the local day-trippers.

Getting There & Away There is a bus stop 50 metres before the beach and from here buses operate to Ras Jebel and Bizerte. Louages also make the trip. In summer the transport gets pretty crowded, particularly around 7 pm when everyone is heading back to Tunis or Bizerte.

Hitching is possible but you need to have patience, as a lot of the cars are already full.

Sidi Ali el Mekki

On the other side of Cap Farina from Raf Raf, Sidi Ali el Mekki is the best beach in northern Tunisia. However, without your own transport it can be a six km walk from the town of Ghar el Melh. Hitching is reliable only on summer weekends, when there are quite a few day-trippers in cars.

The road out to the beach skirts the lagoon of Ghar el Melh, the outlet for the Medjerda River. Although there's little reminder of it, the town has quite a history. In the 17th century it was a pirate hang-out, which the famous English admiral Sir Francis Drake attacked and destroyed. In the 18th and 19th centuries the Ottoman beys fortified the town and turned it into an arsenal in the hope of making the lagoon, connected to the sea by just a small channel, into a large naval base. Their schemes were thwarted by the Medjerda River, which silted up the lagoon. Today the ruins of the forts and port are still visible, and the only boats able to sail in the lagoon are small fishing vessels.

Places to Stay & Eat The only place to stay is in one of the 30 or so grass shelters on the beach. They consist of one room and a shade area in front which is welcome in summer. Like the huts at Raf Raf they are rented for the day by day-trippers, but you can stay overnight if you have something to sleep on. The custodian lives in one of them and keeps

Top: City centre, Ave Habib Bourguiba, Tunis (HF)
Left: Cathedral, Tunis (HF)
Right: Mosque at Tataouine, Tunisia (HF)

Top: Tourist shops, Medenine, Tunisia (HF)
Left: Market scene, Tunis medina, Tunisia (HF)
Right: Sidi Bou Said, Tunisia (HF)

a careful eye on things so your stuff is safe. They cost TD 4 per day, or TD 5 on Sundays, the most popular day.

In summer there is a small shop here which sells very basic provisions such as bread, eggs, a few canned goods, and drinks. It also makes good casse croûtes.

Getting There & Away Buses run infrequently from the Bizerte bus station to Ghar el Melh, and from there it's a matter of walking or hitching the six km to the beach.

Utica

At one stage after the fall of Carthage this port city was the capital of the Roman province of Africa. It was on the banks of the Medjerda River, but as the river silted up, it was reduced from being a fine city into an insignificant farming village.

The ruins today are unimpressive and are a hot one-km walk, signposted to the east from the small settlement of Zana on the main Bizerte-Tunis road. A visit is not really worth the effort unless you have your own vehicle.

Two km from the road on the left is the museum, which houses an extensive collection of bits and pieces found on the site. Some mosaics are displayed outside.

The site itself is a further 500 metres along the road at the bottom of the slope. The only significant ruin is the House of the Cascade, named after the fountains which used to decorate this mansion. The best mosaics, of men fishing from boats with nets and rods, are small; they're protected from the elements by wooden covers which can be lifted. For a small consideration the caretaker will splash some water on them, which really brings them to life. His real pride and joy, however, is the small garden here; he obviously devotes most of his time to this, as visitors to the site don't exactly swarm in every day.

The site is open from 8.30 am to 5.30 pm; entry is 800 mills and a charge of TD 2 is made if you want to take photographs.

Getting There & Away The only way to do this on public transport is to catch a bus or louage going from Tunis to Bizerte or vice versa and ask to be dropped at the turn-off to the ruins. After seeing the site you will have to walk the two km or so back to the road and either hitch or wait for a bus – a lot of work for very little reward.

Menzel Bourguiba

On the southern side of Lake Bizerte, Menzel Bourguiba is a large and uninteresting provincial town. It is a service centre for a sizable military base and the site of a major metallurgical complex.

Places to Stay There is absolutely no reason to stop here, but if you get stuck the *Hotel Younes* (☎ (02) 60 057) is a couple of km out of the town centre on the shore of the lake. The only way to get there is by taxi. Rooms cost TD 14 for a double, supposedly with breakfast, which somehow never seems to materialise. It is the main drinking establishment in Menzel Bourguiba and is quite pleasant in the evenings with its outdoor terrace by the water, although in summer the mosquitoes also find it very pleasant and a good hunting ground.

North Coast

Further from Bizerte towards Tabarka along the north coast are a couple of secluded seasonal settlements. However, unless you have a vehicle these places are hard to get to and, what is more, there is really no reason to visit them.

Sidi Mechrig Sidi Mechrig has a few permanent residents as well as families who camp here for the summer. You will need to have all your own supplies if you are contemplating coming here, because although there is plenty of water, there are no provisions of any sort for sale.

The people who stay in Sidi Mechrig buy their things in Sejenane, 17 km inland on the Bizerte-Tabarka road. The coast here can make an interesting diversion, although you'll need your own transport; otherwise, you can ask around in Sejenane for lifts.

Cap Nègre The track to Cap Nègre branches off the Sidi Mechrig track about one km after leaving the main road. Once a small village living off the trade in coral, it is now deserted.

TABARKA

The last town along the coast before the Algerian border, Tabarka is small, scenic and friendly. It is becoming increasingly popular: people have discovered the beautiful little bay and beach which are watched over by an impressive-looking fort built by the Genoese, but the town is still a relaxed backwater.

The Carthaginians were the first to use the port. It really flourished under the Romans, who built the causeway connecting the small island with the mainland. Some of the mosaics found in the town have been displayed in the Bardo Museum in Tunis.

Tabarka was also part of the string of pirate haunts along the Barbary Coast in the 1700s. In 1741 it was annexed by the bey of Tunis. It's most recent claim to fame, however, is the fact that Bourguiba was forced to spend a short time here in exile in 1952.

Today the town owes its existence partly to the red coral which is found just offshore; it is also a shipment point for the tonnes of cork taken from the forests of the Khroumirie Mountains, which rise sharply behind the town.

Apart from climbing up to the fort, or walking around the bay to the unusual rock formations known as Les Aiguilles ('the needles'), there's little to do except walk along the tree-lined main street (called Ave Habib Bourguiba, just to be original), checking out the coral jewellery in the shops, or lie on the beach.

There's a tourist office on Ave Habib Bourguiba, near the roundabout, which is open from 9 am to noon and 4 to 7 pm.

Places to Stay

Accommodation is at a premium, especially in summer when you'll be lucky to find a room after noon. This is no problem if you are prepared to sleep on the beach; otherwise Ain Draham (26 km inland) offers the only other possibility.

The cheapest place is the *Hotel Corail* and even this is no bargain at TD 12 for a double. It's on Ave Habib Bourguiba, about halfway between the roundabout and the *Hotel de France* (☎ (02) 44 577), which is the only other accommodation alternative. The latter costs TD 16 for a double and, although it's no great shakes, it does its best to cash in on the fact that Bourguiba spent time in the hotel.

Up on the hill, the three-star *Hotel Mimosas* (☎ (02) 44 376) has a commanding position and is the place to stay if you can afford the TD 35 they charge for a double with bath and breakfast.

Places to Eat

About the best place in town is the restaurant of the *Hotel de France*, although it might take a minute or two to get over the shock you get on entering the restaurant – strategically placed right in the middle of the doorway is the biggest, ugliest and most ferocious-looking stuffed wild boar you would ever want to see. Although it is a bit moth-eaten these days, it is still bloody awful. For added effect there are other assorted porcine bits around the walls. The four-course set menu for TD 4 is not bad value.

Right opposite the Hotel de France, the *Restaurant Khemis* has good calamari and passable spaghetti. The *Restaurant Triki*, on Rue Farhat Hached, just off Ave Habib Bourguiba, does good fish for TD 1.800.

Getting There & Away

Bus The SNTRI buses leave from Rue du Peuple, one block back from the Hotel Corail. Regional buses go from outside the customs house *(douane)* down at the beginning of the causeway.

There are connections with Ain Draham, Bizerte, Jendouba and Tunis.

Taxi The louages leave from the main street at the entrance to town, opposite the turn-off to the Hotel Mimosas.

To/From Algeria It's possible to hitch to the border and, once across it, to the town of El Kala. Here there are hotels, a youth hostel and transport connections on to Annaba, from where you can get a direct bus to Algiers, El Oued or Constantine.

AIN DRAHAM

From Tabarka the road starts winding upwards almost immediately, and there are some spectacular views back towards the coast. All along this stretch as far as the village of Babouch there are young boys selling pine nuts, rather aggressively (and at times dangerously): they stand out in the middle of the road, almost daring the vehicles not to stop.

At Babouch there is a turn-off to the Algerian border. This is 13 km away and can be reached by taxi, but there is the problem of crossing the 10 km or so of neutral territory before the Algerian post. It may be possible, if time-consuming, to hitch. The turn-off leads also to Hammam Bourguiba – a three-star thermal springs resort tucked in a small valley. Charges here are TD 22/29 for singles/doubles with breakfast.

The town of Ain Draham itself clings to the side of a hill almost 1000 metres above sea level. The elevation makes it quite a bit cooler than the plains or the coast, although in winter it means that deep snow is quite common.

The town used to be popular with hunters in the days of the French administration. Today leisure activities are a lot more peaceful, and Tunisians come here to relax and escape the summer heat.

There is a bank and a post office here.

Places to Stay & Eat

Accommodation is very limited, as most local tourists stay here for a week or more and rent out entire villas. The *Youth Hostel* is at the top of the hill on the road to Jendouba.

The only other place is the scenic *Hotel Beauséjour* (☎ (08) 47 005) but it will very likely be full in summer. Rooms, if you can get them, cost TD 7.500/10 for singles/doubles with bath and breakfast. The building itself is covered with creepers, and its past association with game hunting is very evident thanks to all the skins and skulls hanging on the walls.

Seven km along the road to Jendouba is the *Hotel Les Chênes* (☎ (08) 47 211), which is in the middle of a cork forest. It is an old hunting lodge and, again, there are several stuffed 'trophies' around the walls. Rooms cost TD 14.500/19 for singles/doubles with bath and breakfast; however, you're better off paying for pension complète, as there is nowhere else to eat. They do allow you to camp in the grounds and use the hotel facilities for a couple of dinar per person.

In Ain Draham itself there are a couple of basic restaurants in the main street. You can get casse-croûte and plates of assorted fried food (egg, chips, chillies) – certainly no gourmet delights here. If you can't face that try the restaurant in the *Hotel Beauséjour*, but expect to pay at least TD 5 per person.

Getting There & Away

Bus Buses leave from the intersection at the bottom of town near the petrol station, 300 metres down from the hotel and youth hostel. There are infrequent buses to Tabarka and Jendouba, and one air-conditioned SNTRI bus per day direct to Tunis.

Taxi Louages leave from the top of the hill, outside the youth hostel. They are far more frequent than the buses but only run to Tabarka and Jendouba.

BULLA REGIA

This Roman site is most famous for being the place where the Romans went underground. That is to say, they built their villas with one storey above ground and another below to escape the heat. The site was inhabited before Roman times; the Regia in the name refers to the royal Numidian kingdoms.

After the Romans moved in the residents

became wealthy, living off the revenue generated by the rich grain country of the Medjerda Valley.

Bulla Regia lies three km east of the Ain Draham-Jendouba road, and is six km north of Jendouba. Visiting it is easy enough and it is one of the best sites in the country. Making your way from Jendouba out to the site and back again will take you half a day.

The Ruins

The entrance to the site is just to the left of the Memmian Baths, the most extensive of the remaining above-ground buildings.

The three main underground houses are kept locked, so make sure you ask for the keys. The caretaker seems quite happy to let you take them and return them when finished. The site is open daily from 8.30 am to 5.30 pm, and entry is TD 1. There is a TD 2 charge for taking pictures. Most of the major points of interest are labelled with yellow signs.

The Memmian Baths on the right are impressive in size, and some of the mosaics have remained intact. The street in front of them leads to the theatre, which has loads of atmosphere; it still has a mosaic of a bear in the centre of the stage.

Following the street along to the left of the theatre brings you to the forum, which has the Temple of Apollo on the north side and the capitol to the east.

A path along an overgrown water channel takes you to a spring which is fenced off; this has a pump house which supplies Jendouba with water. From here it's a matter of scrambling over a bank to the left until you come to another excavated street. The Palace of Fishing, to the right, is one of the houses kept locked; it has a basement with fountain. Signposted just to the north-east, the House of Amphitrite (also locked) has a beautiful mosaic of Poseidon and Amphitrite surrounded by cupids.

Back next door to the Palace of Fishing is the residence known as the Palace of the Hunt. Its basement is the most impressive of the three houses, as it has a colonnade around it.

The museum outside the site across the road from the entrance doesn't have anything in it and so, logically enough, is closed.

Getting There & Away

From Jendouba you can catch a local bus heading for Ain Draham and ask for Bulla Regia. This will drop you at a signposted intersection six km north of Jendouba, from where it's a three-km walk to the site. Hitching along this stretch is easy enough, as there is quite a bit of local traffic as well as small louages.

JENDOUBA

Jendouba is dull in the extreme. Its only redeeming feature is that it's a handy base from which to visit Bulla Regia. Perhaps the most remarkable thing about the whole place is the stork's nest on top of the police station chimney.

If you are heading for Algeria it is possible to pick up the Trans-Maghreb Express train here, which runs daily to Algiers.

Life revolves around the central square, which is 100 metres north of the old main road through town. (The new road actually skirts the town to the south.) Around the square, complete with garden and fountain, you'll find the post office, bank and police station. All the hotels are nearby.

Being an important provincial town, Jendouba has branches of all the major Tunisian banks.

Places to Stay – bottom end

The *Pension Saha en Noum* is the best bet at TD 3.500 per person. It is on Blvd Khemais el Hajiri, not far from the square. Avoid the claustrophobic *Pension es-Saada*; it is about as attractive as a prison and has no washing facilities.

Places to Stay – middle

The town's premier establishment is the two-star *Hotel Atlas* (☎ (08) 30 566), just behind the police station. Despite the austere air, it is quite comfortable; for a room with washbasin and bidet you pay TD 9.200/13.100, which includes breakfast.

Places to Eat

There are a couple of restaurants about 100 metres east of the main square. The *Restaurant le Golfe* has a reasonable selection, and the nearby *Restaurant Carthage* is also not bad.

The nightlife is limited to the pleasant outdoor beer garden of the *Atlas Hotel* – not a bad place to be on a hot summer evening.

Getting There & Away

Bus The bus station is over the railway line on the western edge of town. There are regular connections with Ain Draham, Ghardimao, Le Kef, Tebersouk and Tunis.

Train The railway station is just off the main square, near the police station. There are five trains daily to Tunis, and five to Ghardimao, one of the latter which (at 3.40 pm) continues on to Algiers via Annaba and Constantine.

Taxi Louages for Ghardimao leave every few minutes from the station on Blvd Sakiet Sidi Sousse, towards the main road from the square. For Tunis, they leave from Rue 1 Juin 1955, 50 metres along from the Pension es-Saada.

GHARDIMAO

If anything, Ghardimao is even more deadly boring than Jendouba – it really is the end of the line. It's certainly not worth a special trip, but you may find yourself coming through here on the way to Algeria.

Places to Stay

Just like the rest of the town the *Thubernic Hotel* (☎ (08) 45 043) is totally lacking in atmosphere, but there is no alternative. It has no sign, but is the two-storey building opposite the railway station. Rooms cost TD 8.400 for a double.

Getting There & Away

Both the buses and the louages leave from next to the railway line, about 200 metres towards Jendouba from the station.

There are frequent louages to Jendouba, and there is one bus daily direct to Tunis.

To/From Algeria The daily Trans-Maghreb Express crawls through here at around 4 pm every day. Don't be fooled by the name: although it conjures up romantic images of a great railway journey clear across the top of the African continent, it is in fact a slow and crowded trip requiring numerous changes, and is something of an endurance test.

The best bet, if you are heading for Algeria this way, is to take the train as far as Annaba, the first town of any note on the Algerian side. You could just go to Souk Ahras but, apart from the interesting countryside (which you see from the train anyway), there is stuff-all to do there; if you do stop at Souk Ahras, there are buses to Constantine, Annaba and El Oued, as well as hotels if you get caught overnight.

DOUGGA

Another of Tunisia's excellent Roman sites, Dougga has a commanding position on the edge of the Tebersouk Mountains. It is six km along a bitumen road from the small town of Tebersouk and three km up a dirt track from the even smaller town of Dougga, which now houses the residents who were moved from the ancient site to protect the ruins from further decay.

If you haven't yet had an overdose of Roman ruins, this one is well worth visiting. It does, however, require a bit of effort, as there is no cheap accommodation in the immediate vicinity and public transport only takes you to within three km of the site. The best place to base yourself for a visit is the town of Le Kef, 60 km to the west.

Most of the excellent mosaics from this site are in the Bardo Museum.

History

The town of Thugga was already well established in the Punic era, and the unusual monument just below the Roman ruins (known as the Libyco-Punic Mausoleum) dates back to the 2nd century BC.

In early Roman times Thugga became one of the capitals of one of Rome's allies, a Numidian king by the name of Massinissa.

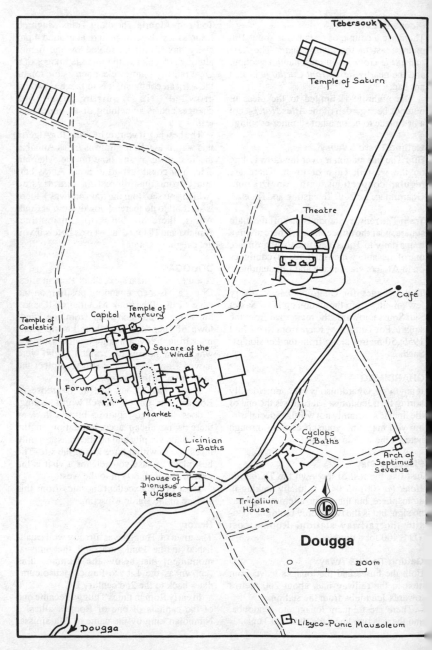

Tebersouk

Temple of Saturn

Theatre

Café

Temple of Caelestis

Temple of Mercury

Capitol

Square of the Winds

Forum

Market

Cyclops Baths

Arch of Septimus Severus

Licinian Baths

House of Dionysus & Ulysses

Trifolium House

Dougga

0   200m

Dougga

Libyco-Punic Mausoleum

Its fortunes followed the familiar pattern of Roman towns in North Africa: great prosperity in the 2nd to 4th centuries followed by a steady decline during the Byzantine and Vandal occupation. Its prosperity was aided by its ample fresh-water supplies as well as by its nearby rich agricultural land and marble quarries.

The Ruins

The site is open daily from 8.30 am to 5.30 pm; entry is TD 1.

Theatre Having shaken off the persistent would-be guides at the entrance, the first monument you come to is the restored theatre on the right. Built in 188 AD by one of the city's wealthy residents, Marcus Quadrutus, it could accommodate an audience of 3500 on its 19 tiers.

Temple of Saturn A track up to the right just past the theatre leads to the Temple of Saturn, which was erected on the site of an earlier temple dedicated to the ancient Semitic god Baal.

Square of the Winds Back at the theatre, the track leads past the site administration office to an unusual winding street (the Romans were great ones for straight lines), which brings you out at the irregularly shaped Square of the Winds. On the paving an enormous inscription not unlike a compass lists the names of the twelve winds. It is still possible to make out some of the names, including Africanus (the sirocco). The Temple of Mercury borders the square to the north, while the market and capitol border it to the south and west respectively.

Capitol The capitol is a remarkable monument – one of the finest in Tunisia. It was a gift to the city in 166 AD from two members of the (obviously) wealthy Marcia family. The inscription carved on the portico records that it was dedicated to the gods Jupiter, Juno and Minerva. Six enormous fluted columns support the portico, which is some eight metres above the ground. The frieze has an

unusually unweathered carving depicting the apotheosis of the emperor Antonius Pius, who is shown being carried off in an eagle's claws.

Inside the capitol was an enormous statue of Jupiter, fragments of which are now in the Bardo Museum in Tunis.

The Byzantines were responsible for the fortifications that intrude on the forum and the capitol here. They filched the stones from various buildings, including the forum, in order to build them.

Temple of Caelestis About 100 metres out to the west among the olive trees is the Temple of Caelestis with its unusual (for North Africa, anyway) semicircular courtyard. It was dedicated to the cult of Juno Caelestis, who was in fact the Roman version of the Carthaginian god Tanit. The sanctuary was built early in the 3rd century and was funded by a resident who was made a *flamen* (a Roman priest) in 222 AD.

House of Dionysus & Ulysses South of the forum a track runs through an old residential area to the Licinian Baths on the left, accessible through a service entrance. The House of Dionysus & Ulysses is on the right. At one time this was a sumptuous residence. It was here that the mosaic of Ulysses mesmerised by the sirens was found (it's now in the Bardo Museum).

Trifolium House The road curves around further, and below it to the right is the Trifolium House. Despite what any guide might tell you about it having been a mansion, it was in fact the town brothel. The name comes from the clover-leaf shape of the main room.

Cyclops Baths Next door are the Cyclops Baths, named after the mosaic found here. The baths are largely in ruins, except for the horseshoe-shaped row of latrines just inside the entrance. The Romans were obviously of the opinion that having a crap should be a communal experience.

Arch of Septimus Serverus Below the baths is the derelict Arch of Septimus Serverus, which was erected in 205 AD when Thugga became a municipality.

Libyco-Punic Mausoleum A track to the south-east leads down to the Libyco-Punic Mausoleum, which is one of the only surviving examples of pre-Roman architecture. According to an inscription, it was erected in memory of a Numidian leader, Ateban, in the 3rd century BC. In 1842 when the British Consul removed the important inscription from it the whole bloody thing collapsed. The inscribed stone was taken to England (where it is now the property of the British Museum) and the funerary tower was rebuilt.

Getting There & Away
The ruins of Dougga are three km up a track from the village of Dougga on the main Tunis-Le Kef road. You can reach it either by walking from here or by going to Tebersouk, six km from the site, and hoping you can hitch from there; the first option is the better one.

The track up to the site is signposted by the Mobil station at the far end of the village. You can save yourself a bit of the walk by cutting through the middle of the village and asking the locals for directions. It's a solid hour's walk but, as long as the weather is not stinking hot (it invariably is in summer), it is an easy uphill grade and you will often have local people for company.

Car drivers should note that the track up from Dougga village gets very rough just below the ruins; you are better off going round via Tebersouk.

Taxi If you are coming on a louage from Le Kef, get off at Dougga. If you arrive in Tebersouk from somewhere else and can't get a lift to the site, take a local louage to Dougga township and walk from there.

TEBERSOUK
This small town sees its fair share of tourists, but no-one actually seems to stop; they are all in a hurry to get to Dougga and on to the next place. Not a bad plan really, as there is stuff-all here.

Places to Stay
The only reason you might want to stop here is to have a base for visiting the ruins at Dougga. The place to stay is the two-star *Hotel Thugga* (☎ (08) 65 713), down by the main road. It is quite OK at TD 15.600/25 for singles/doubles with full board, and is popular with tour groups at lunch time.

Getting There & Away
There are louages running frequently to the village of Dougga (not the ruins), and less often to Beja, Jendouba and Tunis.

LE KEF
This is a picturesque village perched up on the side of a hill overlooking some fine agricultural land. Although it has little in the way of conventional attractions, its location and friendly residents make it a very pleasant place to spend a day or two. In summer its 800-metre elevation means it is significantly cooler than the plains, although it also means that it gets snow in winter.

There is at least one bank here for changing money.

Kasbah
The kasbah dominates the town from the top of the hill. Although it is in a very bad state it is still worth a wander around, and there are some excellent views over the town and surrounding countryside. Until quite recently it was inhabited by the army. There is usually someone hanging around to show you the various points of interest (Turkish mosque, prison cells, gates and walls of various vintages) if your French is up to it.

Museums
Immediately below the kasbah is a small museum housed in what was originally a basilica and then later on a mosque. The museum exhibits are not exactly riveting but entrance is free.

There is another regional museum, which is in a building which previously housed a *zaouia* (a religious fraternity based around a marabout), in a small square not far from the presidential palace. The emphasis is on the nomadic Bedouin and there are some well-displayed exhibits including a tent, some crude utensils, jewellery, weaving looms showing the unusual weaving technique, and agricultural implements. The museum is open from 9 am to noon and 3 to 7 pm Tuesday to Saturday, and 9 am to 2.30 pm Sunday; it's closed Monday. Entry is 800 mills – worth a look.

Places to Stay
The lack of both local and foreign tourists in Le Kef is reflected in the accommodation available; there are only a couple of basic but adequate places.

The modern *Hotel Medina* (☎ (08) 20 214), at 18 Rue Farhat Hached, is immaculately clean and the staff are friendly. It's in the centre of town, about 20 minutes' walk uphill from the bus station. Rooms cost TD 6.500 for a double including cold showers.

Just off Ave Habib Bourguiba, the *Hotel La Source* is the next choice; it has definitely seen better days. The tiny rooms face onto a tiny glassed-in courtyard and the sickly yellow paint job doesn't help either. The front rooms are only a few metres from the minaret across the road, so be prepared for the early morning call. Rooms are overpriced at TD 7.500 for a double with shower.

Although it looks mildly promising from the outside, the *Hotel Auberge* (☎ (08) 20 036) close by cannot really be recommended. The dark and gloomy entrance leads to an equally dark and gloomy bar, and the hotel rooms are not much better. Avoid it if possible.

Places to Eat
As with the hotels, there's little choice. The best place is the small, popular *Restaurant el Hanaa*, 200 metres along Ave Habib Bourguiba, opposite the white and ugly multistorey Banque du Sud building. They have good half chickens for TD 2 and couscous for TD 1.200.

The *Restaurant Venus* has pretensions, is poor value and the owner certainly doesn't win any prizes for friendliness. Tunisian salad is a ridiculous TD 1 and other dishes are similarly overpriced.

Getting There & Away
Bus & Taxi Transport centres around the bus station, 20 minutes' walk downhill from the centre. Shared taxis shuttle between the town centre and the main intersection at the bottom of the hill, passing the bus station on the way.

Buses leave regularly for Ain Draham, Kasserine and Tunis. Louages are frequent, and go to Tunis, Kasserine, Jendouba and Sakiet Sidi Youssef on the Algerian border, from where there are taxis to the town of Souk Ahras.

Train The railway station is right at the bottom of the hill, about one km from the town centre. There is one train daily to Tunis.

Central Tunisia

The central coast of Tunisia has some excellent beaches and, consequently, quite a bit of tourist development. Sousse and Monastir are the major centres but, just a bit further south, the beautiful village of Mahdia is right off the tourist track.

Further south again is Sfax, an interesting regional centre. The Kerkennah Islands just offshore from here are easily accessible, and are a great place to escape the crowds and slow down a bit.

Once you leave the coast and head inland, you are among the olive trees – millions of them! The Romans were the first to plant them and the practice has been revived. In fact, olive oil and olives are both important exports today.

Kairouan, the fourth holiest city in Islam, lies on the plains only a couple of hours from Sousse; tradition has it that seven visits here have as much merit as one visit to Mecca. The city was the capital of the first Arab

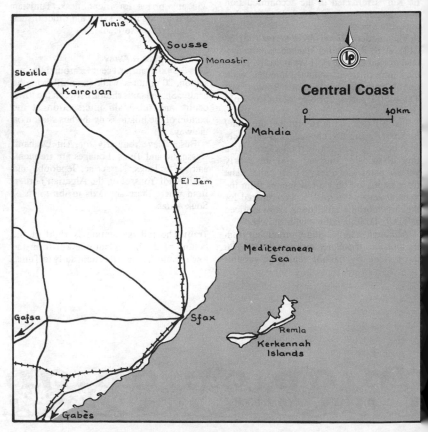

dynasty in North Africa, and today is the most interesting city in the country.

Other attractions of the area are the massive and remarkably well-preserved Roman amphitheatre at El Jem in the olive country, and the ruins of yet another Roman city, Sufetula (Sbeitla today), out on the hot plains near Kasserine, the dull provincial capital.

Sousse

Although Sousse has a large port and is a major industrial centre, it also has an interesting medina and kasbah, and the beach, although crowded in summer, is not at all bad.

It is also a city that is extremely popular with the tour companies, and they bring their clients here in droves in summer. The strip of beach to the north of the town centre has virtually one hotel after another, but you can escape this easily if you want, as quite acceptable accommodation can be found in the medina.

One of the most unusual features of the town today is the way the main Tunis-Sfax railway line runs right along the centre of the main street; the relative calm is well and truly shattered whenever a train comes through. As there are no flashing lights, boom gates, bells or other warning devices of any kind, it's worth a precautionary look when crossing the road to make sure you don't become a decoration on the front of the 4.08 to Sfax.

History

Sousse has been a popular spot for centuries. It was an important Phoenician town before Carthage was even founded, and Hannibal, as leader of the Carthaginian forces, used it as his base against the Romans in the Second Punic War in 218 BC.

It was later occupied by the Romans, Vandals and Byzantines, each of whom gave it a different name. In the 9th century it became the main port of the Aghlabid dynasty based in Kairouan; it was taken over again in later years – first by the Normans in the 12th century, then by the Spanish in the 16th.

Its most recent problems were in WW II, when it was being used as a German port and was bombed heavily by the Allies; however, it has all been restored since then.

Information

Tourist Offices The national tourist office (☎ (03) 25 157) is at 1 Ave Habib Bourguiba, right on the central square, Place Farhat Hached. There is an informative noticeboard inside the office with all the bus and train information, and other items of local interest. The woman staffing the office speaks excellent English and is very helpful. It is open Monday to Thursday from 8.30 am to 1 pm and 3 to 5.45 pm, and on Friday and Saturday, in the mornings only.

The local syndicat d'initiative (☎ (03) 20 431) is across on the other side of the street, in the small, white-domed building.

Money There are plenty of banks along Ave Habib Bourguiba and up by the beach. One branch of the STB on Ave Habib Bourguiba is open long hours in summer.

Post & Telecommunications The main post office is also right in the thick of things, on Ave de la République just along from Place Farhat Hached.

There's a telephone office in one of the small streets near the Claridge Hotel. It is possible to dial direct, or through the operator, between 8 am and 11 pm daily.

Medina

The main monuments in the medina are the *ribat* (a sort of fortified monastery) and the Great Mosque, both in the north-eastern corner of the medina, not far from Place Farhat Hached.

The area surrounding the Great Mosque and ribat is thick with tourist stalls (complete with the obligatory stuffed camels), and the number of tourists that pass through here is reflected in the prices.

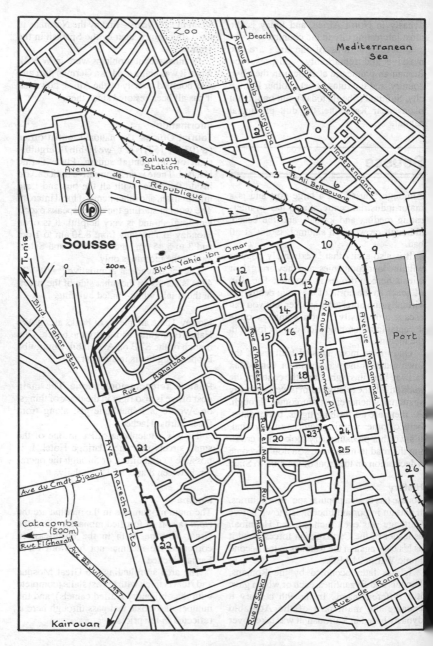

1	Restaurant le Marmite
2	Restaurant de la Jeunesse
3	Tourist Office
4	Claridge Hotel
5	Telephone Office
6	Restaurant Le Bonheur
7	Main Post Office
8	Syndicat d' Initiative
9	Buses to Monastir & Mahdia
10	Place Farhat Hached
11	Hotel Ahla
12	Ribat
13	Restaurant Populaire
14	Great Mosque
15	Hotel Gabes
16	Hotel Medina
17	Residence Fatma
18	Hotel Amira
19	Hotel Zouhour
20	Restaurant Medina
21	Restaurant Hannibal
22	Museum
23	Bab Jedid
24	SNTRI Office
25	Louage & Bus Station
26	Trains to Monastir

Ribat The ribat was built in the 9th century; its primary role was that of a fort to protect the local Muslim population from threats, both from the sea and inland. When the men weren't involved in hostilities they would pursue Islamic study. The design and decoration are extremely simple, no doubt intended to be conducive towards religious study. Small cells surround the arcaded courtyard and steps lead up to the roof, where it's possible to walk right around the ribat.

A narrow winding staircase leads to the top of the watchtower, from where there are excellent views over the city and into the courtyard of the Great Mosque just below. Entry costs 800 mills and there's a further charge of TD 2 for photography.

Great Mosque The Great Mosque is also a fairly simple affair. Built in the 9th century, it has undergone 17th-century renovation and 20th-century restoration. The courtyard is open to visitors from 9 am to 1 pm Monday to Saturday; it's closed on Fridays. Entry is

300 mills. Modest dress is essential, but if your garb fails to meet the required standard it is possible to rent a gown for a couple of hundred mills from one of the shops opposite the entrance.

Museum
The Rue d'Angleterre is the main thoroughfare of the medina; it eventually brings you out on the southern edge of the medina at Bab el Khabli. From here it's a 15-minute walk up the hill to the kasbah and museum. Make sure you get outside the medina before heading up the hill, as there is no access from inside and it means a long walk around to Bab el Gharbi to get out again.

The museum, laid out in the rooms around the citadel courtyard, has some excellent, well-presented mosaics including some from the Christian catacombs in Sousse. There are also funerary objects and stelae from these catacombs, which you can visit; however, as they are over-restored and are a km or two away, they are not worth it. The museum and catacombs are open from 9 am to noon and 3 to 6.30 pm in summer, and 9 am to noon and 2 to 5.30 pm in winter; they're closed on Mondays. Entry is TD 1 to the museum, 800 mills for the catacombs.

Other Attractions
The main beach, at the northern end of Ave Habib Bourguiba, is only a short walk from the centre. It is quite a decent strip of white sand but is backed by high-rise hotels and apartments. At the height of summer it can get ridiculously crowded.

Further north is the much vaunted Port el Kantaoui, a large tourist development touted as 'the garden and pleasure port of the Mediterranean with typically Tunisian architecture', etc etc – my advice is to steer well clear of it. If you want to visit it there's a 'Noddy' train which runs every hour on the hour from the northern end of Ave Habib Bourguiba to Port el Kantaoui. The fare is TD 2 return, or TD 1.200 one way.

Places to Stay – bottom end
As usual the cheapies are in the medina, but

there's not much to choose from. The pick of the rock-bottom places is the *Hotel Gabes*, at 12 Rue de Paris. It is clean, quiet and well kept, and costs TD 5 per person. Hot showers are free. Further along the same street, at No 48, is the slightly sleazy *Hotel Zouhour*. It is like a castle inside, with stairways and passageways leading in all directions. The best rooms are at the top, as these have windows which open outwards rather than onto the courtyard, but they are a bit on the small side. Single/double rooms cost TD 4/5, and there are no showers in this place.

Places to Stay – middle

Things improve rapidly in this category. The *Hotel Amira* (☎ (03) 26 325), inside the medina on the eastern edge near Bab Jedid, is not a bad place. It costs TD 12.5/17 for a double with bath. Breakfast is included, and you can have it served to you outside on the upstairs terrace.

The *Hotel Medina* (☎ (03) 21 722), right by the Great Mosque, has a nice airy and cool lounge room in the centre and is popular with younger tour groups; the locals are attracted to the smoky and sleazy air-conditioned bar at the back. Rooms are clean and cost TD 10/14 for singles/doubles with bath and breakfast.

Just around the corner from the Amira is the *Residence Fatma* (☎ (03) 22 198), which is usually heavily booked but you may be lucky. Rooms cost TD 7.500/11 for a double with breakfast.

Lastly, outside the medina on Ave Habib Bourguiba, the *Hotel Claridge* (☎ (03) 24 759) is a very good one-star hotel in the old style. They charge TD 11.500/16 for a large room with shower, and breakfast in the café next door is included.

Places to Stay – top end

The top-end resort hotels are all along the two main streets in the north of town, Blvd Hedi Chaker and Blvd de la Corniche, and stretch all the way to Port el Kantaoui. Most are geared to the package-tour industry and are fully booked for the season.

Some of the cheaper ones include: *Said* (☎ (03) 28 900) at TD 15/22, *Nour Justinia* (☎ (03) 26 381) for TD 18.500/29, and the *El Hana Beach* (☎ (03) 26 900), which charges TD 23.500/34.

Places to Eat

In the medina, the *Restaurant Medina* is in the street which leads up from Bab Jedid. The menu is in Arabic only, but they do good casse-croûtes and other Tunisian food. They also make one small concession to hygiene by keeping everything in a fly-proof cabinet. Another good local place is the *Restaurant Populaire*. It doesn't have a sign in English, but is opposite the front of the Great Mosque. The food is very good, especially the tajine, but you have to pay for your meal before sitting down.

Just inside the main western gate of the medina is the *Restaurant Hannibal*, which serves good couscous and freshly squeezed orange juice.

There are a couple of cheap local places in a small side street just opposite the Claridge Hotel. One is the *Restaurant de la Jeunesse*, which is very reasonably priced and does excellent hot chips.

As you'd expect given the number of tourists, there are plenty of restaurants, although none offer anything out of the ordinary. Menus are often in three or four languages and the waiters can speak any or all of them. Most restaurants are along Ave Habib Bourguiba and Place Farhat Hached. One that is quite good is the *Restaurant Le Bonheur*, on Place Farhat Hached, which has excellent grilled tuna steaks at TD 8 for two.

In the street parallel and to the west of Ave Habib Bourguiba is the curiously named *Restaurant le Marmite*. Because it is slightly out of the way, the prices are cheaper than those found in restaurants on the main streets – TD 4 for a grilled steak, for instance.

Just off Ave Habib Bourguiba in a side street next to the Hotel Claridge, there's a stall which sells a mixed fruit juice for 300 mills; it contains all sorts of mysterious things, but tastes great.

Getting There & Away

Air You'll find Tunis Air (☎ (03) 25 232) at 5 Ave Habib Bourguiba.

Bus The SNTRI bus office is on Ave Mohammed Ali, not far from Bab Jedid. The buses of the local authority also leave from here. There are daily departures to:

Destination	Time	Fare
Gabès	5½ hours	6.750
Jerba	6 hours	9.650
Kairouan	1½ hours	1.850
Kebili	7½ hours	9.400
Matmata	7 hours	7.580
Sfax	2½ hours	3.670
Tataouine	9 hours	9.120
Tunis	2½ hours	4.060

For services within the Sousse region (to Monastir and Mahdia) buses leave from the end of Place Farhat Hached near the port entrance. To Mahdia, there are 16 buses daily from 7 am to 9.30 pm and the trip takes two hours.

Train The railway station is right in the middle of town, so train is the most convenient way to arrive. The medina and hotels are only five minutes' walk from here.

There are seven trains daily for the two-hour trip to Tunis. Air-conditioned 2nd-class costs TD 3.320. For Sfax there are four departures per day (two hours, TD 3.040), and for Gabès, two per day (four hours, TD 5.420), one of which goes on to Metlaoui (for Tozeur).

There are also local trains, which run on a fairly recently completed line down to Monastir and Mahdia from near Bab Jedid. For Monastir they run almost hourly from 6 am to 7.20 pm and cost 500 mills. For Mahdia the services are much less frequent: three daily, the first not until 2.20 pm.

Taxi Louages for all over the country leave from the station near Bab Jedid on Ave Mohammed Ali. There are regular departures for Kairouan, Kasserine, Mahdia, Sfax and Tunis.

Car Rental The car-rental companies with branches here include: Avis (☎ (03) 25 901), Blvd de la Corniche; Budget (☎ (03) 24 041), 63 Ave Habib Bourguiba; Europcar (☎ (03) 26 252), Blvd de la Corniche and Hertz (☎ (03) 25 428), Ave Habib Bourguiba.

MONASTIR

Situated on a headland some 15 km south of Sousse, Monastir must have at one stage been a pleasant little village. Today it has become a national showpiece, mainly because it was Bourguiba's birthplace and it is here that he has chosen to be buried.

The monuments in the centre include the Bourguiba family mausoleum with its twin cupolas, the 8th-century ribat, which overlooks the sea and the 9th-century Great Mosque.

Saturday is market day in Monastir and on this day the area around the bus station becomes jam-packed with stalls and people. Although Monastir is not really worth an overnight stop, it does make a pleasant day trip from Sousse.

Ribat

The ribat here has been almost totally rebuilt, so lacks authenticity, but it still has quite an interesting atmosphere. It has been used as a film set on more than a couple of occasions. Two films that have had scenes shot here are *Life of Brian* and *Life of Christ*. There are excellent views of the town and coastline all the way back to Sousse from the top of the tower. Entry is TD 1; it's closed Mondays.

Costume Museum

This small museum is right next to the tourist office (☎ (03) 61 960) in the medina, and is worth a quick wander through. It's open daily, except Sunday, from 9 am to noon and 2 to 5.30 pm; entrance is free.

Places to Stay

The only cheap accommodation in Monastir is the *Youth Hostel*, which is close to the bus station, behind the music school. A bed costs TD 4 and breakfast is available for 700 mills. Other than this it's all resort hotels, which run the gamut from cheaper places like the *Hotel Yasmin* (☎ (03) 62 511) at TD 14.800/26 up to the *Club Med* (☎ (03) 31 155) which charges upwards of TD 52 per person.

Places to Eat
The *Restaurant El Medina*, right in the centre of the medina, has a good range of local dishes, while the small *Restaurant Ridha* by the bus station is also good.

Getting There & Away
Air The Tunis Air office (☎ (03) 62 550) is in the Complexe Habib on the foreshore near the ribat. The Air France office (☎ (03) 61 316) is at the airport.

Monastir's international airport is at Skanes, eight km north towards Sousse. Although most of the international flights are direct charters from Europe, Tunis Air has scheduled flights to Amsterdam, Brussels, Frankfurt, Luxembourg, Lyons, Nice, Paris and Rome.

On the domestic network, there are flights to Tunis (twice weekly) and Jerba (three times weekly).

Bus The bus station is at the western edge of the medina. There are regular departures for Sousse, Mahdia and other towns in the surrounding area.

Train The train station is also on the western edge of the medina. There are almost hourly departures for the 45-minute trip to Sousse (500 mills) and three daily to Tunis (three hours).

Taxi The louages leave from the bus station. Demand often exceeds supply so it is a matter of making a dive for a door handle.

MAHDIA
Mahdia is one of the few towns on this section of coast which has managed to escape being turned into a tourist resort. It's a beautifully relaxed place, with a small medina stuck out at the end of a little promontory, 60 km or so south of Sousse.

History
The town has an important history dating back to 916 AD, when the first Fatimid ruler, Obeid Allah, made it his capital. He was a self-declared *Mahdi*, 'one who is guided' (to convert the world to Islam). He belonged to the Shiite sect, considered heretical by the Sunni majority, and therefore needed a place that was easily defended. Mahdia fitted the bill neatly, as it is on a high promontory. In order to defend the town a massive wall, in places up to 10 metres thick, was built right across the neck of the spit, with just one easily guarded gate giving access.

However, in 968 the Fatimids realised their dream of becoming caliphs in Cairo and from that time on the town decreased in importance. It was still important enough for the Christians to invade in the 11th century, followed by the Normans in the 12th and the Spanish in the 16th. When the Spanish left they blew the walls down, only to have the Ottoman Turks partially reconstruct them.

Information
There is a small tourist office (☎ (03) 81 098) just inside the main gate, Skifa el Kahla, and the guy here tries to be helpful. The post office is near the Grand Hotel in the new part of town, 500 metres' walk from the Skifa el Kahla.

There are a few banks, mostly along the foreshore road on the harbour side of the promontory.

The Friday market and the daily fish market are held in the large white building opposite the fishing harbour.

Medina
The medina starts with the massive gate, Skifa el Kahla, which at one time was part of the 10-metre-thick wall that blocked off this narrow part of the promontory. The narrow vaulted passageway had various iron gates which could be lowered to block the entrance to the medina.

Once inside, the tourist office is straight

ahead on the right. On the inside of the wall here are steps leading up to the top of the gate, from which you can get a good perspective of the town and see how well defended it was.

The narrow, cobbled main street first leads to a small Museum of Silk on the right, identifiable by a small nameplate by the door (which seems to be permanently closed). The street then leads past a hammam on the left. It eventually opens out onto an immaculate small square, complete with shady trees, vines and cafés. By day the old men sit around in the shade drinking coffee; later on the square livens up considerably, with all the men coming out for their evening coffee and game of dominoes.

The main street then continues and comes out at a larger square dominated by the Great Mosque. This is a 20th-century recreation of the original built by the Mahdi in the 10th century and it is a very simple construction. Its only major feature is the unadorned entrance, a characteristic of Fatimid design.

On the highest point of the headland is the Borj el Kebir, which was built in the 16th century and has been heavily restored. It is not worth the 800 mills entry, as there is nothing to see inside and the views from the ramparts are not that much better than from on the ground.

The road past the fort leads through an enormous cemetery to the lighthouse on the end of the headland; down to the right is what is left of the old Fatimid port, today used as a mooring for a few fishing boats.

Weaving cotton sheets and exquisite cloth for weddings on hand looms is widespread throughout the old city, and the click-clack of the shuttles is often the only sound disturbing the torpor which sets in on hot summer afternoons. Many of these small workshops have a definite air of the Dickensian workhouse about them, with poor lighting, cramped conditions and no ventilation. The weavers are usually more than willing to break the boredom and explain the finer points of their craft. Wedding material is full of gold thread and has to be ordered at least 12 months in advance.

The water here is a clear blue and swimming is definitely possible, either from the rocks outside the Hotel El Jazira or from the beach about three km further along the coast.

Place to Stay – bottom end

The family-run *Hotel El Jazira* (☎ (03) 81 274) is not the friendliest place in the world, but the price is reasonable, especially given the views. It is right on the water on the northern side of the headland, about 50 metres inside Skifa el Kahla. Some of the rooms look straight out over the water, although the best view is to be had from the bathroom. Rooms cost TD 6 and there are hot showers. There's a table and chairs on the roof.

Places to Stay – middle

The two-star *Grand Hotel* (☎ (03) 80 039) is about 500 metres from the main gate along the Sousse road, which is the main road to the right as you come out of the gate. The hotel has a nice shaded garden, with pergolas covered in bougainvillea and even cute little cubicles where you can sit in privacy. Rooms cost TD 7/10 for a single/double with bath and breakfast.

The *Hotel Rand* (☎ (03) 80 448) is further again from the centre. From the Grand Hotel, take the left fork and then turn left after about 200 metres at the first major intersection; the hotel is on the right. At TD 4/6 for a single/double it's not bad value but its location makes it inconvenient.

Places to Stay – top end

Out along the beach about three km north of town is the *Hotel Sables d'Or* (☎ (03) 81 137); this is a one-star resort hotel that is nevertheless fairly low key. The beach here is clean and uncrowded; there are shade shelters on it, and small yachts and sailboards for hire. Rooms cost TD 13/20 for bed and breakfast, or TD 18/30 for pension complète. There are blue-and-white service taxis which run out past here from the corner near the market for 300 mills per person.

Places to Eat

There's not a lot of choice here, but there's one small place which is extremely popular at lunch times and serves excellent food. This is the *Restaurant El Moez*, between Skifa el Kahla and the market. Run by a very jolly fat fellow who welcomes you with open arms, it serves the best shakshuka (vegetable stew) in the country and also has excellent fresh fish. In the evening the selection is more limited.

Getting There & Away

Bus Buses leave from the kiosk near the market up by the entrance to the fishing harbour. There are regular departures to Sousse and Monastir, and less frequent departures to Kairouan and Tunis.

Train The relatively new railway station is on the other side of the Esso station from the louages. The line from Monastir was only opened in 1987, so the station is very modern and comes complete with marble floors and potted plants.

There are three departures daily for the 75-minute journey to Sousse, but there's nothing between 6 am and 1 pm. These trains go on all the way to Tunis. The total journey time to Tunis is three hours.

Taxi The louage station is right by the Esso station at the opposite end of the wide open space to the bus station. It is only about 300 metres from the centre. There are departures for El Jem, Kairouan, Monastir, Sfax and Sousse.

EL JEM

If it wasn't for the fact that El Jem has a very well-preserved Roman amphitheatre which is not much smaller than the Colosseum in Rome, this otherwise unremarkable town would certainly be low on the list of priorities for any visitor to Tunisia – its setting on the flat plains is dull and the summer heat is oppressive.

The amphitheatre sticks up in the middle of the town, and the tourists come flocking to see one of the most impressive Roman monuments in North Africa – it's well worth a visit.

From the 2nd century AD onwards, ancient Thysdrus prospered as the centre of an olive-growing region; it was a town with sumptuous villas adorned with some brilliant mosaics.

In 238 AD at the age of 80, Gordian was declared emperor of Rome here, and the amphitheatre is a legacy of his reign. It suffered badly in the 17th century when the guts were blown out of one side of it in order to flush out some dissidents who had taken refuge within the walls. Not only did this completely demolish a large section, it also destabilised the rest of it; some fairly hasty and none-too-professional repairs were done to stop the whole thing collapsing.

The seating capacity is estimated to have been around the 30,000 mark, although none of the seats remain today. Under the arena two long passageways were uncovered, and it is believed that these held the animals, gladiators or other unfortunates who would get thrust into the ring to do battle and provide entertainment for the masses.

The amphitheatre is enclosed by a small fence and there's an entry charge of TD 1.500. Around the entrance are the usual hangers-on who always appear wherever there are tourists in numbers – camel drivers, souvenir sellers, guides, etc etc, and the number of Land Rovers that come through here from Sousse 'on safari' fully laden with all the gear, is really quite amazing.

About 500 metres south of the amphitheatre, along the road to Sfax, is the museum. This houses yet more mosaics, all found on the site right behind the building, which was an area of particularly rich villas. Some of the mosaics have been left *in situ* while the best have been moved into the museum. It is open from 8.30 am to noon and 2.30 to 6 pm in summer, and 8.30 am to noon and 2 to 5.30 pm in winter; entry is TD 1, and there's a further charge of TD 2 if you want to take photographs.

Across the road from the museum are the

ruins of more houses and another amphitheatre, this one much smaller and barely recognisable.

Places to Stay & Eat

Although there is a hotel in town, it takes only a couple of hours to see the amphitheatre and museum, so the best thing is to carry on to another destination later in the day. The railway station won't look after baggage but the guy at the entrance to the amphitheatre will keep an eye on it for a while.

The only accommodation in El Jem is the *Hotel Julius* (☎ (03) 90 044), right on the main road by the railway station. Rooms are arranged around a pleasant courtyard and cost TD 7.500/13 for a single/double; it fills up early in summer.

There are a couple of small restaurants along the main street between the hotel and the museum, but don't expect anything more exotic than brochettes.

For coffee and tea, there are a few cafés around the square directly opposite the railway station.

Getting There & Away

Bus The SNTRI bus office is on the right just before the museum. The only departures are the buses in transit, so in summer it will be difficult to get a seat. The train is a better bet.

Train The railway station is only about five minutes' walk from the amphitheatre and is right in the centre.

For trains south, there are four daily to Sfax (one hour) between 10.20 am and midnight; two of these go on to Gabès (three hours), while the midnight one goes all the way to Metlaoui (six hours, change in Sfax).

For Tunis, there are five trains which stop on the way from the south: these are at 2.30 and 8.15 am, and 1.15, 2.15 and 7.15 pm. The trip takes three hours.

Taxi The louages leave from the street just opposite and to the right of the train station.

Demand often exceeds supply here and it can be a bit of a scramble to get a seat. There are frequent departures to Sousse, Sfax, Kairouan and Mahdia, although things dry up a bit in the afternoon.

Kairouan

Historically, this is the most important town in the country. It ranks behind only Mecca, Medina and Jerusalem in Islam. The medina, with the Great Mosque, is compact and interesting and there are other sights around the town.

With a population of 100,000, Kairouan is the fifth-largest city in the country. It's the centre of a major fruit-growing region and is also well known for the traditional carpetweaving which is carried out here.

Because of its importance, however, Kairouan sees more than its fair share of tourists. As a result the medina is overflowing with tourist shops, and some of the merchants have started resorting to a bit of good old Moroccan-style aggression to get business. It's easy to cope with all this, however.

History

Founded in the second half of the 7th century by Aqbar ibn Nafi, Kairouan is where Islam first took hold in the Maghreb. It became the capital of the Aghlabid dynasty in 800 AD, and it was under these rulers that the Great Mosque and other buildings of religious significance were constructed.

The Fatimids conquered the city in 909. When they moved their capital to Mahdia, Kairouan went through a period of decline, reaching a low point in 1057 when the Beni Hilal Bedouin tribe destroyed the city at the behest of the Fatimid ruler Mustansir.

Although Kairouan was largely rebuilt in the 13th century, it was never to regain its position of political pre-eminence. However, as a religious centre it was and still is the most important place in the country.

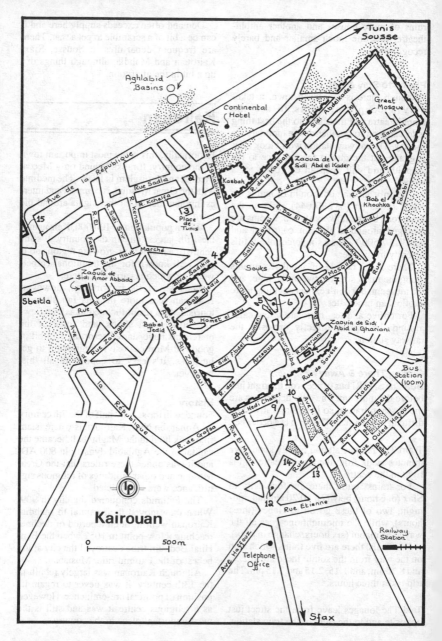

Kairouan

0   500m

1	Hospital
2	Hotel el Menema
3	Market
4	Bab Tunis & Louages
5	Medina Hotels
6	Bir Barouta
7	Mosque of the Three Doors
8	ONAT Emporium
9	Hotel Sabra
10	Tourist Office
11	Bab ech Chouhada
12	Main Post Office
13	Hotel Tunisia
14	Hotel Splendid
15	Zaouia of Sidi Sahab

Information

Tourist Office The tourist office (☎ (07) 21 797) of the national tourist body is right at the entrance to the old city, opposite Bab ech Chouhada (Gate of the Martyrs). Tickets for the main sites can only be bought from here. For TD 1.500 you get a combined ticket, which is valid for two days and gets you into the six major monuments around the city and the Islamic Art Museum at Raqqada, on the road to Sfax. The office is open daily from 8.30 am to 5.30 pm.

Money There are plenty of banks for changing money, including one just inside Bab ech Chouhada and a couple more on Ave Habib Bourguiba, just around the side of the tourist office.

Post & Telecommunications The main post office is 100 metres or so south of Bab ech Chouhada, at the roundabout on the corner of Ave de la République and Rue Farhat Hached. It is open from 8 am to 6 pm Monday to Saturday in winter, and 7.30 am to 12.30 pm Monday to Saturday in summer.

There is a small telephone office on the Sfax road, just south of the roundabout by the post office. It has a few payphones and is open 8 am to 10 pm daily.

Hammam There's a hammam in the Hotel Sabra which is open daily until 3 pm for men.

A bath costs 500 mills, or TD 1.500 with massage.

Medina

The walled medina is the central part of the city; the new French section spreads away to the south and follows the usual orderly plan. The wall itself is pierced by a number of entrances, the main ones being Bab ech Chouhada to the south and Bab Tunis in the north wall. A 100-metre section in the north wall near the kasbah has been removed to ease the traffic congestion and give the tour buses access to the Great Mosque.

In summer the place is crawling with tour groups, so it's best to get out and about early before they whiz in from Sousse; late afternoon is also a good time. This is also the best way to do it, as Kairouan gets bloody hot in the middle of the day.

The main street of the medina is, you guessed it, Ave Habib Bourguiba. It is wall-to-wall souvenir shops selling every imaginable souvenir from tacky stuffed camels to really beautiful carpets. There are numerous cafés and the odd restaurant as well.

Great Mosque The Great Mosque is in the north-eastern corner of the medina and is the principal monument. The building that you see today dates from 670 AD, although it has been restored more than once since then.

From the outside it is extremely plain, lacking in decoration of any kind, and in fact looks more like a fort. Although it has eight gates, only one of the four on Rue Brahim ben Lagleb along the west side is open today for non-Muslims.

The marble-paved courtyard is surrounded by an arched colonnade and is dominated by the square minaret on the northern side. The marble paving slopes towards the centre, where there is a decorated drain hole down which the collected rainwater falls into the 9th-century cisterns below. There are a couple of wells in the courtyard and, over the centuries, the grooves in the lips of these have been worn in by the ropes which were used to haul out the buckets of water.

It is thought that the lowest level of the 35-metre minaret dates from the 8th century, making it the oldest standing minaret in the world.

The main entrance to the prayer hall is beneath the portico with the cupola, one of five on the mosque. The large wooden doors are fairly recent, dating back to the last century; the carved panel above the doors is particularly fine. The 400 or so pillars within the prayer hall have been filched from various Roman sites throughout the country including Carthage and Sousse. At the far end of the hall it is vaguely possible to make out the precious 9th-century faïence tiles behind the *mihrab* (prayer niche in the mosque wall which indicates the direction of Mecca), which were imported from Baghdad along with the wood for the *minbar* (pulpit) next to it.

The mosque is open daily except Friday. For people not considered suitably dressed there are robes available at the entrance.

Mosque of the Three Doors Heading back through the lanes of the medina you'll come to the Mosque of the Three Doors, on Rue de la Mosquée not far from Ave Habib Bourguiba. Although it has just been restored it is not open to the public, but is of interest for the rare 9th-century Arab inscriptions carved in the façade.

Zaouia of Sidi Abid el Ghariani Closer again to Ave Habib Bourguiba is the Zaouia of Sidi Abid el Ghariani, one of the monuments on the ticket. Recently restored, the building dates from the 14th century and contains some fine wood-carving and stucco work. The custodian here is a very willing talker, and will guide you around pointing out the finer points (in French of course) such as the cedar ceiling and the new and old stucco. There is a carpet shop close by in the same street and the owner will try to lure the unwary visitor in, with the assurances that his shop is in fact the zaouia.

Bir Barouta The biggest tourist trap in the whole city is a well, known as Bir Barouta. It is on Ave Habib Bourguiba in the centre of the medina, at the top of a set of stairs through a high arched doorway. In quite a confined space here a poor mangy old camel trudges around and around all day, while the tourists file in and out, taking the obligatory photo and leaving the obligatory tip. The well's popularity stems from the fact that it is supposedly connected to Mecca, so to drink the water is supposed to do wonders for you.

Other Attractions

To get to the other two monuments requires a bit of foot slogging. The Zaouia of Sidi Sahab and the Aghlabid Basins are both on the Tunis road north of the medina. It takes a couple of hours to see both of them.

The Zaouia of Sidi Sahab was built in honour of Abu Zama el Belaoui, a saint and friend of the Prophet who is renowned for always carrying three hairs from the Prophet's beard around with him. For this reason he became known as the Prophet's barber, which explains the other name of this zaouia – the Mosque of the Barber.

A very highly decorated passageway leads off the white courtyard into the main courtyard of the zaouia, which is also highly decorated with tiles and stucco work. In a room off to the left is the tomb of the designer of the Great Mosque, while the saint's tomb is in the room on the far side of the courtyard. Non-Muslims are allowed to enter as far as the courtyard only.

As at the Great Mosque, robes are available at the entrance. This is the third of the monuments on the ticket.

The Aghlabid Basins are a km to the north-east of the Mosque of the Barber, along Ave de la République. These two cisterns were originally built in the 9th century and were filled by an aqueduct from a spring some 30 km away; they were some of the many which once used to supply the town with water. The larger of the two is over 130 metres in diameter and the perimeter wall has curious buttressing. In the centre are pillars which used to hold a pavilion where the rulers could come to relax in the cool on summer evenings. They were heavily restored about 20 years ago and are all concrete, but are still worth a quick look.

Ten km south of Kairouan is the Raqqada Islamic Art Museum, which is well worth a visit. To reach it you'll have to take a bus from near the post office to the university, and then walk the remaining couple of km. There are buses at 8, 9, 10 and 11 am, and at noon. The museum is open daily, except Monday, from 9 am to 2.30 pm.

Places to Stay – bottom end

The best place in town is outside the medina opposite Bab ech Chouhada. This is the big, clean *Hotel Sabra* (☎ (07) 20 260), which is popular and conveniently located; it charges TD 4/7 for singles/doubles including breakfast and free hot showers – a good place.

There are a couple of places in the medina. The *Hotel Barouta*, on the square on Ave Habib Bourguiba, is noisy and barely adequate; rooms cost TD 3 per person.

A better bet is the *Hotel Marhala* (☎ (07) 20 736) at 35 Souk el Belaghija, one of the covered souks off Ave Habib Bourguiba right in the heart of the medina. This place is an old hostel and offers something a little different from the average medina hotel. The rooms are tiny, however, and those on the roof get unbearably hot in summer. Rooms cost TD 4.500 per person. To find the hotel, head through the big arch with crenellated top, on the right on Ave Habib Bourguiba coming from Bab ech Chouhada. It's easy to miss during business hours, as it is obscured with all sorts of stuff from the shops selling souvenirs. The hotel is about 50 metres along on the left.

Places to Stay – middle

The *Hotel el Menema* (☎ (07) 20 182) is a fairly new place a couple of blocks north of Bab Tunis. The rooms are all arranged around a covered courtyard but some also have windows to the outside. Charges are TD 10/18 in single/double rooms with bath,

TD 1 less without bath; these prices include breakfast.

There are also a couple of good places just south of the medina. The two-star *Tunisia Hotel* (☎ (07) 21 855) on Ave de la République has big, cool rooms which cost TD 10.500/17 with bath and breakfast. Close by is the three-star *Hotel Splendid* (☎ (07) 20 041), where a room with bath and breakfast will set you back TD 13/18. This place is popular with tour parties from the resorts on the coast.

Places to Stay – top end

The *Continental Hotel* (☎ (07) 21 111) is on Ave de la République, right opposite the Aghlabid Basins. It has definitely seen better days, but is air-conditioned and charges TD 22.500/34 for singles/doubles with breakfast in the low season, rising to TD 25.500/38 in the summer. It's no real problem to just stroll in and use the pool, regardless of whether you are staying there or not.

Places to Eat

The fact that most tourists come here just for a day trip is reflected in the fact that there are very few restaurants. One that is quite good is the *Restaurant Faïzour*, well signposted but tucked away in the corner of the small square on Ave Habib Bourguiba. You can sit outside in the evening. Be precise about what you order, or they may try to bring out all sorts of stuff and add it to the bill.

As usual, there are numerous cafés in the medina, but one with a little more atmosphere than usual is the *Café Errachid*, housed in an old part of the medina, near the Hotel Marhala.

There are a couple of other Tunisian restaurants along Ave Habib Bourguiba.

Things to Buy

Kairouan is one of the major carpet centres in the country, so if you are in the market for one this is a good place to do your shopping. The ONAT emporium/museum on Ave Ali Zouaoui not only has an excellent display of old rugs but also sells new ones. You can get a good idea of prices and what is available, although the prices here are certainly not the cheapest around. It is open daily from 8.30 am to 1 pm and 1.30 to 5.45 pm.

All carpets for sale which have been inspected and classified by ONAT carry a label and seal on the back. Ones without this label may be of dubious quality, so don't buy indiscriminately.

Getting There & Away

Air The Tunis Air office (☎ (07) 20 422) is on Rue Khawarezmi, not far from the tourist office.

Bus The bus station is to the south-east of Bab ech Chouhada, about 10 minutes' walk away. Both the SNTRI and the regional buses leave from here.

There are regular departures to Sousse, Sfax (four daily, TD 2.430), Kasserine, Nabeul (three daily, TD 4.440), Gafsa and Tunis (three daily, TD 7.630).

Taxi Louages to all points north, south, east and west leave from the vacant lot just outside Bab Tunis. There are departures for Tunis (two hours, TD 4.300), Gafsa, Kasserine and Sousse. Note that the only transport to Sfax is by bus.

SBEITLA

Stuck right out in the middle of nowhere, Sbeitla is quite a good Roman site, although it is not really on the way to or from anywhere in particular. If you have your own vehicle it is worth a detour; for those without, stop off if it's on your route; otherwise don't make a special trip to see it.

The site lies only 500 metres or so from the lifeless town of Sbeitla, 40 km east of Kasserine and 120 km south-west of Kairouan.

The history of the Roman town of Sufetula is not well known, especially during the period from the 2nd to the 4th century AD, the height of Roman prosperity in North Africa.

Things to See

From the town the first monument you come across is the restored Triumphal Arch of Diocletian, among the eucalypt trees to the right of the road. The site entrance, however, is a further couple of 100 metres along, between a couple of Byzantine forts.

Once inside, the ruins of interest are off to the left – there is a well-trodden path which is easy to follow. The walled forum is still easy to identify, but the dominant structures are the three temples on the north side. Although they have been largely reconstructed, they provide one of the best examples of how the centres of towns were dominated by temple buildings.

Out behind the temples are the ruins of a couple of churches. The first is a basilica with three aisles and the second a Byzantine cathedral with five aisles. Just on the forum side of the latter is a beautifully restored baptistry, complete with mosaics which include colourful floral and cross motifs.

Back towards the river (oued), the theatre is in a bad way; at one time it must have been fantastic with its position right above the bank of the oued.

Opposite the entrance to the site is a small museum which even the custodian tells you is not worth it – sound advice.

Places to Stay

If bad luck or bad management finds you looking for a bed here, you do at least have a choice. The *Hotel Bakini* on the main street in the township would do in a pinch.

For something better there's the fancy *Hotel Cillium* (☎ (07) 70 106), 500 metres beyond the site on the Kasserine road. This place is designed with tourists in mind and this is reflected in the prices: TD 15.600/21.900 for rooms with bath and breakfast. One big advantage is that there is a swimming pool; also, the hotel overlooks the Roman site.

Getting There & Away

Transport centres around the dusty bus station, 200 metres south of the main intersection. You can't miss it; this is only a small town.

There are bus and louage connections with Tunis, Kasserine, Tozeur, Kairouan, Dahmani and Le Kef.

Sfax

With a population of over 375,000, Sfax is the second-largest city in the country, and is a major port. Exports which are shipped from here include phosphate from the Gafsa region and olive oil from the thousands of groves near the coast.

As a place to visit, Sfax is not exactly riveting. However, the walled medina is worth a wander around in, if only to see what a medina is like before it gets filled with souvenir shops. Also, the folk museum set in a typical 17th-century house is excellent.

The new city is really devoid of interest, but ferries from the port here give access to the nearby Kerkennah Islands. These are an ideal place to escape to and do nothing for a few days, mainly because there is nothing to do there except swim on the mediocre beaches or rent a bicycle and explore a bit.

Information

Tourist Office The syndicat d'initiative (☎ (04) 24 606) is in the small green-roofed pavilion in a small square on Ave Habib Bourguiba. As usual it is of very little use, and this is compounded by the fact that the office is only open in the mornings.

Money There are plenty of banks for changing money along Ave Habib Bourguiba and Rue de la République.

Post & Telecommunications The post office is the enormous edifice on Ave Habib Bourguiba which occupies the entire first block from the railway station. The entrance for posting letters and parcels is the small door on Ave Habib Bourguiba under the 'Rapide Poste' sign. It is open Monday to Saturday from 8 am to 6 pm and Sunday

from 9 to 11 am. There is an international telephone counter inside the post office, and it's possible to either dial direct or go through the operator.

Hammam The Hammam Sultan is close to the Museum of Popular Traditions in the heart of the medina. It is open for women from noon to 4 pm, and for men from 4 pm to midnight. A bath with massage is TD 1.500.

Medina

The walls of the medina originally dated from the 9th century, but what you see today is a mixture from many periods.

The main access from the new city is through Bab Diwan in the middle of the southern wall. The main street through the medina, Rue Mongi Slim, is incredibly narrow and is little more than a footpath.

About a third of the way along is a small street to the right (next to No 54) which leads to the well laid-out Museum of Popular Traditions; this is set in a 17th-century mansion, Dar Djellouli, at 5 Rue Sidi Ali Nouri. The house alone is worth a visit, with its beautiful carved wood and stucco work. The exhibits help give a better grasp of everyday life in the times of the beys – costumes, jewellery and household implements. The display of calligraphy is especially interesting. The museum is open daily, except Monday, from 9 am to 4.30 pm; entry is 800 mills and there's a TD 1 charge if you want to take photos.

Just outside the north gate, Bab Jabli, is the fairly recently constructed market, the southern wall of which is lined with the butchers' stalls – don't venture in if you can't stand the sight of butchered animals. Most stalls have the head of the animal prominently displayed, presumably so you can see what sort of a beast it was, and the stalls sell everything from tongues to testicles.

Ville Nouvelle

The focal point of the ville nouvelle is the very formal main square, Place Hedi Chaker,

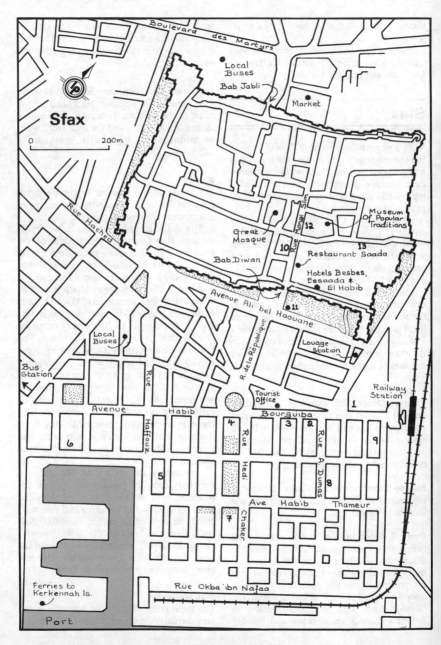

Sfax

0   200m

Boulevard des Martyrs

Local Buses
Bab Jabli
Market

Rue Hached

Museum Of Popular Traditions

Rue Mongi Slim

Great Mosque
12
10
Bab Diwan
Restaurant Saada
13

Hotels Besbes, Essaada & El Habib

Avenue Ali bel Haouane
11

Local Buses

R. de la République

Louage Station

Bus Station

Rue Haffouz

Tourist Office

Avenue   Habib   Bourguiba

Railway Station
1

4
Rue Hedi

3   2
Rue A. Dumas

9

6

5
8

Ave   Habib   Thameur

7
Chaker

Ferries to Kerkennah Is.

Rue Okba ibn Nafaa

Port

1	Main Post Office
2	French Consulate
3	Hotel Sfax Centre
4	Town Hall & Museum
5	Restaurant Chez Nous
6	Market
7	Hotel Leo Oliviers
8	Hotels de la Paix & Alexander
9	SNTRI Buses
10	Hotel Medina
11	Louages to Gafsa & Libya
12	Hotel Andalous
13	Hamman Sultan

with its statue of Bourguiba, and the town hall with its clashing dome and clocktower.

In the town hall itself is the Museum of Antiquities, which has a few mosaics and other bits and pieces of only passing interest – you can easily pass this one up.

Places to Stay – bottom end

Once again, the medina offers a choice of cheapies. The *Hotel Besbes* (☎ (04) 27 271) is about 50 metres inside Bab Diwan to the right in amongst a group of cheap hotels. It's friendly, if a little gloomy, and small rooms cost TD 3.500 for a double. The *Hotel Essaada* (☎ (04) 20 892) next door is similar, although unfriendly, while the *Hotel El Habib* (☎ (04) 21 373), on the other side of the road, has doubles for TD 9.

There are a few more cheapies on Rue Mongi Slim. The *Hotel Medina* at No 53 charges TD 6 for a double and 500 mills for a shower. It's not a bad place but lacks privacy. The *Hotel Andalous* (☎ (04) 20 903), also on Rue Mongi Slim, is a typical medina dive but is cheap at TD 2.500 for a bed.

Places to Stay – middle

The best place in this category is the *Hotel Alexander* (☎ (04) 21 911), at 21 Rue Alexandre Dumas. It is good value for money at TD 9.500/15 for single/double rooms with bath and breakfast included.

Almost next door to the Alexander is the somewhat run-down *Hotel de la Paix*

(☎ (04) 21 436). Not long ago this was an excellent place to stay, but these days it is overpriced at TD 7/10 for basic rooms, and TD 9/12 with bath; breakfast is not included.

Places to Stay – top end

If you can afford it, the place to stay is the classy *Hotel Les Oliviers* (☎ (04) 25 188), on Ave Habib Thameur, two blocks south of the town hall. It is a grand old building which still has an air of elegance. Rooms cost TD 16.500/25 for singles/doubles with bath and breakfast, TD 2.500 more with air-conditioning. The hotel has a good bar and also a swimming pool.

Sfax's newest monster is the four-star *Hotel Sfax Centre* (☎ (04) 25 700), on Ave Habib Bourguiba, which is popular with the tour groups. Rooms cost TD 36/49 with air-conditioning; there's a swimming pool and all the other frills.

Places to Eat

For cheap Tunisian food, there are a few good places just inside Bab Diwan. To the right is the clean *Restaurant Tunisien*, where a main meal costs around TD 1.200. There are a couple of others up to the left of Bab Diwan.

The small and cosy *Restaurant Saada* on Rue Mongi Slim also has quite reasonable food and friendly service.

For just a tea or cold drink there are plenty of cafés on Place de l'Indépendance, behind the tourist office. For a beer the best place is the bar in the Hotel Les Oliviers, although you do pay a little over the odds here.

For a minor splurge the *Restaurant Chez Nous*, on Rue Patrice Lumumba towards the port, is worth a try. It has a fairly extensive menu and also serves alcohol. Expect to pay around TD 5 per person, plus drinks.

Getting There & Away

Air The Tunis Air office (☎ (04) 28 628) is at 4 Ave de l'Armée. Air France (☎ (04) 42 500) has an office at 15 Rue Taieb M'Hiri. There are weekly flights to Paris with both Air France and Tunis Air.

Bus The SNTRI office is almost opposite the railway station, at the eastern end of Ave Habib Bourguiba. There are departures for Gabès (five daily), Jerba (two daily), Medenine (three daily) and Tunis (four daily). Booking in advance is advisable, although this is not always possible, as most buses are actually only stopping in transit.

For regional buses to Gafsa and places south, there is a station about 15 minutes' walk west of the town hall. In summer it's a hot and dusty place, and the Gafsa buses get impossibly crowded. There are departures for Gafsa at 12.30, 1.45 and 2.45 pm; the fare is TD 5.500.

Train The railway station is right at the eastern end of Ave Habib Bourguiba and is a grand affair. There are five departures daily to Sousse (two hours) and Tunis (four hours) and two to Gabès (two hours).

Taxi Most louages leave one block north of the post office in a shady square. There are departures here for El Jem, Gabès, Kairouan, Sousse and Tunis. The exception is the louages for Gafsa, which leave from the carpark just outside and to the east of Bab Diwan. There are also plenty of Libyan shared taxis here, in the unlikely event that you are heading there.

Car Rental The following agencies have offices in Sfax: Avis (☎ (04) 24 605), Rue Tahar Sfar; Europcar (☎ (04) 26 680), 16 Ave Habib Bourguiba; and Hertz (☎ (04) 28 626), 47 Ave Habib Bourguiba.

Sea The ferries for the Kerkennah Islands leave from the port (☎ (04) 23 615), a 15-minute walk from the town hall. There are four departures daily (for times, see the Tunisia Getting There & Away section for the Kerkennah Islands). In summer, if you are taking a vehicle across and want to get on the first or second ferry, it is necessary to join the queue around 6 am to be assured of a place. Passage is free for passengers; for a car you'll pay TD 4.500. The crossing takes about 1½ hours.

Kerkennah Islands

This group of islands lies only 25 km off the coast from Sfax, but the pace of life is definitely a gear or two lower than on the mainland. If you want a place to do nothing for a couple of days, this isn't a bad choice. However, if it's a tropical island paradise you're after, this definitely isn't it: the palm trees are all very shabby, the whole place is extremely dry and the highest point is about three metres above sea level.

There are two main islands, Ile Gharbi and Ile Chergui, connected by a small causeway dating back to Roman times. Ile Gharbi has little more than the ferry port at Sidi Youssef, from which it's a 16-km drive to the causeway. Chergui has a bit more to offer – a few tourist resorts on the north coast at Sidi Fredj and the small village of Remla, the 'capital' of the islands. Despite a small amount of tourist development, the tourists are staying away in droves and the calm of the islands remains undisturbed.

Fishing is the main activity of the islanders. The water gets deep very slowly, which makes swimming pretty hopeless. However, it has enabled the locals to develop a unique fishing method whereby they make large traps out of lines of palm fronds stuck in the sea bed in a V shape. The fish are then driven into this large funnel and into a small trap at the end of the V. At least half the vehicles on the ferries from Sfax are trucks and pick-ups loaded with palm fronds for the traps.

El Attaya is a small village right at the far tip of Ile Chergui, 12 km from Remla. If the weather is not too scorchingly hot, it is a pleasant walk (catch a bus there or back) or bike ride.

The islands are a real backwater and it is only very recently that facilities such as a bank have been established there. The bank is 50 metres from the Hotel El Jazira, towards the water.

Places to Stay

The only conventional hotel is the very basic

Hotel El Jazira (☎ (04) 81 058) in Remla. It is quite clean, friendly, has showers and is right by the bus stop. Single/double rooms cost TD 8/12 including breakfast. The hotel is also the main social point on the islands, as it has the only bar (750 mills for a beer) and one of the few restaurants.

The resort places of the 'Zone Touristique' at Sidi Fredj are inconveniently located; you need to take them on a full-board basis, as there are no nearby restaurants. They are all quite expensive and don't offer particularly good value, especially as the beaches are only mediocre.

The *Hotel Cercina* (☎ (04) 81 228) is the most convenient if you are on foot, as it is only 200 metres from the bus stop. The only problem is that the 'rooms' are horrible little claustrophobic concrete shacks which are let out for a ridiculous TD 27 for a double with full board. It should be possible, however, to bargain this down to TD 10 with breakfast only.

A much better place is the enormous *Club des Iles* (☎ (04) 81 521), a few 100 metres further along. Although it would be rare to find the place more than 25% full, the managers are not prepared to bargain, and charge the full whack of TD 17 per person with meals, or TD 14 with breakfast only. If you just want to use the beach for the day the fee is a totally ridiculous TD 5 per person! They rent bicycles here for TD 3.200 per day (you don't need to be staying at the hotel), and they also have a minibus which meets the ferries.

Further along the beach are two more places, the *Hotel Farhat* (☎ (04) 81 236), which charges TD 23.500/34, and the *Hotel Grand* (☎ (04) 81 266), where you'll pay TD 23.400/36 for accommodation on a full-board basis.

Places to Eat

Well, sadly, when it comes to places to eat, there's really not a lot to choose from. The best bet is the *Restaurant La Sirène*, by the waterfront down the road next to the Hotel El Jazira. It has a shady terrace and reason-able food, although its opening hours are very irregular. There is another restaurant with the same name further up the street near the El Jazira but it is not as good.

The only other place is the restaurant of the *Hotel El Jazira*, which is passable but nothing special.

For sweet snacks and drinks there is the usual assortment of patisseries and cafés.

Getting There & Away

Four ferries cross daily between Sfax and Sidi Youssef in summer. Departures from Sfax are at 7 and 10.30 am, and 1.30 and 4.30 pm; from the islands the departures are at 8.30 am, noon, 3 pm and 6 pm. The crossing takes about 1½ hours, and is free for passengers; cars cost TD 4.500. In summer there are usually six departures per day to cope with the extra demand.

Getting Around

Bus There is a small bus network which connects the towns of the islands, and there are always at least two or three to meet each ferry. One has the sign 'Hotel' in the window and goes via Sidi Fredj, from where it's a one-km walk to the Farhat and Grand hotels, and 500 metres to the Club des Iles. For Remla, take any of the buses. There is also a minibus which runs right to the resorts but costs TD 1.500 per person, as against 300 mills on the public buses.

In Remla the bus station is right next to the Hotel El Jazira. There are a couple of buses daily to El Attaya but, as there's nothing much after about 3 pm, be careful that you don't get stranded there. If you do, there is a bit of local traffic and hitching is possible.

Buses from Remla to the ferry leave one hour before the ferry departures; there is a list posted in the bus station window.

Bicycle The lack of any hills higher than one metre makes bicycle the ideal way of getting around. Bikes can be hired at the Club des Iles in Sidi Fredj at the rate of TD 3.200 per day.

Southern Tunisia

The attractions in the south of the country are many – the Saharan oasis towns of Nefta and Tozeur, the shimmering chotts, the troglodyte dwellings of Matmata, the *ksour* (fortified strongholds) around Tataouine, and the resort island of Jerba, supposedly the land of the Lotus-Eaters. There's enough to keep you busy for at least a week or two, and if you are heading for Algeria and the Sahara proper you'll more than likely be coming through this way.

This area lies on the fringe of the Sahara and so, as you may well imagine, gets pretty damn hot in summer – so hot in fact that it can be a real effort to move. If you are here at this time of year it makes a lot of sense to adopt the local habit of disappearing indoors during the heat of the day. Of course the climate down here also means that while you might be shivering your butt off in Europe in winter, the temperature here will still be a very bearable 15°C or so.

Chott el Jerid

The Chott el Jerid is an immense salt lake covering almost 5000 sq km, which is dry for the greater part of the year. The surface becomes incredibly blistered and cracked, and shimmers in the heat. There is a made road on a two-metre-high causeway right across the middle of it, and there are regular buses making the crossing between Kebili and Tozeur – a worthwhile trip. It is quite weird to drive across and see the water that has collected on either side of the road: because of the chemicals present it may be pink on one side and green on the other. It is even more weird to come across small cafés and souvenir stalls by the side of the road at regular intervals! Mirages are also a common occurrence, and if you have picked a sunny day to cross you're bound to see some stunning optical effects.

The oasis towns of Tozeur and Nefta are right on the edge of the chott and are welcome patches of green in what is otherwise a totally barren area. The oases rely wholly on the fresh spring water, which gushes out and makes quite intensive agriculture possible. The main crop is the incredibly succulent *deglat nour* ('finger of light') dates, which are harvested in November – a good time to visit the area, as the weather is moderate and there is plenty of activity. Many local villagers work in other parts of the country but return home every year for the date harvest.

GAFSA

Gafsa is the major regional service town of the area, mainly for the phosphate mines which are in the surrounding hills. It holds very little of interest for the average visitor, although the hills and, especially, the Seldja Gorge, to the south-west on the Tozeur road, are well worth a visit.

Information

There is a small tourist office (☎ (06) 21 664), in the small, dusty square by the Roman pools, but its opening hours are erratic.

There are branches of all the major banks in and around the centre, and the post office is on Ave Habib Bourguiba, one block west of the main street, Ave Taieb M'Hiri. For international phone calls there is a small office on Rue Hocine Bouzaiane, off Ave Taieb M'Hiri. There is no operator, but direct-dial calls can be made with ease. It is open daily from 7 am to 10 pm.

Roman Pools

These twin pools are easily located at the southern end of Ave Habib Bourguiba. There is little to see, but there is a pleasant café next to one, and it's easy to while away an hour

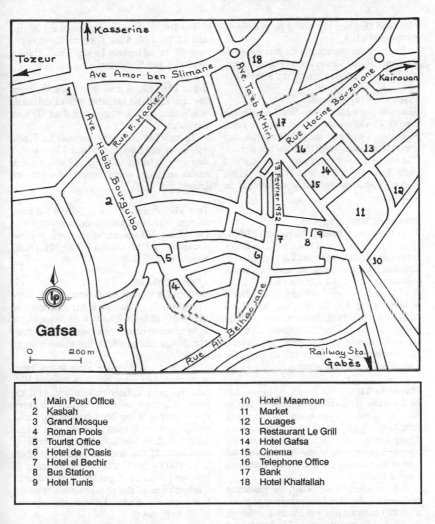

1	Main Post Office	10	Hotel Maamoun
2	Kasbah	11	Market
3	Grand Mosque	12	Louages
4	Roman Pools	13	Restaurant Le Grill
5	Tourist Office	14	Hotel Gafsa
6	Hotel de l'Oasis	15	Cinema
7	Hotel el Bechir	16	Telephone Office
8	Bus Station	17	Bank
9	Hotel Tunis	18	Hotel Khalfallah

or so while watching the young boys jumping off the house roofs into the pool.

Right by the entrance to the pools is a small museum which houses, among other things, a couple of large mosaics from ancient Capsa. It is worth a quick look and is open from 8 am to noon and 2 to 6 pm; it's closed Monday. Entry is free.

Places to Stay – bottom end

The cheap accommodation is all in the area of the bus station. Pick of the bunch is the *Hotel el Bechir* (☎ (06) 23 239) on Rue Ali Belhaouane, just around the corner from the bus station. Rooms here cost TD 4 and are a decent size, although the toilets are a bit on the nose. The *Hotel de l'Ousis*, close by, is older and shabbier but would do in a pinch; rooms cost TD 5.

Right by the entrance to the bus station is the *Hotel Tunis*. This is another cheap place, at TD 3 per person; showers are 300 mills.

Places to Stay – middle

The best place here is the *Hotel Khalfallah* (☎ (06) 21 468) on the main street, Ave Taieb M'Hiri. It's just past the police station, and about 10 minutes' walk from the bus station. The rooms are very clean and have attached bath. The rate is TD 9/12 with breakfast, although this is definitely negotiable in winter.

Places to Stay – top end

The multistorey *Hotel Gafsa* (☎ (06) 22 676) is right in the centre of town and is a major landmark. Rooms here cost TD 17.5/25 with attached bath and breakfast, and the central location makes this a popular place.

The other top-end offering is the *Hotel Maamoun* (☎ (06) 22 501), on Ave Taieb M'Hiri. It's also in the centre of town, on the corner of Rue Hocine Bouzaiane. This is a three-star hotel and so is quite comfortable and boasts a swimming pool. The charge for rooms is TD 21/30 with breakfast.

Places to Eat

Gafsa lacks good restaurants, and if you're here on a Friday the pickings are especially thin, as many places seem to be closed then. There are a few basic places around the central square outside the bus station, the best of these being the *Restaurant Carthage* (closed Fridays).

For something a bit better, the basement restaurant in the *Hotel Gafsa* is very popular, probably because it serves alcohol, although the food is also pretty good. The *Restaurant Le Grill* behind the market also looks promising, but it too is closed on Fridays.

Getting There & Away

Bus The bus station is right in the centre of town, the entrance being next to the Hotel Tunis. There are ticket windows for pre-booking, and even boarding announcements.

For Tozeur there are departures at 7.30 am, and 12.30, 4.30, 5 and 6.30 pm. Other destinations served include Le Kef, Tunis, Gabès, Metlaoui and Kasserine.

Train The railway station is a few km from the centre, across the other side of the oued; you'll need to take a taxi – less than TD 1 on the meter.

There is just one departure daily for Tunis, via Gabès and Sfax, at 8.30 pm. There is also one train to Metlaoui daily at 6 am, but it is easier and more convenient to take a bus or louage.

Taxi The louage station is behind the Esso station, which is on the main street opposite the Hotel Maamoun. There are regular departures for Metlaoui (TD 1.150), Tunis, Kasserine and Tozeur.

AROUND GAFSA

Metlaoui & the Seldja Gorge

There is little of interest in the drab town of Metlaoui, 42 km south-west of Gafsa, but it is the place to come for a visit to the spectacular Seldja Gorge which lies to the west of the town.

The best way to make a trip to the gorge is to catch the *Lizard Rouge*, a restored 19th century train upholstered in red, laid on purely for the tourists. It doesn't run every day – only if it has been booked by a tour group – so you'll need to check with Transtours Tunisie in Metlaoui, the agent handling bookings. If the train is running it costs TD 7.700 for the 1½-hour return journey. If you want to do it independently try and hitch a ride on one of the phosphate trains which run regularly from Metlaoui through the gorge to Redeyef.

Places to Stay

Metlaoui has just one hotel, the *Hotel Ennacim* (☎ (06) 40 271), a km or so out of town on the road to Tozeur.

Getting There & Away

There are regular buses and louages between Tozeur and Gafsa, and these all pass through

Top: Restaurant window, Tataouine, Tunisia (HF)
Left: Underground dwelling, Matmata, Tunisia (HF)
Right: Old granary, Medenine, Tunisia (HF)

Top: Fishing boats, Jerba, Tunisia (HF)
Left: Beach backed by Genoese fort, Tabarka, Tunisia (HF)
Right: Whitewashed buildings of Sidi Bou Said, Tunisia (HF)

Metlaoui. The louage fare to Tozeur is TD 1.200.

TOZEUR

This is the major town of the chott area and so has developed into something of a tourist centre – the number of Land Rovers and buses that come through has to be seen to be believed. This is 'accessible Sahara' and, although you really have to get into Algeria to appreciate the enormous extent of this desert, there are enough dunes and pictur - postcard oases in this area to make it a compulsory stop for any package tour – a fact reflected in the number of souvenir shops which have sprung up.

These shops are colourful affairs, mainly because of all the rugs for which the area is well known. It's not a bad place to buy rugs, but quality and price vary enormously, so do a bit of comparing before buying.

Despite the pressures and prosperity which tourism brings, the town maintains a laid-back atmosphere and is indeed a pleasant place to pass a few days.

Information

There are two tourist offices in Tozeur. The local syndicat d'initiative (☎ (06) 50 034) is on Place Ibn Châabat, right near the corner of Ave Farhat Hached. There is also a branch of the national tourist office (☎ (06) 50 088) on Ave Abdulkacem Chebbi, next door to the Hotel Djerid, about 10 minutes' walk from the post office. This is by far the more useful of the two offices.

Money There are a couple of banks by the main intersection on the Nefta road.

Post & Telecommunications The post office is on the main square by the market (which is busiest on Thursdays).

There's small telephone office just around

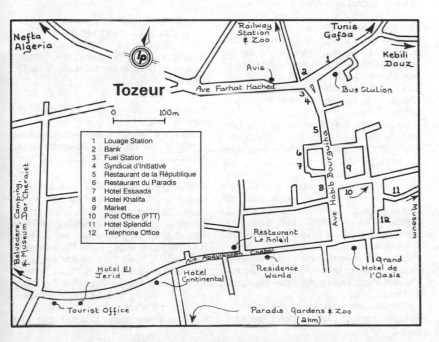

Tozeur

1	Louage Station
2	Bank
3	Fuel Station
4	Syndicat d'Initiative
5	Restaurant de la République
6	Restaurant du Paradis
7	Hotel Essaada
8	Hotel Khalifa
9	Market
10	Post Office (PTT)
11	Hotel Splendid
12	Telephone Office

the corner from the post office, open daily from 8 am to 9.30 pm. There are payphones only here.

Things to See

The oasis is the main attraction and, although it is enormous, it can be explored successfully on foot. For those who don't want to walk, there are camels for hire by the Hotel Continental.

The best walk is to take the track heading south off Ave Abdulkacem Chebbi signposted to 'Paradis Garden & Zoo'. It's a two-km walk to the luxuriant date garden where vendors sell luridly-coloured syrups of banana, rose, pomegranate and pistachio extract, all of which you can taste – for TD 1 per glass! The zoo is quite interesting but, as usual, the animals are kept in depressingly small cages; entry is TD 1.

Another walk takes you out along a sandy track to a group of rocks known as Belvedere. These are out past the main tourist office, and from here you get one of the best views out over the chott. There is a small spring-fed pool which usually has enough water in it for a swim, and there's a small campsite. The ground around here is littered with sand roses, which you would have to buy elsewhere. This walk through the *palmeraie* (an oasis-like area) takes a solid couple of hours out and back, so carry a supply of water.

This second walk takes you past the new and impressive Museum Dar Cheraiet, one km west of the tourist office along Ave Abdulkacem Chebbi. A lot of work and thought has gone into the displays here, which include a comprehensive small-arms collection – with an inlaid pistol with the butt in the shape and profile of a dog's head, replete with real yellowed teeth! – jewellery, costumes and even a model of a hammam. It's well worth a visit. Entry is TD 2.500 and the museum is open daily from 8 am to 11 pm. Descriptions are in French, Arabic and English. There's also a café and an expensive restaurant here.

There is another museum in the old part of town, signposted past the Hotel Splendid.

The 300 mills entry is hardly worth it: they have only a few bits and pieces on display, which have been collected from the surrounding area. This old section of town is worth a wander around in; the architectural style is quite unusual.

In the north of town near the railway station is another zoo which is, if anything, even more depressing than the Paradis. It even has live scorpions housed in cigarette packets – 'just the thing for the mother-in-law' touts the attendant.

Places to Stay – bottom end

The best bottom-end place to stay is the *Hotel Khalifa* (☎ (06) 50 068), on Ave Habib Bourguiba, opposite the market. Although this place is fairly new the workmanship is diabolically poor. It is, however, kept quite clean and is a friendly place. Rooms cost TD 5 per person, including breakfast. Hot showers are 600 mills. They also have bicycles for hire for TD 5 per day, or 750 mills per hour.

Next best is the *Hotel Essaada* (☎ (06) 50 097), right in the centre just off Ave Habib Bourguiba. It is quite basic but clean and friendly, although the rooms are very small; beds cost TD 2.500 and hot showers are 500 mills.

Youth Hostel Tozeur also has a *Youth Hostel* (☎ (06) 50 514) but it is only for the dedicated. It is in the usual inconvenient location – at least 1½ km out of the centre on the Tunis road. A bed in a dorm costs TD 4.

Camping The campsite in Tozeur, known as *Camping Belvedere* is out in the oasis, by the rocks of the same name. Facilities are limited but it is quite shady. Washing facilities consist of a spring-filled pool and the toilet is a smelly hole in the ground. Tea and coffee are available from the caretaker but you'll need to have your own food. On foot it takes about half an hour to walk from the tourist office. The charge is TD 1.500 per person.

There is another campsite at Degache, 16 km from Tozeur on the road to Kebili. This one charges TD 2 to pitch a tent, and TD 3.500 for a bed in a double room.

Places to Stay – middle

A good place in this category is the *Residence Warda* (☎ (06) 50 597), which has very friendly management. Rooms cost TD 6.300/9.600 with bath and breakfast; air-conditioning is an extra TD 3.

The *Hotel Splendid* (☎ (06) 50 053), right in the centre, has a certain faded elegance, although it's not fantastic value. The best rooms are upstairs at the front and cost TD 9.100/13.200 for singles/doubles with bath and breakfast, and TD 3.500 extra with air-conditioning.

Places to Stay – top end

As might be expected, Tozeur has a couple of top-end hotels, both of which are on the edge of the palmeraie along Ave Abdulkacem Chebbi.

The three-star *Hotel Continental* (☎ (06) 50 411) charges TD 19/27 for singles/doubles with breakfast, while a bit further along, the *Hotel El Jerid* (☎ (06) 50 488) is somewhat cheaper at TD 17.500/26. Both hotels are popular with tour groups and in summer you may have trouble finding a vacant room.

Places to Eat

For cheap food and friendly service you can't beat the *Restaurant du Paradis*, just a couple of doors along from the Hotel Essaada. They have good soups and salad as well as all the other usual things, and the tables outside are a pleasant place to sit on a warm evening.

On Ave Abdulkacem Chebbi near the Residence Warda is the *Restaurant Le Soleil*, which serves excellent local food of a pretty good standard – their tajine is very good.

The only other place is the *Restaurant de la République*, in an arcade off Ave Habib Bourguiba near the mosque, which has similar stuff but is more expensive.

For a real blash out try the restaurant out at the Museum Dar Cheraiet. It is very flash and the prices are surprisingly reasonable: TD 2 to TD 2.500 for an entree, TD 4 to TD 8 for main courses. The café upstairs at the back of the building is a good place to go in the evenings as there are performances by local musicians, and you can try a *nargileh*. It also overlooks the oasis, which is illuminated at night.

A local breakfast speciality is a kind of deep-fried doughnut which is very filling and guaranteed devoid of any flavour or nourishment.

There are plenty of cafés and a couple of patisseries along Ave Habib Bourguiba. For fresh juices, try the patisserie right opposite the main mosque.

Getting There & Away

Air The Tunis Air office (☎ (06) 50 038) is on Ave Habib Bourguiba in the centre of town. The airport is four km from town. There are weekly flights to Paris, while on the domestic routes there are flights to Jerba (twice weekly) and Tunis (three times weekly).

Bus The bus station for both regional and SNTRI buses is on Ave Farhat Hached near the intersection with Ave Habib Bourguiba. There are two air-conditioned SNTRI buses to Tunis daily, one of which comes from Netta; buy tickets the day before. The trip takes seven hours and costs TD 10.950.

Regional buses operate regularly but infrequently to Gabès, Gafsa, Kebili and Nefta. The uniformed employees who hang around the station know all the departures and are not totally unhelpful. The 9.30 am bus to Nefta goes all the way to Hazoua at the Tunisian border post. See the Nefta section for full details about tackling this border crossing.

Train The railway station is in the north of town but, due to lack of demand and a minor problem with a bridge being washed away, passenger services have been discontinued and trains from Sfax only run as far as Metlaoui, 50 km to the north.

Taxi The louage station is almost opposite the bus station, in a small yard just off the street. There are regular departures to Nefta (20 minutes, 600 mills), Degache, Metlaoui, Gafsa, and occasionally to Kebili.

Car Rental There is an Avis office (☎ (06) 50 547) on Ave Farhat Hached.

NEFTA

Twenty-three km west of Tozeur is Nefta, the last town before the Algerian border. To some extent it is a smaller version of Tozeur but it does have a religious significance as well. This is the home of Sufism in Tunisia and there are a couple of important sites here.

Sufism

The mystical Islamic sect of Sufism was formed by ascetics who were concerned to achieve a mystical communion with God through spiritual development rather than through the study of the Koran. This brought them into conflict with the religious orthodoxy but, because they were prepared to make concessions to local rites and superstitions, they were able to attract large numbers of people who had not embraced Islam. The Sufis also believed in the miraculous powers of saints, and saints' tombs became places of worship. A particular aspect of Berber Sufism in North Africa is maraboutism – the worship of a holy man endowed with magical powers.

Literally hundreds of different Sufi orders sprang up throughout the Islamic world. The differences between them lay largely in the rituals they performed and how far they deviated from the Koran. They were regarded with a good deal of suspicion, which was exacerbated by some of their peculiar devotional practices such as eating glass and walking on coals (which they did in order to come closer to God).

The Sufis held positions of power in Tunisia; with the breakdown of Almohad rule in the 13th century they held influential positions, particularly in rural areas.

Information

There is only one main street, Ave Habib Bourguiba (just for a change), which is the main Tozeur-Algeria road. The bank, post office, tourist office and bus station are all on the east side of the *corbeille* (gully). The bank here reportedly will not cash American Express travellers' cheques. There is a ring road around the north of the town and it gives access to the two flash hotels.

The tourist office is just by the ring road,

on the right as you enter the town from Tozeur. The guy there is quite helpful but loses interest rapidly if you decide not to rent a camel (TD 2 per hour).

The post office is on the left, just where the road descends to cross the corbeille.

Things to See

The palmeraie here cuts right through the middle of the town, and the corbeille is about 30 metres deep and is quite spectacular. The old part of town lies on the far (west) side, while the new French part is on the near side. At the head of this small valley, water gushes out of the ground, and there are bathing pools for both men and women.

At the head of the corbeille is the Zaouia of Sidi Brahim, where this saint and some of his followers are buried.

Despite the town's attractive setting, there is really very little to do here other than wander in the palmeraie and old town. If you are not going on to Algeria, it can easily be visited in a day (or even a morning) from Tozeur.

Places to Stay & Eat

Nefta's cheapest hotel is the *Hotel de la Liberte* in the old souk on the far side of the corbeille. It has no sign so you'll have to ask directions. It's a friendly place, and basic rooms cost TD 3 per person.

The best value is the *Hotel Marhala* (☎ (06) 57 027), one of the three excellent places run by the Touring Club de Tunisie (the others are at Matmata and Jerba). It is on the west side of town, about 20 minutes' walk from the bus station, and is actually an old brick factory – it's better than it sounds. The rooms are a bit on the small side but are spotless, comfortable and have a shower. Singles/doubles cost TD 5/6.900 with breakfast, or TD 8 per person for full board – good value.

Next up the scale is the *Hotel Mirage* (☎ (06) 57 041), near the northern tip of the corbeille. It's not far from the Zaouia of Sidi Brahim, around the ring road past the enormous four-star *Sahara Palace* (☎ (06) 57 046), a genuinely ugly construction.

The sum total of Nefta's eateries is a few basic restaurants on Ave Habib Bourguiba near the bus station and the hotel restaurants. One of the better ones is the *Restaurant du Sud*.

There is a café, up on the edge of the corbeille near the Hotel Mirage, where the views are good and the drinks cold.

Getting There & Away

Bus The bus station is on the north side of Ave Habib Bourguiba, about 100 metres past the tourist office. There is one SNTRI bus daily to Tunis (eight hours) and a few regional buses to Tozeur.

Taxi The louages leave fairly regularly from opposite the bus station for the 20-minute ride to Tozeur (600 mills). There are also occasional departures for Hazoua on the Tunisian border.

To/From Algeria The Algerian border is at Hazoua, 36 km south-west of Nefta. There is one bus daily from Tozeur at 9.30 am, and this leaves Nefta at 10 am. Infrequent louages to Hazoua leave each day. There is no bank on the Tunisian side of the border.

Between the two border posts is a four-km stretch of neutral territory which you may have to walk across – be prepared with hat and water. There are occasional Algerian shared taxis and tourist vehicles but you can't rely on them.

At the Algerian post you have to declare your money and fill in a currency form. To save hassles later, read the information on money in the Algeria section *carefully* before you reach this border. It is a very easygoing crossing and the officials are friendly. There is a bank on the Algerian side at Bou Aroua but it is closed more often than it is open. If that's the case and you need to change money, you can change small amounts of cash (officially) at the customs office.

From the Algerian border post there are shared taxis to the town of El Oued, a further 80 km along a good bitumen road. The drivers accept either Tunisian dinar (TD 5), or Algerian dinar (AD 50). It is also possible to hitch along this stretch but traffic is very light along the first 27 km until the road joins the Tébessa to El Oued road.

KEBILI

This small regional town at the eastern edge of the Chott el Jerid really has nothing to recommend it apart from its hot-spring baths on the road to Douz.

Facilities include a post office and bank (open for changing money from 9 am to noon only).

The baths are about a km from the centre of town. The men's pool is right by the roadside and is really pleasant, with a couple of cafés around it. The pool for women is about 150 metres upstream and is screened by palm fronds stuck in the ground. The slightly sulphurous water gushes out of the ground at high temperature, a couple of hundred metres further up from the women's pool.

Places to Stay

The basic *Hotel l'Oasis* is about 10 minutes' walk from the centre on the Tozeur road. It is very spartan and only has cold showers but is otherwise OK. Rooms cost TD 5/6.250 for singles/doubles, or TD 2.500 for a bed in a shared room.

The only other place is the somewhat up-market *Hotel des Autriches* (☎ (05) 90 233). This is a km or so into the palmeraie; it's signposted (to 'Fort des Autriches') off to the left near the military base on the Douz road, a total of about 30 minutes' walk from the bus station. It is quite a pleasant place, with a swimming pool and terrace. Rooms are TD 11.900/18.700 for singles/doubles with breakfast.

Places to Eat

Considering the small size of the town, there are a surprising number of restaurants. The *Restaurant Les Palmiers*, right in the centre by the bus station, does fairly good stuff. The *Restaurant l'Oasis* is out on the Tozeur road near the hotel of the same name. There are a couple more places right by the louage station.

Getting There & Away

Bus The bus station is in fact just an office in the main street, right near the junction of the Douz, Gabès and Tozeur roads.

From here there are buses (either minibuses or regular-sized ones) to Douz at 11 am and 2, 4 and 6 pm; there are others passing through on the way from Gabès as well.

There are also regular departures for Tozeur and Gabès.

Taxi All the louages leave from a street next to the old military compound in the centre of town. Just look for the old rusty steel tower (not the post office tower).

Louages leave throughout the day for Gabès, Douz and occasionally Tozeur.

DOUZ

Although it tries to promote itself as 'the Gateway to the Sahara', Douz doesn't suffer from the tourist masses anywhere near as badly as Tozeur does.

It is in fact a very laid-back little oasis village and, with the other oases to the south, it can be a pleasant place to pass a couple of days.

There is a new bank for changing money near the main intersection on the Kebili road, and opposite it is quite a good map of the town on a small signboard.

The centre of the town, for what it's worth, is the market square, 100 metres from the bus station. Around the square are a few desultory souvenir shops which have a fair range of rugs bearing local designs. Thursday is market day and so a good day to be in the area. The market square becomes a hive of activity and you need to get there early before the tour groups arrive. Down a small alley on the far side of the square is an animal market, which is interesting and doesn't have the crowds.

Douz is now the base for some of the seminomadic tribes of the Nefzaoua, the name given to this south-eastern region of the country.

The best way to explore the palmeraie is to walk out along the road to the Marhala and Saharien hotels, and keep going to the Place du Festival, which is set on the edge of the dunes. As the name suggests, this is the centre of activities during the Sahara Festival in December/January (during which time the town gets packed out). It takes about 30 minutes to walk to the palmeraie from the centre. Alternatively, you can hire camels from behind the tourist office – there are literally dozens here, but you may have a hard time dragging the owners away from the TV in the café at the tourist office.

The road to Zaafrane and El Faouar heads off to the south from next to the cemetery, almost opposite the louage station.

Places to Stay – bottom end

There are three cheapies, all in the centre near the souk and the bus station. Best of the bunch is the friendly *Hotel 20 Mars*, which has its rooms around a courtyard; there are free hot showers. The hotel used to be above the café of the same name in the corner of the market square; although there are still rooms there, you'd do best to avoid them.

The squalid *Hotel du Calme* is by the post office and should be avoided if at all possible. The other cheap place is the *Hotel l'Oasis*, just opposite the entrance to the market square.

All these places charge around TD 3.500 for a bed.

Places to Stay – middle

Signposted out along the road to the south of the town are the *Hotel Marhala* (☎ (05) 95 315) and the three-star *Hotel Saharien* (☎ (05) 95 339). Both have swimming pools and are set in the middle of the palmeraie. If you are staying out here and don't have your own transport you are more or less obliged to eat at one of the two hotels, as it is a long, dark walk into the village at night.

The Hotel Marhala is the cheaper of the two and costs TD 7.500/11.900 for singles/doubles with bath and breakfast. The Saharien has a more pleasant setting with a bit more shade and costs TD 9.500/14.500 for singles/doubles (room only).

Places to Eat

Well, for a couple of dinar you can get as full as a fat girl's socks in Douz. It is no gourmet's paradise, but there are a couple of choices. Because lunch is the main meal of the day, however, most of the restaurants don't have much left by the time dinner rolls around.

Between the Hotel 20 Mars and the bus station is the *Restaurant El Acil*, which has the usual standards. The *Restaurant de l'Oasis* at the hotel of the same name is very average.

Getting There & Away

Bus The bus station is the small kiosk just by the main intersection in the centre – you can't miss it as there are usually one or two buses parked nearby. There is a timetable outside it, but as it's all in Arabic it's of little use.

The buses are a bit hard to pin down. There is a daily air conditioned SNTRI bus to Tunis at 5 am.

There are small, 20-seater minibuses which run right to El Faouar at the end of the road, and there are also a couple of departures daily to Gabès.

Taxi The louage station is about 50 metres around towards the telecommunications tower from the bus station. There are plenty of departures for Kebili, but they're less frequent for Gabès and Tozeur. The easiest thing is to take one to Kebili and then another from there.

AROUND DOUZ
Zaafrane & Beyond

The small oasis town of Zaafrane lies some 12 km south of Douz, right on the edge of the Grand Erg Oriental. This is where you really get to the start of the desert.

It is one of the few villages in the country where you can still see the traditional goat-hair tents of the seminomadic people of the Nefzaoua. Most of the inhabitants actually live in concrete-block houses and have the tents set up outside, often to give shade to the family's mules, camels or goats.

The town is busiest during the date harvest in November; for the rest of the year, many of the people migrate to the east and Douz slips back into the torpor that grips any desert town for much of the time.

The road continues on past other small oases as far as El Faouar, home to yet another nomadic tribe. According to the advertising signs by the side of the road near Zaafrane, there is apparently a hotel in El Faouar.

Getting There & Away The usual practice is to stand on the corner in Douz and wave down any passing vehicles. The fare to Zaafrane is 550 mills, although you may be lucky and get a free lift. The flow of traffic dries up around 4 pm and there is never anything much on Friday afternoons.

Fridays aside, it is quite a busy road and hitching out to the end to El Faouar should present no problems. The place to wait for lifts in Zaafrane is by the busy well in the middle of the village.

There are two minibuses daily which make the run from El Faouar to Douz.

Gabès

There's very little reason to stay in this modern town on the coast. It has been heavily industrialised and the pollution in both the air and water is noticeable. The town has two supposed attractions, the beach and the oasis.

The beach is raved about because it stretches so far, but it's smelly and unattractive; the oasis is nothing special either. Despite this, dozens of tour buses disgorge their daily loads on the edge of the palmeraie, the waiting calèches (horse carriages) take the tourists through and the buses pick them up at the other end by the depressing zoo and crocodile farm.

Information

Tourist Office The tourist office (☎ (05) 70 254) is in the small building in the middle of the intersection of Ave Habib Thameur and

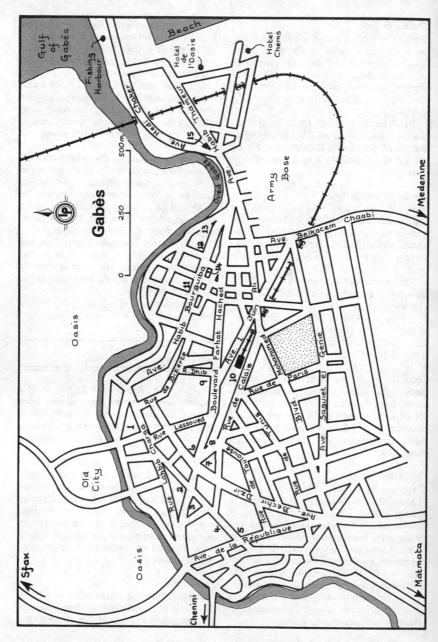

1	Market
2	Hotel Restaurant Ben Nejima
3	Bus Station
4	Medina Hotel
5	Bus to Chenini
6	Artisonat
7	Post Office
8	Louage Station
9	Youth Hostel
10	Railway Station
11	Hotels Regina & Keilani
12	Hotel de la Poste
13	Atlantic Hotel
14	Restaurant à la Bonne Table
15	Tourist Office

Ave Hedi Chaker, down towards the waterfront. The guy running it is reasonably helpful and there is a complete list of bus departures posted on the door.

Money There are a couple of banks along Ave Habib Bourguiba.

Post & Telecommunications The enormous post office is on the corner of Blvd Farhat Hached and Ave Bechir Dzir. The telephone office is through the side entrance; it is simple to make international calls from here. It is open Monday to Saturday from 8 am to 6 pm.

Newspapers The small Tabac Nefoussi Abdallah on Ave Habib Bourguiba, just down from the Hotel de la Poste, often has English, German and French newspapers, even if they are up to a week old.

Things to See
To get to the palmeraie, head west along Ave Habib Bourguiba to the oued, and then turn left and then right across the oued. The road twists and turns through the oasis until you finally come out at El Aouadid, a small outlying town.

The crocodile farm and zoo are another km or so to the south; they are built at the site of a small Roman dam which has been reconstructed. This is where the tour buses come

to pick up their passengers after the carriage ride through the palmeraie and so, not surprisingly, a few entrepreneurs have set up stalls selling all sorts of junk at inflated prices. Don't waste your money on the zoo.

A path (negotiable by bicycle) heads off around the back of the dam and winds around through the palmeraie to the Chellah Club, a hotel tucked away in the palms. It's about a 20-minute walk and you can continue on along the creek to the end of the valley. Climb up the small escarpment out of the valley for a view of the surrounding area.

From the Chellah Club, the road leads back to the village of Chenini and the main Gabès-Jerba road. To do the circuit on a bicycle takes an easy half day.

Places to Stay – bottom end
The best budget place is the *Hotel de la Poste* (☎ (05) 70 718) on Ave Habib Bourguiba. It is above a café of the same name and the entrance is in the side street. It's good value at TD 7 for a double with washbasin and there are cold showers.

Right opposite the bus station is the *Hotel Marhaba*. It's noisy and none too appealing, but is conveniently located. Beds cost TD 3 per person.

Place to Stay – middle
On Ave Habib Bourguiba there are two hotels virtually side by side, both of which offer decent value. The *Hotel Regina* (☎ (05) 72 095) is marginally the better of the two; the rooms are a little less gloomy than those at the *Hotel Keilani* (☎ (05) 70 320), where they are arranged around a courtyard and have little ventilation. They both charge TD 7.500/9.500 for singles/doubles with bath and hot water.

Also near the bus station on Ave Habib Bourguiba is the *Hotel Restaurant Ben Nejima* (☎ (05) 71 062), on the corner of Rue Djilani Lahbib. Although the front rooms are noisy, the others are quite good and cost TD 5.400 per person with bath and hot water.

If you want to stay in the oasis, the *Chellah Club* (☎ (05) 70 442) is about five km from the centre of town in the middle of the palmeraie. The setting is pleasant, but there is little to see or do and it's a pain to get to. Bungalows cost TD 11.250/16.250 for singles/doubles including all meals, which isn't bad value.

Places to Stay – top end

Right on the beach are the two top-end places, the *Hotel Chems* (☎ (05) 70 547) and the *Hotel de l'Oasis* (☎ (05) 70381). The Chems is the cheaper of the two; its high-season rates are TD 24/38 for air-conditioned singles/doubles with bath and breakfast.

Places to Eat

One of the few pleasant surprises of Gabès is the tiny *Restaurant à la Bonne Table*, on Ave Habib Bourguiba, almost opposite the Hotel de la Poste. It has good food: there's an excellent dish called Chicken Farci, which is roast chicken with an unusual spicy stuffing and a plate of sauce.

The *Hotel Restaurant Ben Nejima*, near the bus station, is not too bad and does all the usual dishes.

Things to Buy

There is a large government-run ONAT artefact showroom right opposite the post office on Blvd Farhat Hached. It has the usual range of quality carpets and other handicrafts. Opening hours are 8 am to noon and 3 to 6 pm.

Gabès is a major centre for the production of straw goods – baskets, hats, fans and mats – and the souks here are a good place to buy things.

Getting There & Away

Air The Tunis Air office (☎ (05) 71 250) is in the centre of town on Ave Habib Bourguiba.

Bus The bus station is a small crowded carpark at the western end of Blvd Farhat Hached, about 10 minutes' walk from the hotels on Ave Habib Bourguiba. The booking office is right in the far corner and

has a listing (in Arabic only) above the door. The SNTRI office is just across the road.

There are daily departures for Gafsa (three daily); Jerba (five daily); Kebili (four daily, two hours, TD 3.500); Kairouan (two daily); Matmata (four daily, one hour, TD 1.200); Medenine (six daily, one hour); and Sfax (six daily).

There are at least five SNTRI buses daily to Tunis, but most of them are coming from points further south and are often full in the summer; in winter getting a seat is not a problem.

Train The railway station is just off Ave 1 Juin, about five minutes' walk from Ave Habib Bourguiba. There are two trains daily to Tunis (at 3.25 and 10.40 pm) for the five-hour journey. The only trains travelling further than Gabès go to Metlaoui (4.50 am, two hours).

Taxi The louage station is the big dusty expanse just along from the post office. There are departures for Kebili, Medenine, Sfax and Tunis, although things quieten down considerably as the afternoon wears on.

Surprisingly, there are no louages operating between Gabès and Matmata.

Car Rental The major agencies here are: Avis (☎ (05) 70 210), Rue 9 Avril; Budget (☎ (05) 70 930), 57 Ave Farhat Hached; Europcar (☎ (05) 74 720), 12 Ave Farhat Hached; and Hertz (☎ (05) 70 525), 30 Rue Ibn el Jazzar.

Getting Around

Bicycle Hire The small cycle and moped shop a couple of doors along from the Hotel de la Poste towards the souk will usually rent out bikes for TD 2 for half a day. It's the best way to see the palmeraie, but make sure they don't give you an old broken-down clunker with minor defects such as no brakes and a swivelling seat.

Matmata

In an attempt to escape from the extreme heat the Berbers of the Matmata area went underground some centuries ago, and it was so successful that they have stayed there ever since.

Their homes are all built along the same lines: a central (usually circular) courtyard is dug down about six metres out of the very irregular terrain, and the rooms are then dug out from the sides. The main entrance is usually through a narrow tunnel which goes

out of the courtyard to ground level. Some of the larger houses had two or three courtyards, all connected, and these have now been turned into unique hotels.

Because there are only a few buildings above ground, there doesn't appear to be much to the town. The TV aerials and parked cars, however, are a giveaway that there is more here than first meets the eye. A quick walk around soon reveals literally dozens of these craters. It feels very voyeuristic to be peeking over the rims at the residents going about their business; they must be utterly sick and tired of being perved at like goldfish

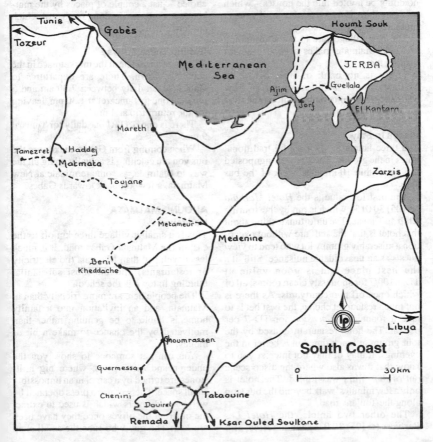

South Coast

0   30km

in a bowl every day of the year. On the whole, the 5000-odd locals are not all that friendly, which is understandable.

As you might imagine with this unusual life style, Matmata is well and truly on the tour-group itineraries, and the town even has its own Hollywood-style sign on the side of the hill as you approach. Every day at least five buses roll up and the hordes troop around. Fortunately, none of them choose to stay overnight, so in the early morning and late afternoon it's possible to wander around and have the place fairly much to yourself. Because of the exposure to tourism you will no doubt be invited into the houses – which you may think is a nice gesture until you get pressured to buy handicrafts.

The best villages are in the surrounding area and Matmata makes a good base for visiting them.

There is no bank or post office in Matmata; these facilities are all at New Matmata, five km or so back along the road to Gabès.

Places to Stay

The three hotels in town are all traditional holes in the ground. They're well signposted and are within 10 minutes' walk of the bus stop.

The best for value is the *Hotel Marhala* (☎ (05) 30 015), which is run by the Touring Club de Tunisie. The unfortunate thing about this hotel is that the staff are without exception a miserably grumpy lot who tend to view guests as an unavoidable nuisance. Still, it's the best place and is good value at TD 4.100/7 for spotlessly clean rooms, all of which open off two courtyards. As there is not much restaurant choice, the best bet is to take a room *demie-pension* for TD 7 per person. The hotel restaurant is used by the tour groups at lunch time but is better in the evenings. It may or may not interest you to know that it was also where the disco scene out of *Star Wars* was filmed. The hotel is only a few minutes' walk beyond the bus stop along the Toujane road.

The other two hotels, the *Hotel Les Berbiers* (☎ (05) 30 024) and the *Hotel Sidi Driss* (☎ (05) 30 005) are not as good as the Marhala and charge around TD 3.500 per person.

Youth Hostel There is also a *Youth Hostel* in the town but as it's a modern above-ground construction it does not have the appeal of the other places. It is cheap, however, and may be a good fall-back if the other places are full. It costs TD 2.500 for a bed and is right up towards the entrance to the town.

Places to Eat

Apart from the hotels, there is very little choice – just a couple of places by the marketplace on the main drag, neither of which are terribly inspiring.

Getting There & Away

The buses terminate at the marketplace in the centre of town. There are departures to Gabès (seven daily between 7.30 am and 5 pm) and one to Tamezret at 1.30 pm, leaving for the return trip at 4 pm.

There is one SNTRI bus daily for Tunis at 9 pm.

When coming from Gabès, make sure the bus you are catching is actually going all the way to Matmata, as some terminate at New Matmata, a few km back towards Gabès.

AROUND MATMATA
Haddej

This is a smaller village three km off to the east of the Matmata-Gabès road. It is much less developed than Matmata (no electricity or restaurants) and the most substantial building in town is the school.

The people here are more friendly than in Matmata, and an invitation into a family home is liable to be genuine rather than motivated by the chance to make a bit of money.

You can get someone to show you the underground olive press, where big mill-stones are turned by a camel in an impossibly small space. There is also a press operated by weights and levers which is used to extract the oil from the olives once they have been crushed. The guy who runs the small shop and post office can arrange for someone to take you there.

Getting There & Away The easiest way to get to Haddej is to catch a Gabès bus from Matmata for the four km to the village of Tijma, which is nothing more than the turn-off to Haddej. From there it's a three-km walk to Haddej; there is the occasional vehicle.

If the weather is favourable, it is an excellent walk back to Matmata along the mule track which cuts direct through the hills. It'll take you about 1¼ hours at a steady pace. Just ask the locals in Haddej to point it out to you, as it's not obvious where it starts. Once you are on it, it's well trodden and easy to follow.

Tamezret

This is an above-ground village which sees very few tourists. It's an interesting place, but the bus schedule makes it difficult to spend more than a couple of hours there unless you can get a lift or are invited to stay.

Getting There & Away The bus leaves Matmata at 1 pm and returns around 4 pm. The trip takes about one hour for the 10 km journey.

Toujane

Toujane is built right on the edge of the range of hills, on the rough track which runs from Matmata to Medenine. It is an isolated place but sees its fair share of tourists, as the Land Rovers rumble through here on their way to Matmata.

The road is of more interest than the village itself, as it runs through some pretty wild country, much of it covered by esparto grass which the locals gather and use for making all sorts of things, from mats to mule harnesses.

Getting There & Away There is no scheduled transport along this route but you may be able to organise a lift from the Hotel Marhala, as this is where most people stay.

Despite what you may be told, the Matmata-Medenine road *is* negotiable *with care* by even the smallest of the rented cars, although the rental companies would no doubt have a fit if you told them that was where you intended going.

The Ksour

Medenine and Tataouine are both fairly standard provincial towns but they're the centre of the ksour area of the south.

A ksar (plural: ksour) is a fortified stronghold and consists of many *ghorfas* – arched structures built to store grain, often three or more storeys high. The Berbers originally built just the ghorfas (for storage) but, with the Arab invasion, they were forced to make more defensive structures and the ksour became widespread. They were usually built on an easily defendable position such as on top or against the side of a hill.

Today the ksour are mostly falling into ruin but some are being put to good use – the one at Medenine has been restored and is now a tourist market, while at Metameur an enterprising young Tunisian has restored a three-storey ghorfa and turned it into a cheap hotel.

If you are going to only one place, Medenine has the better accommodation alternatives; however, the effort of getting down to Tataouine and the Berber villages around it is well worthwhile.

With your own vehicle you can make an interesting loop from Medenine to Beni Kheddache, Ksar Haddada, Ghoumrassen, Guermessa, Chenini, Douiret and Tataouine. It would take one long day, or you could stop the night at Ksar Haddada where a ksar has been turned into a hotel (the *Ksar Haddada*, ☎ (05) 69605)). The roads around here are usually not in fantastic condition and are poorly signposted – getting lost is not that difficult, but there are small villages and houses dotted around where you can ask directions. It doesn't rain very often, but when it does many of the roads become impassable.

MEDENINE

Medenine is unexciting in the extreme but not a bad place to stop if the need arises. The skyline is dominated by the gigantic regional hospital, which seems totally out of proportion to the rest of the town. In the days when the Libyan border was closed it was a real backwater, but these days it is much busier, and seemingly every second car has Libyan licence plates.

There is a ghorfa fairly close to the centre of town, just before the Hotel Les Palmiers. It has been done up and now houses a dozen or so souvenir shops. Although it is very colourful with all the rugs hanging up it is something of a tourist trap, as the tourist buses which don't make it any further south all call in here.

The fruit and vegetable market is held in the streets up the hill behind the ghorfa and is also colourful.

There are a couple of banks along Ave Habib Bourguiba, a very original name for a main street, which is basically the Gabès-Zarzis road. The Tataouine road leads off to the south by the bridge, and on it are the post office and the town's two-star hotel.

Places to Stay – bottom end

The *Hotel Les Palmiers* (☎ (05) 40 592) is friendly and basic and costs TD 2.500 per person, but there are cold showers only. It is just past the ghorfa; from the bus station, walk downhill to the roundabout and then left for 200 metres to the hotel – a five-minute walk.

More convenient is the *Hotel Essaada* on Ave Habib Bourguiba, uphill from the bus station opposite the Esso station. Rooms cost TD 2.500 per person. Slightly further up the hill is the noisy *Hotel El Hana* where rooms cost TD 4 per person.

Right opposite the ghorfa is a string of shops, and above one is the *Hotel Salaam*, which is overpriced at TD 5 per person, although this is definitely negotiable.

Places to Stay – middle

The *Hotel Sahara* (☎ (05) 40 007) is over the bridge and around to the right, next to the post office. The rate is TD 9/12 for rooms with bath attached, and breakfast.

Places to Eat

The *Restaurant Carthage* is opposite the bus station. The food is quite adequate, but the place gets no prizes for friendliness.

There are a couple of shops selling casse-croûtes, and there's another restaurant in the same street.

The restaurant in the *Hotel Sahara* is the best in town and you can get wine with a meal here.

Getting There & Away

Bus The bus station is in the centre of town on Rue 18 Janvier.

There are four buses daily to Tataouine between 9.30 am and 5 pm. To Jorf, for the ferry to Jerba, buses leave at 5.30 and 8 am and 3 and 5 pm.

There are buses which take you all the way to Houmt Souk but, as they go via Zarzis, they take a good deal longer.

Taxi Louages leave from the small side street directly opposite the bus station. There are departures for Ben Guerdane, Tataouine, Jorf and Zarzis.

AROUND MEDENINE

Metameur

The attraction of this small village, six km from Medenine and one km off the main Medenine-Gabès road, is the old ghorfa on the high point of the village.

The town itself dates back to the 15th century but the ghorfas are obviously later constructions. In one of the courtyards near the mosque, a ghorfa in one corner has been restored and turned into a unique low-key hotel. It's easy to recognise by the bright whitewash and the yellow doors. It is quite isolated and would be perfect if you just wanted a spot to escape to and do nothing in for a few days. The only problem is that the owner seems totally disinterested in solo travellers, and is abrupt in the extreme. Don't arrive here expecting to be able to stay. If you can persuade him to give you a room, they are quite cheap, and other meals can be arranged; otherwise it's a matter of bringing food from Medenine, as there is nothing much in the village.

Getting There & Away The cheapest way to get to Metameur is to hitch out along the Gabès road. The turn-off to Metameur is well signposted off to the left and you can see the village not far off.

There are local shared taxis which run to the neighbourhood villages; these are Peugeot 404 pick-ups with a painted red licence plate on the tailgate. A lift in one from the Metameur turn-off into Medenine costs 200 mills.

The back road to Matmata through Toujane runs through here, so it may be possible to hitch. Practically the only people using this road, however, are other tourists in rental cars.

Joumaa
This is a magnificent hill-top site, 36 km south-west of Medenine. The village, visible from the road where the bus stops, is built on a spur and appears to be just a blank wall.

Inside, however, are a couple of streets, a mosque, a courtyard and water tanks.

Getting There & Away There are buses from Medenine at 8.15 and 10 am, and they return from Joumaa at 10 am and 2 pm; the trip costs 800 mills.

Beni Kheddache
From Joumaa you can continue on to Beni Kheddache, a market and administrative village in the hills with a low-lying ksar. It has been largely demolished but what remains is still in use.

There is no accommodation here but there are a couple of restaurants. There are regular minibuses back to Medenine.

TATAOUINE
The other major centre of the ksour region, Tataouine is largely an administrative town with little of interest. It is, however, a friendly place and the best time to be here is

Monday or Thursday because that's when the market is on.

It would be much improved as a base for exploring the nearby ksour if it had some decent budget accommodation.

The post office is at the end of the main street, tucked in beneath the jebel – just look for the radio tower. There are a couple of banks in the streets nearby.

Things to See
The Ksar Megabla is within walking distance; it's a couple of km from the centre, signposted to the right off the Remada road. It takes about an hour to walk up to it, and there are good views of the town and surrounding area. The ksar itself is not in the best condition – in fact you need to be a bit careful when poking about in the courtyard. The villagers still keep their livestock in the cells.

Places to Stay & Eat
The budget hotel situation here is a bit grim. The better of the two places available is the *Hotel Ennour*, about 500 metres from the centre on the main Medenine road. It is certainly nothing special and charges TD 2.500 per person.

The other cheapie is the *Hotel Elksour*, right in the centre, but it is dirty and uninviting.

If you can afford it, by far the best place is the two-star *Hotel La Gazelle* (☎ (05) 60 009) up near the post office. Rooms with bath, hot water and breakfast cost TD 11.250/16.250 in summer; in winter the price drops to TD 8 for a single.

There are a couple of restaurants worth a mention. The small one on the left just down the street directly in front of the post office is quite friendly, and they do a good couscous for TD 1. The place has no name in English but has a chef painted on the window, giving the thumbs-up sign.

Further along the same street, near the statue, is the *Restaurant B Moussa*. This is the best place in town, with good food and prices.

Getting There & Away
Bus The bus station is on Rue 1 Juin 1955, pretty much in the centre of things.

There are buses to Medenine at 6.30, 8 and 9.30 am, and at 2.30 pm. The 9.30 am bus continues on to Zarzis and Houmt Souk.

For Ghoumrassen, there are departures at 10.30 am and 4.30 pm. The afternoon bus leaves Ghoumrassen at 7.30 am the next day for the return trip.

There is one SNTRI air-conditioned bus to Tunis daily at 9 pm.

Taxi The louages leave from the same street as the buses. Things are much busier in the mornings. There are daily departures for Ghoumrassen, Medenine, Remada, Tunis, and Zarzis.

AROUND TATAOUINE
Chenini
Don't miss this place. It is a Berber village perched on a narrow escarpment on the edge of the mountains, 18 km west of Tataouine.

The houses themselves consist of a cave room, which has a fenced courtyard out the front with maybe a couple more rooms. On the peak of the ridge is an old ksar which is largely in ruins. It was originally a fort built to defend the local inhabitants from the invading Arabs but it later became a granary.

On a saddle between the ksar and the other more substantial ridge is a beautiful white mosque. The whole setting is superb, and the village has a commanding position over the plains to the north.

Chenini is very much on the Land Rover trail, but if you can get out here in the early morning the light is excellent and you should have the place to yourself.

Just around from the mosque and below the ksar, one of the enterprising locals has turned his house into an informal museum and for a small consideration will show you around.

Places to Stay & Eat The *Relais Restaurant* is at the bottom of the hill by the carpark. It specialises in lunch-time banquets for the tour groups. It is possible to stay here if you don't mind roughing it, which in this case means sleeping on the floor or the roof.

Getting There & Away This is the real snag. There is no public transport to Chenini, so it's a matter of hitching or chartering a louage.

Hitching is OK but can be slow, as most of the vehicles coming out this way are tour-group Land Rovers which usually have up to 11 people crammed in anyway!

To charter a louage, ask around with the drivers in Tataouine. It shouldn't cost more than TD 10 for the round trip and it's quite possible that the driver will act as guide when you get there. An hour is the minimum time necessary for a leisurely scramble around, so make sure the driver knows that you want to stay at least that long.

Douiret
This is really something, perched as it is on a hill with its dazzling whitewashed mosque. The village is inhabited in parts and is a fascinating place to wander around.

The site is very well preserved, and from above you can get a good view of the layout of the houses. The main buildings for animals front onto the road, then there's a walled courtyard, and then the living quarters are built 10 metres or so into the rock.

There are several camel-powered olive presses – just look for the telltale black streaks down the hill sides.

Getting There & Away As usual in this neck of the woods, transport is a bit of a hit-and-miss affair. There is a village *camionette* (Peugeot 404 pick-up) which makes the run from Tataouine but it can be hard to track it down – ask around the louages at Tataouine.

Failing that you can catch a louage to Dabbab and hitch from there; you may be in for a long wait, as there is very little traffic along this road. You will get there in the end, however.

Ksar Ouled Soultane
This is the best preserved of the ksour, and also the most difficult to get to. Buses and

camionettes from Tataouine run as far as Maztouria, passing the ksour of Beni Barka and Kedim on the way.

From Maztouria the road to Remada turns to dirt; after eight km there's a signpost for Ksar Ouled Soultane and from here it's a further three km.

Although not built on a particularly big rise, the ksar is visible for miles around and was obviously easily defendable. The ghorfas rise to four levels in two courtyards and the climb to the top of the stairs can be dizzying.

This is the best place to visualise the ksar as a storage place and not just as a ruin. There are a couple of small shops and a café in this town, which sees only a handful of tourists.

Ghoumrassen

This is the largest of the southern Berber villages and is the only one regularly accessible by public transport. It is surrounded by rocky cliffs on all sides and there are cave dwellings dotted all over the place.

The most interesting aspect of the place is that many of the dwellings have only recently been deserted; wandering through some of them, in which utensils and tools are still lying around, it's easy to get the feeling that the owners are going to return any minute and catch you snooping. Bring a torch if you have one; even matches would be a help in exploring some of the deeper dwellings.

There is a bank and a couple of restaurants but no place to stay, so it is necessary to return to Tataouine.

Getting There & Away There are infrequent buses and louages to and from Tataouine.

Jerba

Well, if the locals are to be believed, Jerba is the mythical land of the Lotus-Eaters, where Ulysses was delayed on the way back from the scrap at Troy. If that's the case, then the island today is populated by the descendants of these people, who lived 'in indolent forgetfulness, drugged by the fruit of the legendary honeyed-fruit'. The fruit is variously thought to have been hashish, jujuba or the lotus. Fantasy or not, it makes a good exotic story to draw the tourists with.

The low-lying island is in the Gulf of Gabès. Its southerly location gives it a climate much envied by the people of Europe – so envied in fact that it has become a major tourist destination complete with international airport and resort hotels. In the summer months, the place is crawling with tourists – you're better off visiting out of season, when it's cheaper and facilities are less in demand.

The architecture of Jerba is very distinctive. The island is dotted with square whitewashed houses (known as *menzels*) which, from the outside, look more like small fortresses. It is unlikely you will be invited inside at any stage unless you are lucky enough to befriend a local resident – there have been too many foreigners here for the locals to get any thrill out of inviting someone in for a tea. This is not to say they are unfriendly – just reserved.

Jerba has an area of about 500 sq km, and is connected to the mainland by a ferry from the south-western tip; there's also a causeway in the south-eastern corner which links it with the town of Zarzis, another place which is cashing in on the tourist dollar (or yen, or kroner, or whatever). As well as this, there are daily flights to Tunis and direct charter flights to points all over Europe.

Since the highest point on the island is less than 30 metres above sea level, Jerba lends itself to exploration by bicycle or, better still, moped. Both can be hired in the main town of Houmt Souk.

The bulk of the local people belong to the heretical Kharijite sect of Islam. There used to be a sizable Jewish community but this diminished greatly in number with the formation of the state of Israel.

The Kharijite sect was popular among the Berbers in the 7th century; when the Fatimids wiped them out in the early 8th century, Jerba was one of the few pockets to survive. It is the Kharijites who are largely responsible for the huge number of mosques on the island – 213 in all.

History

The Phoenicians were the first to realise the potential of a virtually land-locked gulf and were the first of many invaders to occupy the island over the next 2500 years.

In Roman times it became an important commercial centre and the causeway connecting it to the mainland was built. Since the Romans left, the island has been occupied by Spaniards, Barbarossa pirates, Italians and then, in the 1500s, by the Turks.

HOUMT SOUK

The main town of the island, Houmt Souk, is on the north coast. The 6500 residents depend fairly heavily on tourism for their livelihood; the other, more traditional source of income is the fishing industry.

Out of season it's an easy-going place; the few hotels and restaurants are virtually deserted and the shopkeepers don't even bother hassling for a sale.

Information

Tourist Offices The local syndicat d'initiative (☎ (05) 50 195) is on the main street (Ave Habib Bourguiba would you

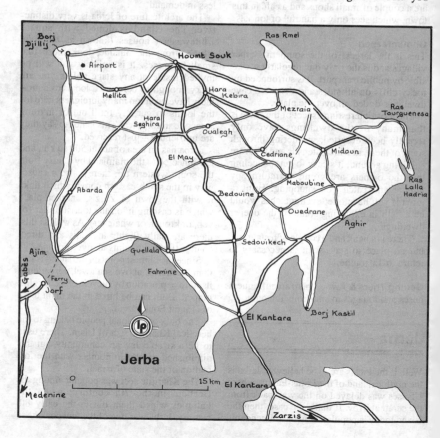

believe?) and is set back from the road. The staff have a hand out map of the island and are also quite helpful with enquiries. It is open in the mornings and afternoons.

The office of the national tourist body (☎ (05) 50 016) is about 15 minutes' walk from the centre and is really not worth the effort. It is part of a complex which includes a fancy restaurant and other facilities, and is open from 8.30 am to noon and 3 to 5.45 pm.

Money There are a number of banks on Ave Habib Bourguiba and around the squares just off it. There is always one bank rostered to be open on Saturdays and Sundays. The local syndicat d'initiative has a current list.

Post & Telecommunications The main post office is also on Ave Habib Bourguiba. There is an international telephone office around the side, although you may have to fight your way in as it gets extremely crowded at times.

Souk

Houmt Souk is compact enough to make seeing everything on foot quite practical. The old souk is the centre of things and consists of a tangle of narrow alleys and a few open squares with cafés. The place is full of souvenir shops and, although the prices are high, there is some excellent quality stuff for sale.

There are a few old *foundouks*, which used to provide lodging for pilgrims and the merchants of the camel caravans; some of these have been turned into excellent cheap hotels. The rooms are on two floors around a central courtyard, in the middle of which is a large cistern which provided water for the guests and animals. One of the hotels, the Arischa, has converted the cistern into a very small swimming pool.

Islamic Monuments

There are a few interesting Islamic monuments around the town but they are all closed to non-Muslims. Just on the edge of the souk, the Zaouia of Sidi Brahim has the tomb of the 17th-century saint. Today it is used as a

place of prayer. On the other side of the road is the multidomed Mosque of the Strangers. The 18th-century Mosque of the Turks is north of the souk; it has a distinctly Turkish minaret.

Museum of Popular Arts & Traditions

About 200 metres out along Ave Abdelhamid el Cadhi is the Zaouia of Sidi Zitouni, which now houses the Museum of Popular Arts & Traditions. This has quite a good range of local costumes as well as other bits and pieces. One room still has the original terra-cotta-tile ceiling. The museum is open daily, except Monday, from 9.30 am to 4.30 pm; entry is 800 mills. The ticket office is the small traditional weaver's hut near the main entrance.

Borj el Kebir & Around

From the Mosque of the Turks, the main street is lined with beautiful shady eucalypt trees and leads to the fort on the water's edge. Known as the Borj el Kebir, the fort was originally built by the Aragonese (members of an independent kingdom in north-eastern Spain) in the 13th century, and was extended in the 16th century under the Spanish. Later the same century the Turks captured the fort and massacred the Spanish garrison. The skulls of the victims were stacked in a pile a couple of 100 metres along from the fort, and this macabre tower of skulls stood for over 200 years until the soldiers were given a formal burial. The site is still marked by a monument.

The fort itself is good for a quick wander around, if only for the views along the coast. It is open the same hours as the museum.

The fishing harbour is only a little further along. It is a hive of activity during the day, when the nets are mended in preparation for the evening's outing.

Places to Stay – bottom end

The cheapest hotels (including the youth hostel, which for once is not a bad place to stay) are old converted caravanserais, which provide good accommodation.

Pick of the bunch is the *Hotel Marhala*

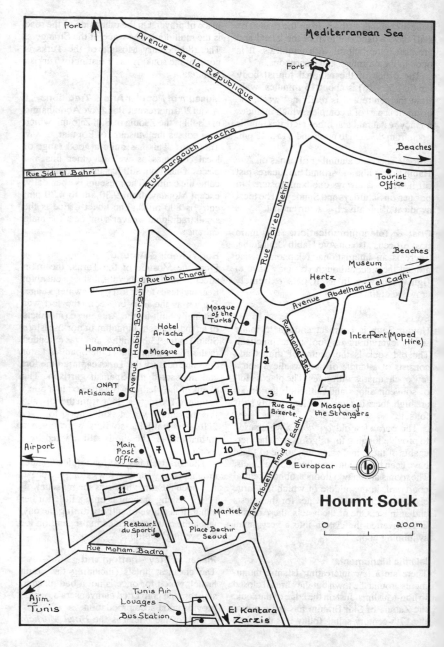

Mediterranean Sea

Port

Fort

Avenue de la République

Beaches

Rue Sidi el Bahri

Tourist Office

Rue Dardouth Pacha

Rue Taïeb Mehiri

Beaches

Museum

Hertz

Avenue Abdelhamid el Cadhi

Rue ibn Charaf

Mosque of the Turks

InterRent (Moped Hire)

Hotel Arischa

Rue Monest Bey

Hammam

Mosque

1
2

ONAT Artisanat

5

3 4

Rue de Bizerte

Mosque of the Strangers

Avenue Habib Bourguiba

6

9

Airport

8

7

10

Main Post Office

11

Ave. Abdelh Amid el Cadhi

Europcar

Houmt Souk

0   200m

Market

Restaurt du Sportif

Place Bechir Seoud

Rue Moham. Badra

Ajim
Tunis

Tunis Air
Louages
Bus Station

El Kantara
Zarzis

1	Hotel Marhala
2	Youth Hostel
3	Hammam
4	Zaouia of Sidi Brahim
5	Hotel Sable d'Or
6	Place Sidi Abdelkader
7	Place Mongi Bali
8	Hotel Sindbad
9	New Hotel
10	Place Hedi Chaker
11	Syndicat d'Initiative

(☎ (05) 50 146), another one in the chain of three run by the Touring Club de Tunisie. As usual the standard is excellent, and it is not bad value at TD 6/10 per person with breakfast. In winter it is a bargain at TD 4.500 per person. Cold showers are free but for a hot one you pay 800 mills. The rooms are all arranged around the traditional colonnaded courtyard.

The *Hotel Arischu* (☎ (05) 50 384) is just north of the souk and is another caravanserai. It costs much the same as the Marhala at TD 6/8.700 for a single/double with breakfast, slightly less in winter. In this place the central cistern has been turned into a tiny swimming pool.

The *New Hotel* (☎ (05) 50 756) is the cheapest at TD 3.500 per person; it's not that bad, it's just that the other places are better. Close by is the *Hotel Sable d'Or* (☎ (05) 50 423), which is also not bad for TD 5 per person.

On Place Mongi Bali in the centre, the *Hotel Sindbad* (☎ (05) 50 047) is a bit run down and overpriced at TD 6 per person, although this is definitely negotiable in winter.

Youth Hostel The *Youth Hostel* (☎ (05) 50 619) is housed in the fondouk next to the Hotel Marhala. The staff are friendly, and the hostel is open throughout the day until at least 10 pm. In summer this may be the only place with a vacancy. Beds cost TD 2.500.

Camping The only campsite is attached to the *Hotel Sidi Slim* (☎ (05) 57 023), one of the resort hotels on the eastern corner of the island. It is on a decent beach, so if you just want to spend a few days doing nothing it's not a bad place to be; otherwise, it can be a bit isolated. The Sidi Slim is on the coast, south-east of Midoun.

Places to Stay – middle & top end
All the resort hotels are scattered along the north-eastern coast of the island, along the Sidi Mahares beach. Prices in summer are generally high across the board, but there are a few places which really drop their prices out of season.

Top of the range is the *Dar Jerba* (☎ (05) 57 191), which is a totally over-the-top construction complete with cinemas, conference halls, and beds for over 2000 people – just the thing for a quiet getaway? There are even tricycles that you can hire to explore the complex! The place is in fact four hotels rolled into one and prices range from TD 18 to TD 51 for a single. Much more sensible is the *Hotel Tanit* (☎ (05) 57 132), further around the coast, where rooms cost TD 23/32.500 with breakfast (dropping to an affordable TD 11.500/15 in winter). The *Hotel Medina* (☎ (05) 57 233) with its excellent beach is also good. Charges here are TD 31/46.500 for singles/doubles, which drop to TD 15.500/21 in winter.

Other beach hotels which are moderately priced are the *Hotel Al Jazira* (☎ (05) 57 300), the *Hotel Yati* (☎ (05) 57 016) and the *Hotel Sidi Slim* (☎ (05) 57 023), which also has the campsite.

Places to Eat
Around Place Hedi Chaker are three or four tourist-oriented restaurants. The menus are posted outside, usually in four languages, and there is not a great deal to choose between them – they are all good and have much the same prices. The prices are also aimed at the tourists – expect to pay about TD 6 (or more) per person. Beware of the owners who try and get you to have a 'special

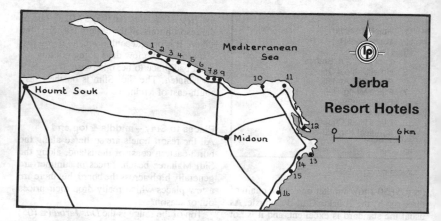

Jerba

Resort Hotels

Mediterranean Sea

Houmt Souk

Midoun

0   6 km

1   Ulysses
2   Mimosas
3   Al Jazira
4   Strand
5   Medina
6   Les Sirènes
7   Abou Nawas
8   Palm Beach
9   El Bousten
10 Dar Jerba
11 Yati
12 Tanit
13 Jerba Menzel
14 La Douce
15 Calypso
16 Sidi Slim

meal', as the price will be pretty bloody special as well unless you clarify beforehand just how much you are prepared to pay.

One place with a similar menu but cheaper prices because of its less central location is the *Restaurant Central* on Ave Habib Bourguiba near the bus station.

The main Tunisian restaurant, where a meal costs about half as much as the other places, is the *Restaurant du Sportif* on Ave Habib Bourguiba.

If you are staying out at the hotel strip you will have to eat out there as well because the area is not well served by the buses, and taxis are not cheap.

Getting There & Away

Air The Tunis Air office (☎ (05) 50 586) is at the southern end of Ave Habib Bourguiba, a block in front of the bus station. Tunis Air has daily flights to Tunis at 6 am in winter. In summer there are up to three flights daily and you need to book in advance to get a seat. Tickets for the 40-minute flight cost TD 21 one way.

Jerba is also an international airport and in the summer months there is a constant stream of charter flights coming and going from Europe. You may be lucky and score a seat on one of these, but you would have to do the rounds of the resort hotels and get in touch with the company reps.

There are also scheduled Tunis Air flights to cities in Europe, although some of these operate only from April to October. They include: Frankfurt (Tuesday); Geneva (Sunday); Lyons (Friday); Marseilles (Thursday); Paris (Thursday, Saturday, Sunday); and Zürich (Saturday).

Bus The uncharacteristically well-organised bus station is at the southern end of Ave Habib Bourguiba. All the scheduled departures are listed on a board above the ticket windows.

There is a nightly SNTRI bus to Tunis, and local departures to Zarzis, Medenine, Tataouine and Gabès.

Taxi The louages leave from just outside the bus station. There are departures for Zarzis, Gabès and Tunis.

Many of the mainland louage services go only as far as Jorf. From there you need to catch the ferry across, and then a bus or louage to Houmt Souk. Some services do go all the way but they usually do so via Zarzis, which makes the trip a good deal longer.

Car Rental Jerba is a popular place to hire cars for trips around the island and to sights around the south of the country. All the major companies have offices both in town and out at the airport, where the phone number for them all is (05) 50 233.

The offices in town are: Avis (☎ (05) 50 151), Ave Mohammed Badra; Budget (☎ (05) 50 185), Rue 20 Mars 1934; Europcar (☎ (05) 57 191), Hotel Dar Jerba; Hertz (☎ (05) 50 196), Ave Abdelhamid el Cadhi; and Topcar (☎ (05) 50 536), Rue 20 Mars 1934.

Getting Around the Island
To/From the Airport The airport is eight km from the centre of Houmt Souk, signposted out past the village of Mellita. There is one bus daily at 6.30 am, which is obviously useless if you are catching the 6 am flight to Tunis.

The taxis congregate in the middle of Ave Habib Bourguiba, near the Tunis Air office. They have meters, and the run out to the airport shouldn't cost more than TD 2.

Bus There are local services which connect the larger towns of the island, but the coverage is erratic and trying to use the buses successfully can be a frustrating experience.

There is a timetable and a colour-coded route map of the services around the island above the ticket windows in the bus station.

Taxi The Peugeot taxis can be hired for the day for trips around the island or just to specific places on the island. A daily charter shouldn't cost more than TD 25.

The taxis are forever cruising the hotel strip for fares into Houmt Souk. In summer

demand far exceeds supply, and it can be difficult to get hold of one in Houmt Souk, especially in the early afternoon when things close up for a couple of hours and everyone is returning to Sidi Mahares.

Bicycle & Moped Bikes are available for rent from any of the hotels in Houmt Souk. In fact they just act as agent and take a small cut. Some of the bikes are in pretty poor shape, so make sure you get a decent one.

The amount you can see by bicycle in a day is very limited, as the island is too large to see the lot. If there were places to stay in the other towns you could make a great three or four-day circuit, but unfortunately this is not possible at the moment unless you sleep out somewhere. Another factor conspiring against cyclists is the strong winds which often prevail; trying to ride into them is no joke.

Rental costs are 800 mills per hour, TD 3 per half day and TD 4 for a full day.

Mopeds are a much better bet for seeing the whole island; in half a day you can cover pretty well the whole thing, although a full day makes for a much more leisurely trip. Again, the hotels act as agents, or you can get them direct from InterRent. They cost TD 3 per hour, TD 10 for half a day (six hours) and TD 14 for a full day.

When riding a moped you are not covered by any insurance. Be extremely careful, especially out in the smaller villages inland where young children, wayward cyclists and suicidal dogs can be a real hazard.

A guy named Moncef Bourguiba also rents bicycles and mopeds. His shop is on the Route Touristique, 13 km east of Houmt Souk near the big hotels.

AROUND THE ISLAND
Midoun
This is the second major town of the island and is best known for its busy Friday market. Most of the items on sale are really only tacky tourist rubbish, but a few local stalls set up to sell fruit and vegetables.

Foreigners far outnumber locals here on Fridays. It's not unusual for a tour group on horseback to make a total nuisance of themselves and come pushing their way through the crowds.

The women of this area dress distinctively in white *sifsaris* which have a border of bright embroidery. They also wear small straw hats with a coloured ribbon tied to the back.

Hara Seghira

Once an exclusively Jewish settlement, Hara Seghira lies just off the main Houmt Souk-Zarzis road. With the mass migration of Jews to Israel the population is now predominantly Muslim, but there are still a number of synagogues.

The most important Jewish synagogue is El Griba, signposted a km south of the town. It is a major place of pilgrimage during the Passover festival. The site is believed to date back to pre-Christian times, although the present building dates back only as far as early this century. The inner sanctuary is said to contain one of the oldest *torahs* in the world.

The site was apparently chosen after a stone fell from heaven; it is also said that an unknown woman turned up and performed a miracle or two in helping the builders.

It is open to the public but you need to be modestly dressed, and men have to don *yarmulkes* (skullcaps) on entering. Donations are compulsory but you don't have to leave much.

Guellala

This is a tiny village on the south coast which is known for its pottery. In the past the pottery was sold on the mainland but these days almost all of it is sold on site.

The dozen or so workshops and galleries line the main road. They all sell much the same stuff, which unfortunately falls into the 'tacky souvenir' category with ease.

From Guellala there is a dirt track which skirts around a bay, where the local fishing people paddle around in waist-deep water, to the village of Ajim, where the ferries connect with the mainland.

Ajim

There are no attractions in Ajim, but if your transport goes only as far as Jorf on the mainland you'll have to catch a louage from here to Houmt Souk.

The ferry dock is about 500 metres from the centre and the ferries run 24 hours a day, although the frequency drops in the middle of the night to about once an hour.

West Coast

There is very little along the whole western coastline. There's just one dirt track, which hugs the swampy coast all the way.

The ruins of the 18th-century Turkish fort Borj Djillij are out past the airport, but you needn't waste your time trying to get out here unless you have a moped and an overpowering passion for ruined Turkish forts.

Glossary

This glossary is a list of Arabic (a), Berber (b) and French (f) words commonly used in the three Maghreb countries.

Words followed by a capital letter in brackets are those which are used principally in one country – Algeria (A), Morocco (M) and Tunisia (T).

Adrar (A) – mountain.
Agadhir – escarpment.
Aid – see **Eid**.
Ain – see **In**.
Akhbar (a) – great.
Al – see **El**.
Allah (a) – God.
Andalous – Muslim Spain and Portugal

Bab (a) – gate.
Babouche (M) – traditional leather slippers.
Bali (a) – new.
Baraka (a) – divine blessing or favour.
Barbary – European term used to describe the North African coast from the 16th to 19th centuries.
Basilica – type of Roman administrative building; later used to describe churches.
Beni (a) – tribal name .
Berbers – indigenous inhabitants of North Africa.
Bey – provincial governor in Ottoman Empire.
Borj (a) – fort.
Burnous (a) – traditional full-length cape with a hood, worn by men throughout the Maghreb.

Capitol – main temple of Roman town, usually situated in the forum.
Casse-croûte (T) – French bread stuffed with some or all of the following: olives, tuna, egg, sausage, chips and oil.
Chechia (T) – term for the traditional red felt hats, only worn by the older generation these days.

Chott (a) – salt lake.
Couscous – semolina, staple food of North Africa.

Daira (A) – Algerian equivalent of a local government.
Dar (a) – house.
Dey – title given to commanders of Turkish janissaries.

Eid (a) – feast.
El (a) – the article 'the'; can change according to the first letter of the following word, eg **Ech, Es, En, Et.**
Erg (a) – sand 'sea' or region.

Forum – open space at centre of Roman towns.
Fouggara (a) – system of underground water channels used to supply an oasis; found mainly near Adrar in Algeria.
Foum (a) – gorge, defile.
Foundouk (a) – caravanserai.

Gare routière (f) – bus station.
Ghar (a) – cave.
Ghorfa (a) – room; used in Tunisia to describe grain storage rooms in a ksar.
Guerba – waterbag made from the skin of a goat or sheep, seen hanging on the side of many Saharan vehicles; they look the part, but certainly add a bit of flavour to the water and are not very efficient, as they rely on evaporation (water loss) to keep the contents cool.

Hajj (a) – pilgrimage to Mecca; hence **Hajji**, one who has made the pilgrimage.
Hammada – stony desert.
Hammam – Turkish-style bathhouse with sauna and massage; there's at least one in virtually every town in the Maghreb.
Harira (M) – bean soup.

Ibn (a) – son of.
Imam – Islamic prayer leader.
In (a) – water-source, spring.

Janissaries – the elite of the Turkish army.
Jebel (a) – hill, mountain.
Jedid (a) – new.
Jezir (a) – island.
Jemaa (a) – mosque.
Jemil (a) – camel.

Kasbah – fort, citadel; often also the administrative centre.
Kef – cliff.
Kissaria – commercial centre of medina.
Koubba – sanctuary, marabout.
Ksar (a) – (pl: **ksour**) fortified stronghold found predominantly in the south of Tunisia.

Maghreb (a) – west (lit: where the sun sets); used these days to describe the area covered by Morocco, Algeria and Tunisia.
Marabout – holy man or saint; often used to describe the mausolea of these men, which are places of worship in themselves.
Mechouar – royal assembly place.
Medersa (a) – college for teaching theology, law, Arabic literature and grammar; widespread throughout the Maghreb from the 13th century.
Medina (a) – city; used these days to describe the Arab part of modern towns and cities.
Mellah – Jewish section of medina.
Mihrab (a) – prayer niche in wall of mosque indicating direction of Mecca.
Minbar (a) – pulpit in mosque; the imam delivers the sermon from one of the lower steps because the Prophet preached from the top step.
Moulay (M) – ruler.
Mozabite – a Berber inhabitant of the M'Zab, the name given to the area around Ghardaia in Algeria.
Muezzin (a) – mosque official who sings the call to prayer from the top of the minaret.

Oued (a) – river.

Palmeraie – oasis-like area around a town where date palms, vegetables and fruit are grown.
Pasha – high official in Ottoman Empire.
Piste (f) – a track, often a couple of km wide, in the Sahara.

Ras (a) – headland.
Reg – stony desert.
Ribat – monastery and fort in one.

Sebkha (a) – saltpan.
Sherif – descendant of the Prophet
Sidi (a) – honorific reserved for saints and holy men.
Sifsari (T) – off-white robe worn by Tunisian women.
Souk (a) – market.
Sufism – mystical strand of Islam; adherents concentrate on their inner attitude in order to attain communion with God.

Tajine (M) – stew, usually with meat as the main ingredient.
Tassili – the word for plateau in the Touareg language, Tamahaq.
Tizi – mountain pass.
Touareg – nomadic Berbers of the Sahara, sometimes known by romantics as the Blue Men, because of their indigo-dyed robes which gives their skin a bluish tinge; however, these days the cloth comes ready-dyed from Europe.

Ville Nouvelle (f) – towns built by the French, generally alongside existing towns and cities of the Maghreb.
Vizier – another term for a provincial governor, usually in the Ottoman Empire.

Wilaya (A) – province; there are 43 of them Algeria.

Zaouia – religious fraternity based around a marabout.
Zeriba (A) – house built of reeds and grass; found in southern Algeria.
Zitouna (a) – olive tree or grove.

Index

Dear traveller

Prices go up, good places go bad, bad places go bankrupt ... and every guidebook is inevitably outdated in places. Fortunately, many travellers write to us about their experiences, telling us when things have changed. If we reprint a book between editions, we try to include as much of this information as possible in a Stop Press section. Most of this information has not been verified by our own writers.

We really enjoy hearing from people out on the road, and apart from guaranteeing that others will benefit from your good and bad experiences, we're prepared to bribe you with the offer of a free book for sending us substantial useful information.

Thank you to everyone who has written and, to those who haven't, I hope you do find this book useful – and that you let us know when it isn't.

Tony Wheeler

Morocco and Tunisia have so far been politically quiet compared to Algeria. The Algerian elections in December 1991 were won in a landslide victory by the Islamic opposition party, the Front Islamique du Salut (FIS). In response to this, the military-dominated Higher Security Council appointed a five-person presidency with a mandate to rule under a state of emergency until 1993, which was followed by riots. The titular head of the new ruling committee was Mr Mohammed Boudiaf, who was subsequently assassinated in the coastal city of Annaba in June 1992. Since the appointment of the Higher Security Council the FIS has issued statements denouncing the military takeover.

The Morocco Stop Press was written by Tony Wheeler, after he researched the country for Lonely Planet's new guide book *Mediterranean Europe on a shoestring*. The Algerian Stop Press was compiled from letters sent to us by the following travellers: Stephen-Andrew Lee & Barbara Benoit (C), Brian Stewart (AUS) and Dennis Ward (AUS).

MOROCCO
Money & Costs
The current official exchange rate is US$1 to Dr 8.66.

Time
Moroccan Time is GMT year round. In summer when daylight saving time is in force in Europe, Morocco is one hour behind British summertime and two hours behind Spanish summertime. The rest of the year it's on the same time as Britain, one hour behind Spain.

Getting There & Away
Air Royal Air Maroc now has regular Montreal-New York-Casablanca flights but it will still probably be much cheaper to arrive via London.

Boat Beware of the rush home in July when Moroccans from all over Europe converge on the Spanish ferry ports and cause monumental traffic snarls. Pedestrians usually have no problem finding space on the ferries (it's car space which is in short supply), but the coastal road to Algeciras can be blocked for hours at a time.

Tangier
The Museum of the American Legation in the medina is well worth a visit – a fine and immaculately kept old building with numerous interesting old pictures and other mementoes of the city. The *Restaurant*

Mauritania has closed but on Rue du Commerce *Restaurant Grece* and *Restaurant Andalus* are good budget alternatives.

Asilah

Restaurant Alcazaba has closed but many other new restaurants have sprung up in this town which previously suffered from a shortage of restaurants. Try *Restaurant El Oceano* and *Restaurant Noujoum* near the excellent *Restaurant Al Kasaba*. *Salon de Thé Ifrane*, near the grands taxis stop, is a popular place for a mint tea and a session of people-watching.

Rabat

Just beyond the popular *Restaurant de la Jeunesse* in the medina are the similar *Restaurant de l'Union* and *Restaurant de la Liberation*. Behind the Balima Hotel on Zenkat Tanta is *Pizza La Mama* with excellent pizzas costing Dr 39 and they also have cold beer. *Restaurant Saïdoune*, across from the Hotel Terminus on Ave Mohammed V, offers Lebanese food at reasonable prices.

Fès

Sandwitchs Amin (great spelling!) is a good place for cheap food on Rue Kaid Ahmed, beside the market on Boulevard Mohammed V in the ville nouvelle. *Café Khozama* on Ave Mohammed es Slaoui offers a variety of food including pizzas. The stylish *Café Restaurant Mounia* still has great food but they seem to have misplaced their wine list. At *Brasserie Le Marignan* you can actually get a cold beer at the outside tables, as a change from the usual gloomy Moroccan bars.

Only grands taxis will go out to the airport and it's hard to beat them down to a reasonable price.

Meknés

La Coupole Restaurant, right across the street from *Rotisserie Karam* in the new town, is a good place to eat. Although the main grands taxis station is in the old town, it is not necessary to trek all the way out there, as there are smaller stations in the new town. The silver Mercedes with black roofs are grands taxis – the petits taxis are smaller blue and yellow cars.

Marrakesh

Close to Djemaa el Fna and right behind the post office the very popular *Hotel Ali* (tel 44 4979) has rooms at Dr 70/90 or Dr 85/120 including breakfast, or you can get a bed on the roof terrace for Dr 30 including breakfast. There's a popular restaurant and the hotel is a gathering point for High Atlas trekking trips. The same people run the *Hotel Farouk* (tel 43 1989) close to the railway station at 66 Ave Hassan II in the ville nouvelle. Rooms here are Dr 90/120 including breakfast. The *Iceberg Restaurant*, between the Hotel Foucald and the Grand Hotel du Tazi in the Djemaa el Fna area, has excellent food on its Dr 60 fixed price menu.

ALGERIA

The border between Algeria and Mali at Borj Mokhtar is apparently open according to the latest reports we have received from travellers, but unfortunately it is not safe to travel in Mali from the border to Gao. The Tuaregs and other bandits roam the countryside, and convoys along the 550 km trip from Borj Mokhtar to Gao can be robbed up to five times. It is not a recommended route.

The Algerian/Niger border is closed according to the latest reports. This virtually closes the overland route. It might be worth while to enquire about taking the Mauritania route which up to now has been closed.

According to travellers who hitchhike across Algeria it is better to get rides in smaller vehicles rather than the large trucks, which get stuck more often in the sand and drive at slower speeds. Large trucks like a Mercedes can apparently take twice or three times as many days to cover the same distance as a Peugeot 504.

Another recommendation for people who drive their cars across the Sahara is that they might want to take some posters of

Ferraris, or even some toy cars as gifts for customs officers. This is apparently an almost definite way of getting your car through customs without it being taken apart!

Travellers' Tips & Comments

There is a good restaurant on the road into In Salah called *The Skier* and there is a picture of someone skiing on the sign outside. There you can rent skis to ski down the sandy slopes of the creeping sand dune, however, there is only one set of skis and one pair of boots – you need to bargain for the rental price. I still don't know why we did it, but there was a huge throng of people gathered to watch the crazy Canadians ski down the dune and then trudge back up with the skis over their shoulders – the sun was as hot as hell!

Stephen-Andrew Lee & Barbara Benoit – Canada

Keep in touch!

We love hearing from you and think you'd like to hear from us.

The Lonely Planet Newsletter covers the when, where, how and what of travel. (AND it's free!)

When...is the right time to see reindeer in Finland?
Where...can you hear the best palm-wine music in Ghana?
How...do you get from Asunción to Areguá by steam train?
What...should you leave behind to avoid hassles with customs in Iran?

To join our mailing list just contact us at any of our offices. (details below)

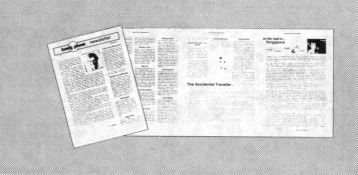

Every issue includes:

* *a letter from Lonely Planet founders Tony and Maureen Wheeler*
* *travel diary from a Lonely Planet author - find out what it's really like out on the road*
* *feature article on an important and topical travel issue*
* *a selection of recent letters from our readers*
* *the latest travel news from all over the world*
* *details on Lonely Planet's new and forthcoming releases*

Also available Lonely Planet T-shirts. 100% heavy weight cotton (S, M, L, XL)

LONELY PLANET PUBLICATIONS
Australia: PO Box 617, Hawthorn, 3122, Victoria (tel: 03-819 1877)
USA: Embarcadero West, 155 Filbert Street, Suite 251, Oakland, CA 94607 (tel: 510-893 8555)
UK: Devonshire House, 12 Barley Mow Passage, Chiswick, London W4 4PH (tel: 081-742 3161)

Guides to Africa

Africa on a shoestring

From Marrakesh to Kampala, Mozambique to Mauritania, Johannesburg to Cairo - this guidebook has all the facts on travelling in Africa. Comprehensive information on more than 50 countries.

Central Africa - a travel survival kit

This guide tells where to go to meet gorillas in the jungle, how to catch a steamer down the Congo...even the best beer to wash down grilled boa constrictor! Covers Cameroun, Central African Republic, Chad, The Congo, Equatorial Guinea, Gabon, São Tomé & Principe, and Zaïre.

East Africa - a travel survival kit

Detailed information on Kenya, Uganda, Rwanda, Burundi, eastern Zaïre and Tanzania. The latest edition includes a 32-page full-colour Safari Guide.

Kenya - a travel survival kit

This superb guide features a 32-page 'Safari Guide' with colour photographs, illustrations and information on East Africa's famous wildlife.

West Africa - a travel survival kit

All the necessary information for independent travel in Benin, Burkino Faso, Cape Verde, Côte d'Ivoire, The Gambia, Ghana, Guinea, Guinea-Bissau, Liberia, Mali, Mauritania, Niger, Nigeria, Senegal, Sierra Leone and Togo.

Egypt & the Sudan - a travel survival kit

This guide takes you into and beyond the spectacular and mysterious pyramids, temples, tombs, monasteries, mosques and bustling main streets of Egypt and the Sudan.

Morocco, Algeria & Tunisia - a travel survival kit

Reap the rewards of getting off the beaten track with this practical guide.

Zimbabwe, Botswana & Namibia - a travel survival kit

Exotic wildlife, breathtaking scenery and fascinating people...this comprehensive guide shows a wilder, older side of Africa for the adventurous traveller. Includes a 32-page colour Safari Guide.

Lonely Planet Guidebooks

Lonely Planet guidebooks cover every accessible part of Asia as well as Australia, the Pacific, South America, Africa, the Middle East, Europe and parts of North America. There are five series: *travel survival kits*, covering a country for a range of budgets; *shoestring guides* with compact information for low-budget travel in a major region; *walking guides*; *city guides* and *phrasebooks*.

Mail Order

Lonely Planet guidebooks are distributed worldwide. They are also available by mail order from Lonely Planet, so if you have difficulty finding a title please write to us. US and Canadian residents should write to Embarcadero West, 155 Filbert St, Suite 251, Oakland CA 94607, USA; European residents should write to Devonshire House, 12 Barley Mow Passage, Chiswick, London W4 4PH; and residents of other countries to PO Box 617, Hawthorn, Victoria 3122, Australia.

Indian Subcontinent
Bangladesh
India
Hindi/Urdu phrasebook
Trekking in the Indian Himalaya
Karakoram Highway
Kashmir, Ladakh & Zanskar
Nepal
Trekking in the Nepal Himalaya
Nepal phrasebook
Pakistan
Sri Lanka
Sri Lanka phrasebook

Africa
Africa on a shoestring
Central Africa
East Africa
Kenya
Swahili phrasebook
Morocco, Algeria & Tunisia
Moroccan Arabic phrasebook
South Africa, Lesotho & Swaziland
Zimbabwe, Botswana & Namibia
West Africa

Mexico
Baja California
Mexico

Central America
Central America on a shoestring
Costa Rica
La Ruta Maya

North America
Alaska
Canada
Hawaii

Europe
Eastern Europe on a shoestring
Eastern Europe phrasebook
Finland
Iceland, Greenland & the Faroe Islands
Mediterranean Europe on a shoestring
Mediterranean Europe phrasebook
Scandinavian & Baltic Europe on a shoestring
Scandinavian Europe phrasebook
Trekking in Spain
USSR
Russian phrasebook
Western Europe on a shoestring
Western Europe phrasebook

South America
Argentina, Uruguay & Paraguay
Bolivia
Brazil
Brazilian phrasebook
Chile & Easter Island
Colombia
Ecuador & the Galápagos Islands
Latin American Spanish phrasebook
Peru
Quechua phrasebook
South America on a shoestring
Trekking in the Patagonian Andes

The Lonely Planet Story

Lonely Planet published its first book in 1973 in response to the numerous 'How did you do it?' questions Maureen and Tony Wheeler were asked after driving, bussing, hitching, sailing and railing their way from England to Australia.

Written at a kitchen table and hand collated, trimmed and stapled, *Across Asia on the Cheap* became an instant local bestseller, inspiring thoughts of another book.

Eighteen months in South-East Asia resulted in their second guide, *South-East Asia on a shoestring*, which they put together in a backstreet Chinese hotel in Singapore in 1975. The 'yellow bible' as it quickly became known to backpackers around the world, soon became *the* guide to the region. It has sold well over half a million copies and is now in its 7th edition, still retaining its familiar yellow cover.

Today there are over 100 Lonely Planet titles – books that have that same adventurous approach to travel as those early guides; books that 'assume you know how to get your luggage off the carousel' as one reviewer put it.

Although Lonely Planet initially specialised in guides to Asia, they now cover most regions of the world, including the Pacific, South America, Africa, the Middle East and Europe. The list of *walking guides* and *phrasebooks* (for 'unusual' languages such as Quechua, Swahili, Nepalese and Egyptian Arabic) is also growing rapidly.

The emphasis continues to be on travel for independent travellers. Tony and Maureen still travel for several months of each year and play an active part in the writing, updating and quality control of Lonely Planet's guides.

They have been joined by over 50 authors, 48 staff – mainly editors, cartographers, & designers – at our office in Melbourne, Australia and another 10 at our US office in Oakland, California. In 1991 Lonely Planet opened a London office to handle sales for Britain, Europe and Africa. Travellers themselves also make a valuable contribution to the guides through the feedback we receive in thousands of letters each year.

The people at Lonely Planet strongly believe that travellers can make a positive contribution to the countries they visit, both through their appreciation of the countries' culture, wildlife and natural features, and through the money they spend. In addition, the company makes a direct contribution to the countries and regions it covers. Since 1986 a percentage of the income from each book has been donated to ventures such as famine relief in Africa; aid projects in India; agricultural projects in Central America; Greenpeace's efforts to halt French nuclear testing in the Pacific and Amnesty International. In 1991 $68,000 was donated to these causes.

Lonely Planet's basic travel philosophy is summed up in Tony Wheeler's comment, 'Don't worry about whether your trip will work out. Just go!'